Motor Development in Children:
Aspects of Coordination and Control

NATO ASI Series

Advanced Science Institutes Series

A Series presenting the results of activities sponsored by the NATO Science Committee, which aims at the dissemination of advanced scientific and technological knowledge, with a view to strengthening links between scientific communities.

The Series is published by an international board of publishers in conjunction with the NATO Scientific Affairs Division

A	Life Sciences	Plenum Publishing Corporation
B	Physics	London and New York
C	Mathematical and Physical Sciences	D. Reidel Publishing Company Dordrecht and Boston
D	Behavioural and Social Sciences	Martinus Nijhoff Publishers Dordrecht/Boston/Lancaster
E	Applied Sciences	
F	Computer and Systems Sciences	Springer-Verlag Berlin/Heidelberg/New York
G	Ecological Sciences	

Series D: Behavioural and Social Sciences – No. 34

£82.25

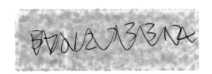

Motor Development in Children: Aspects of Coordination and Control

edited by

M.G. Wade

Department of Physical Education
Southern Illinois University
Carbondale, Illinois
U.S.A.

H.T.A. Whiting

Department of Psychology
Interfaculty of Human Movement Sciences
The Free University
Amsterdam
The Netherlands

1986 **Martinus Nijhoff Publishers**
Dordrecht / Boston / Lancaster
Published in cooperation with NATO Scientific Affairs Division

Proceedings of the NATO Advanced Study Institute on "Motor Skill Acquisition in Children", Maastricht, The Netherlands, July, 1985

Library of Congress Cataloging in Publication Data

```
NATO Advanced Study Institute on "Motor Skill
   Acquisition in Children" (1985 : Maastricht,
   Netherlands)
   Motor development in children.

   (NATO ASI series. Series D, Behavioural and
social sciences ; no. 34)
   "Proceedings of the NATO Advanced Study Institute on
"Motor Skill Acquisition in Children," Maastricht, the
Netherlands, July 1985"--T.p. verso.
   "Published in cooperation with NATO Scientific Affairs
Division."
   Companion volume to : Themes in motor development.
   Includes bibliographies and indexes.
   1. Motor ability in children--Congresses.  2. Child
development--Congresses.  I. Wade, Michael G.
II. Whiting, H. T. A. (Harold Thomas Anthony), 1929-
III. North Atlantic Treaty Organization.  Scientific
Affairs Division.  IV. NATO Advanced Study Institute
on "Motor Skill Acquisition in Children" (1985 :
Maastricht, Netherlands)  Themes in motor development.
V. Title.  VI. Series.  [DNLM: 1. Child Development--
congresses.  2. Motor Skills--in infancy & childhood--
congresses.  WE 103 N2786  1985m]
BF723.M6N37  1985        155.4'12              86-16425
ISBN 90-247-3389-8
```

78339

155.412

ISBN 90-247-3389-8 (this volume)
ISBN 90-247-2688-3 (series)

Distributors for the United States and Canada: Kluwer Academic Publishers, 101 Philip Drive, Assinippi Park, Norwell, MA 02061, U.S.A.

Distributors for the UK and Ireland: Kluwer Academic Publishers, MTP Press Ltd, Falcon House, Queen Square, Lancaster LA1 1RN, UK

Distributors for all other countries: Kluwer Academic Publishers Group, Distribution Center, P.O. Box 322, 3300 AH Dordrecht, The Netherlands

Printed in The Netherlands

CONTENTS

Foreword

This book is divided into sections. Each section is devoted to a particular issue in Motor Development and comprises two or more contributions. The order of presentation mirrors the order of presentation at the Institute and thus is not entirely fortuitous! Nevertheless, it does not reflect any value judgement on the part of the editors as to the importance of any one issue in comparison to others addressed in the book.

This volume is to be seen as a companion volume to *'Themes in Motor Development'* in which the more specific topics presented during the Institute are published. Together, the two volumes provide both a general and theme specific approach to this expanding field of knowledge.

PREFACE

Books and conferences, on what in North America is euphemistically termed motor development, have been few and far between in the past 25 years. This is not to say that the study of how children acquire and develop motor skills has not been a subject on which scientists have focused their attention. In the United States in the 1930's and 1940's, Bayley (1935) and Gesell and Amatruda (1947) described and scaled the rates at which young children acquired motor skills. In Europe, the development of childrens' motor behaviour was of theoretical interest to Piaget (1952). Nevertheless, we feel that it is true to say that the study of motor skill acquisition in children has been overshadowed, certainly in the past 25 years, by the attempts of human movement scientists to establish the basic theory of action as it relates to the broad aspects of motor learning, control and coordination. As Wade (1976) noted, there has been no real theorising in motor development. This deficiency could be attributed to the fact that the field of motor learning was, at that time, trying to establish its own theoretical position – only since the late 1960's and early 1970's have theoretical models to predict and describe how motor skills are acquired become apparent (e.g. Adams, 1971; Schmidt, 1975).

Although considerable developmental research on motor skill acquisition exists (see for example reviews by Wade, 1976), publications specifically focusing on the topic have been meagre. A landmark conference organised by Connolly - funded by the CIBA organisation - produced a publication in 1970 called 'Mechanisms of Motor Skill Development' and a conference held at the University of Iowa in 1980 - sponsored by the Big Ten Committee on Institutional Cooperation - produced a publication in 1982 edited by Kelso and Clark (1982) entitled "The Development of Movement Control and Co-ordination". Both of these books cast the study of motor skills in a more theoretical light by asking questions as to *how* children acquire motor skills rather than describing what it is they acquire.

With respect to the study and focus of motor skills research within the framework of NATO Advanced Study Institute programmes, only the Institute on Motor Behaviour held in France in 1979 and co-directed by Stelmach (USA) and Requin (France) is of central concern. Nevertheless, given the considerable interest, both in Europe and North America, in theorising and active experimentation over the past 15 years, it seemed to the Co-directors of the ASI that it was high time that another conference, focusing on developmental issues, was held. Subsequently, a successful application was made to the NATO Scientific Committee. This led directly to the conference in Maastricht held in July 1985.

It was decided to develop the ASI along the lines of central issues in motor development with invitations being sent to senior scientists to provide keynote lectures each day on a specific topic and to have other participants react or present research material addressing related themes. The response to invitations was overwhelming to the point that in this volume are included

only the keynote lectures and the reactions. A second volume entitled
'Themes in Motor Development' is devoted to the theme presentations. In
this sense, the second publication is very much a necessary and companion
volume to the one presented here.

The conference opening lecture entitled "Motor Skill Acquisition in
Children: Perspective and Problems" was presented by Connolly (UK). In
his address, Connolly attempted to review the theoretical issues facing the
field and presented a taxonomic analysis of some of the research directions
which he felt needed to receive further scientific inquiry. Connolly's
presentation was followed by that of Butterworth who addressed similar
issues. Prechtl (Netherlands) in addressing the issue of prenatal onset of
motor patterns presented interesting video tapes demonstrating very
convincingly that much of the skill development in young children is present
and exhibited by the infant as it develops in the womb. This was followed
by Fentress's (Canada) lecture on the "Development of Coordination".
Fentress, an animal ethologist, presented evidence that re-emphasised the
importance of coordination in animals for the organisation of the research
effort with human subjects.

An important issue that developed during the period of the institute,
and in fact grew to a climax with the final presentation of Kugler, was the
current controversy in psychological theorising that contrasts a cognitive
perspective of the development of control and coordination with a more
radical realist perspective, which rejects the traditional notion of some
central executor or other heuristic mechanisms purported to control important
parameters of movement. These ideas were elaborated on in presentations on
perception and action by Pick (USA), Von Hofsten (Sweden), and Lee (UK)
and on cognition and action by Newell (USA). The more traditional notion of
the role of cognition and its relationship to motor skill actions was argued
by Mounoud (Switzerland).

The presentation by Trevarthen (UK) discussed influences of the
developing brain on mature brains by the process of intersubjectivity.
Intersubjectivity was viewed by Trevarthen as the transmission and sharing
of the control of motor coordination by 'subjects'. On the final day, Paillard
(France) presented an address on recent developments in brain research and
how contemporary knowledge of the living brain relates to the development
of control and coordination. The Epilogue lecture by Kugler (USA) attempted
an overview of the conference and proposed the perspective of direct realism
and how this might accommodate not only the direct realism between
perception and action but also a view of cognition within a realist framework.
A realist theory of cognition would anchor its predicates around properties
as opposed to logical propositions, hypotheses, or inferences. It does not
deny the latter but makes them parasitic on the properties.

All of the presentations in this volume contain at least one or two
reactions with Kugler's summary address at the end being an attempt to
provide some overall balance and perspective to the topics covered in the
ten working days of the conference. The director and codirector wish to
thank all of the participants, senior lecturers and students for their thoughtful presentations and comments and for the endurance that they showed over
the ten day working conference. Many of the participants had not met each
other prior to convening in Maastricht, and it was gratifying to both the
director and co-director that in a very short while, individuals from all over
the participating NATO countries quickly became friends and participated in

intense discussion and exchange of ideas which is the very essence of the NATO Advanced Study Institute programme.

The environment in which the institute prospered was in large part due to the hard work of the staff of the Hotel Maastricht and of the conference secretariat provided by Mrs. Irma Reijnhout of the Free University of Amsterdam. In addition, to thanking Mrs. Reijnhout for her hard work the directors would also like to recognise the work of Ms. Pat Terneus of Southern Illinois University for the organising effort that she put in regarding the North American participants. In addition to the funding received from the NATO Scientific Committee, the directors would also like to recognise the funding provided by the *National Science Foundation* (Grant nr. 8505988) that provided travel support for the United States participants.

Mrs. Irma Reijnhout took on the thankless task of typing all the manuscripts and preparing the book for publication. The fact that it is in press so quickly is largely due to her efforts. We express our sincere appreciation as well as that of the publishers.

The present volume provides an up-to-date perspective on the current status of motor skills research as it relates to children and in that sense builds on the earlier volumes published by Connolly (1970) and Kelso and Clark (1982). It remains to be seen what the level and impact of the theorising presented in this volume will have on the theorising and research activities of those interested in motor skill acquisition in children in the ensuing decade. The effects of this will perhaps be assessed by another Advanced Study Institute towards the end of the present century!

M. G. Wade
Carbondale, IL

H.T.A. Whiting
Amsterdam, Netherlands

XIV

References

Adams, J.A. (1971). A closed-loop theory of motor learning. *Journal of Motor Behavior, 3,* 111-150.
Bayley, N. (1935). The development of motor abilities during the first three years. *Monographs of the Society for Research in Child Development, 1,* 1-26.
Connolly, K.J. (1970). *Mechanisms of motor skill development.* New York: Academic Press.
Piaget, J. (1952). *The origins of intelligence in children.* New York: International University Press.
Wade, M.G. (1976). Developmental motor learning. In J. Keogh and R.S. Hulton (Eds.), *Exercises and sport sciences reviews, 4,* 375-394.
Gesell, A. & Amatruda, C.S. (1947). *Developmental diagnosis* 2nd Edition. New York: Harper and Row.
Kelso, J.A.S. & Clark, J.E. (1982). *The development of movement control and coordination.* New York: Wiley and Sons.
Schmidt, R.A. (1975). A schema theory of discrete motor skill learning. *Psychological Review, 82,* 225-260.

XV

INVITED DELEGATES
(who contributed to this volume)

Bard, C.
Université Laval
Faculté des Sciences de l'Education
Cite Universitaire
Quebec
Canada G1K 7P4

Beek, P.J.
Vakgroep THLOK
Interfaculteit Lichamelijke Opvoeding
Vrije Universiteit
De Boelelaan 1081
1081 HV Amsterdam
The Netherlands

Butterworth, G.
Department of Psychology
The University of Southampton
Southampton S09 5NH
England

Clark, J.E.
Department of Physical Education
University of Maryland
College Park
MD 20742
U.S.A.

Connolly, K.
Department of Psychology
University of Sheffield
Sheffield
England

Fentress, J.C.
Department of Psychology
Dalhousie University
Malifax
Nova Scota
Canada

Hay, L.
Centre National de la Recherche Scientifique
31, Chemin Joseph-Aiguier
13274 Marseille
Cedex 02
France

Hofsten, C. von
University of Umea
Department of Psychology
S-90187 Umea
Sweden

Hopkins, B.
Academisch Ziekenhuis
Instituut voor Ontwikkelingsneurologie
Oostersingel 59
9713 LZ Groningen
The Netherlands

Kugler, P.N.

Crump Institute
UCLA
Los Angeles
CA
U.S.A.

Lee, D.N.

University of Edinburgh
Department of Psychology
7, George Square
Edinburgh EH8 9TA
Scotland

Mounoud, P.

Université de Genève
Faculté de Psychologie et des Sciences
24, Rue Général Dutour
1211 Genève 4
Switzerland

Newell, K.M.

University of Illinois
Room 1, ICBD
51 Gerty Drive
Champaign, Ill 61820
U.S.A.

Paillard, J.

Institut de Neurophysiologie
C.N.R.S.
31, Chemin Joseph-Aiguier
14274 Marseille, Cedex 2
France

Pick, H.L. Jr.

Institute for Child Development
51 E. River Road
Minneapolis, MN 55455-0345
U.S.A.

Prechtl, H.F.R.

Department of Developmental Neurology
University of Groningen
Groningen
The Netherlands

Roy, E.

Department of Psychology
1501 Mt. Sinai Hospital
600 University
Toronto
Canada M5G 1X5

Smyth, M.M.

Department of Psychology
University of Lancaster
Lancaster, LANCS
England

Thelen, E.

Department of Psychology
Indiana University
Psychology Building
Bloomington, Indiana 47405
U.S.A.

Trevarthen, C.   Department of Psychology
                        University of Edinburgh
                        7, George Square
                        Edinburgh EH8 9TA
                        Scotland

Wade, M.G.   Department of Physical Education
                        Southern Illinois University
                        Carbondale
                        Ill. 62901
                        U.S.A.

Wall, A.E.   Department of Physical Education
                        University of Alberta-Edmonton
                        Alberta
                        Canada T6G 2E1

Whiting, H.T.A.   Vakgroep Psychologie
                        Interfaculteit Lichamelijke Opvoeding
                        Vrije Universiteit
                        De Boelelaan 1081
                        1081 HV Amsterdam
                        The Netherlands

Wieringen, P.C.W. van   Vakgroep Psychologie
                        Interfaculteit Lichamelijke Opvoeding
                        Vrije Universiteit
                        De Boelelaan 1081
                        1081 HV Amsterdam
                        The Netherlands

Wolff, P.H.   Children's Hospital
                        300 Longwood Avenue
                        Boston, MA 02115
                        U.S.A.

Zelaznik, H.   Department of Physical Education
                        Purdue University
                        West Lafayette
                        IN 47907
                        U.S.A.

SECTION 1

MOTOR SKILL ACQUISITION IN CHILDREN:
PERSPECTIVES AND PROBLEMS

A PERSPECTIVE ON MOTOR DEVELOPMENT

K.J. Connolly

INTRODUCTION

I first reviewed the literature on the development of motor skills in the late 1960's (Connolly, 1970). At that time there was little current research or even interest in the subject though it had a substantial past. Over the past 15 years the picture has changed greatly, to the substantial past can be added a promising, even exciting future. The evident increase in interest in motor development, of which this Advanced Study Institute is a reflection, is a consequence of several things. Some of the important factors stem from practical concerns such as the rehabilitation of disabled children, or the emergence of physical education as an academic discipline. Other factors spring from more theoretical concerns, the burgeoning of the neurosciences, the growing interest among psychologists in the concept of action, and of course over the 1970's a widespread interest in the developmental sciences. It is plain from the literature (see for example, Kelso & Clark, 1982) that there are now a good number of theories available about aspects of motor development, and the data base has also grown greatly.

Motor development is an extensive topic and we run the risk of being swamped with data and experimental results. It seems to me that progress in research comes as often by finding better questions as it does by finding answers to questions, and the precision of our questions is not unconnected with our overall orientation to a subject. I shall not attempt to provide a summary review of the more recent work on motor skill development but instead focus on one or two features of development. The concept of development is concerned with changes in the structure and function of organisms. Not all changes are correctly described as developmental, there are for example, changes of a cyclical kind and changes which are a consequence of injury. The meaning of change reserved for development has to do with the orderly appearance of new structures and processes. The emergent form has to last for an unspecified though reasonable period of time and the new state is considered to be more adapted to the organism's current needs than the preceding one.

Developmental changes are directional and some, though not all, are irreversible. In the case of the mental and behavioural development of children a fundamental question implicit in much of our thinking is concerned with what respects, and to what extent, and under what conditions does the psychological development of individuals proceed towards some universal and uniquely definable destination. Another way of putting this question is to ask how far it is possible to determine and define in advance the final goal or destination towards which improvements in ability and capacity are proceeding. The question links on the one hand to the historical evolution of features characteristic of the species and on the other to the ontogeny of individuals.

Much of our thinking about development is based on the implicit assumption that we are dealing with orderly changes directed towards an ideal, predetermined end state. In some way the characteristic development- al changes seem fixed by the end state itself. There is a widely held implicit assumption that the child is growing towards some better adapted form; it is a comforting assumption though quite what it entails is unclear.

In considering the general patterns of change, which in broad terms are well known, we can identify four problems which require explanation. First we must be able to account for the normal ontogenetic changes in behaviour which appear to be universal. Typically we have thought of these as being produced by some interactive process between the environment and a phenomenon called maturation. Psychologists for the most part have considered maturation to be the process by which particular behavioural competencies and capacities emerge as a result of the growth and different- iation of the central nervous system. Maturational competencies of course require that certain environmental conditions be met if they are to be realised. The second problem which requires explanation has to do with variations in behaviour between individuals which arise in a specific context during development. The third issue concerns variations in behaviour and competence within an individual which are observed in different contexts during the same developmental epoch. A particular skill or competence may be used in one situation but not decontextualised and generalised to other appropriate situations for some time. The fourth problem concerns the explanation of fairly extreme deviancy, these are conditions which are often described clinically and which sometimes result in disability and handicap. The central issue can be summarised simply, we need a way of thinking about a seeming paradox which is that development entails at the same time marked similarities and marked variation between individuals.

We know, both from our own observations and from descriptions in the literature that the behaviour of the young is in many ways less complete and less competent, in the sense of being less efficient, than that of the adult. The development of behaviour is thus seen as a process of elaboration and refinement as the child matures. Any failures in this process, or serious difficulties in the form of extensive delays, present as clinical cases. In the study of development the mature form of a response, process or function is usually used as a yardstick by which to assess the immature form. However it is important to realise the limitations and dangers of viewing the developing organism as an immature form of the adult. The rules of behavioural organisation in infant and adult differ not just quantitatively but also qualitatively. The processes by which the rules of behavioural organisation are transformed at different stages in development also gives rise to fundamental changes. Put simply, it is essential to appreciate that the child is not a miniature adult, and to assume that the same parameters are important in understanding the performance both of child and adult may be seriously misleading.

Science is concerned with the understanding and explanation of natural phenomena. Broadly speaking this entails two different but related activities: the systematic collection of facts about the world and the construction of theories to account for these observations. However the relationship between facts and theory is not quite as simple or straightforward as has sometimes been supposed. There is an implication that first we collect the facts and then having done so we devise a theory to account for them. The theory is then in turn subjected to further scrutiny and empirical test. If the test fails to support the explanation the theory is discarded or at least modified. But the relationship between the collection of data and the construction of theory is not so clear cut. Before we have theories to explain our observations of nature – the facts that we gather – we have implicit notions about what it is important to observe, describe and measure. The relationship between theory and facts is in itself interesting and important for it is here that fundamentally important choices are made.

When we consider the adequacy of a theory to account for observed facts it is not really critical experiments which determine whether the theory is retained so much as the ability of the theory to deal with the totality of the data in a particular discipline, and the acceptance at a particular time of certain kinds of explanations. Of course the availability of alternative theories is also an important factor. It goes without saying that scientific progress depends both on the systematic accumulation of facts and on the devising of theory to explain, illuminate, and create them. Theory serves to focus available data and also to guide the direction in which new data collecting takes place. Theory thus varies from some precisely articulated explanation where the relevant variables and their relationships to each other are clearly specified, to some much vaguer orientation towards what is believed to be important, that is to a way of loosely conceptualising the matter in hand. Both of these are important and both are features of the scientific endeavour. Both have to be examined and re-examined, refined, changed, and sometimes discarded. I shall concern myself largely with our implicit, often vague, sometimes misleading, conceptual framework for studying development.

MATURATION AND BEHAVIOURAL DEVELOPMENT

Among the pioneers of this approach to accounting for developmental changes in behaviour are Shirley (1931), McGraw (1945), Gesell (1954) and Bayley (1970). Gesell perhaps did more than anyone to develop a theoretical statement of the maturationist position. He laid emphasis on biological factors because he saw these as providing both the impetus and the direction for development. Whether structure determines function, or function determines structure is an old question in developmental psychology. Gesell's concern with the structure-function relationship followed Coghill (1929) who considered that structure must be present and developed before function can take place.

In observing that development progressed through an orderly sequence of stages, Gesell believed that the sequence itself was fixed by biological factors which emerged through the evolutionary history of the species. The rate of progression through the sequence of stages was considered a function of an individual's genotype but the broad pattern itself was one typical of the species. Thus Gesell dealt with two striking and apparently paradoxical features of development, similarity and variation between individual members of the species. It is sometimes assumed that the environment was considered to be relatively unimportant but such an assumption is mistaken. The environment was seen as supporting and sustaining the individual as development unfolded. Biological factors however were the central controlling

agents. This position allowed for observations such as catch-up in growth.
If a child suffers undernourishment or illness his growth may be retarded
but when adequate nutrition is restored or the illness cured growth
accelerates until the process 'catches-up' to the growth curve of normal
healthy controls (McCance, 1962; Prader et al, 1963; Tanner, 1963, 1970).

The normative approach in child development pioneered by Gesell
relies on obtaining characteristic age descriptions; age being used as a
rough indication of developmental status, and often as a proxy measure of
process. Individual differences, the significance of which Gesell emphasised,
were seen to reflect both genetic differences and the differential effects of
environmental variables. Maturational forces however were seen to control
development, the environment having a supportive but not causal role. On
the basis of his observations Gesell stressed the self-regulatory properties
of the growth matrix which served to demonstrate the power of internal
regulatory mechanisms. In fact Gesell did not believe that the course or
pace of development could be appreciably changed by altering the
environment. Investigations which employed the method of co-twin control
(Gesell & Thompson, 1929) were used to explore the possibilities of such
manipulation and the results revealed modest effects, though it must be
said that the means of operationalising and measuring change are crucially
important and in these investigations not above criticism.

Development is concerned with changes in the pattern of organisation
which an organism exhibits in its morphology, physiology and behaviour.
It follows therefore that in studying development we are interested not only
in the final state to which a system arrives but also and especially in the
course by which it gets there. The route or pathway of change is particularly interesting and a knowledge of it may well point us towards an understanding of the processes by which the end point is attained, and indeed
the functions of certain structures and behaviours at different points in
ontogeny.

Any explanation of behavioural development must take into account
four general points which are as follows.

1. The human infant at birth is generally immature, for example in
terms of motor behaviour, though in respect of some systems it is capable
of very competent and quite precise actions. The baby's capacity to control
sucking movements, and to track a moving object with the eyes (Kaye, 1967;
Barton et al, 1971) are examples of highly developed motor control systems
which are functional early in post-natal life. It is clear that the infant's
behaviour is adapted to the demands of its environment and that behaviour
and environment change hand in hand. Ontogenetic adaptations have been
the subject of close scrutiny by Oppenheim (1981, 1984) and are plainly
very important.

2. Over an extensive period of time, in the case of the human infant
more than 3 or 4 years, a range of behaviours will make their appearance
in an orderly fashion and over a time scale which is fairly well known (see
for example, Frankenburg & Dodds, 1967).

3. There are marked similarities between individuals superimposed on
which is a quite wide range of individual differences. The extent and
nature of the observed differences is of course partly dependent on the
means of measurement employed.

4. There is a gradual increase in the range and complexity of behaviour

which an individual shows.

Descriptions of behavioural change give rise to a variety of questions generally having to do with the nature and origins of what is to be explained. Consider two examples of skilled motor action commonplace amongst 8 year old children in the Netherlands; walking and writing. By the age of 8 just about every normal healthy child will have some mastery over both these skills. On the face of it these two common skills appear to differ in a fundamental way. All normal children irrespective of culture will come to walk without any specific form of training, whereas we know that writing is a skill which must be specifically taught. One of these actions appears to be biologically fixed, the other culturally fixed. In Gesell's terms the skill of walking is internally impelled and directed whereas hand-writing is a learned skill. Learning is not here used to imply a state to which biological changes and capacities are unrelated, indeed ideas such as 'readiness' to learn or acquire a given skill are of obvious relevance.

Differences of this kind, albeit rather exaggerated in order to make my point, have been classified in terms of innate/acquired or instinctive/ learned behaviours. Walking would be towards the innate end of the dimension and writing towards the learned. Whatever position is adopted the essential concern is with understanding the origin of behaviours and the nature of behavioural change. Psychologists have tended to see behavioural development in terms of opposing pairs of explanations. Maturation has often been linked with physical growth, behavioural change being a consequence of structural change, and sharply contrasted with learning.

Definitions of learning usually explicitly exclude maturation, for example, Kimble (1967). Notions such as innate, learned, and maturation are readily swept up into the language of genetical versus environmental causes and then quite quickly into tangled confusion. Although it has been frequently asserted that the nature/nurture dichotomy is now a dead issue it clings to life and influence with remarkable tenacity.

A central concern in genetics is the relationship between phenotypic characteristics and genotypes, and it is here that confusion begins, partly from the loose way in which language is used. The gene is perceived as the bringer of order and as such is endowed with the power of controlling, regulating, dictating, etc. The genome is seen as providing the plan or blueprint and the environment the materials with which the plan is actualised. Although this constructional analogy has the advantage of emphasising the essential contribution of both genes and environments it is nevertheless misleading. The idea of genetically controlled differences is not at all the same thing as genetically controlled characters. Characters can be affected by genetic differences and by environmental differences but they are created by gene-environment coaction. Genotypes and phenotypes covary but so also do environments and phenotypes.

When we speak of an abnormality being genetically determined what this means is that the genotype and phenotype covary while the environment remains in the normal (that is typical for the species) range. Broadly the phenotypic invariance, observed in the appearance of sequences of behavioural development is generally attributed to genetic information or genetic control. Similarly if we observe a normal phenotype under abnormal environmental circumstances then this is also construed as evidence of genetic control. Again it is invariance in the phenotype and not variance which provides the basis for such a conclusion. The implicit logic is that since environmental variation did not lead to a difference then genes must be responsible for keeping ontogenesis on the right track.

If the process of maturation is not genetically controlled, in the sense of being predetermined by the read-out of some literal code, then what is this apparently fundamental process? What we are seeking to explain and understand is the broad similarity in the course of developmental change shown by members of the same species. To be sure there are individual differences in the pattern whereby say walking develops but the similarities across cultures, ethnic groups and so forth are evident. There are thus species typical patterns of development such as those described by Shirley, (1931), McGraw (1945), Gesell (1954) and Bayley (1970).

The term *species typical* is a description (Oyama, 1982) not a shorthand for a theory or process. It is based on the presumption of a normal range of genotypes and environments and it refers, without implications about the processes involved, to the *relatively* constant *pattern* of change and outcome. As Oyama points out, this is not at all the same as the genetical concept of heritability which refers to phenotypic variation in populations which is genetic in origin. Species typicality refers not to properties of populations but to qualities of individuals. Seen as species typical patterns of change maturation is a description and not an explanation. By definition such a pattern is quite stable across the normal range of environmental and genetic variation associated with the particular species in question. So in the case of walking, whether a child is strapped to a cradle board or not will have little effect on the appearance of independent locomotion. Environmental differences of this kind have no large general effects on either the end point or the pattern of development.

The idea of species typicality is free from polarities of the 'innate' or 'learned' kind but it does encompass the coherence and broad predictability of normal development. Development is not encoded in the sense of being preformed but it is guided by qualities of the genotype (which are conventionally seen as internal factors) and the surround (external factors). The unusual, the aberrant and the pathological are thus no less an orderly function of the genome than are the common range of outcomes.

CONCEPTIONS OF DEVELOPMENT

If maturation is a description of characteristic behaviour patterns and forms of development exhibited by a species then we still have to search for the general processes or mechanisms which underlie these changes. In embryology there are basically two alternative formulations of development; the preformationist and the epigenetic. The preformationist idea assumes a gradual conversion of latent to manifest differences as development proceeds. The end states and the routes by which these end states are attained are specified in the genome. The notion plainly has links with behavioural concepts such as instinct, or perhaps more fashionably behaviour said to be 'genetically programmed'. The alternative to the preformationist position is the epigenetic. This assumes that a system starts from a relatively chaotic, lowly organised condition. Those features of the organism which appear later are not pre-existing in the genome but are gradually expressed by developmental processes. To understand outcomes it is necessary to understand processes; the outcome is not preordained but depends upon transactions between different states of organisation and environments as development proceeds.

The epigenesis of behaviour can be broadly divided into two classes, predetermined epigenesis and probabilistic epigenesis (Gottlieb, 1983). In the case of predetermined epigenesis the development of behaviour is explained entirely in terms of processes such as the growth, migration and connection of neurones. Fundamentally the idea is that the nervous system matures in some encapsulated fashion so that a sufficiently comprehensive account of this provides an explanation for the emergence of a given behaviour. Function may of course be necessary to maintain systems and behaviours intact. In the case of probabalistic epigenesis use and experience not only facilitate neural and behavioural development they may also exert an inductive function. The key assumption is that in the case of predetermined epigenesis there exists a one-way relationship between structure and function, structure gives rise to and determines function. In contrast probabalistic epigenesis permits a two-way exchange, not only does structure affect function but function can influence and change structure (Gottlieb, 1976).

THE ROLE OF EXPERIENCE

There appear to be three ways in which experience can contribute to species-typical behaviour (Gottlieb, 1983). The simplest effect of experience on the development of the nervous system or behaviour is where it serves to maintain an already developed state. The best known examples are related to the atrophy of neural tissue in sensory systems that are deprived of stimulation. For example the investigations of Chow, Riesen and Newell (1957) who reared infant chimpanzees in darkness and observed degeneration of the retinal ganglion cells. A good deal of the behaviour and neural hardware which has been assumed innate (in that it seems to make its appearance and be perfected without experience) may be dependent on experience for its functional maintenance.

The second way in which experience exerts an effect is on temporal aspects of development. More precisely experience serves to facilitate or accelerate the attaining of certain states or endpoints. It is important to appreciate that the behaviour in question will eventually make its appearance without this specific facilitative effect of experience. An example of facilitation is provided by the observations of Zelazo, Zelazo and Kolb (1972) on primary walking in young infants. They reported that prolonged practice in the reflexive stepping of newborns from birth to 2 months accelerated the appearance of independent walking towards the end of the first year.

The third way in which experience can effect development is by induction. In this case the absence or presence of a particular stimulus or experience determines whether a given species typical neural feature or behaviour will manifest itself later in development. Imprinting in precocial birds is perhaps the most widely known phenomenon which appears to reflect the inductive function of experience. Here an early experience brings about a normal later state of affairs, in this case a social attachment (Bateson, 1978, 1979).

GENERAL PRINCIPLES AND MODELS OF DEVELOPMENT

The descriptive principles of development tend to be the same irrespective of whether we are considering the development of an organ, such as the liver or the brain, or a whole organism, such as a rat or a child. Developing systems differentiate that is to say they progress from relatively simple homogeneous states to relatively more complex heterogeneous states. Generally speaking as an organism's development proceeds its behaviour becomes more differentiated, that is to say its behavioural repertoire increases. The infant's capacity for more finely differentiated movements increases as does his cognitive competence and range of social behaviour in the manner outlined by Gesell and others (see, Gesell & Amatruda, 1965; McCarthy, 1966; Bayley, 1970; Hartup, 1983). Later behavioural and neural differentiation builds on earlier changes so that integrated hierarchies form. The sequence in which behavioural changes follow each other in any species is remarkably constant; there plainly is a species typical pattern as for example in Piaget's descriptions of the stages of cognitive development in children (see Piaget, 1970). The existence of a pattern or the description of stages however carries no implications about developmental processes.

Concepts such as instinct and maturation invoked as causal explanations of behaviour are unsatisfactory and indeed often seriously misleading. Development refers to a process of change a regulated, controlled process of change in the form of organisation of a system. Such change is influenced by structures and events outside the organism as well as by internal regulative processes. In effect the external structures and events (the environment) and the internal regulative processes (genetic programmes) are welded together into a common process. The emergence of phenotypes should not be thought of as stemming from interactions between genes and environments, or the organism and its experience, because this implies a separateness which is misleading. Conjointly they form a unity which creates an organism's structure and behaviour, these are in fact emergent properties. Modifications of the genotype or the environment produce a different unity which may or may not lead to changes in phenotypes. The sources of developmental change are in fact transactions between organised systems and environments.

THE EPIGENETIC LANDSCAPE

A way of conceptualising development is offered by Waddington's (1957) epigenetic landscape. This is not an explanation of development but a model, that is a metaphor, in Braithwaite's (1953) terms an example of 'as-if' thinking. The epigenetic landscape illustrated in Figure 1 is a representation in three dimensions of the properties of a system which involves many dimensions. Waddington employed the metaphor; to discuss general properties of embryogenesis, I think it is relevant also to behavioural development.

If a ball is placed towards the rear of a sloping surface such as that illustrated in Figure 2 it will roll forward until it reaches some final end state at the bottom, front edge, of the landscape. Such end states might represent say the eye or the spinal cord while differential initial conditions might be represented by the bias on the ball as it runs over the surface. The metaphor of the ball (which represents the developing phenotype) moving

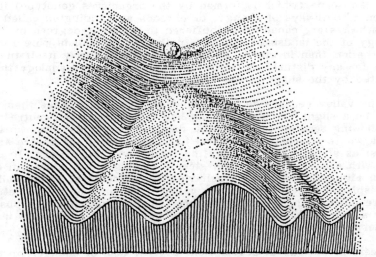

Fig. 1. A portion of an epigenetic landscape. From Waddington (1957).

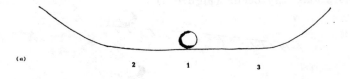

(a)

2 1 3

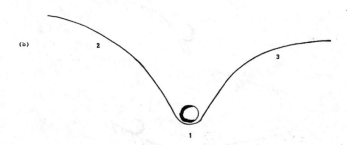

(b)

2 3

1

Fig. 2. Cross-section of two chreods or developmental pathways. In (a) alternative positions, 2 and 3 on either side of ball are just as stable as position 1. The chreod is weakly canalised. In (b) positions 2 and 3 are much less stable than position 1 which is strongly canalised.

over the landscape (which is formed by the organism's genotype) illustrates the notion of pathways of change, or chreods as Waddington called them. These pathways are canalised or buffered to different degrees by the morphology of the landscape. In some pathways the ball is more resistent to perturbation than in others so that within the pathway itself there is a tendency for any disturbance to be compensated. In the analogy this is represented by the shape of the valley, Figure 2.

If the valley has a wide bottom and gently sloping sides then there will only be a slight tendency for the ball to return to the centre of the valley following some disturbance and displacement. This is shown in Figure 2a where alternative positions to either side of the centre are in effect just as stable. The self-righting tendency is very weak. In contrast a valley with a narrow bottom and steeply sloping sides, shown in cross-section in Figure 2b has strong self-righting tendencies. If the ball by some bias is displaced up the side of the valley it will in due course return to the centre position in the valley bottom. Major disturbance may push the ball over a watershed into another valley but so long as it stays in this valley the pathway which it follows is tightly specified.

At certain periods in development a great deal of change appears to take place rapidly whereas in other periods the rate of change seems to be much less. This too can be represented in the analogy by the slope of the landscape. The steeper the slope the more rapidly will the ball travel down the pathway. Changes in the profile of the chreod indicate how accelerations and decelerations may occur (Figure 3).

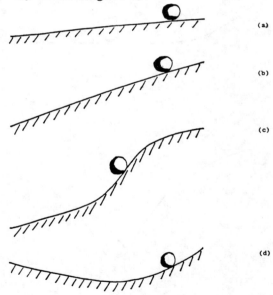

Fig. 3. Various chreodic profiles which give different rates of developmental change, (a) a gentle slope, slow rate of change (b) steeper slope, quicker rate of change (c) feature with sudden acceleration (d) feature leading to deceleration.

Development is a controlled process and the evident equilibrium is dynamic
in nature. There is a stability about changing systems but it is a dynamic
stability. This equilibrium Waddington called homeorhesis, which comes from
the Greek and means to flow. The adult condition, at least for certain
phenotypes, is one of a relatively steady state where development continues
but where the rate of change is slower.

An obviously important question is how the landscape is formed and
how it changes during the life history of the organism. Figure 4 is
Waddington's attempt to express this visually.

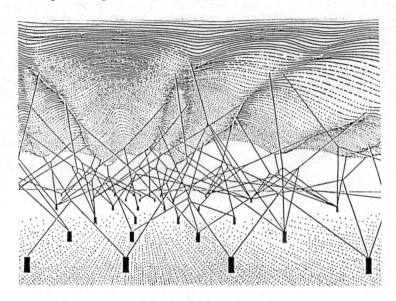

Fig. 4. System of interactions underpinning the epigenetic
landscape. The pegs represent genes, and the guy
ropes between the genes and the plastic surface
represent the products of the genes. From Waddington
(1957).

The diagram shows the underside of the landscape. Imagine it as a flexible
sheet of some plastic material such as polythene, which is held down in a
particular way by ropes attached to pegs. The pegs represent genes and
the tension on the guy ropes represents the chemical products of the genes.
As the diagram shows, the course and slope of a particular valley is
affected by the contribution of many genes. In this representation a change
on any single guy rope is unlikely to have a major catastrophic effect on a
pathway because of the inter-relationship of many genes. The epigenetic
landscape is formed by the action of an organism's genome, different genes
in different locations will, so to speak, affect the shape of the landscape.
However, it is important to appreciate that this does not result in any
fixed static form. The landscape itself is dependent not only on the genome
but also on the environments in which the genes are located, changes in
the micro-environment may result in changes in gene action which in turn

lead to a reformation of the landscape. A reformation of the landscape means that new chreods are formed.

Each cell in an embryo contains an identical set of genes yet cells follow different developmental courses as tissues and organs are different-iated and integrated. Depending on the chemical environment of the cell, which is in turn influenced by the presence and nature of other cells, different processes are turned on and off. These regulating processes are not fully understood but they are certainly complex. An example of a control system is provided by the operon model of Jacob and Monod (1961). This was devised to account for certain cellular processes in prokaryotes (such as bacteria). In higher organisms the process of control and trans-action may be different (Britten & Davidson, 1969) but this model serves my purpose of illustrating gene control circuits and the role of the environment.

The system is made up of a regulator gene, an operator gene and a number of structural genes; the relationship between these is shown in Figure 5.

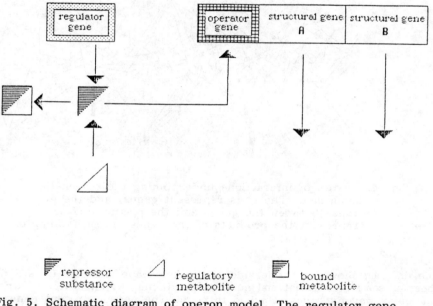

| repressor substance | regulatory metabolite | bound metabolite |

Fig. 5. Schematic diagram of operon model. The regulator gene produces a repressor substance which binds preferentially with regulatory metabolite. In the absence of the regulatory metabolite the repressor binds with the operator gene and inhibits its activity. The operator gene activates the structural genes which code for polypeptides. When the operator gene is inactive the structural genes are also inactive.

Structural genes are responsible for specifying polypeptides. The regulator genes produce substances called repressors that bind chemically, with certain metabolic products or, if these are not available, with an operator gene. Operator genes are located close to the structural genes and together these form the operon. The operator is the critical starting point for transcription of RNA from the DNA of the structural genes. If the operator is activated then the structural genes are active, if the operator is inhibited then the structural genes are switched off. If the appropriate regulatory metabolite becomes available either from exogenous sources or by the function of another operon the repressor will bind preferentially to this and so permit the synthesis of the enzymes of the operon to proceed. The regulatory metabolite serves to turn the operon on and its absence turns it off. Interactions among operons can provide mechanisms for relatively permanent changes in gene functioning and the inter-relationship of quite simple control circuits enables complex processes to be controlled.

Turning again to the model of the epigenetic landscape it is possible to show how gene control circuits, the functioning of which is linked to the micro-environment of the genes, can by their action change the form of the landscape. Figure 6 shows a small portion of a landscape and the buffered pathway which it specifies. Changes in the micro-environment (action of repressors) affect gene activity and gene products, these effects are represented in the landscape by releasing the tension on some of the guy ropes which results in a new chreod being created as shown in Figure 7. In this metaphor it is now possible to see how genes and environments together, but not separately, create developmental pathways and hence phenotypes. Micro-environments and macro-environments of course map in many and changing ways. At some times in some locations crucial events will take place, at other times these same events may have no consequences, or they may have different consequences for the organism.

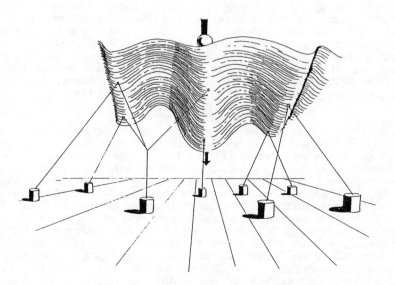

Fig. 6. Underside of small section of epigenetic landscape with
central chreod indicated by arrow.

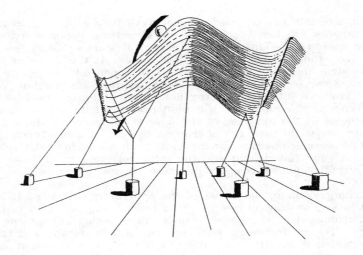

Fig. 7. Same section of landscape but with tension on central
guy rope (variation in gene product) relaxed which
creates new chreod indicated by arrow.

The epigenetic landscape also provides a means of illustrating another
general property of development which is that a given endpoint can be
attained by different routes. Using another geographical metaphor we can
see this plainly enough. A road map of Northern Europe will show that
there are many road connections between most cities, for example Maastricht
and Aachen. There are some principal routes, motorways and trunk roads,
and numerous secondary roads and lanes by which it is possible, should
one so wish, to travel between cities. The most efficient, by which I mean
shortest and fastest, route is likely to involve a motorway or main highway
and down this the bulk of the traffic will normally flow. However many
alternative pathways are available, the route differs but the end point does
not.

Robson (1970) described the course of locomotor development in a
group of children who did not follow the normal, that is more usual pattern
of crawling, described by McGraw (1945). These children, whose gross
motor performance (measured against a population matched for age, sex and
socio-economic status) was delayed followed a pattern of 'shuffling', described
by Peiper (1963). The children were characterised clinically as having a
mild to moderate hypotonia and although their motor behaviour during the
first year was judged 'abnormal' they all walked and on follow-up their gait
measurements were normal. Robson also reported some evidence that this
pattern of development occurred within families which suggests that the
difference may well be due to genetic differences. Independent walking in
these children was achieved by a different route to that followed by the
majority of infants. This example of equifinality (different routes to the
same end state) can be represented in an epigenetic landscape as in Figure
8. Here two routes are shown whereby the ball can travel down the landscape to the front edge. One route is shorter and more direct, and the
topography of that route is different from the other which is considerably

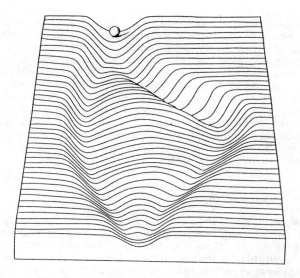

Fig. 8. Epigenetic landscape with two alternate pathways to
same endpoint, illustrates principle of equifinality.

longer. If the ball takes the shorter route it eventually arrives at the
same endpoint. The shorter route here represents the more common pattern
of development of independent walking as described by McGraw (1945) while
the longer route represents the 'delayed' pattern described by Robson.

Waddington (1973) suggested that there are two kinds of chreods,
what he called generative and assimilative, which come into existence in
contrasting ways. Generative chreods make their first appearance as
definite coherent statements which are then elaborated into a series of
details. If a small piece of tissue is transplanted from the leg limb bud of
a chick embryo onto the wing limb bud it elaborates its basic theme - a
toe grows on the tip of the wing. A basic fundamental theme is first stated
and the details appear later. In a musical analogy Waddington likens this
to a piece which begins with a melodic theme which is then elaborated into
a concerto or fugue. In the case of an assimilative chreod a number of
isolated and apparently unrelated bits and pieces are brought together and
coordinated into an organised whole. Waddington illustrates this with
another example from experimental embryology involving two species of
newts and the formation of the eye. If the lens is transplanted from the
embryo of a larger and faster growing species into the eye cup of another
smaller species an adaptation takes place. The large, faster growing lens
begins to grow more slowly (an effect of the eye cup) and the eye cup
begins to grow more rapidly (an effect of the lens). The final result is an
eye with a fairly normal relationship between lens and eye cup. The musical
analogy to go with this is traditional jazz where each player begins independently of the others but they eventually gell and the group begins to
work together in harmony.

Waddington offers an interesting speculation in terms of the development
of two kinds of skilled motor action. Babies he points out do not have to be
specifically taught much about walking. Before they can support their own

18

weight they make coordinated movements which foreshadow walking (Thelen & Fisher, 1983). When further growth of muscles, skeleton, etc. has proceeded far enough they need minimal help to start walking, earlier disorganised movements are assimilated and the walking pattern appears almost fully fledged (Sutherland et al, 1980). From walking the pattern begins to act in a generative manner, the same basic components are employed in running, skipping and so on. This he contrasts with swimming where unlike fish he argues man does not have much of an inbuilt system of coordinations (though see McGraw, 1939). In the case of swimming a much more extensive task of assimilating components of coordinated activity is necessary, the movements of arms, legs and of course breathing must all be brought together into a unified scheme of action.

CONCLUSIONS

I must stress that the scheme I have described is a metaphor, it tells us nothing about the mechanisms or processes involved, rather it is a way of thinking about development and maturation. Developmental processes are probabalistic, some highly probable, others less so. Because order is so evident in development we often tend to think of it as a relatively closed system but, as Waddington's scheme shows, this is a mistake. There are two ways of ensuring an invariant outcome. The first is by what some would label as strict genetic control. In this case the outcome is relatively insensitive to the conditions under which it occurs; in terms of the metaphor we are dealing with a chreod strongly canalised against perturbations. The other means of ensuring an invariant outcome is by a system sensitive only to environmental factors which are all invariant in the animal's ecological niche.

The two methods are not unconnected though the first relates primarily to the range of genotypes in the species, the second to the environments occupied by the species, and of course these change during development, often dramatically as between uterine and extra-uterine life. It is important to realise that both genotypes and environments are inherited. In man selection has produced a very powerful means for modifying and extending phenotypes on the basis of learning and experience, namely culture. The distinction between learning and development which traditionally psychologists have sought to make is neither very clear nor very helpful. In fact I would go further and deny that such a distinction makes sense. Maturation as species specific patterns of behaviour has to encompass not only internal factors but also the surround, it is intimately connected with external factors.

When we consider skilled motor actions there appears to be something similar to the gene/environment coaction that I have discussed. In Bernstein's (1967; see also Whiting, 1984) formulation, a task (or a motor problem) results from the interaction of the system with its external surround. The exact circumstances associated with a task (be it standing, walking, throwing, or manipulating a tool) vary and so the exact nature of a solution must vary. Changes in relevant characteristics of the environment, or the field of external forces, or the organisation of the biological system require a new organisation of movement to achieve the required action. There is a similarity between the rules and solutions on the one hand and the motor problems on the other; our observations on the emergence of skilled action patterns, the descriptions of behaviour change, are a reflection of these congruences. As

Higgins (1985) puts it, "Movement patterns are ongoing adaptive re-presentations of system-surround encounters...The movement form that emerges is the one most likely to exist given the task, the system and the surround - it is an integrated expression of the unity of the organism and environment".

References

Barton, S., Birns, B., Ronch, J. (1971). Individual differences in the visual pursuit behaviour of neonates. *Child Development, 42,* 313-319.

Bateson, P.P.G. (1978). Early experience and sexual preferences. In J.B. Hutchison (Ed.), *Biological determinants of sexual behaviour.* Chichester: Wiley.

Bateson, P.P.G. (1979). How do sensitive periods arise and what are they for? *Animal Behaviour, 27,* 470-486.

Bayley, N. (1970). Development of mental abilities. In P.H. Mussen (Ed.), *Carmichael's manual of child psychology, Vol. 1.* New York: Wiley.

Bernstein, N.A. (1967). *The coordination and regulation of movements.* Oxford: Pergamon Press.

Braithwaite, R.B. (1953). *Scientific explanation.* Cambridge: Cambridge University Press.

Britten, R.J., Davidson, E.H. (1969). Gene regulation for higher cells: a theory. *Science, 165,* 349-357.

Chow, K.L., Riesen, A.H., Newell, F.W. (1957). Degeneration of retinal ganglion cells in infant chimpanzees reared in darkness. *Journal of Comparative Neurology, 107,* 27-42.

Coghill, G.E. (1929). *Anatomy and the problem of behaviour.* Cambridge: Cambridge University Press.

Connolly, K.J. (1970). Skill development: Problems and plans. In K.J. Connolly (Ed.), *Mechanisms of motor skill development.* London: Academic Press.

Frankenberg, W.K., Dodds, J.B. (1967). The Denver developmental screening test. *Journal of Pediatrics, 71,* 181-191.

Gesell, A. (1954). The ontogenesis of infant behaviour. In L. Carmichael (Ed.), *Manual of child psychology* (2nd Ed.). New York: Wiley.

Gesell, A., Thompson, H. (1929). Learning and growth in identical infant twins: An experimental study by the method of co-twin control. *Genetic Psychology Monographs, 6,* 1-124.

Gesell, A., Amatruda, C.S. (1965). *Developmental diagnosis* (2nd Ed.). New York: Harper & Row.

Gottlieb, G. (1976). Conceptions of prenatal development: behavioural embryology. *Psychological Review, 83,* 215-234.

Gottlieb, G. (1983). The psychobiological approach to developmental issues. In P.H. Mussen (Ed.), *Handbook of child psychology, Vol. 2.* New York: Wiley.

Hartup, W. (1983). Peer relations. In P.H. Mussen (Ed.), *Handbook of child psychology, Vol. 4.* New York: Wiley.

Higgins, S. (1985). Movement as an emergent form: Its structural limits. *Human Movement Science, 4,* 119-148.

Jacob, F., Monod, J. (1961). On the regulation of gene activity. *Cold Spring Harbor Symposia on Quantitative Biology, 26,* 193-209.

Kaye, H. (1967). Infant sucking behavior and its modification. In L.P. Lipsett and C.C. Spiker (Eds.), *Advances in child development and behavior, Vol. 3.* New York: Academic Press.

Kelso, J.A.S., Clark, J.E. (1982) (Eds.), *The development of movement control and co-ordination.* Chichester: Wiley.

Kimble, G.A. (1967). *Foundations of learning and conditioning.* New York: Appleton.

McCance, R.A. (1962). Food, growth and time. *Lancet ii,* 671-675.

McCarthy, D. (1966). Language development in children. In L. Carmichael (Ed.), *Manual of child psychology* (2nd Ed.). New York: Wiley.

McGraw, M. (1939). Swimming behavior of the human infant. *Journal of Pediatrics, 15,* 485-490.

McGraw, M.B. (1945). *The neuromuscular maturation of the human infant.* New York: Columbia University Press.

Oppenheim, R.W. (1981). Ontogenetic adaptations and retrogressive processes in the development of the nervous system and behaviour: a neuroembryological perspective. In K.J. Connolly and H.F.R. Prechtl (Eds.), *Maturation and development: Biological and psychological perspectives.* London: SIMP, Heinemann.

Oppenheim, R.W. (1984). Ontogenetic adaptations in neural development; toward a more 'ecological' developmental psychobiology. In H.F.R. Prechtl (Ed.), *Continuity of neural functions from prenatal to postnatal life.* London: SIMP, Blackwell.

Oyama, S. (1982). A reformulation of the idea of maturation. In P.P.G. Bateson and P.H. Klopfer (Eds.), *Perspectives in Ethology 5.* New York: Plenum Press.

Peiper, A. (1963). *Cerebral function in infancy and childhood.* New York: Consultants Bureau.

Piaget, J. (1970). Piaget's theory. In P.H. Mussen (Ed.), *Carmichael's manual of child psychology, Vol. 1.* (3rd Ed.). New York: Wiley.

Prader, A., Tanner, J.M., von Harnack, G.A. (1953). Catch-up growth following illness or starvation. *Journal of Pediatrics, 62,* 646-659.

Robson, P. (1970). Shuffling, hitching, scooting and sliding; some observations on 30 otherwise normal children. *Developmental Medicine and Child Neurology, 12,* 608-617.

Shirley, M.M. (1931). *The first two years. Vol. 1. Postural and locomotor development.* Minneapolis: University Minnesota Press.

Sutherland, D.H., Olshen, R., Cooper, L., Woo, S.L.Y. (1980). Development of mature gait. *Journal of Bone and Joint Surgery, 62A,* 336-353.

Tanner, J.M. (1963). The regulation of human growth. *Child Development, 34,* 817-847.

Tanner, J.M. (1970). Physical growth. In P.H. Mussen (Ed.), *Carmichael's manual of child psychology, Vol. 1.* (3rd Ed.). New York: Wiley.

Thelen, E., Fisher, D.M. (1983). The organisation of spontaneous leg movements in newborn infants. *Journal of Motor Behavior, 15,* 353-382.

Waddington, C.H. (1957). *The strategy of the genes.* London: George Allen & Unwin.

Waddington, C.H. (1973). The development of mind. In A.J.P. Kenny, H.C. Longuet-Higgins, J.R. Lucas and C.H. Waddington (Eds.), *The development of mind.* Edinburgh: Edinburgh University Press.

Whiting, H.T.A. (Ed.) (1984). *Human motor actions: Bernstein reassessed.* Amsterdam: North Holland Publishing Co.

Whiting, M. (1939). Swimming of behavior of the human infant. *Journal of Pediatrics, 15,* 485-490.

Zelazo, P., Zelazo, N. & Kolb, S. (1972). "Walking" in the Newborn. *Science, 177,* 1058-1059.

SOME PROBLEMS IN EXPLAINING THE ORIGINS OF MOVEMENT CONTROL

G. Butterworth

1. INTRODUCTION

Although enormous progress has been made in studying sensory perception in the human infant, (see Butterworth, 1981; Bower, 1982; Spelke, 1983) little thought has been given to the implications of such research for explaining the origins of motor development. Yet if we are agreed on the perceptual sophistication of the neonate this may have consequences for our theories of motor development too. Here I propose to discuss recent research on the proprioceptive control of movement in early infancy in the context of two major examples: the control of posture through vision and the kinaesthetic control of directed arm movements in the neonate.

It has been traditional to consider sensory and motor processes as distinct systems that only become related in development by long apprenticeship. It is only in recent years that the inherent relationships within and between sensory and motor processes have been studied in babies. On the sensory side a great deal of progress has been made in describing the intersensory coordinations that exist between e.g. seeing and hearing, or between vision and touch from the neonatal period (Butterworth, 1981; Spelke, 1983). Yet on the motor side we are still left with an image of the newborn as simply an immature, reflexive organism whose actions are generally characterised as involuntary responses to gross aspects of physical stimulation.

Such assumptions about action control in early infancy are more limited than the evidence warrants. More than a century ago Preyer (1888)* suggested a fourfold classification of activity in early infancy. The activities of babies were thought to be either impulsive, reflexive, instinctive or ideational. This classification may be useful in considering the behavioural repertoire of the neonate in the discussion that follows and it may be worthwhile considering his classification in greater detail:

Impulsive movements are spontaneous, purposeless, uncoordinated and arise from an overflow of energy. They are caused he said:

> ...without previous peripheral excitement, exclusively
> by the nutritive and other organic processes that go
> on in the motor centres of the lowest rank.

---

* I am indebted to John Morss for historical information on motor behaviour in the neonate.

Of the *reflexive movements* Preyer lists, such as crying or sneezing, most are well coordinated responses to strong physical stimulation and characteristically, the reflex response promptly follows the sensory stimulus that elicits it. The importance of the reflexes to his account is that their inhibition in development precedes the intentional control of action. His first evidence for intentional control of action comes with the acquisition of control over the upright head posture, an example to be elaborated further on in this chapter.

The third category comprises the *instincts* and these are the least numerous. All instinctive movements must be preceded by a disposition to respond. A sensation and an emotion must precede the response and supply the motor impulse. Among the instinctive movements he describes are sucking and the manual grasping of objects. Another of Preyer's examples, also to be pursued in this chapter, concerns hand- mouth coordination in the first few months of life.

Preyer's final category consists of the *ideational* movements. He says that to determine as exactly as possible the date of the first imitative acts is of especial interest in establishing the origins of motor control through "higher" mental processes because:

> ...even the most insignificant imitative movement
> furnishes a sure proof of activity of the cerebrum
> (p. 282).

In order to imitate one must first perceive through the senses, secondly have an idea of what has been perceived, third execute a movement corresponding to this "idea"*. Preyer gives examples of imitation of lip pursing and tongue protrusion in the child in the third and fourth months of life which then "disappear" until the ninth month before they can be elicited. This category of movements is particularly interesting since he argues that however often imitation may appear to be involuntary, when it was executed for the first time it must have been executed with intention i.e. voluntarily. When the child imitates, it already has a will. This assertion is particularly interesting in the light of recent discoveries by Maratos (1972), Meltzoff (1981) and Vinter (1984) that suggest that imitation of lip pursing, tongue protrusion and certain manual gestures may be innate.

As a result of what follows we may wish to consider whether Preyer's fourfold categorisation of the movement patterns of the young baby may help us better to understand the variety of control processes that may co-exist even in the behaviours of the neonate. This may widen our horizons on the variety of psychological mechanisms that may be implicated in movement control from the earliest age.

---
*
Preyer's use of the term "idea" here is not intended to imply that young infants can think if they can imitate. It is meant to differentiate control of activity through cognitive processes that involve the cerebral cortex. Contemporary use of Preyer's terminology need not require acceptance of his model of "lower" and "higher" centres in the nervous system. However the phenomenon of neonatal imitation does suggests that abstract perceptual mechanisms are available.

2.   VISUAL CONTROL OF POSTURE IN THE PRE-LOCOMOTOR INFANT

The first step is to consider the extent to which patterns of activity may be governed by complex properties of sensory stimulation in the young infant. One example is the defensive response of newborn babies to a looming stimulus that has been produced by accelerated expansion of a delimited portion of the visual field, as if on a collision course with the baby (Bower, Broughton & Moore, 1970a; Ball & Tronick, 1971; Yonas et al, 1984). That is, the baby seems to defend its own body against the approaching object, a phenomenon that may indicate that the infant innately differentiates between self and object and that a particular visual event may give rise to fear and defensive behaviour at birth. Research on looming therefore provides one example of how structured sensory stimulation may enter into the control of action in early infancy. In Preyer's scheme, we would have to consider this an instinctive response since the sensory stimulation elicts both a disposition to respond (the emotion of fear) and an appropriate, goal directed defensive response.

Further evidence comes from studies of visual proprioceptive control of posture in infancy. Gibson (1966) coined the term "visual proprioception" to draw attention to the role of vision in providing information for self movement through perspective transformations of the retinal image that arise when an observer is specified by total motion of a structured visual array, outward from a stationary central point. Under conditions of the natural ecology (where the surroundings may be considered stable) such a flow pattern can only arise when the observer is moving; hence it is sufficient to specify the distinction between "self" and "the world". Gibson argued that the optic flow patterns is a structured form of sensory information. The developing child need only attend to the available information; there is no necessity to construct the invariants, or to learn what the visual flow pattern specifies as a result of extensive experience of locomotion. His theory suggests that posture and locomotion are controlled through visual proprioception and that this control system may be innate. Until the early 1970's there was little empirical information on the origins of visual proprioception. It seemed possible that optic flow patterns might equally become informative through the infant's developing mobility (and hence be learned) as to be inherently informative, as Gibson maintained.

Lee and Aronson (1974) were the first to show that infants use visual information to monitor their posture. Babies who had recently learned to stand were tested standing on a rigid floor, within a moveable room comprising three walls and a ceiling. The infants faced the interior end wall and the whole structure, except the floor, was moved so that the end wall slowly approached or receded. Babies compensated for a non-existent loss of balance signalled by the optic flow pattern (generated by the movement of the surroundings) and consequently fell in the direction appropriate to the plane of instability specified by the misleading visual flow pattern. If the end wall moved away from the baby, the infant fell forward and if the wall moved toward the baby, the infant fell over backward.

Subsequent studies demonstrated that vision does not acquire its proprioceptive function as a result of motor development. Butterworth and Hicks (1977) found that infants too young to walk would nevertheless compensate for visually specified instability when seated in the moving room. Butterworth and Cicchetti (1978) showed that length of experience of the sitting or standing posture in babies was negatively correlated with susceptibility to misleading visual feedback. The maximum disruption by discrepant visual feedback occurred during the period of three months after each posture was acquired and declined thereafter. The research has been extended to pre-locomotor infants by Pope (1984) who showed that even before babies can crawl they are responsive to discrepant visual feedback. He investigated the role of visual proprioception in the maintenance of a stable head posture in infants as young as two months, when supported in an infant chair. Babies too young to be able to sit without support and who are certainly not capable of independent locomotion nevertheless will make directionally appropriate compensatory movements of the head under con-ditions of discrepant visual feedback. In fact, Pope (1984) showed that the onset of independent locomotion by crawling, at about 6 months, actually coincides with a relative decline in susceptibility to the effects of misleading visual feedback in the moving room.

The pattern of high susceptibility to the optic flow pattern with the acquisition of head control, and later the seated posture is repeated when the child starts to walk. With the onset of bipedal locomotion, the infant once again becomes very unstable in the face of misleading visual feedback as control over the unfamiliar standing posture is acquired. After about three months of extreme instability, there is a decline in the effects of moving the room as a degree of autonomous control is gained. Pope also showed that information arriving in the periphery of vision is particularly implicated in postural control since movement of just the central portion of the visual field does not generate instability in babies who have recently learned to stand (Pope, 1984).

Thus, far from independent locomotion giving rise to meaningful optic flow patterns, the infant appears to make use of the optic flow pattern as a means of gaining control over the body in its succession of postures. The obvious moving room experiment that still needs to be published is with neonates but there is a good reason to suppose that the infant's sensitivity to the optic flow pattern will prove to be innate*.

What are the implications for the origins of motor control processes? Studies of the kind discussed above go to the heart of the matter, since they force us to consider the role of sensory perception in the genesis of control. The obvious implication is that the optic flow pattern is inherently informative about movements of the infant in relation to the environment. From the earliest age the infant seems to make use of the optic flow pattern to maintain the head under a stable posture. It is as if the optic flow is a form of pre-structured feedback, informing the perceiver about the relation between his or her own motion and the environment. On the other hand, it is clear that the very young infant has no objective, reflective self knowledge. In the "moving room" studies, even though the infant is

---

* Francois Jouen (University of Paris, personal communication) has evidence for visual-vestibular interactions among one months infants which may support the argument that visual-proprioceptive control of posture is an innate, intrinsic coordination. Scania de Schonen (University of Marseilles, personal communication) reports that it is possible to elicit the stepping reflex in a newborn baby placed in a "moving room".

objectively stable, postural compensations are made to the misleading visual feedback. It is not until infants are about 15 months of age that they have developed sufficient reflective self awareness to turn to see "who has made the room move" (Butterworth & Cicchetti, 1978). Until then the infant behaves as if completely dependent on the information currently available to perception.

What kind of a control mechanism is this? In terms of Preyer's fourfold classification we may wish to describe it as a reflexive process, since it is not until relatively late in development that we observe the acquisition of mechanisms capable, at least in part, of over-ruling the misleading sensory input to which the infant involuntarily responds. However, to do so might be to ignore the fact that under normal conditions, the optic flow pattern would occur only under circumstances where the infant has moved. Since we have suggested that the meaning of the optic flow pattern is not something that is learned, we might wish to argue that it is inherently goal directed. There is something teleological about it, since it serves to maintain a stable posture. The optic flow pattern is not a stimulus that gives rise to a reflex response in the traditional sense. Rather it both provides a motive for corrective behaviour (by informing about loss of postural stability) and is also goal directed in that it specifies when a well controlled posture has been achieved (see also Dewey, 1896). In Preyer's terminology it is an instinctive mechanism whose ultimate purpose, we may conjecture, lies in the control of locomotion.

3.   HAND-MOUTH COORDINATION

I should now like to consider another example of neonatal behaviour. This is the phenomenon of hand-mouth coordination which we have been studying with a view to establishing what kind of control mechanism may be involved*.

In the spontaneous activity of the newborn baby movements of the arms often result in contacts of the hand with the head, face and mouth. Some of these movements result in the hand being placed in the mouth. The question is whether this is accidental, perhaps the result of a series of chained reflexes, or whether the infant may be deliberately attempting to bring the hand to the mouth? Again, a variety of explanations have been put forward for the tendency of the newborn infant to bring the hands constantly around the head. Preyer considered them impulsive, haphazard movements caused by an overflow of nervous forces. Millicent Shinn (1900) also commented on these movements; she called them spontaneous and argued that none showed the least volition. In recent years Kravitz et al (1978) have suggested that hand to mouth movements may be a kind of tactual self exploration. As far as the hand-mouth movement is concerned at least two kinds of reflexive mechanisms might be involved. In the rooting reflex the baby turns the mouth toward tactual stimulation of the cheek and in the Babkin reflex the mouth opens when the palm of the baby's hand is pressed. So it could be that the infant, in the course of random movement of the arms, may self-stimulate the rooting reflex after contacting the cheek, or perhaps by clenching the hands tightly the Babkin reflex may be elicited and the hand may subsequently enter the mouth accidentally. Piaget (1953) also noticed the almost continuous

---

* I am indebted to Brian Hopkins, Chris Henshall, Sharon Johnston and Noraini Abd-Fattah for assistance with this study.

movements of the arms in the first few weeks of life and suggested that these were impulsive movements that serve to exercise the innate grasping reflex. With constant repetition he suggested that these movements may differentiate into the primary circular reactions involved in tactile exploration of the face in the second month of life. None of these authors described the arm movements as goal directed or intentional.

In an attempt to understand the mechanism we filmed the spontaneous motor activity of 17 newborn babies (mean age 79 hours) using a split-screen video system. The infants were placed on their backs and filmed for approximately 5 minutes. The video-recordings were then analysed by two observers acting independently who noted the first episode in which the hand came into the region of the face and nineteen subsequent episodes. For each infant the posture of each hand at the beginning and end of the episode (open, intermediate, closed), of the mouth just before contact, (open, closed), and of the head and body was noted (facing left, right, at the midline).

The episodes fell into four categories: direct movement of hand to mouth (15%), movements stopping short of the face and resulting in no contact (22%), movements going to the mouth after contact with the face (20%) and contacts with the face that did not terminate in the mouth (43%). Statistical analyses revealed that the mouth was significantly more likely to be open throughout the arm movement in the case where the hand goes directly to the mouth than in the three other classes of arm movement. This suggests that the mouth "anticipates" arrival of the hand, even before the arm starts to move. Other analyses revealed that visual guidance of the hand to the mouth may not be necessary for this coordination, since the eyes are equally likely to be closed as open just prior to contact with the mouth. Once the hand touches the mouth it is withdrawn and there is little evidence of sucking the fingers or for "self comforting" behaviours. There was no evidence for self stimulation of the Babkin reflex prior to these episodes, since neither hand is clenched. Finally, the active hand is invariably ipsilateral to the orientation of the head and right or left handed movements to the mouth are equally probable.

The hand can also find the mouth after contact with the perioral region or more distantly removed parts of the face. This category of movement is similarly organised to the direct movement to the mouth, except that the mouth opens wide only after manual contact with the face. There is no evidence of rooting after contact, the head is invariably held still and the hand moves immediately in the direction of the mouth. Again, the majority of movements are ipsilaterally coordinated with the head posture and there is a tendency for right handed movements to predominate. This category of movement does not appear to be reflexive either, it simply seems less "well aimed" than the former.

The majority of movements contact the face without finding the mouth. In this category approximately half the movements are cross lateralised with head posture, i.e. the head is facing in the opposite direction from the active hand. These movements have the hallmarks of unskilled, rather confused actions, as if the components of a successful act are available but are inappropriately sequentially organised.

How are we to characterise this unexpected coordination of hand and mouth? There is clearly an impulsive or spontaneous element in the general pattern of arm movements observed but guidance of the hand to the mouth cannot be considered as reflexively triggered; rather it has all the

29

characteristics of a goal-directed act which only occasionally fulfills its
intended outcome because it is unskilled. The coordination falls in Preyer's
instinctive category since the mouth is clearly the goal of quite a proportion
of the arm movements even though no particular emotional state accompanies
this activity. Alternatively, we may wish to describe the behaviour as an
intentional action pattern, since the fact that the mouth opens before the
arm moves suggests that the mouth actually anticipates the arrival of the
hand rather than simply acting as the terminus for the movement. Certainly,
Bower et al (1970b) felt it appropriate to describe their study of neonatal
visually elicited reaching as a demonstration of intention; reaching with the
hand to the mouth seems an analogous case. Perhaps this dilemma as to
whether the action is goal directed or intentional might be solved by Baldwin's
concept of circular reaction in which the hand-mouth coordination comprises
an innate precursor of a functional unit of behaviour. The interpretation I
favour is that hand-mouth coordination may be an early form of targeted
reaching that might be a precursor of later self-feeding activity. This innate
behaviour pattern may be developmentally related to later behaviours, just as
it has been argued the stepping movements in the newborn may be developmentally embedded in later voluntary walking (Zelaso, 1983). Of course, behaviour
patterns observed in the neonate may also have served some functions in
utero and it has not yet been conclusively demonstrated that there actually
is continuity between earlier and later forms of similar behaviours.

4.   NEONATAL IMITATION

Preyer's fourth category comprises the ideational movements. This is a
particularly interesting category because recent research suggests that
imitation of tongue protrusion, mouth opening, lip pursing and various hand
movements may be innate. The original discovery of neonatal imitation was
extended by Meltzoff and Moore (1977) and this research has recently been
replicated by Vynter (1984) at the University of Geneva. Thus we have independent sources of evidence for neonatal imitation, a motor behaviour that
Preyer felt certain involved sensori-motor coordination and volition. Whether
neonatal imitation is "elicited" by the conditions of sensory stimulation that
apply in imitation tasks and can thus be described as an instinctive, goal-
directed activity or whether it is an intentional behaviour, is a moot point
and so it is difficult to pin down in terms of Preyer's scheme. However, it
is possible to understand the phenomenon in terms of our previous discussion
of proprioception. Mounoud and Vynter (1981) suggest that an innate body
schema may authorise the match between visual input and motor output in
imitation tasks.

Meltzoff (1981) has suggested that the ability to imitate "invisible"
gestures, such as tongue protrusion must require an abstract ability to
relate the properties of visual sensory input to motor output. This ability
is similar, he argues, to that involved in detecting the equivalence of
information across sensory modalities. In a series of converging studies he
showed that infants in the first month of life can relate visually perceived
shapes to the same shapes perceived through oral-tactual exploration. At
some abstract level of description vision and tactual exploration yield
equivalent information for shape. In a similar study Kuhl and Meltzoff (1982)
have shown that infants also perceive the equivalence between certain
characteristics of auditory stimulation and mouth shape in a "lip reading"
task. Infants in the second month of life prefer to look at a videorecording

of a person speaking where the perceived sound is appropriate to the shape of the mouth producing the sound. Again, Meltzoff argues that the infant perceives abstract information in the two displays that is equivalent across modalities of perception.

5.   CONCLUSION

All of these examples can be understood in terms of our earlier discussion of proprioception and kinaesthesis. Phenomena such as these reinforce Gibson's (1964) assertion that proprioception is best understood as a general form of self-sensitivity, regardless of the modality in which information arrives. In our example of hand-mouth coordination the fact that the hand can find the mouth without visual guidance suggests that the coordination is based on kinaesthetic information alone. It may be that an innate body schema underlies the coordination of hand and mouth and enables the infant to bring one into contact with the other. In the case of visual proprioception it is clear that stability of the body posture is to some degree specified in the optic flow pattern, so again a postural schema may be involved in mapping visual information to motor activity. Finally, it has also been suggested that neonatal imitation can be explained if sensory information maps onto a unified body schema in the neonate (Mounoud and Vynter, 1981). The concept of the body schema is a familiar one in psychology but it is nevertheless difficult to define. Bairstow (1986, this volume) captures the essential characteristics admirably. He defines the body schema as a superordinate representation at the interface between sensory and motor processes that both externally and internally specify a posture. This definition unifies the various strands of research discussed above. Perhaps we should now explore the characteristics of the body schema in infancy so that we may be in a position to determine whether in the newborn infant, behaviours may occur that are not merely reflexive or impulsive. Goal directed behaviours or even intentional activities may also be a part of our innate endowment that we have overlooked until now.

31

References

Bairstow, P. (1986). Postural control. In H.T.A. Whiting and M.G. Wade (Eds.), *Motor skill development in children: aspects of coordination and control*. Dordrecht: Martinus Nijhoff.
Ball, W. & Tronick, E. (1971). Infant responses to impending collision, optical and real. *Science, 171*, 818-820.
Bower, T.G.R. (1982). *Development in Infancy*, 2nd. Edition. San Francisco: Freeman.
Bower, T.G.R., Broughton, J. & Moore, M.K. (1970). Infant responses to approaching objects: an indicator of response to distal variables. *Perception and Psychophysics, 9*, 193-6(a).
Bower, T.G.R., Broughton, J. & Moore, M.K. (1970). Demonstration of intention in the reaching behaviour of the neonate. *Nature, 228*, No. 5272(b).
Butterworth, G.E. (1981). The origins of auditory-visual perception and visual proprioception in human infancy. In R.D. Walk and H.L. Pick Jr. (Eds.), *Intersensory perception and sensory integration*. New York: Plenum Press.
Butterworth, G.E. & Cicchetti, D. (1978). Visual calibration of posture in normal and motor retarded Down's syndrome infants. *Perception, 7*, 513-525.
Butterworth, G.E. & Hicks, L. (1977). Visual proprioception and postural stability in infancy: a developmental study. *Perception, 6*, 255-262.
Dewey, J. (1896). The reflex arc concept in psychology. *Psychological Review, 3*, 357-370.
Gibson, J.J. (1966). *The senses considered as perceptual systems*. Boston: Houghton-Mifflin.
Gibson, J.J. (1982). The use of proprioception and the detection of propriospecific information. In E. Reed and R. Jones (Eds.), *Reasons for Realism: Selected essays of James J. Gibson*. New Jersey: Lawrence Erlbaum.
Kravitz, H., Goldenberg, D. & Neyhus, A. (1978). Tactual exploration by normal infants. *Developmental Medicine and Child Neurology, 20*, 720-726.
Kuhl, P. & Meltzoff, A. (1982). The bimodal perception of speech in infancy. *Science, 218*, 1138-1141.
Lee, D. & Aronson, E. (1974). Visual proprioceptive control of standing in human infants. *Perception and Psychophysics, 15*, 529-532.
Meltzoff, A.N. (1981). Imitation, intermodal coordination and representation in early infancy. In G.E. Butterworth (Ed.), *Infancy and Epistemology: An Evaluation of Piaget's Theory*. Brighton: Harvester.
Meltzoff, A.N. & Borton, T.W. (1979). Intermodal matching by human neonates. *Nature, 282*, 403-4.
Meltzoff, A.N. & Moore, M.K. (1977). Imitation of facial and manual gestures by human neonates. *Science, 198*, 75-8.
Mounoud, P. & Vinter, A. (1981). Representation and sensori-motor development. In *Infancy and Epistemology: An Evaluation of Piaget's Theory*. Brighton: Harvester.
Piaget, J. (1953). *The origins of intelligence in the child*. New York: Routledge.
Pope, M.J. (1984). Visual proprioception in infant postural development. Unpublished Ph.D thesis, University of Southampton.
Preyer, W. (1888). *The Senses and the Will*. New York: Appleton.
Shinn, M.W. (1900). *The biography of a baby*. Boston and New York: Houghton-Mifflin.
Spelke, E.S. (1983). Cognition in infancy. Occasional Paper # 23 Center for Cognitive Science, Massachusetts Institute of Technology.

Vynter, A. (1984). Imitation, representation et mouvement dans les premieres mois de la vie. Unpublished Ph.D thesis, University of Geneva.

Yonas, A., Petterson, L. & Lockman, J. (1984). Sensitivity in 3 and 4 week old infants to optical information for collision. *Canadian Journal of Psychology, 33,* 268-276.

Zelaso, P.R. (1983). The development of walking: new findings and old assumptions. *Journal of Motor Behavior, 15,* 99-137.

A KNOWLEDGE-BASED APPROACH TO MOTOR SKILL ACQUISITION

A.E. Wall

In a recent article, my colleagues and I outlined an heuristic approach to motor development which stressed the importance of knowledge about action in the skill acquisition process. In that article, we noted that up until recently most studies of motor development had essentially been cross-sectional studies of children's motor performance with age, sex and a few trials as the major independent variables (Wall, McClements, Bouffard, Findlay & Taylor, 1985). Furthermore, when developmental studies did examine the skill acquisition process the interaction between the knowledge base of the learners and the task-to-be-learned was rarely systematically considered. In presenting our ideas on a knowledge-based approach, we argued that motor development should be viewed from a holistic perspective especially if it was to guide our remedial strategies in adapted physical education. This paper will extend some of the ideas outlined in that paper and attempt to demonstrate the crucial role that the learner's knowledge base plays in the skill acquisition process. The paper is divided into three major sections. The first reviews some of the main ideas in a knowledge-based approach to motor development. The second section deals with some major developmental factors that influence the acquisition of motor skills; while the final section briefly notes some of the major principles underlying a knowledge-based approach to motor skill acquisition.

STRUCTURAL CAPACITY

Knowledge about action can be differentiated into two major categories: structural capacity and acquired knowledge. Structural capacity refers to the anatomical and physiological potential that a person inherits. It includes the skeletal, circulo-respiratory, digestive, endocrine, neuromuscular and sensory systems of the body. Clearly, these highly inter-related systems are intimately involved in the development and control of action. However, as a study of the process of human evolution shows, the human brain is certainly the most important organ in the skill acquisition process (Holloway, 1983).

Recent studies in the neural sciences have shown that physical changes in the brain and neuromuscular system underly the learning of all voluntary actions. The building block for this learning is the neuron. The brain contains approximately 10^{12} neurons; this enormous number of highly inter-connected nerve cells facilitates the storage and control of knowledge in predictable and consistent ways. Furthermore, the structure of the nervous system is such that specific functions are localised within a particular region or group of regions in the brain; and nerve impulses from various sensory surfaces, including the skin, retina, tendons and joints, etc., are transported to precise topological locations within it. A similar topological representation is also responsible for the motor commands that underly voluntary and involuntary actions. It has been shown that even the most simple behaviour requires the involvement of countless nerve cells. Quite often these cells perform very similar functions; in fact, such parallel processing underlies the flexibility and reliability of function which is so characteristic of the brain and neuromuscular system (Kandel & Schwartz, 1985). Most importantly, these structural characteristics of the brain and neuromuscular system uniquely prepare humans for learning and development in all knowledge domains. The ultimate development of this neurological network depends on learning; without sufficient learning experiences the full potential of the human brain will not be reached (Prechtl, 1981).

Clearly, skill acquisition has a physical basis even though it is not possible to document, at this time, exactly how such physical processes support the learning of complex motor skills (O'Donovan, 1985). Certainly there have been major strides made towards that end; however, as Kandel (1985) notes co-operation is needed between the behavioural and biological sciences if we are to fully appreciate the mechanisms underlying learning and development in the cognitive-motor domain:

> ...the boundary between behaviour and biology is arbitrary and changing. It has been imposed not by the natural contours of the disciplines, but by lack of knowledge. As our knowledge expands, the biological and the behavioural disciplines will merge at certain points, and it is at these points of merger that our understanding of mentation will rest on particularly secure ground. For as we have tried to show in this book, the merger of biology and cognitive psychology is more than a merger of methods and concepts. Ultimately, the joining of these two disciplines represents the emerging conviction that a coherent and biologically unified description of mentation is possible (p. 832).

Most of the ideas discussed in this paper stem from a behavioural approach to skill acquisition; however, they are made in conjunction with an appreciation of the complex biological systems that underly learning and development.

ACQUIRED KNOWLEDGE

Acquired knowledge refers to the knowledge that is gained through experience which increases with development. As Figure 1 shows, acquired knowledge about action can be categorised into three major types: procedural, declarative, and affective. In addition, metacognitive knowledge and skills can also be differentiated. It is to a discussion of each of these different types of knowledge about action that we now turn.

PROCEDURAL KNOWLEDGE ABOUT ACTION

Procedural knowledge refers to the storage of action schemas that control the execution of skilled actions (Wall et al, 1985; Norman & Shallice,

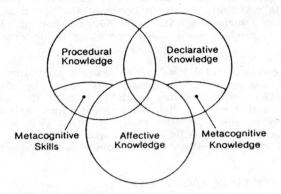

Fig. 1. Types of knowledge about action.

1980). In the knowledge-based approach, schemas are viewed as packets of knowledge that store information in a generalised manner. As such, they facilitate the storage and flexible use of large amounts of information. Furthermore, perceptual, decision-making and response execution schemas can be linked together to control complex skills. At each stage of an action sequence, considerable flexibility is provided by the use of control schemas that access relevant information from lower-level schemas (Kozminsky, Kintsch & Bourne, 1981). Such control schemas can access both declarative and procedural knowledge consciously or automatically. Thus, factual information on the rules of the game, pertinent biomechanical factors, or key contextual cues can readily influence the initiation or control of an action. In the same way, control schemas can access general or specific procedural knowledge about visual search, attention deployment, memory retrieval and executive processes. Thus it is postulated that procedural knowledge, stored in schema form, underlies the instantiation of all aspects of an action sequence including the stimulus identification, perception, decision-making, response selection and execution, and the evaluation of intrinsic and extrinsic feedback (Singer, 1980; Norman & Shallice, 1980; Gallistel, 1981; Stelmach & Diggles, 1982).

Acquired procedural knowledge, in schema form, operates within an heterarchial system that makes use of a myriad of feedforward and feedback systems (Parker, 1981; Wolfe, 1983). As noted earlier, human evolution has ensured that motor skill acquisition will be influenced by both top-down and bottom-up processing (Greene, 1972; Arbib, 1980). At the same time, such flexible processing occurs within the constraints established by the anatomical and neuro-physiological features of the body. Recent developmental studies have demonstrated how such constraints influence the early acquisition of procedural knowledge about action (Thelen, 1981; Thelen & Fisher, 1983; von Hofsten, 1983).

A fundamental observation in the skill acquisition process is that deliberate attentional control is required at certain times in it. In fact, Fitts (1964) and Gentile (1972) postulated that motor skills are usually acquired in three distinct phases: cognitive, associative and autonomous. The cognitive or "getting the idea of the movement" phase requires the involvement of considerable cognitive resources, whereas the associative and autonomous phases are more automatically controlled. Such conscious cognitive control is relatively costly in terms of the speed and fluidity of a given performance (Norman & Shallice, 1980; Kinsbourne, 1981), furthermore, by definition, novices are usually operating in just such a costly control mode.

Finally, the developmental level of a person's procedural knowledge about action base may be viewed in terms of the quantity and quality of automatised skills that he or she has available to meet the tasks of a given domain. Hence, a skilled person with a large repertoire of automatised skills can more efficiently handle a broader range of tasks than a person with less skills. Furthermore, the skilled person will have to use deliberate attentional control much less often than a novice to meet such demands.

DECLARATIVE KNOWLEDGE ABOUT ACTION

Declarative knowledge about action refers to factual information stored in memory that can influence the development and execution of skilled action. As children grow older, they begin to appreciate the morphological, biomechanical and environmental constraints under which they are operating. This movement-related knowledge about the self, others, and physical objects within the environment is a major product of cognitive-motor development.

As their declarative knowledge base increases children begin to attach expanded conceptual meanings to their actions and these, in turn, stimulate the use and control of their actions. During the preschool years, declarative knowledge about action is essentially nonverbal. However, as children develop more knowledge about their actions, the actions of others, and the effects of their actions on objects and other people , they begin to use language to describe them. This movement vocabulary is particularly important when caregivers use language to guide the motor learning process.

Perhaps one of the most important aspects of declarative knowledge about action is the information that children acquire about their own body and how it operates in space. Pick and his colleagues have shown that children can handle progressively more complex spatial tasks as they grow older. They note that children acquire multiple reference systems for describing the way they move in three dimensional space. Starting with relatively simple egocentric coding of manipulatory tasks, children go on to use geocentric reference systems which ultimately lead to the flexible use of more sophisticated mental representations about space (Pick & Lockman, 1981). As noted above, very early in life children begin to attach verbal labels to describe their self-referential spatial system and use this declarative knowledge in making decisions about their movements in spatial environments (Olson, 1975).

Bruner (1983) describes a number of initial cognitive endowments that underly language acquisition in children. These include predicting the environment, getting to goals with the aid of another, and using abstract rules to reach desired ends. He stresses that children acquire these prelinguistic skills through countless physical interactions within their social environment. As he so aptly states, "the child must master the conceptual structure of the world that language will map - the social world as well as the physical" (p. 39). Clearly, a child's procedural knowledge base will play a major role in this important language acquisition process. In fact, Huttenlocker, Smiley and Charney (1983) report that actions are among the first class of concepts that are expressed and children seem to develop them in a relatively systematic fashion.

Bruner (1983) also describes a series of studies that examine the development of attentional control in young children. He reports that as children develop their cognitive-motor skills, they learn to use verbal cues, changes in the intonation of the voice of a parent, and contextual cues to direct their attention. Much of this attentional control is acquired in game-like interactions between the parent and the child. Thus, the continuous interaction among action, gestures, and language gives rise to language and the powerful role which it will eventually play in the conscious control of action.

AFFECTIVE KNOWLEDGE ABOUT ACTION

Affective knowledge about action refers to the subjective feelings that children store about themselves in various action situations. Such feelings develop from the thousands of interactions that children have with objects and other people in a variety of action environments. As they grow older, children develop varying degrees of movement competence. Competent children experience a greater number of success experiences than less skilled children simply because they more readily handle the increasingly difficult tasks which they meet as they grow older. Such positive experiences generate feelings of confidence that motivate children to try even more challenging tasks which further increases their skill level and general movement competence (Griffin & Keogh, 1982). These success experiences generate feelings of confidence and eventually result in the development of a positive self concept (Harter, 1978, 1981, 1982). In contrast, less-skilled children experience more failure and, in turn, may develop negative feelings about themselves in action situations. In fact, children who face inordinate amounts of failure often exhibit characteristics of learned helplessness which is characterised by a lack of motivation, minimal persistence in the face of difficulties, and a general apathy to involvement in challenging situations (Dweck, 1980; Gibson, 1980; Weisz, 1979). Such negative personal feelings can certainly adversely affect the skill acquisition process.

Smith (1978) sheds further light on the development of affective knowledge from the perspective of attribution theory. As people grow older they develop relatively consistent attributions for their success or failure in action situations. Learners usually attribute their success or failure to four main factors: the internally-controlled ones of personal effort and ability or the externally-controlled ones of task difficulty and luck (Rotter, 1966; Weiner, 1974). Task difficulty and personal ability are rather stable factors while luck and personal effort are less predictable.

Smith reports that Weiner (1974) and others (Diggory, 1966; Fontaine, 1974) have categorised people into those with high and low achievement needs. People who consistently experience success are usually those with high achievement needs. In contrast, people who often experience failure are usually placed into the low achievement needs group. Of special importance to us is the fact that people with high achievement needs generally attribute their success to personal effort and ability, or to a task which was within their capability. On the other hand, they view failure as being due to insufficient effort on their part, an internal factor which they can change if they feel it important enough to do so. In contrast, individuals with low achievement needs generally do not have a clear set of attributions for their success; that is, when they actually do succeed at a task they are unable to attribute clear reasons for their success. However, when they fail, which they quite often do, they attribute it to their low ability. Unfortunately, this attribution is a fairly stable one that leads to less personal effort because such effort is thought to have little influence on their success or failure.

Clearly, the nature of a learner's affective knowledge base will play a major role in the skill acquisition process. If a person has developed attributions that lead to little personal effort being exerted or, even worse, simply not trying to analyse or attempt a task, then learning will certainly be adversely affected. More importantly, such negative behaviour can become cumulative resulting in a vicious circle that may lead to learned helplessness and other developmental problems (Gibson, 1980; Wall, 1982).

METACOGNITIVE KNOWLEDGE ABOUT ACTION

Wellman (1984) contends that as children grow older they develop a fairly extensive set of concepts about how their mind works. In fact, he suggests that children use their knowledge about what they know to develop a theory of mind that is an essential product of development. Such knowledge has been referred to as metacognitive knowledge. Metacognitive knowledge refers to what one knows or does not know. It is knowing about knowing. Wellman suggests that children become aware of five general classes of metacognitive knowledge. Let us consider each of Wellman's classes of knowledge about cognition as they will be of value in a subsequent discussion of metacognitive knowledge about action.

As children grow older, they begin to realise that mental processes exist; that is, they become aware of the fact that they have a mind. Clearly, an important aspect of this awareness will be related to their physical body and how they control it. As they gain experience, they begin to distinguish between different types of cognitive processes. They recognise that people can remember, dream, reason and create mental images; and of special importance for the motor domain, they learn that they can mentally plan and rehearse future actions. They also become aware of the types of variables that affect their cognitive processing. In the same way, they become cognisant of the factors that influence their memory performance and the execution of skills in the motor domain. Children also develop an understanding of how different cognitive processes affect each other and how they can be integrated to handle different types of tasks. This under-standing is especially important in the motor domain, as skilled action requires the use of different types of knowledge about action. Finally, they learn to appreciate their own mental states. Wellman suggests that they know when they know and when they understand, and they also know when they don't know or don't understand. They also become aware of when they are fantasising, dreaming, and imagining. This final class of knowledge is of crucial importance in the monitoring and control of cognitive as well as cognitive-motor activities; as such it becomes procedural in nature and might be better classed as metacognitive skill as will be done later in this paper.

As mentioned above, metacognitive knowledge refers to knowing about what one knows or does not know. In the action domain, it is knowing about knowing how to move. As such it is a higher form of declarative knowledge that develops as children become aware of what they can and cannot do in a wide variety of action situations.

As noted above, children develop fairly sophisticated theories of how their mind operates. A crucial aspect of this metacognitive knowledge base is related to the proficiency with which they can perform the cognitive-motor skills in their repertoire. They also become aware of the declarative knowledge that they have about their bodies and the environments in which they use it. And, perhaps more importantly, they know how they feel about themselves in different action situations. In short, they develop meta-cognitive knowledge about their procedural, declarative and affective knowledge about action. In turn, this metacognitive knowledge will be especially valuable in situations where metacognitive skills are required. It is to a discussion of metacognitive skills within the action domain that we now turn.

METACOGNITIVE SKILLS

Metacognitive skills are responsible for the executive control of cognitive activity. Brown (1977) suggests that efficient metacognitive control requires that learners: appreciate their capacity limitations so they are able to predict what they can and cannot do; know when and how to use heuristic problem solving strategies and know in which situations that they will be effective; readily analyse the demands of a given task and characterise it in relation to their knowledge base; choose and use suitable problem solving strategies; monitor and control the operation of the strategies used; and evaluate the success or failure of the entire problem solving process in relation to the demands of the task.

As an example of the above process, let us consider one of the most important metacognitive skills - planning. Pea (1982) describes planning as a heterarchial process that involves both top-down and bottom-up processing. He contends that developing a plan requires that alternative plans be considered, and the results of each alternate plan must usually be considered prior to its execution. As planning continues, it might be necessary to modify the initial goal in relation to the feedback received. He stresses that planning is an iterative process that depends upon the knowledge base of the person and the effectiveness of the planning process. Clearly, in novel situations, conscious planning requires a person to evaluate the skills and understandings that they have in their repertoire. Thus, there is a close connection between a person's metacognitive knowledge base and the use of higher-level metacognitive skills like planning.

Recent studies of metacognitive development show that such higher-level self-regulatory skills increase with age and experience (Brown, 1975, 1977; Brown & De Loache, 1978; Flavell, 1976; Flavell & Wellman, 1977; Kopp, 1982; Wellman, 1977). Very little research has been completed on metacognitive skills within the motor domain; however, it seems clear that such metacognitive skills must also develop within the motor domain. Research on the development of such skills is certainly needed if we are to fully appreciate the skill acquisition process.

In the initial sections of this paper we adumbrated a knowledge-based approach to motor development; however, before considering the implications of such an approach for the developmental study of skill acquisition, let us examine a number of recent observations about development in the cognitive domain that have considerable relevance for the acquisition of motor skill. Specifically, we will consider the importance of expert-novice differences, domain-specific knowledge, and motivation in learning.

MOTOR DEVELOPMENT AND SKILL ACQUISITION

As outlined above, a knowledge-based approach views motor development from a broad perspective that emphasises the importance of a child's procedural, declarative, affective, and metacognitive knowledge about action. In doing so, it also stresses the heterogeneity of development and the importance of domain-specific knowledge. Before considering some of the implications for learning that arise from the knowledge-based approach, let us examine a number of factors which influence the organisation and control of knowledge in the motor domain.

EXPERT-NOVICE DIFFERENCES AND DOMAIN-SPECIFIC KNOWLEDGE

In a classic developmental study of children's memory, Chi (1978) found that young children who played tournament chess were much better able to recall chess positions than naive adults, even though on a control task the adults obtained significantly higher digit-span results than the children. In the same vein, Allard, Graham and Paarsalu (1980) in a study of expert-novice differences in basketball found that the skilled players remembered more structured offensive and defensive situations than their less-skilled peers; however, no differences were found between the two groups on the recall of unstructured situations. Jones and Miles (1978) also found that advanced tennis players were better able to predict where a ball would land than beginners could. All three of these studies underline the importance of considering domain-specific knowledge about action.

In addition to the above expert-novice differences, other studies show how expertise in a specific domain influences the learning of a given task. For example, in a series of experiments on verbal learning, Chesi, Spilich and Voss (1979) have shown that domain-specific knowledge about baseball influences the acquisition of new information. Dividing their subjects into experts and non-experts in baseball, they studied the effect such expertise had on a variety of learning parameters. When people with expertise in baseball were given normally-ordered baseball passages to read they recalled significantly more information than their low knowledge counterparts; however, the opposite was true when they read a visual scene passage that was not related to baseball. The conceptual framework for these experiments is based on the notion that "sequential baseball information should be recalled better by HK individuals than LK individuals because of the greater ability of the former to relate sequences of states and actions of baseball-related information" (p. 266). As noted above, the reading recall data supported this hypothesis, however, an even more important prediction was that the high knowledge group would be able to use context better than their peers in recalling logical sequences of baseball-related information. Again, this hypothesis was clearly supported. The authors argue that "baseball knowledge involves the existence in long-term memory of patterns (or rules for generatin|

patterns) of actions which produce changes in game states" (p. 271-2); furthermore, this domain-specific knowledge is of considerable help when solving problems related to the reading of baseball passages as it provides a context from which to consider the sequence of action that is occurring within a game.

The results of the above studies support the differences between experts and novices that have been found in the "chunking" of chess patterns (Chase & Simon, 1973) and the use of strategies in the game of "Go". Furthermore, such domain-specific differences have been found in the way experts approach problem solving in the following knowledge domains: physics (Simon & Simon, 1978), radiological diagnosis (Lesgold, Feltovich, Glaser & Wang, 1981) and political science (Voss, Greene, Post & Penner, 1984). In all of these domains, experts were able to use their domain-specific knowledge to generate more effective problem solving strategies than their less-informed peers (Siegler, 1983b). Clearly, this is an important finding that supports some of our earlier contentions about the relationship among precedural and declarative knowledge and metacognitive skills; it also suggests that such metacognitive skills as planning, monitoring, and evaluating are directly influenced by the domain. specific knowledge of the person (Glaser, 1984).

LEARNING AND DOMAIN-SPECIFIC KNOWLEDGE

Siegler (1983a) in an important paper on cognitive development emphasises the influence existing knowledge has on the learning process. He reports a number of studies that investigated the use of rules in children's understanding of time, speed, and distance, and their value in problem solving situations. He notes that as children acquire more knowledge they begin to use more specific strategies in accessing and integrating knowledge. Conversely, "children's reasoning across different concepts is more homogenous when they have little knowledge about the concepts than when they have more" (p. 269). Thus, as children increase their domain-specific knowledge, if learning and instructional strategies are to be effective they should be directly related to the knowledge bases of the children. As Seigler points out, this is exactly what expert teachers do in helping children learn, they adjust questions, priorise learning objectives, and correct errors in relation to the knowledge level of their students (Collins & Stevens, 1982).

Before moving to the next section of this paper, we should reflect on the relevance of the above studies for the learning of procedural skills. It seems logical that if the procedural and declarative knowledge that baseball experts have acquired about their sport facilitates the acquisition of specific information when reading about baseball, then it would seem equally reasonable to investigate how such declarative knowledge might affect the acquisition of procedural skills within such a domain. Again, we know that "getting the idea of an action", or developing an "image of achievement" is an important initial phase in skill learning (Gentile, 1972; Whiting, 1980). Furthermore, these initial steps in learning are facilitated when the task-to-be-learned can be placed into a meaningful context. Thus, a rich declarative base in a given sport might enhance the learning of specific skills simply because such knowledge might provide a better context for learning and problem solving. Unfortunately, such studies relating declarative and metacognitive knowledge and skills with instruction in the learning of motor skills have not been completed.

In addition to the above observations on the role of a declarative knowledge base, we know that skilled athletes have automatised more skills than novices; however, they also have acquired a greater declarative knowledge base about action, appreciate and control their feelings during performance and appropriately use such metacognitive skills as planning, monitoring, and trouble shooting in learning and performance situations. Clearly, more research needs to be done on how these expert-novice differences affect the acquisition of motor skills. In doing such research, it will be essential to specify the nature and extent of the domain being studied and the knowledge bases of the people involved.

METACOGNITIVE SKILLS AND LEARNING

Metacognitive skills are concerned with the control and effective use of stored knowledge through the selection, control and monitoring of a person's cognitive processes. Within the motor domain, most voluntary actions are initiated to fulfil specific situational demands. Whether one is walking across a room, playing a violin, steering a car, or returning a tennis service, actions are characterised by their goal-directed nature. No matter how beautiful the spatial-temporal pattern of a given action might be, it is of little value unless the kinematic response results in the desired goal being reached. Hence, higher-level executive processes are central to the control and execution of skilled action. Effective metacognitive control of cognitive processes underlying stimulus identification, response selection and response programmming can ensure that voluntary actions optimally meet the demands of a situation.

From an evolutionary perspective, it is the quality and efficiency of metacognitive and cognitive processes that differentiate man from the primates and lower animals (Oakley, 1967). Furthermore, from a development-al perspective, the development of such generic metacognitive skills as predicting, planning, and monitoring allow people to control and enhance their own learning. Such metacognitive skills develop slowly with age and experience. The use of such self-regulatory skills can make dramatic differences in the rate of learning; however, certain conditions must be met if such metacognitive interventions are to be effective. Let us consider some of these conditions.

Learning and development in the motor domain depends on the demands of the task at hand, the developmental level of the learner, and the nature of the environment in which the learning is to take place. If the demands of the task require accurate motor responses to fast changing stimuli such as hitting a baseball in a game-like practice situation, then the novice learner must have at least minimal skill in the selection, initiation and execution of the basic response patterns of hitting before metacognitive skills can effectively enhance learning and performance. Prediction rules, knowledge of pitching tendencies, cues for judging the type of pitch that might be thrown will all be of little value if the novice learner has not initially acquired the appropriate response execution skills. Granted, metacognitive skills associated with getting the idea of the movement will be of some help; however, more likely than not, such a novice learner would be simply over-whelmed by the physical demands of the situation and withdraw from it. Clearly, it is essential that metacognitive strategies be matched to the developmental skill level of the learner if they are to be of any value.

As mentioned earlier, metacognitive skills may be under conscious control or automatised so that they operate unconsciously. The more skilful a learner is in a specific situation the more likely he or she will be to use both types of metacognitive processing. Again, the demands of the task and situation will affect the type of metacognitive skills that will be used. Skilled athletes all relate countless conscious rules and hints that they use to enhance their learning and performance, however, they also recognise that such conscious processes are best used prior to or after a performance rather than during the execution of skilled action. A practical observation that demonstrates the crucial role that metacognitive control plays in learning and performance.

MOTIVATION, METACOGNITIVE SKILLS, AND TASK DIFFICULTY

Perhaps, the most important reason for considering the role of meta-cognitive skills is the intimate relationship they have with the motivation of the learner. Experienced instructors know that the effectiveness of a suggested metacognitive strategy will largely depend on the learner's willingness to use it. The motivational state of a learner largely determines the degree to which such skills as planning, predicting, monitoring and evaluating will be used. As mentioned in our discussion of affective knowledge about action, motivated learners are more likely to strategically enhance their learning by systematically controlling their own learning. Individuals with learned helplessness will usually not want to use self-initiated metacognitive skills. Even in situations where an instructor encourages such a learner to voluntarily use metacognitive skills, the chances of them being used will be slight. Experimental studies with mentally handicapped adolescents and our clinical work with physically awkward children indicates that such motivational difficulties can be a major developmental problem (Gibson, 1980; Wall et al, 1985).

Smith (1978) makes a number of important points about task difficulty, motivation, and learning that are relevant to this discussion. He notes that task difficulty must always be viewed from the perspective of the individual learner. Generally, a learner will have a subjective expectancy of success or failure on a given task, he or she will be optimally motivated when the subjective expectancy of success versus failure is about 50/50. Clearly, an important role of the teacher or coach, or for that matter skills researcher, is to break down tasks-to-be-learned into manageable parts of simplified wholes. Smith stresses that "by simplifying the skill-to-be-learned we not only make it more understandable but we may redefine it as a skill task that is subject to learner control, rather than a chance task in which the learner feels relatively helpless" (p. 11). Thus, experienced teachers may help less-confident learners use more powerful metacognitive strategies by presenting tasks in progressively more difficult learning sequences.

A KNOWLEDGE-BASED APPROACH TO SKILL ACQUISITION

In the initial section of this paper, it was suggested that an holistic approach to motor development was needed if our theories of skill acquisition were to be of value in physical education and adapted physical education. Whether one considers procedural, declarative, affective or metacognitive knowledge about action, there are wide individual differences in development due to age, sex, intelligence, and socio-cultural differences that must be recognised in the skill acquisition process. Large differences in metacognitive skill and the conscious control of action can also be found within any group of children. In addition to underlining the importance of individual differences, this approach stresses the interaction that occurs among the different types of knowledge about action during the skill learning process. A number of implications arise from this approach for the skill acquisition process, let us examine some of them at this point.

NEED FOR AN ANALYSIS OF THE TASK-TO-BE-LEARNED

When conducting research on the skill acquisition process, it will be necessary to carefully consider the demands of the task-to-be-learned. In doing so, it will be important to remember that the demands of a task vary with the skill and developmental level of the learner. As noted earlier, tasks that are not within the capabilities of a given child may have adverse effects on the motivation of the learner. Thus, a careful examination of task demands must be made in relation to the learner's knowledge base. Questions that might be asked are: Does the task require mainly procedural, declarative, or metacognitive knowledge? Is the task a novel or familiar one? Is controlled or automatic processing required? Does the task require mainly perceptual, cognitive, or response-loaded processing? Is it to be learned in a closed or open environment? Where will it ultimately be used, in a competitive, stressful, or cooperative environment?

As one considers such questions, it becomes clear that they can only be answered in relation to the knowledge-base of a learner or group of learners. Thus, in contrast to many information processing approaches to skill acquisition that often only emphasise the processes involved in learning, a knowledge-based approach recognises the interaction between the developmental level of the learner and the processes that will be needed to learn and perform a given task.

NEED TO EVALUATE THE LEARNER'S KNOWLEDGE BASE

A knowledge-based approach to skill acquisition recognises the importance of evaluating the child's knowledge base prior to prescribing skills for instruction. In doing so, it challenges the notion of simply assigning subjects to treatment groups on a random basis and then implementing a given instructional programme. The literature on expert-novice differences certainly supports the need to carefully evaluate the skills and knowledges of a particular group before implementing any instructional programmes. We need to develop means to accurately measure the developmental level of the learner and the different types of knowledge about action that are needed for the learning of a given task.

LANGUAGE AND SKILL ACQUISITION

As outlined earlier, a knowledge-based approach recognises the importance of declarative and metacognitive knowledge in the selection, control, and evaluation of skilled actions. Such knowledge is especially imporant during the early stages of skill acquisition when the conscious control of action is of crucial importance. Studies of the skill acquisition process must examine the interaction between declarative and metacognitive knowledge in the learning of procedural skills. For example, do specific terms or action words limit the value of the instructions that are given to learners? More generally, to what degree does a learner's declarative knowledge base limit their use of instructions, feedback, and self-control techiques in the learning process?

METACOGNITIVE SKILLS AND SKILL ACQUISITION

Metacognitive skills vary with the extent and specificity of a learner's knowledge base; recent studies in cognitive development show that these self-regulatory skills can have a dramatic affect on learning. Unfortunately, very few motor development studies have considered the role of these executive processes in the skill acquisition process. Studies are needed on the interaction among declarative, procedural, and metacognitive knowledge about action with special attention to the role that metacognitive skills play in the skill acquisition process.

A knowledge-based approach to skill acquisition also recognises the relative stability of development and the role of domain-specific knowledge in development (Macnab, 1979). When we consider the developmental level of children in the motor domain, we immediately note very broad differences in knowledge and skill due to the past experiences of the children. In contrast to scholastic achievement in which a fairly homogeneous curriculum is often taught, the play and sport experiences of children fluctuate dramatically due to age, sex, intelligence, family, and socio-cultural factors. These heterogenous play and sport experiences often result in the acquisition of domain-specific knowledge that must be considered in our studies of skill acquisition. Again, such a view underscores the importance of initially assessing the knowledge base of the children involved in our developmental studies of skill acquisition.

46

References

Allard, F., Graham, S. & Paarsalu, M.E. (1980). Perception in sport: Basketball. *Journal of Sport Psychology, 2,* 14-21.

Allard, F. & Starkes, J.I. (1980). Perception in sport: Volleyball. *Journal of Sport Psychology, 2,* 22-33.

Arbib, M.A. (1980). Interacting schemas for motor control. In G.E. Stelmach and J. Requin (Eds.), *Tutorials in motor behavior.* New York: North-Holland Publishing.

Brown, A.L. (1975). The development of memory: Knowing, knowing about knowing, and knowing how to know. In H.W. Reese (Ed.), *Advances in child development.* New York: Academic Press.

Brown, A.L. (1977). Development, schooling and the acquisition of knowledge about knowledge. In R.C. Anderson, R.H. Spiro and W.E. Montague (Eds.), *Schooling and the acquisition of knowledge.* Hillsdale, NJ: Erlbaum.

Brown, A.L. & De Loache, J.S. (1978). Skills, plans, and self-regulation. In R.S. Siegler (Ed.), *Children's thinking: What develops?* Hillsdale, NJ: Erlbaum.

Bruner, J.S. (1983). *Child's Talk.* New York: Norton.

Chase, W.G. & Simon, H.A. (1973). Perception in chess. *Cognitive Psychology, 4,* 55-81.

Chi, M.T.H. (1978). Knowledge structures and memory development. In R. Siegler (Ed.), *Children's thinking: What develops?* Hillsdale, NJ: Erlbaum.

Chi, M.T.H. & Koeske, R.D. (1983). Network representation of a child's dinosaur knowledge. *Developmental Psychology, 19,* 29-39.

Chiesi, H.L., Spilich, G.J. & Voss, J.F. (1979). Acquisition of domain-related information in relation to high and low domain knowledge. *Journal of Verbal Learning and Behaviour, 18,* 257-274.

Collins, A. & Stevens, A.L. (1982). Goals and strategies of inquiry teachers. In R. Glaser (Ed.), *Advances in instructional psychology.* Hillsdale, NJ: Erlbaum.

Diggory, J. (1966). *Self-evaluation: Concepts and Studies.* New York: Wiley.

Dweck, C.S. (1980). Learned helplessness in sport. In C.H. Nadeau, W.R. Halliwell, K.M. Newell and G.C. Roberts (Eds.), *Psychology of motor behaviour and sport- 1979.* Champaign, IL: Human Kinetics.

Fitts, P.M. (1964). Perceptual-motor learning. In A.W. Melton (Ed.), *Categories of human learning.* New York: Academic Press.

Flavell, J.H. (1976). Metacognitive aspects of problem solving. In L.B. Resnick (Ed.), *The nature of intelligence.* Hillsdale, NJ: Erlbaum.

Flavell, J.H. & Wellman, H.J. (1977). Metamemory. In R.V. Kail Jr. and J.W. Hagen (Eds.), *Perspectives on the development of memory and cognition.* Hillsdale, NJ: Erlbaum.

Fontaine, G. (1974). Social comparisons and some determinants of expected personal control and expected performance in a novel situation. *Journal of Personality and Social Psychology, 29,* 487-496.

Gallistel, C.R. (1981). Precis of Gallistel's The organization of action: A new synthesis. *The Behavioral and Brain Sciences, 4,* 609-650.

Gentile, A.M. (1972). A working model of skill acquisition with application to teaching. *Quest, 17,* 3-23.

Gibson, B.J. (1980). An attributional analysis of performance outcome and the alleviation of learned helplessness on motor performance tasks: A comparative study of educable mentally retarded and non-retarded boys. Unpublished doctoral dissertation, University of Alberta.

Glaser, R. (1984). Education and thinking: The role of knowledge. *American Psychologist*, *39*, *2*, 93-104.

Greene, P.H. (1972). Problems of organization of motor system. In R. Rosen and F.M. Snell (Eds.), *Progress in theoretical biology* (Vol. 2). New York: Academic Press.

Griffin, N.S. & Keogh, J.F. (1982). A model for movement confidence. In J.A.S. Kelso and J.E. Clark (Eds.), *The development of movement control and coordination.* New York: Wiley.

Harter, S. (1978). Effectance motivation reconsidered: Toward a developmental model. *Human Development*, *21*, 34-64.

Harter, S. (1981). The development of competence motivation in the mastery of cognitive and physical skills: Is there still a place for joy? In G.C. Roberts and D.M. Landers (Eds.), *Psychology of motor behaviour and sport- 1980.* Champaign, IL: Human Kinetics.

Harter, S. (1982). The perceived competence scale for children. *Child Development*, *53*, 87-97.

Holloway, R.L. (1983). Human brain evolution: A search for units, models and synthesis. *Canadian Journal of Anthropology*, *3*, 215-230.

Huttenlocher, J., Smiley, P. & Charney, R. (1983). Emergence of action categories in the child: Evidence from verb meanings. *Psychological Review*, *90*, 72-93.

Jones, C.M. & Miles, T.R. (1978). Use of advance cues in predicting the flight of a lawn tennis ball. *Journal of Human Movement Studies*, *41*, 231-235.

Kandel, E.R. (1985). Cellular mechanisms of learning and the biological basis of individuality. In E.R. Kandel and J. Schwartz (Eds.), *Principles of neural science.* New York: Elsevier.

Kandel, E.R. & Schwartz, J. (1985). *Principles of neural science.* New York: Elsevier.

Kinsbourne, M. (1981). Single-channel theory. In D. Holding (Ed.), *Human Skills.* New York: Wiley.

Kopp, C.B. (1982). Antecedents of self-regulation: A developmental perspective. *Developmental Psychology*, *18*, 199-214.

Kozminsky, E., Kintsch, W. & Bourne, L.E. Jr. (1981). Decision making with texts: Information analysis and schema acquisition. *Journal of Experimental Psychology: General*, *110*, 363-380.

Lesgold, A.M., Feltovich, P.J., Glaser, R. & Wang, Y. (1981). The acquisition of perceptual diagnostic skill in radiology (Tech. Rep). Learning Research and Development Center, University of Pittsburgh.

Macnab, R.B.J. (1979). A longitudinal study of ice hockey in boys aged 8-12. *Canadian Journal of Sport Sciences*, *4*, *1*, 11-17.

Mischel, H.N. & Mischel, W. (1983). The development of children's knowledge of self-control strategies. *Child Development*, *54*, 603-619.

Norman, D.A. & Shallice, T. (1980). Attention to action: Willed and automatic control of behaviour. (Tech. Rep.). San Diego: University of California, Center for Human Information Processing.

Oakley, K.P. (1967). Skill as a human possession. In N. Korn and F. Thompson (Eds.), *Human Evolution.* New York: Holt, Rinehart & Winston.

O'Donovan, M.J. (1985). Developmental regulation of motor function: An uncharted sea. *Medicine and Science in Sports and Exercise*, *17*, *1*, 35-43.

Olson, D.R. (1975). On the relations between spatial and linguistic processes. In J. Eliot and H.J. Salkind (Eds.), *Children's spatial development.* Springfield, IL: C.C. Thomas.

Parker, D.E. (1981). The vestibular apparatus. *Scientific American*, 118-135.

48

Pea, R.D. (1982). What is planning development the development of? In
D. Forbes and M.T. Greenberg (Eds.), *New directions in child
development: Children's planning strategies*. San Francisco: Josey-Bass.

Pick, H.L. & Lockman, J.J. (1981). From frames of reference to spatial
representations. In L.S. Liben (Ed.), *Spatial representation and
behavior across the lifespan*. New York: Academic Press.

Prechtl, H.F.R. (1981). The study of neural development as a perspective
of clinical problems. In K.J. Connolly and H.F.R. Prechtl (Eds.),
Maturation and development: Biological and psychological perspectives.
London: Heinemann.

Rotter, J.B. (1966). Generalized expectancies for internal versus external
control of reinforcement. *Psychological Measurement, 80,* 1-28.

Siegler, R.S. (1983a). Five generalizations about cognitive development.
American Psychologist, 263-277.

Siegler, R.S. (1983b). How knowledge influences learning. *American
Scientist,* 631-640.

Simon, D.P. & Simon, H.A. (1978). Individual differences in solving
physics problems. In R. Siegler (Ed.), *Children's thinking: What
develops?* Hillsdale, NJ: Erlbaum.

Singer, R.N. (1980). Motor behaviour and the role of cognitive processes
and learner strategies. In G.E. Stelmach and J. Requin (Eds.),
Tutorials in motor behavior. New York: North Holland Publishing.

Smith, M.F.R. (1978). Attribution, achievement motivation, and task
difficulty in physical education. Paper presented at the B.C. Conference
on the Teaching of Physical Education, Victoria, B.C.

Stelmach, G.E. & Diggles, V.A. (1982). Control theories in motor behavior.
Acta Psychologica, 50, 83-105.

Thelen, E. (1981). Rhythmical behaviour in infancy: An ethological
perspective. *Developmental Psychology, 17, 3,* 237-257.

Thelen, E. & Fisher, D.M. (1983). The organization of spontaneous leg
movements in newborn infants. *Journal of Motor Behavior, 15, 4,* 353-
382.

von Hofsten, C. (1983). Catching skills in infancy. *Journal of Experimental
Psychology: Human Perception and Performance, 9, 1,* 75-85.

Voss, J.F., Greene, T.R., Post, T.A. & Penner, B.C. (1984). Problem
solving skill in the social sciences. In G.H. Bower (Ed.), *The
psychology of learning and motivation* (Vol. 18). New York: Academic
Press.

Wall, A.E. (1982). Physically awkward children: A motor development
perspective. In J.P. Das, R.F. Mulcahy and A.E. Wall (Eds.), *Theory
and research in learning disabilities*. New York: Plenum.

Wall, A.E., McClements, J., Bouffard, M., Findlay, H. & Taylor, M.J.
(1985). A knowledge-based approach to motor development: Implications
for the physically awkward. *Adapted Physical Activity Quarly, 2,* 21-42.

Weiner, B. (1974). *Cognitive views of human motivation*. New York:
Academic Press.

Weisz, J.R. (1979). Perceived control and learned helplessness among
mentally retarded and non-retarded children: A developmental analysis.
Developmental Psychology, 15, 311-319.

Wellman, H.M. (1977). The early development of intentional memory
behaviour. *Human Development, 20,* 86-101.

Wellman, H.M. (1984). The development of concepts of the mental world.
Behavioral and Brain Sciences, 7, 4, 651-652.

Whiting, H.T.A. (1980). Dimensions of control and motor learning. In G.E.
Stelmach and J. Requin (Eds.), *Tutorials in motor behavior*. New York:
North-Holland Publishing.

Whiting, H.T.A. (1982). Skill in sport - A descriptive and prescriptive appraisal. In J.H. Salmela, J.T. Partington and T.O. Orlick (Eds.), *New paths of sport learning and excellence*. Ottawa: Canadian Coaching Association.

Wolfe, J.M. (1983). Hidden visual processes. *Scientific American*, 94-103.

SECTION 2

PRENATAL ONSET OF MOTOR PATTERNS

PRENATAL MOTOR DEVELOPMENT

H.F.R. Prechtl

1.   INTRODUCTION

Until recently our knowledge of early motor behaviour in the human
was based on observations of the newborn infant. It is clear that the
neonatal repertoire does not appear *de novo* at birth but is preceded by a
prenatal developmental course. However, as the newborn's repertoire was
seen merely as a set of primitive reflexes, the interest was focussed
primarily on the onset of these reflexes in the prenatal period. Viable
preterm infants, providing a possibility to investigate fetal neural functions
extra-uterinely, have been included in such reflex studies. For still younger
ages one was restricted to experiments with aborted fetuses. When surviving
for a few minutes in a warm bath they were systematically stimulated to
study their responses to tactile stimuli. The concept of an essentially passive
nervous system - a product of the experimental procedures commonly
employed in neurophysiological studies - has prohibited due attention being
given to spontaneous motor activity. It was also insufficiently realised that
the kind of stimulation the fetus was exposed to, was totally unbiological,
as such stimuli never occur under normal conditions. These studies
demonstrated nevertheless an amazingly early onset of many reflexes, which
are known to be also present in postnatal life. However, the high rate of
fetal movements felt by every expecting mother should have raised queries
about the reflex origin of fetal motility.

2.   METHODS OF FETAL STUDIES

Scientific interest in embryonic and fetal motility has a long history.
Probably one of the first scientists was Swammerdam in Holland who
observed with his new microscope elegant movements of the embryos of
snails. He described his observations in his book "Bible of Nature". Somewhat later embryonic movements were seemingly rediscovered by v. Leeuwenhoek (1695) in mussels.

With a big leap to the end of the 19th century, an outstanding
contribution was made by Preyer (1885) with his book "Die specielle Physiologie des Embryo". Not only did he make extensive observations and
experiments on chick embryos, but he also devoted more than 30 pages to
observations on the human fetus. He appreciated the spontaneous nature of
fetal movements and said: "The sometimes quick, sometimes slow, mostly
uncoordinated extension and flexion of arms and legs of the newly born are
nothing else than a continuation of the intra-uterine movements" (p. 161,
translated from German edition). With this observation he put fetal movements
in the perspective of a developmental continuum from prenatal to postnatal

life.

The twenties and thirties of this century have seen a great effort to study the operatively removed human fetus in his responses to tactile stimulation. Minkowsky (1928), an adult neurologist in Zürich started such experiments, followed by the comparative anatomists Davenport Hooker and Tryphina Humphrey in the United States. They stimulated systematically fetuses during the few minutes of survival and made film recordings of their responses. Their lifework has been beautifully summarised in Hooker (1952) and Humphrey (1978) and needs no repetition here. The theoretical framework of these studies was traditional reflexology with very little concern for the spontaneous activity of the developing nervous system.

What had entered the textbooks on early motor development by the seventies was mainly based on these reflex studies. The situation changed only with the introduction of a new non-invasive technique which permitted prolonged and repeated visualisation of the undisturbed fetus in utero: real-time ultrasound. During the last 10 years, ultrasound equipment has improved rapidly in the quality of resolution and dynamics. What is still inadequate is the size of the visualised field. Fetuses become too large during the second half of pregnancy to be observed in toto with one transducer. The use of two transducers is still a stop-gap until larger linear array equipment becomes available.

After the pioneering work by Reinold (1971, 1976) there are three larger sonographic studies of fetal movements available, mainly from the eighties. Birnholz et al (1978) described the emergence of particular movement patterns based on observations of several minutes. Their terminology is said to be based on reflex patterns described by Hooker (1952). There are, however, differences with the spontaneously generated movements seen with ultrasound. The second extensive investigation was carried out by Ianniruberto and Tajani (1981) on ten thousand fetuses between 8 and 42 weeks of gestation. Only brief descriptions of the different types of movements are provided, based on Milani-Comparetti's system of motoscopy (1967) for the diagnosis of neurological abnormalities in post-natal development. Unfortunately, the latter descriptions are very global and brief and do not provide a suitable instrument for general use in fetal studies.

The third group of sonographic investigations of fetal movements comes from a close cooperation between obstetricians and a developmental neurologist (De Vries et al, 1982, 1984, 1985). The design was different from the previous studies as only a small group of 12 fetuses was longitudinally followed weekly in a one-hour continuous observation, recorded also on video tape. Analysis was carried out off-line from re-played videotapes. This strategy greatly facilitates a detailed analysis of the movement patterns and the rate and sequence of their occurrence. In addition, they allow for an assessment of the movement quality which may change in the compromised fetus and in those with congenital defects of the nervous system. The following descriptions in this chapter will be mainly based on the results from these studies.

3.   CLASSIFICATION OF FETAL MOVEMENTS

Whenever a proper description of fetal movements is attempted, a classification of these movements becomes a crucial issue. The most obvious and simple distinction is in terms of fast or slow, and large or small movements. Such descriptors have in fact been used (Reinold, 1971) but this was when the development of ultrasound equipment was just beginning. It soon became clear that the complexity of fetal movements cannot be captured by such elementary categorisations.

Our own attempts in the Groningen studies (De Vries et al, 1982, 1984, 1985) are based on a long experience of infant observations and neurological examinations (Prechtl, 1977; Prechtl et al, 1979). My personal hope at the beginning of our ultrasound investigations of fetal movements was that familiarity with motor patterns in the preterm and fullterm infant might help us to recognise the same pattern in the fetus. It came as a surprise that the repertoire of fetal movements consists exclusively of motor patterns which can also be observed in postnatal life. All fetal motor patterns can be also seen postnatally, some only again weeks after birth. The reverse is of course not true as there are behaviour patterns in the newborn which are not available to the fetus. An example is the Moro-response and the vestibulo-ocular reflex, which cannot be elicited in the fetus (personal observation). This seems to be due to a blocking of vestibular responses during intra-uterine life, a very reasonable strategem since it prevents the fetus moving every time the mother turns.

The striking similarity between fetal movements and many postnatal movement patterns greatly facilitates a comprehensive and consistent descriptive classification and terminology of fetal motility. It remains puzzling how movements can be executed in such a similar way before and after birth even though the physical differences between the intra-uterine and the extra-uterine environment are considerable. Peripheral sensory control must play a negligible role in these movements.

4. TYPES OF FETAL MOVEMENTS

A great effort was made to make the listing of fetal movements as exhaustive and comprehensive as possible and to leave no movements un-labeled. The more important ones will be described in the following:

Startles are quick, generalised movements which always start in the limbs and often spread to trunk and neck. The duration of a startle is one second or less. Usually they occur singly but sometimes they may be repetitive. They can be super-imposed incidentally on a general movement.

General movements are also gross movements but they are slow and involve the whole body. They may last from a few seconds to a minute. What is particular about them is the indeterminate sequence of arm, leg, neck and trunk movement. They wax and wane in intensity, force and speed. Despite this variability, they must be considered as a distinct pattern, easy to recognise if they occur again.

Hiccup. A phasic contraction of the diaphragm, often repetitive at regular intervals. A bout may last up to several minutes. In contrast to the startle, the movement always starts in the trunk, but may be followed by involvement of the limbs.

Breathing movements. Fetal breathing movements in the fetus are paradoxical. Every contraction of the diaphragm (which leads after birth to an inspiration) causes an inward movement of the thorax and a simultaneous movement of the abdomen outwards. The sequence of "breaths" can be either regular of irregular. No amniotic fluid enters the lungs during breathing movements. Isolated breaths may resemble a sigh.

Isolated arm or leg movements. An arm or a leg may be moved in isolation without other parts moving. The speed may vary and so does the amplitude of the movement.

Twitches are quick extensions or flexions of a limb or the neck. They are never generalised and are not repetitive.

Cloni are repetitive, tremulous movements of one or more limbs. Their rate is about 3 per second. There are rarely more than 3-4 beats in normal fetuses.

Isolated hand movements. The fingers may flex or extend together repetitively or in isolation. Some hand postures may resemble hand gestures seen in later life. The hand may also rotate outwards, or inwards (supination or pronation).

Hand-face contact. The hand may accidentally touch the face either by an arm movement in the direction of the face or by a head movement in direction of the hand. Hand-mouth contact occurs but it is often difficult to judge where precisely the hand makes contact.

Retroflexion of the head. The backward bending of the head may vary in speed from slow to jerky. The head may remain in retroflexed position from 1 sec. to a minute, often accompanied by an over-extension of the spine.

Lateral rotation of the head. The head is rotated from the midline to a lateral position or vice versa. This movement occurs in isolation. The speed is usually slow; the amplitude may vary.

Rhythmical side to side movements of the head. As in postnatal rooting, the regularity is not accurate. The movements are slow and may cover a range of 180 degrees.

Anteflexion of the head. This forward bending of the head is usually slow but always consists of a lift-off from the surface the fetus is resting on.

Opening of the mouth. Amplitude and speed may vary. Occurs in isolation. Sometimes tongue protrusion can be observed.

Yawn. A slow opening of the mouth is followed by open position of several seconds and a quick closure.

Rhythmical mouthing. Small and rhythmical quiver of the jaws without opening of the mouth. Occurs in bursts of 5-10 movements which have a rate of about 4-5 per second.

Sucking. Bursts of rhythmical jaw movements with a rate of about one per second and of varying length. Sometimes they are followed by swallowing, indicating that the fetus is drinking amniotic fluid.

Stretch. This complex motor pattern consists of over-extension of the spine, retroflexion of the head, abduction, external rotation and elevation of the arms. The movement lasts several seconds and occurs singly.

Rotation of the fetus. The rotation may occur along the longitudinal axis or the transverse axis of the fetal body. These movements are always forceful. Alternating leg movements, when the feet are contacting the uterine wall, may result in a somersault over the head. Rotation around the saggital axis are initiated by either a rotation of the head or of the hip.

Eye movements. Slow, rapid and repetitive (nystagmoid) eye movements can be distinguished. The displacement of the eye ball can be seen as a flicker of the echo behind the orbit or better as shifts in the position of the echoes of the lenses.

5. THE EMERGENCE OF FETAL MOVEMENTS

There is general agreement in the literature that the first fetal movements can be observed at a postmenstrual age of 7-8 weeks (Van Dongen & Goudie, 1980; Ianniruberto & Tajani, 1981; De Vries et al, 1982). Interestingly enough this is the same age at which Hooker (1952) was able to elicit the first responses in aborted fetuses. Perioral stimulation with a Frey's hair was followed by a lateral bending of the head. The first spontaneous movements in the intact fetus and observed by sonography have a different character. They include limb movements and flexion and extension of the vertebral column.

What we (De Vries et al, 1982) originally called "just discernible movements" are now believed to be general movements. This conclusion comes from observations with more advanced ultrasound equipment. Nevertheless a more detailed investigation of these very early movements remains to be done, until a final conclusion can be reached.

By eight to nine weeks, quick startles and slow general movements are distinguishable, followed at nine weeks by hiccups and isolated arm and leg movements (see Fig. 1). From ten weeks onwards rhythmical breathing

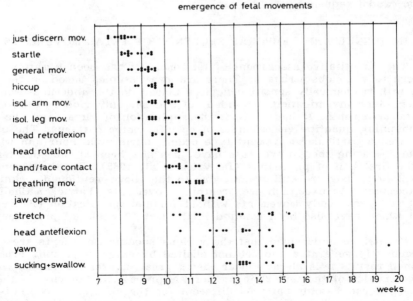

Fig. 1. Postmenstrual ages of fetuses at which a certain motor pattern was observed for the first time (n= 12). From De Vries et al, 1984).

movements can be observed, the head can be rotated to lateral positions
and back or be retroflexed together with an over-extension of the back.
By ten and a half weeks jaw opening, anteflexion of head and the complex
stretch movements are added to the repertoire. Yawns and rhythmical
sucking and swallowing follow at 11 and 12 weeks.

The scatter of the dots in Figure 1, each dot representing an individual,
differs for the different movements. Some have a range of less than 2 weeks,
the others scatter more widely. A certain dispersion of the ages can be
expected from the variation in interval between actual timing of conception
and the first day of the last menstruation (to which we relate ages here),
and from the limitation in resolution imposed by the one observation per
week. The movements with a broader scatter all occur less frequently (see
below) than those with a small scatter. Since they appear rarely (e.g. one
or two times per observation) their first onset may have been missed
accidentally in the one hour lasting observation. What remains surprising is
the very early onset of so many different specific movement patterns. An
early period with only amorphic random movements, preceding the
differentiation of distinct motor patterns, does not exist.

It may not surprise that many ages of first appearance of certain
movement patterns are younger in this study than described by others (for
details see comparative table in De Vries et al, 1984). These corrections of
the ages of onset shed interesting light on some concepts of early fetal
motility. They show that jerky and twitchy movements do not precede slow
and tonic movements but both occur for the first time at about the same age.
Generalised movements of trunk and limbs (startles and general movements)
appear only two or three days earlier than isolated limb movements. Arm
and leg movements have a simultaneous onset and thus do not follow a
cranio-caudal sequence.

6.   INCIDENCE AND TEMPORAL SEQUENCE OF FETAL MOVEMENTS

The quantitative assessment of fetal motility has been a matter of
concern to many obstetricians. There are many studies based on recordings
made with mechanically sensitive devices placed on the abdominal wall of the
mother. Such investigations provided, of course, only global measurements
of fetal movements. It had to await the application of ultrasound observations
for obtaining quantitative measures of specific motor patterns. The question
how often a particular movement type occurs during one hour and what
temporal spacing these movements have, has now been answered, at least
for the first half of pregnancy (De Vries et al, 1985). For the second half
of gestation, data are still scarce, due to the above mentioned technical
shortcomings. An exception are breathing movements (Patrick & Challis,
1980) and gross body movements without further specification (Patrick et al,
1982) which have also been counted in the last 10 weeks of pregnancy.

It must be understood that the various specific movements are
endogenously generated and are not elicited by external stimuli. From the
obtained results it is already clear that a great diversity exists in the
characteristics of the underlying generator processes. Not only is the rate
of the generated motor patterns different for the different movements, it is
also their temporal sequence which shows a great variety. The picture
becomes even more complex when the developmental course is taken into
account. For example, general movements increase in incidence from 8 to 10

weeks, reach a plateau of 10-15% of time at this age which is then maintained for the rest of the intra-uterine period (Fig. 2). Even after birth the same amount of general movements is observed in neonates. In contrast to this

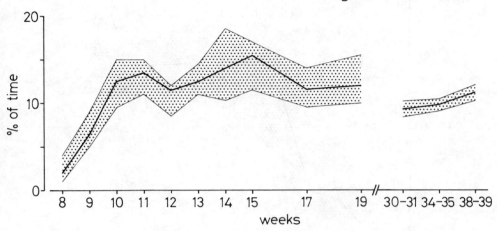

Fig. 2. Percentage of observation time spent in general movements
(median and interquartile range; n= 12). In the right hand
part data in mean and SE from Patrick et al (1982).

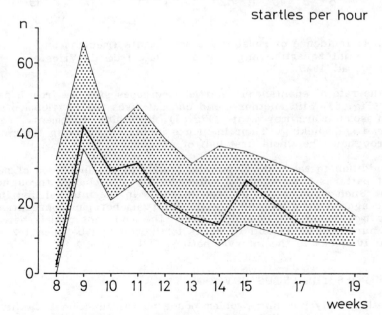

Fig. 3. Incidence (median and interquartile range) of startles
(n= 12). Data from de Vries et al, 1985.

60

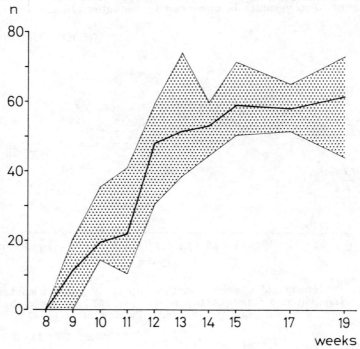

Fig. 4. Incidence of isolated arm movements (medians and
interquartile range; n= 12). Data from de Vries et
al, 1985.

pattern the rate of spontaneous startles decreases steadily from a peak at
9 weeks (Fig. 3). Still another trend characterises the developmental
course of isolated arm movements (Fig. 4), breathing movements, rotations
of the head and sucking. Their incidence increases following their early
onset throughout the whole first half of pregnancy.

In addition to these developmental trends in the incidence of particular
movement patterns their temporal sequence may also change throughout
gestation. Such changes can be seen in shifts in the interval distributions,
related to age. A good example are the intervals between consecutive
breathing movements. At 10 and 11 weeks the modal interval is between
2-3 sec. but shifts at 14 and 15 weeks to the interval between 1-2 sec. and
at 17 and 19 weeks to the interval between 0-1 sec.

7.   WHY DOES THE FETUS MOVE?

A still greatly puzzling problem concerns the functional significance of
fetal motility. Why does the fetus move so frequently and in so many
different ways?

First of all it must be realised that embryonic motility is found in all species studied so far, including invertebrates. The mechanisms of fetal motility must be considered to be a fundamental property of the developing nervous system. There may be certain additional qualities to the fetal movements of vertebrates. The development of muscles, joints and even the fine structure of the central nervous system itself may depend to a certain degree on this neural activity and its motor effects. How much such mechanisms play a role in human fetal development is far from being understood.

What is known, however, is the anticipatory character of many of the fetal motor patterns. When they emerge after two or three month gestation they are coordinated right from their onset. Whatever their effects during prenatal development may be, many motor patterns such as breathing movements, yawns, stretches, eye-movements or side-to-side-movements of the head reach their full adaptive function only after birth. At that time they are no longer only endogenously generated but come under afferent control. To make them adaptive, they must be elicitable at the appropriate moment in the adequate situation. The sensory trigger becomes mandatory.

There exists another set of fetal movements which undoubtedly possess an adaptive function during intra-uterine life. The fetus changes his position and orientation from time to time in the uterus, probably to prevent adhesions and stasis. Two different motor patterns are responsible for these postural changes. One is a rotation along the longitudinal body axis, initiated by a lateral turning of the head or the hips, and the other consists of alternating leg movements which produce a somersault if the legs are properly positioned against the uterine wall. Positional changes may occur up to 20 times per hour during the first half of pregnancy. With progressing gestation the number of changes decreases in rate, probably due to spatial restriction rather than to a decrease in the incidence of movements capable of bringing about a change in position.

A word of caution is necessary. Recently there have been attempts to over-interpret the meaning of many fetal movements and to attribute intentional behaviour to the fetus and likewise to the newborn infant. Such interpretations go far beyond the available evidence and are purely speculative. By the same token there is an over-concern with the capacity of the fetus to respond to external stimulation accompanied by a simultaneous neglect of the rich repertoire of spontaneous movements. It becomes necessary in fetal investigations to put things into the right proportions. Moreover, if stimulation experiments are carried out, mostly in fetuses near term, the effects of behavioural states on the responsivity to stimuli of various modalities have to be taken into account. Behavioural states develop in the human fetus around 36 weeks post-menstrual age (see Prechtl, 1985) and show the same input-output relationship as after birth in the neonate (see Prechtl, 1974).

8.   THE POSTNATAL FATE OF FETAL MOVEMENTS

It is already clear from what has been said before, that many fetal movement patterns continue after birth and reach their full adaptive functions postnatally. This is especially evident in the cases of breathing movements, eye movements, stretches, finger flexions and rhythmical side to side movements of the head. As far as fetal movements are specific intra-uterine adaptations such as the alternating leg movements or the rotation along the midsaggital axis, their survival in the postnatal period is merely a residual from fetal life. It may be said that there exists a striking continuation of the fetal repertoire into postnatal life, a topic which has been extensively dealt with in a previous publication (Prechtl, 1984). A unique situation seems to exist in the human when compared with other primates (Prechtl, 1986). The human newborn infant is remarkably poorly adapted to the requirements of the extra-uterine environment. His muscle power is poor, the postural control of head and limbs in the field of gravity is weak or even absent, social behaviour is at its best rudimentary, vision is limited and goal directed movements lack necessary precision. The young infant continues unchanged with many fetal movement patterns such as the alternating leg movements (known postnatally as stepping movements) or the writhing character of general movements (Hopkins & Prechtl, 1984). These obvious signs of incompetence continue until about the end of the second month when a major transformation of the behavioural repertoire and sensory capacities occurs. I hasten to add that there are certain adaptations shortly after birth but they involve exclusively vital functions, namely respiration, circulation and nutrition. Without these adaptations the human species would not have survived.

References

Birnholz, J.C., Stephens, J.C., Faria, M. (1978). Fetal movement patterns: a possible means of defining neurological developmental milestones in utero. *Amer. J. Roentgenol., 130*, 537-540.

Dongen, L.G.R. van, Goudie, E.G. (1980). Fetal movement patterns in the first trimester of pregnancy. *Brit. J. Obstet. Gynaecol., 87*, 191-193.

Hooker, D. (1952). *The prenatal origin of behaviour*. University of Kansas Press: Lawrence.

Hopkins, B., Prechtl, H.F.R. (1984). A qualitative approach to the development of movements during early infancy. In H.F.R. Prechtl (Ed.), *Continuity of Neural Functions from Prenatal to Postnatal Life*. Oxford: Blackwell Scientific Publications Ltd., Clinics in Developmental Medicine, no. 94.

Humphrey, T. (1978). Function of the nervous system during prenatal life. In Uwe Stave (Ed.), *Perinatal Physiology*. New York: Plenum.

Ianniruberto, A., Tajani, E. (1981). Ultrasonographic study of fetal movements. *Semin. Perinatol., 5*, 175-181.

Leeuwenhoek, A. v. (1697). Letter dated Delft Sept. 10, 1697. *Phil. Trans., 19*, 790-799.

Milani-Comparetti, A., Gidoni, E.A. (1967). Pattern analysis of motor development and its disorders. *Develop. Med. Child Neurol., 9*, 625-630.

Minkowski, M. (1928). Neurobiologische Studien am menschlichen Foetus. *Hand. Biol. Arbeidsmeth. Abt. V. Teil 5B*, 511-618.

Patrick, J., Campbell, K., Carmichael, L., Natale, R. & Richardson, B. (1982). Patterns of gross fetal body movements over 24-hour observation intervals during the last 10 weeks of pregnancy. *Am. J. Obstet. Gynecol., 142*, 363-371.

Patrick, J. & Challis, J. (1980). Measurement of human fetal breathing movements in healthy pregnancies using a real-time scanner. *Semin. Perinatol., 4*, 275-286.

Prechtl, H.F.R. (1974). The behavioural states of the newborn infant (a review). *Brain Res., 76*, 1304-1311.

Prechtl, H.F.R. (1977). *The neurological examination of the full-term newborn infant*. Second revised and enlarged version. London: Heinemann. Clinics in Developmental Medicine, vol. 63.

Prechtl, H.F.R. (1984). *Continuity of neural functions from prenatal to to postnatal life*. Oxford: Blackwell Scientific Publications Ltd. Clinics in Developmental Medicine, no. 94.

Prechtl, H.F.R. (1985). Ultrasound studies of human fetal behaviour. *Early Human Developm., 12*, 91-98.

Prechtl, H.F.R. (1986). New perspectives in early human development. *Europ. J. Obst. Gynecol. Repr., 21* (in press).

Prechtl, H.F.R., Fargel, J.W., Weinmann, H.M., Bakker, H.H. (1979). Posture, motility and respiration in low-risk preterm infants. *Develop. Med. Child Neurol., 21*, 3-27.

Preyer, W. (1885). *Die spezielle Physiologie des Embryo*. Leipzig: Grieben.

Reinold, E. (1971). Beobachtung fötaler Aktivität in der ersten Hälfte der Gravidität mit dem Ultraschall. *Pädiatrie und Pädologie, 6*, 274-279.

Reinold, E. (1976). Ultrasonics in early pregnancy. Diagnostic scanning and fetal motor activity. In *Contributions to Gynaecology and Obstetrics*. *Vol. 1*. Basel: Karger.

Vries, J.I.P. de, Visser, G.H.A. & Prechtl, H.F.R. (1982). The emergence of fetal behaviour. I. Qualitative aspects. *Early Human Develop., 7*, 301-322.

64

Vries, J.I.P. de, Visser, G.H.A. & Prechtl, H.F.R. (1984). Fetal mobility in the first half of pregnancy. In H.F.R. Prechtl (Ed.), *Continuity of neural functions from prenatal to postnatal life*. Oxford: Blackwell Scientific Publications Ltd. Clinics in Developmental Medicine, no. 94.

Vries, J.I.P. de, Visser, G.H.A. & Prechtl, H.F.R. (1985). The emergence of fetal behaviour. II. Quantitative aspects. *Early Human Develop.*, *12*, 99-120.

THE MATURATION AND DEVELOPMENT OF FETAL MOTOR PATTERNS

Peter H. Wolff

Prechtl's summary of observations on fetal motor development has identified a number of issues with implications for developmental theory that extend well into the postnatal period. For example, the observations challenge traditional answers about the developmental mechanisms that transform antecedent behaviours into qualitatively new patterns whose functions cannot be predicted from, or reduced to, their antecedent components. It also presents a novel perspective on enduring debates about motor development, as either an autochthonous maturational process, or as the linking of reflexes by exteroceptive stimuli, or as the spontaneous emergence of novel properties in self organising systems.

The development of fetal motor patterns

On the basis of their organisational features, timing characteristics and spatio-temporal coordinates, Prechtl and his colleagues have described fifteen distinct motor patterns, and have classified these according to their short and long term functional significance. Despite minor individual differences in absolute maturational rate, the sequence in which these motor patterns emerge was found to be invariant across individuals. Furthermore, fetal movements that later comprise the motor repertory of the full term neonate were found to be fully formed by the 15th-16th week of postmenstrual age. With the possible exception of general movements, in other words, the patterns of fetal motor activity do not change qualitatively during the last half of pregnancy (i.e., they do not develop). Such evidence is consistent with at least one traditional hypothesis about early motor development that holds that the direction and rate of behavioural development are controlled by intrinsic maturational timetables, whereas exercise, experience, proprioception and intrauterine stimuli make few if any contributions. Such a conclusion is also compatible with independent findings by Prechtl and his colleagues to the effect that there are striking similarities in the onset and quality of movement patterns between fetuses and preterm infants of the same postmenstrual age, in spite of marked differences in the gravitational force fields in which the respective motor patterns must operate (Prechtl et al, 1979; De Vries et al, 1984). However, an extensive body of experimental and clinical evidence indicates that exercise, repetition and proprioceptive feedback as well as feed-forward mechanisms profoundly influence the development and coordination of motor patterns in animals, in infants, children and adults (Bernstein, 1967; Stelmach, 1976). Therefore, it would be extremely unlikely that the same variables do not play a role in the development of fetal motor activity or that the latter matures in splendid isolation. In contrast to non-mammalian vertebrates, for example, the mammalian fetus shows no significant delays between the onset of spontaneous fetal movements and its capacity to respond to exteroceptive stimuli (Gottlieb, 1976). By extrapolation from experiments on non-mammalian vertebrates, it can therefore not be concluded that the development of human fetal movements in stringently controlled by endogenous programs of maturational timetables which operate independent of experience or exteroceptive stimulation. In fact, Prechtl's observations on the prenatal development of behavioural states provide indirect support for the contrary conclusion that fetal movements *are* modified by their activity. For example, towards the end of pregnancy, eye movements, general movements, heart rate patterns and other coordinated movements are sufficiently synchronised so that distinct ensembles of behaviour patterns, which are analogous to the behavioural states described for full term neonates, can be identified (Nijhuis et al, 1984). Assuming that fetal behavioural states, like those of full term infants, are the emergent properties of dynamically interacting motor patterns acting as organised wholes (Wolff, 1984), one would expect that long before such behavioural states can be recognised as distinct entities, two or more concurrently active repetitive motor patterns will become partially synchronised and will give rise to dynamically stable new coordinated patterns. Instead of the conclusion that individual prenatal motor patterns remain developmentally invariant throughout the last half of pregnancy which is based on their morphological similarities, it is likely that the interaction among two or more distinct motor patterns will modify their temporal and other biomechanical properties (Holst, 1935; Belen'kii et al, 1967). While there is at present no systematic evidence on fetuses to substantiate this claim, related data on limb interaction in non-mammalian vertebrates, mammals and human infants, children and adults justify the generic hypothesis which pertains to all living systems, that the dynamic interaction among patterned movements will, under specifiable conditions, induce novel patterns which possess qualitatively different properties than those of the elements from which they emerge. Such a hypothesis would predict that two or more simultaneously active motor patterns in the fetus will exhibit the same kinds of relative coordination, mutual entrainments and other dynamic interactions which can be shown to play an important role in the motor coordination of infants, children and adults (Kelso & Tuller, 1983; Greene, 1972; Peiper, 1963; Dreier et al, 1979). The hypothesis also predicts that the systematic comparison of motor patterns in fetuses and premature infants of equivalent post-menstrual age in terms of their temporal variables should demonstrate significant differences in their reciprocal timing relationships as a function of the variations in gravitational force fields.

The functional significance of fetal motor patterns

In keeping with established conventions in ethology (Gould, 1982), Prechtl and his colleagues classified the various types of fetal movements by their inferred short or long term adaptive significance. Some fetal motor patterns were classified as having evolved specifically for adaptation to an intrauterine environment but of serving no purpose thereafter. The concept of ontogenetic adaptations (Oppenheim, 1981; Hamburger & Oppenheim, 1982), which is implied by this category, was introduced to developmental investigations as a *caveat* against uncritical applications of the epigenetic hypothesis to all behaviour patterns of the immature organism. The hypothesis posits that all earlier behavioural forms anticipate the direction of development towards an adult steady state (reproductive competence), and that all earlier behavioural forms are integrated into later stages of behavioural organisation in order to achieve that end state. The concept of ontogenetic adaptations was instrumental in redirecting developmental investigations to the possibility that at least some early motor processes have no long range adaptive significance for the adult but are nevertheless important as transient adaptations during self-limited periods of the growth cycle. This, I believe, was the sense in which Prechtl implied the concept of ontogenetic adaptations in his functional taxonomy.

Given the confusion in developmental psychology that is likely to arise as it comes to terms with major advances of developmental neurobiology, it is, however, possible that the concept of ontogenetic adaptations will, like other useful terms in the past, become hypostatised (Pepper, 1942). Once hypostatised, the concept of ontogenetic adaptations could then become a convenient escape clause to explain otherwise unexplained discontinuities of motor development, in this way shortcircuiting any systematic analysis of the many ways in which fetal motor activity can influence postnatal motor development even when there are no obvious linear continuities of morphology. "Critical experiments" necessary to test the assumption that ontogenetic adaptations are totally deleted from the developmental process can obviously not be performed on humans. Even in species where such experiments are ethically permissible, however, it would probably be as difficult to prove that early behavioural forms contribute *nothing* to later motor coordinations, as it would be to substantiate the epigenetic claim that *all* antecedent conditions prepare the way for, and are incorporated by, later developmental states. For example, the exercise and repetition of fetal motor patterns might lay the foundations for later motor coordinations – not in terms of the skeleto-muscular units and motor programs of the movements themselves, but in terms of "operational principles" such as serial order control (Lashley, 1951) or load compensation (Fentress, 1976) that derive from the earlier practice of motor activities. Such functional principles might then be exported to entirely different movement patterns while the observed fetal movements are in fact deleted from the repertory. Such an alternative would imply that a functional taxonomy of fetal motor patterns can be misleading when inference about functional continuities or discontinuities are based on superficial analogies of form and when the equally likely possibility is ignored that evolution has selected for physiologically plausible mechanisms or operational principles that are shared across different classes of motor behaviour (Gould, 1977).

A related issue which is not pertinent to Prechtl's discussion where the term never arose, but which is nevertheless mentioned frequently by others as a critical point in motor coordination that must be overcome before development of the full term infant can proceed, involves the notion of "primitive reflex" (Capute et al, 1978; Touwen, 1984). The term implies that "the reflex" is the primary unit of motor coordination. It also implies a model of central nervous system development in which earlier motor patterns are inhibited in hierarchic layers by higher control centres but are preserved in their original form rather than being transformed by schema formation. If not properly inhibited, such primitive reflexes will interfere with the acquisition of more adaptive motor patterns. However, once inhibited, primitive reflexes can also re-emerge in the adult when neuropathology, for example, strips away layers of inhibitory mechanisms (Paulson & Gottlieb, 1968). Uncritical acceptance of the primitive reflex concept as a theoretical basis for developmental neurology has, as others already have commented, led to very questionable diagnostic and clinical practices (Touwen, 1984). The possibility that mechanisms of motor coordination which were elaborated by the exercise of early motor patterns are nevertheless maintained and refined throughout the growth years should, however, not be dismissed outright, simply because the primitive reflex concept is misleading.

While investigating the temporal organisation of nutritive and non-nutritive sucking patterns in human infants (Wolff, 1968, 1972) I also examined the oral praxis of pre-senile and functionally decorticate adult patients. In full term infants, non-nutritive and nutritive sucking patterns could easily be differentiated according to their respective patterns of serial organisation, and these were closely related to their different functions. Healthy infants after six months, children and adults performed *nutritive* sucking patterns for extended periods without fatigue, whenever the nipple provided fluid. By contrast, they (including normal adults who were fully acquainted with patterns of non-nutritive sucking in infants) could not reproduce the non-nutritive sucking pattern on a blind nipple, fatigued rapidly and showed gross variability of inter-response intervals. Similarly, senile adults who were still responsive to their social and physical environment had no difficulty reproducing the nutritive sucking pattern but never sucked in the expected non-nutritive mode on a blind nipple. In effect, decorticate patients were the only adults who exhibited both nutritive and non-nutritive sucking patterns. They were remakably proficient in both modes; they performed at about the same frequency and with the same stability of rhythm as full term infants and they did so without evidence of fatigue.

From such findings one might conclude that the behavioural regression which occurs after decortication had removed higher cortical inhibitory centres and, when the regression was severe enough, had released the "non-nutritive sucking reflex" in its original form. However, the comparative developmental analysis of oral motor patterns was, in my experiments, limited to variables of serial order control. If the analysis had been extended to include variables of force, muscle tonus, reciprocal activation and the co-ordination of sucking with other skilled actions, the results might have led to the very different conclusion that development transformed fetal and infantile motor patterns so radically that the non-nutritive sucking pattern of the young infant is eliminated by ontogenetic adaptations. The second alternative proposed above assumes that some important functional characteristics of the fetal motor patterns continue to operate throughout the growth years and are appropriated by different classes of motor patterns when other functional characteristics of fetal motor activity are lost to ontogenetic adaptation or are so radically transformed that they become unrecognisable. For reasons already alluded to, however (see also below), it is operationally impossible to make any categorical distinction among these proposed alternatives concerning the fate of early motor patterns. Therefore, it may also be more productive to investigate actual processes of motor development in the transition from prenatal to postnatal life than to argue categorically either that primitive reflexes are the self-evident and logical basis for early clinical intervention or alternatively that the concept primitive reflexes is rank nonsense.

Another category of functional types which was included in Prechtl's review of prenatal motor patterns, assumed that some fetal movements have no obvious intrauterine function but prepare motor coordinations which will be vital for postnatal adaptation. Such preparatory functions should therefore confer reproductive advantage on the species. Respiratory and eye movements, for example, serve no conceivable direct function as long as the fetus remains in the uterus. Nevertheless, they are spontaneously active by at least fifteen weeks of postmenstrual age. The functional taxonomy proposed by Prechtl suggests that these fetal motor patterns may, as preparatory exercises, strengthen existing movements and fine tune the coordination of components into complex motor patterns which will make them functionally competent as soon as they are needed after birth. Parenthetically, if at least some fetal motor patterns can be shown to "prepare" postnatal adaptations by repetition and exercise, such a finding would imply that fetal motor patterns, like postnatal motor actions, are in fact modified by their own activity and are therefore not developmentally invariant during the second half of pregnancy.

The category of *general movements* is of particular interest for a functional classification of types because these motor patterns are assumed to serve at least two and possibly more pre- as well as post-natal adaptive functions. General movements therefore raise theoretically important but problematic procedural questions concerning the appropriate criteria for assigning particular functions to specific motor patterns. As prenatal ontogenetic adaptations, general movements prevent adhesions and prevent the stasis of skin circulation, maintain joint mobility and perhaps enhance muscle tonus. While general movements also comprise a major portion of the infant's motor repertory until at least the fifth month after birth, their postnatal adaptive functions are not clear. Evolutionary and ethological considerations would argue against any skeptical conclusion to the effect that this major category of movement patterns has no function but is simply there. In contrast to traditional assumptions in the child development literature, however, mass activity of the infant apparently does not provide the non-specific matrix from which new and discrete motor patterns gradually differentiate (Irwin & Weiss, 1930; Hopkins & Prechtl, 1984). On the other hand, it has been proposed on the basis of longitudinal studies (Hopkins & Prechtl, 1984) that the postnatal exercise of general movements may calibrate proprioceptive control of the limbs, and particularly of the arms. From this proposal it remains unclear, however, whether proprioceptive fine tuning of the arms, which obviously does occur during development, is a serendipitous effect of non-specific general movements, or whether general movements were in fact adapted by evolution exactly for this purpose.

As already suggested, there are no self-evident rules for adjudicating among competing hypotheses about the functional significance and evolutionary purpose of prenatal motor patterns, for deciding whether the short and long term adaptive significance of ontogenetic adaptations differs in principle from those of primitive reflexes, or for deciding which particular fetal motor patterns are and are not involved in later processes of motor coordination. As long as theoretical guidelines do not exist which would constrain evolutionary speculations about the adaptive significance of behaviour for the developing individual, any motor pattern and all of its presumed operational principles could in effect serve a wide range of short and long term adaptive purposes. However, many of these purposes can only be inferred after the fact (Oppenheim, 1981).

An alternative strategy for the systematic developmental analysis of fetal motor patterns may therefore be useful, which is in the end not required to appeal to criteria of self-evidence for classification. It starts with the premise that patterns we recognise as motor types are not ontological entities with prescribed adaptive functions, but "emergent properties" resulting from the interaction of different combinations of neuro-motor units, and inducing novel ensembles with greater or lesser internal cohesion or "self equilibrating" tendencies (Kugler et al, 1980; Turvey et al, 1978). The functions of these ensembles are not prescribed *a priori,* and can only be inferred *a posteriori*. Moreover, the function of a particular motor pattern is not fixed inexorably but varies systematically with the context to which it is applied. Thus the functional significance of early motor patterns is prescribed by their context rather than by their morphology. Simply labeling fetal or neonatal motor activity as the emergent property of "self organising systems" obviously achieves nothing more than to confuse an already complex issue with obscure jargon. Nevertheless, as a metaphor for guiding research, rather than as an explanatory concept, it leads to empirically testable hypotheses about early motor development that can be stated in a coherent theoretical framework. It calls attention to functional dynamics *among* component movements as one possible mechanism of developmental transformations that does not appeal to extrinsic executive agencies, motor programs or maturational timetables in order to "explain" development (Kelso & Tuller, 1983). The dimension of functional dynamics has generally been neglected in conventional studies of early motor development (Thelen, 1985). The alternative hypothesis also redirects the developmental analysis of fetal movements from untestable speculations about short and long term adaptive functions to a theory-based investigation of the mechanisms by which one fetal motor pattern modulates the frequency, timing and spatiotemporal coordinates of other movements; and of the process by which qualitatively new motor patterns are induced during the dynamic interaction of two or more concurrent movement patterns.

The spontaneous causation of movement

The formulation proposed here to the effect that fetal motor patterns are emergent properties of self organising systems is intimately related to the conception of motor patterns as "spontaneous" phenomena. In contrast to behavioural psychology and reflex notions of neurology, theoretical biology has long recognised that the spontaneity of behaviour is an inherent property of all living organisms. As early as 1928, von Bertalanffy, for example wrote:

> Spontaneous activity is a consequence of the fact
> that the organism as an open system is able to
> maintain a state distant from equilibrium and to
> extend the existing potentialities either in spon-
> taneous activity or in responding to stimuli.
> Biological, neurophysiological, behavioural and
> psychological evidence equally show that spontaneous
> activity is primary; that stimulus response is a
> repetitive mechanism superimposed on it. The organism
> is not therefore a robot or an automaton; rather,
> originally holistic behaviour becomes progressively
> - and never completely - mechanised (Bertalanffy,
> 1934).

In general, this description is, I believe, consistent with a number of contemporary formulations in theoretical biology which hypothesise that all living organisms conform to principles of irreversible thermodynamics (Turvey et al, 1978; Bertalanffy, 1968).

Under specified conditions of behavioural state, all normal and many pathological fetuses or newborns will exhibit "spontaneous" motor patterns that are not provoked by any known exteroceptive stimulus (Wolff, 1966;

Prechtl, 1968). Many spontaneous motor patterns in turn exhibit rhythmic or near periodic temporal patterns whose base frequencies are specific to each motor type. Such observations argue strongly against competing hypotheses concerning the causes of behaviour which posit, for example, that the intra- or extra-uterine environment is furnished with carefully timed stimulus sequences which are capable of triggering each of these "spontaneous" motor patterns according to its own periodicity but without any evidence of "cross talk". The improbability of such an alternative is increased by the fact that external Zeitgeber with the appropriate timing characteristics have never been identified. While spontaneous causation is probably the more plausible explanation for most fetal movement patterns, this conclusion in no way negates parallel observations to the effect that the same motor patterns can also be produced by exteroceptive stimuli (Birnholz, 1984, see also below). However, what kinds of mechanisms may be implied by the term spontaneous remains unclear.

Jeannerod's history of brain physiology and brain-behaviour relation-ships (Jeannerod, 1985) indicates that spontaneity of action traditionally has been advanced as the direct antithesis to a competing hypothesis which posits the reflex as the basic unit of movement and assumes that motor development is ultimately dependent on external stimuli whereas input-output relationships are essentially linear. Thus the concept of spontaneous motor activity challenges any perspective on behavioural adaptation which rejects or ignores the inherent transfer function of the behavioural stages and rejects the self-equilibrating characteristic of living organisms. Experimental studies in developmental neurobiology, for example, demonstrate that neurons in cell culture will aggregate to construct physiologically competent neural networks which will fire spontaneously, as well as responding to afferent input (Crain, 1976). Concretely, therefore, a sufficient density of nerve cells or other living interactive elements (Katchalsky et al, 1974) can be conceived of as inducing new dynamically stable systems whose properties could not be predicted from a linear addition of properties of the separate components.

Similarly, contemporary neurology assumes that the repetitive motor activities which mark grand mal seizures result from the hypersynchronisation among populations of neural cells, and that the intrinsic interaction among a sufficient density of metabolic units is a sufficient cause for organised motor activity. Extrapolating from such well established phenomena of clinical neurology, one might further assume that similar endogenous mechanisms are sufficient causes for non-pathological spontaneous motor activity. Neurologists have, however, recognised that seizures do not occur simply by spontaneous generation and that organismic and environmental variables usually contribute significantly to the induction of seizure activity. Only as the seizure becomes self-organising does the organism become immune to further environmental influences (Fentress, 1976). Thus the causation of seizure activity is neither spontaneous nor dependent on exteroceptive stimuli.

Observations on full term and preterm infants indicate that the behavioural state variable is a critical dimension to be considered in any coherent model of spontaneous motor activity. Behavioural state accounts for the biased distribution of spontaneous motor actions as well as for the non-linear relation between stimulus and discrete motor responses. By varying the intensity of stimulation for elicited motor patterns in full term neonates, I could show, for example, that motor patterns which occur spontaneously with relatively greatest frequency in one behavioural state were also most easily elicited in that state as responses to stimuli of low intensity, whereas stimulus intensity had to be substantially increased to elicit the same motor pattern in other behavioural states where such motor patterns do not occur spontaneously (Katchalsky et al, 1974). In a sense one might therefore conclude that stimuli facilitate but do not cause motor patterns in a particular state; and that spontaneous movement patterns are not "spontaneous" in any ultimate sense but are responses to internal shifts or perturbations in the dynamic stability of component elements comprising a behavioural state. The probability, frequency and intensity of particular motor patterns as spontaneous phenomena or as responses to stimulation are always a function of the behavioural state. Moreover, the spontaneous occurrence of fetal motor patterns under some organismic conditions in no way precludes their provocation by exteroceptive stimuli under other conditions (Birnholz, 1984).

The alternative proposed here assumes that spontaneous causation of motor patterns does not differ in principle from afferent causation of the same motor event. Spontaneous movements cannot be attributed to autochthonous pattern generators or instinctual energies as necessary and sufficient causes. Similarly, motor responses to discrete exteroceptive stimuli are not reducable to direct reflex relationships and the state variable always intervenes as a non-linear transfer function between input and output. The same state variable comprises the organismic condition whose fluctuations presumbly "induce" spontaneous motor activity. The finding that the same motor pattern can either be provoked by exteroceptive stimulation or be induced as an emergent property of transient state fluctuations thus eliminates the need for making categorical distinctions between stimulus-elicited and spontaneous motor patterns.

As an alternative hypothesis for the causation of fetal motor patterns this formulation proposes that the interaction of a sufficient density of motor components will confer dynamic stability on the ensemble as a coherent whole (Fentress, 1976; Belen'kii et al, 1967; Katchalsky et al, 1974). In turn, each ensemble or behavioural state confers different non-linear input-output relationships on the infant's spontaneous motor patterns. The strategic advantage that might derive from such an alternative is its ability to account for the induction of behaviour patterns and for motor development in terms of mechanisms that do not invoke extrinsic executive agencies as their causation.

In sum, the detailed naturalistic observations on fetal movement patterns presented by Prechtl afford a unique opportunity for re-examining a number of cherished assumptions about early motor organisation and development, and for exploring whether other metaphors and theoretical models will bring our knowledge about basic mechanisms of motor development further in those domains where traditional theoretical solutions are no longer productive.

73

References

Belen'kii, V.Y., Gurfinkel, V.S. & Pal'tsev, Y. (1967). Elements of control of voluntary movements. *Biophysics, 12*, 135-141.
Bernstein, N.A. (1967). *The Coordination and Regulation of Movements.* London: Pergamon.
Bertalanffy, L.V. (1934). *Modern Theories of Development.* New York: Harper (1928).
Bertalanffy, L.V. (1968). *Organismic Psychology and Systems Theory.* Barre, MA: Clark University Press.
Birnholz, J. (1984). Fetal neurology. In R.C. Sanders and M. Hill (Eds.), *Ultrasound Annual 1984.* New York: Raven Press.
Capute, A.J., Accardo, P.J., Vining, P.E.G., Rubenstein, J.E. & Harryman, S. (1978). *Primitive Reflex Profile.* Baltimore: University Park Press.
Crain, S.M. (1976). *Neurophysiological Studies in Tissue Culture.* New York: Raven Press.
Dreier, T., Wolff, P.H., Cross, E.E. & Cochran, W.D. (1979). Patterns of breath intervals during non-nutritive sucking in full-term and 'at risk' preterm infants with normal neurological examinations. *Early Human Development, 3/2*, 187-199.
Fentress, J.C. (1976). Dynamic boundaries of patterned behavior: inter-actions and self-organization. in F.P.G. Bateson and R.A. Hinde (Eds.), *Growing Points in Ethology.* Cambridge: Cambridge University Press.
Gottlieb, G. (1976). The roles of experience in the development of behavior and the nervous system. In G. Gottlieb (Ed.), *Development and Neural and Behavioral Specificity.* New York: Academic Press.
Gould, S.J. (1977). *Ontogeny and Phylogeny.* Cambridge, MA: Harvard University Press.
Gould, J.L. (1982). *Ethology: The Mechanisms and Evolution of Behavior.* New York: Norton.
Greene, P.H. (1972). Problems or organization of motor systems. In R. Rosen and F. Snell (Eds.), *Progress in Theoretical Biology.* New York: Academic Press.
Hamburger, V. & Oppenheim, R.W. (1982). Naturally occurring neuronal death in vertebrates. *Neuroscience Commentaries, 1*, 39-55.
Holst, E.V. (1935). Uber den Prozess der Zentra-nervosen Koordination. *Pfluger's Arch. Ges. Physiol. Mensch. Tiere, 236*, 149-158.
Hopkins, B.J. & Prechtl, H.F.R. (1984). A qualitative approach to the development of movements during early infancy. In H.F.R. Prechtl (Ed.), *Continuity of Neural functions from Prenatal to Postnatal Life.* Oxford: Blackwell Scientific.
Irwin, O.C. & Weiss, A.P. (1930). A note on mass activity in newborn infants. *J. Comp. Psychol., 14*, 415-428.
Jeannerod, M. (1985). *The Brain Machine.* Transl. Urion D. Cambridge: Harvard University Press (in press).
Katchalsky, A.K., Rouland, V. & Blumenthal, R. (1974). Dynamic patterns of brain cell assemblies. *Neuroscience Res. Progr. Bull., 12*, 1.
Kelso, J.A.S. & Tuller, B. (1983). A dynamical basis for action systems. In M.S. Gazzaniga (Ed.), *Handbook of Cognitive Neuroscience.* New York: Plenum Press.
Kugler, P.N., Kelso, J.A.S. & Turvey, M.T. (1980). On the concept of coordinative structures as dissipative structures. I. Theoretical lines of convergence. In G.E. Stelmach and J. Requin (Eds.), *Tutorials in Motor Behavior.* New York: North Holland Publishing.
Lashley, K.S. (1951). The problem of serial order in behavior. In L.A. Jeffries (Ed.), *Cerebral Mechanisms in Behavior.* New York: Wiley.

Nijhuis, J.G., Martin Jr., C.B. & Prechtl, H.F.R. (1984). Behavioral states of the human fetus. In H.F.R. Prechtl (Ed.), *Continuity of Neural Functions from Prenatal to Postnatal Life*. Oxford: Blackwell Scientific.

Oppenheim, R.W. (1981). Ontogenetic adaptations and retrogressive processes in the development of the nervous system and behavior: a neuroembryologic perspective. In K.J. Connolly and H.F.R. Prechtl (Eds.), *Maturation and Development: Biological and Psychological Perspectives*. London: Heinemann Medical.

Paulson, G. & Gottlieb, G. (1968). Developmental reflexes: the reappearance of fetal and neonatal reflexes in aged patients. *Brain, 91,* 37-52.

Peiper, A. (1963). *Cerebral function in infancy and childhood*. New York: Consultants Bureau.

Pepper, S.C. (1942). *World Hypotheses*. Berkely: University of California Press.

Prechtl, H.F.R. (1968). Polygraphic studies of full term newborn infants. II. Computer analysis of recorded data. In M.C.O. Bax and R.C. Mackerth (Eds.), *Studies in Infancy*. London: Heinemann-Spastics International.

Prechtl, H.F.R., Fargel, J.W., Weinmann, H.M. & Bakker, H.H. (1979). Posture motility and respiration in low-risk preterm infants. *Develop. Med. Child Neurol., 21,* 3-27.

Stelmach, G.E. (1976). *Motor Control: Issues and Trends*. New York: Academic Press.

Thelen, E. (1985). Developmental origins of motor coordinations: leg movements in human infants. *Develop. Psychobiol., 18,* 1-22.

Touwen, B.C.L. (1984). Primitive reflexes - conceptional or semantic problem? In H.F.R. Prechtl (Ed.), *Continuity of Neural Functions from Prenatal to Postnatal Life*. Oxford: Blackwell Scientific.

Turvey, M.T., Shaw, R.E. & Mace, N. (1978). Issues in the theory of action: degrees of freedom, coordinative structures and coalitions. In J. Requin (Ed.), *Attention and Performance (VII)*. Hillsdale, NJ: Lawrence Erlbaum Associates.

Vries, J.I.P. de, Visser, G.H.A. & Prechtl, H.F.R. (1984). Fetal motility in the first half of pregnancy. In H.F.R. Prechtl (Ed.), *Continuity of Neural Functions from Prenatal to Postnatal Life*. Oxford: Blackwell Scientific.

Wolff, P.H. (1966). *The causes, controls and organization of behavior*. New York: International University Press.

Wolff, P.H. (1968). The serial organization of sucking in the young infant. *Pediatrics, 42,* 943-956.

Wolff, P.H. (1972). The interaction of state and non-nutritive sucking. In J.F. Bosma (Ed.), *Third Symposium on Oral Sensation and Perception*. Springfield, Il: C.C. Thomas.

Wolff, P.H. (1984). Discontinuous changes in human wakefulness around the end of the second month of life: a developmental perspective. In H.F.R. Prechtl (Ed.), *Continuity of Neural Functions from Prenatal to Postnatal Life*. Oxford: Blackwell Scientific.

SECTION 3

DEVELOPMENT OF COORDINATION

DEVELOPMENT OF COORDINATED MOVEMENT: DYNAMIC, RELATIONAL AND MULTILEVELED PERSPECTIVES

John C. Fentress

1.   INTRODUCTION

The ideas of movement, co-ordering and development represent some of
the most fundamental, fascinating and indeed mysterious properties of
behavioural and neurobiological systems. How is it possible for an organism
to stream its actions in space and time, to be controlled through systems
that are both self-ordered and interactive, or to differentiate these integrative
capacities during subsequent phases or early ontogeny? These are questions
that faced all members of the present *NATO Advanced Study Institute on Motor
Skill Acquisition in Children,* although in many specific guises, preferences
of emphasis, specialised topics, etc.

My goal in the present contribution is to probe certain implications of
ideas in movement, co-ordering and development, with special reference to
how these notions might be joined together in future thought and experimentation. To do this I shall work toward establishing a framework that is
explicitly *dynamic, relational* and *multileveled* in its organisational
properties. While such a framework is more complex than those which involve
questionable assumptions of static, isolated and single dimensional events, it
has the advantage of realism, and is empirically tractable. I shall attempt to
illustrate the value of this framework through reference to some of the
research conducted by me, my colleagues and students on socially and
individually coordinated movements in non-human mammals. One of the
benefits to me in participating in this *Advanced Study Institute* was my
realisation that many animal and human oriented researchers are struggling
with very similar problems. These problems have both conceptual and
empirical roots, with broad-ranging implications for how we think about and
do research on coordinated action.

In subsequent chapters, Esther Thelen and Howard Zelaznik will have
the opportunity to "react" to the framework provided here, and to comment
further on possible connections between animal work and recent studies of
early coordination in human infants, plus psychological approaches to human
performance. These include their own elegant studies on the development of
kicking and locomotor movements (e.g. Thelen, 1985; Thelen & Fogel, in
press), and attentional/cognitive processes (e.g. Zelaznik, 1985; Zelaznik &
Hahn, 1985).

2.   THE FRAMEWORK

The reasons for working within the proposed framework are simple. By
way of introduction it is sufficient to say that we do not yet have a

satisfactory taxonomy of either the phenomenology or machinery of behaviour, movement systems included. We are a long way from any "periodic table" in which logical cohesions among defined "elements" can be inferred; the negative result can be rather akin to neurobehavioural alchemy (Figure 1: cf. Jacob's (1976) sympathetic discussion of the relations among early biology and alchemist thought).

AIR
WATER
FIRE
EARTH

Fig. 1. The original caption reads, "The Periodic Table", Sidney Harris, Copyright *American Scientist*. The point is that we do not have any single obvious basis for behavioural taxonomy.

2.1. Why dynamics, relations, and multiple levels?

2.1.1. Dynamics

Movement and development each refer most basically to changes in time; i.e. process. However, our language system tends to compartmentalise observations into static images. While for many purposes derived concepts such as "units", "modules" and "stages" serve well to highlight important categories of events, they can obscure rather than reveal the operation of underlying dynamic processes. From his perspective as a theoretical physicist, David Bohm has phrased his concerns with the broad idea of movement in the following terms:

> Whenever one thinks of anything, it seems to be apprehended either as static, or as a series of static images. Yet, in the actual experience of movement, one senses an unbroken, undivided process of flow, to which the series of static images in thought is related as a series of "still" photographs might be related to the actuality of a speeding car (Bohm, 1980, p. ix).

Now, classes of movement, or classes of developmental events, are obviously recognised by their relatively stable (consistent) characteristics, and it is a legitimate enterprise to categorise and label them on this basis. Indeed, it is to be expected that there are at least relatively stable (e.g. anatomical) substrates that give rise to repeated episodes of movement. It is the relation of these relatively stable and more dynamic attributes of movement that lies at the heart of the matter (Fentress, 1984; Fentress & McLeod, 1986 - see also chapters by Thelen and by Kugler, this *Advanced Study Institute*).

The image of vortices in a stream, noted by Bohm (1980), conveys a good initial sense of the problem; i.e. a vortice is a recognisable category of dynamic movements of fluids. These movements can reflect a stream's (etc.) more stable structural characteristics (cf. anatomy) that are often far removed from the locus of the vortice itself, as well as changes in water level (cf. "drive"!) etc. Stabilities in biological systems are always relative. In a recent review of neural specificity in development, Easter, Purves, Rakic and Spitzer have thus emphasised, "a dynamic process of rearrangement of connections rather than simply a wiring of rigidly identified elements" (1985, p. 508).

2.1.2. Relations

Neither animals nor the movement patterns they express exist in a vacuum. To define either organisms or their movements we obviously draw a conceptual boundary between them and other structures/events. But this does not mean that either organisms or particular categories of movement we define are immune to influences from their surround. In some sense we are all aware of this, but the host of potential complexities that the surround can bring into our conceptualisations is something rarely dealt with in explicit terms. I shall be arguing as the paper progresses that the concept of *co-ordering* , properly considered, brings us face to face with these complexities. In brief, contextual as well as component events must be taken into account.

By way of illustration, for most biologically oriented investigators problems of co-ordering begin with the concern for adaptive relations between organism and environment. While organism and environment are, necessarily, defined in opposition to one another, neither can be fully understood without reference to the other. The evolutionary biologist, Richard Lewontin, has summarised the extreme degree to which our categories of environment depend upon our categories of organism in these terms: "In fact, we only recognise an 'environment' when we see the organism whose environment it is" (1983, p. 280). A closely analogous point was made by the psychologist J.J. Gibson (1979) when he spoke of different "affordances" provided by a given environment for organisms with different inherent capabilities and limitations (see also E.J. Gibson, 1982, for an extension of this framework into a more explicitly developmental context).

The point can easily be lost in abstractions, or (a worse fate still) be ignored altogether. To help set the stage for some of the subtleties that we shall have to deal with later, let me make brief reference to the thoughts of a small number of respected workers from other fields.

In their recent popularised book on physical order, Ilya Prigogine and Isabelle Stengers, summarise the current state of intellectual struggle in these terms: "Today physics has discovered the need to assert both the distinction and interdependence between units and relations. It now recognizes that, for an interaction to be real, the "nature" of the related things must derive from these relations, while at the same time the relations must derive from the 'nature' of the things" (1984, p. 95). In a second popularised book, from the perspective of physical chemists, Manfred Eigen and Ruthild Winkler make the analogous point that in basic biochemical reactions: "the partners are always somehow changed by the encounter" (1981, p. 84). *This is co-ordering parexcellence;* the properties of "pieces" are potentially as much a function of their relations as are the properties of relations a reflection of their chemical components.

Such perspectives can, of course, appear daunting (and perhaps even irrelevant) to workers who view nature in terms of isolated compartments, that can be arranged together more or less as beads on a string. Even our mathematics, as the above authors note, rest upon such notions (there is no such thing at present as a "bootstrap logic"). Here we begin to sense some limitations in our application of compartmentalised models to complex (e.g. biological) systems. The mathematician, Martin Gardner, makes the point well: "In mathematics it is possible to draw sharp, precise lines that divide mathematical entities into two classes. A geometrical structure is either superposable on its mirror image or not superposable. An asymmetric structure is right-handed or left-handed. Every integer is odd or even. There is no integer whose status in this respect is dubious. But in the world itself, except on the subatomic level of quantum theory, dividing lines are almost always fuzzy. Is tar a solid, or a liquid? Is chartreuse yellow, or green? Most physical properties lie on continuums - spectrums that fade imperceptibly from one end to the other. No matter where you bifurcate them, there will be objects so near the dividing line that ordinary language is not precise enough to enable one to say whether the objects belong on one side or the other" (1979, p. 117).

The challenge is to avoid the pseudo-precision of compartmentalised perspectives, while also acknowledging the need to fragment our observations for heuristic purposes. Needless to say, this involves an intellectual tightrope. Coordinated movements imply, at several levels, rules of relation among events that are also independently ordered. Since order itself is defined by rules of relation (Bohm, 1980), the boundary between order and co-order contains subtleties that force our thought to cross complementary levels of organisation.

2.1.3. Multiple levels

The idea of an organism is that of an entity whose parts are co-ordered. Stated somewhat differently, and in a more broadly appropriate abstract sense relevant to the themes of this *Institute,* coherences amongst "co-ordered" events make for processes of a higher order. Individual "motor units" are co-ordered to produce individual muscle contractions, agonist and antagonist muscles combine to move individual limb segments, limb segments are coordinated in space and time even in the most simple actions, and these actions together produce the functionally coherent sequences of movement that we seek to understand. The first essential point is that studies of coordinated movement (and the development of movement) necessitate awareness that nature must be sliced at a number of complementary levels. Each of these levels can have its own special rules. Attempts to generalise across levels (not to mention movement "types", ages, species, etc.) deserve caution in their pursuit.

Perhaps less obviously, even basic parameters of movement, such as *change versus stability* or *continuity versus discontinuity* can appear very different once these levels or order, and co-order, are crossed (Fentress, 1984). At other times there are phenomena that are clearly important at one

level that can be irrelevant at another – such as in temperature and
pressure that refer only to aggregates of molecules, not to single molecules
at all. In the words of von Holst and von Saint Paul (1963), a "level
adequate terminology" is an essential part of the enterprise.

On the other hand, we need to seek principles that may transcend
particular levels of organisation, and also principles that may help us to
find regularities that occur when we do cross these different levels of
organisation, species, etc. Partially for these reasons, we in our laboratory
have chosen to examine behavioural development in both social (canids) and
individual (rodents) contexts. Many of the presentations at the present
Advanced Study Institute show the merit of such multileveled approaches,
and this volume as a whole is a testimony to the value of bringing workers
from specialised levels and perspectives together.

For the ethologist, such struggles have a long history. For example, as
illustrated in Figure 2 (next page), four complementary time frames and
three major levels of analysis can be used to summarise important thrusts
in current ethological research. It is upon the separations and links among
the resulting 12 cells that pose particularly important challenges (cf. Fentress,
1984; Fentress & McLeod, 1986). Although different temporal windows and
analysis levels may be especially germane to other disciplines in the
behavioural and brain sciences, the general importance of these considerations
remains.

There is a growing awareness of the necessity of these considerations,
of multiple and complementary levels, in many fields of behavioural and
neural science. In his penetrating analysis of visual perception, David Marr
thus reflected on the need to complement single neuron analyses with
questions of function and operational algorithms. His statement is of general
importance for problems of integrated (coordinated) functioning in bio-
behavioural systems:

> There must exist an additional level of understanding
> at which the character of the information-processing
> tasks carried out during perception are analysed and
> understood in a way that is independent of the particular
> mechanisms and structures that implement them in our
> heads. This... (referring here to earlier neurobiological
> recording studies)...was what was missing – the analysis
> of the problem as an information-processing task. Such
> analysis does not usurp an understanding at the other
> levels – of neurons or of computer programs – but it
> is a necessary complement to them, since without it
> there can be no real understanding of the function of
> all those neurons (Marr, 1982, p. 19; cf. Fentress,
> 1983a, b).

F.H.C. Crick (1979) makes a similar plea for reconciling complementary
levels of analysis (e.g. "black box" and neuronal), and the difficult
challenges that face the investigator in attempting to do so:

> ...our entire way of thinking about such problems
> may be incorrect (p. 130) ...The brain is clearly so
> complex that the chances of being able to predict its
> behaviour solely from a study of its parts is too

remote to consider (p. 133).

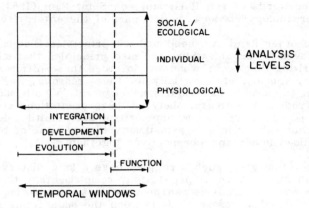

Fig. 2. Some temporal windows and analysis levels relevant to studies of coordinated movement, yielding a 12 celled matrix. ("Function" here refers to projections from the behaviour to its subsequent consequences; the other temporal frames reflect events antecedent to the behaviour. All divisions are heuristic, not absolute).

2.2. Coordination(s) considered further

Thus far coordination has been alluded to but not defined. Indeed, what does it mean to say that a certain action is "well coordinated" while another is not? We all recognise, at some level, that a skilled athlete or wild animal can show remarkable feats of coordinated movement, and most of us would agree that many of these skilled actions improve during development. But we may not always be talking about the same thing. How, then, do we coordinate our thoughts about coordination?!

I gained the impression during the present *Advanced Study Institute* that many special definitions of coordination were being employed. Here I shall attempt to distill three of the main ones (Figure 3).

2.2.1. Coordinates

The first definition is Cartesian, the ordering of events along two or more dimensions. Thus the position of a limb in space, even during static posture, is *co-ordered* along $\underline{X}$, $\underline{Y}$, and $\underline{Z}$ axes (e.g. "length", "width" and "height" of an abstracted spatial cube). In movement, there is a co-ordered change of position in time, which we can plot for these spatial dimensions. The simplest plot here is velocity, but velocity changes can also be co-ordered with time, which we call acceleration. In each case there is essentially a single point or event that we can examine along a variety of abstracted coordinates. The properties that can be abstracted for even a single limb segment are of course multiple, such as when we speak of the planar, conical and rotational movement properties of that limb segment

Eshkol & Wachmann, 1958; Harries, 1983). Common concepts of coordination do enter here, such as when we speak of jerky versus smooth limb segment movements. When we shift our coordinates these judgments can change; a given limb segment may move jerkily through space as defined by a referent external to the animal or child, but smoothly in reference to a proximal limb segment. It is important to keep these referents clear.

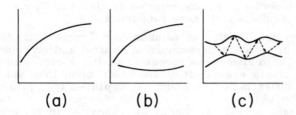

Fig. 3. Three aspects of coordination: (a) "coordinates", (b) "cohesions", (c) "co-orderings". See text for details.

2.2.2. Cohesions

Within a single limb segment we can ask how abstracted properties of movement, such as its planar and rotational aspects, cohere together. Or, we can ask how the movement properties of two or more limb segments are co-ordered, how one abstracted action (e.g. kicking) is organised in space and time with respect to another (e.g. biting), or how the movements of two or more animals in a social encounter are coordinated. Here we take our individual coordinate plots for two or more items of interest and ask how rule-given *their correspondence* is (e.g. can changes in one plot be "predicted" by changes in the other, are they symmetrical or antisymmetrical, etc.?). The qualities and quantities of these cohesions can change not only with age, but also with the descriptive/analytical procedures that we bring to bear upon our observations. Further, increased cohesions along certain dimensions may be accompanied by reductions in the cohesions along others. We see, then, that coordination is far from being a unitary event.

2.2.3. Co-orderings

Here the issue is whether the properties of movement (or development) that we separate from one another for initial analyses not only cohere to a greater or lesser extent, but also influence one another's "individual" properties (arrow in Figure 3(C)). Once we accept that mutual influence as a possibility, then we at least become sensitive to arbitrary distinctions that we might otherwise make between "pieces" of behaviour and the "relations" among these pieces. In most modular views of behavioural and brain functioning, systems of organisation are (necessarily) viewed as being "informationally encapsulated" (Fodor, 1983) in the sense that their intrinsic organisational properties are not attributable to extrinsic influences only. There are, however, *degrees of encapsulation* that are possible, these may be defined along a number of potential channels of influence, and both the degrees and channels of influence may change in time. In developmental systems the distinction between *regulative* and *mosaic* properties (Ede, 1978; Purves & Lichtman, 1985) is often employed to evaluate just how "open" versus "closed" these systems are, with respect to defined variables at particular developmental phases, etc. The fact that behavioural and biological

84

systems appear to be *both* open and closed (interactive *and* self-organised, Fentress, 1976a) remains a particularly fascinating and ubiquitous problem.

2.3. Summary

Behaviour is a multidimensional, richly connected, time machine. To understand behaviour it is necessary to isolate its relevant dimensions and to see how these are interconnected in time and across expressive spaces defined at complementary and cooperative levels. The idea of co-ordering in such a machine implies all of these properties.

The primary task is that of establishing *boundaries*, descriptively first, and then in terms of parameters of control and/or function (Figure 4). Boundaries are the divisions we recognise in the world, which in turn define relations among events; they are based upon the dual criteria of similarities and differences. As Bohm has captured in a pithy phrase: *"To be confused about what is different and what is not, is to be confused about everything"* (1980, p. 16). Pertinent questions, in brief, are: a) *where* to place boundaries, c) the precise *dimensionality* to be used in constructing the boundaries, d) the issue of relative *permeability* of the constructed boundaries to external influences (open versus closed systems), e) the extent to which bounded systems *overlap* with one another, f) the degree to which bounded systems *mutually influence* one another's individually defined properties, and g) the relative *stability* of the systems in question.

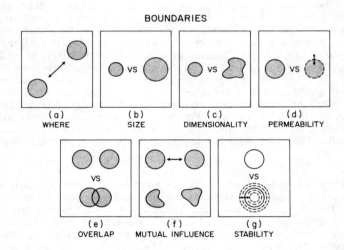

BOUNDARIES

(a) WHERE   (b) SIZE   (c) DIMENSIONALITY   (d) PERMEABILITY

(e) OVERLAP   (f) MUTUAL INFLUENCE   (g) STABILITY

Fig. 4. Considerations in the construction of descriptive and
analytical boundaries.

Co-ordering can in this way be seen as a set of dynamic constraints among systems that have their own ordering properties. Precisely where one draws the line between systems that are ordered as opposed to being co-ordered is at the hub of the problem. This becomes a particularly difficult problem, either to conceptualise or analyse, when one entertains the possibility that the properties of these separately abstracted orders are in part a reflection of their co-ordering. I submit that it is precisely here, as viewed from the context of both singularly and multiply defined transformations, that our attention should be drawn.

A useful way to conceptualise these problems is to ask the extent to which underlying control systems, as reflected in movement, a) are continuous versus discontinuous in their operational properties, and b) represent a balance between dynamic and stabilising processes (Fentress, 1984). Each of these questions can be asked at a number of levels of organisation as well as across diverse time frames, for any specific aspect of motor and other forms of behavioural organisation (Figure 2). Often it is useful in considering problems of movement coordination and its development to evaluate material along a spiral or "swirl" that cuts across the time frames and levels of analysis that are the focus of any particular study (Figure 5). In this way organisational principles and their transformations can be compared to one another.

The next sections of this contribution will be devoted to illustrating these ideas with reference to specific aspects of coordinated movement in non-human mammals. I shall then conclude with a few thoughts as to how such a dynamic, relational and multileveled framework may be used to join studies of integrated performance with the developmental events that make this performance possible.

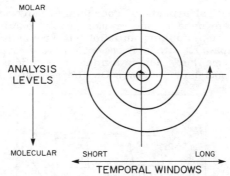

Fig. 5. The "swirl" approach to analysis levels and temporal windows, in which changes along these two dimensions are viewed together.

3.   DESCRIPTIVE MEASUREMENTS

In studies of coordinated movement and development it is clear that "what you measure is what you get". The criteria by which we slice the events in which we are interested necessarily constrain any insights that we may obtain. Ethologists have thus traditionally made the distinction between descriptions of movement *function* (consequence) and descriptions of movement *form* (Hinde, 1982). Terms such as fighting, or grooming, or kicking provide summary statements about what the behaviour accomplishes, but in themselves such terms do not reveal the detailed *form* of the accomplishment, which may vary widely. Similar functions can often be accomplished through movement patterns that differ considerably in their form. This is not to say there are no connections between function and form, nor even that the line between them is always easy to draw; it is merely a caution that movement (including its development) can be sliced in many different ways that yield different clarities.

Issues of *continuity-discontinuity*, *change-stability*, *levels* and *time frames* each come into play. The problems of *coordination amongst measures*, and thus amongst selected parameters of performance, follow directly. Our descriptions are critical to subsequent questions about control, such as defined in terms of the interplay between self-organisational and interactive properties of the systems we thereby abstract for our analyses.

Co-orderings among processes that are more or less continuously distributed can, in their sum, lead to clearly separable *combinations* (consequences) that have a greater structural stability than do any of the processes in isolation, thereby yielding a translation between form and function (cf. Bohm, 1980). Conversely, relatively discrete events may, in *their* sum, produce combinatorial functions that are more continuously ordered than are their constituents. We should be ready to expect surprises at every turn.

3.1. Socially coordinated movements

3.1.1. General considerations

There are critical aspects of coordinated movement that can be under- stood only with reference to one or more social partners (see also accompany- ing chapters by Brian Hopkins and Colwyn Trevarthen). Thus it is often useful to start broadly, with a framework that incorporates selected properties of movement of each individual in explicit relation to the movements of its social partner(s). On the assumption that social organisms

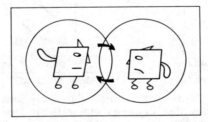

Fig. 6. Socially coordinated movement and mutual adjustments.

adjust their movements with respect to one another (as in a dance), rules of regularity may in this way be highlighted that would otherwise escape notice. While it may often be useful to abstract the occurrence of social movement patterns into a set of more or less discrete "acts" and their interconnections (both within and between participants), documentation of the "flow pattern" that connects the individuals together in space and time can be equally valuable. In this way, for example, relative invariants among changing profiles of actions, individually considered, can become manifest (Golani, 1976).

3.1.2. Wolf social behaviour as illustration

Moran *et al* (1981) found it convenient to assay certain social
interactions in wolves *(Canis lupus)* by taking the longitudinal axis of each
animal in a dyad and describing it in relation to the longitudal axis, point
of nearest opposition (head, neck, tail, etc.), and distance (heuristically
defined in terms of wolf lengths!) of its partner. The three coordinates
together were used to construct a social interaction "cube". Any one or all
of the *relationally defined* coordinates could remain constant even though
the animals were in active motion as defined from a fixed point in the
environment (e.g. camera), and indeed did remain so for extended periods
during supplanting interactions - due to the mutually compensatory actions
of the participants. Further, there were loci within the interaction "cube"
that were the focus of many interactions, while other loci were rarely if
ever occupied. The three *relational dimensions* were not fully independent
of one another, meaning that knowledge of one or two could be used to
estimate the positions along the other(s). In a word, the dimensions were
co-ordered. Finally, trajectories between fixed points throughout the cube
appeared to be restricted along a finite number of paths, indicating that
rules of transition between loci were also rule governed. The point of
emphasis is that each of these rules is anchored in the *relations* among
movements of the partners, and each could in principle be accomplished
through a wide array of actions defined from a fixed point in the environment.

One way to think of social behaviour, then, is in terms of movement
patterns in which the regularities are defined in terms of the *combined
actions* of oneself and one's partner. What about the developmental course
of such socially constrained movements? Havkin (1977; Havkin & Fentress,
1985) has obtained evidence that young wolves are often remarkably
oblivious to the movements of their peers, even when direct contact between
the animals is made. Thus, a three week old wolf pup may continue to eat
when its brother or sister paws at it, or bites its tail. The earliest phases
of socially coordinated movements are marked by a loose symmetry in mutual
contacts, a pattern that gradually differentiates into highly symmetrical and
asymmetrical contacts. Many of these contacts, again necessarily defined in
terms of the *relations* among movements of the social participants, result
in one of the animals losing its balance. Initially (three- five weeks or so)
the falling animal typically hits the substrate quite suddenly on its side.
Later the animal may role more gently onto its back, and still later
(approximately seven weeks) the falling animal may propel itself forward in
an anterior to posterior roll, thus both maintaining control of its head
region and breaking the grip (usually on the neck) of its partner. It is
clear that as development progresses, the animals become much more
sophisticated from a biomechanical point of view - often moving, for example,
into a perpendicular orientation to the long axis of their social partner as a
preliminary to toppling the partner to the ground. A complex set of leg,
trunk and head movements become employed with increasing sophistication.
The animals begin to *anticipate* not only the actions of their partners, but
also the *consequences* of these actions as well as of their own movements.
That is, they now make adjustments that are appropriate to the future events
in a feedforward sense.

Many aspects of wolf social organisation are also dependent upon
ritualised patterns of communication that incorporate postures and movements
primarily involving the lips, ears, hackles, tail and overall body attitude
(Schenkel, 1947). A complementary level of description, therefore, involves

the emergence of these singularly defined movements and their integration within the individual (McLeod & Fentress, 1985). In addition, the contextual specificity of both singular and combined actions, as well as their effectiveness, are important considerations (Fentress & McLeod, 1986). As illustration (McLeod & Fentress, 1985) vertical raising of the tail becomes a good indicator during the fourth and fifth postnatal weeks that the "displaying" animal will bite its partner, but same-aged peers may not yet respond to these potential warning signals. Our data to the present suggest that future insights into such problems of communicatory movements and their ontogeny will have to take into account not only the details of individually defined movements, but also pay particular attention to the various *combinatorial sequences* of these movements, as well as their more broadly defined *expressive contexts*. An additional interesting property of the early social interactions in wolves is that gestures such as tail wagging at the initiation of a sequence may be resolved in either playful or aggressive sequelae. As the animals get older, and establish specific relationships with others within their group, sequences tend to become more predictable.

When we think about social behaviour it is not surprising to form the perspective of one individual changing the behavioural properties of another. There is no reason not to suspect that similar phenomena occur for "socially coordinated" movements *within the individual*, though it is less common for investigators to adopt this perspective in explicit terms.

3.2. Movement coordination within the individual

3.2.1. General considerations

Movement involves trajectories that can be described in reference to coordinates external to the organism as well as in terms of other loci upon the organism's own body. In creatures with clearly demarcated limb segments the distinction between these frames of reference and their complementary value for a complete documentation are obvious once considered. As illustration a speaker can stand before an audience with legs and trunk held in a fixed position, and sweep the upper arm in an arc (Figure 7(a)). There is little ambiguity to the question (a), "Did my arm move?", as indeed the arm did change its position *both* with reference to the audience and to the performer's own trunk. The ambiguity can be seen when either (b) the limb is held in a fixed position with reference to the body as the body swivels in reference to the audience, or (c) when the limb is held in a fixed position with respect to the audience and the body turns in reference to the arm. Similar considerations arise if we next evaluate (d) problems of movement of the forearm with reference to the upper arm, etc. (Figure 7).

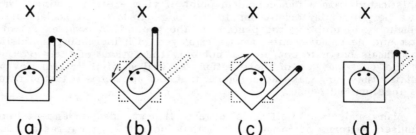

Fig. 7. Four ways to move one's arm (X refers to fixed point in the external environment. See text for other details).

Other forms of movement description may most usefully be applied to particular problems, such as when a given limb segment makes contact with another part of the body – as in the facial grooming movements observed in numerous rodent species (Fentress, 1972, 1981). Here the same point of contact may occur through limb segment movements that follow distinct trajectories, and (if the point contacted at one body locus is the focus of interest) that may occur in conjunction with several contact points in other body segments (such as in scratching the nose with either the hand, fore-arm or upper arm). Important questions concern which properties of movement remain relatively invariant, and which vary (often necessarily to maintain other system invariances, e.g. in response to perturbations).

As pointed out by Eshkol and Wachmann (1958; see also Golani, 1976, and Harries, 1983) it is important to recognise that for an organism with rigid body segments, movements of each segment defined in reference to its neighbor traces an arc along the surface of a sphere – thus linear movements involve the compensatory interactions among two or more segments. These authors also indicate the value of separating planar, conical and rotational properties of movement across one or more limb segments. Bernstein (1967; and others) makes the complementary argument that a given form of movement, even for a single limb segment (frame of reference defined) can occur through a number of different patterns of muscular contraction, etc. Obviously it is often useful to abstract categories from combinatorial properties of movement, to avoid becoming bogged down in too much detail, but the fact that these categories are abstractions should not be allowed to slip too far from our consciousness (Fentress, 1973, 1976).

3.2.2. Rodent grooming behaviour as illustration

Self-grooming movements are common in many rodent species, and involve sequential contacts between different body segments. These grooming sequences occur in predictable contexts. Thus adult rodents commonly groom during transitions between protracted quiet and active states, after initial exploration of novel environments, etc. (Fentress, 1983b). Often these transitions can be referred to a number of abstracted state variables (cf. chapter by Prechtl, this *Study Institute*), such as those involving arousal, conflict, and the like. In young rodents transitions into grooming are more likely than in normal adults to depend also upon the animals' concurrent posture and the similarities in *form* between certain grooming movements and other motor patterns, including those used in locomotion or even swimming (Fentress, 1983b, 1984).

The normal sequential structure of grooming is cephalocaudal, with movements involving contacts between the forepaws and face preceding contacts to the torso region. Perceptually it is possible to abstract these movements into a number of action classes based upon multiple criteria such as amplitude of limb segment movements, their coupling in time, their contact loci, etc. (Fentress & Stilwell, 1973). These movements are arranged into descriptive sequential hierarchies, wherein individually defined actions form clusters that are also ordered in time. Indeed, the sequential regularities among these higher-order clusters are often more apparent than is their detailed internal composition, thus suggesting that different rules of constraint and flexibility may be operative within different levels of the descriptive hierarchy. Another way to state this is that sequential analyses devoted solely to the lower level actions show loci of nonstationarity (cf. Attneave, 1959).

For the development of these action sequences a reasonable first question is whether the basic movements emerge prior to their various sequential combinations. Answers here are somewhat ambiguous (Fentress, 1981). There are many subtle changes in form of the actions that occur at approximately the same time that higher-order blockings are achieved. It is also clear that "form" itself is a multidimensional concept, involving individual limb segment kinematics as well as overall limb trajectories, and that each of these descriptions is somewhat separable from the form of contacts between e.g. the forepaws and the face (thus yielding "function"). Additionally, the forms of different phases of adult rodent grooming sequences differ in a number of structural properties, such as their internal flexibility versus stereotypy - as measured across trials and also animals (Berridge & Fentress, in press). Finally, for a proper developmental assessment of these properties it is important to insure that one's data are not confounded by such factors as muscular strength, or the inability of an animal to maintain a posture that is prerequisite to the movement in question (Fentress, 1984; *cf:* Thelen, 1984; Woollacott, this *Study Institute).*

Ilan Golani and I (Golani & Fentress, in press) have recently addressed some of these problems by placing newborn to two-week old mice into a specially designed mirror chamber that both provided the animals with postural support and allowed us to film their movements at high speed from orthogonal perspectives. When supported in this way even newborn mice will show forelimb movements that are very similar to those normally found only in later grooming, although contacts between the forepaws and face are irregular, and the co-ordering of actions within and between limb segments is clearly imperfect. (The fact that the criterion for "grooming" in this developmental context now refers primarily to similarities (although not identities) in movement *form* in comparison to adults (e.g. synchronous lifting of the forepaws toward the face) rather than in terms of *function* (effective and regular contact pathways of the forepaws across the face), serves to highlight not only that multiple criteria can be used to classify a behaviour, but also that these criteria may segregate during the course of development, thus imposing often difficult taxonomic decisions upon the investigator; cf. von Hofsten, this *Study Institute).*

We found that during the first 100 hours or so postnatally, infant mice in the grooming chamber showed a rich variety of movements of the forepaws toward the face, even though the face itself was contacted only on an irregular basis. Between approximately 100 and 200 hours the contacts on the face were reliably produced, but the contact pathways were restricted to the rostral region, most grooming "sequences" involved but a single symmetrical stroke of the two limbs, and the head did not participate actively in the grooming behaviour. Beyond 200 hours the head began to make a number of movements in coordination with the forelimbs, and together the forelimbs plus head produced reliable and protracted sequences of contact pathways through a flexible combination of individual movement components. By this time the complex sequential ordering rules of clearly defined strokes seen in adults began to appear in unambiguous form.

4. INTEGRATIVE PROCESSES

The network of integrative processes underlying movement production involves a number of complementary levels (Fentress, 1983a, b, 1984). During the 'course of movement development the relative salience of different levels as well as foci of control may undergo important transformations (Fentress, 1984; von Hofsten, Lee and Paillard, this *Study Institute*; Prechtl, 1984 and this *Study Institute*; Thelen, 1985 and this *Study Institute*). How do we account for the operation of these integrative processes as they link together, and across developmental time-frames?

For the present contribution the two terms *network* and *process* are critical. The first refers to the intimate interlocking of events that can be understood only imperfectly by their study in isolation. The second emphasises the dynamics of organisation which are critical both to moment to moment performance and its developmental course.

4.1. Contextual evaluations of integrative processes

As a general principle of both behavioural and neural development, the range of influences upon a given system tend to enlarge as the organism grows older (e.g. Purves & Lichtman, 1985). While there are undoubtably important exceptions to this (or any other!) general principle as applied to particular specific instances in detail, it provides a useful guideline for organising our thoughts. Thus we have seen in the context of motor performance that in the production of early motor patterns young wolves tend to show incomplete coordination with respect to their adjustments to a social partner, even though there is a clear coherence among properties of coordinated movement defined at the level of the individual animal. Analogously, young rodents show clear rudiments of coordinated forelimb grooming movements prior to the time that these are linked in a functionally coherent way to the broader context of sequential contacts between the forepaws and the face.

The selective elicitation of motor patterns provides some of the most useful data for contextual controls. That is, why does an animal perform one action at one time, and another action at a different time? Few would doubt that full answers to such questions demand some evaluation of the broader surround (context) within which a given action occurs.

As illustration, grooming behaviour in adult rodents tends to occur in transitions between protracted active and inactive states, such as just before or just after settling into the nest. Grooming also occurs frequently during transitions between alternative active states, such as feeding and subsequent locomotion. Indeed, grooming is in many respects a prototypical "transition behaviour", occurring when the choice between other patterns of movement are in a somewhat ambiguous state (Fentress, 1983b).

4.1.1. Relations among action classes

A question of interest that follows from this is whether factors primarily relevant to these other functionally defined classes of action have systematic influences upon either the probability or form of grooming behaviour. An affirmative answer is to be anticipated, if for no other reason than that organisms cannot do everything at once. Thus factors that affect one class of actions are likely to have ramifications elsewhere. The next question, then, is whether there are rules of null influence, negative influence and possibly even positive influence among movements that serve different functions.

Here we see the importance of both relational and dynamic perspectives. To summarise a large volume of data briefly (cf. Fentress, 1973, 1976a, 1983a, b, 1984), given that an animal is in the appropriate behavioural "set" (cf. Evarts, Shinoda & Wise, 1984; Prechtl, 1974) early and/or moderate activation of pathways that normally contribute to other classes of action may produce at least momentary facilitation of the "set" behaviour. Stronger activation along these same behaviourally defined pathways are more likely to lead to suppression, as if in these latter conditions the *focus* of activation becomes more tightly constrained to motor patterns within a given functional class. The behaviour becomes restructured along the specific pathways activated. A general perspective that can account for these diverse data is that early and/or weak activation of a number of control pathways can produce relatively diffuse excitation, whereas stronger activation along these same behaviourally defined pathways restricts alternate functions. This can be viewed as control systems that operate through excitatory foci with inhibitory surrounds. The core of excitation is initially broadly focused with a weak and restricted inhibitory surround, whereas with stronger activation the core becomes more tightly focussed and the inhibitory surround spreads further.

The upshot of this dynamic view is that the boundaries which define "different" behavioural systems may overlap to varying degrees, and that the precise parameters and consequences of this overlap among qualitatively distinguished action classes change with changes in quantitative and/or temporal parameters of activation (cf. Todor & Lazarus, this *Study Institute*).

While these principles may suggest rather complex statistical analyses in normal adult animals, they can often be seen in a much more simplified form both in young animals, and in animals which have developed perseverant motor stereotypies (Fentress, 1976a, 1983b). As illustration of the first point, in the study of mouse grooming development by Golani and Fentress (in press) we found that, once the infant mouse was placed into an appropriate sitting posture, a wide variety of events (such as pinching the tail lightly) would facilitate the posturally set grooming behaviour. Stronger stimuli would typically block grooming, such as through the elicitation of conflicting postures (as in orienting toward the pinched tail). The influences of "arousal" upon the kicking movements of human infants (Thelen, 1985; this *Study Institute*) provide an analogous picture.

With respect to perseverant motor stereotypies, a number of animals will develop characteristic motor patterns if they are kept for protracted periods of time under stressful or environmentally impoverished conditions (Fentress, 1976a; cf. Berkson & Callagher, this *Study Institute*). These motor stereotypies can in many respects "take over" most of the movement time of the animals. Again a number of moderate intensity disturbances will increase the probability of these actions still further, whereas higher intensity disturbances will often produce a reorientation toward or away from the source of stimulation. Interestingly, the initial reaction to a high intensity stimulus may be facilitation of the perseverant behaviour, before subsequent blocking. The motor stereotypies also often show a post-stimulus rebound. Such observations argue strongly for the proposition that stimulus events take some time to reach their maximum effectiveness, and also that the decay functions of these stimuli can be assessed quantitatively (cf. Heiligenberg, 1976; Posner, 1978). Different specific parameters are to be anticipated for different classes of stimuli and motor patterns, and the stimuli themselves may summate to varying degrees. It is for these reasons that experimental studies of integrated movement *must* combine considerations of quantitative, temporal and qualitative variables (Fentress, 1976a, 1983a, b).

4.1.2. Contextual relations in sensorimotor sequences

In nature sensory events impinge upon the organism against a changing background of the organism's internal state. The same stimulus can thereby produce very different outcomes. As a simple illustration, Fentress (1968a, b) found that the same overhead moving stimulus would elicit predominantly either fleeing or freezing responses in voles (small rodents) as a function of the animals' locomotory state. Voles that were locomoting at the time of the stimulus presentation or that had been locomoting a short time before were most likely to flee. Those who had been sitting still for several seconds or longer were most likely to freeze. Grooming behaviour often followed either of these two actions. The probability of grooming during the first several minutes after the overhead stimulus was greatest when the initial reaction was not too severe. Grooming that was in progress when the stimulus began was normally disrupted. This disruption was occasionally preceeded by an initial acceleration of one or two grooming strokes.

Early flexible phases of facial grooming are often observed when the animals are "relaxed" in their home cages, but are less common when the animals are engaged in active exploration or during initial recovery from an environmental disturbance. Within a protracted facial grooming sequence there are often phases that are variable and others, containing many of the same basic strokes, that are highly stereotyped (Berridge & Fentress, in press; Woolridge, 1975). As for other motor actions, grooming sequences involve a dynamic balance between central states and responsiveness to various sources of sensory input. Part of the responsiveness depends upon the locus and strength of the stimulus, part depends upon the sequential phase of grooming, and part depends upon the broader context(s) within which the behaviour occurs.

Following complete facial grooming sequences, rodents typically groom their bellies and then their backs (Fentress, 1972). That this sequence reflects a central predisposition can be shown by placing a drop of water or other mild irritant on an animal's back. Given that the stimulus is mild, the animal will initiate grooming with its face in the normal sequence. Stronger stimuli (such as ether) will override this sequential predisposition. Central and peripheral events are in dynamic balance.

During the most stereotyped phase of facial grooming, animals exhibit a reduced sensitivity to potential disruptions by either phasic loading of the limbs or chronic removal of normal tactile input from the face. In an early collaborative study, Michael Woolridge and I found that phasic pulling of the forelimbs from the sides of the face (via stretch threads attached to solenoids) disrupted slow but not rapid phases of facial grooming in mice (see Fentress, 1981, 1984). More recently, Kent Berridge and I have demonstrated that trigeminal deafferentation of the facial region in rats also disrupts variable phases of grooming, but leaves the stereotyped phase essentially intact (Figure 8).

Facial grooming in rats often occurs postprandially upon the infusion of various taste substances into the mouth via chronically implanted oral cannulae (technique devised by Grill & Norgren, 1978). When these substances elicit aversive responses, grooming often occurs *during* the infusions. Note that these grooming actions also point toward central programming mechanisms since the face may not be soiled at all. After deafferentation, paw licking and forelimb strokes showed marked modifications (e.g. in smoothness and amplitude distribution) during the variable phases of postprandial grooming, but not during the infusion of aversive tastes. In contrast, tongue movements were more noticeably affected during ingestion than during postprandial grooming. These data could not be accounted for entirely upon the basis of difference in movement form in the infusion and postinfusion contexts observed in the same rats prior to trigeminal surgery; therefore contextual influences of a higher order of abstraction must be taken into account.

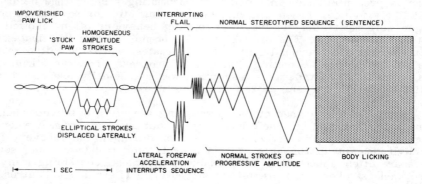

Fig. 8. Early phases of grooming in rats are complex and highly variable. These are followed by a stereotyped sequence ("sentence") of tight elliptical strokes around the mouth, succeeded by progressively larger strokes oriented to the face, and then body licking. Trigeminal deafferentation (shown) can produce a number of disruptions of the early complex phase during postprandial grooming, but leaves the stereotyped phase essentially intact. Left and right sides of animal on opposing X axes. See related details in text (from Berridge & Fentress, in press).

4.2. Contextual hierarchies in movement development

The fact of contextual factors in the control of movement patterns suggests the existence of processes that operate at a number of levels, a full understanding of which in the human case must take into account concepts such as programming demands, attention, etc. (cf. commentary by Howard Zelaznik, this *Study Institute*). Lower-order contextual associations can be seen in the performance of individually abstracted items in a variety of adult movement sequences, including rodent grooming. Careful study of these "simpler networks" (Fentress, 1976b) can, in principle at least, help clarify *themes* and *rules* of organisation that may apply to more complex instances as well. I, and many other authors (e.g. Dawkins, 1976; Fentress, 1983b, 1984) have pointed out that the concept of hierarchical order is a multifaceted one, ranging from descriptive taxonomies only, to ideas about direction and sequence of control process, to implications about an underlying "command" structure, to thoughts about priorities in expression, breadth versus detail of contribution, etc. Common to most of these diverse ideas, however, is an implicit notion that the rules are essentially "fixed" and "unitary" in their operation. I think that we have reason to question this notion even for different phases of a given motor performance; we certainly should throw it out when viewing movement (and other behavioural properties) within a developmental context.

Let me illustrate this from the context of the shifting ramifications of movements at a single limb segment that can occur over a short time scale (cf. Eshkol & Wachmann, 1958; Golani, 1976). Suppose I stand with my arms outstretched over my head, and move my wrist. The ramifications of this movement are minimal as reflected in other body joints. Now, suppose I am holding myself up by a chinning bar, or on a tree branch. In this case movements as the wrist joint will swing my entire body (unless various compensatory movements are produced). In Eshkol-Wachmann (1968) notation, movements of a limb segment that carry along other limb segments are defined as "heavy", while those which are strictly localised are defined as "light". Of course there can be gradations, but the basic point that movements of one limb segment can have either widespread or localised ramifications throughout the body, depending upon circumstances, is clear. Nervous systems, through rules of operation that we do not yet understand, have the ability to operate within such shifting frameworks - even if our concepts of their operations do not!

To come back to the idea of "co-ordering", it becomes apparent that under some circumstances it is advantageous to the organism to compensate for movements of one segment, and to ignore these movements when they are relatively unimportant. Now obviously terms such as importance bring with them a whole host of implications that we do not yet fully understand, but in rough outline the point is clear. It also suggests fascinating avenues for future research into the developmental substrates of integrated movement. For example, if young organisms do not compensate for initially localised movement perturbations in an obvious way (based upon adult criteria) does this mean that they "can not", or that they "need not"?

An interesting example of mutual compensation among rapidly co-ordered movements that is common to most mammals, including ourselves, is that of "co-articulation" in which the detailed *form* of one movement segment, or phase, reflects the broader context(s) within which it occurs (with human speech being the perhaps most obvious case; Studdert-Kennedy, 1983). This adjustment in form based upon one's articulatory neighbors can provide a considerable economy in movements, for by knowing what one has done and is about to do one can adopt an optimal strategy of present action. It has long been known that rodents when they groom do something akin to co-articulation, (Fentress, 1972; Fentress & Stilwell, 1973). A given "stroke-type" may be both recognisable yet predictably different in fine detail from one set of sequential neighbors to the next. Fine-grained analyses make it clear that these adjustments can contribute substantially to the overall smoothness of the animals' performance.

As in the case of children's speech, young mice do not show this adult-characteristic smoothness in their grooming movements; i.e. individual strokes are separated from one another by marked pauses (Fentress, 1981; see also Fentress & McLeod, 1986 for a broader review). It is only later that these individually articulated strokes fuse together into a single coherent unit. The same general principle is true for early movements *within* a single abstracted stroke. Thus, rotational and planar aspects of the movements of a single limb segment are produced smoothly and concurrently in adult mice, but are often separated in young animals (Golani & Fentress, in press).

A more interesting case occurs when one considers the consequences of perturbing one aspect of movement during various aspects of its performance. A characteristic of flexibly co-ordered movements is that other aspects may (within limits) compensate for such perturbations, leaving the functional effectiveness of the overall movement intact. Even with a broken arm we can brush our teeth by compensating for the lack of mobility in the arm through movements of the head. Similarly, mice that have restricted mobility of one of their forelimbs may succeed in making "appropriate" (i.e. normal) symmetrical contact pathways between the forepaws and face through the adjustment of other body segments (Golani & Fentress, in press). Young mice are less able to do this. (Try calling the attention of a young child so that her head turns to the side as she is part way through the process of lifting her spoon full of potatoes to her mouth!)

Clearly there are limitations to such adjustments in adult organisms as well, and these limitations may be more or less manifest under differing overall conditions of performance (see also the commentary by Howard Zelaznik, this *Study Institute*). Actions that are performed very rapidly may be less flexible in their means-ends relations, thereby failing to achieve a goal during unexpected perturbations (e.g. observations on the responses of rodents to both phasic and tonic changes in afferent information during rapi versus slow phases of grooming, noted above). In animals that have developed abnormally stereotyped and perseverant movement patterns the loss of flexibility in the face of environmental perturbations can be most marked, especially during rapid execution of these stereotypies (Fentress, 1976a, 1983b; cf Berkson & Callagher, this *Study Institute*). Normal executive ("hierarchical") control appears to be disturbed in such instances.

There is, of course, some implication in such statements that we, as observers, in a sense "know" what the organisms *should* do; i.e. we understand its hierarchical priorities. Such a proposition is fine as long as we are open to exceptions that may give us more realistic expectations in the future. Thus, Ilan Golani and I were initially surprised to find that when a single forelimb was pulled outward from the face (via a string) during a grooming bout, the other forelimb also sacrificed its contact with the face to maintain spatially symmetrical movements with its neighbor (Golani & Fentress, in press). A lesson from such observations is that behaving organisms have *multiple* constraints that they must deal with in coordinated action. The relative priorities among these constraints deserve explicit empirical testing under specified conditions. These conditions can change with behavioural state, developmental phase, etc.

4.3. Summary

The main points of this section are that the integrative processes which underlie coordinated action are multiple, that they can be viewed in terms of greater or lesser predominance, and (most importantly) that they represent contextual sensitives that operate to varying degrees within a dynamic framework. This dynamic frame can refer to momentary transitions as well as to longer-term developmental events. Even the very description of these events and their context(s) of expression provide many challenges that have received inadequate attention. In terms of processes of control we see that temporal, quantitative and qualitative variables each contribute to what, in sum, is a biologically critical balance between interactive and self-organisational processes of movement coordination.

All of the data discussed thus far are compatible with the notion that during relatively early and weak forms of behavioural activation the systems involved are imperfectly (i.e. broadly) differentiated, only to tighten their focus with more complete activation. Under these latter conditions the systems become more immune to influences from their surround, just as they become more effective in blocking alternative forms of expression (Fentress, 1973, 1983a). If restriction of focus, as well as power of command, are part of our normal definitions of hierarchy, then even this hierarchy must have its dynamic aspects. What we are left with is some sense of "flow patterns" in coordinated movement, with variable networks of connection among these patterns. The picture is one of special challenge to students of development, a topic to which we shall turn next, albeit in necessarily brief outline form.

5. DEVELOPMENTAL TRANSFORMATIONS

Perhaps the most obvious, and also most poorly understood, issue in the development of coordinated action is how the organism's genetically based potentialities and constraints play against the diverse roles of experience during subsequent phases of ontogeny (Connolly, this *Study Institute*; see also Fentress & McLeod, 1986). Transformations in movement form and its underlying control processes have recently begun to attract skilled workers in a number of behavioural and neurobiological disciplines (e.g. Oppenheim, 1982; Prechtl, 1984). Yet we still have difficulty in isolating the most fundamental questions. Here four major points that appear to deserve further consideration will be outlined briefly.

5.1. Experience and the emerging phenotype

The organism is transformed into a different creature at each phase in its development. This means both that it is subjected to different sets of experience, and that the consequences of any given experience may vary greatly. At each phase it is important to emphasise that the organism does not simply "copy" the details of its future action from the details of the experiences that it receives; throughout development pre-existing states lead to a number of transformations of these experiences in the sense of amplifying their importance, diminishing their importance, and modulating their message. There is, for example, good reason to suspect that far from merely providing simple "instructions" to the developing organism, experience can serve to enhance or diminish pre-existing biases (perhaps in part as a function of the potency as well as quality of the experience), "select" among alternative developmental pathways that are in some sense already encoded, etc. (Fentress, 1984; Fentress & McLeod, 1986).

Experience, in the broad sense of the term, also provides what we might call the "contextual affordances" for behavioural expression. Thus we have seen that an organism may have capabilities that are normally not observed due to the fact that it fails to obtain the necessary supports for expression (cf. accompanying chapter by Thelen). The behaviour that we observe, then, is the joint product of the history of experiences as they play against a changing phenotype, as reflected within environmental affordances of greater or lesser adequacy (Figure 9).

These contextual affordances may not only serve the function of providing momentary support for the organism, but also play back upon the developing phenotype. Both they and the phenotype tend to become more complex as the organism matures, each incorporating a wider and wider range

98

of variables (cf. Purves & Lichtman, 1985, chapter 15). The behaviour that we observe is a very indirect reflection of all of these processes, and its consequences can feedback not only upon the developing phenotype but also upon the environment in which subsequent phases of behavioural expression are incorporated (cf. Connolly, this *Study Institute*).

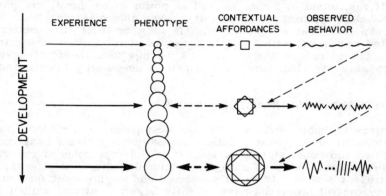

Fig. 9. During the development of behaviour, routes of experience, the existing phenotype, and contextual affordances all change (see text).

5.2. Differentiation and integration as necessary partners

There is an interesting dichotomy in the biological and behavioural literature in which biologically oriented investigators (e.g. neuroscientists; see for example, Cowan, 1978) tend to emphasise the progressive refinement (differentiation) of phenotypic states, whereas behavioural scientists (e.g. ethologists; see for example, Hinde, 1982) are more likely to emphasise the progressive combination (integration) of events that previously occurred separately. It is now clear that both of these processes operate together, sometimes with one being the more obvious (from a given perspective!), and sometimes the other being so. Few workers today would accept a hard and fast dichotomy between the processes of differentiation and integration, but only relatively recently has the importance of recognising the limitations in such previously dichotomised lines of thought been addressed explicitly (e.g. Fentress & McLeod, 1986; Thelen, 1985). Clearly organisms, whether animal or human, need to refine particular aspects of their performance at particular phases of development, just as they must master the ability to synthesise these aspects into various functionally coherent combinations (Figure 10).

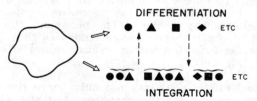

Fig. 10. From relatively homogenous beginnings, there is both separation (differentiation) and recombination (integration) of action patterns

As I have also attempted to demonstrate in this chapter, certain properties of behaviour may be undergoing refinements while other properties may be undergoing synthesis with still others (see also, Fentress, 1984 and Fentress & McLeod, 1986; plus references included in each). And as this volume clearly shows, one must also be careful not to place too much emphasis upon the notion of "progressive", for development also contains a number of relatively stable points, goes through various apparent reversals in terms of behavioural expression, etc.

5.3. Developmental networks

A question that I started this chapter with is how do we best deal with "systems that are both self-ordered and interactive" (see also Kugler, this *Study Institute*; Kugler, Kelso & Turvey, 1980)? One answer, of course, is to seek out especially important rules of constraint among events that might otherwise be defined separately. Here, in many respects, is the nub of everything that I have attempted to express thus far. Given that there are multiple cohesions and separations among events, each of which is most appropriately graded as *more-or-less* rather than as *all-or-none*, the connections vary in terms of the ramifications of experience at different phases of development.

If a given system is completely self-ordered, then one should not expect any measurable influences from outside sources, other than perhaps accelerating or decelerating events that are already in progress. If a system is interactive, then obviously one would assume that there are important connections between its state and the states of other defined systems. The importance of these considerations for developmental processes is that the lines of important connection among behaviourally defined events may shift during ontogeny, including those events that are relevant to an understanding of the ramifications of one or another experience (Figure 11).

DEVELOPMENTAL NETWORKS

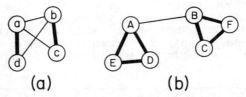

(a)   (b)

Fig. 11. Networks of connection among emerging behavioural systems may change in their strength and focus, thus changing ramifications of experience during successive phases of development ((a) and (b) respectively).

One reason this is important is that it is easy to think of generalisations among experimental events as occurring always at the same level, such as that involving movement form. But, it is equally possible that there are other rules of generalisation that occur in terms of what we might call *functional categories*, such as among physically distinct motor actions used in fighting or grooming, etc. Given that both the forms and functions of coordinated movements can be transformed during development, it is not at all obvious either where or to what extent we should expect the consequences of experience to generalise. Given that processes of differentiation and integration among movement (and other) control systems operate more or less together, it is not to be unexpected that links between "a" and "d" plus "c" are strongest during one phase of ontogeny, whereas later links between "A" + "E" + "D" form one differentiated/integrated unit, relatively separate from "B" + "C" + "F", which form another. As illustration, given that grooming movements in young mice are more closely associated in their contexts of elicitation with movements similar in form but different in consequence than are grooming movements in older mice, might we expect a preponderance of generalisation of the consequences of experience on the basis of formal similarities in movement in earlier developmental phases than in later phases, which are perhaps more obviously linked to commonalities of function - more or less independent of form? Such questions are important, even though they have rarely been asked.

5.4. Bootstrapping pieces and relations

There is a final topic that deserves more explicit treatment. This is akin to the notion of "bootstrapping" in physics (e.g. Gardner, 1979), although it has only rarely surfaced in studies of motor coordination or development. The important notion is that not only are "relations" determined by the properties of the "pieces" from which these relations are comprised, but also that the properties of the resultant relations may affect the properties of their constituent pieces.

From a simple physical point of view, it is not possible to envision interactions among elemental properties that do not also change these elemental properties, at least to some (potentially measurable) extent (cf. Eigen & Winkler, 1981). One can envision this in terms of a biological "game board" in which the properties of any one of the pieces (in terms of the moves it is allowed to make) are influenced by the relations of this piece, present or historical, to other pieces upon the board (Figure 12).

This, of course, does not imply a total lack of internal constraint; rather the expression of any such internal constraint is bounded by extrinsically defined events. Thus in Figure 12 the squares and circles always move in diagonal directions, whereas the diamonds and triangles move either vertically or horizontally. It is the particular direction (and one could also add, extent) of movement along these constrained dimensions that are subject to variation via the influence of neighboring symbols.

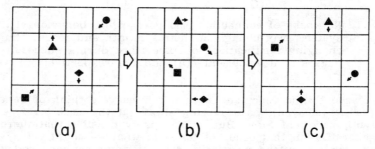

(a)   (b)   (c)

Fig. 12. Suggestion that properties of "pieces" (symbolised by
         figures and arrows of allowed movement) may be affected
         by their positions, mutual "relations", and perhaps history
         ((a)-(c) represent subsequent time-frames ("moves")).

6. SUMMARY

In this chapter I have attempted to look at some of the prevailing themes of motor coordination and its development, especially with reference to a framework that stresses the dynamic, relational, and multileveled nature of behavioural performance at different phases of ontogeny. I have of necessity emphasised animal studies, especially those conducted by me and individuals with whom I have worked closely. At the same time, I have attempted to offer arguments that may be applicable to investigators who concentrate upon the details of motor coordination in our own species, especially with respect to the developmental substrates of these remarkable abilities that we all enjoy.

We do not at present have any fully satisfactory way of dealing with either changing events or their rules of interconnection in space or time. Nor do we have but the dimmest appreciation of challenges that necessarily confront us if we are ever to understand the intertangled processes that underlie these observable events. The present *NATO Advanced Study Institute on Motor Skill Acquisition in Children* not only highlighted major academic problems that we must seek to understand further, but also set a stage upon which future investigations can grow, and in their turn, be tested. Let me conclude with a few caveats and suggestions. The first caveat is that each species in nature is likely to follow its own specialised operations for both the performance and development of behaviour. Thus while animal studies may suggest principles to be investigated in the human species, they cannot be applied without corresponding studies in man. Secondly, each abstracted class or property of movement is likely to have important specialised features, even when studied at the level of a single individual. Thus it is critical that different classes of coordinated action, as well as their occurrence in various contexts, be isolated to test the extent to which present generalisations are applicable. Thirdly, we do not yet have any single analytical or conceptual framework that appears superior in all of its aspects to others. Here one can but suggest that workers strive to examine their material from a number of perspectives, so that the extent to which these perspectives appear satisfactory can be compared directly. Finally, I am aware that by offering terms such as dynamic, relational, and multileveled, I might be viewed to move from the necessary traditional tidiness of static, compartmentalised and single level approaches to coordinated action in pursuit of a framework that may appear difficult to test with traditional rigor.

I think that this is a mistaken perception. It is mistaken in the first instance in that tidiness and relevance are not synonymous. It is mistaken in the second instance in that complexity and rigor are not necessary antonyms. There is no reason why dynamic, relational, and multileveled perspectives cannot be brought to severe empirical test. I have tried to suggest several such tests here. For example, I anticipate that in both an integrative and developmental context, system inputs become more restricted along functionally defined channels with their strength of activation, that most systems we study can change their organisational boundaries and relations to other such systems in rule governed ways, and that once strongly formed these same systems will become progressively immune to further redirections from outside influences. There is every reason to expect that such propositions can be applied to problems of development and co-ordination more fully than they have been to the present. The last thing we want to do in our studies of coordinated action development is to accept operational analogues of chemical alchemy as a substitute for genuine understanding.

ACKNOWLEDGEMENTS

I gratefully acknowledge NATO support which helped defray my expenses to attend the *Advanced Study Institute* in Maastricht, plus support from the Canadian MRC and NSERC. The invitation to attend, and hospitality offered by Professors M.G. Wade and H.T.A. Whiting, are very much appreciated. Other ASI participants, many of whom I had not had the pleasure to meet before, also provided much intellectual stimulation. I also benefited from the opportunity to discuss some of the ideas presented here at the Neurosciences Institute of the Neurosciences Research Program. Finally, my thanks to W.G. Danilchuk, J. and J. Lord, and H. Parr, each of whom assisted in various phases of manuscript preparation.

References

Attneave, F. (1959). *Applications of information theory to psychology*.
New York: Holt, Reinhart and Winston.

Bernstein, N. (1967). *Coordination and regulation of movements*. London:
Pergamon Press.

Berridge, K.C. & Fentress, J.C. (in press). Contextual control of
trigeminal sensorimotor function. *Journal of Neuroscience*.

Bohm, D. (1980). *Wholeness and the implicate order*. London: Routledge &
Kegan Paul.

Cowan, W.M. (1978). Aspects of neural development. *International Review
of Physiology. Neurophysiology III, 17,* 149-190.

Crick, F.H.C. (1979). Thinking about the brain. *The brain: A Scientific
American book*. New York: W.H. Freeman (original article in September
1979 issue of *Scientific American*).

Dawkins, R. (1976). Hierarchical organization: A candidate principle for
ethology. In P.P.G. Bateson and R.A. Hinde (Eds.), *Growing points in
ethology*. Cambridge, England: Cambridge University Press.

Easter, S.S., Jr., Purves, D., Rakic, P. & Spitzer, N.C. (1985). The
changing view of neural specificity. *Science, 230,* 507-511.

Ede, D.a. (1978). *An introduction to developmental biology*. New York:
John Wiley.

Eigen, M. & Winkler, R. (1981). *Laws of the game*. London: Allen Lane.
(first published (1975) as *Das Spiel: Naturgesetze steuern den Zufall*.
Munich: R. Piper).

Eshkol, N. & Wachmann, A. (1958). *Movement notation*. London: Weidenfeld
& Nicholson.

Evarts, E.V., Shinoda, Y. & Wise, S.P. (1984). *Neurophysiological
approaches to higher brain functions*. New York: John Wiley.

Fentress, J.C. (1968a). Interrupted ongoing behaviour in voles *Microtus
agrestis* and *Clethrionomys britannicus)*: I. response as a function of
preceding activity and the context of an apparently 'irrelevant' motor
pattern. *Animal Behaviour, 16,* 135-153.

Fentress, J.C. (1968b). Interrupted ongoing behaviour in voles *Microtus
agrestis* and *Clethrionomys britannicus)*: II. extended analysis of
intervening motivational variables underlying fleeing and grooming
activities. *Animal Behaviour, 16,* 154-167.

Fentress, J.C. (1972). Development and patterning of movement sequences
in inbred mice. In J. Kiger (Ed.), *The biology of behavior*. Corvallis,
Oregon: Oregon State University Press.

Fentress, J.C. (1973). Specific and non-specific factors in the causation of
behavior. In P.P.G. Bateson and P. Klopfer (Eds.), *Perspectives in
ethology*. New York: Plenum Press.

Fentress, J.C. (1976a). Dynamic boundaries of patterned behavior: Inter-
action and self-organisation. In P.P.G. Bateson and R.A. Hinde (Eds.),
Growing points in ethology. Cambridge, England: Cambridge University
Press.

Fentress, J.C. (1976b) (Eds.), *Simpler networks and behavior*. Sunderland,
Massachusetts: Sinauer Associates.

Fentress, J.C. (1981). Sensorimotor development. In R.N. Aslin, J.R.
Alberts and M.R. Petersen (Eds.), *The development of perception:
Psychobiological perspectives*. New York: Academic Press.

Fentress, J.C. (1983a). The analysis of behavioral networks. In J.P. Ewert,
R.R. Capranica and D.J. Ingle (Eds.), *Advances in vertebrate neuro-
ethology (NATO ASI Series)*. New York: Plenum Press.

Fentress, J.C. (1983b). Ethological models of hierarchy and patterning of species-specific behavior. In E. Satinoff and P. Teitelbaum (Eds.), *Handbook of Behavioral Neurobiology: Motivation*. New York: Plenum Press.

Fentress, J.C. (1984). The development of coordination. *Journal of Motor Behavior, 16*, 99-134.

Fentress, J.C. & McLeod, P. (1986). Motor patterns in development. In E.M. Blass (Ed.), *Handbook of behavioural neurobiology: Developmental processes in psychobiology and neurobiology*. New York: Plenum Press.

Fentress, J.C. & Stilwell, F.P. (1973). Grammar of a movement sequence in inbed mice. *Nature, 244*, 52-53.

Fodor, J.A. (1983). *The modularity of mind*. Cambridge, Massachusetts: The MIT Press.

Gardner, M. (1979). *The ambidextrous universe*. New York: Charles Scribner's Sons.

Gibson, E.J. (1982). The concept of affordances in development: The renascence of functionalism. In W.A. Collins (Ed.), *Minnesota Symposium on Child Psychology, Vol. 15: The concept of development*. Hillsdale, N.J.: Lawrence Erlbaum Associates.

Gibson, J.J. (1979). *The ecological approach to visual perception*. Boston: Houghton Mifflin.

Golani, I. (1976). Homeostatic motor processes in mammalian interactions: A choreography of display. In P.P.G. Bateson and P.H. Klopfer (Eds.), *Perspectives in Ethology, Vol. 2*. New York: Plenum Press.

Golani, I. & Fentress, J.C. (in press). Early ontogeny of face grooming in mice. *Developmental Psychobiology*.

Grill, H.J. & Norgren, R. (1978). The taste reactivity test: I and II. *Brain Research, 143*, 263-297.

Harries, J.G. (1983). *Language of shape and movement*. Tel Aviv: The Movement Notation Society.

Havkin, G.Z. (1977). *Symmetry shifts in the development of interactive behaviour of two wolf pups (Canis lupus)*. Unpublished M.A. Thesis, Dalhousie University, Halifax, Nova Scotia.

Havkin, Z. & Fentress, J.C. (1985). The form of combative strategy in interactions among wolf pups (*Canis lupus*). *Zeitschrift für Tierpsychologie, 68*, 177-200.

Heiligenberg, W. (1976). A probabilistic approach to the motivation of behavior. In J.C. Fentress (Ed.), *Simpler networks and behavior*. Sunderland, Massachusetts: Sinauer Associates.

Hinde, R.A. (1982). *Ethology: Its nature and relations with other sciences*. New York: Oxford University Press.

Holst, E. von & Saint Paul, U. von (1963). On the functional organization of drives. *Animal Behaviour, 11*, 1-20. (first published in German, *Naturwissenschaften, 47*, 409-422.

Jacob, F. (1976). *The logic of life: A history of heredity*. New York: Random House. (first published as *La logique du vivant: une histoire de l'héridité*. Paris: Editions Gallimard).

Kugler, P.N., Kelso, J.A.S. & Turvey, M.T. (1980). On the concept of coordinative structures as dissipative structures: I. Theoretical lines of convergence. In G.E. Stelmach and J. Requin (Eds.), *Tutorials in motor behavior*. New York: North-Holland.

Lewontin, R.C. (1983). Gene, organism and environment. In D.S. Bendall (Ed.), *Evolution from molecules to men*. Cambridge, England: Cambridge University Press.

Marr, D. (1982). *Vision*. New York: W.H. Freeman and Company.

McLeod, P.J. & Fentress, J.C. (1985). Communicative posturing and its early development in timber wolves. *Proceedings 19th International Ethological Conference, 1:* 100 (Abstract).

Moran, G., Fentress, J.C. & Golani, I. (1981). A description of relational patterns during 'ritualized fighting' in wolves. *Animal Behaviour, 29,* 1146-1165.

Oppenheim, R.W. (1982). The neuroembryological study of behavior: progress, problems, perspectives. In R.K. Hunt (Ed.), *Current topics in developmental biology, Vol. 17, Neural Development.* New York: Academic Press.

Posner, M.I. (1978). *Chronometric explorations of mind.* Hillsdale, New Jersey: Erlbaum.

Prechtl, H.F.R. (1974). The behavioural states of the newborn infant (a review). *Brain Research, 76,* 185-212.

Prechtl, H.F.R. (1984). Continuity and change in early neural development. In H.F.R. Prechtl (Ed.), *Continuity of neural functions from prenatal to postnatal life.* Spastics International Medical Publications. Oxford: Blackwell Scientific/Philadelphia: J.B. Lippincott Co.

Prigogine, I. & Stengers, I. (1984). *Order out of chaos: man's new dialogue with nature.* New York: Bantam Books.

Purves, D. & Lichtman, J.W. (1985). *Principles of neural development.* Sunderland, Massachusetts: Sinauer Associates.

Schenkel, R. (1947). Ausdrucks-Studien an Wolfen. *Behaviour, 1,* 81-129.

Studdert-Kennedy, M. (1983) (Ed), *The psychobiology of language.* Cambridge, Massachusetts: The MIT Press.

Thelen, E. (1985). Developmental origins of motor coordination: Leg movements in human infants. *Developmental Psychobiology, 18,* 1-22.

Thelen, E. & Fogel, A. (in press). Toward an action-based theory of infant development. In J. Lockman and N. Hazen (Eds.), *Action in social context.* New York: Plenum Press.

Woolridge, M.W. (1975). *A quantitative analysis of short-term rhythmical behaviour in rodents.* D. Phil. Thesis, Oxford University.

Zelaznik, H.N. (1985). Theoretical issues in attention and performance. *Psychology of Motor Behavior and Sport 1985.* Gulf Park, Mississippi: NASPSPA (Abstract).

Zelaznik, H.N. & Hahn, R. (1985). Reaction time methods in the study of motor programming: the precuing of hand, digit, and duration. *Journal of Motor Behavior, 17,* 190-218.

DEVELOPMENT OF COORDINATED MOVEMENT: IMPLICATIONS FOR EARLY
HUMAN DEVELOPMENT

E. Thelen

1.   A DYNAMIC, RELATIONAL, AND MULTILEVEL PERSPECTIVE

I first became acquainted with John Fentress and his work when I was
a graduate student in animal behaviour and interested in the organisation of
motor patterns in much simpler beasts than human babies. I can remember
the "aha!" sensation when I read the first Fentress paper, a feeling that
has been wonderfully repeated over the years; John Fentress generates more
ideas in a single paper than many can produce in a career. It is a great
honor, therefore, to comment upon his paper and to use many of his
principles derived largely from animal work (as I have done before!) to build
a scheme of early motor development especially addressed to humans.

In my view, Fentress's signal contribution over the last decade has
been his ability to break away from the prevailing ethological and neuroethological models of behaviour to ask questions about the fundamental nature
of movement and its development. This meant a significant advance over the
"fixed action pattern", with the implications (however denied by post-
Lorenzian ethologists) of neat little packets of movement, inevitably released
and precisely performed to consumate a motivational or drive force. Fentress
has also led the way in interpreting the more reductionist studies of isolated
neural networks into a larger behavioural framework (Fentress, 1976).

Because Fentress is proposing principles of great power, richness, and
generality, his framework, unlike many other schemes derived from animal
models, is as useful for thinking about human motor development as it is for
nonhuman animals. However elegant the framework, it is not a *simple* entry
into the problems of behaviour and development. But this complexity is
entirely justified. As one who has toyed with the more simple models derived
from classical ethology or motor programming notions, I can report that they
are utterly unsatisfactory for explaining the richness and dynamic structure
of movement as it unfolds in real and developmental time.

Fentress offers three principles of organisation of behaviour and its
development: that they are *dynamic, relational,* and *multileveled.* By
reorganising that behaviour is dynamic, he gives primacy to changes of form
over time, both as movement is called for in everyday tasks and as
behaviour changes during ontogeny. Basic to both time frames are questions
of what gives behaviour its stability within the dynamic processes of change.
The relational aspect emphasises that both elements *within* the organism
and *between* the organism and the surrounds are *co-ordered,* that is, that
they are known by their interactions. Thirdly, that the matrix of co-order is
multileveled, and while our interpretation of any behaviour is necessarily
level-dependent, we must also seek rules that transcend various levels and
perspectives.

The problem for Fentress, and for all of us who adopt these somewhat abstract concepts, is to go beyond the warm fuzziness of global principles to explaining real-life behaviour in real-life animals without resorting to "everything is related to everything else" generalisations. Systems principles as used by Fentress and myself have had a long history in developmental psychology (see Kitchener, 1982; Overton & Reese, 1973; Reese & Overton, 1970; Sameroff, 1983; Werner, 1957 for reviews). The fact that such theories have not been widely accepted, despite their obvious (to the converted!) intuitive elegance and biological relevance, lies, at least in part, with the difficulty of breaking into complex systems for empirical analysis (Levins, 1970). That is, how do we isolate the multidimensional elements contributing to behaviour outcome and once studied, how do we integrate our results back for a more organic understanding? I would argue, for example, that even Piaget, who stands as our most "organic" developmental theorist, is less appreciated for the systems aspects of his theories such as the global and hard-to-operationalise notion of equilibration than for the details of his structure of knowledge. Thus, while many may acknowledge at a theoretical level that animals are dynamic, relational, and multileveled, complexity appears to dictate research programs where the behaviours are isolated, the variables reduced, and the contexts simplified.

One long-held criterion for good theory is the generation of testable hypotheses. Historically, holistic or systems theories, including that of Fentress, have been less successful at meeting this criterion than more uni-dimensional models - those derived from S-R and information processing approaches, for example. The difficulty lies in the complexity of the beast and the unpredictability of knowing, when the system is poked, the nature of the global reverberations. Some theoretical biologists have suggested that in the study of complex systems we in fact subordinate the goal of predictability and focus on the goal of explanation (Levins, 1970).

We can accomplish a level of understanding of the dynamic, relational, and multileveled nature of behaviour by a two-pronged research strategy. First, we need descriptive studies of animals in real-life situations to map the co-orderings of elements and their surrounds. We know virtually nothing about the rules by which animals, and especially humans, build the postures and movements of everyday functional acts (see Reed, 1985 for elaboration of this point). This in itself is a formidable task. Studies of coordination require extremely tedious mapping of segments in time and space (see for example, Golani, 1976; Pellis & Pellis, 1983) and the job is made even more daunting when several or many ages must be compared. Once some parameters of the parts and the whole are established, we may begin to dissect the dynamic relations, sliced, as Fentress puts it, at a number of levels.

We can look at Fentress's own work on grooming behaviour in mice as a stellar example of the power of such a stretegy to begin to tackle this immense task. By analysing in great detail the temporal and spatial characteristics of grooming sequences in adult and young mice, Fentress (1978) could describe the co-orderings of movement and their ontogeny using the metaphor of a musical composition. Development could then be envisioned as individual *notes* (strokes of the limb) being assembled into sequential *melodies* nested and rearranged within an ever-more ordered *score*, characteristiced by *timing, rhythmicity* and *rules of transposition*. Whatever the limitations of this particular analogy, it has captured the variability-within-stability theme that is the heart of dynamic approaches. Within this descriptive framework, then, Fentress has performed a number of manipulations

- preturbations of the system - to identify mechanisms of control and change. These have included changing postural context (Fentress, 1978) and surgical interventions (Berridge & Fentress, 1985; Fentress, 1973) to assess organic and contextual contributions to these coordinated acts.

2. SYSTEMS PRINCIPLES IN REAL AND DEVELOPMENTAL TIME

In the remainder of this chapter, I wish to show how principles introduced by Fentress are fully concordant with a model of early human development, with an emphasis on motor activity and to offer some preliminary ideas how systems approaches can tackle some seemingly intractable developmental problems. The sources of this approach are twofold. First are the powerful insights into motor problems recently formulated by the so-called "Connecticut School" (e.g. Kelso et al,1980; Kugler et al, 1980). This *dynamical approach* to motor control and coordination derives, in part, from the work of Soviet movement physiologist, N. Bernstein (1967), and heavily from systems theory in physics and biology (Haken, 1977; Prigogine, 1980). Second, are the applications of systems approaches to embryology (e.g. Goodwin & Cohen, 1969). Kugler, Kelso and Turvey (1982) provide a theoretical rationale for extending dynamic principles of real time behaviour to the motor development domain, and Thelen and Fogel (in press) elaborate a more specific developmental model, supported by examples from various aspects of infant behaviour.

In our statement, Thelen and Fogel sought to define those systems properties which organise behaviour in both the real (movement) time domain and the developmental time span, and I briefly summarise from the longer discussion cited above. First, because both moving and developing organisms are cooperative systems (with dynamic, relational, and multileveled elements), order, and co-order are viewed as *emergent* properties of those relations. That is, order is derived from the relations of the elements at many levels, such that the assembly of the units results in an *increase in complexity*. This is in contrast to strict hierarchical models, where complexity resides in the highest, or executive levels, and is distributed, as instructions, to lower levels. Second, across both time scales, there are components of the system which preserve *stability* of form and components that allow for *flexibility* in the face of functional demands. And thirdly, systems theories predict that the *transitions* from one stable phase of organisation to another may not be linear or continuous. Small continuous changes in one element may have system perturbations that may cause the organism to shift into a qualitatively different behavioural topography.

There are three additional assumptions discussed by Thelen and Fogel that are essential for translating general systems ideas into the developmental domain. These are that in a developing system the contributing components may not mature in a synchronous fashion; their rates of change may vary dramatically. Thus, at any point in time an animal may have an immature motor system and highly developed sensory capabilities, or have one sensory system advanced and the others more retarded (Turkewitz & Kenny, 1982), or even one highly selective neural tract accelerated in function (Anokhin, 1964). Nonetheless, the behavioural outcome at that point in time is a product of the dynamic, relational, multileveled interaction of those systems, what-ever their individual maturation level. From this we predict that components may compete with, inhibit, or facitate each other, with implications for behavioural performance. Secondly, in the developmental sphere, any one

110

subsystem or component may act as the *rate-limiting* factor (Soll, 1979). Whatever the developmental readiness of the other components, new developmental forms arise only when the slowest component matures. From this we predict that certain elements of behavioural performance may appear "early", either disassociated from the mature function or even used for another function. Finally we emphasise that at every stage in the life cycle, it is *function*, rather than instructions, that drives behaviour. Specific tasks may thus be met by a variety of behaviours, depending on context and maturational state.

The challenge of systems approaches now lies in their empirical utility. Will such dynamic, relational, and multileveled approaches better explain developmental phenomena than other prevailing models? Will these principles allow us to generate both *post hoc* integrating schemes and testable hypotheses that will span many aspects of motor development, in different ages and subject populations?

3. A SYSTEMS ACCOUNT OF THE DEVELOPMENT OF LOCOMOTION

The development of upright, independent locomotion has been perhaps the single best-studied motor skill (e.g., Burnett & Johnson, 1971; Forssberg, 1985; McGraw, 1932, 1940; McGraw & Breeze, 1941; Shirley, 1931; Statham & Murray, 1971; Sutherland et al, 1980). Nonetheless, the prevailing explanations for the development of human locomotion have been primarily unidimensional. The emergence of this skill has been attributed to cortical maturation (McGraw, 1932, 1940; McGraw & Breeze, 1941), the evolution of pattern generation (Forssberg, 1985), or the development of a particular stage of cognitive development (Zelazo, 1983). Implicit in these formulations is that development, and motor performance, are *instruction driven* , and that the impetus for both developmental change and movement in real time lies in some executive - be it the spinal cord, motor cortex, or some locus of cognitive functioning. In the model I develop here, I adopt the dynamic perspective (Kelso & Tuller, 1984) that motor coordination is not an iconic representation of instructions. Rather, the topography of movement emerges fundamentally from the organisation of the limbs and joints into functional units assembled for specific tasks and operating within particular environmental constraints. Specifically, I propose the existence of an early, very generalised *coordinative structure* or constraint on the possible co-orderings of the joints of the legs, which leads to a highly patterned output. This coordinative structures undergoes elaboration and differentiation during development that allows more flexible assemblies of the joints. At any point in ontogeny, however, movements in time and space are not specified by this pattern generation process alone, but by the systems outcomes of interacting components, each with its own developmental course and acting *within definite constraints and opportunities afforded by the context*.

4. COMPONENTS OF LOCOMOTOR SKILL

For the sake of this heuristic model, I have identified eight hypothetical "components" contributing to locomotor skill. Note that the isolation of components is at least partially artifactual because of their intimate interconnectivity - visual flow sensitivity is both functionally and anatomically part and parcel of postural control and vice-versa. Nonetheless, we can

envision separate developmental timetables for these components, just as we
may envision asynchrony to the elements *within* these arbitrarily chosen
components. In Figure 1, I plot these hypothetical developmental timetables
– with the caution that these are extrapolated from sometimes very scant
data!

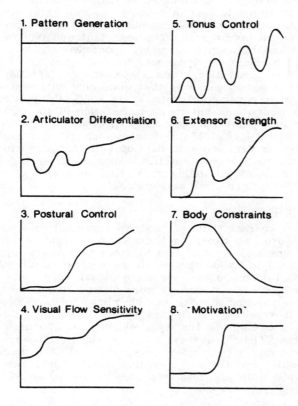

Fig. 1. Hypothetical components of locomotor development, plotted
as a function of age.

4.1. Pattern generation

From the earliest postnatal days, and likely even much earlier (Heriza,
1985; Prechtl, this volume), human infants and fetuses perform coordinated
movements. Behaviours such as rooting, sucking, hand-mouth contact, and
other early reflexes, and facial expressions, as well as many spontaneous
movements of limbs and trunk are not random assemblies. Rather, they are
recognisable synergies that may span many body segments, although the
linkages between the segments may be more loosely linked than in mature
movement. Coordination within the joints of the legs appears to be an especially
early ontogenetic acquisition in humans as well as other animals (Bekoff, 1981;
Provine, in press). Thelen and Fisher (1982, 1983) described highly
synchronous excursions of hip, knee, and ankle joints in newborn "stepping"
and supine kicking. Identical movements were described by Heriza (1985) in

premature infants as young as twenty-eight weeks gestational age, and
these may well be the same leg activities discovered by Prechtl in young
fetuses and reported at this conference.

The existence of highly coordinated leg movements in such young
infants and fetuses suggests that in humans, as well as in other mammals,
pattern generation *per se* can be accomplished by the neuromuscular system
without higher cortical involvement. The important question for developmental
studies is the relation between these early spontaneous coordinative
structures and later voluntary movement. My colleagues and I have proposed
that newborn pattern generation is not a specialised adaptation, but reflects
an underlying autonomous mechanism that undergoes differentiation and
integration with other developing systems. As such, this pattern generation
is not iconic with locomotion, but is a manifestation of the dynamic product
of muscles linked in a particular way and expressed in a particular context
(see Thelen, Kelso & Fogel, 1985 for further elaboration). Both the muscle
synergies and their control contexts develop and change during the first
year in ways which allow a more specific locomotor patterning to be produced.
Thus, this model assumes, as in Figure 1, that some form of pattern-
generation is available from birth and underlies subsequent motor development.

4.2. Articulator differentiation

One important characteristic of newborn coordinative structures is their
seeming global nature. All three leg joints move in tight synchrony (Thelen
& Fisher, 1983); arm and hand extend together toward an object (von
Hofsten, (1984) head and shoulders rotate as a piece (Bullinger, 1982). In
order for functional action to emerge, these global constraints on the degrees
of freedom of the system must become more differentiated. That is, knee and
ankle must be able to work in more flexible phase relationships with one
another, just as in reaching the fingers must extend, then flex to grasp
while the arm is extending. In the legs, within-joint synchrony is tightest
at about one-month (Thelen, 1985a), but over the first year, both more
isolated and more complex patterns emerge, although in a nonlinear fashion.
Similarly, the undifferentiated and co-active muscle firing patterns seen in
young infants evolve into progressively more reciprocal activation (Gatev,
1972; Thelen, 1985a).

4.3. Postural control

At birth, human infants have minimal ability to support the body
segments against the force of gravity (Casaer, 1979). Beginning with head
control, antigravity responses develop slowly over the first year, as
reflected and in behavioural adjustments to vestibular, proprioceptive and
visual stimuli (Barnes et al, 1978), but it is only recently that these
reactions are being studied in controlled experiments. Woollacott (in press)
found some instances of appropriate neck extensor muscle responses to
platform translations in infants as young as 4 months under normal visual
conditions, and consistent correct responses in darkness. Sitting infants of
8-14 months showed clear directionally specific neck and trunk muscle
responses. While an 8 month-old did not have leg, trunk, and neck responses
to platform sway while supported in the standing position, some proprioceptive
responses were apparent by 10 months, and correct responses available in
the legs, but not trunk and neck by 14 months. It is difficult to know in
postural support, as in other developing systems, whether the "wiring" is
in place before performance is detected, but is masked by inadequate
strength to lift the head of stiffen the legs or by competing sensory systems,

or whether sensory inputs are mapped on muscles by a period of trial and error learning (Woollacott, in press). Nonetheless, some elements of postural support are apparently in place before independent locomotion, although they likely do not reach their mature form for several years (Shumway-Cook & Woollacott, 1985).

4.4. Visual flow sensitivity

Although humans use a combination of visual, proprioceptive, and vestibular responses to maintain stable posture (Nashner, 1981), vision is especially crucial in regulating locomotion (Gibson, 1979). Two developmental issues can be raised. First, when do infants become sensitive to visual flow, and second, when do they use it to regulate their movements? It seems likely that sensitivity to kinetic information in the optic array is acquired within the first few weeks of life, as behavioural responses to a looming object have been described in 6-9 day-old infants (Yonas & Granud, 1984). Both sitting and standing infants control posture by optic flow (Butterworth & Hicks, 1977; Lee & Aronson, 1979). In a recent study, Stoffregen et al (1985) showed that infants used optic flow to control equilibrium during walking as well. Adults and older children use peripheral optic flow in preference to central flow to control posture (Stoffregen, in press). However, this preference was not seen in new walkers, who were disturbed equally by perturbances in the centre field as the peripheral field. These authors concluded that peripheral preference developed only after erect locomotion. Like the recruitment of appropriate muscle synergies for postural support, it appears that some ability to recognise and adjust to optic flow is mature long in advance of locomotion, but that the system becomes increasingly refined only after locomotor behaviour is exhibited.

4.5. Tonus control

In his classic studies of prone progression, Gesell (1939) describes twenty-two "stages" characterised by either flexor or extensor dominance of posture. Gesell suggested that the maturation of antagonist muscle groups is not linear or synchronous, but follows a spiralling path he labelled "reciprocal interweaving". Studies in my laboratory have confirmed this uneven developmental course in supine kicking. Kicks in newborn infants are initiated largely by simultaneous activation in both flexors and extensors, with flexor strength predominating. The extension phase of the kick, in contrast, is largely a passive relaxation, with the leg recoiling from the strong flexor contraction (Thelen & Fisher, 1983). By about five months of age, the character of the kick changes from a strong flexor thrust, to both active flexor and extensor thrusts. At about this age, infants also show extensor elements in posture. This new extensor phase can be detected electromyographically by muscle bursts at the initiation of both phases. However, only at about 7 months can fragments of reciprocal activation be seen, and even at one year leg movements may have some coactive control (Thelen, 1984; 1985a). Similar asymmetries are apparent in bilateral tonus control (Gesell, 1939; Thelen et al, 1983).

Thus, at any point in development, the contribution of flexor or extensor, or right or left muscles may not be balanced. Since movement expression is a result of the relative dynamic balance between these antagonistic forces, the tonus of the muscles is one crucial determinant of the behaviour pattern we observe, whatever the underlying pattern generation.

114

4.6. Extensor strength

In addition to developing neurological control of their muscles, infants also gain in actual strength. The muscles of the newborn infant are small, watery, and have few nuclei (Eichorn, 1979), but change in both size and composition during the first year (Mastaglia, 1974). There are likely complex interactions between maturational factors and function, which is known to affect both muscle and bone strength. To develop a strong and stable base of support for bipedal locomotion, infants need especially to developed strong muscles in legs and trunk, and to balance flexor and extensor influences. I have argued previously that relative weakness of the plantar flexors of the ankle (toe-pointing muscles) not only accounts for many of the pecularities of early gait, but also may act as the rate-limiting factor in standing and walking (Sutherland et al, 1980; Thelen, 1984). Again, whatever the neurological preparation for a behaviour, its expression can be limited by muscle strength.

4.7. Body constraints

Newborn infants are terribly designed for bipedal locomotion. Their heads are too large, trunks too long, centre of gravity too high, legs too short, and shoulders too narrow, and they rapidly become very fat. As growth proceeds, the body proportions and composition changes in a direction that favors upright stance and locomotion (Thelen, 1984). The scale and composition of the moving segments, as well as their linkages, impose important constraints on movement outcome. Although little is known about the relation between these scale factors and performance, it is clear that biodynamic considerations can determine patterned outcome.

4.8. "Motivation"

By motivation I mean the infants ability to recognise the task at hand, and to desire to act upon it. In the case of locomotion, this means moving forward toward a recognised and desired goal, be it something in the physical environment or a social partner. In Figure 1, I have sketched the hypothetical motivation curve as reaching a high level sometime in the middle of the first year. At this time infants will self-propel themselves towards objects if given proper postural support and artificial mobility, such as in a wheeled crawler or walker, and some infants learn to roll over or hitch on their stomachs towards toys even earlier. At the very least we can say that the perceptual systems recognise goals and some motor systems can be recruited in service of those goals long before independent locomotion is possible.

5. THE SYSTEMS PRODUCT

One way of understanding a dynamic, relational, and multileveled system is to try and identify the components and their interactions. In the case of voluntary locomotion, it is clear that the contributing elements have very different developmental profiles; some elements are "ready" far in advance of our target behaviour and others mature only after locomotion is achieved. Within each component, development is not linear, but shows times of acceleration and retardation. No one element alone "is" or "controls" locomotion, and it is unlikely therefore, that we could point to a "locomotion" centre somewhere which is switched on at about 12 months and which "causes" infants to walk. Upright locomotion cannot occur unless all of these components are appropriately mature. It is nonetheless important to identify which components are indeed rate-limiting, that is, which factors constrain the final appearance of the behaviour. My colleagues and I have suggested previously that it is primarily postural control and balance, and especially extensor strength that are rate-limiting for bipedal locomotion. This means that the other components are sufficiently developed so that the maturation of balance and strength serves to shift the entire system into an emergent mode. After erect locomotion is achieved, however, it becomes increasingly skilled and refined, as contributing elements both continue to mature and also become more highly integrated with each other.

This systems approach is useful not only for understanding the milestone behaviour of independent walking, but also for clues to what underlies the sometimes tortuous path of the development of leg coordination in general throughout the first year. In Figure 2, I outline the observed types of coordination of the legs seen when infants are both supine and upright during the first year and the possible functional outcomes of those modes of coordination.

In both postures, infants appear to have at least four overall phases of coordination. First, is the newborn phase of highly obligatory muscle synergies, with a predominantly simultaneous coordination of the joints within each limb and a loosely coupled alternating coordination between the limbs. At about one month, these synergies begin to dissolve, with more individuation of joints within a limb and unstable and asymmetric coordination between the limbs. A first phase of reintegration occurs at about five months, when strong bilaterally simultaneous movements emerge. The period from 7 to 12 months is characterised by both more joint individuation, and their reintegration into the complex phasings of crawling and walking.

What produces these identifiable phases of leg coordination if not simply instructions from an executive in the developing central nervous system. Figure 3 depicts the parallel developmental course of the hypothetical components as a layering in three-dimensional space. The system as a whole is enclosed by a bracket representing context, which includes the task at hand, as well as the physical constraints and supports of the immediate environment. At any point in time, and within these contextual constraints, we can draw an imaginary line through the layered plates to represent the interactions of the components. Behaviour is the systems product of the maturational status of the components within the task space. No one level by itself determines the behaviour, but when in dynamic combination, one element may support, facilitate, inhibit, or mask expression of another element. Over time, these relations shift and flow, depending on the rate of development of the contributing units. Because of the systems nature of the resulting movement, however, even small changes in one component may shift the topography of the entire behavioural outcome.

How can we dissect these systems interactions? In the remainder of this Chapter, I offer three examples from my laboratory where a systems explanation is explored for some of the coordinative outcomes presented in Figure 2. Specifically, my colleagues and I have manipulated or perturbed one of the contributiong components to simulate naturally occuring changes and thus determine the effects on movement outcome.

116

	Obligatory synergies simultaneous interjoint alternating interlimb	Dissolution dissociated interjoint asymmetric interlimb	New synergies	Joint individuation + reintegration
Type of coordination — Supine	Newborn kicking	Lateralised Unstable	Simultaneous kicking	Little or no kicking unless aroused
Type of coordination — Upright	Newborn stepping	Little or no stepping	"Jumping"	Elicited steps — Supported Walking — Independent Walking
Movements in utero				
Age, in months		3	6	9 — 12
McGraw's "stages"	A / B	B		C / D / E
Functional or task consequences	"Exercise" → / "Expressive" →	Exploration →	Turning over	Postural Support Crawling — Standing

Fig. 2. Types of coordinative patterns of the legs in upright and supine postures during the first year. These are compared to McGraw's classic stages of locomotor development and suggested functional uses of the legs.

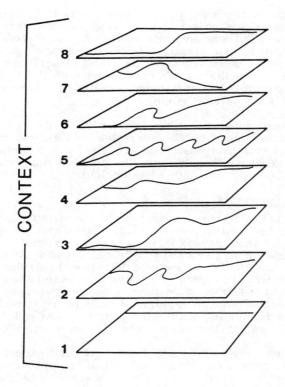

Fig. 2. The hypothetical components of locomotor development shown
as a layered system, with parallel, but interacting
developmental profiles. Outcome at any point in time is
context dependent, indicated by the whole system bracket.

5.1. The disappearance of newborn stepping

Developmentalists have long been intrigued with the apparent loss of
the newborn infant stepping response at about 2 months of age. The
traditional explanation for this behavioural regression has been that the
pattern generation was either lost or inhibited by developing cortical centres
(McGraw, 1940; Peiper, 1963). This explanation is especially problematic
given that pattern generation in the form of kicking is not suppressed when
infants are supine, nor when they are exercised in upright stepping
(Zelazo et al, 1972). This paradox is more easily resolved from a dynamic,
relational and multileveled perspective than from a single-causal view. As
Thelen & Fisher (1982) have suggested previously, rapid increases in body
fat in proportion to muscle during the first three months result in fat, but
not strong,legs. This body constraint may make it difficult for infants to
lift their legs when in the biomechanically taxing upright position. In
contrast, these leg movements can be performed when the load is decreased
by the supine posture or when the legs are strengthened by exercise.

Thelen, Fisher and Ridley-Johnson (1984) tested this hypothesis by manipulating the load on the legs. In one experiment, the stepping response of four-week-old infants was observed when small weights were attached to their legs. Infants stepped less and with weaker flexion movements when their legs were weighted. In contrast, infants of the same age whose legs were submerged in water increased both the rate and amplitude of stepping. In fact, submersion – reducing the effect of gravity on the legs – produced step rates in three-month-old infants (who normally step very little) equal to newborn rates in a comparable group.

Thus, the pattern generation while necessary, is not sufficient. Performance is multidetermined by the interaction of available patterns with body constraints and in a particular context – here the differential effects of gravity. As muscle strength increases, the physical constraints are lessened, and infants again may step while upright.

5.2. Leg movement asymmetry

A second example of interacting systems is the striking asymmetry seen in leg movements at 1-4 months (Gesell, 1939; Thelen et al, 1983). When placed supine, infants show marked bilateral asymmetry, but the lateral preference is inconsistent and transient both within and between infants. Usually, lateralised movements are assumed to reflect hemispheric differences in cortical or subcortical structures. We previously raised the possibility, however, that such asymmetries could be of more peripheral origin. Specifically, that the interaction between rapid, and perhaps asymmetrical changes in leg mass with the fluctuating tone and strength of the muscles could disrupt the bilateral organisation of the legs (Thelen et al, 1983).

Recently, Thelen, Skala and Kelso (1985) provided experimental support for the position that peripheral factors can influence symmetry of movements. They added small weights to one leg of six-week old infants and compared the rate, laterality, and kinematics of their supine kicks when both right and left leg were weighted to an unweighted baseline. In each case, adding weight to the legs shifted the laterality of kicking such that the weighted leg decreased in number of kicks and the unweighted leg increased so as to maintain the baseline kick rate. In addition, when one leg was weighted, the amplituded and velocity of the unweighted leg increased. We interpreted these results as infants having a bilateral system sensitive to the dynamics of each leg. That is, that infants could detect and respond to the dynamic condition – the mass or stiffness – of the limbs. In a systems model, this means that fluctuating changes in these parameters, in dynamic relation with the underlying pattern generation, will determine movement outcome. When growth, tone, and strength changes are stabilised, the underlying symmetry of movement can again be expressed. As before, neither pattern generation alone nor any other component taken by itself determines the movement we observe. The outcome is truly emergent from the relationships of the elements.

5.3. Systems and the emergence of upright stepping

I had suggested previously that stability in the upright posture likely both balance and strength - were the rate-limiting factors in upright locomotion. In particular, infants need to be stable on one leg so that the opposite leg can swing up and forward to propel the body. Because in bipedal locomotion, the centre of gravity is both shifted forward and from side-to-side during the step cycle, maintaining stability is an especially difficult biomechanical problem. Many of the long-recognised deficiencies of early gait such as increased cadence, decreased stride length, wide-base of support, external rotation- can be traced to unstable support. These deficiencies improve gradually only after months of walking experience, presumably as a result of both practice and maturation.

Deborah Cooke and I have recently suggested that elements of the coordinative patterns of erect locomotion may also emerge as a result of stance stability (Thelen & Cooke, 1985). One way in which mature locomotion can be distinguished from newborn stepping is the more complex phasing of hip and knee as the swing is initiated. In newborn and immature walkers, both hip and knee flex simultaneously as a result of active muscle contraction. In more mature gait, the swing of the leg is more pendular, and as the leg is extended backward, knee flexion precedes the start of flexion of the hip. What triggers this change of coordinative patterns?

In fact, in order for one leg to be stretched backward, the infant must have sufficient stability to shift and maintain the centre of gravity over the opposite leg. Normally, this is acquired with development. However, when I placed seven-month-old infants, who normally took no or very few steps when supported upright, on a small, motorised treadmill, all infants performed regular, alternating stepping with mature-like phasic patterns of hip and knee (Thelen, 1985b). These same infants performed the more immature pattern in steps without the treadmill and in supine kicks.

By placing infants in a biomechanical context facilitative of more mature coordination, the step system was shifted into a new movement topography. Presumably, the treadmill did nothing to change the maturational status of the underlying pattern generation. Rather, the treadmill substituted for the as yet not ready, rate-limiting components of postural control and strength. A similar postural facilitation for the development of interlimb coordination has been recently reported by Clark, Phillips and Whitall (Clark & Phillips, 1985; Whitall et al, 1985). They showed consistently more mature interlimb coordination patterns in new walkers when they were supported than when they walked independently. These authors concluded that the coordinative structures underlying bilateral coordination were in place in early walking, but were masked by the infant's adjustments to control upright posture. Again, by experimentally substituting for the rate-limiting component, more mature patterns emerge without the necessity of changes in an executive function.

6. CONCLUSION

Traditional descriptive or information processing approaches have not been satisfactory in explaining the mechanisms of change underlying the development of coordinated leg movements. Human motor development, like that of the mouse, is multidetermined and dynamic. Thus, while we may choose to isolate and study only one element of action development, a complete story must involve a more integrative scheme. Infants, like mice, never act as isolated central nervous systems or computers, but as organisms motivated by tasks, acting in physical and social worlds, and constrained by their morphology. Systems approaches allow us to ask how these many levels act together to perform functional goals, and at the same time point out the subsystems where small changes have holistic consequences. John Fentress has drawn a road map toward these goals that those of us in human motor development would do well to follow.

120

ACKNOWLEDGEMENTS

I would like to thank D. Cooke, C. Heriza, D. Niles and K. Skala for assistance and support in conducting some of the research reported here, and D. Niles and B. Ulrich for their comments on the manuscript. Supported by grants from the National Science Foundation and the National Institutes of Health.

References

Anokhin, P.K. (1964). Systemogenesis as a general regulator of brain development. *Progress in Brain Research, 9,* 54-86.

Barnes, M.R., Crutchfield, C.A. & Heriza, C.B. (1978). *The neurophysiological basis of patient treatment. Volume 11: Reflexes in motor development.* Morgantown, West Virginia: Stokesville Publishing.

Bekoff, A. (1981). Embryonic development of the neural circuitry underlying motor coordination. In W.M. Cowan (Ed.), *Studies in developmental neurobiology: Essays in honor of Viktor Hamburger.* New York: Oxford University Press.

Bernstein, N. (1967). *Co-ordination and regulation of movements.* New York: Pergamon Press.

Berridge, K.C. & Fentress, J.C. (1985). Trigeminal-taste interaction in palatability processing. *Science, 228,* 747-750.

Bullinger, A. (1982). Cognitive elaboration of sensorimotor behaviour. In G. Butterworth (Ed.), *Infancy and epistemology: An evaluation of Piaget's theory.* New York: St. Martin's Press.

Burnett, C.N. & Johnson, E.W. (1971). Development of gait in childhood: Part II. *Developmental Medicine and Child Neurology, 13,* 207-215.

Butterworth, G. & Hicks, L. (1977). Visual proprioception and postural stability in infancy. A developmental study. *Perception, 6,* 255-262.

Casaer, P. (1979). *Postural behaviour in newborn infants.* London: Spastics Society and William Heinemann.

Clark, J.E. & Phillips, S.J. (1985). The organisation of upright locomotion. Paper presented at the biannual meeting of the Society for Research in Child Development, Toronto.

Eichorn, D.H. (1979). Physical development: Current foci of research. In J.D. Osofsky (Ed.), *Handbook of infant development.* New York: John Wiley.

Fentress, J.C. (1973). Development of grooming in mice with amputated forelimbs. *Science, 179,* 704-705.

Fentress, J.C. (Ed.) (1976). *Simpler networks and behavior.* Sunderland, Mass.: Sinauer.

Fentress, J.c. (1978). Mus musicus: The developmental orchestration of selected movement patterns in mice. In G.M. Burghardt and M. Bekoff (Eds.), *The development of behavior: comparative and evolutionary aspects.* New York: Garland STPM Press.

Forssberg, H. (1985). Ontogeny of human locomotor control. I. Infant stepping, supported locomotion and transition to independent locomotion. *Experimental Brain Research, 57,* 480-493.

Gatev, V. (1972). Role of inhibition in the development of motor co-ordination in early childhood. *Developmental Medicine and Child Neurology, 14,* 336-341.

Gesell, A. (1939). Reciprocal interweaving in neuromotor development. *Journal of Comparative Neurology, 70,* 161-180.

Gibson, J.J. (1979). *The ecological approach to visual perception.* Boston: Houghton Mifflin.

Golani, I. (1976). Homeostatic motor processes in mammalian interactions: a choreography of display. In P.P.G. Bateson and P.H. Klopfer (Eds.), *Perspectives in ethology.* New York: Plenum.

Goodwin, B.C. & Cohen, M.H. (1969). A phase-shift model for the spatial and temporal organisation of developing systems. *Journal of Theoretical Biology, 25,* 49-107.

Haken, H. (1977). *Synergetics: An introduction.* Heidelberg: Springer-Verlag.

Heriza, C. (1985). The organisation of spontaneous leg movements in premature infants. Paper presented at Bienniel Meeting, Society for Research in Child Development, Toronto.

Hofsten, C. von. (1984). Developmental changes in the organisation of pre-reaching movements. *Developmental Psychology, 20,* 378-388.

Kelso, J.A.S., Holt, K.G., Kugler, P.N. & Turvey, M.T. (1980). On the concept of coordinative structures as dissipative structures: II. Empirical lines of convergence. In G.E. Stelmach and J. Requin (Eds.), *Tutorials in motor behavior.* New York: North-Holland.

Kelso, J.A.S. & Tuller, B. (1984). A dynamical basis for action systems. In M.S. Gazzaniga (Ed.), *Handbook of cognitive neuroscience.* New York: Plenum Press.

Kitchener, R.F. (1982). Holism and the organismic model in developmental psychology. *Human Development, 25,* 233-249.

Kugler, P.N., Kelso, J.A.S. & Turvey, M.T. (1980). On the concept of coordinative structures as dissipative structures. I. Theoretical lines of convergence. In G.E. Stelmach and J. Requin (Eds.), *Tutorials in motor behavior.* New York: North-Holland.

Kugler, P., Kelso, J.A.S. & Turvey, M.T. (1982). On the control and co-ordination of naturally developing systems. In J.A.S. Kelso and J.E. Clark (Eds.), *The development of movement control and co-ordination.* New York: John Wiley.

Lee, D.N. & Aronson, E. (1974). Visual proprioceptive control of standing in human infants. *Perception & Psychophysics, 15,* 529-532.

Levins, R. (1970). Complex systems. In C.H. Waddington (Ed.), *Towards a theoretical biology, Vol. 3.* Chicago: Aldine.

Mastaglia, F.L. (1974). The growth and development of the skeletal muscles. In J.A. Davis and J. Dobbing (Eds.), *Scientific foundations of paediatrics.* London: Heinemann.

McGraw, M.B. (1932). From reflex to muscular control in the assumption of an erect posture and ambulation in the human infant. *Child Development, 3,* 291-297.

McGraw, M.B. (1940). Neuromuscular development of the human infant as exemplified in the achievement of erect locomotion. *Journal of Pediatrics, 17,* 747-771.

McGraw, M.B. & Breeze, K.W. (1941). Quantitative studies in the development of erect locomotion. *Child Development, 1,* 267-303.

Nashner, L.M. (1981). Analysis of stance posture in humans. In A.L. Towe and E.S. Luschei (Eds.), *Handbook of behavioral neurobiology, Vol. 5. Motor coordination.* New York: Plenum.

Overton, W. & Reese, H. (1973). Models of development: Methodological implications. In J. Nesselroade and H. Reese (Eds.), *Life-span developmental psychology: Methodological Issues.* New York: Academic Press.

Peiper, A. (1963). *Cerebral function in infancy and childhood.* New York: Consultants Bureau.

Pellis, S.M. & Pellis, V.C. (1983). Locomotor-rotational movements in the ontogeny and play of the laboratory rat. *Rattus norvegicus. Developmental Psychobiology, 16,* 269-286.

Prigogine, I. (1980). *From being to becoming.* San Franscisco: W.H. Freeman.

Provine, R.R. (in press). Behavioral neuroembryology: Motor perspectives. In W.T. Greenough and J.M. Juraska (Eds.), *Developmental psycho-neurobiology.* New York: Academic Press.

Reed, E.S. (1985). Applying the theory of action systems to the study of motor skills. Paper presented at symposium on Complex Motor Behavior, University of Bielefeld.

Reese, H.W. & Overton, W.F. (1970). Models of development and theories of development. In L.R. Goulet and P.B. Baltes (Eds.), *Life-span development psychology: Research and theory*. New York: Academic Press.

Sameroff, A.J. (1983). Developmental systems: Contexts and evolution. In P.H. Mussen (Ed.), *Handbook of child psychology. 4th. ed. Volume I. History, theory, and methods*. New York: Wiley.

Shirley, M.M. (1931). *The first two years: A study of twenty-five babies. Volume I. Postural and locomotor development*. Minneapolis: University of Minnesota Press.

Shumway-Cook, A. & Woollacott, M.H. (1985). The growth of stability: Postural control from a developmental perspective. *Journal of Motor Behavior, 17,* 131-147.

Soll, D.R. (1979). Timers in developing systems. *Science, 203,* 841-849.

Statham, L. & Murray, M.P. (1971). Early walking patterns of normal children. *Clinical Orthopaedics, 79,* 8-24.

Stoffregen, T. (in press). Flow structure versus retinal location in the optical control of stance. *Journal of Experimental Psychology: Human Perception and performance.*

Stoffregen, T., Schmuckler, M., Gibson, E., Gurin, C. & Tien, G. (1985). Development and use of peripheral optical flow in stance and locomotion in young walkers. Paper presented at the Biennial Meeting of the International Society for the Study of Behavioural Development, Tours, France.

Sutherland, D.H., Olshen, R., Cooper, L. & Woo, S.L.Y. (1980). The development of mature gait. *Journal of Bone and Joint Surgery, 62,* 336-353.

Thelen, E. (1984). Learning to walk: Ecological demands and phylogenetic constraints. In L.P. Lipsitt (Ed.), *Advances in infancy research, Vol. 3.* Norwood, N.J.: Ablex.

Thelen, E. (1985a). Developmental origins of motor coordination: Leg movements in human infants. *Developmental Psychobiology, 18,* 1-22.

Thelen, E. (1985b). Treadmill-elicited stepping in seven-month-old infants. *Child Development,* in press.

Thelen, E. & Cooke, D.W. (1985). The relationship between newborn stepping and later locomotion: A review and a new interpretation. Submitted for publication.

Thelen, E. & Fisher, D.M. (1982). Newborn stepping: An explanation for a "disappearing reflex". *Developmental Psychology, 18,* 760.775.

Thelen, E. & Fisher, D.M. (1983). The organization of spontaneous leg movements in newborn infants. *Journal of Motor Behavior, 15,* 353-377.

Thelen, E., Fisher, D.M. & Ridley-Johnson, R. (1984). The relationship between physical growth and a newborn reflex. *Infant Behavior and Development, 7,* 479-493.

Thelen, E. & Fogel, A. (in press). Toward an action-based theory of infant development. In J. Lockman and N. Hazen (Eds.), *Action in social context*. New York: Plenum.

Thelen, E., Kelso, J.A.S. & Fogel, A. (1985). Self-organising systems and infant motor development. Submitted for publication.

Thelen, E., Ridley-Johnson, R. & Fisher, D.M. (1983). Shifting patterns of bilateral coordination and lateral dominance in the leg movements of young infants. *Developmental Psychobiology, 16,* 29-46.

Thelen, E., Skala, K. & Kelso, J.A.S. (1985). The dynamic nature of early coordination: Evidence from bilateral leg movements in young infants. *Developmental Psychology,* in press.

Turkewitz, G. & Kenny, P.A. (1982). Limitations on input as a basis for neural organisation and perceptual development: A preliminary theoretical statement. *Developmental Psychobiology, 15,* 357-368.

124

Werner, H. (1957). The concept of development from a comparative and organismic point of view. In D.B. Harris (Ed.), *The concept of development*. Minneapolis: University of Minnesota Press.

Whitall, J., Clark, J.E. & Phillips, S.J. (1985). Interaction of postural and oscillatory mechanisms in the development of interlimb coordination of upright bipedal locomotion. Paper presented at the North American Society for the Psychology of Sport and Physical Activity, Long Beach, Mississippi.

Woollacott, M.H. (in press). Children's development of posture and balance control: Changes in motor coordination and sensory integration. In D. Gould and M. Weiss (Eds.), *Advances in pediatric sport sciences: Behavioral issues*. Champaign, Ill: Human Kinetics publishers.

Yonas, A. & Granud, C.E. (1984). The development of sensitivity to kinetic, binocular, and pictorial depth information in human infants. In D. Ingle, D. Lee and M. Jeannerod (Eds.), *Brain mechanisms and spatial vision*. Amsterdam: Martinus Nijhoff Press.

Zelazo, P.R. (1983). The development of walking: New findings and old assumptions. *Journal of Motor Behavior, 15,* 99-137.

Zelazo, P.R., Zelazo, N.A. & Kolb, S. (1972). "Walking" in the newborn. *Science, 177,* 1058-1059.

ISSUES IN THE STUDY OF HUMAN MOTOR SKILL DEVELOPMENT:
A REACTION TO JOHN FENTRESS

H.N. Zelaznik

First, let me state that it is a pleasure to be allowed to respond to
the paper by John Fentress. Second, since my primary research and
scholarly interests do not revolve around the motor developmental theme of
the conference, it is challenging to try to make recommendations and
comments concerning the study of motor development as it pertains to John's
paper, and the Advance Study Institute as a whole.

In terms of the major message of John's paper, there is little to quibble
with. The theme that the study of motor development, or motor behaviour,
in general involves the examination of the co-ordering relationships among
many different levels of analysis is an important consideration in the
conduction of research in motor development. In addition, John argues,
rather convincingly, that one must study the stable aspects of behaviour
along with the dynamic, to develop a complete picture.

My reaction to John's paper is three fold. First, being a researcher
involved in the examination of the control of movement via motor programs
(Keele, 1968; Langley & Zelaznik, 1984; Schmidt, 1975, 1982; Zelaznik,
1981), a discussion of issues of development raised by John will be presented
to contrast the motor program theorist's approach to problems of development
compared to an ethologist such as John Fentress. Second, the idea of
context dependent control, the "pieces - relation" problem shall be explored
in terms of development of human motor skills within the context of closed
and open skills. Recommendations for future developmental research questions
will be posed. Finally, at John's instigation an attempt will be made to
discuss the meaning of coordination.

THE DEVELOPMENT OF SKILL VIA MOTOR PROGRAMS

One of the most widely utilised constructs in motor behaviour research
is the motor program. The program is thought to be a set of instructions
for movement, organised ahead of its execution, and in which feedback is
utilised to insure its correct execution, but not to select a different motor
program (see Keele, 1968 and Schmidt, 1982 for a thorough discussion).
During the past ten years theorising about motor programs has grown to
include the notion of how a program can control more than one specific
action. This work has resulted in the generalised motor program construct
(Pew, 1974; Schmidt, 1975; 1982).

The generalised motor program is theorised to be capable of controlling
movements within the same class of actions. To be capable of such feats the
program contains invariant features that do not change across different

instances of movement within that class, and mutable parameters that provide the specific information for the program to execute a particular movement.

Within this framework development can be seen as the acquisition of patterns of motion that display certain invariant features across similar actions that differ in scale. The performer then develops a library of stored motor programs that are utilised in the performance of various actions. The programs are retrieved at the appropriate time, and then tailored via response specifications to produce a specific action (see Schmidt, 1975; Zelaznik, 1981 for some perspectives on this theme). While to my knowledge, little research has utilised this approach with children (see Shapiro & Schmidt, 1982 for a discussion of experiments utilising this framework in the development of schema), we can examine the study of the learning of motor programs in adults.

One of the most thorough investigations of the learning of motor programs comes from work by Shapiro (1977, 1978). In her experiments subjects practiced a rotational movement of their right forearm that involved the execution of a series of reversals; Some of her subjects had to "hit" the reversal points at particular times, in other words they were required to learn a spatial-temporal pattern. Other subjects were required to "hit" these reversal points at any time they were comfortable with, but to complete the entire sequence in 2000 ms (the spatial-temporal pattern, if correctly performed also would be completed at 2000 ms).

First, Shapiro searched for sequential dependencies during the learning process. Did the subjects appear to first perfect the early segments prior to the mastery of the entire pattern? In other words were the "elements" of the task acquired prior to the higher-order temporal pattern? The answer appears to be no. Through a series of correlational analyses on several kinematic measures it appeared reasonable to assume that both the spatial-temporal, and spatial subjects were learning the "elements" in parallel with the whole. This kind of result is consistent with John's observation that the perfection of individual grooming strokes occurs in parallel with the emergence of the higher-order temporal patterns of grooming.

Second, after considerable training, Shapiro required that her subjects perform the reversal movement task as quickly as possible, and ignore the previously acquired temporal constraints. It was clear that subjects could speed up the movement, as indicated by a 300 ms decrease in overall movement duration. However, both sets of subjects utilised the same temporal structure acquired during training. Thus, an imposed timing pattern (the spatial-temporal group) or an intrinsically acquired one (spatial group), behaves as an invariant feature. This kind of experiment (see also Summers, 1975) suggests that learning involves the acquisition of invariant features. With a small (large) inferential leap one can claim that development of motor skills also involves the acquisition of generalised motor programs that exhibit invariant characteristics.

A series of experiments by Langley and Zelaznik (1984) suggests that the above mentioned approach is an oversimplification. One group performed a barrier knockdown task which required that the last barrier be contacted at a certain elapsed time (spatial group), and another group were required to contact each barrier at a particular time interval (spatial-temporal group). In addition, there were two different kinds of spatial-temporal groups. Both groups performed two versions of this task. For one group the two tasks possessed the same relative timing, and for the other group the two versions possessed different relative timings.

As expected, the group that performed two different relative timings produced more error during training than either the spatial-temporal or the spatial group. Furthermore, the spatial group performed with the least error. After training, subjects were transferred to a new version of the task that had a different relative timing than any of the training tasks. The spatial-temporal group that trained with different relative timing patterns performed with the least amount of error. Of greater interest was the subjects' capability to *change* their acquired temporal patterns to fit the new demands of the transfer task.

The Langley and Zelaznik (1984) experiments suggest that relative timing need not be an invariant characteristic and that the context of learning and the demands of transfer determine whether relative timing remains invariant. This suggests that learning (and thus development) involves the acquisition of various sources of information, one of which can be an invariant relative timing base, that is then utilised by the performer to meet the demands of the task. When a subject can get by with utilising a lower level strategy, such as maintain relative timing, he/she will. Thus, this kind of work hints that the study of development by following the canons of generalised motor program theory might be limiting.

Can one examine the development of skill within the context of motor program control? It is here that John's work makes the greatest contribution to human motor skill development. One must take a multi-level approach to human motor skill development. It is proposed that as a first approximation, this multi-level approach consists of an examination of the relationship between environmental demands and control of simple movements. This is viewed as a beginning in an examination of the pieces-relation problem. To perform such activity involves the examination of control from a taxonomic perspective.

TAXONOMIC CONSIDERATIONS FOR MOTOR SKILL DEVELOPMENT

John is correct; we do not have a periodic table of the elements of movement. It still is undetermined whether an overam throwing motion provides the basis for many throwing skills (see Wickstrom, 1977). These kind of taxonomies that classify only movement are limiting. Taking up John's suggestion for a multi-level approach to understand development, the taxonomy proposed by Gentile and her students will be considered in the study of motor development.

In this taxonomy (Gentile, Higgins, Miller & Rosen, 1975; Spaeth-Arnold, 1981) three important characteristics of movement are analysed. First, whether the environment is stable or changing. This distinction is the open-closed skill one (Poulton, 1957). Second, whether the performer is moving or stationary, and third whether the task demands spatial or spatial and temporal accuracy. How might this taxonomy be helpful for the understanding of motor skill development. Let us concentrate upon the open-closed skill distinction.

A motor program theorist such as Schmidt (1975) believes that the main difference between open and closed skills concerns the issue of *when* the action is initiated. In an open skill the environment provides the trigger, while in a closed skill the subject moves at his/her discretion. Thus, one could posit that an open and closed version of the same movement would show the same kinematic invariances, with the only difference being the external versus internal trigger. However that is not readily apparent. Work by David Lee (see this volume) suggests that vision provides a continuous update for the control of action. It could be the case then that there is a fundamental difference in open versus closed skill movement control. Such a finding would be consistent with the approach taken by John Fentress in that it would show that the environmental constraints operate to change the control at perhaps a kinematic level. How then can this approach be utilised from a developmental framework?

The proposed approach is simple, have children of various ages (better yet - do it longitudinally) perform a skill in a closed and open environment. For example they can perform a striking movement to a ball placed upon a stand or to a ball propelled at them. Kinematic analysis on both movement patterns across ages will reveal what aspects are consistent within closed -open tasks, across closed-open tasks, ages, and then across all three levels, should be revealing.

Suppose the interval between the step and beginning of bat swing is found to be invariant in stationary hitting but not in pitched ball hitting. For example, Turvey (1977) claims that data from Hubbard and Seng (1954) show that the step of a swing is modulated by the pitch. By examining this modulation by hitting balls,that are stationary from a number of locations compared to pitched balls one can ascertain the kind of coupling between the environmental demands and the kinematics. Is this coupling invariant across different developmental ages? If such is the case, and only the "degree" of skill improves, not the "kind" then one can make the case for the discovery of a fundamental characteristic, an invariant, in the development of control.

It also would be enlightening to discover features that are not invariant across open and closed skills or ages. Studying the development of any invariances across age changes also would be important in that it would provide evidence for experiential effects on development and learning. The search for these kinds of invariances are different from what a motor program theorist at this time would study. We might consider these types of studies as attempting to discover what Golani (1976) calls relational invariances.

Some of this research has begun, although its aim is different. Halverson and Roberton (Roberton, 1982; Halverson, Roberton & Harper, 1973) have begun to map out the stage changes in the development of forceful throwing. We are very sympathetic to the approach they have taken and view our suggestions for research as expansions on their research program. However keeping our perspective on development of motor programs it is clear that more detailed kinematic descriptions are required. Furthermore, most of the previous investigations are involved in the examination of the task being performed in a closed environment. We believe that the closed situation enhances the chance to "discover" invariances which might not be found in the open environment.

This research program can help answer some questions posed by critics of motor program theory. Specifically, Kugler, Kelso and Turvey (1982) argue that it is unrealistic to expect the spatial-temporal form of a movement to be preserved during development. Their logic is based upon physical principles. For example, if you constructed a bridge of a particular size and then had to construct a bridge that was larger the engineer could not just scale up the former's linear dimensions. They argue that this is true because the strength of the bridge will increase with the square of its linear dimension but the weight of the bridge will increase with the cube. Thus, the two bridges that have the same geometric shape will have non-proportional strengths. In conclusion a good engineer would design a new bridge with a different form. The inference from this work is that one might not find invariances in the motor patterns across development ages since children are growing and as such the form of the "old bridge" will not suffice the "newer and bigger" one.

First, the proposed work will allow for an empirical examination of this hypothesis. Second, we are not convinced that such an argument is necessarily true. The following arguments are based upon John's point about multi-level analysis. At a particular level of analysis Kugler et al are correct in stating that different size bridges might produce different invariant features and perhaps different forms. A trip to New York City might suggest otherwise. There are many suspension bridges in New York that cover vastly different distances. However, it is clear that they are all of the suspension bridge type and as such do maintain an invariant form. Thus, at one level of analysis, all of the bridges in New York might be classified as having a different form, but on a different level of analysis we would all agree (I hope) that suspension bridges appear to have many characteristics in common. Kugler et al are correct in realising that one cannot just scale up the dimensions of a bridge. And thus, one cannot scale up the motor programs instructions.

The above analysis is only true if and only if one holds to the tenets that the motor program is coded in terms of muscular instructions. This is a straw person (formerly called a straw man). The program is viewed as an abstraction, and then parameters are added to scale the program to a specific task. Why couldn't the rule for parameter specifications be non-linear.

In summary this section attempted to provide a framework for the study of motor development in children that could discover which variables are dependent upon physical characteristics of children at various levels of maturational development, and which characteristics cut across changes in body size, height, and a host of other physical variables.

ISSUES IN COORDINATION

In the Compact edition of the Oxford unabridged dictionary the fourth definition of coordination provided states that coordination is the:

> Harmonious combination of agents or functions towards
> the production of a result; said *esp.* in *Phys.* in
> reference to the simultaneous and orderly action of a
> number of muscles in the production of certain complex
> movements (p. 552).

We have checked other sources, however none provides any further insight than the previously quoted definition. John discusses three levels of co-ordination: coordinates, cohesions and co-orderings. We believe that the latter begins to attack the real problem of coordination.

In the above dictionary definition coordination is seen as being useful towards the production of a result. We therefore view coordination as the co-ordering or units of action in which the individual units will sacrifice their own integrity to maintain a particular goal. Kelso (1984) demonstrates that during a speech movement, if the lower lip is perturbed, the upper lip compensates to maintain an invariant opening between the lips. We would define this as an example of coordination. In mice grooming, John demonstrates that the co-ordering involves maintaining a constant distance between the front paws. So that if one paw is perturbed the other compensates to keep a fixed distance. Thus coordination can be thought of as the rule of co-ordering pieces of behaviour. Data from Kelso, Southard and Goodman (1979) point out that in the co-ordering of two handed movements, the rule appears to be to maintain a common timing of the two hands (see Marteniuk & Mac-Kenzie, 1984 for an alternative discussion).

My intuitive hunch is that children have more coordination rules than adults and that the process of development involves the breaking down of some of the coordination rules and of course the establishment of others. Let me provide one anecdotal example. My 20 month old son enjoys playing the piano (he plays the Minute Waltz in 57 seconds). Sometimes he reaches up and strikes the keys (his definition of playing) only with one hand. Careful observation of his other hand shows that he is performing "imaginary" key strokes identical to his playing hand. In this case the coordination rule is what one hand does so does the other. I am sure that adults performing the same task would not perform these imaginary key strokes for the non-playing hand. Thus, this simple rule of co-ordering must not be obeyed in mature actions.

However, adults have more elaborate rules of co-ordering. Klapp (1979) shows that finger and speech movements are performed in harmonic relation. In some more detailed work by Kelso, Tuller and Harris (1981) and Smith, McFarland and Weber (under review) it is demonstrated that the intensity of finger and speech movements are coupled, as are the temporal patterns. Thus, two distinct anatomical and physiological systems as the manual and speech control systems are, appear to be co-ordered on a very high level.

CONCLUSIONS

John's paper highlights some very important issues for the study of motor development. He points out that the control that one observes is in many ways context dependent. Furthermore the view of context needs to cut across different levels of analysis. This theme served as the major focus for my reaction in that I tried to show how the motor program construct might be utilised in the study of motor development. The major point was that the proper taxonomic system needs to be employed in order to examine the relations between context and control. Finally some very speculative thoughts on the notion of coordination were presented.

References

Gentile, A.M., Higgins, J.R., Miller, E.A. & Rosen, B.M. (1975). The structure of motor tasks. *Mouvement, 7,* 11-28.

Golani, I. (1981). The search for invariants in motor behavior. In K. Immelmann, G.W. Barlow, L. Petronovich and M. Main (Eds.), *Behavioral Development: The Bielefeld Interdisciplinary Project.* Cambridge, England: Cambridge University Press.

Halverson, L., Roberton, M.A. & Harper, C. (1973). Current research in motor development. *Journal of Research and Development in Education, 6,* 56-70.

Hubbard, A.W. & Seng, C.N. (1954). The visual movements of batters. *Research Quarterly, 25,* 42-57.

Keele, S.W. (1968). Movement control in skilled motor performance. *Psychological Bulletin, 70,* 387-403.

Keele, S.W. (1981). Behavioral analysis of motor control. In V.B. Brooks (Ed.), *Handbook of Physiology: Motor Control.* Washington, DC: American Physiological Society.

Kelso, J.A.S. (1984). *Higher order relational invariances in action patterns: A dynamic analysis.* Paper presented at Generation and Modulation of Action Patterns, Bielefeld, Federal Republic of Germany, October 22-24, 1984.

Kelso, J.A.S., Southard, D.L. & Goodman, D. (1979). On the coordination of two-handed aiming movements. *Journal of Experimental Psychology: Human Perception and Performance, 5,* 229-238.

Kelso, J.A.S., Tuller, B. & Harris, K.S. (1981). A "Dynamic Pattern" perspective on the control and coordination of movement. In P.F. Mac-Neilage (Ed.), *The production of speech.* New York: Springer Verlag.

Klapp, S.T. (1979). Doing two things at once: The role of temporal compatibility. *Memory and Cognition, 7,* 375-381.

Kugler, P.N., Kelso, J.A.S. & Turvey, M.T. (1982). On the control and co-ordination of naturally developing systems. In J.A.S. Kelso and J.E. Clark (Eds.), *The development of movement control and co-ordination.* New York: John Wiley & Sons.

Langley, D.J. & Zelaznik, H.N. (1984). The acquisition of time properties associated with a sequential motor skill. *Journal of Motor Behavior, 16,* 275-301.

Marteniuk, R.G., MacKenzie, C.L. & Baba, D.M. (1971). Bimanual movement control: Information processing and interaction effects. *Quarterly Journal of Experimental Psychology, 36A,* 335-365. *The Compact Edition of of the Oxford English Dictionary* (1971). Oxford, England: Oxford University Press.

Pew, R.W. (1974). Human perceptual-motor performance. In B.H. Kantowitz (Ed.), *Human information processing: Tutorials in performance and cognition.* Hillsdale, NJ: Lawrence Erlbaum.

Poulton, E.C. (1957). On prediction in skilled movements. *Psychological Bulletin, 54,* 467-478.

Roberton, M.A. (1982). Describing 'Stages' within and across motor tasks. In J.A.S. Kelso and J.E. Clark (Eds.), *The development of movement control and co-ordination.* New York: John Wiley & Sons.

Schmidt, R.A. (1975). A schema theory of discrete motor skill learning. *Psychological Review, 82,* 225-260.

Schmidt, R.a. (1982). *Motor control and learning: A behavioral emphasis.* Champaign, IL: Human Kinetics.

Shapiro, D.C. (1977). A preliminary attempt to determine the duration of a motor program. In D.M. Landers and R.W. Christina (Eds.), *Psychology of motor behavior and sport (Vol. 1).* Urbana, IL: Human Kinetics.

Shapiro, D.C. (1978). *The learning of generalized motor programs.* Unpublished doctoral dissertation, University of Southern California.

Shapiro, D.C. & Schmidt, R.A. (1982). The schema theory: Recent evidence and developmental implications. In J.A.S. Kelso and J.E. Clark (Eds.), *The development of movement control and co-ordination.* New York: John Wiley.

Smith, A., McFarland, D.H. & Weber, C.M. (1985). *Interactions between speech and finger movements: An exploration of the dynamic pattern perspective.* Manuscript under review.

Spaeth-Arnold, R.K. (1981). Developing sport skills. *Motor Skills: Theory into Practice, Monograph 2.*

Summers, J.J. (1975). The role of timing in motor program representation. *Journal of Motor Behavior, 7,* 229-242.

Turvey, M.T. (1977). Preliminaries to a theory of action with reference to vision. In R. Shaw and J. Bransford (Eds.), *Perceiving, acting and knowing.* Hillsdale, NJ: Lawrence Erlbaum.

Wickstrom, R.L. (1977). *Fundamental Motor Patterns* (2nd Ed.), Philadelphia: Lea & Febiger.

Zelaznik, H.N. (1981). The effects of force and direction uncertainty on choice reaction time in an isometric force production task. *Journal of Motor Behavior, 13,* 18-32.

SECTION 4

PERCEPTION AND ACTION

PERCEPTION AND REPRESENTATION IN THE GUIDANCE OF SPATIALLY COORDINATED BEHAVIOUR*

H.L. Pick, Jr. and C.F. Palmer

Often the study of motor development is carried out at a level of analysis that emphasises movements of specific limbs (e.g., the stereotypies investigated by Thelen, 1981) or the performance of very simple acts (e.g., reaching investigated by von Hofsten). In the present paper the development of spatially coordinated behaviour will be discussed in a much more functional sense. How does the spatial layout of the environment come to guide people's behaviour? While spatial layout seems most relevant for knowing where one is and where one is going the description here also implicates spatial information in communication and even object recognition.

Reed's (1982) concept of action system will be used as a point of departure for the present discussion. According to his view the study of action involves ascertaining how available information is used to modulate actions. That includes determining "what the perceived task of an agent is, and how perceptually accessible control variables actually modulate overall behaviour" (Reed, 1982, p. 110). The emphasis on task and perceptual control variables implies that action systems are functionally organised aspects of behaviour in which the detailed anatomy of particular movements is not critical. One is reminded of the classical behaviourist experiments with rats swimming a maze that they had previously learned by running. In this way formally very different (limb) movements may involve the same action system and formally very similar movements may involve different action systems as, for example, a raising of the hand in preparation to strike, to scratch one's head or to gesture to someone.

In Reed's analysis he identified several action systems with very general but distinct functions. These included a basic orienting system, one which had to do with maintaining orientation with respect to gravity (and on which all other action systems depend), an investigatory system, a manipulative or performatory system, an expressive system, etc. The present discussion concerns primarily what Reed called the locomotor system although other action systems are implicated as well. The locomotor system involves the use by an organism of the various means and mechanisms at their disposal to move from one place to another. Part of the analysis of the locomotor system involves studying how the actual movement is modulated once one knows where they are going. This is the type of analysis carried out by researchers such as David Lee. Another aspect of the analysis of the locomotor action system concerns what information an organism uses to know where to go and how that information is organised.

It is the thesis of this discussion that one's locomotion is guided both perceptually by current sensory information and cognitively by previously acquired information. We want to discuss the development of the use of both

these kinds of information. Then we would like to describe an example of
how the interaction of these two types of guidance may depend on early
visual experience.

Perceptual Guidance

The interpretation of spatial stimuli can be altered radically depending
on the task in which the subject is engaged. This is illustrated by an
experiment on identification of simple stimuli differing only in orientation
(Rieser & Pick, 1976). Subjects were taught to identify by letter names
tactually inscribed lines traced on their stomach. Thus a vertical line might
be identified as "a", a horizontal as "b", a left diagonal as "c", etc.
Training was given with subjects standing upright until they were proficient,
i.e., fast and accurate. Then they were asked to identify these same lines
while lying on their side, so that an objectively vertical line was now
horizontal with respect to their body axis, and so on. Subject's judgements
were invariant whether standing up or lying on their side when considered
with reference to their body axes. A second group of subjects were asked
to make very similar identifications of bars fixed in various orientations.
Again they were trained standing upright until they could reach out, grasp
a bar of a given orientation, and quickly and accurately identify it. In this
case judgments made subsequently while lying on their side were invariant
with respect to gravity. Apparently a geographic frame of reference is used
for identifying an object in the world, while an egocentric frame of reference
is used for identification of scratches on one's skin.

More relevant to the development of spatially coordinated behaviour and
the manipulative vs. the locomotor action system is a study by Lockman
(1982) of detour behaviour in young infants. Lockman showed babies between
the ages of 7 and 12 months an attractive object and then hid it by passing
it over a high barrier and placing it on the other side. The baby was then
permitted to try to retrieve the object. The barrier was too high for the
baby to reach over. The problem was presented to the baby in two ways.
One was in the form of a reaching problem. The barrier was set on a high
chair and the baby could reach around the side of the barrier. The other
way was in the form of a locomotor problem. The barrier was set on the floor
and the baby needed to crawl around the end of the barrier. The babies were
all crawling well before they solved either the reaching or the locomotor
problem. However, the reaching problem was solved on the average of a
month earlier than the formally similar locomotor problem. A baby would
skilfully reach around the end of the barrier when confronted with the
reaching problem but would engage in a frontal attack on the barrier when
faced with the locomotor problem. Here it would seem again that the nature
of the task determines what information the baby uses to attain the object.
Attaining an object by reaching and attaining it by locomotion while formally
very similar apparently involve different action systems which are developing
at different rates.

In studies of spatial cognition a developmental trend has often been
found with younger children being more egocentrically oriented and older
children and adults being more geographically oriented. That is, younger
subjects seem to use body relevant reference systems in guiding their
behaviour and older subjects geographic frames of reference. One illustrative
study was reported by Acredolo (1976). In her study children between the
ages of 3 and 7 years were brought into a small room which was relatively

bare except for a table on one side and a window at the end opposite the door. The layout is depicted in Figure 1. The child was walked to a corner of the table at the side of the room and was then blindfolded. The child was then walked in a circuitous route back to the door *or* to the window where the blindfold was removed. The child was finally asked to return to the place where the blindfold had been put on. Sometimes unbeknownst to the child during its walk the table was moved to the other side of the room.

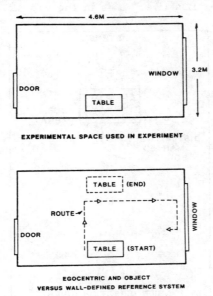

EXPERIMENTAL SPACE USED IN EXPERIMENT

EGOCENTRIC AND OBJECT
VERSUS WALL-DEFINED REFERENCE SYSTEM

Fig. 1. Layout and example of procedure of Acredolo's experiment on frames of reference.

How does the child know the place where the blindfold was put on? It is possible to consider three different frames of reference for defining place in this situation. It could be defined egocentrically in terms of whether one went to the left or right side when first entering the room. It could be defined in terms of objects in the room, in this case, the table. Or it could be defined in terms of the walls of the room. As far as the child is concerned these might form a continuum from proximal to distal reference systems. By sometimes moving the table and sometimes not; by sometimes ending the walk at the door and sometimes at the window it was possible to pit all combinations of two reference systems against the third. For example, suppose the table was moved to the other side of the room during the blindfold walk which ended at the window. An egocentrically defined response would be to go to the right-hand side of the room. This would also be congruent with a response based on an object- (table-) defined reference system. If the child went to the original side of the room it was presumably responding in terms of a more distal wall-defined reference system (see Figure 1). In fact, with increase of age there was a trend toward responding in terms of more distal reference systems. The youngest children responded most egocentrically, and the oldest children tended to respond more in terms of the walls.

138

In a more recent study (Elicker, Crayton, Pick & Plumert, in preparation) a spatial orientation task was integrated with a communication task. Children again between the ages of 3 and 7 years were asked to communicate in words alone (i.e., without gestures), the location of a trinket hidden in an array of cups. The child was at one end of a small room and the listener was sitting next to the array of cups at the other end of the room as depicted in Figure 2. The child could describe the location of the hidden trinket in egocentric terms (i.e., it is in the cup closest to me, in the

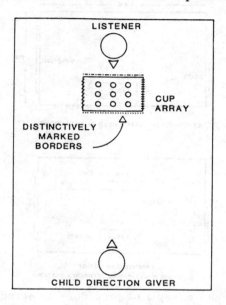

Fig. 2. Layout for experiment combining spatial orientation and communication.

column to my right), or in allocentric terms (i.e., it is in the cup furthest from you in the column on your left), or in some cases in terms of geographic markings (i.e., it is in the corner cup near the red tape and the yellow tape). In this case even the three year olds did not respond egocentrically. Apparently the fact that this spatial task was embedded in a communication task elicited from them, use of allocentric or geographic frames of reference. In terms of the action system concept, engaging a communication (semantic action system according to Reed's nomenclature) action system elicits perceptual guidance by different information than engaging the locomotor system as in Acredolo's study.

The same sort of trend from egocentric to geographic responding has been reported in the spatial behaviour of infants. In these studies infants are typically conditioned to look at one side of the room as opposed to the other upon presentation of an auditory signal. After such training the infant is moved to the other side of the room and rotated 180 degrees. The conditioned stimulus is presented once again. Younger babies e.g., 6-month olds tend to look in the same egocentric direction. By 16 months or so babie will look in the same geographic direction. Why should this developmental trend appear so much earlier in this case than in Acredolo's study described previously with 3 to 7 year olds? Again it may be the question of the action system engaged. The infants are employing what Reed has termed the investigatory system. Babies will learn to look in particular directions to find interesting sights. This is a capacity which develops very early as evidenced by the relatively highly developed control of eye movements in infancy (Aslin, 1981; Haith, 1980) and hence it is not surprising that action derived from that system would be more sophisticated.

The sensitivity of communicative behaviour to spatial layout information is also manifest in another way. When speaking with a listener at different distances the intensity of a constant vocal output decreases as the square of the distance of the distance of the listener. To what extent does a speaker compensate for this physical fact? Johnson, Pick, Siegel, and Garber (1981), found that speakers as young as 3 years of age and adults increased their vocal intensity as the distance of the listener increased but not nearly as much as the inverse square law would predict. Adults increased their intensity slightly but not significantly more than young children. But it is interesting to note that the increase was sufficient for communication across the distances used (2 to 8 metres). Analogous adjustments may be made by deaf signers (Holmes, Pick, Siegel, Uchiyama, in preparation).

With the examples above it was hoped to illustrate how the use of perceptual spatial information modulates behaviour of various action systems. However, behaviour is also organised on the basis of previously acquired information. This fact is recognised in theories and studies of the execution of motor behaviour emphasising the concept of motor programs (e.g., Schmidt, 1982). Although some aspects of planning of action can be studied through examination of choice of motor program, there has been relatively little concern with the organisation of information on which these choices are based. Consideration of how spatial information is mentally represented is one way of thinking about this issue with regard to spatially coordinated behaviour.

Cognitive Guidance

It is commonly acknowledged that in moving about our environments we learn how to get from one place to another and after greater or lesser familiarity with an area we can take new routes or give instructions for travel to people who are unfamiliar with the area. Just how is the information to do this organised? How does the ability to do this develop? To answer such questions a common technique is try to infer the nature of the structure and organisation of spatial knowledge from the kinds of operations that can be accomplished on the information that a person has. Hazen, Lockman, and Pick (1978) tried to apply this technique with children ranging in age from 3 to 6 years. Children were taught a route through a set of rooms such as is illustrated in Figure 3 and then they were tested on their ability to perform some operations on the spatial knowledge they had acquired. Each room was square with a curtain door in each wall. The routes through the house were in the form of a u-shape or a zig-zag as illustrated in Figure 4. The youngest children were taught the routes in a four-room "house" and the older children in a six-room house as depicted. Each room was identical except for a distinctive toy animal on the floor which was used to identify the room, e.g., one room was the elephant room and another the horse room. The child's task was to learn the path through the room, that is in each room to know which direction to go to get to the next room. In addition they had

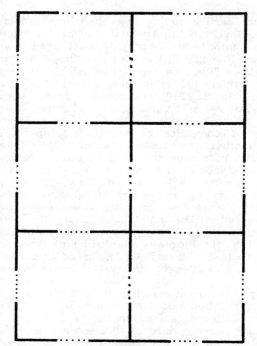

Fig. 3. Configuration of rooms for Hazen, Lockman, and Pick study. Dotted lines represent curtain doors.

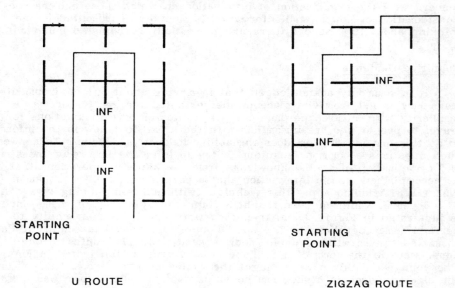

U ROUTE   ZIGZAG ROUTE

Fig. 4. Paths through animal "house". See text.

to learn to anticipate which animal "lived" in the next room. The children were trained until they could do this correctly twice in a row. Then they were given a series of tests of their spatial knowledge.

The first test was to reverse their route through the "animal house" indicating as they went through, which animal lived in the next room they were coming to. The second test was to make a "spatial inference" indicating what room lay behind doors through which they had never passed. These are the doors marked "inf" in Figure 4.

Children of all ages were able to reverse their route correctly. That is, in each room they could correctly indicate which door they should go through next on the route back to the start. However, the youngest children were deficient in naming the animal who would be living in the next room. Both the 3 and 4 year olds were poor at making the spatial inferences. This began to improve by 5 years of age but didn't reach a high level of accuracy until the age of 6. These results might be interpreted to suggest that even the youngest children here at least have a sensori-motor representation of the route which they can reverse. To the extent that the animal label for the room represents a verbal symbol identifier they don't seem to have enough of a command of this level of representation to reverse the order of labels. The ability to make spatial inferences may reflect configurational knowledge of the layout. Good performance on this test does not occur until the age of 6 although it is present to some degree at the age of 5. (This is not to say that under no conditions will younger children have configurational knowledge. In very familiar spaces such as children's own homes younger children have been found capable of making spatial inferences. It is likely the case that what develops is not an absolute ability to make spatial inferences or induce configural knowledge from serial information but rather the speed or ease with which this is done. It is probable that in very complex spaces most adults would learn a route in terms of right and left turns long before they induced the overall configuration).

In this study the organisation of spatial knowledge was inferred on the basis of operations of reversal and inference. Another common operation for inferring the organisation of spatial knowledge is the ability to imagine perspective changes. Many of these kinds of operations seem visually relevant. That is, if one had a visual image or some sort representation isomorphic to a visual image all these obtained operations would be possible. Indeed, one is tempted to suggest that all mental spatial representations are visual in nature. A thought experiment which argues against that idea implies that at least in some cases there is an organisation of knowledge which might be better considered a motor representation. Consider the typewriter keyboard. Skilled typists have difficulty responding to such questions as what are the keys from right to left on the lower row. This would seem to have to be easy if they were reading off a visual representation. Yet in a very real sense they know the keyboard, in a very real motor sense. If they are given to type the characters in the order in which they appear in the lower row typists whip them off very quickly. If they do answer the verbal question response is usually very slow and they report imagining moving their finger to each key before responding. It is interesting to conjecture about the nature of this motor representation*. Again it would be a good candidate for study by ascertaining the kinds of transformations that could be tolerated. It is not a representation that permits of easy intermanual transfer as many motor programs do, e.g., handwriting. On the other hand one could imagine relatively easy adaptation to some range of scale changes, i.e., interkey distances. Not withstanding the last part of this discussion, many of the spatial representations of humans seem to be visual in nature. The final topic we would like to address in this discussion is the role of early visual experience in using cognitive spatial representations to guide behaviour.

Interrelation of Perceptual and Cognitive Guidance of Behaviour

So far the discussion has considered perceptual guidance of spatially coordinated behaviour and cognitive guidance more or less separately. However in natural spatial situations and in life experience perceptual information and cognitive information are not separate. We often *know* a great deal about spatial layouts that we are perceiving. Our ability to make cognitive operations on spatial information may depend on prior perceptual experience. How do perceptual and cognitive processes involved in spatial behaviour interact in development?

One aspect of this question can be approached by asking how relative reliance on perceptual and cognitive information in guiding spatial behaviour might change with age. An illustration of this approach is provided in a study by Smith, Hakke and Pick (in preparation). Children between the ages of 16 and 24 months of age were taken on a circuitous walk away from a parent. The walk ended near but out of sight of the parent. The children were then asked to find their way back to their parent by themselves. The older children almost all chose a direct path over which they had no prior experience. The younger children almost all reversed the longer original path. So far this simply illustrates the same kind of result described earlier – ability to make spatial inferences increases with age and younger children can reverse spatial motor patterns. However, in a follow-up study with 16-month olds immediate perceptual information was provided along with the cognitive route knowledge the children apparently had. The parent called to the child as they were asked to find their way back. Some of the children now took a direct path back. But many children continued to rely on their route knowledge and reversed the original path. In some of these cases the parent's voice was very motivating and the child rushed back, but over the long circuitous route. Presumably ability to use this so-called cognitive route knowledge develops later than ability to respond to direct perceptual information. However, it seems that once this cognitive knowledge is available there is a strong tendency to rely on it in such situations as described here.

---

*
On reflection, there is considerable evidence against the idea that all spatial imagery is visual. Empirically, there are a number of studies of congenitally blind subjects which demonstrate ability to perform mental operations on spatial representations. See Warren (1984) for a general review. For example, congenitally blind subjects show the same kinds of temporal functions as sighted subjects when asked to make compatative judgments which involve mentally rotating representations of stimuli, e.g., Marmor and Zaback (1976) and Carpenter and Eisenberg (1978). More anecdotally, many people are able to perform the intricate motor movements involved in tying knots but would be unable to visualise this process.

A second aspect of the question of interrelation of perceptual and cognitive guidance of behaviour concerns the role of perceptual experience in cognitive information processing. Although, as suggested above, not all mental spatial representation is visually relevant or dependent. Vision richly and pervasively provides spatial information throughout the lives of seeing persons. As also noted above many characteristics of our spatial knowledge seem visual in nature and in many cases blind subjects are not as good in spatial tasks even as sighted objects performing without vision (e.g., Rieser, Lockman & Pick, 1980).

An obvious strategy for investigating such questions is by comparing sighted and congenitally blind subjects. Although blind subjects often are less able than sighted subjects to perform such experimental tasks as making spatial inferences or practically making detours, exactly what underlies their difficulty is not known. Rieser and his colleagues (Rieser, Guth & Hill, 1982) performed an intriguing study comparing congenitally blind and sighted subjects in their ability to make spatial inferences from actual and imagined viewpoints.

Blindfolded sighted subjects and congenitally blind subjects were taught to walk from a home base to each of six locations: A, B, C, D, E, and F and to return to the home base. After this training they were asked to stand at home base and point as rapidly and accurately as possible to each of the 6 locations. In a subsequent test condition they were asked to imagine walking to one of the 6 locations in the room and from that imagined location point at the other 5 locations. In a second test condition they were actually walked to one of the 6 locations and were asked to point at the other 5 locations. For the sighted subjects' responses were quick and accurate when pointing from the original home base *and* when pointing from the location to which they had actually been walked. However, their responses were slow and relative inaccurate when pointing from an imagined location. The responses of the congenitally blind subjects were also fast and accurate when pointing from home base but their responses were slow and inaccurate *both* when pointing from a new imagined and a new actual location. Actually walking to a new· location facilitated pointing for the sighted over simply imagining the new location, but it didn't help the blind. Moreover, the sighted in the imaginary condition, and the blind in the imaginary and walking conditions, reported having to concentrate very hard and almost calculate the new spatial directions. For the walking condition the sighted subjects reported that making judgments was very easy, just like at home base; they simply knew where things were.

For sighted subjects but not for blind, walking facilities keeping track of where things are in relation to themselves even though the things are out of view. What about the lack of early visual experience might account for this difference? Possibly the existence for the sighted subjects of optical flow patterns everytime they move their head throughout their walking lives would sensitise them to the relative movement of objects as they move around their environment. This constant correlation may be so pervasive that even when there is no visual information during a walk, a sort of virtual flow pattern occurs. Its almost automatic effect results in sighted people main-taining updated information about where things are in relation to themselves.

Conclusion

The invoking of optical flow patterns to explain these effects of early visual experience raises the question of the relation of the present analysis to James Gibson's (1979) theory of perception (and action). Gibson was extremely uncomfortable with explanations which involved contructivist concepts such as mental representations. He tried to explain as much as possible of our behaviour by perception rather than by memory or other cognitive processes. In the case of knowing where things are when they were out of sight, he wanted to argue for the possibility of perceptual information. Gibson referred to Michotte's observations that *phenomenally* one could see an object after it had entered a tunnel and while it was out of sight passing through the tunnel. In interpreting this possibility Gibson convincingly argued that when an object disappears out of sight behind an occluding object there is information that it is not going out of existence but that it is going behind something else. An object going out of existence might explode or evaporate, etc., a very different kind of event specified by a very different kind of information. Although Gibson doesn't develop the argument for location of objects there may well be information for where occluded objects are especially when they go out of sight by virtue of movement of the observer. The optical flow pattern specifies where an observer is in relation to the visible objects in the world. And as one moves through the world the images of objects at different distances have different relative velocities. This pattern of optical flow could be extrapolated to occluded objects for whose continued existence there was information. Extending such an argument to a completely occluded (non)visual world, as when the eyes are closed, is a considerable leap but Gibson's analysis provides a point of departure.

Initially in the present paper the importance of current perceptual information for guiding action was emphasised. The main point was that different tasks, engaging different action systems, drew selectively on different aspects of the available information. We perceive in order to act, in analysing the inter-relation of cognitive and perceptual guidance of spatial behaviour the guidance of action was shown to depend in some cases on prior perceptual experience (perhaps of optical flow patterns which themselves are generated by action). We act in order to perceive. It does indeed seem difficult to separate perception and action.

ACKNOWLEDGEMENTS

*Preparation of this chapter was supported by Program Project Grant Number HD-05027-15 to the Institute of Child Development and by the Center for Research in Human Learning of the University of Minnesota.

References

Acredolo, L.P. (1976). Frames of reference used by children for orientation
 in unfamiliar spaces. In G.T. Moore and R.G. Golledge (Eds.),
 Environmental knowing. Stroudsberg, PA: Dowden, Hutchinson & Ross.
Aslin, R.N. (1981). Development of smooth persuit in human infants. In
 D.F. Fisher, R.A. Monty and J.W. Sanders (Eds.), *Eye movements:
 Cognition and visual perception*. Hillsdale, NJ: Erlbaum.
Burton, A.W. (1985). The development of phasing ability in children.
 Unpublished manuscript, University of Minnesota.
Carpenter, P.A. & Eisenberg, P. (1978). Mental rotation and the frame of
 reference in blind and sighted individuals. *Perception and Psychophysics,
 23*, 117–124.
Gibson, J.J. (1979). *The ecological approach to visual perception*. Boston:
 Houghton-Mifflin.
Haith, M.M. (1980). *Rules that babies look by*. Hillsdale, NJ: Erlbaum.
Hazen, N.L., Lockman, J. & Pick, H.L., Jr. (1978). The development of
 children's representations of large-scale environments. *Child Development,
 55*, 482–491.
Johnson, C., Pick, H.L., Jr., Siegel, G.M. & Garber, S.R. (1981). Effects
 of interpersonal distance on children's vocal intensity. *Child Development,
 52*, 721–723.
Lockman, J.J. (1984). The development of detour ability during infancy.
 Child Development, 55, 482–491.
Marmor, G.S. & Zaback, L.A. (1976). Mental rotation by the blind: Does
 mental rotation depend on visual imagery? *Journal of Experimental
 Psychology: Human Perception and Performance, 2*, 515–521.
Pick, J.L. & Rieser, J.J. (1982) Children's cognitive mapping. In M. Potegal
 (Ed.), *Spatial abilities*. New York: Academic Press.
Pick, H.L., Jr. & Teulings, H.L. (1983). Geometric transformations of
 handwriting as a function of instruction and feedback. *Acta Psychologica,
 54*, 327–340.
Reed, E. (1982). An outline of a theory of action systems. *Journal of
 Motor Behavior, 14*, 98–134.
Rieser, J.J., Guth, D. & Hill, E. (1982). Mental processes mediating
 independent travel: Implications for orientation and mobility. *Journal of
 Visual Impairment and Blindness, 76*, 213–218.
Rieser, J.J., Lockman, J.J. & Pick, H.L., Jr. (1980). The role of visual
 experience in knowledge of spatial layout. *Perception and Psychophysics,
 28*, 185–190.
Schmidt, R.A. (1982). More on motor programs. In J.A.S. Kelso (Ed.),
 Human motor behavior: An introduction. Hillsdale, NJ: Erlbaum.
Thelen, E. (1981). Rhythmical behavior in infancy: An ethological perspective.
 Developmental Psychology, 17, 237–257.
Warren, D.H. (1984). *Blindness and early child development*. New York:
 American Foundation for the Blind.

Perception
+
Action
Memory?
can they be
Separated.

MOVEMENT INVARIANCES IN CULTURE-SPECIFIC SKILLS

H.T.A. Whiting

PERCEPTION AND ACTION

The problem for a theory of action is not so much to explain how we begin to act on the environment but, rather, how we change from one action to another over time, i.e. how we move from one steady state to another. We are involved in a living narrative whose unfolding is a record of our actions. From such a perspective it is not difficult to find sympathy for Pick and Palmer's wish to move away from discussions about movements of specific limbs or the performance of very simple acts, and to concentrate attention on the development of spatially coordinated behaviour in a much more global and functional sense. I have, in the past, been moved by similar motives, to comment on the very limited perspectives provided by traditional approaches to motor learning (Whiting, 1980, 1984a). The restricted nature of the actions selected for the majority of laboratory studies of motor learning as well as the excessive concern of such studies with 'outcome' measures at the expense of the movements themselves severely constrains their interpretative scope. This emphasis has, for example, as Carroll and Bandura (1982) suggest, led to a neglect of the problem of how complex movement patterns are acquired.

Since the latter topic is to be a focus of attention in this paper, a questioning of the generality of Pick and Palmer's contention that 'action systems are functionally organised aspects of behaviour *in which the detailed anatomy of particular movements is not critical*'*, is already signalled.

Perception and action are intimately linked (if not confounded) in every-day life situations. We act to perceive and we perceive to act. While both processes may, to some degree, be usefully separated in the laboratory this should not lead us into believing that, in so doing, researchers are necessarily contributing much to an understanding of everyday functioning. The perception/action link has, perhaps, been most appropriately addressed by Neisser (1976) in his conception of an action/perception cycle in which actions provide new information which, in turn, can be used to modify further actions. Adoption of this kind of conceptual framework would be more likely to lead to agreement with Gibson (1979) that in researching human actions we could more profitably shift our focus away from efferent commands or their consequences to the question of how organisms – in Reed's (1982) terms – use available information to modulate their actions. Pick and Palmer clearly wish to embrace such a conceptual framework, particularly the concept of action systems expounded by Reed (1982) in his outline of a theory of action. While Reed's standpoint is an attractive one, and I will have cause to invoke it as we proceed, it does prompt a number of additional questions which,

* Author's italics.

following this introduction, I will want to address. Reed's standpoint is a recognition that movements are seldom simply reactive but, are functionally adaptive, functionally specific and context sensitive. The question then becomes - to cite Bransford and Shaw (1977) - no longer the *how* of psychological processing, but the what.

In coming, now, to recognise this kind of position, we should not be complacent. Psychologists, all too often, forget, or ignore, their psychological history. That the position here being sketched has a rich history is to be deduced from Ricoeur (1966) who, in expanding on some of the 1934 reflex notions of Goldstein, points out that:

> ...if the subject knows the conditions of the experiment
> in advance his artificially provoked reflexes are modified.
> Thus, we cannot rightly speak of reflexes apart from the
> method by which they have been obtained...

In developing his argument into the field of, what he calls 'initial skills' (i.e., those skills available, at birth or shortly there after), Ricoeur comes closer to the position of Pick and Palmer on the functionality of action systems and leads in a similar direction to that which they wish to take:

> ...initial skills are not chains of invariable movements,
> but are already supple forms, structures with variable
> contents, as habits will be later - they have been called
> 'kinetic melodies'.
> They do not respond to simple stimuli (through even
> reflexes might never respond to a simple and invariable
> stimulus), but to discriminated aspects (qualities, forms
> etc.), which already represent a complex perceptive
> organisation.

Skill, is, thus, not produced by a stimulus, in the double sense that it is governed by perceived objects or events and not by physical stimuli and it requires that the subject be able to detect an affordance appropriate to his present course of action. Voluntary movement is 'appropriate' movement. Blondel (writing in the 30's) sought the criterion of voluntary movement not in its psychological antecedents, but in its opportuneness, that is, in its social convenience (Ricoeur, 1966). As I have stressed elsewhere (Whiting, 1980), the criterion of appropriateness has, also, to be learned. What the actor considers an appropriate solution to a motor problem at a particular stage of learning may well be inappropriate as more competence is acquired.

Perhaps it is not surprising that Bernstein (Whiting, 1984b) whose fundamental research on human actions was, in the '30's , already well established, should be more easily influenced by these, for him, more contemporary studies. Even in his early work was to be discovered an attempt to substitute the analysis of action in terms of efferent commands from cortex to motor neurones by an analysis based on the selective use of information both about the environment and about the actor's ongoing movements. Bernstein was, also, not slow to appreciate the similarities between perceptual and motor activities. As long ago as 1935, he drew attention to what he termed 'a circumstance of great and immediate interest' in the structural analysis of movements, namely 'the fact that topological peculiarities in visual perception display marked similarities to some signs of idiosyncracies in the topology of motor organisation'. While, since that time, the perception of movement has been extensively pursued, notably by Johansson and Cutting and their co-workers (Johansson, 1950, 1973, 1978; Cutting, 1981, 1983; Cutting & Kozlowski, 1977; Cutting & Profitt, 1981) its significance for action has seldom been stressed. This issue will be returned to more forcibly later.

The precise nature of the information that has a steering function or the role of information pick-up in skill learning is, of course, a matter for extended research programmes which take this issue as their starting point. Clearly, Pick and Palmer wish to set such investigations forward in the context of spatial orientation. Our own interest, while embracing some similar concerns, has been somewhat different. In the first place, it has not been addressed specifically to children and in the second it has been concerned primarily with culture-specific skills - particularly those in a sport context. There are, however, as already indicated, points of similarity and points of debate. Before introducing this work, it is necessary, therefore, to pursue further some of the issues already lightly touched upon and further elaborated in the paper of Pick and Palmer.

THE STUDY OF ACTION

It is useful, to begin by reconsidering Reed's (1982) contention that the study of action is 'the study of how available information is used to modulate actions', together with Pick and Palmer's rider, thereto, that action systems are functionally organised aspects of behaviour *in which the detailed anatomy of particular movements* is not critical. While, strictly speaking, neither the standpoint of Reed or that of Pick and Palmer excludes learning one is left with the impression that many of the statements made are performance oriented and directed to phylogenetic skills (e.g. locomotion), i.e. established phylogenetic action systems are the starting point for such considerations. The limitation, in this respect, is both the comparative neglect of the acquisition of culture-specific skills as well as of the developmental history of the organism which has led to the establishment of such systems - a developmental history which may well have recourse to other systems of control than those operating when the system is relatively autonomous. In this respect, what Fitts and Posner (1967) - in their three-stage model of skill development - refer to as the *cognitive stage* of skill learning has seldom received attention. Instead, the focus has been on relatively autonomous systems and how they might be modulated by perceptual information. As we shall see later, this can lead to anomalies in the interpretation of how the system works.

The contention of Pick and Palmer that locomotion is guided both perceptually by current sensory information and cognitively by previously acquired information is very interesting in this respect as it gives a hint of a possible rapprochement between the action system approach and the motor system approach (Beek, Meijer & Whiting, 1985). To illustrate, McLeod, McLaughlin and Nimmo-Smith (1985) point out that the idea, represented in a variety of forms in different theories, is that practice leads to the development of specific devices or programmes for carrying out actions. Such devices may, in Fodor's (1983) terms, have become 'informationally encapsulated', i.e. capable of producing appropriate output on the basis of a specific input only, needing no interactions with general purpose cognitive facilities. The important point being made is that actions which, at an earlier stage of development, might rely (solely) on cognitive mediation come to rely much less so as competence develops.

The over-concern in the motor skill literature with relatively simple actions which quickly become autonomous (in the sense that the actor need no longer assign much attention to them) and the methodological concern to balance performance levels of subjects (often so that they are asymptotic) before the experiment proper begins, denys the actor's developmental history. This is not to say that the study of performance *per se* is not interesting but merely to reiterate that learning has become something of a Cinderella topic.

For example, in the Hazen, Lockman and Pick (1978) study on spatial orientation to which they refer is to be read:

> Children were taught a route through a set of rooms
> ...and *then** they were tested...The children were trained
> until they could do this correctly twice in a row. *Then**
> they were given a series of tests of their spatial knowledge.

That Pick and Palmer are not disinterested in the learning process *per se* is clear when, in relation to spatial orientation, they raise the questions:

> How is the information to do this organised?
> How does the ability to do this develop?

Nevertheless, the approach is different from that which might ensue if the question 'what kind of information is used for spatial orientation at various stages of learning' was posed.

To return, now, to Pick and Palmer's contention that with respect to action systems the detailed anatomy of particular movements is not critical. While the cited, classical work on maze-running by rats would give credence to their contention, the question must be raised as to how general is their statement when, for example, one moves from phylogenetic to more rule-bound culture-specific skills in which the detailed anatomy of particular movements may well be critical?

These signalled deficiencies in current approaches to theories of action are, as already suggested very pertinent to the student of skill acquisition, since they point to the very limited attention paid, in the literature, to the very early cognitive stage of skill learning when, it is suggested, movement 'form' is beginning to be established (Tyldesley & Whiting, 1975).

The deficiency is further apparent in the much-researched schema theory of motor learning (Schmidt, 1975), which takes as its departure point the prior existence of abstract general motor programmes, defined in terms of relational parameters (c.q. relative timing, relative force etc.), but provides no explanation as to how such programmes become established. Shapiro and Schmidt (1982) were moved to recognise, in this respect that '...a motor learning theory that does not explain how programmes are learned will fall considerably short of providing an understanding of the motor learning

* author's italics.

process'.

It is these kinds of consideration together with the learning model put
forward by Tyldesley and Whiting (1975) which has led to the interest of
the author's group in the early stages of skill learning. This interest has
centred, lately, around both discrete actions as exemplified by the forehand
drive in table-tennis and cyclical actions as exemplified by slalom-type ski
movements on a skill simulator.

In the methodology employed in the group, a general standpoint has
been taken. The contention is that the outcome of an attempt to solve a
motor problem as measured by overall achievement (some global measure)
cannot stand alone as a dependent variable in motor learning experiments i.e.
we must not only have measures of outcomes but how they are achieved. At
different stages towards the development of competency more attention may
be placed on the *end* rather than on the *means* and vice versa. Recently,
for example, in a study of the learning of the tennis service by novices –
significant positive correlations between form and outcome only became
apparent after an extended period of practice (Emmen, Wesseling, Bootsma,
Whiting & Van Wieringen, 1985). In a more general way, then, since
movements can be characterised by a whole host of parameters – not
necessarily related – the measurements used to index motor performance
should reflect this diversity. Only by this kind of analysis can a
comprehensive description of the performance be built up and a more
integrated view of the manner in which a learner acquires a movement
sequence be provided. Our approach has been one of what we call 'operational
analysis' (Whiting, 1970) i.e., the multi-dimensional abstraction of information
about the movements/postures of learners/performers in *relatively* unstructured dynamic situations.

The value of such multi-dimensional approaches has been repeatedly
shown (e.g., Tyldesley & Whiting, 1975; Bootsma, Den Brinker & Whiting,
1985; Den Brinker & Van Hekken, 1982; Den Brinker, Stäbler, Whiting &
Van Wieringen, 1985a, b) and has recently been illustrated in the (unpublished) study of Warren, Lee and Young (1985). These workers were
able to show that, while in principle, a number of gait parameters might be
influenced by information pertinent to running over irregular terrain, it was
in fact flight time, probably by adjustment of the vertical impulse, that was
varied – presumably being modulated by the optical variable *tau*.

Some of our most interesting recent work, in the present context, has
its roots in the earlier studies of Tyldesley and Whiting (1975) on Operational
Timing. These studies were based on operational analyses of semi-structured
table-tennis situations in which the forehand drive of subjects at levels from
novice to international were studied. The kinds of reference system utilised
by subjects, in a less general sense than that addressed by Pick and Palmer,
was one of the topics of interest. It is useful, therefore, to recall Wohlwill's
(1981) comments that such reference systems are not absolute but, are a
function of situational factors, such as the presence or absence of landmarks,
the demands of a particular task and the individual's experiential history. We
will return to these comments at various times in what follows. At this stage,
it is sufficient to note that a table-tennis situation contains many landmarks.
Our own concern with the experiential history of the individual is reflected in
the range of playing ability studied and, more recently, in our attention to
the early learning stage (Fitts & Posner's, 1967, cognitive stage). Potentially
different demands of different tasks have been considered by studying both

discrete and cyclical actions.

In the Tyldesley and Whiting (1975) research, on the basis of an extensive study of a very small group of subjects, the spatial and temporal consistency of the movement patterns of both intermediate and expert players was demonstrated. Figure 1 shows examples of the space-time displacements of the wrist (although data on the elbow or shoulder might equally well have been substituted) of both an intermediate and an expert player while carrying out an attacking forehand drive. The lack of consistency in the movement patterns of novices, studied under similar conditions, meant that there were no reproducible movement patterns available for comparison.

From just the expert and intermediate results, it is possible to indicate that a form of timing is being used that Tyldesley and Whiting (1975) refer to as 'operational timing'. Through the initiation point (IP) location (spatial IP) and time (temporal IP) may differ, the completed movement pattern always lasts a uniform length of time.

Thus, while the 'programme' is running, the mode of operational timing can be said to be occurring to an accuracy of ± 4 msec (in the expert) without, apparently, conscious attention to a time perception process. Such a 'programme' would provide, in Pick and Palmer's terms, a guidance function in the sense of a relatively consistent spatio-temporal frame of reference. In as far as operational timing is a reflection of the bringing under control of an important unit of an action system, it is of fundamental importance. It should not, however, be allowed to detract from the ultimate controlling influence of the initiation point and its prediction. A consistent movement pattern initiated at a wrong instant in time is unlikely to provide an appropriate solution to a motor problem. Perceptual processes must remain the critical mechanisms in the reduction of temporal uncertainty. Timing on the output side can only assist in giving expression to central decisions in a reliable and consistent fashion. The information on which such central decisions are made is as important as the analysis of the movement itself. Ultimately, of course, it is the perception/action link which is sought.

It is to be noted, further, from Figure 1 that while it is possible to overlay the ballistic portions of the displacement (and also velocity) curves for the intermediate player, for anatomical data points such as wrist, elbow and shoulder joint centres in a way that virtual coincidence is achieved (thus operationalising 'operational timing') such a manipulation involves a shift on both the spatial and temporal axes. These results show that an identical movement pattern (to the external observer) in terms of displacement and velocity is being achieved but, that this pattern is being initiated at variable positions (spatial IP) in space and, at slightly different temporal instances (temporal IP) on each stroke. With some experts, variability is restricted to the temporal IP dimension. It should be noted that commencing an identical pattern of movement at different times could result in a displacement difference at ball/bat (b/b) contact. This would only result in an error if the 'outcome' tolerance band for the task is narrow. If, for example, a top-spin loop shot had been required, then the displacement tolerance for correct contact would be reduced, and the initiation of the ballistic action would have had to have been more accurate, both spatially and temporally. One of the situational factors affecting reference systems to which Wohlwill referred.

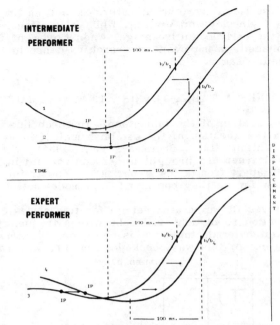

Fig. 1. A diagrammatic reconstruction of the shifts necessary to
overlay the ballistic portions of an intermediate and an
expert performer's movement patterns. For clarity,
displacement traces only are shown, but similar shifts are
required to overlay the velocity traces, key:
b/b - time of bat/ball contact
IP - initiation point.

On the basis of these kinds of analysis, and bearing in mind the
limited number of subjects on whom the analyses were based, Tyldesley and
Whiting (1975) were led to speculate that errors will arise in novices as a
result of an inability to:
  i) select the required 'motor programme'
 ii) run the correct motor programme consistently
iii) spatially predict the initiation point (spatial IP)
 iv) temporally predict IP (temporal IP).
In more general terms, this model is a specification of the invariances that
are likely to become established as learning proceeds. with transitions through
the skill levels, errors type i and ii, it is proposed, would drop out first
and then type iii until the expert will be faced solely with a problem of
temporal prediction of *when* to start a movement sequence which is both
spatially and temporally constrained.

While we would, now, be a little more cautious in ascribing consistency
of performance to motor programmes *per se,* the model proposed by
Tyldesley and Whiting was found to be a useful departure point for a series
of experiments recently carried out, in the author's laboratories by Bootsma,
addressed to the cognitive stage of skill learning (Bootsma, Den Brinker &
Whiting, 1985). The choice of this learning stage was dictated both by

deficiencies in the motor learning literature as well as by the learning model put forward by Tyldesley and Whiting. While it is often recognised in the literature that the early cognitive stage, when movement forms are first becoming established, is important, research evidence in that respect is, as already indicated, meagre.

LEARNING TO MAKE A TABLE-TENNIS ATTACKING FOREHAND DRIVE

In the continuation of the table-tennis research line, we were particularly interested in the question of the establishment of invariances (Bootsma, Den Brinker & Whiting, 1985; Bootsma & Valk, 1984). What movements/ postures of the learner are brought under control and in what order when a player is left, apart from a few experimental constraints, to 'discovery learning'. In how far do they conform to the model outlined?

Figure 2 gives the apparatus set-up for this series of studies. A Sitco R-IIs ball projection robot delivered balls with a frequency of 40 per minute to a, former, Dutch female table-tennis champion, *who then played the ball towards the player*. In this way, ecological validity was maintained and, also,

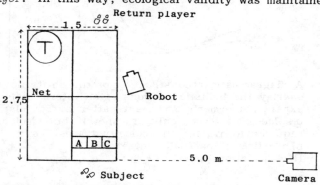

Fig. 2. Table-tennis apparatus set-up.

this procedure proved to be a more accurate means of delivering the balls to subjects.

Five male Dutch top table-tennis players, including the national champion, were filmed. The analyses included movement outcomes (not to be discussed here) operationalised as the number of hits on target per block of 40 trials, together with a number of space-time variables derived from a frame by frame analysis of the films. This data was used for comparative purposes in a later learning study in which novices were used as subjects.

TOP PERFORMERS

Five male top table-tennis players were required to play four blocks of 40 attacking forehand drives. In the fourth block, a minimum of seven drives were filmed – all such drives were in response to balls being projected into target area B. The results for the variables of interest are summarised in Table 1. B/b was defined as the X/Y coordinates of the bat at the moment of ball/bat contact expressed in cms to the table surface (Y) or the leading

Table 1. Means and standard deviations of 5 first division players
averaged over seven strokes for a number of variables.

	$\overline{X}$	S.D.
X coordinate b/b (cms)	32.53	6.45
Y coordinate b/b (cms)	40.53	2.18
Y coordinate (spatial) IP (cms)	108.11	3.67
Y coordinate (spatial) IP (cms)	19.11	2.82
Movement time (msec)	146.40	17.80

edge (X). Spatial IP was determined by the X/Y coordinates of the bat at
the moment that the forehand drive was initiated. Movement time (an
operationalisation of Operational Timing) was the time between IP and B/b.
An analysis of variance of the standard deviations showed no changes in
the variability over the whole length of the stroke. The results reflect to
a large extent the findings of Tyldesley and Whiting (1975). The high level
of consistency over all variables is noteworthy in this respect. A standard
deviation of only ± 18 msecs for the duration of the ballistic portion of the
stroke (operational timing) is particularly impressive given that the results
are averaged over 5 players. If the records of the individuals were to be
inspected, one of these would be seen to have a S.D. of ± 4 msecs. In
summary, players produced strokes with similar time durations, with similar
trajectories from similar spatial initiation points. In this way, virtually only
one degree of freedom remains - the temporal initiation point. Operational
timing together with spatial consistency of IP is very efficient in the sense
that the visuo-motor problem is reduced to a temporal decision. Whether
this temporal problem is solved on the basis of *tau* or whether it is related
to certain landmarks (e.g., a point of singularity such as the point of zero
vertical acceleration in the flight-path of the ball) and/or velocity information
is an open question - a question being pursued within our research group
at the present time. Preliminary data, reported below, from an ongoing study,
raise some doubts about exclusive reliance on tau.

TIME TO CONTACT

Under similar conditions, to those of the experiments just reported, an
expert table-tennis player was required, after a relevant warming up period,
to make a series of forehand drives in response to balls projected at a
constant, high, velocity. The whole series of strokes was filmed (as
previously). Subsequently, the player was required to repeat the procedure
with his dominant eye masked (If tau is the significant variable guiding
action, performance should be equally good under monocular as under binocular conditions). Prior to filming, the player was allowed 40 practice strokes
under this condition. The fact that playing with one eye masked is not novel
is to be gleaned from the fact that players at this level regularly play
'friendly' tournaments with 'one-eye masked' players playing against players
with normal vision.

The results of the analysis are given in Table 2. Significant differences
are apparent for movement time (IP to b/b) - operational timing - longer
in the 'one-eye masked' condition, with increased variability; time from ball

bounce on table to b/b - shorter in the 'one-eye masked' condition, subjects strike the ball earlier in time; temporal IP - shorter in the 'one-eye masked' group, probably reflected also in the shorter ball bounce to b/b mean but, much more variable.

While this raises questions for the primacy of tau, there is still the possibility that tau is only one of the information sources used in such semi-structured situations. Since, under both conditions, the total flight time of the ball is similar, it follows that under the monocular condition the stroke is initiated (IP) when the ball is in a different spatial position than under the binocular condition. If, therefore, IP were to be determined not by *tau* but by some ball spatial cue (as suggested by Tyldesley, 1979) the interesting question shifts from *tau* to misperception of the spatial position of the ball under the monocular condition.

One possibility is provided by Von Hofsten (1985) in pointing out that retinal expansion may inform the catcher of time to contact and in which direction the hand should be moved but not how far from the eye the object is going to arrive. It could be a large object moving slowly and passing close by. To determine the scale of the event, the catcher needs veridical information about the motion of the object, at least at some point during its approach.

Table 2. Means and standard deviations on a number of parameters of a first division player under conditions of monocular and binocular vision.

Condition:	Binocular vision		Monocular vision		Significance
	$\overline{X}$	S.D.	$\overline{X}$	S.D.	
Flight time (msec)	523.64	6.0	522.8	7.7	N.S.
Landing position (m) from proximal edge of table	.452	.95	.471	.07	N.S.
Movement time (msecs)	81.9	2.7	89.43	9.1	$p < .05$
Ball bounce to b/b (msecs)	205.93	15.1	192.6	13.3	$p < .05$
Temporal IP (msecs)	647.67	15.8	625.97	9.2	$p < .05$

NOVICE PERFORMERS

Ten novice players were trained for five consecutive days. Film recordings were made in the manner previously described. From Figure 3 is to be seen that the mean duration of the strokes increased from day 1 to day 3 and decreased again on day 5 of training. ($F(2,18) = 13.93$, $p < .001$). The movement time of the top players was notably shorter and more consistent. More interestingly, the variability in movement times for the novices did not change over days - no significant differences were found. Apparently novice subjects have not yet reached the stage of operational timing. Unfortunately, the present analysis did not permit an assessment of

157

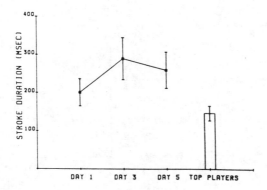

Fig. 3. Means and S.D.'s of stroke duration of novices on days
1, 3 and 5 of training together with similar data for top
players.

movement form. It might, however, be predicted that at this stage of
training no clearly established form would be present.

From Figures 4 and 5 is to be seen that novice players bring their
spatial IP closer to the near edge of the table over training and also closer
to the surface of the table (height above table) with a corresponding
reduction in the variability of both these indices of spatial IP.

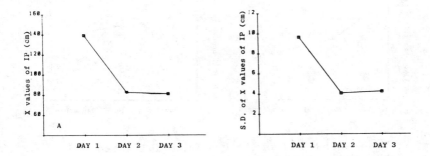

Fig. 4. Means and S.D.'s of the spatial IP expressed in cm to
the leading edge of the table.

Apparently, novice subjects quickly reduce their spatial orientation
degrees of freedom by establishing a relatively stable spatial IP with respect
to the leading edge of the table.

Consistency in temporal IP is reflected both in the consistency of
movement duration (shown to be relatively variable) and in the consistency
of the temporal aspect of b/b contact. The latter (Fig. 6) is reflected in
the time interval between ball bounce and b/b contact. While this becomes
less variable over training days, inconsistency in movement duration still

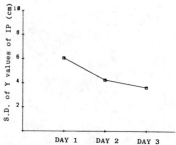 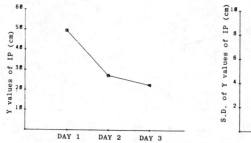

Fig. 5. Means and S.D.'s of the spatial IP expressed in cm to
the surface of the table.

means that there is considerable temporal IP uncertainty. This, as Tyldesley
and Whiting (1975) predicted, will only become less variable after players
have moved to an operational timing mode following an extensive period of
practice.

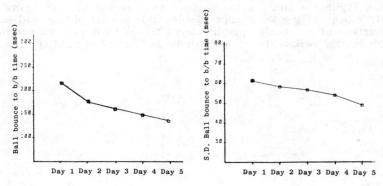

Fig. 6. Means and S.D.'s of the time interval between ball
bounce and b/b contact in msec.

These results would suggest that, contrary to the predictions of
Tyldesley and Whiting, the spatial invariance of IP is beginning to be
established before stroke duration becomes consistent.

In summary, what the work of Tyldesley and Whiting (1975), and that
reported here, illustrates is that there are, in contrast to the position
eschewed by Pick and Palmer, functionally organised aspects of behaviour
in which the structure of the movements, at least at the kinematic level is
crucial. Such a statement may need to be qualified in the sense that it may
be restricted to culture-specific skills (such as sports skills) which take
place in a dynamic environment involving fast moving objects and people with

fine constraints on speed and accuracy being imposed by a complex rule-structure within which the player is required to operate. It might well be that the only way to successfully operate under such conditions is to *contain* some of the numerous degrees of freedom by the acquisition of spatial and temporal invariances. If this should prove to be the case, it is clear that we are less likely to become aware of such possibilities by studying, only, the movements of very young children and the development of their phylogenetic skills.

An interesting observation, on which we are now working, stems from these findings. In order that players be able to reproduce consistent movement patterns – such as those exhibited by top players – in response to variable information about space-time characteristics of the ball, it is necessary for them to vary their dynamic posture quite considerably. It is also an accepted fact in racquet games that the most efficient strokes are made from a stable postural base (i.e. two feet on the ground well spaced horizontally and lengthwise). This is evidenced by observation of any table tennis match in which high calibre players are involved, they are continually on the move, until such time that they are in position to play a stroke, then the stable stance becomes apparent. In contrast, novices produce inconsistent movement patterns from relatively static postural conditions. It seems likely that the coordination to be learned involves the organisation of the degrees of freedom of the active limb within a dynamic postural base. While, following Bernstein (Whiting, 1984b), it may be necessary for novices to freeze certain degrees of freedom (for example in the postural control mechanisms) while they pay attention to other aspects of motor control, ultimately, however, these must, as Bernstein suggests be converted to a controllable system:

> This is because (as extensive work on children,
> sportsmen and also hemiparetic subjects and amputees
> has shown) fixation eliminating the redundant degrees
> of freedom mentioned above is employed only as the
> most primitive and inconvenient method, and then
> only at the beginning of the mastery of the motor
> skill, being later displaced by more flexible, expedient
> and economic methods of overcoming this redundancy
> through the *organisation* of the process as a whole.

The studies on the learning of table-tennis strokes (coordinative structures) are continuing in the Department and will soon encompass the assessment of movement form. At the same time, cognisant of the fact that different tasks may make different demands on subjects, parallel work is being carried out on the cognitive stage of learning cyclical actions.

THE LEARNING OF SLALOM-TYPE SKI MOVEMENTS

In a whole series of previous studies addressed to the early cognitive stage of learning slalom-type ski movements on a ski-simulator (Figure 7) attention has been paid to:
1) the multidimensionality of the task. It has, for example, been shown that amplitude, frequency and fluency of the movement of the ski-simulator platform are good indices of learning in that they show (with the exception of the frequency measure on the first day of training) pre-post test, and day-by-day, increments in performance (Den Brinker & Van Hekken, 1982).

2) that providing feedback about *amplitude* and requiring subjects to concentrate their attention on this parameter leads to superior learning, as indexed by the three parameters amplitude, frequency and fluency of performance (Den Brinker, Stäbler, Whiting & Van Wieringen, 1985a). Giving feedback about *frequency* while maintaining high frequency levels leads to significantly lower amplitude attainment while providing feedback about *fluency* leads to a significantly lower levels of frequency.

3) Only tenuous support for the advantages of variable over constant practice (defined in terms of the strengths of the simulator springs) and then only for the fluency parameter (Den Brinker, Stäbler, Whiting & Van Wieringen, 1985b).

4) The disadvantages of training at a high prescribed frequency (in terms of the parameter amplitude) and how these might be offset by gradually increasing the frequency imposed (Van Emmerik, 1985).

The study I now wish to address is concerned with imitation or, more appropriately, the effect of the availability of a dynamic model on the acquisition of a complex cyclical action. If, as Pick and Palmer propose, Reed's (1982) contention that the study of action is the study of how people use available information to modulate their actions is taken seriously and, if it is recognised that most human actions are socially mediated, the importance of an understanding of observational learning to a theory of action is apparent

While 'discovery learning' in which the learner tries to provide appropriate solutions to the problems posed, often plays a role in the acquisition of novel motor skills, such learning is much more often socially mediated. Verbal mediation and/or demonstration by a 'teacher', Carroll and Bandura (1982) point out, in providing a model for response production, usually plays a leading role in skill acquisition. Central to Bandura's (1977) social learning theory of imitation is the role of symbolic representation. He proposes two such systems – a spatial (imaginal) and a verbal. Verbal mediation by, for example, establishing categorical similarities, enables people to very quickly 'represent' and retain 'model' behaviour. But, as Williams (1985) suggests, while it is clear that people can match the movements of others and produce similar movements themselves, it is not particularly helpful merely to know that this is achieved by means of the 'construction of a central representation that serves as an internal model for response production' (Bandura, 1977).

The research line on imitation currently under way in the author's group was prompted not only by the discussion above, but was already signalled in the 'image of the act' theory of Whiting and Den Brinker (1982). These authors make a distinction between what Pribram (1971) labels the 'image of achievement' i.e., 'the learned anticipations of force and changes in force required to perform a task rather than an abstract model of external space' and what Whiting and Den Brinker (1982) refer to as the 'image of the act'. Such images are specifications of the essential 'form' of a movement, defined in terms of topological rather than metrical parameters, necessary for the solution of a particular motor problem. Thus, the 'image of the act' specifies the 'form' of the movement rather than the pattern of neuromuscular activity to be used in operationalising that form. An operationalisation of the image of achievement is provided in the Chapter (of this book) by Roy, in which he discusses the imaging of the tension in the musculature of the foot independent of the movement form.

In most learning situations, inaccuracies in both images are likely to be encountered since, in a novel skill area, the actor has not only to discover an appropriate movement form but, in attempting to solve the motor problem posed he has to try, however inadequately, to overcome the external forces that present themselves. Whiting and Den Brinker (1982) propose that the best way for an actor to enhance one or the other image would be to keep the requirements of the other image as stable as possible so that attention does not need to be shifted between the two. More particularly, they propose that the formation and enhancement of the 'image of the act' will best be promoted by so structuring the learning situation in the early cognitive stage that the field of external forces to be overcome remains relatively constant so that the actor can direct his attention to establishing a reliable and appropriate 'image of the act'.

The paradigm used for this study is very similar to that used in the previous studies to which reference has already been made. The ski-simulator (Fig. 7) consists of a platform designed to ride over a pair of bowed metal 'runners' but which, because of the spring system beneath the simulator, returns to the central resting position after being disturbed in a sideways direction. Attached to the centre of the platform is a bank of light-emitting diodes the movement characteristics of which are picked up, and registered via a SELSPOT system. It is this signal which is used to generate data about

Fig. 7. Ski-simulator apparatus.

amplitude, frequency and fluency of the movement of the platform. For methdological and analytic details, the reader is referred to Den Brinker and Van Hekken (1982).

The experiment to be discussed here was addressed to the role of imitation in the early (cognitive) stage of acquiring the gross motor cyclical action of slalom-type ski movements on the ski-simulator. More specifically, it was concerned to discover which parameters (amplitude, frequency, fluency) of the movements of the platform operated by the subject - and, ultimately, (in subsequent studies) which characteristics of his dynamic posture - are affected by the presence of a dynamic model.

EXPERIMENTAL DESIGN

Two groups of N= 20 (per group) were assigned to either a 'discovery learning' condition or to a condition in which, during training trials, the presence of a dynamic video model (trained to a high level of performance on all parameters) was available. Subjects practised on five successive days, each daily session consisting of six one and a half minute practice sessions interspersed with one and a half minute rest periods. Each training period was preceded and followed by a test period during which subjects from both groups performed under similar conditions i.e. without the availability of a model. Subjects in both groups were instructed to learn to make large amplitude, high frequency, fluent movements on the simulator.

RESULTS

Analyses comprised the means and standard deviations of the three parameters amplitude, frequency and fluency. Analyses of variance showed that the group who had the benefit of the presence of a dynamic video model during training had superior overall mean fluency scores and showed less overall variability in both the fluency and the frequency of their movements.

DISCUSSION

The results demonstrate the superior skill level of the group who had the advantage of the availability of a dynamic model during training. That fluency of movement should be considered an important criterion of skilled behaviour is confirmed by Vincke (1984). As she points out, when initially confronted with a novel skill to perform, subjects will move slowly and with tense muscles. After a period of practice, performance of the skill will take less time and the movement will become 'smoothed'.

It is interesting to note that the availability of a dynamic model on the skill level of subjects, as indexed by the fluency of their movements, is superior to providing feedback about fluency *per se*. It will be recalled, in the experiment of Den Brinker, Stäbler, Whiting and Van Wieringen (1985a) that feedback about fluency did not lead to superior performance in terms of fluency than provision of feedback about the parameters amplitude or frequency but, resulted in depressed frequency of movement in comparison with the other two feedback conditions. In the present experiment, not only was the fluency of the group having access to a dynamic model superior to the control group, but, this was not at the expense of frequency of movement.

There remains the possibility that the results are artefactual in the sense that while topological and metrical variables are mathematically distinct, it does not mean that, under certain circumstances, they might not be related. Thus, subjects may not pick up from the model information about fluency per se, but, they might come to adopt the topological movement form of the model. If a particular movement form were to impose a constraint(s) on the level of fluency achieved, this could account for the current findings. The difficulty of addressing this issue empirically has, in the past, been limited by the difficulty of experimentally determining and manipulating movement form. This possibility has now been resolved to some degree in the author's

laboratory (Valk, 1984) and is currently being alborated upon. Future
experimentation in this line should clarify this issue.

In as far as we are confronted, from birth onwards, with dynamic
models exhibiting various degrees of competency in both phylogenetic and
culture-specific movement skills it is important to examine the kinds of
constraint on learning and performance that such models impose. These
may range from social facilitation, i.e. information that makes subjects aware
of possibilities while not restricting the kinds of solution they may provide
to the problem posed, to imitation in the sense that the subject tries to
reproduce the movement characteristics of the model with whom he is
confronted. Unfortunately, there is all too little information available on
the effect of imitation on pre-speech, on the acquisition of gestures or on
the acquisition of phylogenetic movement forms - such as walking and running. Nevertheless, in everyday life situations we are able to identify,
and sometimes specify, the chracteristic movement styles of top sportsmen
and dancers, the similarity between the movement forms of children and
their parents or between apprentice and craftsman. On what information
are such judgements made? More importantly, what is the relationship
between the information provided by a dynamic model and the movement
characteristics of the performer who, either deliberately or unconsciously,
comes to acquire similar characteristics? It is hoped, in a continuation
of this line of work to begin to provide answers to these kinds of question.

CONCLUSION

To return now to the more general issue of learning addressed earlier
in the paper. Problems inherent in the motor programme concept of Schmidt
(1975) were there, signalled. Leaving aside the theoretical problem of
representation, i.e. whether there are motor programmes which are centrally
represented or, alternatively, whether there are such things as coordinative
structures which arise, spontaneously, on some principle of self-organisation
not requiring representation of any kind, there still remains a very practical
problem. One is left, from either viewpoint, with the nagging impression
that novice skill learners first establish motor programmes or coordinative
structures and only when these are consistently established do they learn to
discover the appropriate parameters to tune such structures to environmental
contingencies. Such a conception is surely a denial of the experiential
history of the subject en route to the establishment of such structures?

Here, it is preferred to look upon the establishment of complex movement
forms as being the outcome of a problem-solving approach, iterative in nature
Each time the actor is confronted with a motor problem in the environment,
either fortuitously or under the instigation of someone who artificially
structures the environment, he provides what for him is the best solution
at that time, based both on the information which he considers to have a
steering function as well as on his current movement repertoire. Through
providing successive solutions to motor problems of a similar kind, over a
considerable period of time, stable movement forms emerge. In discovering
successively more finely specified affordances in the environment he learns
to make his movement solutions more and more appropriate. In this sense,
the actor has fewer and fewer degrees of freedom in providing a solution to
the problem. At the same time, his perception also becomes costrained in the
sense that the 'free' attention that characterised him as a naive actor comes
to be controlled as the nature of the affordances which have a steering
function become more clearly specified and more attention demanding.

    Recently, Von Hofsten (1985) has suggested that it seems reasonable
to assume – in an evolutionary context – that perception and action evolved
together. It is maintained here that the ontogenetic development of perception
action systems must be seen in the same light. Thus, to paraphrase Von
Hofsten, the problem to be solved is not primarily, how perception makes
contact with action, but how different perception/action systems come to
be established.

References

Bandura, A. (1977). *Social learning theory*. Englewood-Cliffs, N.J.: Prentice-Hall.

Beek, P.J., Meijer, O.G. & Whiting, H.T.A. (1985). *Specifying differences:* Some remarks on ecological theories of actions, their putative irreconciability. Proceedings of the International Psychological Society, Acapulco, Mexico.

Bootsma, R.J. & Valk, P.J.L. (1984). *, Operational analyses of motor skills:* Acquiring new movement patterns. Proceedings of the Sport and Science Conference, Bedford, England.

Bootsma, R.J., Brinker, B.P.L.M. den & Whiting, H.T.A. (1985). Complexe bewegingshandelingen op sport gebied. *Nederlands Tijdschrift voor Psychologie* (in press).

Bransford, J. & Shaw, R. (Eds.) (1977). *Perceiving, acting and knowing:* Towards an ecological psychology. Hillsdale, N.J.: Erlbaum.

Brinker, B.P.L.M. den & Hekken, M.F. van. (1982). The analysis of slalom-ski type movements using a ski-simulator apparatus. *Human Movement Science, 1,* 91-108.

Brinker, B.P.L.M. den, Stäbler, J.R.L.W., Whiting, H.T.A. & Wieringen, P.C.W. van. (1985a). The effect of manipulating knowledge of results on the learning of slalom-type ski movements. *Ergonomics* (in press).

Brinker, B.P.L.M. den, Stäbler, J.R.L.W., Whiting, H.T.A. & Wieringen, P.C.W. van. (1985b). A multidimensional analysis of some persistent problems in motor learning. In D. Goodman, R.B. Wilberg and I. Franks (Eds.), *Differing perspectives in motor learning and control*. Amsterdam: North-Holland.

Carroll, W.R. & Bandura, A. (1982). The role of visual monitoring in observational learning of action patterns: making the unobservable, observable. *Journal of Motor Behavior, 14,* 153-167.

Cutting, J.E. (1981). Six tenets for event perception. *Cognition, 10,* 71-78.

Cutting, J.E. (1983). Four assumptions about invariance in perception. *Journal of Experimental Psychology: Human Perception and Performance, 9,* 310-317.

Cutting, J.E. & Kozlowski, L. (1977). Recognising friends by their walk: gait perception without familiarity cues. *Bulletin of the Psychonomic Society, 9,* 353-356.

Cutting, J.E. & Profitt, D.R. (1981). Gait perception as an example of how we may perceive events. In R.D. Walk and H.L. Pick (Eds.), *Intersensory perception and sensory integration*. New York: Plenum.

Emmen, H.H., Wesseling, L.G., Bootsma, R.J., Whiting, H.T.A. & Wieringen, P.C.W. van. (1985). The effect of video instruction methods on the learning of the tennis service by beginners. *Journal of Sports Sciences* (in press).

Emmerik, R.E.A. van. (1984). Het effect van oefentempo op het aanleren van een groot motorische vaardigheid. Doctoral dissertation, Department of Psychology, IFLO, The Free University, Amsterdam, The Netherlands.

Fitts, P.M. & Posner, M.I. (1967). *Human performance*. Belmont: Brooks/Cole.

Fodor, J. (1983). *The modularity of mind:* An essay on faculty psychology. Cambridge, Mass.: MIT Press.

Gibson, J.J. (1979). *The ecological approach to visual perception*. Boston: Houghton-Mifflin.

Hazen, N.L., Lockman, J. & Pick, H.J. Jr. (1978). The development of children's representations of large-scale enrivonments. *Child Development, 49,* 623-636.

Hofsten, C. von. (1985). Catching. In H. Heuer and A.F. Sanders (Eds.), *Perception and action*. Amsterdam: North-Holland.

Johansson, G. (1950). *Configurations in event perception*. Uppsala: Almquist & Wiskell.

Johansson, G. (1973). The visual perception of biological motion and a model for its analysis. *Perception and Psychophysics, 14,* 201-211.

Johansson, G. (1978). Visual event perception. In R. Heid, H.W. Leibowitz and H.L. Teuber (Eds.), *Handbook of sensory physiology: VIII - Perception.* New York: Springer- Verlag.

McLeod, P., McLaughlin, C. & Nimmo-Smith, I. (1985). Information encapsulation and automaticity: Evidence from the visual control of finely timed actions. *Attention and Performance* (in press).

Neisser, U. (1976). *Cognition and reality.* San Francisco: Freeman.

Pribram, K.H. (1971). *Languages of the brain.* New Jersey: Prentice-Hall.

Reed, E. (1982). An outline of a theory of action systems. *Journal of Motor Behavior, 14,* 98-134.

Ricoeur, P. (1966). *Freedom and nature:* The voluntary and the involuntary. Illinois: North-Western University Press.

Schmidt, R.A. (1975). A schema theory of discrete motor skill learning. *Psychological Review, 82,* 225-260.

Shapiro, D.C. & Schmidt, R.A. 81982). The schema theory: recent evidence and developmental implications. In J.A.S. Kelso and J.E. Clark (Eds.), *The development of movement control and coordination.* New York: Wiley.

Tyldesley, D.A. & Whiting, H.T.A. (1975). Operational timing. *Journal of Human Movement Studies, 1,* 172-177.

Valk, P.J.L. (1984). Effecten van oefentempo op de ontwikkeling van de bewegingsvorm bij het aanleren van een groot motorische vaardigheid. Doctoral dissertation, Department of Psychology, IFLO, The Free University, Amsterdam, The Netherlands.

Vincke, M.H. (1983). Control of limb stiffness. Ph.d thesis, Department of Medical Physics, University of Utrecht, The Netherlands.

Whiting, H.T.A. (1970). An operational analysis of a continuous ball-throwing and catching task. *Ergonomics, 13,* 445-454.

Whiting, H.T.A. (1980). Dimension of control in motor learning. In G.E. Stelmach and J. Requin (Eds.), *Tutorials in motor behavior.* Amsterdam: North-Holland.

Whiting, H.T.A. & Brinker, B.P.L.M. den. (1982). Image of the act. In J.P. Das, R.F. Mulcahy and A.E. Wall (Eds.), *Theory and research in learning disabtlities.* New York: Plenum.

Whiting, H.T.A. (1984a). The concepts of adaptation and attunement in skill learning. In O.G. Selfridge, E.L. Risland and M.A. Arbib (Eds.), *Adaptive control of ill-defined systems.* New York: Plenum.

Whiting, H.T.A. (Ed.) (1984b). *Human motor actions: Bernstein reassessed.* Amsterdam: North-Holland.

Williams, J.G. (1985). Movement imitation: Some fundamental processes. Ph.D. thesis, University of London, England.

Wohlwill, J.F. (1981). Experimental, developmental, differential: Which way the royal road to knowledge about spatial cognition. In L.S. Liben, A.H. Patterson and N. Newcombe (Eds.), *Spatial representation and behaviour across the life-span.* New York: Academic Press.

THE EMERGENCE OF MANUAL SKILLS

C. von Hofsten

1. THE EMERGENCE OF MANUAL SKILLS

The manual system develops extensively during the first year of life By the end of the first year the infant can pick up most kinds of objects including very tiny ones, examine them and manipulate with them. How is this rapid development achieved? In the present paper, I will examine this problem from a Perception-Action perspective.

2. PERCEPTION-ACTION SYSTEMS

It is reasonable to assume that perception and action evolved together. Evolution seems to work mainly by solving specific action problems for the animal demanding specific perceptual skills rather than designing general capacities. In lower animals this is rather obvious. According to Arbib (1981) the frog may be said to possess a number of specific visual systems working in parallel: one for threat avoidance, one for barrier negotiation, etc. In humans, the tie between perception and action is undoubtedly less rigid than that. However, the point is that problems of motor skills and perception in humans may be better understood in the context of the actions for which they evolved.

In this perspective, describing the information that drives the motor system becomes as important as the description of the motor system itself. In the past, problems of motor skill have often been studied without considering their specific ties to perception. It is not that the motor system has been studied in isolation of any controlling stimuli but rather in ignorance of the possibility that different stimuli might drive the system in qualitatively different ways.

The study of timing and anticipation in children offers good examples of this. Although most papers on this topic make references to the extra-ordinary timing in various kinds of ball skills, the situation typically studied is quite different. Dorfman (1977), for instance, used a task in which the subject was to direct a cursor dot on a oscilloscope screen to intercept a moving target dot. This was done with the aid of manual slide control. The absolute timing error of the 6-7 years old in this task was 121 msec and the variable error 129 msec. In another study, Dunham (1977) had subjects lifting a foot off a spring switch in coincidence with the arrival of a rolling ball at a target flag. The performance in this task was much better than that in Dorfman's task. The absolute and variable errors were both around 40 msec. for seven-year-old subjects. However, these errors are still about three times larger than the maximum timing error allowed for catching even a lightly thrown ball (Alderson, Sully & Sully, 1974). As seven-year-olds can master that task with little difficulty one must conclude that the sensori-motor processes involved in the catching of moving targets are much more precise than those involved in the timing tasks of Dorfman (1977) and Dunham (1977). The aim of those studies were to learn about skilled behaviour. If the perception-action systems involved in motor skills are as specific as I have suggested above and as empirical results indicate, then there is little hope in learning much about, for instance, catching from studying the performance in artificially constructed interception tasks like those described above.

Evidence favouring the perception-action approach also comes from pathology. Hemiplegia following stroke has commonly been described as a purely motor disturbance. However, Lee, Lough, and Lough (1983) found that the ability of hemiplegic patients to reach out and grasp a target was heavily dependent on the stimulus condition. When they were given the task of grasping an approaching target, they performed much better than when asked to grasp a stationary one. Movements were faster and smoother. Bilateral coordination was also finer under the former conditions. The difference in time of arrival of the hands at the ball was both shorter and less variable.

The view that motor skills are made up of rather specific, biologically given, perception-action systems has important implications for the study of motor skill development. The problem is not any more how the motor system makes contact with perception but how the different perception-action systems differentiate into the sophisticated perceptuo-motor control of the adult. An important task will be to identify the specific innate perceptuo-motor adaptations. They should appear early because they constitute the very foundation for motor skill development.

3.   THE EMERGENCE OF COORDINATIVE STRUCTURES FOR MANUAL ACTION

Neuro-anatomical knowledge of the structures that control the movements of the upper limbs have mainly been gained through elaborate studies on the rhesus monkey by Kuypers and his associates (Kuypers, 1962, 1964, 1973; Lawrence & Kuypers, 1968a,b; Lawrence & Hopkins, 1972, 1976). The manual system of the rhesus monkey is in several respects similar to the human one. It has an opposing thumb and an index finger which can be moved independently of the other fingers.

3.1. The cortical system

This system projects directly to the motoneurons of the distral extremity muscles. It seems to be responsible for independent finger movements. Lawrence and Kuypers (1968) showed that the interruption of both pyramidal tracts initially severely affected independent movements of the hand and that a permanent loss of individual finger movements occurred. The monkey could not move the index finger anymore without also moving the rest of the fingers and could not any longer pick up a pellet from a small depression.

The authors attribute the complete loss of independent finger movements to the cortico-motoneuronal connections. Other observations support this conclusion. For instance, direct cortico-motoneuronal connections are present in animals which possess individual finger movements but not in others (see e.g., Kuypers, 1973). They occur in increasing numbers in the raccoon, rhesus monkey, chimpanzee, and man. They are largely lacking in for instance rat, goat, cat, and dog.

3.2. The subcortical systems

Lawrence and Kuypers (1968b) found it appropriate to distinguish between two subcortical systems: one ventromedial and one lateral grouped according to their termination in the spinal grey matter. Lawrence and Kuypers studied how interruption of these two systems affected the motor control of the limb in monkeys with prior bilateral interruption of the pyramidal tracts.

The animals with lesions of the lateral brainstem system produced an impairment of independent hand movements and an impaired capacity to flex the extended thumb. Initially the lesioned animals could not reach out to pick up pieces of food by closure of the hand. However, movements involving the whole limb and the body, like in walking and climbing, were only minimally affected. After some recovery these animals regained the capacity to close the hand but only as a part of a total arm movement.

Interruption of the ventromedial pathways produced severe impairment of axial and proximal extremity movements and the maintenance of body posture (Lawrence & Kuypers, 1968). When the monkey finally could sit and walk they were unsteady. Head and trunk would slump forward and when approached with food, the animals showed an immobility of the head, trunk, and limb. However, despite these impairments they could pick up pieces of food with their hands if the limbs were appropriately supported and brought to the food.

In summary, the ventromedial pathways seems to be especially concerned with the maintenance of erect posture and the integration of movements of trunk and limbs. The lateral brainstem pathways would superimpose upon this control the capacity for independent use of the extremities, particularly the hands. The cortical system, finally, exerts control over the distal part of the arm, hand, and the individual finger movements.

3.3. Development

Lawrence and Hopkins (1972, 1976) found that the direct cortico-motoneuronal connections were not yet established in the newborn rhesus monkey and that the two subcortical systems seemed relatively undifferentiated. Earliest reaching for food occurred around 4 weeks of age. The aim was rather inaccurate and the arm movements unsteady so that the hand frequently missed the food. If the food was grasped at all it was done by closure of the fingers altogether and the subsequent releasing of it in the mouth when the arm was flexed was reported to be difficult.

At 3 months of age these difficulties had disappeared. Reaching was smooth and accurate and there was no longer any difficulty in releasing the grip. The arm and hand had gained independent status.

Effective removal of the food with the index finger was observed at 3-4 months of age and an adult level of performance was judged to be present at around 8 months. The development of independent finger movements was observed to occur very much in parallel to the establishment of direct cortico-motoneuronal connections. The number of connections increased markedly up to 8 months of age. Complete interruption of both pyramidal tracts at 4 weeks of age did not affect the early development of reaching. However, independent finger movements never appeared. Apparently, the direct cortico-motoneuronal connections are crucial for such movements. Other parts of the brain do not seem to be able to take over the control.

4.   PATTERNS OF COORDINATION IN THE PREREACHING INFANT

The newborn human infants do perform coordinated arm and hand movements but they seem to be rather wholistic in character like those of the newborn rhesus monkey. Many of them are flexion and extension synergies which engage all the muscles of the limb. For instance, if the hand of the infant is pulled, the arm, hand, and fingers will all flex in a traction reflex. In the well known Moro reflex, arms, hands, and fingers will first extend synergistically and then flex synergistically in an embrace pattern. However, neonates' movements are not stereotyped. On the contrary, not two movements look exactly the same. Fractionated movements may actually also be performed, like opening the hand without extending the arm or extending some digits without extending others.

Little is known about what information drives the motor system in the newborn. Knowledge has mainly been gained in connection with the standardized neurological testing procedures (see e.g., Prechtl, 1977 or Brazelton, 1973). The focus has been on reflexes and the stimuli used has mostly been tactile, vestibular, and proprioceptive in the traditional sense. Hardly anything is known about visual control which is of such importance later in life. A reason for this ignorance has, may be, been the widespread conviction that vision is not yet connected to the motor system at this age (see e.g., Piaget, 1953, 1954). But the rhesus monkey reached, however awkwardly, toward seen food at only four weeks of age. Converging evidence now shown that also in the case of the human infant vision is connected to the motor system right from the beginning of life. The neonate may indeed, to some extent, visually control the movements of the arm (Trevarthen, 1974; Hofsten, 1982; Rader & Stern, 1982).

Hofsten (1982) studied the arm movements of five days old infants placed in a semireclining seat that supported their waist and trunk but allowed free movements of their arms. A spherical tuft made of bright red, blue, and yellow yarn was moved slowly and irregularly in front of the neonate along a horizontal circular path of 140 cm diameter. The setup is depicted in Figure 1. A moving rather than a stationary object was choosen due to the low resolution of the visual system in the neonate. Dobson and Teller (1978) and Held (1979) estimated the acuity of the newborn to less than one twenieth of the adult's acuity. Therefore there is a risk that a stationary object would be left unnoticed for acuity reasons. A moving target does not run the same risk, since its motion adds potently to the information separating it from the background. All neonates tested, detected the moving target, were attracted by it, and followed it for shorter or longer periods with their eyes and head. This tracking made it also easier to detect whether the infant observed the target or not.

The movements were recorded with two videocameras placed 90 deg. to each other which made it possible to reconstruct the three dimensional

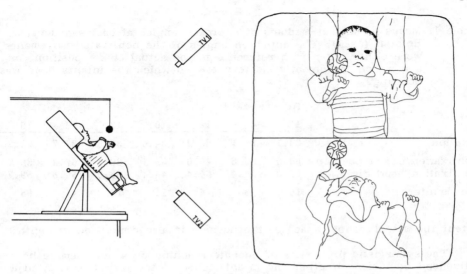

Fig. 1. The left figure shows the experimental setup used to
investigate neonate reaching. The inclination of the chair
was 50 deg. The right figure shows the resulting display on
the video screen (From Hofsten, 1982).

trajectories of the movements. To be able to calculate aiming, the movements
were subdivided into functional units each of which consisted of one
acceleration and one deceleration phase (see Brooks, Crooke & Thomas,
1973). The unit that carried the hand closest to the trajectory of the object
was examined further. This part of the movement should be aimed at the
object if there is visual control but not otherwise.

The result showed that the movements performed while the infant
fixated the object were aimed much closer to the target on the average than
others. The results could not be explained in terms of some coordination
between the head direction and reaching direction. When the infant did not
fixate the object, movements were just as far away from the target when the
head was directed towards it as when it was not. These results were
replicated in a study where eleven infants were followed from the first
week of life, every third week to 19 weeks of age (Hofsten, in preparation).
The main results of that study is shown in Table 1. Table 1 shows that the
movements performed while fixating the target were aimed much closer to it
than those performed while not fixating it. The directedness of the nonfixated movements were calculated in two ways. First, the direction was
calculated relative to the true object position. Second, it was calculated
relative to an imagined object position in the direction of the head. Table 1
shows that these two measures differ very little. Thus, at no age level
could the arm movements performed while the infant fixated the target be
explained in terms of a tendency to reach in the direction of the head.

The studies cited above show that the reaching of newborn infants is
organised in a visual-manual space which is structured at least directionally.
However, as the distance to the target was not varied it is unclear to what

Table 1. Means of subject-medians of approach angles at each age level of
Hofsten (1985). The approach angles of the nonfixated movements
were either taken with reference to the actual object position, or
a point on the object trajectory toward which the infants head was
pointing.

	Age (weeks)						
	1	4	7	10	13	16	19
Fixation	34.1	31.1	28.2	34.6	36.6	27.7	22.2
Nonfixation/object position	60.0	60.6	49.0	45.1	66.4	67.3	56.7
Nonfixation/head direction	55.0	54.4	54.4	44.1	65.9	64.6	59.7
% encounters	10	3	8	11	13	41	68

extent the visual-manual space of the neonate is also structured in depth.

The synergistic properties of neonate reaching does not seem to be
influenced by vision. Whether the infant looked at the target or not, in a
majority of cases the reaching hand would open before or during the
extension of the arm. In the extended phase of the arm the subjects were
never observed to flex the hand to grasp the target, not even when the
hand ended up with the object on its palm. The earliest reaching attempts
of the rhesus monkeys studied by Lawrence and Hopkins (1972, 1976) also
showed some of these characteristics.

At around two months of age the reaching pattern changes dramatically
in the human infant (Hofsten, 1984). At this age the hand was found to be
fisted in almost all forward extended movements of the arm. Visual fixation
of the target did not affect this tendency. Apparently, the extension
synergy is broken up and the hand is gaining independent status. A few
weeks later, the infant will start opening up the hand again when extending
the arm but this time only when fixating the target. This development is
shown in Figure 2.

5.   TWO MODES OF VISUAL CONTROL OF REACHING

Adult reaching can be characterised by two distinct modes of control
(see e.g., Hofsten & Lee, 1982). The first mode is a visuo-proprioceptive
one. It is used during the initial phase of the approach. The seen position
of the target and the felt position of the hand are used to define the
direction and extent of the movement. The initial phase of the reach covers
most of the approach. It has often been called ballistic, not in the sense
that it is launched but in the sense that it is preprogrammed and does not
rely on feedback. The kind of feedback one has in mind then is visual
feedback. Quite correctly, this part of the movement does not seem to rely
on such feedback. However, it is not known but quite feasible that proprioceptive feedback may exert some control over the movement also during
this phase.

When the hand comes close to the target proprioception is not precise
enough to ensure a smooth grasp of the target. Therefore, the reach passes
over into a purely visual mode. The seen position of the hand relative to the

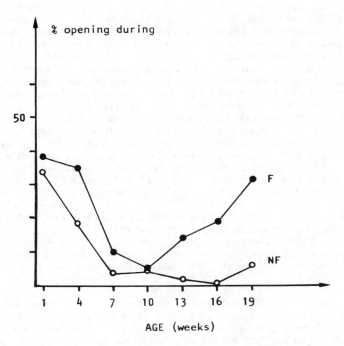

Fig. 2. Forward extended movements during which the hand is
opening up. The figure shows the percentage of such
movements at which the subject is fixating the target (F)
or not (NF) over age (From Hofsten, 1984).

seen position of the target is used to control the final adjustments before
grasping. This part of the reach has often been called guided in contrast
to the first part. Surely, visual information about the position of the hand
guides the movement during this part of the reach. However, even when
vision of the reaching hand is prevented, two distinct phases may still be
seen (Jeannerod & Biguer, 1982).

Different kinds of visual information is needed for the two modes of
control. In the first mode, the subject needs information about the direction
and distance of the target in body-related coordinates. In the second mode,
precise information about relative distance between the reaching hand and
other objects in the visual field is needed.

The visual-proprioceptive mode seems to be the first one to appear in
development. The newborn child does not appear to take advantage of seeing
the reaching hand in relation to the target. Although the forward extensions
of the arm can be divided into steps the steps do not differ in time nor do
they seem to carry the hand progressively closer to the target. The few
encounters with the target is also an indication of this (see Table 1).

Table 1 also shows that toward the end of the prereaching period there
is a systematic and rapid increase in the proportion of encounters with the

target. This development is even more clearly reflected in individual data. For instance, Subject B.W. had 7 forward extensions at 10 weeks of age but none of them encountered the object. At 13 weeks of age he had 8 forward extensions and 4 of them encountered the object. Finally, at 16 weeks of age he had 12 forward extensions and all of them encountered the object. Common behaviour at this age when the target was stationary or moved slowly was to leave the limb extended at the target for a considerable time while making minor adjustments. This kind of behaviour has earlier been described by Piaget (1952) and White, Castle and Held (1964). White et al (1964) writes: "Occasionally, one hand will be raised, looked at, and brought slowly to the stimulus while the glance shifts from hand to object repeatedly". Thus, it seems without doubt that shortly before four months of age the infant starts to be able to use also the purely visual mode of control whereby the seen position of the hand is related to the seen position of the object. McDonnell (1975) has shown that a 4-month-old infant will correct a reach for a target seen through horizontally displacing prisms.

However, at this age, the two modes of reaching are still poorly integrated. Reaches typically consist of several steps or phases which are of equal duration on the average (Hofsten, 1979). The reaching paths are also grossly circuitous (Hofsten, 1979), which indicate that the motor system needs to be better tuned to the information that controls it before reaching becomes adultlike.

During the months to follow this picture changes dramatically. The first step grows in importance. More and more of the approach and the power of the reach becomes concentrated to this step. Subsequent steps will be more and more subordinate to the first one, having less to do with the approach and more with increasing the precision of the reach. At around six months of age the adultlike reaching pattern starts to dominate. From Figure 3 it can be seen that from that age on, most reaches consist of, at most, two movement elements: presumably one visual-proprioceptive "approach" element and one visual-visual "correction" element. Up to six months of age, infants become increasingly dependent on seeing the reaching hand. Lasky (197 had infants reach for an object seen through a horizontally placed mirror. At the proper place underneath the mirror and object identical to the reflected one was placed. In the control condition a panel of clear plastic replaced the mirror. Lasky found that in the control condition, six-month-olds contacted the target 9 times more often and retrieved the object 3 times more often than in the mirror condition.

When infants are still older they seem to become less dependent on seeing the reaching hand. Reaching has become more precise and more auto-matised. The subject might even look away while reaching and does not seem to be as bothered as the six-month-olds when sight of the reaching hand is disrupted (Bushnell, 1982). However, in reaching for small targets, where control of individual finger movements is essential, visual guidance is always a prominent factor in controlling the movements. The fine pincer grasp appearing around nine months of age presupposes delicate visual guidance.

6.   CALIBRATION OF THE APPROACH SYSTEMS

Better integration between the two modes of movement control is probably not the only reason why reaching becomes smoother and more auto-

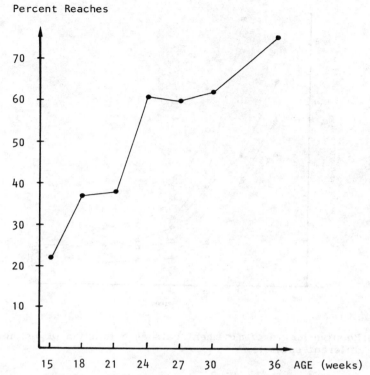

Percent Reaches

Fig. 3. Proportion of total number of reaches with one or two
movement elements for different ages (Redrawn from
Hofsten, 1979).

matic. Another important factor is the more precise attunement between
movements and perception. This development is especially evident during the
first two months of successful reaching. Figure 4 depicts the relative length
of movement paths for five infants studied from $3\frac{1}{2}$ to $8\frac{1}{2}$ months of age.
Figure 3 shows that the straightening out of the reach paths occur mainly
up to around $5\frac{1}{2}$ months of age.

Experience seems to play an important role in this process. Held, Hein
and their associates (see e.g., Held & Hein, 1963; Hein & Held, 1967; Hein,
1974; Bauer & Held, 1975) have shown that deprivation of sight of the
forelimbs of cats and monkeys during the earliest development produces
deficits in visually guided control of these members. More specifically, they
found that visual feedback from selfproduced movements was necessary for
the normal development of visually guided reaching. However, they also
found that only after, at most, a few days of free sight of the limbs the
performance of the experimental animals approached the normal ones, even
if this occurred after as much as six months of deprivation. Bauer and Held
(1975) therefore concluded that it was more appropriate to describe this
kind of learning as a form of calibration of the metrical relation between
space of vision and the motor space than to characterize it as motor learning
in an ordinary sense.

176

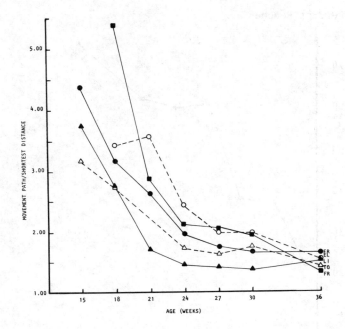

Fig. 4. Relative length of movement path as a function of age for five
different subjects.

There is also another factor that might be of importance in this process.
Good calibration requires precise information to calibrate against. At the
time when successful reaching emerges, the subject starts to have access to
precise binocular information about near space. The sensitivity to binocular
disparity develops very rapidly between three and five months of age. Fox,
Aslin, Shea, and Dumais (1979) found that 3½ months-olds but not 2½ months-
olds would track a moving virtual object specified by binocular disparity in
a dynamic random-dot stereogram. Held and colleges (Birch, Gwiazda & Held,
1982; Held, Birch & Gwiazda, 1980) showed the same developmental trend
using a modified preferential looking technique. They showed a rapid rise
in detecton of fine disparities from 3 months of age to an adultlike level
between 5 and 7 months of age.

7.   GRASPING

When infants first start to encounter objects successfully, they do not
yet grasp them very well. Contact is often made with the back of the hand,
and grasping, if any, is slow and awkward. Hofsten and Lindhagen (1979),
using moving objects to be reached for, found that although the target was
frequently contacted at 15 weeks of age (3½ months), it always slipped out
of the hand and was lost during or before the infant's attempts to grasp it
(see Figure 5). However, development is fast thereafter. At 18 weeks of
age the target was grasped in a majority of reaches. In early grasping,
remarkable knowledge about objects is revealed; knowledge about what
constitutes an object and knowledge about how to adjust to object properties

in order to secure a smooth grasp.

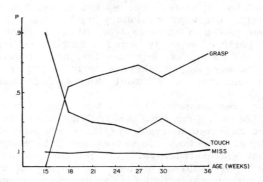

Fig. 5. Type of contact with object. Proportion of total number
of reaches for "grasp", "touch", and "miss" at different
ages (From Hofsten and Lindhagen, 1979).

8. KNOWLEDGE ABOUT OBJECTS

In order to manipulate the world effectively, a child must be able to
structure the perceived world into objects: manipulable units with internal
unity and external boundaries. Are infants able to do this at a time at
which they first begin to reach for what they see? This question was studied
by Hofsten and Spelke (1985) in a series of experiments.

Five-month-old infants were presented with a small object in front of
a larger object and a background surface, arranged in depth so that all
were within reaching distance. The two objects were sometimes adjacent,
sometimes separated in depth (see Figure 6).

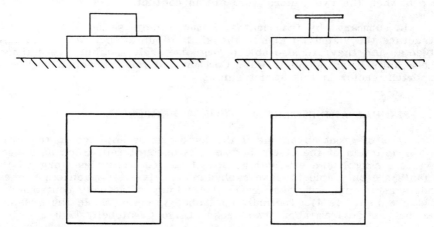

Fig. 6. The two objects used in the study by Hofsten and Spelke
(1985). The left figure shows the adjacent objects situation
and the right figure shows the separated objects situation.

Studies by Spelke and colleagues (see Spelke, 1984 for a review) have earlier shown that prereaching infants perceive two adjacent objects as one unit and two spatially separated ones as two units. The two objects sometimes moved together (or were stationary together against a moving background) sometimes moved relative to each other. Kellman and Spelke (1983) have shown that parts of a partly occuded object that move together are perceived as united. In adults, surfaces that move together are perceived as belonging to the same object whereas surfaces that move independently are perceived as belonging to different objects (Johansson, 1978).

Infants have been shown to have a tendency to reach for the closer of two structures (Yonas & Granrud, 1985). Thus when infants perceived two objects they were expected to reach for the closer one. When they just perceived one object they were instead expected to reach for the outer boundaries of that whole structure, i.e., for the boundaries of the larger more distant object. It could be argued that an appropriate grasp should be organised around an opposition axis intersecting a vertical line through the center of mass (Iberall, Bingham & Arbib, 1985) which in the present case would favor a grasp organised around the larger object. This is also in line with earlier observations. Piaget (1954) noted that his son Laurent at six months of age would reach for a small object dangling in the air, but if the same object was placed upon another bigger one such as a book or a pillow he tended instead to reach for the supporting object. Similar observations were made by Bresson and de Schonen (1976-1977) and Wishart (1979).

It was found that when the objects were stationary and adjacent, infants would reach for the larger, more distant one. When the two objects were stationary and separated in depth, infants would reach for the smaller and closer one. When the two objects moved together or were stationary together against a moving background, reaches were directed towards the boundaries of the larger object. Finally when the objects moved relative to each other, the small object would be grasped even if the two objects were spatially adjacent. Thus, motion had a tendency to take precedence over depth when the two factors were put in conflict.

In summary, by five months, human infants seems to be able to structure the visual world into the kinds of units that we, as adults, call objects, and they are also able to organise their manipulative actions toward these units in an adequate way. Common and relative motion seems to be an important factor in this structuring.

9. MANUAL ADJUSTMENT TO OBJECT PROPERTIES

It is of great advantage if the hand can be adjusted to the form, size and orientation of the object before it is encountered. Such adjustments will secure a smooth and efficient grasp. It has commonly been argued that infants are only able to make such adjustments after much experience and that grasping in early goal-directed reaching is tactually controlled (White, Castle & Held, 1964). Tactually controlled grasping as in the grasping reflex can be elicited from about two weeks of age (Twitchell, 1970).

Visually controlled adjustments of hand orientation to object orientation was studied by Lockman, Ashmead and Bushnell (1984) and by Hofsten and Fazel-Zandy (1984). Hofsten and Fazel-Zandy presented infants, 18 to 34 weeks old, with a vertical or a horizontal rod. The orientation of the reaching hand was measured at each 60 msec. interval during the last 540 msec. of the approach. It was found that even at the youngest age there were signs of adjustment of the hand to the orientation of the object before it was touched. However, at that age the adjustments were rather incomplete. During the months that followed there was a rapid increase in the skill studied.

These findings are in accordance with the idea that information about object orientation is accessible to the manual system when infants start reaching for objects but that the system has yet to be tuned and calibrated before functioning efficiently.

10. CATCHING

Developmental psychologists who have been thinking about the onto-genesis of ball catching have mostly been struck by the complexity of the task. Kay (1970), for instance, suggested that catching ability would appear at the earliest around 5 years of age.

However, in a series of studies I have found that already young infants possess a remarkable capacity to catch objects (Hofsten, 1980, 1983; Hofsten & Lindhagen, 1979). Hofsten and Lindhagen (1979) studied this problem longitudinally in a group of 11 infants. They were 12 to 24 weeks old at the first session, were seen at 3-week intervals until 30 weeks old, and were finally seen at 36 weeks of age. The subjects were presented with an object moving at infant's nose height in a horizontal circular path of 115 cm in diameter. The object passed the infant at a nearest distance of either 11 or 16 cm. It moved at 3.4, 15, or 30 cm/sec and stopped moving when it was grasped. For each condition the object was placed randomly to one side and was then moved back and fourth from one side to the other until the infant grasped it. This procedure was repeated until three reaches were secured or the object had passed in front of the subject at least six times.

We found that from the very age when infants start to master reaching for stationary objects, they will also reach successfully for fast moving ones. Eighteen-week-old infants caught the object as it moved at 30 cm/sec. To be able to catch such an object, at least some predictive ability is necessary. As the length the infant's arm at that age is less than 20 cm, the infant needs to start reaching for the target before it is actually within reach.

To be able to evaluate the predictive skill reflected in these reaches, a quantitative analysis of the three-dimensional trajectories were performed (Hofsten, 1980). The movements were divided into units each consisting of one acceleration and one deceleration phase. The aiming of each unit relative to the meeting point was then calculated. The analysis showed that most reached were aimed for the meeting point right from the beginning, i.e. a predictive strategy was employed. This was true for all age groups (Hofsten, 1980). The predictive reaching was typically performed with the hand contra-lateral to the direction from which the object arrived (See Figure 7).

In the reviewed longitudinal study of infants catching behaviour aiming was studied but not timing. That leaves many questions open related to the principles used by the infant in catching fast objects. To answer some of these questions, a second study was performed that took both aiming and

180

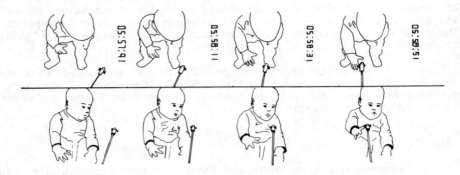

Fig. 7. The performance of a well-aimed reach by L.I. at 21 weeks.
The frame to the far left is the start of the each. The
interval between the frames is 0.2 sec (digital clock time is
shown in the upper right corner of each frame). The
velocity of the object was 30 cm/sec.

timing into account (Hofsten, 1983).

Fifteen, healthy, full-term infants took part in the experiment. At the
time of the study the subjects were between 34 and 36 weeks of age. A
similar set up was used as before. The target moved in a horizontal circular
path of approximately 153 cm in diameter. Velocity and starting position was
systematically varied. Velocity was either 30, 45, or 60 cm/sec. A subgroup
was also tested with 90 and 120 cm/sec targets. The starting position was
either 30, 60, or 90 deg. off the sagittal plane corresponding to 40, 80, and
120 cm from the nearest position to the object.

Aiming was calculated as before. The "best" angle ahead was expressed
as the angle between the position of the object at the start of the movement
unit (A), the position of the hand at the same time (B), and the position of
the object at the end of the reach (C) (see Figure 8). The obtained angle
ahead was expressed as the angle between A, B, and the position of the
position of the hand at the end of the movement unit (D). To estimate timing,

Table 2. The initial aiming and timing of reaches for objects travelling of
30, 45, 60 cm/sec.

Velocity (cm/sec)	n	Initial aiming (deg.)		Timing (msec)	
		β	$\beta-\alpha$	M	SD
30	47	33.9	3.7	9.4	54
45	46	43.4	4.0	4.4	57
60	45	48.9	0.6	-17	59

Note: β is the obtained angle ahead and $\beta-\alpha$ the deviation of the obtained
angle ahead from the "best" angle ahead (see Figure 8), n= number
of reaches analysed, M= mean timing reflecting the systematic timing
error; SD reflects the variable timing error.

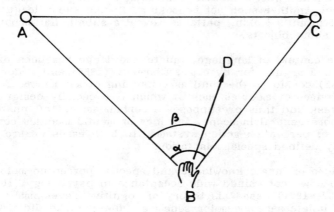

Fig. 8. How the aiming of a movement unit was calculated. A is the
position of the object at the beginning of the step; B is the
hand at the same time; C is the position of the object at the
meeting point, and D the position of the hand at the end of
the step, α is the "best" direction ahead, β is the obtained
direction ahead.

the time at which the reach ended was compared to the time at which the
hand was closest to the target. The end of the reach was thereby defined
as the time after the end of the approach when the hand came to a stand-
still or when its decleration had stopped.

The initial aiming of reaches in the different velocity conditions of the
experiment is shown in Table 2. Table 1 shows that although the required
angle ahead increases with increasing velocity of the target, so does the
obtained angle ahead. The reaches are at all instances directed close to the
meeting point with the target. Table 2 shows the systematic and variable
timing errors. It can be seen that at no velocity was the systematic timing
error greater than 17 msec. The variable timing error was found to be
between 54 and 59 msec.

11. FINAL COMMENTS

The reviewed research shows that the manual system is connected to
and driven by vision at a very early age. Also the neonate's arm movements
may come under visual control. It seems mainly to be sensory and neuromotor
maturation that determines the limits of the manual system and even such a
complex skill as catching is mastered, in principle, as soon as the motor
system is ready for it.

Basic manual skills like reaching, grasping, and catching require elaborate knowledge about space and objects. Infants seem to have such
knowledge. This does not mean that it is generally accessible. On the
contrary, the perception-action approach would argue that it comes in the
form of being able to perform specific tasks. Of course, manual action is not

the only instance where knowledge of objects is of great biological significance. Another such act is looking. Spelke and colleagues (1985) have shown that infant's looking patterns reveal a substantial amount of innate knowledge about objects.

In the context of language, innate knowledge has been extensively discussed and argued for by e.g., Chomsky (1980) and Fodor (1983). Fodor (1983) considers the mind as consisting of a number of special purpose devices or modules each of which is especially designed to perform a certain task and thus presupposes a certain amount of innate knowledge. However more general in scope, the idea of mental modules come close to the notion of perception-action systems. In both cases we are dealing with functionally defined special adaptations.

The idea of innate knowledge and specific perceptuo-motor adaptations has, up to now, not gained wide acceptance in psychology. It is true that Piaget (1952, 1971) based his theory of cognitive development on a limited number of innate sensory-motor schemas. However, he did not grant the young infant very much of this commodity. He even considered the arm and the hand as being unconnected to the vision at birth. From a biological point of view it is peculiar that the idea of innate knowledge has been so difficult to accept in psychology. The animal kingdom is full of examples of this kind of knowledge; beavers know how to build dams, birds how to fly, etc. If some experience can be saved by incorporating basic skills into the system, there will certainly be selective pressure favouring such incorporation.

Learning plays a role but not in the traditional sense. The connections between perception and action does not seem to be established through experience as generally believed. They are prewired into the systems from the start. However, the perceptio-action systems need to be tuned and calibrated. Motor space has to correspond to visual space if the perception-action systems are to function adequately. This kind of learning only seems to work if the subject acts, i.e., only in the context of self-produced movements (Held & Hein, 1963; Hein, 1974). Just seeing the limb being moved does not calibrate the action systems.

Another kind of learning is the continuing differentiation of perception (Gibson, 1969; Gibson & Spelke, 1983). As perception gets more sophisticated so does motor skill. The child will detect new affordances, i.e., new possibilities for actions offered by the objects and events around him or her, which will increase the repertoir of actions and make the control of existing action patterns more efficient. Real skilled action comes with efficient perception. The difference between the medium skilled tennis player and the champion is not so much a question of being able to move faster or more steadily when striking the ball, but of being able to move in the right way to the right place at the right time which in turn relies on picking up the right kind of information about the ongoing event.

References

Alderson, G.J.K., Sully, D.J. & Sully, H.G. (1974). An operational analysis of a one-handed catching task using high speed photography. *Journal of Motor Behavior, 6,* 217-226.

Arbib, M.A. (1980). Perceptual structures and distributed motor control. In V.B. Brooks (Ed.), *Handbook of Physiology, Volume III.*

Bauer, J. & Held, R. (1975). Comparison of visually guided reaching in normal and deprived infant monkeys. *Journal of Experimental Psychology: Animal Behavior Processes, 1,* 298-308.

Birch, E.E., Gwiazda, J. & Held, R. (1982). Stereoacuity development for crossed and uncrossed disparities in human infants. *Vision Research, 22,* 507-513.

Brazelton, T.B. (1973). *Neonatal Behavioral Assessment Scale.* Clinics in Developmental Medicine no. 50. Philadelphia: Heinemann Medical Books.

Bresson, F. & Schonen, S. de. (1976-1977). A propos de la construction de l'espace et de l'object: La pris d'un object sur un support. *Bulletin de Psychologie, 30,* 3-9.

Brooks, V.B., Cooke, J.C. & Thomas, J.S. (1973). The continuity of movements. In R.B. Stein, K.G. Pearson, R.S. Smith and J.B. Redford (Eds.), *Control of posture and locomotion.* New York: Plenum Press.

Bushnell, E. (1985). The decline of visually guided reaching during infancy. *Infant Behavior and Development.* In press.

Chomsky, N. (1980). *Rules and Representations.* Oxford: Basil Blackwell.

Dobson, V. & Teller, D.Y. (1978). Visual acuity in human infants: A review and comparison of behavioral and electrophysiological studies. *Vision Research, 18,* 1469-1483.

Dorfman, P.W. (1977). Timing and anticipation: a developmental perspective. *Journal of Motor Behavior, 9,* 67-79.

Dunham, P., Jr. (1977). Age, sex, speed, and practice in coincidence anticipation performance of children. *Perceptual and Motor Skills, 45,* 187-193.

Fodor, J.A. (1983). *The modularity of mind.* Cambridge, Mass: Bradford Books.

Fox, R., Aslin, R.N., Shea, S.L. & Dumais, S.T. (1980). Stereopsis in human infants. *Science, 207,* 323-324.

Hein, A. (1974). Prerequisite for development of visually guided reaching in the kitten. *Brain Research, 71,* 259-263.

Hein, A. & Held, R. (1967). Dissociation of the visual placing response into elicited and guided components. *Science, 158,* 390-391.

Held, R. (1979). Development of visual resolution. *Canadian Journal of Psychology, 33,* 213-221.

Held, R., Birch, E.E. & Gwiazda, J. (1980). Stereoacuity of human infants. *Proceedings of the National Academy of Science U.S.A., 77,* 5572-5574.

Held, R. & Hein, A. (1963). Movement-produced stimulation in the development of visually guided behavior. *Journal of Comparative and Physiological Psychology, 56,* 872-876.

Hofsten, C. von. (1979). Development of visually guided reaching: the approach phase. *Journal of Human Movement Studies, 5,* 160-178.

Hofsten, C. von. (1980). Predictive reaching for moving objects by human infants. *Journal of Experimental Child Psychology, 30,* 369-382.

Hofsten, C. von. (1982). Eye-hand coordination in newborns. *Developmental Psychology, 18,* 450-461.

Hofsten, C. von. (1983). Catching skills in infancy. *Journal of Experimental Psychology: Human Perception and Performance, 9,* 75-85.

Hofsten, C. von. (1984). Developmental changes in the organization of pre-reaching movements. *Developmental Psychology, 20,* 378-388.

Hofsten, C. von. (in preparation). Visual guidance of arm movements in the prereaching infant: A longitudinal study.

Hofsten, C. von & Lindhagen, K. (1979). Observations on the development of reaching for moving objects. *Journal of Experimental Child Psychology, 28,* 158-173.

Hofsten, C. von & Lee, D.N. (1983). Dialogue on perception and action. *Human Movement Science, 1,* 125-138.

Hofsten, C. von & Fazel-Zandy, S. (1984). Development of visually guided hand orientation in reaching. *Journal of Experimental Child Psychology, 38,* 208-219.

Hofsten, C. von & Spelke, E.S. (1985). Object perception and object directed reaching in infancy. *Journal of Experimental Child Psychology: General, 114,* 198-212.

Iberall, T., Bingham, G. & Arbib, M.A. (1985). Opposition space as a structuring concept for the analysis of skilled hand movements. *Experimental Brain Research Supplement.* In press.

Jeannerod, M. & Biguer, B. (1982). Visuomotor mechanisms in reaching within extrapersonal space. In D.J. Ingle, M.A. Goodale and R.J.W. Mansfield (Eds.), *Analysis of Visual Behavior.* Cambridge: MIT Press.

Johansson, G. (1978). Visual event perception. In R. Held, H.W. Leibowitz and H.L. Tenber (Eds.), *Handbook of Sensory Physiology* (Vol. 8). Berlin/Heidelberg/New York: Springer.

Kay, H. (1970). Analyzing motor skill performance. In K. Connolly (Ed.), *Mechanisms of Motor Skill Development.* London: Academic Press.

Kellman, P.J. & Spelke, E.S. (1983). Perception of partly occuded objects in infancy. *Cognitive Psychology, 15,* 483-524.

Kuypers, H.G.J.M. (1962). Corticospinal connections: Postnatal development in the rhesus monkey. *Science, 138,* 678-680.

Kuypers, H.G.J.M. (1964). The descending pathways to the spinal cord, their anatomy and functions. In J.C. Eccles and J.C. Shade (Eds.), *Organization of the Spinal Cord.* Elsevier.

Kuypers, H.J.G.M. (1973). The anatomical organization of the descending pathways and their contribution to motor control especially in primates. In J.E. Desmedt (Ed.), *New Developments in Electromyography and Clinical Neurophysiology. Vol 3.*

Lasky, R.E. (1977). The effect of visual feedback of the hand on reaching and retrieval behavior of young infants. *Child Development, 48,* 112-117.

Lawrence, D.G. & Kuypers, H.G.J.M. (1968a). The functional organization of the motor system in the monkey. I. The effects of bilateral pyramidal lesions. *Brain, 91,* 1-14.

Lawrence, D.G. & Kuypers, H.G.J.M. (1968b). The functional organization of motor system II. The effects of the descending brainstem pathways. *Brain, 91,* 15-36.

Lawrence, D.G. & Hopkins, D.A. (1972). Developmental aspects of pyramidal motor control in the rhesus monkey. *Brain Research, 40,* 117-118.

Lawrence, D.G. & Hopkins, D.A. (1976). The development of motor control in the rhesus monkey: Evidence concerning the role of corticomotor-neuronal connections. *Brain, 99,* 235-254.

Lee, D.N., Lough, S. & Lough, F. (In press). Activating the perceptuo-motor system in hemiparesis. *Journal of Physiology.*

McDonnell, P. (1975). The development of visually guided reaching. *Perception & Psychophysics, 18,* 181-185.

Piaget, J. (1953). *The Origin of Intelligence in the Child.* London: Routledge & Kegan Paul.

Piaget, J. (1954). *The Construction of Reality in the Child*. New York: Basic Books.

Prechtl, H. (1977). *The Neurological Examination of the Full-term Newborn Infant*. (2nd Edn.) Clinics in Developmental Medicine No. 63. London: Heinemann Meidcal Books.

Rader, N. & Stern, J.D. (1982). Visually elicited reaching in neonates. *Child Development, 53,* 1004-1007.

Spelke, E.S. (1984). Perception of unity, persistence, and identity: Thoughts on infant's conceptions of objects. In J. Mehler and E. Fox (Eds.), *Neonate cognition: Beyond the Blooming, Buzzing Confusion*. Hillsdale, N.J.: Erlbaum.

Trevarthen, C.B. (1974). The psychobiology of speech development. In E.H. Lenneberg (Ed.), *Language and Brain: Developmental aspects. Neurosciences Research Program Bulletin, 12,* 570-585.

Twitchell, T.E. (1970). Reflex mechanisms and the development of prehension. In K.J. Connolly (Ed.), *Mechanisms of Motor Skill Development*. London: Academic Press.

White, B.L., Castle, P. & Held, R. (1964). Observations on the development of visually directed reaching. *Child Development, 35,* 349-364.

Wishart, J. (1979). The development of the object concept in infancy. Unpublished doctoral dissertation, University of Edinburgh.

Yonas, A. & Granrud, C.E. (1985). The development of sensitivity to kinetic, binocular, and pictorial depth information in human infants. In D.J. Ingle, M. Jeannerod and D.N. Lee (Eds.), *Brain Mechanisms and Spatial Vision*. Dordrecht: Martinus Nijhoff Publishers.

PERCEPTION-ACTION COUPLING IN THE YOUNG INFANT:
An appraisal of von Hofsten's research programme

P.J. Beek

1.   INTRODUCTION

        I am pleased to find myself in a position to be able to react to Claes
von Hofsten's paper since I have great sympathy for the perception-action
perspective he adopts. Working, as I am, at the interface between philosophy
and psychology, with a special interest in what has come to be called the
ecological approach to perception and action, the work of von Hofsten on
the development of manual skills provides me - as an instance of ecological
psychology - with a rich source of interesting theoretical problems. Problems
that are repeatedly encountered or which are alluded to in other chapters of
this book; problems that have to do with the kind of description one is willing
to invoke in the study of movement control, coordination and development.
It is clear that this field of study is in a stage of transition. Anything goes!
Cognitive, neuropsychological, biological, ecological and dynamical approaches
have been used to provide a framework for the   evolving field. Ecological and
dynamical approaches tend to dissociate themselves from other perspectives
and, in so doing, give rise to considerable debate. This state of affairs
allows one to discuss work like von Hofsten's from a number of perspectives.
In what follows, that is precisely what I would like to do.

        My aim is two-fold: in the first place, I will indicate some implications
of von Hofsten's work for the study of the development of prehension, making
a few critical remarks as I go along. Secondly, I will indicate the significance
of von Hofsten's work for the development of an ecological theory of action,
again with some critical overtones. I will defend the view that von Hofsten's
insights into the development of manual skills come closer to the ecological
perspective offered by Reed (1982) than to the dynamical perspective
advocated by the Connecticut-school (see, for example, Kugler, Kelso &
Turvey, 1980 and, especially, Kugler, Kelso & Turvey, 1982).

        Of course, this kind of reaction can be nothing more than a bird's eye
view on the place of von Hofsten's research programme in the total field of
study.

2.   IMPLICATIONS FOR THE STUDY OF MOTOR DEVELOPMENT

2.1. The impact of a new methodology

        One of the major implications of von Hofsten's research programme for
the study of the development of prehension lies in the production of a new
set of data on early development which deviate from the traditionally accepted
norms.

Von Hofsten (1980, 1983) has made accurate measurements of the transportations of the wrist and orientation of the hand by babies as they track, or try to intercept, an attractive object passing before them in an horizontal arc at about chest level. Most notably, these data illustrate that the reaching of the neonate is organised in a visual-manual space which is structured at least directionally, and that infants as young as 18 weeks are (in some cases) able to use a visual mode of control for the efficient catching of objects moving at a velocity of 30 cm/second. In earlier studies of prehension, no evidence of such visual control of movements was found during the neonatal period (with the possible exception of that provided by Trevarthen in 1974), whereas visually guided reaching and grasping were generally held to appear about a month or two later (e.g. Bower, 1974; Butterworth, 1981; Lenneberg, 1967).

An explanation of this somewhat surprising fact may be found in the often ignored idea that knowledge is at least partly dependent on methodology. In line with Newell's ideas on task constraints (this volume), it can be plausibly argued that von Hofsten manipulated the constraints of the (experimental) reaching task in a more optimal manner than researchers before him (e.g., Halverson, 1931; Piaget, 1953; White, Castle & Held, 1964; Bruner & Koslowski, 1972). By using moving objects instead of stationary objects, by providing an optimal postural support for the infants (who were placed in a semi-reclining seat that supported their waist and trunk but allowed free movements of their arms) and by using brightly coloured, attractive objects von Hofsten facilitated the expression of the true level of competence. The introduction of moving objects rather than static ones seems to be especially crucial. Not only does a moving target enhance its separation from its background, thereby accommodating the limited visual acuity of the neonate, it also puts constraints on the timing of the reaching, providing a favourable challenge for the infant.

The lesson to be learned from this explanation is - if true - that in order to establish the real limits to the development of prehension, or of any other motor skill for that matter, one has to vary the constraints of the (experimental) task in such a way as to be able to specify optimal conditions.

2.2. Reflections on reflexes

Another, also not sufficiently recognised, implication of von Hofsten's findings on the development of reaching is the light they throw on what is traditionally referred to as the relationship between reflexes and voluntary behaviour. The question posed is how to explain the disappearance of infantile reflex patterns (like the hand-grasp reactions and the asymmetric tonic neck reflex) and the simultaneous emergence of voluntary patterns of grasping movements clearly directed toward the achievement of goals? Over the years, at least two types of answer have been given. On the one hand, there are those who wish to provide explanations based on 'infantile reflexes' as building blocks in the normal development of behaviour (e.g., Gesell & Armatruda, 1947; André-Thomas & Saint-Anne Dargassies, 1952). On the other, the 'infantile reflexes' have been regarded as primitives of the relatively undeveloped nervous system that are gradually inhibited by maturing 'higher' structures (e.g., Hay, 1984). In the latter account, the infant is supposed to acquire, in steps, the ability to modulate and control such triggered movements by means of cognitive and/or perceptual mediation. During old age and in the course of some diseases, these inhibiting mechanisms are sometimes believed to be removed, so that the primitive reflexes reappear.

As far as the ontogeny of reaching is concerned, von Hofsten's findings strongly contradict both these explanations. Neonates show coordinated, organised and (to some extent) controlled movements. Those observations are consistent with those of Prechtl (this volume), who demonstrated that foetuses show, almost from the beginning of life, spontaneous, organised motor behaviour. Just after birth (3-8 days), von Hofsten (1985) recorded signs of adjustment of the hand to the orientation of an object before it was touched. While the synergies were rather holistic they were not stereotyped: a degree of visual perception-action coupling being already present. Infants of 15 to 18 weeks of age already correct their reaching for moving targets on the basis of visual information. Von Hofsten observed a general trend towards greater efficiency between 15 and 36 weeks - and, hence, a trend towards increasingly 'ballistic control' (though never completely without some element of perceptual control during the movement). The infants were all aiming very well at the youngest age, but the younger infants proceeded in smaller steps than the older. Early reaches appear to be overdamped (von Hofsten, 1979, Fig. 11), having a larger number of components than later reaches - suggesting that infants slightly under four months of age lack certain basic coordinative structures, and that it is mainly the mobility aspects of reaching that are developing during the months which follow. That is not to say, however, that the motor behaviour of infants around four months of age is dominated by 'infantile movement patterns'. As a matter of fact, von Hofsten found no evidence at all of triggering. On the contrary, by the time infants can reach out to grasp, they attempt to reach only for objects moving slowly enough to be caught. A moving target is not a trigger for reaching; infants treat objects, travelling with different velocities, differentially. Sometimes infants would 'play' with slow moving objects (3.4 cm/sec), following, touching and retouching them. Infants do not reach automatically for every moving target that passes in front of them. They seem to know, in advance, whether there is a fair chance of success. To have such knowledge, they not only have to be able to correctly perceive the spatial parameters of the surrounding space, and the motion characteristics of the moving object, but also to be able to correctly judge their own capacities when acting in this situation.

Nevertheless, one might argue, with standarised neurological procedures (e.g., Prechtl, 1977) more or less fixed responses can be triggered by tactile, vestibular and proprioceptive stimuli. How are we, then, as students of motor actions, to look upon these reactions? As Touwen (1980) argues, every behavioural expression of activity of the nervous system is a reflection of an age-related structural integrity and the manner in which these behaviours are related to each other via the development of neuronal structures is drawn from our observations. Moreover, it might well be the case that they are not related at all. It is not, therefore, surprising that no one has succeeded in revealing a clear relationship between the disappearance of the hand-grasping reaction and so-called voluntary grasping. On the other hand, it has to be admitted, it is hard, if not impossible, to provide conclusive evidence for the non-existence of such a relationship.

What von Hofsten's research shows, to my mind, is that the knowledge derived from elicited responses in neurological examination - although definitely a valuable device in the diagnosis of developmental defects - is of very limited relevance for the study of the development of action. In fact, this kind of knowledge throws the student of action off the track, since it gives rise to intractable questions, based on the probably false and almost certainly unfruitful assumption that reflexes are the primitives or building-blocks of action.

2.3. The trickiness of developmental neuropsychology

A third, rather tricky issue, I want to address, shortly, is the relationship between the development of (certain) neuronal structures and the development of prehension. Quite rightly, von Hofsten shows interest in the neuronal processes underlying the development of reaching and grasping. By way of justification or partial explanation of the observed behavioural changes, he refers extensively, in his paper, as do others in the field (e.g., Trevarthen, 1984), to the work of Kuypers and his colleagues. Their studies on the development of the separate motor systems and the projections of these to the musculature surrounding the proximal and distal joints of the limbs in the rhesus monkey, show the successive establishment of, respectively, the ventromedial, lateral brainstem and cortico-motoneuronal pathways and their responsibility for the control of successively more distal parts of the trunk-arm-hand-finger-system. The crucial importance of the establishment of the cortico-motoneuronal connections for independent finger control and predictive reaching is especially stressed by von Hofsten.

Nevertheless, some remarks and amplifications should be made in this regard. The question is, to what extent these findings in the rhesus monkey are legitimately applicable to the development of reaching and grasping in the human infant. Little, if anything, is known about the development of the human nervous system in the first half-year of life. There might be some behavioural indications that the neuronal development of the rhesus monkey is in some respects similar to that of man, but on the other hand there are remarkable differences as well, for instance, the relatively early disappearance of the delicate pincer grasp in man. Moreover, the task used by Lawrence and Kuypers (1968a, 1968b), pushing a pellet out of a small dell, is not quite the same as the actual grasping of objects, involving individual movements of the digits.

At this stage, the explanatory status of von Hofsten's references to changes in the nervous system occuring more or less synchronously with the development of behaviour is, in the first place, associative. One has to be careful in this respect: the relationship between the establishment of the cortico-motoneuronal pathways and the occurrence of fine finger-movements seems to be very straightforward, but a necessary condition will certainly not always be a sufficient condition as well.

Probably for reasons of time constraint, nothing is said by von Hofsten about the development of the sensory systems. It would be interesting to know, if von Hofsten's findings on the development of the assumed perception-action coupling for reaching and grasping can in any way be related to neuro-developmental data? According to many (Bronson, 1974; Goldberg & Lee Robinson, 1979; Stein, 1984), for instance, the superior colliculus is a prime functional visual region in the human neonate and an important centre of sensorimotor integration. Most likely, it plays a role in spatial orientation, especially with respect to moving visual objects, and it mediates both the reach and the response to looming objects. What is the precise relationship between von Hofsten's data and the development of the superior colliculus?

Also, the disappearance of grasping at around the second month of (postnatal) life and its reappearance a few weeks later, deserves a neuro-developmental explanation. Lawrence and Hopkins (1972, 1976) suggest that in this period the corticospinal pathways become connected to the cervical motoneurons.

The overall question however remains: what is the nature of the relationship between the nervous system and behaviour? As Gibson (1966, 1979, 1982) and Reed (1982) have convincingly argued, the psychological concepts of sensory and motor cannot be equated, respectively, with the neuro-anatomical structures termed afferent and efferent. The neuro-anatomical definition of sensory system (as receptor elements, cortex, and the afferent pathways that mediate them) fails to accommodate the purposive activity of the perceptual systems (Gibson, 1966), whereas the neuro-anatomical definition of motor systems (as cortex, motoneurons, and the efferent pathways that mediate them) fails to accommodate the adjusting, flexible activity of the action system.

Of course, these insights do not deny that a discipline of neuro-psychology is possible, but they do demand a reconsideration of the relation-ship between neuronal events and facts of behaviour before a neuropsychology, relevant for perception and action, can be established.

3. IMPLICATIONS FOR THE ECOLOGICAL APPROACH TO PERCEPTION AND ACTION

3.1. Support for Reed's theory of action systems

Now, to the significance of von Hofsten's research programme for the development of an ecological theory of perception and action, I will argue that, despite a few minor differences, von Hofsten's work fits best into Reed's (outline of a) theory of action systems (Reed, 1982, 1984a, 1984b). Later, I will indicate some of the implications of this position for other ecological accounts – like the dynamical approach.

In a nutshell, Reed's theory of action systems holds that actions are realisations of affordances. The specificity of an action lies in the meaning-ful changes wrought, that is in its function, not in the patterns of the movements made. Actions are not comprised of physical displacements, but of 'ecologically defined' postures and movements. Posture, in this sense, refers to the maintenance of some persistent orientation of an animal to its sur-roundings, whereas movements are transitions among postures, that is, specific changes in some animal-environment system. Both postures and movements are controlled by perceptual information, they are not triggered or imposed by external and internal commands. Thus, the mature actions of all vertebrates are not triggered movements or responses, but coordinated nesting of postures and movements, under the functionally specific control of that animal's extero- and proprioception.

Just as the notion of specific information lies at the core of Gibson's ecological approach to visual perception, functional specificity is probably the key concept in Reed's action systems theory. Functional specificity is the thesis that animals and human beings achieve their goals not by muscle-contractions or bodily displacements, but by coordinating a series of sub-actions called postures and movements. Quite naturally, therefore, Reed's theory of action systems implies the general hypothesis of an increase in functional specificity during development.

192

Von Hofsten's perspective on the development of a specific perception-action system fits perfectly into this theory. Like Reed, von Hofsten thinks of the relationship(s) between perception and action as being intimately organised in specific perception-action systems, implying that for a specific action specific information is being picked-up (that is, according to Reed, information about both the invariant and variant aspects of the environment and the actions of the self within that environment). Functional specificity refers to a certain actor or a system of acting in which some variations in anatomical or mechanical details are tolerated so long as they serve specific functional uses and if changes in that function lead to a reorganisation of the act. For instance, the fact that von Hofsten's infants at six months of age reach out in a (spatio-temporal) variety of ways to catch a moving object, indicates that they are capable of making adaptive adjustments to the parameters of the task at hand. Thus, one can legitimately speak of a functionally specific action. When von Hofsten measures the kinematic details of the movements performed in the infant's reaching and grasping, such as accelerations, decelerations and directions, he does so simply in order to describe this change in efficiency and effectivity in the development of reaching and grasping, not because the Newtonian concept of movement is considered to be basic for all actions. Von Hofsten's account of the development of reaching and grasping should be interpreted as an increase in functional specificity. He would, therefore, probably be quite prepared to go along with Reed's idea of postures and movements – conceived of as specific modes of resource use – as the basic components of action.

As to the study of perception-action systems, Reed as well as von Hofsten stress the need for ecologically valid experimental set-ups. The first problem for von Hofsten – as for Reed – is to identify the separate perception-action systems, define their areas of operation, and determine their strengths and limitations. Apart from Reed's tentative taxonomy of action systems – involving the basic orienting system, the investigatory system, the locomotor system, the semantic system, the performatory system, and so on – little work has been done in this respect. The empirical question at hand, here, is whether specific actions can indeed be uniquely correlated with the different, specific kinds of information on which the perception-action systems are supposed to be based by definition.

A methodological snake in the grass is, of course, that in borderline cases critical testing is circumvented by equating, too soon, a newly discovered information-basis with a new particular perception-action system. For instance, one can reasonably argue that driving a car on the basis of time-to-collision is a different perception-action system than catching on the basis of time-to-contact, but when von Hofsten (1983) finds that catching of an object that moves pendicular to the line of sight is based on different information than catching an object that moves parallel to the line of sight, does that imply that there are two specific perception-action systems for catching? And, what if different kinds of information turn out to play a role in one action? Logically speaking, questions like these have to be considered before one can attack the developmental problem of how the different perception-action systems differentiate into the sophisticated perceptuo-motor control of the adult.

This discussion brings us to another correspondence between Reed's and von Hofsten's approaches. Both focus, primarily, on the kind of information that regulates action rather than on how precisely action dynamics are controlled and regulated via perception. This is not an absolute omission, it is a matter of degree. Of course, von Hofsten also offers, to some extent, an account of how reaching is controlled, but this account is formulated in terms of a general strategy, not in terms of a parameterisation of a function that constrains the potentially free variables into a behavioural unit, as put forward in the task dynamic approach (see Kugler, Kelso & Turvey, 1980, 1982; Saltzman & Kelso, 1983). Too much emphasis is put on the perception-side rather than on the action-side of perception-action systems. Like Reed, von Hofsten owes more to Gibson and Johansson than to Bernstein. Many questions concerning the solution of typical Bernsteinian problems - like the problem of degrees-of-freedom and the problem of context-conditioned variability - are left unanswered.

Depending on one's inclination, one might stress the need for complementing von Hofsten's research programme with an, in principle compatible, dynamical account of coordination and control.

3.2. Timing

In the previous section, I alluded to a possible implication of von Hofsten's research for an ecological account of timing-behaviour. Recent human ethological research by Thelen (1981) suggests, rather strongly, that the organism possesses a high degree of intrinsic temporal organisation at a very young age. The kicking pattern of an one-month-old displays the same temporal pattern of flexion and extension as the gait of a mature adult. Von Hofsten (1983) makes reference to a different category of timing in showing that infants around 15 weeks of age possess a remarkable capacity to catch moving objects, that is, to time their movements under severe time constraints. His explanation of this performance suggests that the infant has at its disposal a sensorimotor system for anticipatory tracking. More specifically, infants achieve predictive reaching by tracking the object with the hand and at the same speed moving the hand towards it. The resultant of these two vectors is then the path along which the hand is actually carried leading, necessarily, to the desired end-position. The significance of this hypothesis, true or not, is that it challenges the primacy of Lee's time-to-contact ideas.

Von Hofsten (Lee & von Hofsten, 1982; von Hofsten, 1985) argues that time-to-contact, although proven to be a potent determiner of timing-behaviour (Lee & Reddish, 1981; Lee, Lishman & Thomson, 1982) can not be the only one. There are a number of situations in which there is no, or very limited, retinal expansion, while action is still successful: for instance when an object circles around the subject or moves horizontally across the line of vision of the subject at an angle of around 90 degrees. In those cases timing has to be based on some other kind of visual information. With these insights, experimenters will probably be inspired to study the limits of time-to-contact and time-to-collision (instead of contributing to a less valuable empirical expansion of retinal expansion research). In addition to instances in which there is no, or only limited, retinal expansion, one can think of manipulation of the optic array itself, by degreading or obscuring it, and of artificial manipulation of the retinal expansion itself, i.e. by inflating or shrinking balls.

3.3. Maturation versus learning

Now, having come to the last part of my appraisal of von Hofsten's research programme, I want to revisit the maturation-learning debate, so often referred to during the congress. My reasons for doing so, have to do with the fact that the traditional distinction between maturation and learning is quite apparent in von Hofsten's work. Moreover, it is a subject on which ecological psychologists have rather divergent opinions.

In apparent agreement with the positions adopted by Bruner (1973) and Bower (1974), von Hofsten takes a strong nativist position with respect to the determinants of visuomotor development. According to von Hofsten, the perception-action systems of man are biologically given. The orderliness in skilled behaviour comes from internal biological sources and is, so to speak, shaped but not constructed by the environment. It is the result of sensory and neuro-motor maturation with some additional timing and calibration through experience. Since the neonate is prepared to act adaptively in certain contexts, von Hofsten proposes to accept the idea of innate knowledge about the world in psychology.

In the traditional maturation-learning debate, an environmentalist would certainly be inclined to criticise the explicit claim of generality and the tendency to underplay environmental influences in this account of the emergence of motor skills. He might for instance, point to an abundance of neurophysiological evidence gathered in the 70's, supporting the position that environmental factors are far more important in the development of structure and function of the nervous system than assumed in former days (e.g., Braitenberg, 1977; Goldman & Lewis, 1978; Granit, 1977). This evidence led Granit to the conclusion that the brain behaves as if it had been genetically instructed to be maximally open to environmental modification. On this view, the blueprint of the nervous system is genetically given, but its detailed expression is highly dependent on environmental factors. Our hypothetical environmentalist might also offer a sophisticated account of subtle learning processes even during the earliest months of life.

It is however an illusion to think that a distinction between the relative impact of endogeneous and exegeneous factors in the development of co-ordination can be drawn. The two can not be put into sharp contrast. In general, genes seem to offer possibilities rather than fixed patterns. The way in which these possibilities are realised is dependent on the environment, albeit within certain, genetically determined, limits. To cite Waddington (1975), "the capacity of an organism to respond to environmental stresses during development is in itself a hereditary quality". If that is the case, biological disposition and environmental influence, maturation and calibration, can not be distinguished. In recent years this insight seems to be fairly generally accepted.

Quite rightly, in my opinion, von Hofsten looks for a sound evolutionary epistemology for the study of the development of action. Reed is also aware of this necessity, but avoids the thorny issue of genetic determination. Instead, he offers a model of natural selection that is based on phenotype rather than on genotype. Those who promote a dynamical approach will give, or rather will try to give, a thermodynamical account of evolution. Von Hofsten adheres to the idea of innate knowledge which does not explain much; it is a cheap solution - popular since Kant - for the problem of animal-environment synergy. Moreover, I think the term has the wrong connotations: it smacks of something conscious and cognitive. However, better alternatives are hard to think of. It is clear that fundamental, to some extent philosophical questions, also for the development of motor control, have to be answered here.

References

André-Thomas & Saint-Anne Dargassies, S. (1952). *Etudes neurologiques sur le nouveau-né et le jeune nourisson.* Paris: Masson et Cie.

Bower, T.G.R. (1974). *Development in Infancy.* San Francisco: W.H. Freeman.

Bronson, G. (1974). The postnatal growth of visual capacity. *Child Development, 45,* 873-890.

Braitenberg, V. (1977). *On the texture of brains.* Berlin: Springer Verlag.

Bruner, J.S. & Kozlowski, B. (1972). Visually preadapted constituents of manipulatory action. *Perception, 1,* 3-12.

Bruner, J.S. (1973). Organization of early skilled action. *Child Development, 44.*

Butterworth, G. (1981). The origins of auditory-visual perception and visual proprioception in human development. In H.A. Pick and R. Walk (Eds.), *Perception and Experience. Vol. II.* New York: Plenum.

Gesell, A. & Armatruda, C.S. (1947/1969). *Developmental diagnosis.* New York: Harper and Row.

Gibson, J.J. (1966). *The senses considered as perceptual systems.* Boston: Houghton-Mifflin.

Gibson, J.J. (1979). *The ecological approach to visual perception.* Boston: Houghton-Mifflin.

Gibson, J.J. (1982). Notes on action. In E. Reed and R. Jones (Eds.), *Reasons for realism: Selected essays of James J. Gibson.* Hillsdale: Erlbaum.

Goldberg, M.E. & Lee Robinson, D. (1978). Visual system: superior colliculus. In R. Bruce Masterton (Ed.), *Handbook of Behavioral Neurobiology, Vol. I.* New York: Plenum Press.

Goldman, P.S. & Lewis, M.E. (1978). Developmental biology of brain damage and experience. In C.W. Cotman (Ed.), *Neuronal Plasticity.* New York: Raven Press.

Granit, R. (1977). *The purposive brain.* Cambridge, Mass.: MIT Press.

Halverson, H.M. (1931). Study of prehension in infants. *Genetic Psychology Monographs, 10,* 107-285.

Hofsten, C. von. (1979). Development of visually directed reaching: The approach phase. *Journal of Human Movement Studies, 5,* 160-178.

Hofsten, C. von. (1980). Predictive reaching for moving objects by human infants. *Journal of Experimental Child Psychology, 30,* 369-382.

Hofsten, C. von. (1983). Catching skills in infancy. *Journal of Experimental Psychology: Human Perception and Performance, 9,* 75-85.

Hofsten, C. von. (1985). Catching. Report No. 28. Research Group on Perception and Action, Center for interdisciplinary research (ZiF), Bielefeld.

Hofsten, C. von. & Lee, D.N. (1982). Dialogue on perception and action. *Human Movement Science, 1,* 125-138.

Kugler, P.N., Kelso, J.A.S. & Turvey, M.T. (1980). On the concept of coordinative structures as dissipative structures: I. Theoretical lines of convergence. In G.E. Stelmach and J. Requin (Eds.), *Tutorials in Motor Behavior.* New York: North Holland Publishing Co.

Kugler, P.N., Kelso, J.A.S. & Turvey, M.T. (1982). On the control and coordination of naturally developing systems. In J.A.S. Kelso and J. Clark (Eds.), *The development of movement control and coordination.* Chichester: John Wiley.

Lawrence, D.G. & Kuypers, H.G.J.M. (1968a). The functional organization of the motor system in the monkey. I. The effects of bilateral pyramidal lesions. *Brain, 91,* 1-14.

196

Lawrence, D.G. & Kuypers, H.G.J.M. (1968b). The functional organization of the motor system. II. The effects of the descending brain-stem pathways. *Brain, 91,* 15-36.

Lawrence, D.G. & Hopkins, D.A. (1972). Developmental aspects of pyramidal motor control in the rhesus monkey. *Brain Research, 40,* 117-118.

Lawrence, D.G. & Hopkins, D.A. (1976). The development of motor control in the rhesus monkey: Evidence concerning the role of corticomotor-neuronal connections. *Brain, 99,* 235-254.

Lee, D.N. & Reddish, P.E. (1981). Plummeting gannets: a paradigm of ecological optics. *Nature, 293 (5830),* 293-294.

Lee, D.N., Lishman, J.R. & Thomson, J.A. (1982). Visual regulation of gait in long jumping. *Journal of Experimental Psychology: Human Perception and Performance, 8,* 448-459.

Lenneberg, E.H. (1967). *Biological Foundations of Language.* New York: Basic Books.

Prechtl, H. (1977). *The Neurological Examination of the Full-term Newborn Infant. Clinics in Developmental Medicine No. 63.* London: Heinemann.

Reed, E.S. (1982). An outline of a theory of action systems. *Journal of Motor Behavior, 14,* 98-134.

Reed, E.S. (1984a). From action gestalts to direct action. In H.T.A. Whiting (Ed.), *Human Motor Actions: Bernstein Reassessed.* Amsterdam: North-Holland.

Reed, E.S. (1984b). What develops when action develops? Paper presented at symposium on Motor Development in Children Sponsored by Herbert L. Pick & Thomas J. Tighe for the Society for Research in Child Development. Unpublished manuscript, Department of Humanities and Communication, Drexel University.

Saltzman, E.L. & Kelso, J.A.S. (1983). Skilled actions: A task dynamic approach. *Haskins Laboratories Status Report on Speech Research, SR-76,* 3-50. *Developmental Psychology, 17,* 237-257.

Stein, B.E. (1984). Development of the superior colliculus. *Annual Review of Neurosciences, 7,* 95-125.

Thelen, E. (1981). Rhytmical behavior in infancy: An ethological perspective. *Developmental Psychology, 17,* 237-257.

Touwen, B.C.L. (1980). Structuur en functie van het zich ontwikkelende zenuwstelsel. In A. Jennekens-Schinkel e.a. (Red.), *Neuropsychologie in Nederland.* Deventer: Van Loghum Slaterus.

Trevarthen, C. (1974). The psychobiology of speech development. In E.H. Lenneberg (Ed.), *Language and Brain: Developmental aspects. (Neurosciences Research Program Bulletin, 12).* Cambridge, Mass.: Neurosciences Research Program.

Trevarthen, C. (1984). How control of movement develops. In H.T.A. Whiting (Ed.), *Human Motor Actions: Bernstein Reassessed.* Amsterdam: North-Holland.

Waddington, C.H. (1975). *The evolution of an evolutionist.* Edinburgh: University Press.

White, B.L., Castle, P. & Held, R. (1964). Observations on the development of visually directed reaching. *Child Development, 35,* 349-364.

THE PERCEPTION-ACTION PERSPECTIVE: A COMMENTARY ON VON HOFSTEN

J.E. Clark

By the end of the first year of life, the human infant has attained the rudiments of the two major perception-action systems, manipulation and locomotion. For the survival of the species, there is little doubt that these two action systems are crucial. With accurate reaching and grasping, the young infant is capable of feeding herself while the attainment of independent biped locomotion allows her to obtain food from other than her immediate surround. In his paper, von Hofsten (this volume) has focused our attention on the development of the manual action system. In reacting to his paper, I would like not only to extend upon his remarks on the emergence of manual skills, but I would like to incorporate into my discussion the work on the development of locomotion. I have included the latter to demonstrate the similarities between these two important perception-action systems. This has been done with the hope that as we seek a theory or metatheory for the development of motor skills, we will seek common principles which govern both manipulative and locomotor skills.

I have by no means attempted here to articulate a theory for the development of perception-action systems; rather I have chosen to expand on three themes which emerged from von Hofsten's paper and which I felt were important to our further theorising. The first theme, to which von Hofsten alluded and to which I have added my comments, is the nature of the perception-action perspective on the development of motor skills. The second theme I have expanded upon is the emergence of the early patterns of coordination. And finally, I have offered my comments on the nature of developing patterns of coordination.

1. THE PERCEPTION-ACTION PERSPECTIVE ON THE DEVELOPMENT OF MOTOR SKILLS

For decades developmental psychologists, much like their cousins the experimental psychologists, have assumed the dualistic separation of motor and sensory systems. To Piaget (1952) and others such as McGraw (1941) and White and his associates (1964) who have described the development of visually directed reaching, the motor and sensory systems were unconnected at birth. From the work presented here by von Hofsten and that of others such as Bower (1972, 1979), Meltzoff and Moore (1977) and Rader and Stern (1982), evidence has been growing that at birth, vision is *already connected* to the motor system. Indeed, von Hofsten (1982) has shown that as early as 5 days after birth the human infant is capable of directing her arm toward a visually presented target.

It seems reasonable, argues von Hofsten, to suggest that perception and action evolved together and come ready to function together, albeit in a limited fashion. Although one might take issue with such a notion - and surely there is room to do so - I show my own bias for von Hofsten's position by expanding on his points rather than criticising them. I have chosen to do so because I know only too well that for those of us studying gross motor play-game skills, the perception-action perspective is often neglected. Work from our laboratory is a good illustration of the type of research in which the perception-action perspective would appear to be lacking. I have chosen to "pick on" our own work so as not to offend any-one, but I would suggest that ours is not the only example.

In one of the first studies (Clark & Phillips, 1985) on jumping that my colleague, Sally Phillips, and I did, we attempted to identify the develop-mental sequence for the standing long jump, one of the so-called fundamen-tal motor skills (Wickstrom, 1983). Our purpose was to describe the changing patterns of coordination employed by the developing child as she projects her body for maximum distance in a horizontal direction.

We found systematic age-related changes in the patterns of coordination used to create the force for jumping. *So what!* Here we have a contrived task in a constant environment. When we watch children moving in their econiches, do we see them performing a "standing long jump"? I think not. If you do observe such a skill, it is probably in a physical education class. Studying the standing long jump of children *can* tell us about how a child marshalls her multi-segmented body to create the necessary force to project her body horizontally. But does this go far enough? I believe that it does not.

To understand the development of a motor skill, is to understand the nature of the action in the environmental context in which it occurs. What is the purpose of the action? How is it organised to meet this purpose? How is it controlled? In order to answer these questions we must look conjointly at perception and action, rather than ignoring one at the expense of the other.

For as Gibson (1979) wrote, manipulation and locomotion are "...neither triggered nor commanded but controlled (p. 225)". This control or constraint comes from the environment in which the actor is moving. To understand how a movement is organised, we must understand the nature of the mover in her environment. Thus in looking at the standing long jump *only*, we come to understand but a part of the puzzle. What do we know of jump roping or jumping puddles or any of the other body projections the developing child performs in her world of play? How do the internal and external environ-mental constraints change and what is their effect on the movement's organisation?

One example of how we might know more of the puzzle comes from a dissertation done by one of my doctoral students, Ricardo Petersen (1984). In his research, Petersen demonstrated that the pattern of coordination for the standing long jump was similar to that for the vertical jump in children 3, 5, and 7 years. Changing the task demands from the horizontal to the vertical resulted in a reparameterisation of the angle at which the forces were applied, but had little effect on the timing of joint reversals. Looking at Table 1, we can see that both the absolute and the relative time of joint reversals are almost the same for the two jumps. Invariance (albeit stability) was maintained over one level of change in task demands. Of course, those

Table 1. Mean absolute time (ms) and relative time (%) for joint reversals in the standing long and vertical jumps.

Age/Jump	Ankle Absol(rel)time		Knee Absol(rel)time		Hip Absol(rel)time
3 yr olds					
SLJ	146.7	(71.1)	173.3	(83.7)	207.0[1]
VJ	150.0	(73.6)	173.3	(85.3)	203.3
5 yr olds					
SLJ	173.3	(68.5)	180.0	(69.3)[2]	260.0
VJ	177.0	(68.9)	206.7	(79.1)	263.3
7 yr olds					
SLJ	193.3	(91.4)	173.3	(81.4)	210.0
VJ	213.3	(107.0)	176.7	(89.6)	200.0

[1] To calculate relative time, hip reversal was taken as the movement's start and toe off as its end.

[2] Significant difference in absolute time.

who study time-to-collision might have found our data more interesting if we had looked at how the children landed, rather than how they constructed the projection. But I must confess, it was not a question for us. Indeed, that makes the point, for where von Hofsten assumes rather than argues for the perception-action perspective, I have highlighted it knowing that for myself and my colleagues it is not so obvious a perspective. Yet it is undoubtedly one which deserves attention by those who study the gross motor play-game skills.

But I would like to go a bit further in my remarks about a *proper* perspective for understanding motor skill development by promoting the inclusion of the Bernsteinian (1967) biophysical perspective. For just as I believe those who study gross motor skills pay little attention to perception in the perception-action equation, so too do I observe little attention to action by those studying manipulative skill development. In some ways I share Reed's (1982) view that we might be well served in our understanding of motor skills by combining Gibson and Bernstein's perspectives. It is in the spirit of such a marriage of perspectives that I address the second of the themes I have chosen from von Hofsten's paper.

2. THE EMERGENCE OF EARLY PATTERNS OF COORDINATION

When the neonate comes into our world, she comes with a complex bio-dynamic system of over 620 paired muscles and 100 moveable joints. Although each joint is not a potential source for major movements of the body's segment (e.g., joints of the metacarpals), a conservative estimate of the number of degrees of freedom in the human body which might result in the displacement of a major body segment would be 90 or so. In analysing any movement, in our examples here, locomotion or reaching, our attention usually focuses on the limb or limbs, but unless the trunk is stabilised, the infant must regulate almost all of the system's degrees of freedom when she moves. This is a major undertaking especially when this control must be gained in the face of a constantly changing environment.

In looking at von Hofsten's infants and analysing their problem in moving to catch or contact an object from the Bernsteinian or biophysical perspective, there are two fundamental problems which must be solved. The first is the problem of the degrees of freedom and the second is the problem of "peripheral indeterminacy" or context-conditioned variability (Turvey et al, 1982). Bernstein's solution to these problems, as we are aware, was to constrain the degrees of freedom into functional groupings referred to as synergies (Gelfand et al, 1971), collectives (Gelfand & Tsetlin, 1971), linkages (Waterland & Shambes, 1970) or coordinative structures (Easton, 1972; Kelso et al, 1981; Turvey, 1977). The process of coordinating the action is viewed as the function which constrains the free variables into behavioural units while control is the process of assigning values to the variables in the function (Kelso, 1982).

Given the vast problems of managing the multi-segmented biodynamic neuromuscular system, it seems all the more remarkable that the human neonate can even move let alone move in a coordinated manner in what would appear to be an environmentally sensitive fashion. Yet the evidence that von Hofsten has presented here as well as that presented by Prechtl and Thelen (in this volume) would suggest that indeed the human fetus as well as the neonate is capable of very early patterns of coordination.

Clearly, the actions of the young infant are more than random chaos. Both Thelen and von Hofsten describe a synergistic-like organisation which has spatial and temporal regularity. The many degrees of freedom inherent in the limbs seem to be constrained, that is, coordinated. But how does this organisation arise? What are the principles of organisation which govern movement behaviour so early in life? Two explanations seem most evident. The first explains the organisation of action in terms of hardwired neural circuitry such as reflexes or spinal pattern generators. The second and the one to which I would subscribe has been put forth by Kugler, Kelso and Turvey (1980). It requires that no such structural formalism as spinal generators be invoked. From Kugler et al's perspective, the organisation such as that observed in the neonate's repertoire emerges from its biodynamic properties. Coordinative structures are not mechanisms or units to be found as if they were anatomical entities. Clearly there are "hardwired" units, but given the variety of functions required of the upper and lower extremities, *hardwiring* patterns of action only would seem highly restrictive. Why not have a flexible organisation which arises to meet the environmental demands, i.e., to achieve an objective?

It seems so obvious a point that coordination of our multi-segmented body is for a purpose. Constraints bring the action into functional parady with the environment. Constraints not only come from within the system but they also arise from the environment. Our understanding of what and how constraints arise and also how they give shape to our movement organisation.

Clearly, von Hofsten's work has been directed to identifying visual constraints for the infant as she masters reaching. Although his work has offered insights into the characteristics of the optic array which might determine some aspects of manual coordination, I would suggest that the work go one step further and look at how the environmental information is used to *organise* the form of the movement, i.e., the pattern of coordination.

No doubt when you are studying reaching, vision "looms" as a major constraint, but it certainly is not the only constraint. In fact, Jeannerod (1984) has shown that although vision is important in improving movement accuracy, it lacks influence in the pattern of intersegmental coordination. Perhaps at some level of dynamic stability, vision may only serve to *control* the system, not to reorganise it.

But what other sources of information in the environment might act as a constraint on the patterns of coordination? Here I would offer gravity as an important and oft overlooked source of information in movement. Gravity is such a quiet constant in our world that we must remind ourself of its omnipresence by watching astronauts floating about in spaceships. Clearly, gravity constrains our movements. It can help brake a movement as Thelen and Fisher (1983) have suggested in supine kicking. Or it can completely dominate a movement as Hollerbach and Flash (1982) have demonstrated in slow reaching movements.

But what is the nature of the constraint? What happens to the leg action of supine kicking when the body is reoriented to the vertical or reaching when the baby is backlying or seated? Trevarthen (1984) has remarked that the infant seems to account very well for the change in gravity's pull when her orientation is changed in reaching. Similarily, Thelen (1984) has observed invariance in vertical stepping and supine kicking. Over what changes do we see invariance and when do we see change? Here I would suggest that our future work in both locomotion and reaching seek to describe over what changes in the environment does action remain stable and when does it change? I will turn to this latter question as I take up the last and most important theme, changing patterns of coordination.

3.   CHANGING PATTERNS OF COORDINATION

To the developmentalist, one of the first steps in programmatic research is to identify the early perception-action adaptations. In his paper, von Hofsten has summarised the wealth of data he has collected on the early patterns of manual coordination. The next step, and one which he has signalled here, is the process of deriving the principles of change. How might we account for the changes we see in the perception-action system as it develops from the "extension synergy" to the smooth, finely tuned and precise movements of the concert pianist? What changes? Why does the change occur? That is to ask, how is it that new forms arise?

If we return to Thelen's (1985) example of infant stepping, we recall that in the young infant the hip and knee actions were tightly coupled. At 10 months (when the child was supported), the pattern of coordination appeared "transitional", as the timing between the knee and hip joint actions was far less coupled. At 12 months, when the infant was independently walking, the pattern was entirely different. From the tight temporal coupling in infancy, the infant had moved to a new pattern of coordination (a new coordinative structure, if you would). But how did this new form of organisation arise?

One suggestion offered by Thelen (1984) is that physical size is a system-sensitive scaling factor which, when changed, will result in a new mode of organisation. The changing pattern of coordination is not necessarily due to reprogramming the system or maturation of neural networks. Rather the system reorganises itself in response to the changing biodynamics - an increase in size and concomittent increase in muscle mass.

We also might find our answer to how new patterns of coordination emerge by exploring how the system utilises energy. Biological systems are systems of energy. To Morowitz (1979), this energy is a crucial element in the organisation of biological systems. A principle theorem of Morowitz's is that the flow of energy through the system from a source to a sink will result in at least one cycle of the system. Cyclicity, then, is a fundamental endogenous characteristic of the infant's action system. For movement, cyclicity or oscillation is an elegant, simple and unifying element. For even the most complex of oscillations can be described by a series of sinusoidal oscillations superimposed one atop another (known as Fourier's theorem). With a mere handful of sinusoidal oscillations, for example, one can describe the most complex of human motions.

Thus, if energy flows within the system (to either the extensors or flexors of a limb), at least one cycle will result (more than one cycle, if we assume the system is a thermodynamic engine). The newborn need only begin the system with some amount of undifferentiated energy. This would be congruent with Thelen's (1985) observation that what appears to "turn on" rhythmical kicking is the infant's state of generalised arousal. Putting energy in, gets the process started. The resulting movement organisation would not have to be specified - it would emerge as a consequence of the biodynamic properties of the system. Complex coordinated movement may arise from a system which need not yet know how to *control* itself (i.e., assign the proper values to the function).

Indeed, energy, like size, can be seen as a scaling factor - a continuous variable. If we scale the system to some critical value - the system changes qualitatively. Kelso (1984) has given us a rather elegant demonstration of this reorganisation in an experiment in which he asked subjects to simultaneously flex one index finger while extending the other. Asking the subjects to increase speed resulted in a rather abrupt change in the movement's organisation. The index fingers continued to move synchronously but now they flexed and extended together. Scaling on a system sensitive parameter (i.e., energy or speed) resulted in the emergence of a new mode when certain critical regions were exceeded. Within a range of values the system was stable, but as the system approached these boundaries - instability resulted. Crossing the boundaries resulted in a new mode - a new stability.

Returning to our jumping example, I would offer our observations on the age-related changes which occur in the patterns of coordination. Recall that Petersen (1984) found temporal invariance across the tasks of vertical and horizontal jumping in 3-, 5- and 7-year-olds. In that same study, he also looked at adults who were skilled in volleyball and gymnastics and compared their standing long and vertical jumps to their sport-specific jumps - namely, the volleyball spike and the gymnastic dive roll. If sport-specific skills are built upon the fundamental skills (Seefeldt, 1980), we might expect to see similarities between the two skills. Before examining this hypothesis though, let us first examine the temporal relationship between the standing and vertical jumps for the athletes as well as a group of 9-year-olds and average adults.

Table 2. Mean absolute time (ms) and relative time (percent) for joint reversals in the standing, vertical and sport-specific jumps.

Group and Type of Jump	Ankle Absolute (and relative) time	Knee Absolute (and relative) time	Hip Absolute Time	Shoulder Absolute (and relative) time
9 year olds				
Standing long jump	183.3 (88.3)	147.0 (72.5)[1]	203.3[2]	360.0 (167.9)
Vertical jump	197.6 (113.9)	153.3 (89.0)	173.3	360.0 (213.9)
Average adults				
Standing long jump	293.3 (96.5)	251.0 (81.9)	306.7	461.7 (152.8)
Vertical jump	333.3 (100.5)	293.0 (86.9)	335.0	425.0 (128.2)
Volleyball Players				
Standing long jump	273.3 (85.1)[4,5]	198.3 (60.0)[1,3]	326.7[5]	401.7 (125.1)[1]
Vertical jump	266.7 (77.9)	306.7 (87.5)[4,5]	346.7	396.2 (116.1)[4]
Sport specific jump	140.0 (62.2)	131.7 (58.6)	225.0	371.7 (165.6)
Gymnasts				
Standing long jump	201.0 (69.8)[5]	140.0 (48.7)[1,4]	288.3[5]	395.0 (137.0)[1,4,5]
Vertical jump	210.0 (48.6)	185.0 (78.6)	240.0	413.3 (233.4)
Sport specific jump	76.7 (48.6)	125.0 (78.6)	160.0	351.0 (233.4)

1) Significant difference in relative time (SLJ vs. VJ)

2) To calculate relative time, hip reversal was taken as the starting point. Toe off was taken as the end point.

3) Significant difference in absolute time (SLJ vs. VJ)

4) Significant difference in relative time (SLJ or VJ vs. sport-specific jump)

5) Significant difference in absolute time (SLJ/VJ vs. sport specific jump)

Note first that unlike the data for the younger subjects (Table 1), these subjects exhibited shoulder reversal (i.e., they used their arms to assist them in jumping, something the younger subjects did not do) (see Table 2). Secondly, for the 9-year-olds and the athletes, significant differences were found in both absolute and relative timing of joint reversals. For the 9-year-olds, the differences were in the knee joint and for the two athletic groups, the differences were in the knee and shoulder joints.

When we examine the data for the sport-specific skills, we can see that the fundamental skill shares very little temporal similarity with its sport skill. Indeed for the gymnasts, there were significant *differences* in relative timing between the dive roll and the standing long jump for the knee and shoulder. For the volleyball players, their spikes were dissimilar in relative timing for the ankle, knee and shoulder.

What does this mean? In the 3-, 5- and 7-year-olds, the temporal similarities between these two styles of jumping were quite similar, but in the 9-year-olds and the two groups of athletes, the temporal structure was quite different. What has happened? One possible answer might be found by examining our descriptive data on the development of the standing long jump (Clark & Phillips, 1985). Between the ages of 7 and 9 years, we found that children begin to use their arms more "energetically". Indeed, we see active initial retraction of the scapula and increasingly larger amplitudes in arm swings. What we would suggest is that the system becomes unstable with this newly increased arm action and at some point the total pattern of co-ordination changes and a new pattern emerges. The same too would seem to occur with the sport-specific skills where both the volleyball spike and the gymnastic dive roll use the arms in very different ways than in the funda-mental skill. Of course, this is just a "story" for the moment, but it is one we feel is worth pursuing. I offer it here to demonstrate that the changing patterns of coordination we see whether they be in reaching, walking, jumping or hopping should be examined for the constraints which drive the system to instability and then into a new pattern of stability. These constraints may come from a variety of sources in both the internal and external environment.

4.   SUMMARY

In summary, I would reiterate von Hofsten's theme that the perception-action perspective is the appropriate perspective for understanding the development of motor skills. Although he might disagree, I would offer that this might best be accomplished by a marriage of the Gibsonian and Bernsteinian perspectives. Within such a combined perspective, early patterns of coordination are viewed as emergent properties of a biodynamic system requiring only the simplest of energy regulation for their start up and continuation. The changing patterns of coordination so evident in developing systems might well be examined then for those system-sensitive scaling factors which eventually would drive the system to new patterns of organisation. For as developmentalists, we surely seek to understand the principles underlying the changing patterns of coordination.

References

Bernstein, N. (1967). *The coordination and regulation of movements*.
London: Pergamon Press.

Bower, T.G.R. (1972). Object perception in infants. *Perception, 1,* 15-30.

Bower, T.G.R., Broughton, J.M. & Moore, M.K. (1970). Demonstration of
intention in the reaching behavior of neonate humans. *Nature, 228,* 679-
681.

Bower, T.G.R., Dunkeld, J. & Wishart, J.G. (1979). Infant perception of
visually presented objects. *Science, 208,* 1137-1138.

Clark, J.E. & Phillips, S.J. (1985). A developmental sequence of the
standing long jump. In J.E. Clark and J.H. Humphrey (Eds.), *Motor
Development: Current Selected Research, Vol. 1.* Princeton, N.J.:
Princeton Book.

Easton, T.A. (1972). On the normal use of reflexes. *American Scientist, 60,*
591-599.

Gelfand, I.M., Gurfinkel, V.S., Tsetlin, M.L. & Shik, M.L. (1971). Some
problems in the analysis of movements. In I.M. Gelfand, V.S. Gurfinkel,
S.V. Fomin and M.L. Tsetlin (Eds.), *Models of the structural-functional
organisation of certain biological systems.* Cambridge, MA: MIT Press.

Gelfand, I.M. & Tsetlin, M.L. (1971). Mathematical modeling of mechanisms
of the central nervous system. In I.M. Gelfand, V.S. Gurfinkel, S.V.
Fomin and M.L. Tsetlin (Eds.), *Models of the structural-functional
organization of certain biological systems.* Cambridge, MA: MIT Press.

Gibson, J.J. (1979). *The ecological approach to visual perceptions.* Boston:
Houghton Mifflin.

Hofsten, C. von (1982). Eye-hand coordination in the newborn. *Developmental
Psychology, 18,* 450-461.

Hollerbach, J. & Flash, T. (1982). Dynamic interactions between limb
segments during planar arm movements. *Biological Cybernetics, 44,* 66-77.

Jeannerod, M. (1984). The timing of natural prehension movements. *Journal
of Motor Behavior, 16,* 235-254.

Kelso, J.A.S. (1982). Concepts and issues in human motor behavior:
Coming to grips with the jargon. In J.A.S. Kelso (Ed.), *Human motor
behavior: An introduction.* Hillsdale, N.J.: Erlbaum.

Kelso, J.A.S. (1984). Phase transitions and critical behavior in human
bimanual coordination. *American Journal of Physiology, 246,* R1000-
R-1004.

Kelso, J.A.S., Southard, D. & Goodman, D. (1981). On the nature of
human interlimb coordination. *Science, 203,* 1029-1031.

Kugler, P., Kelso, J.A.S. & Turvey, M.T. (1980). On the concept of
coordinative structures as dissipative structures: I. Theoretical lines of
convergence. In G.E. Stelmach and J. Requin (Eds.), *Tutorials in
motor behavior.* Amsterdam: North-Holland.

McGraw, M. (1941). Neural maturation as exemplified in the reaching -
prehensile behavior of the human infant. *Journal of Psychology, 11,*
127-141.

Meltzoff, A.N. & Moore, M.K. (1977). Imitation of facial and manual
gestures. *Science, 198,* 75-80.

Morowitz, H.J. (1979). *Energy flow in biology.* Woodbridge, CT: Oxbow
Press.

Petersen, R. (1984). *The development of movement control parameters in
jumping.* Unpublished doctoral dissertation, University of Maryland,
College Park.

Piaget, J. (1952). *The origins of intelligence in children.* (2nd ed.).
New York: Norton.

206

Rader, N. & Stern, J.D. (1982). Visually elicited reaching in neonates. *Child Development, 53,* 1004-1007.
Reed, E.S. (1982). An outline of a theory of action systems. *Journal of Motor Behavior, 14,* 98-134.
Seefeldt, V. (1980). Developmental motor patterns: Implications for elementary school physical education. In C. Nadeau, W. Halliwell, K. Newell and G. Roberts (Eds.), *Psychology of Motor Behavior and Sport-1979.* Champaign, IL: Human Kinetics.
Thelen, E. (1984). Learning to walk: Ecological demands and phylogenetic constraints. In L.P. Lipsitt and C. Rovee-Collier (Eds.), *Advances in Infancy Research, Vol. 3.* Norwood, NJ: Ablex.
Thelen, E. (1985). Developmental origins of motor coordination: Leg movements in human infants. *Developmental Psychobiology, 18,* 1-22.
Thelen, E. & Fisher, D.M. (1983). The organization of spontaneous leg movements in newborn infants. *Journal of Motor Behavior, 15,* 353-377.
Trevarthen, C. (1984). How control of movement develops. In H.T.A. Whiting (Ed.), *Human motor actions - Bernstein reassessed.* Amsterdam: North-Holland.
Turvey, M.T. (1977). Preliminaries to a theory of action with reference to vision. In R. Shaw and J. Bransford (Eds.), *Perceiving, acting and knowing: Toward an ecological psychology.* Hillsdale, NJ: Erlbaum.
Turvey, M.T., Fitch, H.L. & Tuller, B. (1982). The Bernstein perspective: I. The problems of degrees of freedom and context-conditioned variability. In J.A.S. Kelso (Ed.), *Human motor behavior: An introduction.* Hillsdale, NJ: Erlbaum.
Waterland, J.C. & Shambes, G.M. (1970). Head and shoulder girdle linkage. *American Journal of Physical Medicine, 49,* 279-289.
White, B.L., Castle, P. & Held, R. (1964). Observations on the development of visually-directed reaching. *Child Development, 35,* 349-364.
Wickstrom, R. (1983). *Fundamental motor patterns* (3rd ed.). Philadelphia: Lea & Febiger.

SECTION 5

THE DEVELOPMENT OF INTERSUBJECTIVITY

DEVELOPMENT OF INTERSUBJECTIVE MOTOR CONTROL IN INFANTS

C. Trevarthen

INTRODUCTION: WHAT COMMUNICATING MOVEMENTS DO

Communicating movements have three features of organisation that reveal intrinsic structures and processes of the CNS of vital importance for all motor coordination: 1. They show the temporal patterning inherent in biodynamic control systems of body movement (Bernstein, 1967, 1984). The rhythms of behaviour are dependent on the output of linked physiological or biophysical oscillators (Gallistel, 1980). I shall call this aspect *kinematics*, to describe, not learned elements of gestural expression such as Birdwistell (1952, 1970) wished to identify in his 'kinesics', but the common and largely innate dimensions of neuro-motor dynamics in all kinds of expressive action, including whole body posturing, hand gestures, face expressions and vocalisations. 2. Like other motor actions, communications also vary in intensity, force or power about some modal level of optimal economy or simplicity for a given strength of motivation. This economy of energy, its distribution or entropy, can be regulated by the CNS; and it conveys essential information about the effort and vitality of motivation for movement, and the efficiency of its reafferent control. The information is carried by such features of movement as smoothness, regularity and responsiveness, and depends upon the integrated outcome of confluence in motor centres of activation from both intrinsic (spontaneous) and extrinsic (sensory) neural excitation. I shall call this aspect *energetics*. 3. Finally, different communicating movements have consistent differences in form. The brain generates shapes of expression by transforming the organs of display, organising postural, gestural, facial or vocal settings in distinct categories; not necessarily static because some forms are successions of events as in morse code. These aspects of form in communicating I call *physiognomics*. These three complementary dimensions of expressive movement form a primary level of organisation that is largely innate. They are united by processes that control serial ordering and strategic patterning of movements in adaptive sequences. The development of the latter, higher order, organisation of communication is more dependent on experience and learning.

Communication works because each individual's brain contains representations of the inertia, cohesion, topography, symmetry and polarity of *its* body and how these change with movement, and because brains can, by some means, also represent *other* bodies. Communicating brains can detect invariants in stimulation that identify one kind of objects that are other motivated individuals and they can perceive the various tempos, qualities and discrete forms of expression that each of their body parts can make as messages about motivations.

Motor control is built on the timing of cyclic engagements with the environment (Baldwin, 1894, 1902; Lashley, 1951; von Uexküll, 1957; von Holst, 1973; Neisser, 1976). Proximal and distal parts of the body are activated together in phrases or segments of activity at a certain rate, each act climaxing in a focus of information transfer or assimilation, then relaxing to a pause or equilibrium. This pattern, important for the within-subject self-control of attention, perceptual exploration, learning and skilled movement, is also essential for intersubjective or interactive control between 'self' and 'other'; indeed, motor phrasing appears often to have become accentuated in the evolution of communication, made more regular and salient to assist intercoordination. Turn-taking in communication arises from alternation of observing and expressing states and reciprocal action of the two partners (Buck, 1984).

The levels of human communication that are generated by regulated interactions between subjects, may be divided into: 1. direct interpersonal, 2. sociodramatic or play, 3. cooperative and 4. referential. These require increasing cognitive control because they are increasingly specific with regard to the external conditions for behaviour. That is, they involve the 'communicants' in more and more risky expressive enterprises requiring increasing amounts of experience and knowledge.

The primary aim of communication, even the simplest between organisms with little awareness or intelligence, is to achieve mutual motivation. Inter-actants enter into a trading of signals that will contribute to the form of their future actions. The motives and consciousness of one subject are modified by perception of the behaviour of the other subject. Unlike other kinds of movement where the subject is engaged in action relative to a physical world that is incapable of psychological reaction, communication movements are made with preparation for a possible reaction by another subject to the mental content of the movements. Communication is about mental contents.

In direct interpersonal engagements between humans, expressions of emotion regulate an intimate mutual timing and qualitative attunement of the most fundamental motive states, including perhaps, but not necessarily, autonomic states related to maintenance of vital functions. In play, the forms and energy of actions within a shared context, and the motor style or strategy of capture, mobilisation or transformation of objects, giving them a 'feeling of' evaluation or purpose, must be decoded and reacted to by the players in jokes and games. Displays of orienting, attending, or withdrawal, and expressions of surprise, pleasure, displeasure or other emotion, assist coordination of subjects to each other and to the shared environment. When subjects cooperate they must read one another's minds concerning the reasons and purposes behind doing things with objects or behind acting in the common environment in a particular way. They must contribute matching and complementary acts towards a common purpose in the world.

Linguistic communication goes further; its movements designate and describe or evaluate ideas of objects or events free of present circumstances. The symbols of languages are learned by a process of emotional referencing that gives focal cognitive states (acts, decisions, experiences) value and meaning while they are being shared and this fixes them in a memory of a common code of referential signals. Momentary fusion of motivational adaptations in child and parent, or pupil and teacher, to objects or events in their common world ensures retention in memory of specific words for those things. In this way a common semantics and a shared lexicon are built up. Underneath all syntactic forms of language are the structures that link messages with the interpersonal motives (Lyons, 1977). These structures determine the underlying timing, spatio-temporal sequencing and emotional colouring of linguistic messages, whatever their reference and whatever their medium of expression.

In summarising the developments in communication from birth to the start of language I shall emphasise the role of innate emotions that arise in interpersonal contact. These states of person-to-person response appear to be necessary to organisation of a child's practical intelligence and thinking, which are designed to develop with the aid of sympathetic responses of caretakers. Motivators for communication are, I propose, among the primary morphogenetic regulators of growing cognitive structures in the brain. Developmental psychologists, both behaviourists and contemporary cognitivists, have, with some notable exceptions, been led to overlook this central component of human mental growth by concentrating artificially on the individual child's attainment, as an isolated subject-agent, of rational problem-solving mastery of stimulus information about external physical conditions for moving. At the root of the problem is the artificial separation of cognitions and emotions imposed by a dualistic philosophy.

BODY FORM, MOTOR PROGRAMS, ACTION PLANS AND MAPS FOR THEM IN THE BRAIN

Starting with Bernstein (1967, 1984) we can describe a general force economy for locomotor and tool-using behaviours and attempt to separate intracerebral patterning by neurones of muscle force from the moulding or limitation of movement by the peripheral inertia, elasticity, etc. of the body, or by forces of impact between the external world and the body. We can examine the role of proprioceptive and ex-afferent stimulation in the timing and shape of movements, and seek evidence that the CNS can provide standards of pulse, activity and form for movements independently of patterns in sensory feedback.

In coordinated motor activity, orderly changes of force flow through the mechanisms of the body such that smooth displacements of different members are formed into precisely-timed successions of counter-balanced or synchronised figures of movement. Counteracting forces kept in equilibrium maintain the body at rest, and when the body is in motion its masses are actively propelled within a controlled margin of disequilibrium between the forces round joints. Physical forces arising outside the body and forces inside its peripheral tissues and machinery that are not directly caused by muscle contractions are met by muscle forces that are precisely timed and measured as a consequence of neural excitation. Excessive concentrations of force in the body are avoided by compliant displacements of the parts that would be hit.

Movements have different rates and periodicities depending upon how far they involve only distal body segments, proximal and distal segments or the whole body as one kinetic system. Different fields or modes of afferent regulation, including both proprioceptors and the special distance receptors, can inform about the body or the outside world either separately or in concert. In the end the remarkable efficiency of skillful movements requires synchronisation of all the different body parts to one beat, plus precisely

defined rhythmic sequences of movements in members appropriate to their
various kinetic potentialities (Shaffer, 1982).

Motor coordination requires anticipatory transformations of excitatory
discharge generated from motor centres, and anticipatory timings and
orientations of receptor systems that draw stimulus energy into the
integrative process. As was made clear by the classical researches of
Brown, von Holst, Weiss and Sperry (Gallistel, 1980), the coordination
cannot be explained in terms of triggering of pre-wired reflex sensory-
motor loops driven by stimuli. Neural oscillators, servo systems and
hierarchical control schemes in brain anatomy are needed. In other words,
coordination requires 'biodynamic structures' (Bernstein, 1967/1984) that
generate, control and channel the processing of information from the
environment (Trevarthen, 1978, 1984a).

With or without benefit of concurrent proprioceptive feedback on how
forces are developing in the soft tissues and around joints between bones,
motor programming requires some latent anatomico-functional formula or
image in the CNS of the body and its kinetic future with respect to a
specified goal; this is Bernstein's 'motor image'. There is no other way to
explain the efficiency and regularity of motor coordination, or the flexible
adaptation of muscular activity to solve even simple motor problems, let
alone to serve cognitive 'ideas'. There must be orderly neural systems that
can formulate dynamic *programs* in the present to define future relationships, in body space and body time, between nerve activity exciting
muscles, sensory input giving information on the consequences of this
activity and the resultant form of behaviour.

Bernstein discusses how motor images of the CNS regulate forces of
muscular contraction in kinematic chains with many degrees of freedom to
obtain regular forms of movement that adapt to different environmental
circumstances. He offers the concept of an integrated *ecphorator* or output
drive system that governs the distribution of excitatory activity leaving the
CNS while maintaining appropriate readiness for sensory guidance, as
the conductor of an orchestra urges musicians to contribute their actions on
the beat and with appropriate quality and emphasis while he watches and
listens to the overall effect. Bernstein notes that while jointed limbs move
in synchrony or alternation, there is a programmatic flow of forces from
proximal to distal segments down each limb, doubtless preceded by serial
activation of motor neurones in some somatotopic array within the brain.
The resultant unification and programmatic unfolding of movements is clear,
but it is not necessary that these features arise at one place in CNS
structures. They may be created through mutual assimilation, clustering or
tuning of a number of similar and sympathetic oscillatory regulators (Weiss,
1941; von Holst, 1937, 1973; Hamburger, 1973).

Large scale behavioural projects to exploit the environment require
ecphoresis with regard to a conception of changing circumstances for
movement of the whole organism through time and space, as a conductor is
guided through a musical work by a real or memorised score. This future
plan of body action, preparing adjustments to the heterogenous matter
over or through which navigation will soon take place, must also be conveyed
through ordered neural arrays that can distinguish and relate all the
positions and configurations of the body that may be required. For harmoniou
evolution of the collective forces of movement in the body, and for orienting
and steering the body with reference to the perceived layout of external

media and objects, or any events changing this, an organised matrix of neural body images is indispensible. Thus we are led to the conclusion that efficient motor coordination is a product of neuroembryological events that lay out a pattern of nerve cell networks in the brain to represent an active body in contact with the world and its opportunities or affordances. Arbib (1984) comes to a similar conclusion regarding the basis for motor co-ordination.

In fact, *somatotopic* (body mapping) orderings of neural elements are found abundantly at all levels of the CNS (Trevarthen, 1972, 1974a, 1986a). In integrative centers of brain stem (especially the midbrain reticular formation, cerebellum and tectum), as well as in integrative tissues of the cerebrum, they take the form, not of isomorphic somatotopic reflections of peripheral body structures, but of whole body transformations of these, i.e. *telotopic* (direction mapping) fields (Trevarthen, 1968a, b, 1980a). When stimulated, either naturally by focal sensory input from one patch of cells in any one of a set of equivalent receptor arrays, or artificially by an electric or chemical pulse from a probe inserted in the brain, these teletopic fields produce movements that aim the whole body coherently along one direction from a single orientational reference center on the body's axis of symmetry. Just about every skeletal muscle of the body may be involved in such an orientation. It is also the case that ordered neural fields in the projection systems of the brain are organised prenatally in relation to the bisymmetric, polarised and dorso-ventrally differentiated body (Trevarthen, 1986a).

The hind brain and cerebellum appear to be dedicated to 'computation' of adjustments of the inertial equilibria between moving body parts, taking in proprioceptive and exproprioceptive data on the masses and accelerations of body segments and the whole ensemble to maintain coherent and economical distributions of force and displacement. The cerebellum appears to be a central structure in motor memories that formulate habitual behaviour sequences of maximum efficiency and with the benefit of many proprioceptive and exproprioceptive modalities of perception, including vision. In the neural arrays of parietal cerebral cortex, co-orientations of head and eyes and limbs are related together with respect to one 'extrapersonal' (extra-corporal) space that, with the L/R reversed map of a multimodal telotopic 'behaviour space' in the midbrain, places locations to the left of the body in the right hemisphere, and *vice versa* (Mountcastle, 1975). More ambitious intentional plans, directing the subject through a succession of effective encounters with the world, are evidently formulated with contributions from the basal ganglia, thalamus, supplementary motor area and frontal cortex (Kornhuber, 1974; Goldberg, 1986). These plans are enriched by learned conceptions that are stored in temporal and frontal cortices with strong input from limbic structures (Mishkin, 1982).

Anatomical regularities in the synaptic fields and projection systems of the brain that correlate with the programs and plans for action, give direct evidence of the contribution that neuroembryological processes make to the development of effective and adaptive behaviour. They show that coordinations of movement are the result of phylogenetic adaptation of morphogenesis in the CNS to a living regulation of transactions with the environment, and these anticipatory coordinations, which I call *motives* (Trevarthen, 1982a), provide a foundation for selection of more specific adaptive schemata or structures through learning.

Besides representing potential efforts and displacements of the body, charting body action in a geography of surroundings, brain maps also define a field of evaluative relationships with the world as a resource for life. The anatomical layout of neural systems defines, on the one hand, *orientational* and *appetitive* movements that can vary the placement, configuration and alignment of the body in the world and, on the other hand, *consummatory* moves that can exchange matter between the body and the environment (Trevarthen, 1968a). The body form itself of any land vertebrate is adapted to the requirements of a life of action in reference to a rich and varied mental image of the environment. Rotations of the head, and of the eyes and ears in the head, obtain the necessary telotopic adjustment to an external goal – then transport of the head brings the consummatory organ (mouth) to the goal. Olfactory, gustatory and somesthetic organs surrounding or in the mouth permit judgements to be made as to the quality and value (to the subject's internal economy) of an object to be picked up, bitten, eaten or ejected. In animals with necks, muscles of the head and face have 'capital' importance for orientational, scanning and consummatory movements. The distal parts of prehensile limbs are accessories to the midline consummatory organs. Hands, feet, tails or trunks co-orient with head and eyes and can seize and manipulate, then transport what they hold to the mouth. The consummatory actions associated with reproduction (mating, feeding of the young, etc.) and those involved in fight and attack (biting, clawing, etc.) will obey similar principles of organisation relative to body form (von Holst & von Saint Paul, 1963).

Bernstein, and the same is true for nearly all students of motor co-ordination, does not deal at all with the evaluative aspect of motor transactions between the moving animal and the world. But, for the modern ethologist, as for his predecessor in the 19th Century, the distinctions between exploratory, orienting and consummatory activities are fundamental (Craig, 1918; Tinbergen, 1951). The instinctive behaviour patterns of animals that ethologists study are adapted to produce cycles of engagement and disengagement with the world's resources, including resources, such as gametes, that reside in the bodies of other organisms.

Consummatory actions attempt to have direct control over all effects from the environment that might change the body's state and integrity. They are coordinated with autonomic processes by which the CNS maintains metabolic, reproductive, restorative, and excretive functions of the tissues and vital organs or systems and with 'hedonic' evaluation of the risks and benefits of consummatory acts. The aim and power of moves to affect appetitive approach or defensive withdrawal are regulated by advance assessments that project valences of positive or negative 'reinforcement' into the perceptions of objects in the environment that is yet distant from the body. Both the forms of body movement and their intensity or energy are regulated by internal appetitive or restorative processes that involve the autonomic system and the reticular core of the brain.

The central dynamic of motivation that regulates both the intensity and the aiming of consummatory action was defined by Hess as a balance between environment-directed and self-directed functions. He used electrical stimulation of the brain stem to identify opposing anatomical systems. One produced arousal, increased muscle strength, active psychic alertness and exploration; he called this *ergotropic* and identified it with stimulation of the posterior hypothalamus. The other induced behaviours promoting rest, recuperation, low body activity but high visceral processing, apathy, relaxation and sleep - a state he named *trophotropic* and linked to anterior hypothalamic stimulation. Later work by Hess, Kluver and Bucy, MacLean, Pribram and Olds implicated an extensive system of brain stem and limbic cortex in this same regulation of motivations, appetites and sexuality (Hess, 1964; Olds, 1962; Valenstein, 1973).

For our enquiry into the early postnatal development of intersubjective coordinations, it is important that some order, as in the foregoing, can be put into a description of movements by recognition of the systematic patterns of control which inherent structures in the CNS impose on the body's motor activity. In summary: movements have coordinated timing, somatically programmed unfolding of form and organism-related evaluation of goals. These features give three complementary expressions to the inherent, anatomical and functional organisation of motor control within the brain.

IMPLICIT TEMPORO-SPATIAL UNITY OF ACTION AND ITS INTERMITTENT PLURIMODAL CONTROL BY COMPLEMENTARY PERCEPTUAL SYSTEMS

Typically, then, behaviour is segmented into discrete moves that are adjusted to fit conditions inside and outside the body. A subject takes steps to achieve a particular chain of effects, taking in sensory stimulation intermittently to verify a prediction that the circumstances for action are propitious before movement begins, conveniently supportive of the action once it starts, and capable of satisfying the goal on completion of the act. A cycle of control is established that the CNS can change by varying the motor output in relation to a schema of the expected input.

The rate and volume of input can be varied continuously or intermittently by change in action. A smooth act that applies force against media outside the body with perfect economy of muscular effort requires complete prediction of forces assimilated to the act from the periphery. A misjudgement requires energy-expending correction after sensory detection of the error. When some continuously changing event has to be tracked or matched by movement, errorless action can only be assured if the brain can completely predict the pattern of change; otherwise periodic error correction can be achieved by intermittent moving ahead to meet the event segment by segment, with varying degrees of dependence on sensory feedback.

Most behaviour does not encounter substrates or track events with perfect prediction, and free action is usually not continuous even when all motor problems have been solved and segments of action are smooth and economical. The inevitable intrinsic periodicity of moving is coupled to phasic regulation of perceptual processing.

These simple principles of intentional behaviour raise the question of coordination between receptor modalities that receive stimulation separately from different forms of energy. Every intentional performance is open to regulation by a collection of perceptual modalities. Proprioceptors are more concerned with the internal mechanics of body coordination, some exteroceptors are directed to pick up information about the present or future relationship of body displacement and limb action to the stable outside world, and others are concerned with selecting, identifying and tracking evaluated goal objects that may be in motion relative to the stable background (Lee, 1978, 1980). Interoceptors test for possible effects of materials on the inner functions of the body, nociceptors measure tissue damage, etc.

The regular pulse of whole body action, making steps to displace or
orient in the environment *(total orientations* of the body), will automatically synchronise the beat of input in all modalities stimulated. It will also
drive variations in stimulation along the same profiles of change, as when
the size and intensity of visual and auditory images increase synchronously
and vary in parallel with approach of a single visible and audible thing
towards the subject.

Orienting movements of parts of the body *(partial orientations)* seek
to concentrate sensory input in receptor parts with high resolving power
but limited spatial fields (e.g. the fovea, subtending 3°). When independently mobile receptors make selective telescopic amplification of data from one
small patch of the external world, special muscular activity intervenes to
converge receptor centres on the appropriate piece of information. For
example, bi-foveal fixation, on a small visual target that is motionless or
displacing slowly, to resolve detail subtending a few minutes of arc, is
accompanied by stabilisation of the head, reduction in general body
movements, and fine coordination of extra- and intra-ocular muscle activity
to vary the registration and contrast of two foveal images (see Lee, this
volume). Conjugate eye saccades and vergence and accommodation adjustments
consist of periodic step-like resettings of muscle tensions in or round the
two eyes, and though the steps are accomplished at differing rates (saccadic
eye rotations in about $1/20$ second; vergence, accommodation and head
rotations in about ½ second), all the eye movements are closely coupled.

The oculo-motor neurones must be driven by a coherent neural
oscillator that, furthermore, may command or link up with other oscillators
to synchronise or coordinate with the beat of activity and sensory feedback in other body parts, such as an arm and hand, that can act in precise
concert with the eyes. Movements of hands and eyes at the same moment and
the same place automatically lead to coincidence of focal experiences in
touch, sight and sound. Orienting, approach, capture and inspection of an
object will produce an ordered succession of concentrations of sensory input
in various proprioceptive and exproprioceptive modalities. Consummatory
acts (e.g. picking up something and eating it) involve confluence of
exteroceptive and interoceptive stimulations.

The processes of perceptual or cognitive association that identify
phenomenal goals by which behaviour is directed, and that define the logic
or strategy of effective action, however they may be elaborated or refined
by learning, clearly take origin in such largely inherent motor coordinations
by which the receptors are displaced conjugately relative to the informational
array of stimuli. The CNS also primes reception by changing the thresholds,
resolving capacity etc. of sensory systems so that they will function more
efficiently in picking up information that will assist direction of behaviour.
Intrinsic attention processes are important even in the early stages of
development of sensory tissues. There is recent physiological evidence that
intersensory associations are selected automatically, in both development and
learning, with the aid of an intracerebral reinforcing input to central
perceptual post-synaptic fields where inputs converge, the reinforcement
coming from reticular neurones that also coordinate movements of perceptual
focussing (Singer, 1984; Imbert, 1985). Adaptive space-mapping and
feature-detecting or object-recognising systems are formed by a selective
retention process that accepts votes from inside as well as outside the brain.
In other words, an intrinsic directing of activation or attention guides
perceptual learning, as it coordinates exploratory movements of convergence

between complementary receptors.

The above discovery changes the perspective of research on development and learning, shifting attention from the association of stimulus effects through patterns of experience to questions about the motivating processes that set up intrinsic evaluations and screen stimuli for 'higher order' invariants in stimuli, i.e. invariants that bear no simple relationship to physical dimensions of energy or to the geometric layout of stimulus arrays that can excite ordered fields of receptor cells. Time and space in experience are laid down in the properties and arrangements of interneurones in the central core of the brain, which is already structured at birth (Scheibel, 1984). Patterns and pulses of movement organised in the brain before their afferent consequences are assimilated, serve as a common framework for co-activation of separate parts of the body. Fundamental categories of colour, absolute object size, salient types of sound, supra- or multi-modal structures, textures, and forms of objects identified as separate from their surroundings, can likewise be determined in brain morphogenesis to have specific value in guiding specific forms of action adaptively to their goals in the environment. Certain qualities and configurations of exteroceptive data will be anticipated in inherent motivational and autonomic states that project evaluations on particular forms of experience and define goals for consummatory acts. Finally, slow changes in central motive states, generated in the reticular core of the brain, may set the basis for retrospective and prospective reorganisations of experience, guiding both learning and remembering.

There is much predictable structure in the motivations that underly behavioural transactions between the brain and the world. How much of this is available for communication early in life? Obviously, some patterns of motivation are easier for a partner to follow than others. While simple behaviours consist of short claims of orienting and consummatory steps, in the course of both the learning and the execution of any complex plan of behaviour a subject will perform many cycles of analytical observation and executive commitment. Complex problem-solving behaviours will be built up by the interlocking of separately generated motor programs. Some actions will constitute exchangeable or optional moves in larger frames of movement by which the subject establishes or stabilises a context. These principles of organisation in exploratory and performatory behaviour will extend to the most elaborate intentional performance. They offer an abundance of invariant motor effects that an observer can use to gain some insight into how the performer is thinking about a task and what he is intending to do.

Further specification of the chronography and logic of intelligent behaviour would not be appropriate here. Hopefully the above outline will make clear what is meant by the *a priori* and dependable organisation in actions that an observer might use to get evidence about how brain systems in another person are treating information to control actions. Some of this rich organisation may be present in an infant at birth to facilitate the caretaker's comprehension of the infant's motive states. The infant's brain could also provide a receiver structure that the infant that can use to resonate, mirror or engage with corresponding patterns of output in an adult.

SOME SPECIAL MOTOR PROBLEMS IN ENGAGEMENTS BETWEEN SUBJECTS

To achieve communication, movements (or secretions) of one animal become stimuli for another. But even the simplest sign stimulus in one requires assimilation to a behaviour-releasing mechanism in the other. Nothing will be achieved if the motivation of the latter organism is not changed. In most cases, communicative acts stimulate a multiple awareness; the actor (emitter) has means of perceiving the signal proprioceptively or exproprioceptively, while observers or audience (receivers) can bring their motivation in line with the expressed feeling or purpose by a special kind of exteroception that deserves its own name. We shall call it *alteroception*; an awareness for communication that will depend upon specific cerebral response to the kinematic, energetic and physiognomic aspects of body movements that carry information about motives in another subject.

Let us propose that communication systems have evolved by modification of self-regulatory processes built into organised neural systems. Proprioceptive, interoceptive and exteroceptive functions will be coordinated by the motor structures already discussed. Any perception of the correspondence between the separate proprioception and interception in two selves and alteroception in their communication with each other will depend upon detection of invariants of stimulation that these two avenues of perception share because they relate to the same motive structures.

For communication to work, it is certainly not essential for the signals to sender and receiver to be received in the same modality. The sender may simply emit without gaining any information from reafference, or the signal may be carried as a permanent part of the structure of that species' body. Then the motivation for emitting a move to present the signal will be simply matched or complemented by the effect it has on the motivation of the other animal. Even in such a simple case, effective communication depends upon a pre-established correspondence of forms of motive, each motive having both an effector side (causing a postural setting, orientation or signalling movement) and a receptor side (noticing the relevant signal from another animal) (Figure 1).

In the evolution of more elaborate mental partnerships in higher animals, many features of self-regulatory or autonomic behaviour, and many kinds of consummatory act, including actions of feeding, self-grooming and searching, have become incorporated into 'ritualised' signals of communication (Tinbergen, 1952).

Intersubjectivity, defined as communication between conscious and intending beings, requires coordination between evolving states of attention, changing emotions and cognitive adjustments, including such subtle varieties of mental adjustment as recognition, decision, doubt or rejection. It involves coordination of intentions by means of signals that convey the directions and intensities of actions *before* they are executed, when they are still purposes in the making that can only be detected through their autonomic, attentional and postural antecedents.

We can give some account of how exteroceptive, exproprioceptive and proprioceptive systems collaborate in making possible smoothly coordinated movements of well-conceived locomotion, prehension and the like that will have just the right impact on the world at the right time to control a well-planned progress of behaviour and culminate in intelligently intended actions. To understand communication between intending human subjects we have to add to this a description of how the senses of one being assimilate information onto motor plans that are working to anticipate the replies, evasions, co-

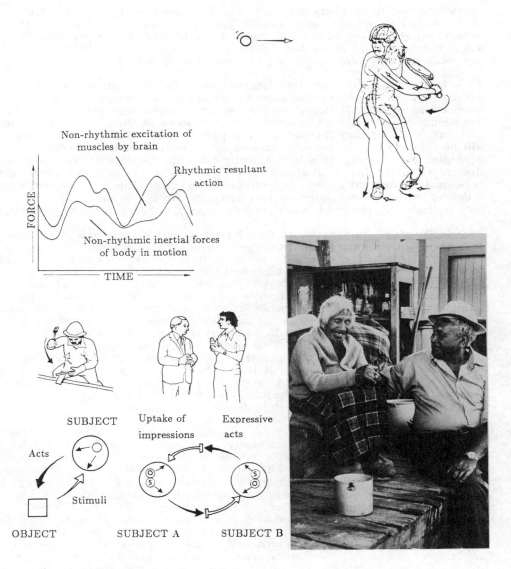

Fig. 1. An individual's control of perception and movement must coordinate events in the body, its brain and their outside world. The brain represents the evolving difference between desired and achieved states of the body's engagement with forces and masses of the environment.

Subject-object and subject-subject engagements are fundamentally different. Two brains/bodies can engage in mutual psychological regulation. In communication A and B each represent both A and B., 'self' (s) and 'other' (o).
(Photo by Marty Friedlander, New Zealand).

operations and antagonisms and such like of another being. Every act of communication anticipates some specific appropriate range of effects on the communicative motives of another, even if the individual who performs the act is not monitoring this effect. Close communication at this level is impossible without joint monitoring of each actor by the other.

We are led to conclude that interpersonal, intersubjective, empathic and cooperative behaviours between human beings are regulated by a special form of organisation of motives in their brains that permits 'mirroring' of each self by another. Motive systems in them are sensitive to patterns of information that designate a partner who, with like sensitivity, will be affected by the gestures and expressions that motives generate. The perceptuo-motor mechanisms of communication must 'represent', and 'organise' the unfolding, not just of the behaviour of one subject, but of an interaction between two coherently motivated selves. Some philosophers, concerned with religious and moral questions, have clearly specified this need, for consciousness of 'self' and 'other' in relationship (Buber, 1937; Macmurray, 196

In language, information is transferred to define ideas and experiences that people in communication cannot perceive from the common pragmatic stuation of objects and of actions being performed. Language makes reference to objects or events that are not present, and such reference has to be drawn out of a linguistic code that is 'in' the language users. Control of communication at this level involves solving many problems of motivational ambiguity – there are many possible states of a subject, many possible actions, many possible interests, recollections, purposes, emotions, as well as an infinity of things that could be referred to outside the present circumstances (Habermas, 1972). As with control of behaviour for a conscious subject planning the effects of movements of different parts of his or her body well in advance of their execution, but even more so, control of intersubjective communication at the level of language will benefit from an economy of 'carrier structure' in motivation. There has to be an intersubjective coordinator like Bernstein's ecphorator.

It is not surprising, therefore, to discover that vocal expressions in speech have the same hierarchical kinematic structure as gestures or head movements with which they may be synchronised (Buck, 1984; Feldstein, 1972; Jaffe & Feldstein, 1970). Kinematics of this behaviour must be set up by a system of pulsemakers or coupled oscillators in the human brain that together provide a necessary temporal foundation for the coordination and control of a motor program that moves several body parts with different dimensions and inertial characteristics. These oscillators, or highly refined levels of the system of coupled oscillators, have been taken over to serve the coordination, and sensory guidance, of the exceptionally rapid movement sequences in communicative interactions between speaking subjects.

As we have seen, intracoordination between the body parts of a moving subject requires more than synchronisation of climaxes of movement. It also requires chaining and grouping of forces to create smooth continuation or strategic interruption of the patterns of movement while they are kept regulated in maximum kinematic simplicity. The same is true for inter-coordination between communicating subjects. It may be impossible for rapid-ly changing purposes, feelings or ideas to be shared between subjects unless the patterning of their movements can be brought into close harmony by a process of resonance or sympathetic tuning. The evidence from analysis of adult interactions is that the coincidence of movement patterns in two communicating persons may be extraordinarily tight and complete (Feldstein & Welkowitz, 1978; Buck, 1984). The movements of speaker and listener may, like those of a dancer and partner, become as closely coordinated as the movements between parts of one body. This matching or resonance in a partnership of action is not achieved by reflexive coincidence - it involves guided predictive tuning and active engagement and disengagement. Mirror coordinative states are set up that share regulation of the movement of both parties between them.

Michotte (1950, 1962) ascribes perception of emotions and intentions to just such an empathy for the intrinsic psychic causes of differently timed actions and expressions, which leads these psychic causes to be perceived directly by a person who sees the actions and expressions. Runeson and Frykholm (1981) have shown that an observer can identify with the effort of someone else picking up an object of unknown weight from the kinematic profile of their movement. This perception can produce an accurate judgement of the weight being picked up when all that is seen is displacement of a set of lights attached to the lifted object. Johansson (1975) demonstrated that light arrays carried by persons moving in the dark are immediately perceived as bodies dancing, walking, turning, etc., their form being directly perceived. It would appear likely that the neural basis for such direct alteroceptive perception of feelings and intentions in movements is closely related to the neural systems that are responsible for perceptuo-motor intracoordinations of one subject, but new channels of reafferent regulation will have been established so that the subject that can tap and draw on invariant evidence for control in the perceived movements of another subject.

Physiognomic resemblance or likeness in form between static expressive configurations of another body and the subject's own body gives a different basis for human empathy. This will have evolved from the somatotopic mapping of body into the nervous system, rather than from mapping in terms of motor kinetics. The physiognomic code of face expressions, voice settings, gestures and postures provides a direct means for transmitting qualities of a steady state of motivation in the integrated core of one brain to another brain. In a sense, expressions of emotion actually regulate the neurotransmitter balance that also changes when a subject's moods or emotions change, thus permitting tuning of neuropharmacological and emotional states between brains. The face or voice of anger can generate fear, and the face or voice of affection can trigger joy, with appropriate accompanying autonomic changes (Ekman, Levenson & Friesen, 1983). This fine tuning of emotional states is also vital for language for it enables the evaluation of objects to be specified and thus is essential to define meanings for symbols of objects.

One function of non-verbal communication is the transmission of emotional states (Buck, 1984), and another is the coordination of timing in movement between people engaged in joint cooperative or competitive action, as when they dance, play sport or fight. Motor coordination in emotional expression is a neglected field. Recently considerable effort has been put into describing the physiognomics of facial expression of emotion (Ekman & Friesen, 1978; Izard, 1979) and variation of voice setting to express feelings has received some attention (Crystal, 1973; Laver, 1980; Scherer, 1981). How feelings are coded in kinematics remains very obscure. Here, poetry and music offer a rich but still mysterious source of data.

Musical communication covers a fascinating range of human expressive action and its perception. Sometimes music expresses clear representations that describe things in the world outside human motives, but all music carries a message of human feeling for movement. All music transforms a simple beat into a rhythmic and melodic stream with which a listener can empathise. There are elaborate traditional forms and rules in music, but common features indicate that humans possess the same basic structures for feeling movement and emotion in sound (Blacking, 1976).

The temporal basis of music is illustrated well by the fragments of performances by Australian aborigines shown in Figure 2. These sounds are made with resonant instruments that have no articulated parts. Hardwood rods mark the beat with sharp clicks. The didjeridu is a long hollow log that is skillfully played by creating a continuous deeply pitched resonance, uninterrupted by breathing, that is varied by rhythmic movement of throat, tongue and lips. Occasional loud 'toots' are made by vibrating the lips as in trumpet playing. It appears that the pulsing beat serves as a framework for intricately varying rhythms. Dramatic development is achieved by varying the setting of the beat (tempo), by slight changes around the beat (rubato), by sharp transformations of rhythm and by an overlay of singing with rapid chanting or long wailing calls with precisely regulated rises and falls in pitch, some very slow and gradual over many seconds.

It is interesting that, in these examples, the most frequent beat is close to the middle range of a metronome (moderato = about 108 to 120 per minute = one beat every 500 to 550 msec; 1/450 msec. is allegro). The underlying rhythms of didjeridu playing are limited by the rate at which deep and middle parts of the vocal apparatus can be oscillated (2-4/sec). Much faster are the intricate rhythms of chanting that performers at corroborees do without musical instruments. In the example shown, rapid speech and nonsense sounds, including periodic bursts of vibration with the tip of the tongue at c.20/sec, make a staccato tapestry of syllables at the upper range of speech articulation rates. But note that the beat of this performance remains close to that of the much more expansive didjeridu performance. I present these exotic examples of complex traditional adult music as a standard for comparison with temporal structures that emerge as universals and absolutes in vocal communication and clapping with infants and mothers (see below).

Any musical performance will exhibit precise control of timing and elaborate regulation of physiognomic or melodic patterns in rhythm, pitch and harmony. In much the same way, human speech, writing and typing exhibit rich variation in physiognomic forms (syllables, words, etc.) carried on an adjustable beat in a limited range with considerable rhythmic variation and changes in emphasis or intention, some according to certain learned rules but most unconsciously determined (Shaffer, 1982). It seems that the regularities represent, on the one hand, important features of inherent coordinative structures in the brains of performing individuals, and, on the other hand, cultivated skills in intercoordination of forms of expressive movement that give these innate features of beat, rhythm and tonal quality special markedness. Intercoordination of musicians, soloists and accompanists, members of an ensemble, conductors and musicians, is based on beat and on variations in rhythmic emphasis, 'size' or effort around the beat (Clayton, 1985). The flow of feelings is also carried by the shifting melodic line, but this, too, is tightly coupled to the beat.

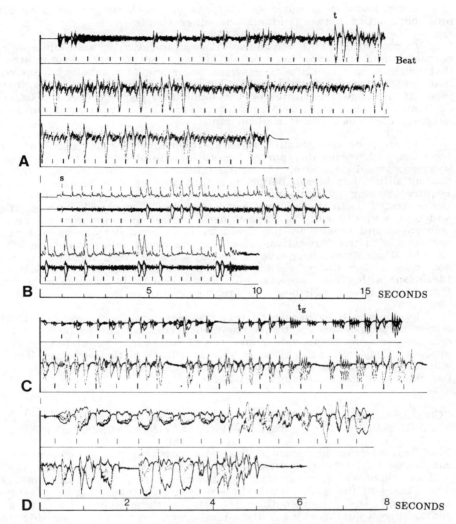

Fig. 2. Aborigine music; body movements and sounds 'in time'.
A: Didjeridu solo. Beat interval accelerates gradually from
525 to 470 msec; loud "toot" noises (t) create rhythmic
patterns round the beat. B: Didjeridu and sticks (s) marking
the beat (interval 450 msec). Overlay of wailing chant lasting
approximately 15 seconds. C: Mouth sounds. Regular beat
interval of 480 msec faintly marked by hand clapping (c).
Elaborate syncopation with bursts of tongue fluttering (tg).
D: Rhythmic mouth sounds, beat interval 456 msec. E:
Sonogram of the portion marked* of the chant in C.
Beat interval 440-450 msec.

In all figures the beat is marked by vertical lines. All
recordings are filtered to remove frequencies below 150 Hz.

These features of music may help us approach the problems of motor intercoordination between infants and other people.

To recapitulate: All psychological communication is built upon a resonance and mirroring between closely matched perceptuo-motor structures that generate and identify expressions according to a scheme of motives that subjects share. Development of advanced communication skills, notably those of language, elaborates on the foundation process, but the basic mechanism evident in animals seems to remain as the core motivator in mature human communication of all kinds.

It might be thought that infants, constrained by limitations of their immature and presumably partly-formed and unreliable central nervous systems, would depend on the crudest kinesic principles for empathic contact with other human beings and that physiognomic resonance will require learning by trial and error. However, recent research has demonstrated a surprising regularity of timing in neonatal communication and that a wide variety of physiognomic indices of motivation can be generated and sensitively perceived by newborns. It looks as though infants are born with the foundations of a complete empathic machinery in effective functional condition. Progressive developments in communication attest a controlled elaboration of cerebral systems for representing coordination of the infant with other subjects, but the general basis appears to be present from birth. It may well begin to function before birth.

Evidence will be presented that the early stages of development in human communication are tightly controlled from within the brain of the child. Developments procede under the direction of a regulated growth process. They are not arbitrarily reinforced associations of experiences gained by chance, or impressions of a design that originates wholly outside the child and enters through social learning.

COORDINATION OF EXPRESSIONS BETWEEN MOTHER AND INFANT IN THE SECOND MONTH: THE FABRIC OF PRIMARY INTERSUBJECTIVITY

The selection in Figure 3 illustrates some expressive behaviours in one female infant 34 days after a late birth (47 weeks Gestational Age), as well as responses of her mother and the resultant intercoordinations. When first placed in the chair the infant was restless, then distressed, struggling, and crying. The mother soothed her with rhythmic sounds and intermittent gentle speech and touching, attempting unsuccessfully to 'over-ride' the crying with regular, long utterances that had a downfalling pitch. Her mother seemed to intend to soothe as well as distract or break open the self-perpetuating complaining. She lifted the infant from the chair, held her close to her body and patted her (3 to 4/second). Then bounced her gently (1.5 to 2.0/second). All the mothers' movements were finely controlled and smooth, giving the infant's body gentle accelerations at regular intervals. The infant became relaxed and still.

In a few minutes the infant, now awake and calm, was placed in the chair. The mother caught her attention with a small suspended ball and the infant attempted to reach. Then the mother attempted to 'chat' with the body. Sitting in front with her eyes about the level of the infant's head, she leaned forward to place her face in front of the baby at c. 35 cm. She began a repeating musical baby talk in a questioning tone, interrupted from

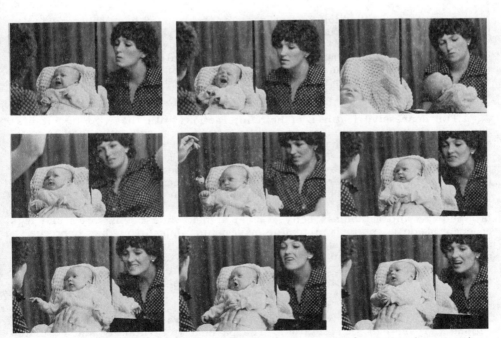

Fig. 3. Mother-infant interaction at one-and-a-half months (see text).

time to time by soft hissing sounds, clicking of her tongue or whistling (4/second). The mother's voice was relaxed and 'breathy'.

Before the sequence shown in Figure 4A the mother of a second infant days of age (47 weeks gestational age) made many utterances each less than a second in length and with pauses of 1 to 1.25 seconds. This is typical baby-talk to a young infant. The illustrated portion shows the regular duration of sounds (0.5 to 0.75 sec.), even spacing (every 1.8 seconds) and the singing modulation of pitch along U-shaped contours. Each rising or falling glide in pitch occupied approximately 0.25-0.3 seconds. The infant's fixed gaze on the mother's face was at first still with intermittent knit brow and jaw drop. Then smile, prespeech, moving arm and hands, raising the right more than the left. Eventually the infant emitted periodic coos – mostly single sounds 0.2 to 0.3 sec. in length.

The interaction illustrated shows precisely timed turntaking, the infant being excited by the beat of mother's repeated utterances to make a reply that was exactly placed to fit in the space between two of the mother's utterances. This resonant coo was articulated by a movement closing the back of the tongue against the soft palate while the mouth was wide open then its release of sound as the lips protruded to make a round tubular cavity. The two sounds (/a gu/), each lasting 200 msec., required precise coordination of a controlled phonation in the speech range (dominant frequency 200-300 Hz) with movements of lips, tongue and jaw. They are evidently made by motor programs basically the same as those used in simple syllables in adult speech. Note, however, that at this age the infant does not articulate vocal emissions with the lips and tip of the tongue, only with the back of the tongue and palate.

After this vocalisation the mother, on the beat of her earlier periodic utterances, imitated the infant's sound with two syllables longer than the infant's and uttered with a falling pitch, then made two more falling sounds at double her previous periodicity. That is, she uttered three sounds in succession leaving no pause or unoccupied beat for the infant. Overlapping with the mother's second vacalisation in this series the infant made a second coo (/gu/).

Two impressive features of both interactions with these young infants are the elaborate coordination of many parts of each subject's body in expressive movements (intracoordinations) and the precise combination of movements between them (intercoordination). The mother moved her face towards the infant as she vocalised and accompanied her utterances with nodding movements of her head and eyebrow movements. She tilted her head and made varied sympathetic expressions when the infant moved, also occasionally touching the infant. The infant observed her with a knit brow, dropped jaw and motionless body, smiled at her while moving arms and legs, cooed or made silent lip and tongue movements while lifting her hands in synchrony with these oral expressions. The right hand was raised high, above shoulder level, and the left hand was held forward or pulled back against her chest or side. This asymmetry of gestures in which the right hand takes the lead has been found to be the most common with infants under 3 or 4 months of age (Trevarthen, 1986b).

Such complexity of behaviour is typical of protoconversational inter-actions (Trevarthen, 1977; 1979a). The pattern of turntaking and regulated coincidences of expression resembles engagement of expressive behaviours

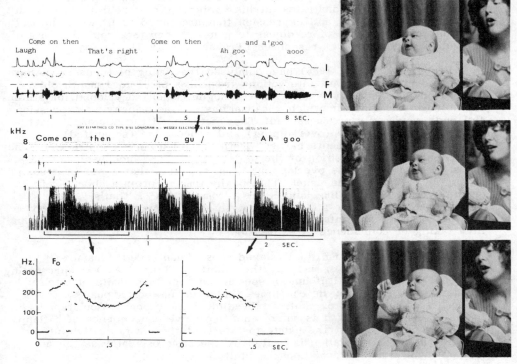

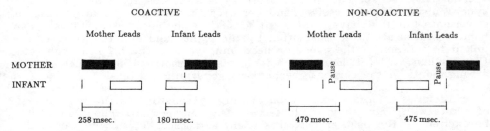

Fig. 4. A: Vocal exchanges between a 6-week-old girl and her mother
(see text).
B: Turn-taking and overlap of sounds in protoconversations,
according to Beebe et al (1985), their times converted
from frames to msec.

between conversing adults (Bateson, 1975; Stern, 1974). The fundamental beat and simpler rhythmic elaborations of relaxed and friendly adult conversations and mother-infant interactions are astonishingly similar (Jaffe & Feldstein, 1970; Beebe et al, 1985). Precise association between the infant's movements demonstrates intrinsic integrity of cerebral control, and the cycles of observing and expression that are tuned to fit what the mother is doing, give evidence of readiness to join with her to accept the form of motivation underlying her responses (Trevarthen, 1985).

Beebe et al (1979, 1985) have analysed the timing of turns in mother-infant and stranger-infant interactions from films of $3\frac{1}{2}$ to 4-month-olds. They used kinesic analysis (an 'adult dialogue model') developed for studies of adult conversations in which vocalisations and accompanying expressions and body movements are measured. They determined the standard onset-onset times for coactive (overlapping) and noncoactive (separated) vocalisations and movements between mothers and infants (Figure 4B). They did not identify the position of the underlying beat, which need not lie at the start of a turn. The overlapping times suggests that a pre-beat sound lasting 18 to 25 msec. is usual. This is the time to utter a short prefix or conjunction syllable like 'and-', 'a-', 'come-', 'ah-', 'that's-', etc. Beebe et al (1985) made statistical analyses that support the conclusion that both mother and infant are actively controlling intercoordinations for turn-taking or coincidence of expressions.

Oller (1981) has identified relaxed coos, (also called 'pleasure vocalisations'), like those made by the infant in Figure 4A, as representing the resonant core sound of human speech, with defined limits of pitch resonance and duration. He concludes that even newborns possess the rudiments of speech motor control. He studied the global articulation in /a gu/ and proved that it is active, not a passive consequence of a floppy tongue dropping against the palate to interrupt the air flow. It would appear that this articulation is limited by the same oscillator as the one that governs similar articulations in adults.

Young infants do not make the more rapid front articulations when voicing. These start to develop with 'canonical babbling' after 5 months. They do, however, when excited to communicate, make rudimentary lip and tongue moves resembling speech articulations. I have called these movements 'prespeech' (Trevarthen, 1974a, 1977, 1985). They are usually made without vocalisations. Prespeech, tongue protrusions and coos are often precisely synchronised with expressive hand gestures that are timed like prereaching movements but that have a different form (Trevarthen, 1974a, 1984a). Early hand gestures are made most often by the right hand and they may be linked to rotation of the eyes, or head and eyes, to the infant's right side (Trevarthen, 1985, 1986a), which indicates asymmetrical anatomical arrangements in the cerebral mechanisms governing expressions.

All forms of infant expression are highly sensitive to the behaviours of adults with whom they are in face-to-face engagement. They may also be excited by the partner becoming silent and immobile, in which case the vocalisations and other behaviours of the infant may express tension, anxiety or distress.

Papousek and Papousek have looked at sonograms and fundamental frequency contours of their own daughter, from birth, and of her mother interacting with her. They trace development of musicality in the control of vocalisation and give a tonal analysis for the mother's singing. Papousek, Papousek and Koester (1985), Papousek, Papousek and Bornstein (1985) and Stern, Spieker and MacKain (1982) have shown how the frequency structure and fundamental frequency contours of infant's calls vary with mood or emotional state, and they describe how the mother controls her voice contours to match or 'control' the infant with intercalated or overlapping utterances. There are now a number of experimental studies reporting discrimination of adult speech sounds, localisation of adult vocalisations, face perception and discrimination of face expressions in infants under 3 months. They show that the intercoordination of expressive movements is regulated by elaborate perceptual skills, including categorical awareness of forms of stimulation that correspond to particular forms of expressive movement (Mehler & Fox, 1984; Field & Fox, 1985; Studdert-Kennedy, 1983).

It has been noted that eye contact is sought even by newborns but is more intercoordinated between infants and adults after two months (Robson, 1967; Jaffe, Stern & Peery, 1973). Stern (1971, 1974) showed how the infant can use making and breaking of eye contact to regulate the communication. Murray found that duration of eye contact is a sensitive indicator of the quality of affective contact (Murray & Trevarthen, 1985). It changes immediately when the mother becomes unresponsive or dis-coordinated with the infant, as it is when adult-adult engagements are disturbed by negative affect.

The infant's capacity to express emotion by face movements has been explored by minute description of face movements of premature and full-term newborns by Oster (1978). She showed that nearly the full complement of facial action components is present at birth and that many coordinated combinations of facial actions, close to those by which adults demonstrate distinct categories of function and other distinct states of mind, may be distinguished. She showed that infants accompany sustained visual fixation with an intent 'knit-brow' expression often linked to relaxed jaw ('jaw drop'). This expression, signifying focussed visual interest, is different from brow movements of anger or sadness even in newborns. It is typically followed by a smile when the infant has been fixating the face of a mother who is speaking gentle, affectionate baby talk (see Figure 3).

A common or universal temporal organisation appears in relaxed and affectionate baby talk in different languages (Waterson & Snow, 1978). That is, mothers of different cultures operate with the same time sense. Further-more, the infant's responses show they use a matching time sense, with an absolute pulse the same as the mother's, both to assimilate her stimulation and to produce behaviour that she will recognise as replying to her.

What mothers say to infants reacting in this way indicates, not only that they expect emotional responses, but also that they perceive the infant's behaviour as expressions of some sort of intent to speak, tell a story, etc. (Trevarthen & Marwick, 1986).

The subtlety of emotional coordination by recognition of temporal, physiognomic and energetic features in such interactions is shown by an analysis of facial expressions of a mother and her 8-week-old daughter who were communicating entirely by means of televised images and sounds emitted by invisible loud speakers (Figure 5). This interaction was maintained by periodic vocal emissions on the part of the mother that were tightly coordinated with head and face movements. As in the previously described

230

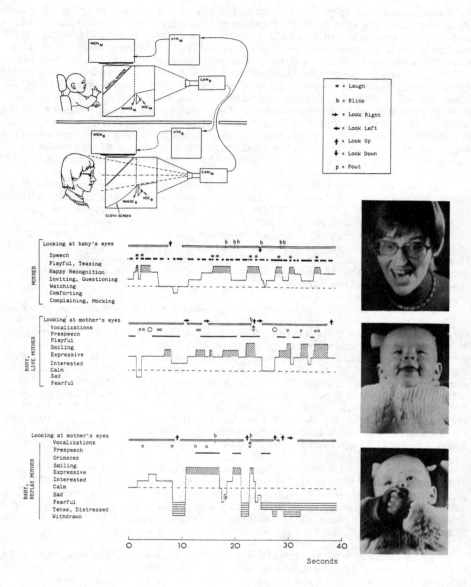

Fig. 5. Above: Mother and Infant communicating by televisual and audio contact alone (Trevarthen, 1985).
Below: Distressed expressions and 'gaze avoidance' of the same infant when the video record of the mother was replayed (Murray & Trevarthen, 1985; Trevarthen, 1985).

interaction, the movements of the mother, as she solicited recognition and reply from her infant, were organised on a regular beat in phrases of rhythmic structure.

In micro-analyses of the behaviours such as the above, reciprocal motor coordination and mutual perception is made evident by the precise form of innumerable actions and reactions and coincidences of movement that relate not only in their kinematics (i.e. both the beat and fluctuations in pitch and intensity) but also in their rhythmic patterns and emotional quality (Trevarthen, 1984b, 1985; Trevarthen & Marwick, 1986). Scepticism in the psychological literature about the infant's capacity to generate coherent changes of expression signifying well-formed and distinct emotions, or to understand a mother's expressions of feeling and communicative intention, is due to prejudice; it is supported by a biassed selection of evidence that represents the behaviours incompletely. Young infants may not regulate their emotions in interaction with external events with the same subtlety or precision as older ones, but they are neither disorganised in emotions nor insensitive. To clear up this problem one strategy is to show that a controlled distortion of the communication, or interference with its controls, causes the behaviours of both parties to change in lawful ways. Such artificial perturbation experiments have the bonus of yielding new forms of coordinated behaviour of a kind that, in more natural circumstances, would have the potentiality for repairing disrupted interactions.

TESTS OF THE EMOTIONAL REGULATION OF MOTHER-INFANT 'PROTOCONVERSATIONS'

Lynne Murray has examined the effects of perturbation on well-established engagements of primary intersubjectivity (Murray & Trevarthen, 1985). She requester the mothers to become immobile, on a cue from the experimenter, for 2 minutes, and to remain silent with expressionless face and steady but unfocussed gaze directed towards the infant. This causes a two- to three-month-old to stare unsmilingly, to make brief forced attempts at expression, with increasing distortion of smiles and efforts to vacalise, grimaces and contorted gestures of arms and hands (Figure 5). The infant increasingly withdraws gaze from the mother. Moreover, the agitated baby makes expressions specifically indicative of distress. These episodes of callapse of happy output or derailments of communication cause concern to the mother and take some time to abate (about 0.5 to 1 minute) after the mother resumes comforting attentions. Tronick et al (1978) obtained similar results with this technique.

In another experiment the videotaped record of 2 minutes of the mother's part in a happy engagement through the double video apparatus was replayed to the infant half a minute after it was recorded. This physical record of patterns in light and sound emitted by a mother interacting with her infant caused immediate decline in the infant's happy expressions and comparable manifestations of confusion and distress to those observed in the 'Still Face' test. There were subtle differences in the quality of distress, which indicate that the infants perceived the two situations differently (Murray & Trevarthen, 1985).

A reciprocal test is possible with this technique. When the video recording of a happy communicating infant is replayed to a mother after a brief delay she fails to perceive that the image of the infant is unreal, but senses a failure of contact. The infant's actions are perceived as strange and unfriendly, and the mother may attribute this to some fault in her own behaviour (Murray & Trevarthen, 1986).

From these tests we may conclude, as indeed we did already from observation of the fine structure of happy real interactions, that mother and infant are both involved in tracking and coordinating the interaction to maintain some state of motivation. If there is no response from the mother, or if her behaviour, though in itself positively expressive, is unrelated (both uncontingent in time and inappropriate in form) to the precise expressions that the infant subject of the test is making, then the motivation for communication changes and its expressions change towards a different physiognomy indicative of agitation, distress, self-awareness, sadness and need for comfort.

Imprecision or inappropriateness of the mother's behaviour is detected by the baby because the baby is making precise predictions about when the mother should respond or emit a signal, and precise predictions about what kind of emotion is an appropriate accompaniment or reply to how the baby is acting. It is simplest to assume that the 'when' of the mother's responses is predicted because the two of them share a regular measure or beat of expressiveness. The 'what kind' question will relate to some physiognomic and energetic code of emotions that they share.

In happy or well-coordinated interactions the mother is attentive to every move of the infant, maintaining attention on the infant's face, especially the eyes, almost without interruption. She seeks to find expressions of communication directed to herself. She generates a regular repeating pattern of intermittent expressiveness, delicately adjusting the emotional quality of her expressions when the infant responds. She often imitates the infant's expressions with a delay of 0.25 to 1 seconds (Trevarthen 1977, 1979). Her behaviour may be compared to that of an accompanist with a singer. As in performance of the musical score for a song with a designated tempo, mother and infant share a standard of time (the beat) and standards of form and expressive quality for the melody. the mother is not behaving as if she is the only party with a sense of time, form and quality in movement, nor is she slavishly taking up the infant's output. However, she does act as if giving active and sympathetic support to the initiative of the infant, as an accompanist does for a singer (Moore, 1943).

Infants show the same sense of time, form and quality in expressions they make with support from the mother and more elaborately coordinated. When an infant is consistently deprived of affective and communicative support from another person positive (happy) expressions decline and self-directed or withdrawn behaviours, resembling those seen acutely after the mother's response is perturbed, are manifested chronically. Neglected infants, deprived of affectionate personal attention, become inactive, depressed and with drawn (Fraiberg, 1980; Stern, 1985). They refuse to feed, lose weight and, *in extremis,* die. At present we do not have sufficiently detailed follow-up studies to make an accurate account of the effects on psychological and emotional development of defective maternal engagement with the infant's motives for protoconversational play. Epidemiological studies and case descriptions suggest there may be effects, but the literature is concerned, almost completely, with supporting or refusing theoretical arguments devised from consideration of adult psycho-pathology and behaviour.

Protoconversational exchanges showing the condition of primary inter-subjectivity in a two-month-old are most strongly developed between the person with whom the infant has formed an affectionate attachment. At this stage attachment is shown in preferential readiness to respond positively to the voice and face of the primary caretaker who is usually the mother. When a stranger attempts to gain response from the infant, a two-month-old is more observant or avoidant, and less likely to smile, vocalise and gesture. Strangers, for their part, keep further back from the infant than the mother, and respond with more caution. This behaviour appears, in many cases, to be a direct consequence of the suspicious unresponding behaviour of the infant. Both timing and expressive quality of the engagement are weaker than in play with the mother.

NEWBORNS IN COMMUNICATION: JUST HOW MUCH DO THEY EXPERIENCE?

The two-month-olds are able to communicate with a mother in face-to-face engagement at a distance, but contact with a newborn is sustained by more intimate means. There is a conspicuous improvement in readiness to focus on and engage with another person's speech and face expressions when the infant is 45 to 46 weeks of gestational age (5 to 6 weeks after a full-term birth). The infant's expressions (smiles, coos and gestures) also become stronger and better coordinated (Trevarthen, Hubley & Murray, 1981). These developments in the cerebral cortex with wide spread effects on perception of events outside the body and on movements (Trevarthen, 1984, 1986b). Before that communication depends more on response to body-contact cues; voice quality and odour or taste.

In the first month, infants can coordinate head and eyes for orientation to a mother's voice, but they are incapable of precisely focussed visual attention and they rarely sustain orientation to face and voice for more than a few seconds. Moreover, they do not respond readily with appropriately matched smiles, vocalisations and gestures in close coordination with a mother's utterances and movements. Nevertheless, in their reactions to a mother's holding and caressing and in their delicate reactions to the prosody and quality of her speech they do demonstrate a remarkable structured sensitivity to her behaviour.

Within minutes of birth infants can show discriminating response to many indices of the mother's presence and to her excited, almost erotic, greeting calls and touching. Recognition of her identity is manifested in preferential alerting and orientation to her odour, voice and touching or holding, and fussing or avoidance when another person makes the same approaches. Recent experimental studies indicate that newborns can see the mother's face and recognise her within hours of birth (Field, 1985). This is presumably learned on the basis of an identification already made by olfactory and auditory criteria of her identity. The sound of a mother's voice have been shown to be recognised immediately or almost immediately after birth, apparently as a result of intra-uterine learning (Alegria & Noirot, 1978; De Casper & Fifer, 1980). A mother's behaviours have clear subdued and evenly paced patterning from first contact at birth and this will assist the infant to learn closer adaptation to her with the help of modalities that work poorly or not at all before birth.

Fetuses show patterned movements of head, trunk and limbs, and of eyes, face and mouth. These movements have the same regulated tempo as spontaneous movements of the same kind by newborns (Prechtl, 1984 ; Trevarthen, 1984). This is evidence for the formation before birth of active motor coordinative systems regulated by neural oscillators and servo systems. The crying of newborns transmits detailed information about the state of core regulatory systems of the brain (Lester, 1984).

Experiments over the last decade prove that newborns, hours old, including those born 2-3 weeks prematurely, not only make spontaneous lip and tongue movements and gesture, but can also imitate mouth opening and lip or tongue protrusions. This shows that the physiognomy of a person's face is identified with the infant's already active face-moving programs. The startling evidence from imitation studies compels us to make a fresh approach to the problem of how human communication originates.

IMITATIONS SOON AFTER BIRTH

Olga Maratos (1973, 1982) carried out the first systematic longitudinal experimental study of imitation. She proved that one-month-olds could imitate tongue protrusion and certain vocalisations that are within their spontaneous repertoire of movements, and she reported a sharp decline in these imitations in the second and third months, an affect she explained as due to differentiation of sensory-motor systems. She also noted that other kinds of imitation were more readily obtained later (Figure 6). Her conclusion was "that the one-month-old possesses a certain notion of his body schema" (1982, p. 97). Meltzoff and Moore (1977, 1983) confirmed that neonates could imitate tongue-protrusion and mouth opening plus three different facial grimaces and a hand gesture. Meltzoff's interpretation focusses on the need for intermodal coordination, eg. between seeing someone else's tongue and feeling proprioceptively one's own tongue doing the same kind of movement (Meltzoff, 1985). Recently Kugiumutzakis (1985) has demonstrated imitation of tongue protrusion and mouth opening by newborns 32 minutes old and his longitudinal measures confirmed Maratos' finding of 'dips' or losses in the capacity or tendency to imitate. He established that different acts are imitated at different ages, which indicates that imitation in young infants is dependent on intrinsically regulated differences in coordination or differentiation of mechanisms of sensory-motor integration (Figure 6). Field et al (1982) and Field (1985) have shown that newborns can imitate consciously acted (and rather exaggerated) face expressions of pleasure, surprise and sadness. They added the important observation that different individuals may have a very different tendency to imitate.

In the phase of primary intersubjectivity (1½ to 3 months after birth) experimental studies of imitation break into the level of communication charact istic of protoconversations with some difficulty. Newborns respond more readily, but in attempts to get maximum response in imitation tests with newborns experimenters have been led to 'control' an ever-expanding set of conditions. Pushed by reductionist reasoning to disprove hypothetical alternative mechanisms suggested by fragmentary behaviours in highly unnatural situations, they try to guide the infant into a strong and sustained orientation to a model action and to obtain a significant contrast between the infant's behaviour before and after the model was presented (Meltzoff, 1985; Kugiumutzakis, 1985). The most successful recent studies have obtained clear correspondence between the infant's expressions and a model expression after the infant, supported in an upright position, has been prepared a 'build up' through rhythmic actions intended to excite responses of arousal,

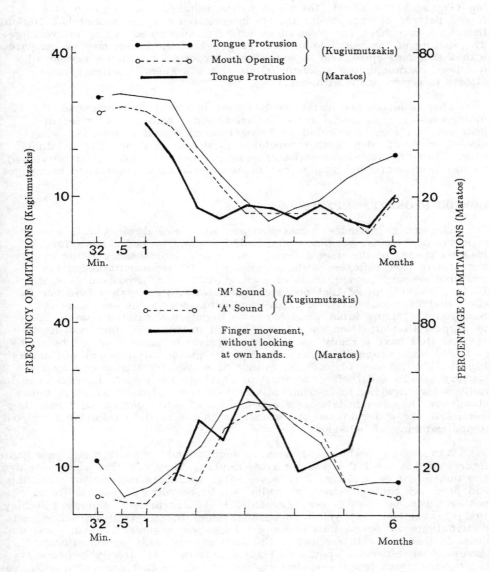

Fig. 6. Imitation by newborns. Data of Maratos (1973, 1982) and Kugiumutzakis (1985).

alertness, and oriented attention. The model movements are like those infants make spontaneously in natural interactions with their mothers, but more exaggerated in form. They are also exaggerated in size and duration in comparison with what adults might be expected to do to infants, though some expressions of adults responding naturally to infants are surprisingly big (Figure 5). In short, the model in the imitation test is given in a forced pattern of engagement that is interrupted and the neonate's imitation, therefore, may have the place of an effort to sustain or regain interchange. The waiting of the model to test for response of the infant may be compared with a still face episode in a perturbation experiment. When a mother who has been communicating suddenly stops and sits silently, infants make efforts to communicate with her.

That neonates can imitate is no longer in doubt, but responses under these circumstances remain unpredictable. With the older infants, imitations are clearly affected by recognition of who the model is, being easiest to obtain with familiar caretaker in situations resembling habitual play. They are like conversation 'repair' procedures, and cannot be viewed as the fundamental building blocks of normal efficiently controlled exchanges.

HOW DO NEONATES IMITATE?

The modern theories of imitation owe much to Baldwin (1902) whose concepts of 'circular reactions' and 'self-imitation' formed a basis for Piaget's theory of the stage-by-stage development of sensory motor co-ordinations from reflexes, with increasing mental representation of the probable sensory consequences of each given form of movement (Piaget, 1954). However, proof that neonates can imitate, and further evidence to show that numerous forms of expressive behaviour in the spontaneous repertoire of young infants can serve as models for imitation, would seem to suggest that attention should be directed to intrinsic motor coordinative systems that have a ready adaptation to certain invariants or constellations of stimulation, especially invariants that the human environment will naturally supply. The problem of imitation cannot be solved by attending only to sensory stimuli and their perceptual processing. We have to unravel neonates' motives for engaging in communicative interactions of many kinds to understand how they can imitate some expressions of other persons and how they can relate the different sensory modalities that give them information related to the matching of behaviours.

Fetuses and newborns show many spontaneous, repeating and coordinated figures of movement that are far from random. They breathe, make nutritive and non-nutritive sucking, face movements, vocalisations, and pre-reaching and precisely conjugated eye saccades can be coordinated with shifts of postural limb movements, etc. (Prechtl, 1984; Trevarthen, Murray & Hubley, 1981; Trevarthen, 1984b). In these behaviours the temporal and anatomical distributions of contractions in many muscles are organised within consistent limits in time and with respect to the body's form. This organisation in movement must depend upon neuro-motor systems that already 'represent' the movements as temporo-spatial events. It may be that none of these move-ments, even at this early stage of development, are completely free of afferent control - somesthetic and mechanoreceptive reafference is a possible contributor to the form of any movement after the embryo stage when the rudimentary motor coordinative structures receive the first terminals from afferent neurones (Oppenheim, 1982). On the other hand, the contribution of afference may vary greatly without disorganising the inherent interneuronal coordination of movements that have adaptive form. Indeed, an unpredictable variety of afferent patterns must be assimilable in such a way that the most effective combinations of sensory stimulation of peripheral neural structures can be selected to confirm and refine established pre-motor organisations in the brain. Inherent biodynamic or coordinative structures are already adapted to the environment in this way for a future behavioural function, or they are necessary to the development of such a function.

For example, a short time after birth both prehensile and expressive movements can either be emitted spontaneously or be triggered by stimuli that the infant can never have experienced before. From the first occasion, within minutes of birth, a movement may be excited which is in some measure appropriate to make use of a stimulus of that kind. A prereaching movement, coordinated with adjustment of the aim of the eye involving head and eye rotations, may be directed with accuracy to within 10° to a real distal visual target, say a slowly displaced object crossing the space in front of the infant (Trevarthen, 1974; 1984b; von Hofsten, 1984). The same coordinated movement may also occur when there is no target in the outside world. The visual stimulus caused by a nearby object of appropriate size is not essential, but it has previledged entry to a coordinated structure that is in the process of formulating one setting aimed at one position in extracorporal space, viz. the salient goal location for a reach-and-grasp movement.

In the same way a face movement that the newborn is capable of co-ordinating spontaneously can be facilitated or activated more strongly by another person who has placed her or himself in front of the baby and spoken softly. What does this mean?

As with the prereaching movement aimed to a thing moving outside the surface of the body, selecting one location in an exteroceptive reaching space that maps onto the whole motor coordinative mechanism of the body (and its proprioceptions), so the expressive movement of another person serves as a goal in an alteroceptive or intersubjectivity space. A stimulus of *that* kind maps onto a motor coordinative mechanism representing, not only the output of communicative expressions of the infant as subject, but also, separately, the invariants of stimulation in an input of expressions from another subject. This is the basis for all intersubjective coordinations, including imitations, which are differently motivated from coordinations adapted to walking (Thelen, 1984) or those adapted to manipulating objects, even in a newborn.

Imitation is thus a special case of communicative identification or mirroring. More commonly the represented 'other' will be acting in complement-ary way to the represented 'self', and the expression of the self will augment and complement the expressions of the other. Thus each subject comes to carry a sequence of functions that represent the changing states of interaction between themselves and another.

Note that in a mature, effective reaching and grasping for an object by an older child or adult the arm and hand are clearly not imitating or matching any attribute of the object - they are nullifying the distance between the subject and the object, and at the same time starting to adapt their form to engulf and support the object or to manipulate it*. As a result of development and learning, the act of reaching to grasp and lift an object, an act seen in outline form in prereaching, becomes more powerful, more complete and more precise - the object's weight and 3-D form are, in time, judged more accurately from a visual impression so that little correction by feedback of somethetic or proprioceptive information is needed when the act is performed and contact made. The efficient movement is a tightened up version of the generalised form produced in the first month, before any of this learning took place. In an important sense the prereaching movements and their successive elaborations are exploratory - they are seeking stimuli in the body and through contact with objects and getting more effective perceptuo-motor control of action (von Hofsten, 1982).

The refined sensitivity that neonates show to the kinematic organisation of adult expressive behaviour can lead to synchronised movements. Condon and Sander (1974) thought that infant arm movements could be entrained to the rhythms of adult speech. They presented evidence of coincidence in climaxes of arm displacement by the infant and syllable or word pronouncement by an adult to support the concept that the infant was imprinted with a temporal patterning that originates in adult speech where it might be the result of social learning and conventional regulation. In this way, an infant, they proposed, is given a foundation for later acquisition of behaviours that have a regular temporal structure, notably speech (see above discussion of protoconversational coordinations).

In Birdwhistle's theory of kinesics (Birdwistle, 1952, 1970), patterns of expressive movement in communication are taken to be learned conventions. The natural conclusion is that synchrony between infant and adult is due to passive entrainment of the inexperienced infant in a structure the adult has learned.

Unlike Birdwhistle, we presume this kind of lining up of temporal patterning in movements arises between adults because they share matching innate neural foundations of time; i.e. matching oscillators. In fact, adult behaviours have, as has been shown above, a consistent, though complex, temporal structure. Communication movements seem to be based on a common absolute time base that is independent of learned cultural constraints. Spontaneous or autonomous movements of neonates have the same regular temporal structure as one level of this motor coordination in adults. The descriptive evidence indicates that temporal intercoordination, producing both alternation and synchrony of moves between infants and adults is the result of engagement between matching motor programs with inherently sympathetic oscillators and control processes built into them.

I believe that physiognomic imitations of the form of facial or hand movement or of vocalisation (which convey information about movements of

---

* If we extend the meaning of the word 'imitate' as Baldwin (1894, 1902) did in his concept of 'self-imitation', to include recreation of a stimulus by repetition of a movement that caused it in the past, then the distinction breaks down. Acting with expectation of a particular kind of stimulation is a circular reaction, afference initiated by a motor excitatory state. Baldwin's thinking is close to Bernstein's and his theory provides a fundamental and necessary concept by which to relate imitation to other kinds of act that enable the subject to control relationships with the body with and with the outside world.

the vocal apparatus) arise similarly, by engagement between matching neuro-motor programs. Infants make discriminations early in life between normal and abnormal face configurations, different forms of face expression (Maratos, 1973; Meltzoff & Moore, 1977, 1982; Field et al, 1982), faces of different individuals (Field, 1985), different vocalisations, voices of different people (De Casper & Fifer, 1980; Mehler et al, 1978), coincident and non-coincident patterns of visible motion and sound variation (Spelke, 1985), visible mouth movements and speech sounds (Kuhl & Meltzoff, 1982). They have, or acquire in a few days or weeks, many capacities that appear to require some representation of coordinations that occur between parts of the body of another person by virtue of the normal motor coordination.

Approached from the perspective of a perceptionist or cognitivist, the psychological process behind being aware of an association between stimuli in different parts of a form, or that between stimuli excited in different modalities (different special sense organs) by a single event requires inter-stimulus or associative links. These have, classically, been assumed to be learned or rationally built up, it being thought that the CNS had only separate S-R channels before learning occurred. But coordinated movements can be the cause as well as the result of regular patterns of interaction between stimuli, whether within or between modalities. The movements of infants show that they are born with many motor coordinative structures. Some of these exist, with selective sensitivity to 'sign stimuli' bridging modalities, even when there can have been no acquired intersensory co-ordination. For example a blind infant may smile spontaneously and also in response to a mother's voice. Sighted newborns may smile when they hear a voice while their eyes are closed. This response is clearly coordinated by something central resembling an emotion of pleasure at recognising a voice sound, and, furthermore, it is an expression that is adapted to the experience of perceiving a particular liked person who may make such a sound.

We have seen that two-month-olds react to sounds and sights of a mother communicating by movements of face, vocal appratus and hands in patterns that resemble coordinations in adult expression, including speech with accompanying gestures. These mannerisms or gestures and their associations could not have been imitated. Infants must possess, as a consequence of prenatal morphogenetic processes, integrated motives to be expressive in these ways when they perceive an affectionately expressive person addressing them with particular combinations of movement (Trevarthen, 1980b, 1982, 1984a). The coordinations will excite sensory effects in many modalities; proprioceptive, exproprioceptive and alteroceptive. All seem to be assimilated in some degree into the process in the infant that coordinates expressive behaviour. These considerations lead to an explanation of neo-natal imitations.

I assume that when a newborn sees a person protrude his or her tongue after this person has excited the infant's interest in his or her face by a build up of movements and/or sounds, a structured motive to communicate is activated. Among the many inputs that can be more or less completely assimilated to this coordinative motivation would be a recognition of the actions of the other person's face. We know that the shape of the face, its configuration or schema can be identified in some of its features because these features (eyes, bisymmetry, redness, warmth, etc.) are salient and preferred in the infant's awareness. The imitation tests prove that certain exaggerated, insistent, repeated strong movements of the expressive system can trigger a response that takes a matching form.

An acceptable communicative response to the expression of some motive for communication will have to come from a limited repertoire of replies. This implies that the person who replies well has identified the expressive value of the movement perceived, and generated a movement to complement it. In most cases the sensory consequences of the reply are different from the sensory effects that caused it, and sometimes they will be in a totally different modality, as when an infant with eyes closed smiles on hearing his mother's voice - he cannot see her voice, and cannot hear his own smile. Their correspondence or fittingness arises because they relate to a structure of amodal, supramodel or intermodal communicative motives that both share. Imitation is a special case of this fitting together. Note that young infants' imitations of expressions by an adult actor made to give exaggerated representation of cardinal emotions may be closer to natural expressions of these emotions than the models were (Field, 1982). The infant is not so much trying to match the model movement as to share that kind of expressive form. He or she has an inner standard of the form of emotion that the model expression refers to.

It is important that immediate, exact imitation of discrete expressions is unusual in communication even with newborns, and that in accurate reproduction of a given model act does not occur at all ages and 'sensitive periods' are different for different kinds of act (Kugiumutzakis, 1985). There are also large individual differences in readiness to imitate. From the data presently available it appears as if constructive, complementary engagement in some new form of communication (e.g. protoconversation with prespeech) may be preceded, a few weeks earlier in development, by a brief period of hightened tendency to imitate (e.g. tongue protrusion and mouth opening). Imitation appears to decline as soon as that form of action becomes well-controlled in interaction with its preferred environment. There is, however, no evidence that direct, immediate imitation of movements is *necessary* for development of forms of communicative expression like those of other persons. In other words, the most constructive form of imitation is voluntary, deferred reproduction of an act in a motivated context that makes it relevant. When the subject takes a communicative role like that of the model, actions of the model perceived at an earlier time may be reproduced to obtain a similar effect. It is the synthesis or cooperative effect that is aimed for, not the actual movements.

We should relate neonatal imitation to the coactions and exchanges that arise at 2 months in 'protoconversation'. When a newborn smiles or moves a hand, this movement has a communicative function in the sense that it is the expression of a state in the brain that already represents an 'other'. Proof of this is the sensitivity with which such movements, adapted in their form to communication, respond to communicative movements of others. Experimental tests of person perception, or discrimination of face, voice, movement or odour stimuli, accumulate to give us an increasingly convincing picture of an awareness of others' movements that goes beyond what the infant can perform. The infant is ready to perceive a wide range of human expressions that can be brought under the infant's control by much simpler signals.

Infants respond appropriately to differences in vocal expression that they cannot come close to emulating. The interactions at 2 months between infant and mother are carried by highly asymmetric behaviours. Their efficient coordination demonstrates that, nevertheless, each subject is adapted to complement the other at a certain level. This must be a consequence of the presence in each of a representation of the other and of the states of intercoordination that the two may achieve together because they share the same communicative code. In the infant this representation is such that a severely limited expressive competence has a broad 'proximal zone of development' in Vygotsky's sense (Vygotsky, 1978) in which the mother's behaviour can support more complex expressions and lead the infant to enriched protoconversational exchanges lasting several minutes. In this zone the infant will develop the fulfilment of rudimentary skills of communication that are, as far as their motives go, there at the beginning.

DEVELOPMENT OF PLAY AND SELF-ASSERTION: DIFFERENTIATION OF EXPLORATORY AND PERFORMATORY ADJUSTMENTS TO OBJECTS OF PREHENSION

In the two years of infancy, large systematic changes occur in the infant's communicative skills and in the kind of engagements that arise with caretakers and other persons. These changes cannot be explained as consequences of conditioning or trial-and-error learning. They are not a simple monotonic accumulation of refinements in motor control or perceptual discrimination, and though they vary with different qualities of support from the human environment, with normal adequate support they show remarkable age-locked regularities. All these features are evidence for an intrinsic control of psychological development by growth and differentiation of critical motivating structures in the child's brain that become facilitated by perceptual engagement with an appropriate environment.

Description of the second of these major changes, subsequent to emergence of Primary Intersubjectivity and communication at a distance, will illustrate the kind of processes that govern development of inter-subjective motor control in relation to behaviour directed to the physical world. All such developments, even when they are clearly precipitated by transformations of motives in the infant, will, because they are conditional on support and stimulation from communication, involve the familiar trusted partner in a change of tactics. Indeed, the developments are seen most clearly if they are viewed as transformations in the relationship between the infant and that most trusted person. It is truly their communication together that develops and much information about the change in the infant can be obtained by observing changes in the mother's behaviour (Sylvester-Bradley & Trevarthen, 1978; Trevarthen & Marwick, 1986).

A wide range of changes in perception and motor coordination give evidence of an extensive remodelling of an infant's psychological mechanism between 3 and 5 months. In this period visual acuity, binocular stereopsis oculomotor reactions of accommodation, vergence and tracking undergo rapid improvement. Control of displacements of the arms increases in parallel with a conspicious growth in mass of the axial and proximal muscles. The oculomotor adjustments that immediately precede reaching to an object become both well-aimed and adjusted to object motion, and the arm and hand movement becomes capable of variation in extent and direction to inter-cept an object, while assimilating proprioceptive information about changing forces due to gravity and the inertia of the limbs. After 12 to 15 weeks from birth, the infant shows increased exploratory interest in surroundings and a keen attraction towards proprioceptive and exteroceptive effects contingent upon limb displacements, often experimenting with these effects in play. At the same time (between 3 and 5 months after birth) there is a marked disinclination to sustain simple face-to-face confrontation with the mother - we have observed a drop from 90% to 40% in the time spent by the infant looking at the mother's face when the two are seated opposite each other and playing together by exchanging vocalisations etc. (Trevarthen, 1983; Trevarthen & Marwick, 1986). This change of motives for orienting and exploring as against communicating marks the end of the period of Primary Intersubjectivity.

The affective range of the infant's expressions changes with this manifestation of independence and interest in looking away from the mother. The baby develops a more vigorous playfulness with laughter and a lively sense of humor that mixes affectionate pleasure with mock-aggressive teasing. The latter is indicated in more 'wicked' face expressions of pleasure, with tight upper lip and forward-jutting lower jaw, and a tendency to laugh in play fighting. Attention to the actions of hands of other persons as well as to their presentation of objects for reaching also increases from three months, in advance of well-controlled reaching and manipulations (Trevarthen, 1983, 1986b). Apparently infants can see what hands can do before they themselves can use hands with good control.

With increased strength of the infant's body and the readiness of the infant to laugh when subjected to rhythmic and suddenly changing movements, adults react by swinging the child about, or moving its limbs vigorously. Doubtless this provides abundant stimulation of the now highly active and reactive proprioceptive system of the rapidly growing baby. 'Body play' also extends the infant's self awareness in the context of communication (Trevarthen & Hubley, 1978).

Although infants are capable only of the simplest articulated vocalisations of short duration at this stage, they can vary the pitch and quality of their calls (Oller, 1981) and they are alert to more complex vocalisations of adults or children more mature than themselves integrating the sights and sounds of people speaking to do so (Kuhl & Meltzoff, 1982). Their quick playful reactions with smiles and laughter stimulate others to make patterns of speech, song or chanting that, backed up by matching rhythms of body movement, provide a rich source of data on the kind of communicative experience that is optimal for the baby.

In the first two months the regular patterns of maternal 'baby talk' vocalisations and comfort sounds or lullabies reflect the patterned sensitivity of the infant to a simple beat, a range of undulating figures of pitch variation a singing style of vocalisation, and a relaxed breathy quality of voicing (Marwick et al, 1984; Trevarthen & Marwick, 1986). In the next 2 months there is a transformation in the quality of play, and in the range of mothers' vocalisations and other expressions of feeling, with introduction by affectionate caretakers and playmates of a vigorous repertoire of baby songs and baby dances (Marwick et al, 1984; Trevarthen & Marwick, 1986). The forms of infant vocalisation seen in primary intersubjectivity are retained, but they become more clearly marked and new forms are added (Oller, 1981). Face expressions show a parallel differentiation without change of their basic forms (Oster, 1978; Oster & Ekman, 1977; Izard, 1978).

Traditional nursery rhymes and chants are not often used by mothers to stimulate infants under 3 months, for the simple reason that they are not much appreciated until after this age. The youngest infants respond to gentler songs and lullabyes, but the older infants enjoy songs with a dancing pattern and lively, playful development. The temporal structures, pitch variations and musical development in baby songs all have remarkable regularity. Figure 7 shows some examples. The main beat appears related to that of baby talk to a younger infant already described. The shifts in fundamental frequency of the mother's voice are of similar rate and range. But the organisation of periods of vocalisation and silence, the rhythmic repetitions and the changes in intensity or tension are much more complex (Marwick et al, 1984). Short 'verses' with a firm regular stress and dancing rhythm are repeated, then there is a build-up with exaggerated emphasis, followed by either a sudden or a gradual termination. The whole of this basic 'sociodramatic' cycle' occupies about 10 to 20 seconds, and it may be repeated many times.

A small corpus of 'baby music' from different cultures immediately reveals universal features. First, the tempo is remarkably consistent. This in turn appears related to cardinal time structure in adult music, based on the beat. It would appear that the pulse and rhythmic variation of these behaviours is an expression of important standards of motor programming in the brain and not caused by any peripheral mechanical constraints inherent in the motor organs. The same beats are made by vocal apparatus and limbs, as when a chant is synchronised with clapping. Expressive features such as these are found in baby music of different cultures that one would expect to be different in sense of music and motor play (Figures 7, 8 and 9).

The performances of aborigine music portrayed in Figure 2 should be compared. Similarities to these mothers singing clapping songs to their infants in three languages are obvious. Note that while the mother's articulations may be of the same high rapidity as the aborigine lip and tongue play, they are regimented inside a much slower rhythmic structure. Every infant became interested in his or her mother's display. Presumably they were caught principally by the steady, bold configurations of sound and movement, though the correlated movements of greater rapidity, when coupled to this context, may also have been discriminated. A process of prediction and recognition, usually described as cognitive but in this instance certainly paralleled by an emotional evaluation that varies predictably, captivates the infant. It often leads to a climax in which the mother provokes laughter by a sudden vigorous movement or 'attack' with a loud sound or rapid staccato rhythm, as in 'pop goes the weasel 'on' peek a boo'.

In the first phase of infancy, communication develops by the mother and infant entering into a mutually supportive engagement that is regulated moment by moment. Reactions of the infant are timed to the beat of the mother's expressions and they reciprocate in close intercoordination. The mother's identity already acts as a consistent motivating element to which the infant manifests preferential attachment, and the mother has a reciprocal feeling of love for her infant that is strengthened by the developments in efficiency and richness of communication and by the positive emotions that the infant shows to her approach. But neither the engagement nor the affectionate attachment are open to adjustment to circumstances outside the immediate coordination of expressive and emotional states. The young infant's expressive behaviour is intrinsically organised in phases or cycles of action and inaction - but there appears to be no active control by the infant of variations in phasing or development.

244

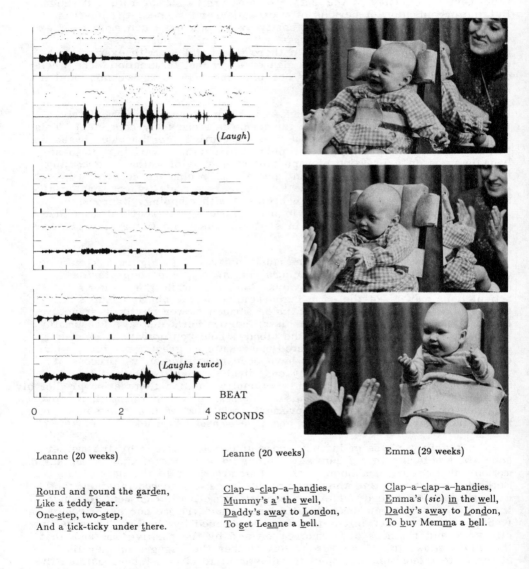

Leanne (20 weeks)　　　　Leanne (20 weeks)　　　　Emma (29 weeks)

Round and round the garden,　Clap-a-clap-a-handies,　Clap-a-clap-a-handies,
Like a teddy bear.　　　　　　Mummy's a' the well,　　　Emma's (sic) in the well,
One-step, two-step,　　　　　　Daddy's away to London,　Daddy's away to London,
And a tick-ticky under there.　To get Leanne a bell.　　To buy Memma a bell.

Fig. 7. Baby songs of Scottish mothers with infants over 3 months of age.

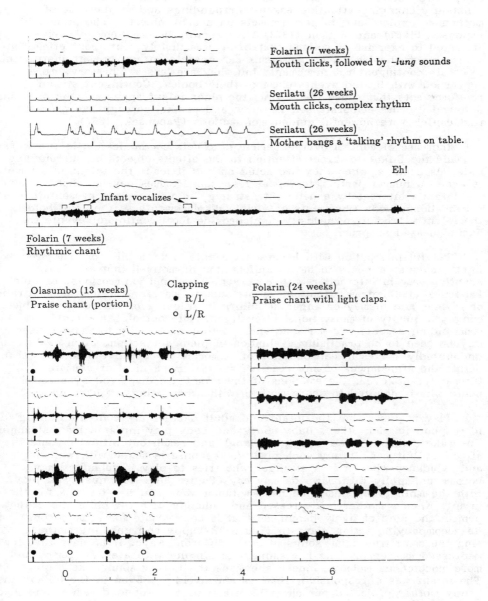

Fig. 8. Italian and African mothers singing to their infants.

After 3 months contacts between them are opened to nearby events as the infant becomes more aware of and visibly attracted towards them. The mother now has to communicate not only with the infant's emotions and expressive motives responsive to and directed towards herself, but with a constantly changing attentiveness to surroundings and an increase of motives to explore and to perform acts on nearby objects. The infant, as Papousek (1967) and Watson (1972) have shown, becomes compulsively attracted to exercise of actions that bring immediately contingent effects in a reactive mechanism. Even newborns can operate an appropriate instrument to obtain contingent reinforcement, but they are less exploratory, more concerned with limited events close to their bodies. Contingent stimuli reinforce acts that cause them, thus the older infant appears to be becoming involved in more elaborate self-imitation and predictive cognitive processes that confer more powerful guidance on actions (Papousek, 1967).

Increase of control over experiences affects communication in two ways. It leads the infant to direct attention to the effects objects or surrounding materials produce when they are acted on and it leads the infant to attempt to excite a human partner to repeat responses. Games develop that attract the infant's interest by a deliberate strategy of varying the presentation of vocalisations, body movements or visible displacements so they will hold the infant's predictive curiosity, and provide focal contingent events that excite pleased surprise.

Playful interaction with impersonal events, like mobiles or triggered light displays, appears to be a manifestation of motives that are fully adaptive only in interaction with a person. Emotional expressions, to which Papousek (1967) drew attention, of pleasure in mastery, serious concentration, or of fear and dismay or anger at failure in tracking or acting on an object, convey a quality of motivational intensity in self-control. An infant commanding reactions of a mobile and reacting emotionally to these consequence may be seen to be practising evaluation of plans for action. Such evaluation undoubtedly serves in consolidation of memories or cognitive strategies that define the affordances of any reactive system, mechanical or animate. Ultimately, however, the emotions of the infant are displayed by a social being who is adapted to share motives with other beings of like mind.

Play requires that the infant and adult partner are contented and glad to respond to each other. Baby songs and body play initiated by a stranger can make a three- to six-month-old laugh and reach out with trust and affection, but usually any such positive response is mixed with watching and avoidance when it is a stranger who tries to play. The infant may become unhappily withdrawn or may cry (Figure 9A). The quality of play with the mother depends upon her emotional state and her feelings for the infant. When a mother is depressed and unhappy with the child she cannot project the kind of lively happiness that is appropriate for a baby song and its accompanying action play. In Figure 9B happy and unhappy mothers sing the same traditional songs in quite different ways. It is clear that the depressed mother projects her sadness in singing with a slower tempo and more monotonous melody. Indeed she made the lullaby sound like a dirge. The infant was unresponsive, restless and avoiding. Even in the lullaby the happy mother projected her cheerful affection. She sounded secure and glad and as she steadily reduced the volume of her singing to a whisper her infant went fast asleep. These songs give us clear data concerning the kind of musical performance which is enjoyable and supportive for an infant.

LULLABY

Olga (6 months)

Nina O, Nina O, Questa bimba a chi la dò?
Se la dò alla Befana, Se la tiene una settimana?
Se la dò a l'uomo nero, Se la tiene un'anno intero?

Fabiana (6 months) Mother depressed.

Nina O, Nina O, Questa bimba a chi la dò?
Se la dò alla Befana, Se la tiene una settimana?
Se la dò a l'uomo nero, Se la tiene una mes intero?

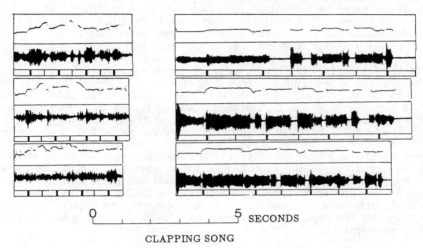

0 _____ 5 SECONDS

CLAPPING SONG

Frederica (5 months)

Batti, batti, le manine,
Che adesso vienne papa,
E ti porta le cioccolatine,
E tu le mangera.

Fabiana (6 months) Mother depressed.

Batti, batti, le manine,
Che thra poco vienne papa,
Ti porta le caremelline,
Fabiana le mangera.

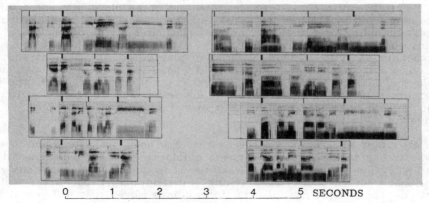

0   1   2   3   4   5 SECONDS

Fig. 9. A: Infants with draw or become distressed with strangers.
B: Italian mothers, one happy, the other depressed, sing
a clapping song and a lullaby, in quite different ways.

248

SELF-AWARENESS AND SHOWING OFF: HEIGHTENED ATTACHMENT AND
FEAR OF STRANGERS: EXPLORATION IN BABBLING, MANIPULATION AND
GESTURE

After 6 months, motivation of infants in all kinds of play manifests
heightened self-awareness. The infant takes more active control over the
effects of moving, including the effects in other people. At the same time
all kinds of action on the world are subject to increasing cognitive control.
In traditional individualistic cognitive approaches of psychology this
development is described as the attainment of a concept of the permanent
object. It may now be described more accurately as attainment of an
increased awareness of the different permanent identities of objects with
many affordances for use by the infant. Object awareness is certainly
present before this age (Bower, 1974; Spelke, 1985).

Tests of infants' abilities to solve problems or make inferences in
situations where a previously recognised and desired object is partly hidden
or becomes completely hidden while the child is observing, show that between
6 and 12 months there are highly significant advances in mental representation
and memory (Bower & Wishart, 1983). Action of the infant may be directed
in such a way that obstacles to the object are circumvented, screens are
removed, hollows are searched etc. Observation of someone else changing
the accessibility and perceptibility of an object can now serve to guide
search and recovery of the object. The infant comes to direct movements not
merely by immediately present information about the place and identity of
objects, or the line of motion an object may be taking, but by a scheme of
the object's existence in a context that may conceal the object from view.
The concept of the object has achieved new 'permanence', independent of
changing perceptions.

Self-awareness shows a parallel advance, and this, with changes in
communication, indicates that the essential development at this age is a
change towards definition of the goal and path of action by 'deferred
imitations' or recollected experiences. Infants in Piaget's Stage III and IV
are manifesting thinking about the fate of objects with increasing imagination
and rational insight, learning to go through strategies for actions that will
reveal objects and their affordances that cannot be directly present in
perception, and gaining an ability to represent the effects of a particular
process of hiding or transformation that eliminates direct perception of the
object. At the same age they also perceive familiar companions as the
occasion for exercise of habitual forms of play. Proof that actions and not
just objects are represented in the child's mind comes from the spontaneous
displays of learned tricks of gesture and expression to strangers who have
never presented the model from which the action was imitated, and who
frequently do not understand or recognise what the infant is doing
(Trevarthen, 1986b) (Figure 10).

An infant who removes a screen that has been placed to hide an object,
or who tracks to the displacements of containers concealing an object the
infant wants, is representing at least the consequences of a previously
experienced act. A successful tracking and manipulation act of the child is
repeated. The insight is a plan of intermediary moves that will reveal the
object again. It develops from a simple repetition of a movement in the
direction of the place where the object disappeared to a movement that takes
account of any transportations of the hiding place by another person. Likewise, when a child, who has learned to 'imitate' hand clapping with a parent,

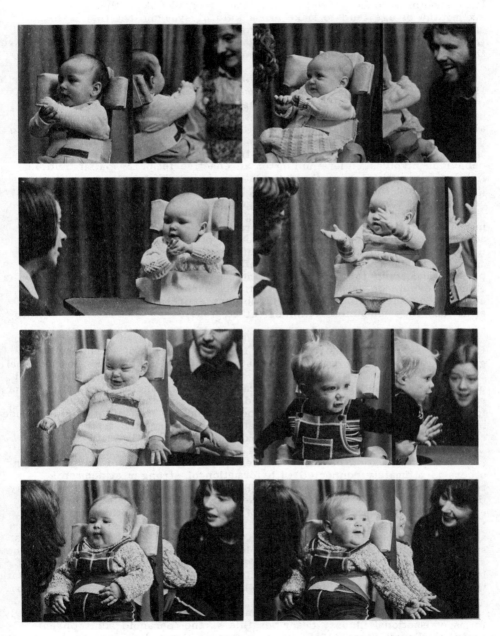

Fig. 10. Showing-off tricks to strangers, who do not understand.

presents this behaviour to a stranger as a friendly of defiant act of communication, this, too, manifests an insight about the act as an intermediary or mediating function. Here it is used to get the reward of attention. It is something to be shared. In the same way all 'jokes' that infants over six months of age tend to make are a kind of symbolic act that is to be shared. They represent both recollection of the self as a presenter and of the other as an audience. They carry a rudimentary conventional value given them by the mental contact established.

Penelope Hubley and I (Trevarthen & Hubley, 1978; Hubley & Trevarthen 1979) have described a major development in communication that takes place when an infant is 9 months of age. We identified it with the beginning of interest in the potentialities of actions that link or combine object-directed and person-directed plans. With this development, infants begin to seek to involve others in their own actions on objects, and they are prepared to modify what they do according to instructions received from others. This behaviour involves understanding of an enactive temporo-spatial field, a field of pragmatic deixis: the articulation of the different perspectives of the infant and the other, an interest in the other's expressions of curiosity or purpose, a following of gaze and gesture to identify focus of another's oriented interest and an imitation of gestures that others use to show and indicate, or of acts that others perform on objects. Now the infant can accept directives about the desired course of manipulative behaviour that uses objects for an arbitrary purpose formulated by the other. Furthermore, at this stage of development infants evaluate objects, events or persons according to the emotions that others express with reference to the objects, events or persons - they actively perform 'emotional referencing', checking on the feelings that their mothers express about objects or situations they encounter (Klinnert et al, 1982).

Up until this stage, the infant has been incapable of sharing a task. Imitations since 5 months have taken the form of ways of vocalising, grimacing, gesturing or posturing that others have given positive emotional evaluation (Trevarthen, 1986b). Now effective acts of communication about objects in the world that the infant can share with another are imitated; or, rather, they are accepted as a shared code of expression by which plans for explorations and object use may be negotiated. The infant begins to use intonational and gestural patterns that have been imitated from the conventionalised acts of meaning of older companions.

This modification of purposefulness to admit sharing of purposes with others is intimately connected with formation of stronger attachments regulated by more intense emotions (Bowlby, 1958; Ainsworth, 1982). Many developmental studies and clinical observations have reported a heightened emotionality at about 7 or 8 months of age, just prior to the emergence of Secondary Intersubjectivity. Anxious fearfulness is manifested to strangers and an angry impatience is displayed when a person to whom the infant is strongly attached fails to act in compliance with the infant's wishes. At the same time self-conscious 'showing off' behaviours increase, both when the infant is confronting his or her own face in a mirror and also in confrontation with other persons (Lewis & Brooks-Gunn, 1979; Trevarthen, 1985, 1986b).

Melanie Klein (Klein, 1952), in a psychoanalytic interpretation of early forms of emotional illness, describes this as the 'paranoid schizophrenic position'. Daniel Stern (1985) in an important theoretical synthesis of psychoanalytic and developmental psychological concepts of infant development describes this period as one of 'intersubjective relatedness' when the infant begins to perceive mental states in others. I consider the changes in intensity of emotion to be connected with development of new motives for cooperating with others, and of control for the exercise of these motives (Trevarthen, 1979b, 1980b, 1982a, 1983). One-year-olds have entered a new range of communications that require helpful, interested attention from partners. They are more skilled but at the same time more dependent on the directives, assistance, evaluations and appreciative responses of others. Many of the infants' signals in this communication are idiosynchratic, peculiar to that child and that family. They are effective because they have been learned in negotiations with the same familiar partners who quickly recognise their meaning. Strangers cannot offer the same support. The responses of the mother to her infant can vary widely and are certainly dependent upon many factors, of temperament, personality, social background, education, health, personality, relationships with husband, parents and other family members, employment, etc. that distinguish mothers. Such differences are shown up in the way mothers talk to infants (Trevarthen & Marwick, 1986).

Michael Halliday (1975, 1978), who described the emergence of proto-language of his son Nigel, was codifying forms of vocalisations that had meaning because they were associated with experiences that had been shared with the parent to whom they were now being uttered. Such a system of communication is completely dependent upon recollection of events and behaviours in a particular maintained companionship. It does not transfer to unfamiliar persons. At this age, deaf infants living in a home where signing is a normal means of communication not only understand the messages intended by some hand movements, but reproduce rudimentary forms of hand signs for action on objects that have become of importance for them in cooperative play (Goldin-Meadow & Feldman, 1977). These signs are usually not recognisible to proficient adult signers using the same language. Though distinct and used deliberately and appropriately, they are protolanguage versions that only the parent can comprehend.

Fearful behaviour towards strangers, of infants who are on the threshold of task sharing and protolanguage in play with their parents, seems to represent a heightened awareness of the inevitable dependence of this kind of communication on the presence of persons who are both familiar and trusted. The emotions of attachment and of fear of strangers are a regulatory mechanism for the exercise of motives that determine sharing of tasks and of ideas about the properties and usefulness of things in a familiar world. To put it another way, the psychological function of perceiving meaningful usefulness in objects depends at first on an established representation of a particular known and trusted person, or a few familiar persons. Out of the representation of the self in affectionate relationship to this other (or these others) causes the motivation to share messages about objects identified and emotionally valued within the relationship. This is the first opening of the child's 'zone of proximal development' (Vygotsky, 1962; 1978) to meanings in a shared material world.

At one year, infants show many behaviours that point towards speech and language, those communicating by hand signing demonstrating that the essential development is more fundamental than the making or understanding of speech as such. Audio-vocal and visuo-manual expressions are equivalent means for communicating meanings. A one-year-old has interest in objects that others find interesting and will modify manipulative performances according to the instructions that others give. Already objects are given value and learned as goals for handling through a process of reference to how others use them. the child uses vocalisations in protolanguage, repeatedly applying the same acquired vocal forms. These protowords are partly imitative of the sounds adults make when they designate a thing, an act or a meaningful gesture with a word. At the same time imitated pointing and other gestures add definition to the communicative purpose of the child.

With the emergence of babbling and protolanguage, lateral asymmetry of cerebral control for hand gestures becomes more marked and in many infants definitive hand preference is clearly manifest at this age (Trevarthen, 1986b). Engagement of interest with others is clearly shown by searching for eye contact with them, timing of expressiveness to fit their speech, and adjustment of posture to follow the goals of their shifting attention (Bretherton & Bates, 1979). The structures involved in such protolinguistic engagements have been evident in less coordinated forms throughout the course of post-natal development to this stage, which we have reviewed.

CONCLUSIONS

Mother-infant communication shows consistent kinematic, physiognomic and energetic features. At the same time both subjects have a great variety of expressions and they show a remarkable capacity for mutual adjustment. Such performance requires that the infant possess special cerebral regulatory structures that govern the patterns and rates of a large number of expressive acts, made by postures, gestures, face movements and vocalisations. The same structures confer a sensitivity to invariants in signals caused by equivalent expressions of the mother than can inform the infant about her motives and emotional states.

In introductory sections it was demonstrated that coordination and control of acts with perceptions requires representation in the CNS of the body's parts, and their temporal and spatial relationships when in movement. In addition there must be cerebral neural arrangements that can specify evaluations of objects relative to essential life functions and that can determine the locations and displacements of objects in the action space outside the subject.

Recent descriptive and experimental studies of infant behaviours proves that the human brain has at birth more structure dedicated to complex mental operations than had been expected in a psychology greatly influenced by empiricist philosophy. Evidently learning to perceive, learning to act with skilful control of body forces and in precise adjustment to external surfaces and objects and learning to comprehend transformations of circumstances in the outside world that are due to causes outside the brain cannot create the fundamental cerebral systems for perception, motor coordination and cognition. These systems have an innate basis - generated among neural arrays before birth - that is capable of selecting stimulus information needed for further developments.

The remarkable precocity of newborns for communication with the emotional and expressive states of other persons, and their immediate readiness to establish a specially close relationship with the mother, or a substitute person offering the same kind of care, indicates that human cerebral perceptuo-motor systems include a great set that has inherent specialisation for engagement with mental control processes in other human subjects.

If a newborn has an active capacity to reciprocate with human emotions and other forms of motivation, including some with evident resemblance to motivation for language, then the newborn can be said to possess both a rudimentary human 'self' and the capacity for 'intersubjectivity'. This self can interact elaborately with another human in the first two months after birth, before the infant can engage in systematic exploratory or performatory actions *vis à vis* the world of physical objects and before the infant can control posture against gravity or perform independent locomotion.

A fundamental component of the mechanism that permits the infant to interact with an adult is a time base. Expressive movements are built up round a beat with a range of tempos that match those that all human adults show and that are spontaneously expressed, and codified, in music and dance. Kinematic forms (rhythms) in human expression, organised round the beat, are regulated by another level of central neural mechanisms, some of which are evidently functional from birth. The physiognomics and energetics of facial and vocal expression appear to derive their organisation from additional inherent structures that translate a great variety of central regulatory states of the brain, the emotional states, into representative patterns of activity in motor neuronal pools of the brain stem that innervate musculature of the face, vocal tracts and hands. Thus the infant can, from birth, indicate the fluctuating balance between different neural and neuro-humoral systems that control ergic against trophic states, exploration and curiosity against rest and withdrawal from stimulation, intense effortful action against relaxed sleep and recuperation. Distinct emotional states of joy, sadness, anger, disgust, fear and concentrated curiosity can be discriminated in the expressive patterns of infants' movements. These inner cerebral motive states, which probably have great importance in the immature brain's regulation of its own development and response to stimuli, respond strongly to signals carried in the movements and expressions of the mother. She, as key member of the infant's human environment, becomes a collaborator in the autoregulation of the growing infant's brain.

As cognitive development brings the infant effective skills for perceiving and identifying objects, and for acting on them with manipulation, the already established emotional partnership with the mother serves as a regulator of knowledge. The infant gains an ability to understand objects and to act on them in cooperation with the consciousness and intentionality of one or a few liked and trusted older human companions. Attachments formed in early months allow communication of intricate learned mental evaluations and plans, including those of language.

It is impossible to understand the more elaborate developments in human communication, including a vast range of cultural, social and moral ideas, without first having at least a general understanding of their basis in inter-subjective regulations that govern expressive movements in early infancy.

SUMMARY

A theory of the intercoordination of movements of expression between persons is developed from a more general theory of motor coordination in individuals for intelligent, adaptive behaviour, and its principles are applied to explain the rapid development of human communication in early childhood. Evidence is presented that the timing, quality and form of expressive movements, and the perception of the expressiveness of others by these same features (alteroception), are built on neuroembryological events that specify forms of communication (states of intersubjectivity) *in utero*. It is proposed that these inborn neural systems motivate the individual's cognitive development and the attainment of social and cultural competence and self-reliance. They require support from a responsive 'human environment' that has matching motivations complementary to the child's needs for interaction.

ACKNOWLEDGEMENTS

Research discussed here has been supported by grants from the Medical and Social Science Research Councils of the U.K. and the Spencer Foundation of Chicago. A study of Nigerian mothers was carried out in collaboration with Professor A.C. Mundy-Castle and staff of the Department of Psychology, University of Lagos. I am indebted to Dr. Maria Luisa Genta, of the Department of Educational Science, University of Calabria, for mother's songs from Southern Italy, and to Mrs. Sereba Agiobu-Kemmer for Nigerian songs. I wish also to thank the mothers who were generous with their time and good will.

References

Ainsworth, M.D.S. (1982). Attachment: Retrospect and prospect. In C.M. Parkes and J. Stevenson-Hinde (Eds.), *The Place of Attachment in Human Behavior*. London: Tavistock.

Alegria, J. & Noirot, E. (1978). Neonate orientation behaviour towards the human voice. *Early Human Development, 1,* 291-312.

Arbib, M.A. (1984). From synergies and embryos to motor schemes. In H.T.A. Whiting (Ed.), *Human Motor Actions - Bernstein Reassessed.* Amsterdam: North-Holland Publishing Co.

Baldwin, J.M. (1894). *Mental Development in the Child and the Race.* New York: Macmillan.

Baldwin, J.M. (1902). *Social and Ethical Interpretations in Mental Development* (3rd Ed.). New York: Macmillan.

Bateson, M.C. (1975). Mother-infant exchanges: the epigenesis of conversational-interaction. In D. Aaronson and R.W. Rieber (Eds.), *Developmental Psycholinguistics and Communication Disorders. Annals of the New York Academy of Sciences, Vol. 263.* New York: New York Academy of Sciences.

Beebe, B., Stern, D. & Jaffe, J. (1979). The kinesic rhythm of mother-infant interactions. In A.W. Siegman and S. Feldstein (Eds.), *Of Speech and Time: Temporal Patterns in Interpersonal Contexts.* Hillsdale, NJ: Erlbaum.

Beebe, B., Jaffe, J., Feldstein, S., Mays, K. & Alson, D. (1985). Interpersonal timing: The application of an adult dialogue model to mother-infant vocal and kinesic interactions. In T.M. Field and N. Fox (Eds.), *Social Perception in Infants.* Norwood, NJ: Ablex.

Bernstein, N. (1967/1984). *The Coordination and Regulation of Movements.* Oxford: Pergamon. (Republished with commentaries in H.T.A. Whiting (Ed.), *Human Motor Actions: Bernstein Reassessed.* Amsterdam: North-Holland Publishing Co.).

Birdwhistell, R.L. (1952). *Introduction to Kinesics.* Louisville, KY: University of Louisville Press.

Birdwhistell, R.L. (1970). *Kinesics and context: Essays on body motion communication.* Philadelphia: University of Pennsylvania Press.

Blacking, J. (1976). *How Musical is Man?* London: Faber and Faber.

Bowlby, J. (1958). The nature of a child's tie to his mother. *International Journal of Psychoanalysis, 39,* 350-373.

Bretherton, I. & Bates, E. (1979). The emergence of intentional communication. In I.C. Uzgiris (Ed.), *New Directions for Child Development, Vol. 4.*

Buber, M. (1937). *I and Thou.* Edinburgh: T. & T. Clark.

Buck, R. (1984). *The Communication of Emotion.* New York: Guilford.

Clayton, A.M.H. (1986). *Coordination Between Players in Musical Performance.* Thesis for PhD, University of Edinburgh.

Condon, W.S. & Sander, L.W. (1974). Neonate movement is synchronized with adult speech: interactional participation and language acquisition. *Science, 183,* 99-101.

Craig, W. (1918). Appetites and aversions as constituents of instincts. *Biological Bulletin, 34,* 91-107.

Crystal, D. (1973). Non-segmental phonology in language acquisition: A review of the issues. *Lingua, 32,* 1-45.

DeCasper, A. & Fifer, W. (1980). Of human bonding: Newborns prefer mother's voices. *Science, 208,* 1174.

Demany, L., Mackenzie, B. & Vurpillot, E. (1977). Rhythm perception in early infancy. *Nature, 266,* 718-719.

256

Ekman, P. & Friesen, W.V. (1978). *Manual for the facial action coding system*. Palo Alto, CA: Consulting Psychologists' Press.

Ekman, P., Levenson, R.W. & Friesen, W.V. (1983). Autonomic nervous system activity distinguishes among emotions. *Science, 211,* 1208-1210.

Feldstein, S. (1972). Temporal patterns of dialogue: Basic research and reconsiderations. In A.W. Siegman and B. Pope (Eds.), *Studies in Dyadic Communication*. New York: Pergamon.

Feldstein, S. & Welkowitz, J. (1978). A chronography of conversation: In defense of an objective spproach. In A.W. Siegman and S. Feldstein (Eds.), *Nonverbal behavior and communication*. Hillsdale, NJ: Erlbaum.

Field, T.M. (1982). Individual differences in the expressivity of neonates and young infants. In R.W. Feldman (Ed.), *Development of Non-verbal Behaviour in Children*. New York: Springer Verlag.

Field, T.M. (1985). Neonatal perception of people: Maturational and individual differences. In T.M. Field, and N.A. Fox (Eds.), *Social Perception in Infants*. Norwood, NJ: Ablex.

Field, T.M., Woodson, R., Greenberg, R. & Cohen, D. (1982). Discrimination and imitation of facial expressions by neonates. *Science, 218,* 179-181.

Field, T.M. & Fox, N. (1985) (Eds.), *Social Perception in Infants*. Norwood, NJ: Ablex.

Fraiberg, S. (1980). *Clinical Studies in Infant Mental Health: The First Year of Life*. London: Travistock.

Gallistel, C.R. (1980). *The Organization of Action*. Hillsdale, NJ: Erlbaum.

Goldberg, G. (1985). Supplementary motor area structure and function: Review and hypotheses. *The Behavioral and Brain Sciences, 8 (4),* 567-616.

Goldin-Meadow, S. & Feldman, H. (1977). The development of language-like communication without a language model. *Science, 197,* 401-403.

Habermas, J. (1972). *Knowledge and Human Interests*. London: Heinemann.

Hamburger, V. (1973). Anatomical and physiological basis of embryonic motility in birds and mammals. In G. Gottlieb (Ed.), *Studies on the Development of Behavior and the Nervous System, Vol. 1.Behavioural Embryology*. New York: Academic Press.

Hess, W.R. (1964). *The Biology of Mind*. Chicago: University of Chicago Press.

Hofsten, C. von (1980). Predictive reaching for moving objects by human infants. *Journal of Experimental Child Psychology, 30,* 369-382.

Hofsten, C. von (1984). Developmental changes in the organization of prereaching movements. *Developmental Psychology, 20,* 378-380.

Hofsten, C. von (1985). Perception and action. In M. Frese and J. Sabini (Eds.), *Goal Directed Behavior: The Concept of Action in Psychology*. Hillsdale, NJ: Erlbaum.

Holst, E. von (1937). Vom Wesen der Ordnung in Zentralnervensystem. *Naturwissenschaften, 25,* 625-631 and 641-647.

Holst, E. von (1973). Relative coordination as a phenomenon and as a method of analysis of central nervous functions. In *The Behavioral Physiology of Animals and Man. Selected Papers of Eric von Holst*. Coral Gables, Florida: University of Miami Press.

Holst, E. von & Saint-Paul, U. von (1963). On the functional organization of drives. *Animal Behaviour, 11,* 1-20.

Imbert, M. (1985). Physiological underpinnings of perceptual development. In J. Mehler and R. Fox (Eds.), *Neonate Cognition: Beyond the Blooming, Buzzing Confusion*. Hillsdale, NJ: Erlbaum.

Izard, C.E. (1978). On the ontogenesis of emotions of emotion-cognition relationships in infancy. In M. Lewis and L.A. Rosenblum (Eds.), *The Development of Affect*. New York: Plenum.

Izard, C.E. (1979). *The Maximally Discriminative Facial Movement Coding System (Max.)*, Newark, Del: University of Delaware, Instructional Resources Center.

Jaffe, J. & Feldstein, S. (1970). *Rhythms of Dialogue*. New York: Academic Press.

Jaffe, J., Stern, D. & Peery, J. (1973). "Conversational" coupling of gaze behavior in prelinguistic human development. *Journal of Psycholinguistics, 2*, 321-329.

Johansson, G. (1975). Visual motion perception. *Scientific American, 323*, 37-88.

Klein, M. (1952). *Developments in Psycho-Analysis*. In J. Rivere (Ed.). London: Hogarth Press.

Klinnert, M.D. et al (1983). Emotions as behaviour regulators: Social referencing in infancy. In R. Plutchik and H. Kellerman (Eds.), *Emotion: Theory, Research and Experience, Vol. 2. Emotions in Early Development*. Academic Press.

Kornhuber, H.H. (1974). Mechanisms of voluntary movement. In W. Prinz and A.F. Sanders (Eds.), *Cognition and Motor Processes*. Berlin, Heidelberg: Springer.

Kugiumutzakis, J.E. (1985). *The Origin, Development, and Function of the Early Infant Imitation*. Uppsala University, PhD Thesis.

Kuhl, P.K. & Meltzoff, A.N. (1982). The bimodal perception of speech in infancy. *Science, 218*, 1138-1141.

Lashley, K.S. (1951). The problem of serial order in behavior. In L.A. Jeffress (Ed.), *Cerebral Mechanisms in Behavior*. New York: Wiley.

Laver, J. (1980). *The Phonetic Description of Voice Quality*. London: Cambridge University Press.

Lee, D.N. (1978). The functions of vision. In H.L. Pick Jr. and E. Saltzman (Eds.), *Modes of Perceiving and Processing Information*.

Lee, D.N. (1980). The optic flow field: The foundation of vision. *Philosophical Transactions of the Royal Society, Series B., 290*, 169-179.

Lester, B.M. (1983). A biosocial model of infant crying. In L.P. Lipsitt and C. Rovee-Collier (Eds.), *Advances in Infancy Research, Vol. 3*. Norwood, NJ: Ablex.

Lewis, M. & Brooks, Gunn, J. (1979). *Social Cognition and the Acquisition of Self*. New York: Plenum.

Lyons, J. (1977). *Semantics (2 volumes)*. Cambridge: Cambridge University Press.

MacMurray, J. (1961). *Persons in Relation*. London: Faber and Faber.

MacNeilage, P.F. (1970). Motor control of serial ordering of speech. *Psychological Review, 77*, 182-196.

Maratos, O. (1973). *The Origin and Development of Imitation in the First Six Months of Life*. PhD Thesis, University of Geneva.

Maratos, O. (1982). Trends in the development of imitation in early infancy. In T.G. Bever (Ed.), *Regressions in Mental Development*. Hillsdale, NJ: Erlbaum.

Marwick, H., Mackenzie, J., Laver, J. & Trevarthen, C. (1984). Voice quality as an expressive system in mother-to-infant communication: A case study. *Work in Progress, NO. 17*. University of Edinburgh, Department of Linguistics.

Mehler, J., Bertoncini, J. & Barriere, M. (1978). Infant recognition of mother's voice. *Perception, 7*, 491-497.

Mehler, J. & Fox, R. (1985). *Neonate Cognition: Beyond the Blooming Buzzing Confusion*. Hillsdale, NJ: Erlbaum.

258

Meltzoff, A.N. (1985). The roots of social and cognitive development:
Models of Man's original nature. In T.M. Field and N.A. Fox (Eds.),
Social Perception in Infants. Norwood, NJ: Ablex.

Meltzoff, A.N. & Moore, M.H. (1977). Imitation of facial and manual
gestures by human neonates. *Science, 198*, 75-78.

Meltzoff, A.N. & Moore, M.H. (1983). Newborn infants imitate adult facial
gestures. *Child Development, 54*, 702-709.

Michotte, A. (1950). The emotions regarded as functional connections.
In M.L. Reymert (Ed.), *Feelings and Emotions*. New York: McGraw
Hill.

Michotte, A. (1962). *Causalite, Permanence et Realite Phenomenales*.
Louvain: Publications Universitaires.

Mountcastle, V.B. (1976). The world around us: Neural command functions
for selective attention. *Neurosciences Research Program Bulletin (Suppl)*,
14, 1-47.

Moore, G. (1943). *The Unashamed Accompanist*. London: Methuen.

Murray, L. & Trevarthen, C. (1985). Emotional regulation of interactions
between two-month-olds and their mothers. In T. Field and N. Fox
(Eds.), *Social Perception in Infants*. Norwood, NJ: Ablex.

Murray, L. & Trevarthen, C. (1986). The infant's role in mother-infant
communication. *Journal of Child Language, 13*, 15-29.

Neisser, U. (1976). *Cognition and Reality: Principles and Implications of
Cognitive Psychology*. San Francisco: Freeman.

Olds, J. (1962). Hypothalamic substrates of reward. *Physiological Reviews,
42*, 554-604.

Oller, D.K. (1981). Infant vocalizations: Exploration and reflexivity. In
R.E. Stark (Ed.), *Language Behavior in Infancy and Early Childhood*.
Amsterdam: Elsevier, North-Holland.

Oppenheim, R.W. (1982). Preformation and epigenesis in the origins of the
nervous system and behavior: Issues, concepts and their history. In
P. Bateson and P. Klopfer (Eds.), *Perspectives in Ethology, Vol. 4:
Ontogeny*. New York: Plenum.

Oster, H. (1978). Facial expression and affect development. In M. Lewis
and L.A. Rosenblum (Eds.), *The Development of Affect*. New York:
Plenum.

Oster, H. & Ekman, P. (1977). Facial behavior in child development. In
A. Collins (Ed.), *Minnesota Symposia on Child Development (Vol. II)*.

Papousek, H. (1967). Experimental studies of appetitional behavior in human
newborns and infants. In H.W. Stevenson, E.H. Hess and H.L. Rhinegold
(Eds.), *Early Behavior, Comparative and Developmental Approaches*. New
York: Wiley.

Papousek, M. & Papousek, H. (1981). Musical elements in infants'
vocalization: Their significance for communication, cognition and
creativity. In L.P. Lipsitt (Ed.), *Advances in Infancy Research (Vol. 1)*.
Norwood, NJ: Ablex.

Papousek, M., Papousek, H. & Bornstein, M.H. (1985). The naturalistic
vocal environment of young infants: On the significance of homogeneity
and variability in parental speech. In T.M. Field and N. Fox (Eds.),
Social Perception in Infants. Norwood, NJ: Ablex.

Papousek, H., Papousek, M. & Koester,L.S. (1986). Sharing emotionality
and sharing knowledge: A microanalytic approach to parent-infant
communication. In C.E. Izard and P.B. Read (Eds.), *Measuring
Emotions in Infants and Children, Vol. 2*. New York: Cambridge University
Press.

Piaget, J. (1954). *Origins of Intelligence*. New York: Basic Books.

Prechtl, H.F.R. (1984) (Ed.), *Continuity of Neural Functions from Pre-
to Post-Natal Life*. Oxford: Spastics International Medical Publications.

Robson, K.S. (1967). The role of eye-to-eye contact in maternal-infant
attachment. *Journal of Child Psychology and Psychiatry, 8,* 13-25.

Runeson, S. & Frykholm, G. (1981). Visual perception of lifted weight.
Journal of Experimental Psychology: Human Perception and Performance, 7,
733-740.

Scheibel, A.B. (1984). The brain stem, reticular core and sensory function.
In I. Darian-Smith (Volume ed.), *Handbook of Physiology Section I, The
Nervous System, Vol. III Sensory Processes, Part I*. Bethesda, MD:
American Physiological Society.

Scherer, K.R. (1982). The assessment of vocal expression in infants and
children. In C.E. Izard (Ed.), *Measuring Emotions in Infants and
Children*. Cambridge: Cambridge University Press.

Shaffer, L.H. (1982). Rhythm and timing in skill. *Psychological Review,
89,* 109-122.

Singer, W. (1984). Learning to see: Mechanisms in experience-dependent
development. In P. Marler and H.S. Terrace (Eds.), *The Biology of
Learning*. Dahlem Conference. Berlin, Heidelberg: Springer.

Spelke, E.S. (1985). Perception of unity, persistence and identity:
Thoughts on infants' conceptions of objects. In J. Mehler and R. Fox
(Eds.), *Neonate Cognition: Beyond the Blooming Buzzing Confusion*.
Hillsdale, NJ: Erlbaum.

Stern, D.N. (1974). The goal and structure of mother-infant play. *Journal
of the American Academy of Child Psychiatry, 13,* 402-421.

Stern, D.N. (1985). *The Interpersonal World of the Infant*. New York:
Basic Books.

Stern, D.N., Spieker, S. & MacKain, K. (1982). Intonation contours as
signals in maternal speech to prelinguistic infants. *Developmental
Psychology, 18,* 727-735.

Studdert-Kennedy, M. (1983). On learning to speak. *Human Neurobiology,
2,* 191-195.

Sylvester-Bradley, B. & Trevarthen, C. (1978). Baby talk as an
adaptation to the infant's communication. In N. Waterson and C. Snow
(Eds.), *Development of Communication: Social and Pragmatic Factors in
Language Acquisition*. London: Wiley.

Tinbergen, N. (1951). *The Study of Instinct*. London: Oxford University
Press.

Tinbergen, N. (1952). "Derived" activities. Their causation, biological
significance and emancipation during evolution. *Quarterly Review of
Biology, 27,* 1-32.

Thelen, E. (1984). Learning to walk: Ecological demands and phylogenetic
constraints. In L.P. Lipsitt and C. Rovee-Collier (Eds.), *Advances in
Infancy Research, Vol. 3*. New York: Academic Press.

Trevarthen, C. (1968a). Vision in fish: the origins of the visual frame for
action in vertebrates. In D. Ingle (Ed.), *The Central Nervous System
and Fish Behaviour*. Chicago: Chicago University Press.

Trevarthen, C. (1968b). Two mechanisms of vision in primates. *Psychologische
Forschung, 31,* 299-337.

Trevarthen, C. (1972). Brain bisymmetry and the role of the corpus
callosum in behaviour and conscious experience. In J. Cernácek and
F. Podovinsky (Eds.), *Cerebral Interhemispheric Relations*. Proceedings
of an International Colloquium held in Smolenice, June, 1969. Bratislava:
Slovak Academy of Sciences.

Trevarthen, C. (1973). Behavioural embryology. In E.C. Carterette and M.P. Friedman (Eds.), *Handbook of Perception, 3*. New York: Academic Press.

Trevarthen, C. (1974a). Cerebral embryology and the split-brain. In M. Kinsbourne and W.L. Smith (Eds.), *Hemispheric Disconnection and Cerebral Function*. Springfield, Ill: Charles C. Thomas.

Trevarthen, C. (1974b). The psychobiology of speech development. In E.H. Lenneberg (Ed.), *Language and Brain: Developmental Aspects, Neurosciences Research Program Bulletin, 12*, 570-585. Boston: Neurosciences Research Program.

Trevarthen, C. (1977). Descriptive analyses of infant communication behaviour. In H.R. Schaffer (Ed.), *Studies of Mother-Infant Interaction: The Loch Lomond Symposium*. London: Academic Press.

Trevarthen, C. (1978). Modes of perceiving and modes of acting. In J.H. Pick (Ed.), *Psychological Modes of Perceiving and Processing Information*. Hillsdale, NJ: Erlbaum.

Trevarthen, C. (1979a). Communication and cooperation in early infancy. A description of primary intersubjectivity. In M. Bullowa (Ed.), *Before Speech: The Beginnings of Human Communication*. London: Cambridge University Press.

Trevarthen, C. (1979b). Instincts for human understanding and for cultural cooperation: their development in infancy. In M. von Cranach, K. Foppa, W. Lepenies and D. Ploog (Eds.), *Human Ethology*. Cambridge: Cambridge University Press.

Trevarthen, C. (1980a). Functional organization of the human brain. In M.C. Wittrock (Ed.), *The Brain and Psychology*. New York: Academic Press.

Trevarthen, C. (1980b). The foundations of intersubjectivity: development of interpersonal and cooperative understanding in infants. In D. Olson (Ed.), *The Social Foundations of Language and Thought: Essays in Honor of J.S. Bruner*. New York: W.W. Norton.

Trevarthen, C. (1982a). The primary motives for cooperative understanding. In G. Butterworth and P. Light (Eds.), *Social Cognition: Studies of the Development of Understanding*. Brighton: Harvester Press.

Trevarthen, C. (1982b). Basic patterns of psychogenetic change in infancy. In T.G. Bever (Ed.), *Regressions in Mental Development: Basic Phenomena and Theories*. Hillsdale, NJ: Erlbaum.

Trevarthen, C. (1983). Interpersonal abilities of infants as generators for transmission of language and culture. In A. Oliverio and M. Zapella (Eds.), *The Behaviour of human infants*. New York: Academic Press.

Trevarthen, C. (1984a). Biodynamic Structures, cognitive correlates of motive sets and development of motives in infants. In W. Prinz and A.F. Saunders (Eds.), *Cognition and Motor Processes*. Berlin, Heidelberg-New York: Springer Verlag.

Trevarthen, C. (1984b). How control of movements develops. In H.T.A. Whiting (Ed.), *Human Motor Actions: Bernstein Reassessed*. Amsterdam: Elsevier (North-Holland Publishing Co.)

Trevarthen, C. (1984c). Emotions in infancy: Regulators of contacts and relationships with persons. In K. Scherer and P. Ekman (Eds.), *Approaches to Emotion*. Hillsdale, NJ: Erlbaum.

Trevarthen, C. (1985). Facial expressions of emotion in mother-infant interaction. *Human Neurobiology, 4*, 21-32.

Trevarthen, C. (1986a). Neuroembryology and the development of perceptual mechanisms. In F. Falkner and J.M. Tanner (Eds.), *Human Growth* (2nd Ed.). New York: Plenum.

Trevarthen, C. (1986b). Form, significance and psychological potential of hand gestures of infants. In J.L. Nespoulous, P. Perron and A. Roch Lecours (Eds.), *The Biological Foundation of Gestures: Motor and Semiotic Aspects*. Cambridge, Mass: MIT Press.

Trevarthen, C. & Hubley, P. (1978). Secondary intersubjectivity: Confidence, confiding and acts of meaning in the first year. In A. Lock (Ed.), *Action, Gesture and Symbol*. London: Academic Press.

Trevarthen, C. & Marwick, H. (1986). Signs of motivation for speech in infants, and the nature of a mother's support for development of language. In B. Lindblom and R. Zetterstrom (Eds.), *Precursors of Early Speech*. Basingstoke, Hampshire: Macmillan.

Trevarthen, C., Murray, L. & Hubley, P. (1981). Psychology of infants. In J. Davis and J. Dobbing (Eds.), *Scientific Foundations of Clinical Paediatrics*. London: W. Heinemann Medical Books Ltd. (2nd. Ed.).

Uexküll, J. von (1957). A stroll through the worlds of animals and men. In C.H. Schiller (Ed.), *Instinctive Behavior*. New York: International Universities Press.

Valenstein, E.S. (1973). *Brain Stimulation and Motivation*. Chicago: Scott Foresman.

Vygotsky, L.S. (1962). *Thought and Language*. Cambridge, Mass.: MIT Press.

Vygotsky, L.S. (1978). *Mind in Society*. In M. Cole, V. John-Steiner, S. Scribner and E. Souberman (Eds.). Cambridge, Mass.: Harvard University Press.

Weiss, P. (1941). Self-differentiation of the basic patterns of coordination. *Comparative Psychological Monographs, 17,* 1-96.

SUBJECTIVE COMMENTS ON THE DEVELOPMENT OF INTERSUBJECTIVITY

B. Hopkins

1. INTRODUCTION

Dennett (1982) has proposed that explanations and predictions of
behaviour can be made by adopting one of three mutually exclusive stances.
One of these he termed the intentional stance*. Most appropriately used
when a system is too complex to be explained by one of the other two
stances, it ascribes to a system the possession of certain information (e.g.
motives) and supposes it to be directed by particular goals. Above all it
assumes that a system evidences some degree of rationality in producing its
behaviour. Such a stance is clearly represented in Colwyn Trevarthen's
research which he has described as the natural history of infant motives
(Trevarthen, 1980a). In one form or another he applies it to each of the
developmental phases he has identified. It is this comprehensive application
of the intentional stance that makes his approach to the early postnatal
development of communicative behaviour a controversial one.

At the descriptive level Trevarthen's developmental account provides
little ground for controversy. For the first year of life he has identified
four phases which take into account the relationships between the infant's
actions directed towards persons and objects. An important point about his
detailed and exquisite descriptions is that the development of communicative
abilities is closely tied to observable changes in the organisation of motor
behaviour. Such changes, particularly in the control of proximal and distal
limb segments, appear to guide or channel striking transformations in early
communication between infant and adult. In contrast to many other
researchers concerned with mother-infant interaction, Trevarthen has not
concentrated on one or two obvious behaviours in the infant's repertoire,
such as looking and smiling, but has rather brought to our attention a
broad spectrum of complex movement patterns that depict with great clarity
the infant's changing communicative abilities. This committment to a natural
history approach, combined with the judicious use of naturalistic experiments,
has revived a neglected research tradition that was originally established by
the likes of Darwin (1872, 1877) and Preyer (1888). As Tinbergen (1963)
has pointed out, contempt for such an approach can only be to the detriment

---

* The other two are the design and physical stances. In the former,
  explanations of behaviour are done solely on the basis of assumptions
  about a aystem's functional design irrespective of its physical make-up,
  a stance compatible with a cybernetic approach to behaviour. In the latter,
  explanations are based on the actual state of a particular system and by
  applying natural laws to it, a stance seemingly in accord with the
  constraints approach to behaviour.

of any science. In the past a neglect of straightforward baby watching has served to promote unrealistic inferences being drawn about what young infants are capable of and how these capabilities might develop. What sort of inferences does Trevarthen draw from his baby watching activities? They are, to say the least, controversial and stem from his adoption of an intentional stance.

Trevarthen holds the view that organisms develop epigenetically through the differentiation of genetic products. Adopting another principle of embryological growth, he suggests that human infants show elaborate pre-functional activities that foreshadow later-occurring abilities (Trevarthen, 1982). Thus, the newborn's spontaneous and reactive movements give evidence of innate programmes preadapted to coordinate later fine and gross motor abilities. During development they become increasingly open to modulation by proprioceptive, exproprioceptive and extereoproprioceptive influences. Such a view is shared in part by other students of motor development (e.g. Thelen, 1985) and is based on there being similarities in the spatiotemporal properties of certain movement patterns between the newborn and the adult. While this epigenetic view serves as a powerful rejoinder to reflexological notions of development, it rests on certain assumptions about the control of developmental change which become questionable if too rigidly held. Some of these assumptions will be examined in the next section.

To use more of Dennett's (1982) terminology, Trevarthen is an iconophile rather than a Gibsonian iconophobe i.e. he assumes the young infant forms images or representations of others, evidence of which is provided by data on the neonatal imitation of certain expressive movements made by adult models (Trevarthen, 1979a). The existence of such a proto-intersubjective ability at this age would lend support to a stance proposing there are two innate strategies for selectively operating on persons and objects. This precursor ability will be examined in section 2. In addition to foreshadowing later motor abilities, neonatal movements are specifically adapted for communication with adults and, like those directed towards objects, demonstrate the rudiments of intentional behaviour. Such behaviour is regulated by two different modes of action (Trevarthen, 1978).or motives (Trevarthen, 1980a) for interacting with persons and objects, each of which is based on distinct neurological mechanisms. This is Trevarthen at his most controversial. Notions such as motives and intentionality constitute what Kuhlenbeck (1967) has referred to as interphenomena: inferred phenomena beyond the reach of direct observation. If not used with considerable circumspection, their application in explaining the behaviour of preverbal infants can lead to accusations of having committed what James (1890) termed the psychologist's fallacy: imputing mental states to an organism that it may not itself possess. With this pitfall in mind, the concept of intentionality as used in infant studies by Trevarthen and others will be examined in section 3. A final topic will be the role of parental behaviour in the development of intersubjectivity which Trevarthen portrays in ways that depart markedly from the more orthodox accounts of mother-infant interaction.

2.   ACCOUNTING FOR DEVELOPMENTAL CHANGE

The concept of epigenesis as currently subcribed to, envisages onto-genetic development as a gradual, goal-directed transformation of the fertilised egg into a reproductively mature adult. The process by which this end state is reached involves precoded instructions built up of DNA (the so-called genetic programme) and an organised cyptoplasm interacting with a series of epigenetic events that are both intrinsic and extrinsic to the organism. During this process, cells not only increase in number but also change in structure and function becoming different from their earlier forms and from each other. This is the concept of differentation which is

> ...perhaps the most indefinite and most loosely applied
> of any concerned with development (Child, 1944, p. 294).

In addition, a basic tenet of epigenesis is that ontogenetic development constitutes a series of causally-related steps. Needham (1959) puts it as follows:

> Development itself, besides being a period of gene action,
> is a period of complex stepwise (epigenetic) reactions in
> which the conditions of one step cause the next (p. 107).

Implicit in this tenet is that each step in development is a preparatory event or prefunctional adaptation for the next step. In an illuminating article, Oppenheim (1982) has traced the history of this embryological growth concept since the 18th. century and shown how it has been assimilated into the study of behavioural and psychological development*. The application of this concept to the development of complex psychological processes such as communication is fraught with pitfalls chief among which is that of 'sort-crossing' (Turbayne, 1971): the production of misleading analogies through the reapplication of concepts at other levels of explanation. As Cutting (1982) has pointed out in his critique of the post-Gibsonian ecological approach, terms cut off from the roots of their disciplinary matrix die out or become something different than they were. It is not at all clear, at least to this reactor, how the development of intersubjectivity is positively analogous to prefunctional adaptations noted during embryological growth as suggested by Trevarthen (1982). The use of organic analogies in developmental psychology has had a long and checkered history starting with Spencer and subsequently applied in controversial ways by the likes of Baldwin, Hall, Gesell, Werner and Piaget. One of the problems in this re-application of embryological concepts is that developmental psychologists have not always paid sufficient attention to the revisions that embryologists have made in their conceptual thinking. One recent example in this respect concerns the genetic or developmental programme concept, a concept which arose as a resolution of the epigenesis-preformationism debate (i.e. a programme regulates the outline of development while the process of epi-genesis sketches in the major details. See Løvtrup, 1974).

The notion of genetic programmes generating the formation of adapted parts has recently been subjected to a re-evaluation by embryologists (Stent, 1981; Webster & Goodwin, 1981; Goodwin, 1982; Newman & Leonard, 1983). This reappraisal has arisen as the nature of such programmes and how they

---

* He has also shown that the present distinction between predetermined and probabilistic epigenesis made in developmental psychology (Gottlieb, 1976) is an unnecessary one, as from the beginning of this century experimental embryologists never held the view that development followed an invariant, predetermined or inevitable course. Rather, they conceived of developmental outcomes as resulting probabilistically from a bidirectional relationship between structure and function.

generate organismic form have remained unresolved problems. In addition, the application of this and other artifactual mechanisms such as referent values in servomechanisms raise the problem of an infinite regress (Dennett, 1982): where do these mechanisms come from and what controls them? Thus, to explain development by recourse to a directing agency such as a genetic programme ultimately leads to a resurrection of the homunculus hypothesis which the concept of epigenesis was supposed to have banished. Given these problems it is not surprising that Webster and Goodwin (1982) have gone so far as to depict the programme concept as "...the last vestige of a mystifying holism (p. 48)". Stent (1981) has argued that the only event of development that is programmatic is the formation of proteins in which amino acids are assembled into a polypeptide chain of a particular primary structure. Here there is an isomorphic correspondence between the arrangement of DNA bases and the sequence of amino acids in the protein molecule. Subsequent events, such as the folding of the polypeptide chain, are not programmatic in this way since they are consequences of the environment in which the protein molecule is found. Development according to this view is a reproducible but non-programmatic process which follows natural laws and not a predefined script somehow encoded in the genes. There is no evidence that a cell changes its state by means of referring to information supplied directly from a genetic programme (Goodwin, 1982). Rather, complex but standard morphological forms emerge from stereotyped interactions between precursor cells with limited repertoires and hetero-geneously distributed extracellular factors (Newman & Leonard, 1983). The take-home message of this dissatisfaction with the programme concept in embryology is that development at whatever level of analysis need not follow the instructions of some mysterious directing agency but only physical laws that bind an organism to its external environment. In the study of the development of coordinated action it is now increasingly recognised that the specification of changes in such action by some central programme leads to an overly narrow (and unrealistic) view of understanding the developmental processes involved (Kugler *et al*, 1982; Fentress, 1984). Such an under-standing cannot be promoted by assuming for a concept an explanatory role in biological change when that concept itself cannot be accounted for other than in terms of a biologically unrealistic metaphor.

One of the most difficult problems in accounting for developmental change is that of establishing functional interconnections between earlier and later occurring events during ontogeny. The strong form of epigenesis assumes that successive events in ontogeny are somehow causally-related to each other with each one representing preparatory-steps-on-the-way towards reproductive maturity. As Oppenheim (1981) has pointed out, such a view of development if too rigidly held ignores a class of recognised events he terms ontogenetic adaptations: transient age-specific structures and functions which are adaptive only for a restricted phase of development and which may be unnecessary or even incompatible with adaptation at later phases*. Oppenheim (1981, 1984) and Prechtl (1981) have presented a number of examples of such transient phenomena that occur during the development

---

* For example, Harré (1974) rejects Bowlby's (1969) view that adult attachments are a continuation of childhood attachment. Accordingly child-hood attachments must disappear before adulthood is possible. While Harré's discontinuity view is an extreme one, it does raise the importance of recognising that considerable differences existing between the infant's and later social worlds.

of non-metamorphic vertebrates. One relatively clear example of an ontogenetic adaptation in mammalian development is that of suckling, which
disappears after weaning to be replaced by a qualitatively different form of
ingestive behaviour. Blass and Cramer (1982) have recently reviewed a
large body of experimental evidence concerned with the effects of physiological, neurological and behavioural manipulations of suckling on the
development of ingestive behaviour in rats. They concluded that suckling
behaviour in the first 12 days is analogous to, but not homologous with,
adult food and water intake. This complex behaviour which involves rooting,
nipple attachment and sucking coordinated with swallowing and breathing
cannot be understood with reference to adult feeding mechanisms. It seems
rather that the two forms of ingestive behaviour follow different developmental
paths which merge briefly at about 25 days until weaning is completed.

While the notion that transient structures and functions constitute age-
specific adaptations with no consequences for later development should not
be overexaggerated (Oppenheim, 1981; Prechtl, 1981), they do raise the
largely ignored issue of what constitute precursors and prerequisites in
development. In descriptive terms a precursor in a developmental sequence
is simply a forerunner or an antecedent to some other event without the
implication that there is a functional interconnection between the two. To
assume such an interconnection is to treat a precursor either as a prerequisite (necessary) condition for a later event or in some way facilitating
its appearance. Additionally a prerequisite precursor can be distinguished
as to whether or not it logically forms a fundamental precursor to some
mature state (i.e. it marks the beginning of a developmental sequence). In
biochemistry, where the scientific usage of the term precursor originated, a
prerequisite precursor has a clear meaning. It is an intermediate compound
or molecular complex in a living organism which when activated physio-
chemically is transformed into a specific functional substance. Usually the
prefixes pre-, pro-, or proto- are used to indicate that a compound is a
precursor in this sense. For example, ergosterol (pro-vitamin D2) is
transformed into vitamin D through its activation by ultraviolet radiation. A
facilitative precursor is one that is not entirely necessary for the completion
of a developmental sequence but if absent may delay or qualitatively affect
progression through this sequence. For example, Ross (1982) reported that
an infant who had undergone neonatal tracheotomy and who remained
decannulated until 21 months of age passed through the normal stages of
speech development, except for babbling. While it is presently acknowledged
that babbling is part of the developmental pathway leading to speech
acquisition (Oller, 1980), it would not appear from this report that it forms
a prerequisite precursor for such an acquisition. However, it is possible
that it facilitates speech development in that this complex motor activity may
constitute a form of 'vocal play' for exploring the limits of the laryngeal and
pharyngeal systems in sound production.

In the study of human behavioural development it is notoriously difficult
to establish functional interconnections between earlier and later behaviours
even when, in terms of subject matter and descriptive analysis, they are
seemingly members of the same developmental sequence. In most cases such
interconnections are assumed on the basis of similarities in form and timing
between earlier and later behaviours. Once such similarities have been
demonstrated it is then further assumed that the earlier behaviour constitutes
a prerequisite precursor for the later one (i.e. the process underlying the
earlier behaviour is a necessary condition for the process underlying the
later one). What is difficult to establish then is a theoretical account which

caters not only for the two sets of processes involved but also how one is transformed into the other. Despite a lack of such theoretical accounts, there is currently widespread acceptance that in many of the processes underlying infant perceptual, motor and communicative behaviour, fundamental precursors to mature abilities can be found. For example, in a series of revealing studies Thelen has shown that spontaneous kicking movements in the supine position (Thelen *et al*, 1981) and elicited stepping (Thelen & Fisher, 1982) in young infants are virtually identical movement patterns with a spatiotemporal structure similar to erect locomotion. One possible conclusion (but not the only one drawn by Thelen*) is that kicking and stepping are manifestations of a common central pattern generator which is later directly incorporated into erect locomotion. In contrast, Forssberg's (1985) recent evidence based on similar sorts of analyses indicates considerable differences in the neural organisation of infant stepping (labelled prewalking by Trevarthen, 1982) and adult locomotion. Specifically he found that neo-natal stepping was more akin to digitigrade locomotion in quadrupeds than to the plantigrade gait of the human adult: there was no heel strike in front of the body, the specific knee-ankle coordination of adults was missing and there was no propulsive force in the ankle extensors. Only after the establishment of independent locomotion was there a gradual transformation of the infantile pattern towards the plantigrade gait. Thus, the plantigrade locomotion of adult man cannot be produced exclusively by the same neural mechanisms that generate neonatal stepping. Using the evolutionary hypothesis of recapitulation with terminal addition, Forssberg concluded that man has retained a spinal locomotor mechanism for the control of quadrupedal locomotion which is ultimately transformed during ontogeny by a newly evolved supraspinal system of locomotory control. Forssberg's findings suggest that infantile stepping and kicking may not be straightforward fundamental precursors to erect plantigrade locomotion but rather are functionally related to the development of crawling. This suggestion implies the testable hypothesis that the spatiotemporal relationships between kicking and arm movements in supine should be similar to those involved in crawling.

The search for the fundamental precursors or origins of linguistic communication is considerably more complicated and less open to testable hypotheses. One of the reasons for this state of affairs is that the constituent abilities of adult communication (e.g. awareness of the purposes of others) are difficult to operationalise in terms of infantile precursors. A widely-used approach to this problem is to examine instead the temporal patterning of adult-infant behaviour for evidence of turn-taking that is supposed to characterise adult vocal interchanges. Kaye (1984), for example, studied in detail the patterning of neonatal sucking and maternal tactile behaviour during breast- and bottle-feeding at 2 days and 2 weeks after birth. He found evidence of a turn-taking pattern becoming more clearly expressed by 2 weeks in that mothers increasingly reserved their behaviour for the pauses between their infant's sucking bouts (see also findings of Alberts *et al*, 1983, indicating the emergence of such turn-taking during the first few feedings after birth). Kaye proposes that this 'dialogue' experience has a clear functional connection with adult conversational turn-taking and may constitute the origins of language acquisition.

Trevarthen considers this proposition to be overly mechanistic. It reduces the origins of interpersonal communication to a simple model of

---

* See Thelen (1985) for interpretations of her findings.

alternating stimulus and response which ignores the expressive content of infant behaviour and the true nature of early receptive abilities (Trevarthen, et al, 1981). Such a model places considerable emphasis on the contingent responsiveness of the mother to the infant's behaviour who in turn is imbued with an innate mechanism for detecting any events that are contingent on his own acts (Watson, 1979)*. For Trevarthen, the human newborn has more than just an awareness of contingencies. There are elaborate movement patterns based on anatomically specified coordinative structures which fore-shadow the syntax and semantics of language as well as evidence of perceptual abilities attuned to the expressive movements of others. The question is, of course, how such putative precursors to intersubjective communication such as prespeech movements and particularly imitation can be present in the newborn. Part of the answer lies with the need to pay greater attention to recent findings concerning fetal behavioural development which point to a striking continuity between prenatal and early postnatal life in many non-vital functions. By means of real-time ultra-sound observations it is now clear that many of the neonatal movement patterns appear for the first time very early in prenatal life and, as Prechtl (1985) has pointed out, on the basis of a minimal neural structure. It is more than likely that complex movement patterns such as prespeech begin their process of assembly during early fetal development. Certainly both slow and quick jaw movements some-times accompanied by tongue movements occur for the first time around the postmenstrual age of 10 weeks (De Vries et al, 1982). The fact that pre-speech movements disappear around the time of the first major transition in spontaneous movements (see Hopkins & Prechtl, 1984) suggests they are based on fetal brain mechanisms which become temporarily linked to particular conditions of elicitation in the postnatal environment.

Evidence for neonatal imitation which Trevarthen (1979a) takes to be a special case of intersubjective mirroring, and a reflection of the cognitive mechanisms on which reciprocal communication is based (Trevarthen, 1984) is more difficult to interpret from the perspective of fetal behavioural development. How newborns can match the movements of others to their own movements (seen and unseen) is currently a topic of considerable controversy, in part because such a possibility runs counter to Piaget's (1962) development-al account of imitation. It should be borne in mind, however, that present research on early imitation has so far been concerned with the imitation of ends and not with the imitation of means which was Piaget's chief concern. Evidence for imitation of discrete movement patterns in the neonatal period (Meltzoff & Moore, 1977, 1983; Vinter, 1984) and up to 6 weeks of age (Jacobson, 1979; Maratos, 1982) is confronted with a number of failures to replicate (Hayes & Watson, 1981; McKenzie & Over, 1983a; Koepke et al, 1983; Abravenel & Sigafoos, 1984; Fontaine, 1984). The even stronger claim that neonates (Field et al, 1982) and even preterms of about 36 weeks gestation (Field et al, 1983) can imitate 3 facial expressions (happy, sad and surprised) has still to be examined by independent researchers**.

----

* The notion of infants possessing an innate awareness of contingencies is generally attributed to Watson. But Preyer (1888) proposed a similar innate ability which he treated as a precursor to the development of self-awareness (p. 191).

**Attempts at replication should take into account 2 possible shortcomings in the Field studies: 1. no control group involving presentation of a facial expression beyond habituation was used. 2. only the occurrence of discrete facial movements (e.g. widened lips), not complete facial expressions, were reported across the three models presented which lessens any claims for exact-class imitation.

Criticisms of failures to replicate concentrate on specific points of procedure (Meltzoff & Moore, 1983): inadequate filming techniques, poor operationalisation of the dependent measures involved and a lack of pretest control of exposure to the experimenter's face. Given the need for a high degree of experimental control points to the rather obvious fact that neonatal imitation is not a robust phenomenon that can be expected to be a noticeable event in the earliest interactions between mother and infant. This point is not an issue of much contention (however, see McKenzie & Over, 1983b). The question is rather about the newborn's highest level of performance under optimal conditions and what this performance suggests in terms of underlying perceptual or cognitive processes.

Whether neonatal imitation involves active intermodal matching together with a supramodal form of representation or some set of releasing mechanisms is not an issue that will be taken up here*. More germane is whether this early type of imitation demonstrates selective responding to persons rather than objects. If this could be shown then there would be some support for Trevarthen's notion of there being two innate modes of action regulating the behaviour of human infants. There seems to be only one published study (Jacobson, 1979) which has addressed this issue in the context of early imitation. It does not support Trevarthen's view of an innate attunement to things social: at 6 weeks a moving pen or ball were as effective as the tongue model in eliciting tongue protusions, and hand movements showed no selective responsiveness to a hand model or a dangling ring. In summary, this and other demonstrations of infant 'imitative' behaviour lead to the parsimonious conclusion that what might be innate is a perceptual sensitivity for movement and optical change over time which does not necessarily involve a capacity for amodal representation**. The question of how the newborn brain can generate such visual sensitivity with so little visual experience and then link what is perceived to matching behaviours of its own is a neurological conundrum of the first order. The establishment of recognisable behavioural states around the gestational age of 36 weeks (Nijhuis *et al*, 1982), and the subsequent transformations they undergo in early postnatal life (Wolff, 1984) is a crucial process of neurological development for understanding how the links between perception and action become increasingly specified. If the development of reciprocal communication depends on anything, then it is on the attainment of stable waking states which themselves depend on a firm basis of active, anti-gravity postural control (von Wulfften-Palthe & Hopkins, 1984).

3.   THE CONCEPT OF INTENTIONALITY

Intentionality is a semantically primitive notion which makes it difficult to reduce it to a more fundamental dimension of meaning (Meiland, 1970). In the past it has been treated as a 'nomological dangler' beyond the reach of

---

* Social facilitation, another ethological concept, seems to be ruled out by the use of cross-modal comparisons which check that there are significantly more responses to an appropriate model than to an inappropriate one (see Meltzoff & Moore, 1983).

**Such an iconophobic interpretation directs attention to the question of what sort of information the infant is picking up. One possibility is that neonates might be sensitive to figural coherence in motion displays as Bertenthal *et al* (1984) have shown for infants as young as 3 months exposed to point-light displays of a walking person.

empirical examination (Searle, 1984). Despite these impediments the concept of intentionality has a long history of use in psychological explanations of human behaviour. In the light of this history it is clear that the concept cannot be readily dispensed with in such explanations. Contemporary technical usage of the concept generally treats intentionality as involving certain mental states and events directed at, about or representing particular other entities and states of affairs (Searle, 1984). It is this directedness of mental states that distinguishes the concept of intentionality used technically from everyday English words as "intend" and "intention". Used in this way it provides no basis for distinguishing intentional action from intentional communication. More importantly in the present context it fails to take into consideration the intentional state of perception.

In developmental psychology the concept of intentionality is most closely associated with Piaget (1952). For Piaget intentional actions are not evident until at least Stage IV of his sensorimotor period around 8 or 9 months of age (i.e. with the coordination of secondary circular reactions). It is only then when the emergence of means – end differentiation that behaviour takes on the characteristics of goal-directed intentionality. In contrast Bruner (1973, 1974) has suggested that the formation of intentional actions precedes their realisation in behaviour: intentionality may be present much earlier but does not become evident because the infant is unable to coordinate movements and postural control so as to reach a goal. Identified with the corollary discharge (Sperry, 1950) and efference copy (Von Holst, 1973) models of motor control, intentional action is treated as consisting of 5 criteria:
1. anticipatory awareness of an outcome of an act;
2. selection of appropriate means for achieving an end state;
3. sustained direction of behaviour during deployment of means;
4. stop order defined by an end state and
5. some form of substitution rule by which alternative means can be used for attaining an end state.
The difference between Piaget and Bruner is that Piaget would only accept criterion 5 as evidence of intentionality. As noted by Harding (1982), Bruner's criterion of anticipatory awareness may be the first step in the development of intentional action and intentional communication.

Trevarthen (1978, 1980a) treats the development of intentionality in much the same way as Bruner but with a different terminology. Intentional behaviour is based on two different sets of innate motives which are realised in two modes of discriminating and relating to the external world: a praxic mode and a communicative mode. For Trevarthen (1980a) a motive is an interior cause of action similar in operation to Piaget's schema or Bernstein's motor images. Through learning they become increasingly specialised and transformed into clearly discernable modes of intentional behaviour. The motives underlying subjectivity generate coordinated acts for dealing with objects (the praxic mode) while those for intersubjectivity are specified for interaction with other persons (the communicative mode). Neither Trevarthen nor other supporters of this qualitative distinction in infant behaviour (Brazelton et al, 1974; Richards, 1974; Bruner, 1975) have ever published empirical evidence in support of it. Indirect evidence derived from research on early imitation has already been mentioned which does not support the thesis that young infants can discriminate between objects and persons. A more explicit test of this thesis was carried out by Frye et al (1983). Using signal detection analysis of observer's ratings of infant behaviour, it was found that 3 month-olds could not be judged as to whether they were with their mother or an object. However, with 10 month-olds this judgement could be reliably made. An analysis of the mean rates of occurrence per 20 sec trial for 5 discrete behaviours also failed to distinguish for both age groups whether the infants were interacting with an object or with their mother. In a more recent study Sylvester-Bradley (1985) compared the behaviour of 9 to 11 week-old infants when interacting with their mother to their behaviour when confronted with a small ball moved across their visual field. The comparison involved behavioural categories thought to distinguish between the praxic and communicative modes. At first sight results tended to support Trevarthen's claim for two distinctive modes of behaviour during the period of primary intersubjectivity: infants opened their mouths, lowered their eyebrows and looked towards significantly more with their mothers than with the ball present. However, these were differences in frequency not in kind. Furthermore, eyebrow raising and tongue protusion were positively and significantly correlated between the two situations. On the basis of these latter two findings, Sylvester-Bradley concluded that the infants had acted 'socially' in both conditions and that there is no justification for the claim that infants are born with the ability to categorise people differently from things.

Trevarthen's assumption of two motives or modes of acting serving as precursors to intentional action and intentional communication does not receive clear support from these empirical evaluations. An alternative assumption is that the origins of intentional behaviour can better be conceptualised in terms of the notion of direct perception*. As Searle (1979, 1980) has pointed out, direct perception (or rather perceiving) is the primary form of intentionality which sense-datum theories have mistakenly denied. Perception is not neutral 'sense-datum' but has an intentionality which is presentational rather than representational. That is to say, the difference between an intentional state (like wanting) and the intentionality of perception is that perception is not a representation of the object but a presentation of it (i.e. when I see an object I directly perceive it and do not represent it to myself). Thus, the intentionality of perception is such that its conditions of satisfaction require an object be there and that the object has a certain kind of causal role in the production of the perception**.

Within the ecological approach (Shaw & Bransford, 1977), perception as a causal process (perception 1) is distinguished from perception as an immediate epistemic act (perception 2). Perception 1 involves processes of physical transmission from receptor to cortex. This process provides causal support for perception 2, the act of perceiving, but does not take part in that act as an epistemic mediator. The importance of this distinction, hinted at by Searle, is illustrated by Shaw and Turvey (1981) in their critique of the cybernetic model of communication. Such a model inevitably introduces discontinuities in the descriptions used and raises the following two puzzles:

---

* Since writing this reaction, my attention has been brought to Breuer's (1985) article which also attempts to root the origins of intentionality in direct perception.

**Searle (1980) also made the distinction between intention-in-action (involving conditions of satisfaction which are implicitly present during intentional action) and prior intention (involving representation of conditions before action begins as in Bruner's stop order). Greenfield (1980) used this distinction to state that the sensorimotor infant shows intention-in-action while the older child is capable of both. However, as Greenfield recognised, even the simplest intentions-in-action are representational as they are analogous to the control features of a thermostat.

how is meaning lost in transmission and how is meaning subsequently recovered? The cybernetic answer is that the mechanical properties of the message which are devoid of communicative meaning are converted into something meaningful in the mind of the receiver. But, as Shaw and Turvey pointed out, this answer causally links two distinct scales of description as if they were logically alike: one is concerned with the act of communicating and the other with the properties of the media that mechanically support this act. Avoiding these difficulties requires distinguishing the causal process of transmission (perception 1) from the epistemic act of apprehending what is perceived (perception 2). Here concern is with the development of perception 2 as the foundation upon which intentional behaviour is based. Developmentally perception 2 involves not only an awareness or apprehension of objects but more fundamentally the ability to demarcate objects in space and time (i.e. to perceive them as unitary objects).

While it is not always necessary to invoke concepts of representation such as motives when referring to intentionality, it is necessary, when dealing with the intentionality of perception, to account for the ontological status of the intentional objects (or conditions of potential satisfaction). In Gibsonian terms this accounting involves defining an intentional object in terms of an affordance i.e. in terms of the possibilities it invites or affords for a particular behaviour (Turvey *et al*, 1981). On this view perception involves not 'just awareness' but instead an 'awareness of' what objects afford (Gibson, 1979). To put it Searle's (1980) way, the intentionality of perception is an awareness of the conditions of a certain kind of presentation. It is in this sense that direct perception involves intentionality. As such it is similar to the concept of intentionality previously held by Act Psychology in which there is a directedness of individuals towards objects, but differs from it in that there is no claim that perception is mentally-mediated. In the ecological approach an awareness or apprehension of an object is lawfully specified by the object's structured energy distributions and not by some internal representation of its properties to which the organism seeks a match in the environment (Turvey *et al*, 1981). Such awareness does not involve a complete description of an object but only a perception of its existence in space and time. Direct perception is then non-propositional in nature (Turvey & Shaw, 1979) in that it does not require the imposition of categorical judgements in order to demarcate objects but rather the pick up of information about their invariant spatio-temporal properties. It is the demarcation of an object from its surround and from other objects that permits the perception of its affordances. The ability to demarcate objects both spatially and temporally, it is argued, forms the perceptual basis on which intentional behaviour develops. Research evidence on neonatal 'reaching' (von Hofsten, 1982) suggests this ability may be present at birth.

Spelke (1982), after reviewing research on object perception in early infancy, suggested two general principles by which such demarcation may be achieved. The connected surface principle refers to the spatial connectedness of surfaces in a three-dimensional layout: two surfaces will be perceived as belonging to the same object if they touch each other directly or through other object surfaces. An object's boundaries are perceived at those points where it is not connected with other surfaces. The common movement principle, adapted from the Gestalt principle of common fate, states that two surfaces will be perceived as belonging to the same object if a movement carrying them from one place to another does not destroy the connection between them. The simultaneous application of these two principles would suggest one way in which the newborns in von Hofsten's (1982) 'reaching' study were able to make the necessary demarcation of the moving object. The same principles may also apply to the perception of certain non-rigid movements which are so prevalent in the social world of young infants (e.g. those in facial expressions). That infants, at least as young as 3 months, perceive a unitary, jointed object in the non-rigid movements of a point-light display of a walking person (Berthenthal *et al*, 1984) has already been mentioned (see page 270). Thus, the origin of all intentional behaviour may reside in one mode of perception based on a set of general perceptual abilities rather than in the two modes which Trevarthen suggests.

Intentional communication involves an awareness of the meanings contained in the actions of others. But how do infants develop the ability to detect such interpersonal affordances as, for example, the ability to pick up information about the meaning of expressive behaviours? On the basis of 4 experiments using the preferential looking paradigm, Walker (1982) concluded that infants around 6 months-old could detect the meaning that was invariant across the optic and acoustic presentations of different expressive behaviours (happy, neutral, sad and angry). Walker's preferred (Gibsonian) explanation was that through increasing perceptual differentiation and abstraction infants become progressively more skilled at detecting invariants specifying significant properties or multimodally presented events. Another explanation is that infants can learn that particular facial patterns (e.g. smile) are typically associated with certain types of voices (e.g. happy). A third explanation, essentially similar to Trevarthen's view, is based on Neisser's (1976) notion of physiognomic perception which assumes innate schemata distinctly sensitive to categorical expressions of emotion and intention in others. A similar notion was put forward by Werner (1948) but he suggested it formed a part of all perceptual acts. None of these explanations is designed to provide an adequate account of how intentional communication develops. Such an account requires an evaluation of what it is that parents contribute to the development of communicative abilities in their infants. Trevarthen's evaluation departs markedly from the more orthodox accounts.

4. ON PARENTAL BEHAVIOUR

One currently popular view on the development of communication borrows heavily from the theoretical edifices of Mead (1934) and Vygotsky (1962). The spontaneous behaviour of young infants is somehow transformed into deliberate actions if the infant is provided with appropriate conditions for learning the consequences of his behaviour. Parents readily interpret their infant's behaviours in terms of their potential meanings while at the same time attempting to 'complete' or 'fulfil' them so that they comply with the imposed interpretations. This view has recently been elaborated upon by Kaye (1984). He treats the infant as serving an apprenticeship to parents who provide age-specific opportunities that guide the attainment of those abilities necessary for intentional communication. Initially there is only complementary interaction in that parents attempt to fit in with the temporal structure of their infant's behaviour. The transition from complementary interaction to reciprocal communication is largely dependent on providing the infant apprentice with experiences in message-sending and message-receiving within various frames or contexts of interaction. For example, in the instrumental frame the parent monitors the infant's behaviour, interprets in terms of an intention and acts upon this interpretation to fulfil that intention.

Such frames are environmental supports for those ability sub-routines that the infant lacks. At the same time they facilitate the acquisition of these sub-routines so that the infant increasingly assumes an executive role in interactions with his parents.

Trevarthen's interpretation of the role of parental behaviour in early development appears almost to involve a reversal of roles. Here it seems that it is the parent who is serving the apprenticeship. Accordingly parents react as agents *subordinate* to acts of babies (Trevarthen, 1979a), are *pushed* by their infants towards a shared understanding (Trevarthen, 1980a), and *track* developments in infant motivation (Trevarthen, 1985). In short, parental behaviour is 'programmed' or drawn along by developmental changes in the infant.

When viewed in terms of broad dimensions of developmental change, particularly with regard to postural control (see van Wulfften-Palthe & Hopkins, 1984), then the strong impression is that infants do engender transformations in parental behaviour. However, while parents undoubtedly undergo 'programming' by developmental changes in the infant, they seem in another sense to remain one (or more) steps ahead of the infant programmer. They have expectancies about their infant's capabilities which go beyond what he can actually do, expectancies that are sometimes translated into action. For example, in a study on the development of mother-infant interaction presently being completed in Groningen, Titia Palthe has noted what Trevarthen (1979b) refers to as 'games of the person' appearing at around 4 months. They do not emerge in a discontinuous fashion. At earlier ages, even as young as 6 weeks, mothers attempt to involve their infants in these games but with little or no success. Why they should do this when the infant does not show the requisite abilities for joining in remains something of a mystery. Perhaps such attempts may serve more than one function. On the one hand as a probing for the presence of a particular competence and on the other to give the infant preparatory exposures to what will become an established routine of communication. In the Groningen study, mothers were not encouraged to use objects when interacting with their infants as one of the major interests was in how changes in visual 'attention' for the mother were related to changes in postural control. Had we done so, then it is likely that 'trailers' to what Trevarthen (1979b) refers to as 'games with objects' would have also appeared in the first 2 to 3 months.

These observations and speculations suggest that parents not only let themselves be subordinated to their infant's acts, but also occasionally take the initiative during face-to-face interaction in a sort of forward-looking subjectivity which helps to canalise the infant's competencies towards an executive role in the process of communication. If there is a motive for intersubjectivity then it is something that initially resides in the parent who transmits it to the infant by selectively amplifying, extending and facilitating his actions as though they had communicative meaning.

As final comment on parental behaviour, it is worth mentioning a new concept introduced and analysed by Stern *et al,* (1985): affect attunement. It is of interest not only because it elaborates on the role of parental behaviour in the development of intersubjectivity, but also because it raises issues about how to describe behaviour. It is a common observation that parents tend to imitate many aspects of their infant's behaviour, but especially facial expressions and vocalisations. In doing so they reflect back to the infant his own behaviour thus enabling him to perceive how he is perceived and thereby fostering the development of self-awareness. Papoušek and Papoušek (1979) have referred to this parental imitation as a biological 'mirror' or 'echo'. Affect attunement is akin to imitation but differs from it in one important respect: what is matched by the parent is not overt categories of behaviour but a quality of feeling perceived as expressed in the infant's behaviour in terms of the dimensions of intensity, timing and shape. In most instances this matching is intermodal in that the modality for the parental expression is different from that of the infant (e.g. infant's vocalisation matched by maternal body movements or vice versa). What is being reflected back to the infant is not traditional affect categories such as 'happy' and 'sad' but a more elusive quality of feeling that is embedded in routine parental responses. Stern *et al* refer to this quality as vitality, a concept which is contained in the Effort Shape analysis of Laban notation. It is a dynamic quality which gives expressiveness to behaviour in terms of exploding, fading, fleeting, surging etc. These vitality affects convey forms of feeling to the infant which eventually lead to a sharing of affectivity rather than just intentionality. In this respect affect attunement is a particular form of intersubjectivity but one that requires the consideration of an additional process of social perception, a process quite unlike that contained in the notion of physiognomic perception.

Most studies of mother-infant interaction have concentrated on describing the content and patterning of the interactions involved. But as Hinde (1976, 1979) has pointed out, there is another dimension of interaction which is perhaps more important than the types of behaviour involved but which is difficult to capture in anything but impressionistic terms: the quality of interaction (e.g. the degree of animation of the interactants). The concept of affect attunement is an attempt to capture this dimension. Unfortunately the language available for describing behaviour in terms of quality is severely restricted, even more so when we try to describe interpersonal relations. Yet is is possible to achieve a high degree of intersubjectivity between observers when, for example, dealing with qualitative changes in the spontaneous movements of young infants (Hopkins & Prechtl, 1984) and with differences in movement quality between healthy and growth-retarded fetuses (Bekedam *et al,* 1985). What seems to be involved is that observers can share an aesthetic appreciation about the qualities of movement (e.g. elegance) which transcend their topographical and scalar properties. As the findings of Stern *et al* demonstrate, the same may apply to the description of development of intersubjectivity in terms of qualities such as vitality affects. Making use of our powers of aesthetic appreciation (in conjunction with those for Gestalt perception) is perhaps an important first step in elucidating what are the relevant dimensions along which an infant becomes socialised. The potential benefit of this way of observing is that it can lead to an initial condition that is crucial for subsequent objective descriptions: what the classical ethologists termed 'getting a feel for the organism'.

CONCLUDING REMARKS

Gesell (1928, 1929) argued strongly (and prophetically) for the role of self-regulation in development which he depicted as

> ...stabilising factors, intrinsic rather than extrinsic,
> which preserve the total pattern and the direction of

the growth trend (Gesell, 1929, p. 319).

Thereagain, in the tradition of experimental embryology at the beginning of the century, Gesell (1933) emphasised the bidirectional relationship between structure and function during all phases of development. This apparent inconsistency in Gesell's developmental thinking can be seen as a result of his attempt to combat the excesses of radical behaviourism which reduced the developing organism to a passive learning machine. His plea for development as a process of self-regulation was in part a debating position which tended to obscure his true theoretical stance, one which recognised that intrinsic and extrinsic factors were closely interwoven during development.

A similar inconsistency can be discerned in the writings of Colwyn Trevarthen that may, as in the case of Gesell, derive from a debating position which opposes accounts of development that reduce it to a few principles of learning. However, Trevarthen deals with the development of complex psychological structures such as intersubjectivity which are dependent on interactions with adults for their fulfilment in ways that do not apply to motor development. His stress on there being innate capacities for intersubjectivity having a developmental continuity with mature forms of communication is very reminiscent of Chomsky's (1965) interpretation of language development. Whereas Chomsky assumed that language development rested on an innate LAD (Language Acquisition Device), Trevarthen assumes that intersubjective development is based on something that might be described as a PAD (Person Acquisition Device). As with the notion of a LAD, the assumption of such a fundamental precursor to mature communication is questionable both on theoretical and empirical grounds.

In terms of many non-vital functions the human newborn resembles an extrauterine fetus. According to this view there has been an evolutionary shortening of human pregnancy, the reasons for which have recently been articulated by Prechtl (1984). The net result of this shortening is a newborn lacking in active postural control and poor in muscle power, particularly in the neck muscles. Compensating for these neurological incompetencies, simply by manually immobilising the head of the newborn, may lead to the release of what Amiel-Tison and Grenier (1980) term liberated motor activity: reaching and grasping movements directed towards an object resting on a surface. What these clinical observations suggest is that newborn action is constrained by limitations in postural control, a view supported by experimental studies with mice (Fentress, 1978) and rats (Bekoff & Trainer, 1979). As emphasised in this reaction, transformations in the mechanisms subserving postural control lead to major changes in the organisation of parental behaviour. For the infant each improvement in postural control results in a tighter coupling between perception and action. In healthy infants around 2 months of age, the first major change occurs in postural control such that looking towards the mother in a semi-upright position can be stabilised and associated with smiling and 'cooing' vocalisations (van Wulfften-Palthe & Hopkins, 1984). It is this change more than any other which brings the infant into the period of what Trevarthen calls primary intersubjectivity and gives his behaviour an unmistakable stamp of intention-ality. Neurological disturbances in the development of postural control could then be one source through which interactional failures can arise. Trevarthen (1974, 1980b) is one of the few who have emphasised the importance of changes in neural functions for the development of communicative abilities in preverbal infants. In this respect alone, he provides a badly needed focus by which more precise hypothesis can be formulated about the development of communication and intentional behaviour.

References

Abravanel, E. & Sigafoos, A.D. (1984). Exploring the presence of imitation during early infancy. *Child Development, 55,* 381-392.

Alberts, E., Kalverboer, A.F. & Hopkins, B. (1983). Motor-infant dialogue in the first days of life: an observational study during breast-feding. *Journal of Child Psychology and Psychiatry, 24,* 145-161.

Amiel-Tison, C. & Grenier, A. (1980). *Neurological Evaluation of the Newborn and the Infant.* New York: Masson.

Bekedam, D.J., Visser, G.H.A., Vries, J..I.P. de & Prechtl, H.F.R. (1985). Motor behaviour in the growth retarded fetus. *Early Human Development, 12,* 155-165.

Bekoff, A. & Trainer, W. (1979). The development of interlimb coordination during swimming in postnatal rats. *Journal of Experimental Biology, 83,* 1-11.

Berthenthal, B.I., Proffitt, D.R. & Cutting, J.E. (1984). Infant sensitivity to figural coherence in biomechanical motions. *Journal of Experimental Child Psychology, 37,* 213-230.

Blass, E.M. & Cramer, C.P. (1982). Analogy and homology in the development of ingestive behavior. In A.R. Morrison and P.L. Strick (Eds.), *Changing Concepts of the Nervous System.* New York: Academic Press.

Bowlby, J. (1969). *Attachment.* New York: Basic Books.

Brazelton, T.B., Koslowski, B. & Main, M. (1974). The origins of reciprocity: the early mother infant interaction. In M. Lewis and L.A. Rosenblum (Eds.), *The Effect of the Infant on its Caregiver.* New York: Wiley.

Breuer, K.H. (1985). Intentionality of perception in early infancy. *Human Development, 28,* 71-83.

Bruner, J.S. (1973). The organization of early skilled action. *Child Development, 44,* 1-11.

Bruner, J.S. (1974). The organization of early skilled action. In M.P.M. Richards (Ed.), *The Integration of a Child into a Social World.* Cambridge: Cambridge University Press.

Bruner, J.S. (1975). From communication to language - a psychological perspective. *Cognition, 3,* 255-287.

Child, C.M. (1941). *Patterns and Problems of Development.* Chicago: University of Chicago Press.

Chomsky, N. (1965). *Aspects of the Theory of Syntax.* Cambridge: MIT Press.

Cutting, J.E. (1982). Two ecological perspectives: Gibson vs. Shaw and Turvey. *American Journal of Psychology, 95,* 199-222.

Darwin, C. (1872). *The Expression of Emotions in Man and Animals.* London: Appleton.

Darwin, C. (1877). A biographical sketch of an infant. *Mind, 2,* 285-294.

Dennett, D.C. (1982). *Brainstorms.* Brighton: Harvester Press.

Fentress, J.C. (1978). Mus musicus: the developmental orchestration of selected movement patterns in mice. In G.M. Burghardt and M. Bekoff (Eds.), *The Development of Behaviour: Comparative and Evolutionary Aspects.* New York: Garland.

Fentress, J.C. (1984). The development of coordination. *Journal of Motor Behavior, 16,* 99-134.

Field, T., Woodson, R., Cohen, D., Greenberg, R., Garcia, R. & Collins, K. (1983). Discrimination and imitation of facial expressions by term and preterm neonates. *Infant Behavior and Development, 6,* 485-490.

Field, T., Woodson, R., Greenberg, R. & Cohen, D. (1982). Discrimination and imitation of facial expressions by neonates. *Science, 218,* 179-181.

Fontaine, R. (1984). Imitative skills between birth and six months. *Infant Behavior and Development, 7,* 323-333.

Forssberg, H. (1985). Ontogeny of human locomotor control. I. Infant stepping, supported locomotion and transition to independent locomotion. *Experimental Brain Research, 57,* 480-493.

Frye, D., Rawling, P., Moore, C. & Myers, I. (1983). Object-person discrimination and communication at 3 and 10 months. *Developmental Psychology, 19,* 303-309.

Gesell, A.L. (1928). *Infancy and Human Growth.* New York: MacMillan.

Gesell, A.L. (1929). Maturation and infant behavior patterns. *Psychological Review, 36,* 307-319.

Gesell, A.L. (1933). Maturation and the patterning of behavior. In C. Murchison (Ed.), *Handbook of Child Psychology* (2nd. Ed.). New York: Russell and Russell.

Gibson, J.J. (1979). *The Ecological Approach to Visual Perception.* Boston: Houghton Mifflin.

Goodwin, B. (1982). Development and evolution. *Journal of Theoretical Biology, 97,* 43-55.

Gottlieb, G. (1976). Conceptions of prenatal development: behavioral embryology. *Psychological Review, 83,* 215-234.

Greenfield, P.M. (1980). Toward an operational and logical analysis of intentionality: the use of discourse in early child language. In D.R. Olson (Ed.), *The Social Foundations of Language and Thought.* New York: Norton.

Harding, C.G. (1982). Development of the intention to communicate. *Human Development, 25,* 140-151.

Harré, R. (1974). The conditions for a social psychology of childhood. In M.P.M. Richards (Ed.), *The Integration of a Child into a Social World.* Cambridge: Cambridge University Press.

Hayes, L.A. & Watson, J.S. (1981). Neonatal imitation: fact or artifact? *Developmental Psychology, 17,* 655-660.

Hofsten, C. von. (1982). Eye-hand coordination in the newborn. *Developmental Psychology, 18,* 450-467.

Holst, E. von. (1973). *The Behavioural Physiology of Animal and Man: The Collected Papers of Erich von Holst (Vol. 1).* London: Methuen.

Hopkins, B. & Prechtl, H.F.R. (1984). A qualitative approach to the development of movements during early infancy. In H.F.R. Prechtl (Ed.), *Continuity of Neural Functions from Prenatal to Postnatal Life.* Oxford: Blackwell.

Hinde, R.A. (1976). On describing relationships. *Journal of Child Psychology and Psychiatry, 17,* 1-19.

Hinde, R.A. (1979). *Towards Understanding Relationships.* London: Academic Press.

Jacobson, S.W. (1979). Matching behavior in the young infant. *Child Development, 50,* 425-430.

James, W. (1890). *The Principles of Psychology.* New York: Holt.

Kaye, K. (1984). *The Mental and Social Life of Babies.* London: Methuen.

Koepke, J.E., Hamm, M,, Legerstee, M.N. & Russell, M. (1983). Neonatal imitation: two failures to replicate. *Infant Behavior and Development, 6,* 97-102.

Kugler, P.N., Kelso, J.A.S. & Turvey, M.T. (1982). On the control and co-ordination of naturally developing systems. In J.A.S. Kelso and J.E. Clark (Eds.), *The Development of Movement Control and Co-ordination.* Chichester: Wiley.

Kuhlenbeck, H. (1967). *The Central Nervous System of Vertebrates (Vol. 1).* Basel: Karger.

Løvtrup, S. (1974). *Epigenetics*. London: Wiley.

Maratos, O. (1982). Trends in the development of imitation in early infancy. In T.G. Bever (Ed.), *Regressions in Mental Development*. Hillsdale, N.J.: Erlbaum.

KcKenzie, B. & Over, R. (1983a). Young infants fail to imitate facial and manual gestures. *Infant Behavior and Development, 6*, 85-95.

McKenzie, B. & Over, R. (1983b). Do neonatal infants imitate? A reply to Meltzoff and Moore. *Infant Behavior and Development, 6*, 109-111.

Mead, G.H. (1934). *Mind, Self and Society*. Chicago: University of Chicago Press.

Meiland, J.W. (1970). *The Nature of Intention*. London: Methuen.

Meltzoff, A.N. & Moore, M.K. (1977). Imitation of facial and manual gestures by human neonates. *Science, 118*, 75-88.

Meltzoff, A.N. & Moore, M.K. (1983a). The origins of imitation in infancy: paradigm, phenomena and theories. In L.P. Lipsitt and C. Rovee-Collier (Eds.), *Advances in Infancy Research, Vol. 2*. Norwood, N.J.: Ablex.

Meltzoff, A.N. & Moore, M.K. (1983b). Newborn infants imitate adult facial gestures. *Child Development, 54*, 702-709.

Needham, J. (1959). *A History of Embryology (2nd. Ed.)*. Cambridge: Cambridge University Press.

Neisser, U. (1976). *Cognition and Reality*. San Francisco: Freeman.

Newman, S.A. & Leonard, C.M. (1983). Against programs - limb development without developmental information. In J.F. Fallon and A.I. Caplan (Eds.), *Limb Development and Regeneration (Part A)*. New York: Liss.

Nijhuis, J.G., Prechtl, H.F.R., Martin, C.B. & Bots, R.S.G.M. (1982). Are there behavioural states in the human fetus? *Early Human Development, 6*, 177-195.

Oller, D.K. (1980). The emergence of the sounds of speech in infancy. In G. Yeni-Komshian, J. Kavanagh and C. Ferguson (Eds.), *Child Phonology (Vol. 1)*. New York: Academic Press.

Oppenheim, R.W. (1981). Ontogenetic adaptations and retrogressive processes in the development of the nervous system and behaviour: a neuroembryological perspective. In K.J. Connolly and H.F.R. Prechtl (Eds.), *Maturation and Development: Biological and Psychological Perspectives*. London: Heinemann.

Oppenheim, R.W. (1982). Preformation and epigenesis in the origins of the nervous system and behavior: issues, concepts, and their history. In P.G. Bateson and P.H. Klopfer (Eds.), *Perspectives in Ethology (Vol. 5)*. New York: Plenum Press.

Oppenheim, R.W. (1984). Ontogenetic adaptations in neural and behavioural development: towards a more 'ecological' developmental psychobiology. In H.F.R. Prechtl (Ed.), *Continuity of Neural Functions from Prenatal to Postnatal Life*. Oxford: Blackwell.

Papousek, H., Papousek, M. (1979). Early ontogeny of human social interaction: its biological roots and social dimensions. In M. von Cranach, K. Foppa, W. Lepenies and D. Ploog (Eds.), *Human Ethology*. Cambridge: Cambridge University Press.

Piaget, J. (1952). *The Origins of Intelligence in the Child*. New York: International Universities Press.

Piaget, J. (1962). *Play, Dreams and Imitation in Childhood*. New York: Norton.

Prechtl, H.F.R. (1981). The study of neural development as a perspective of clinical problems. In K.J. Connolly and H.F.R. Prechtl (Eds.), *Maturation and Development: Biological and Psychological Perspectives*. London: Heinemann.

Prechtl, H.F.R. (1984). Continuity and change in early neural development. In H.F.R. Prechtl (Ed.), *Continuity of Neural Functions from Prenatal to Postnatal Life*. Oxford: Blackwell.

Prechtl, H.F.R. (1985). Editorial: Ultra-sound studies of human fetal behaviour. *Early Human Development, 12,* 91-98.

Preyer, W. (1888). *The Mind of the Child. Part I. The Senses and the Will.* New York: Appleton.

Richards, M.P.M. (1974). First steps in becoming social. In M.P.M. Richards (Ed.), *The Integration of a Child into a Social World.* Cambridge: Cambridge University Press.

Ross, G.S. (1982). Language functioning and speech development of six children receiving tracheotomy in infancy. *Journal of Communication Disorders, 15,* 95-111.

Searle, J.S. (1979). What is an intentional state? *Mind, 88,* 74-92.

Searle, J.S. (1980). The intentionality of intention and action. *Cognition Science, 4,* 47-70.

Searle, J.S. (1984). Intentionality and its place in nature. *Dialectica, 38,* 87-99.

Shaw, R. & Bransford, J. (1977). Introduction: psychological approaches to the problem of knowledge. In R. Shaw and J. Bransford (Eds.), *Perceiving, Acting and Knowing.* New York: Wiley.

Shaw, R. & Turvey, M.T. (1981). Coalitions as models for ecosystems: a realist perspective on perceptual organization. In M. Kubovy and J.R. Pomerantz (Eds.), *Perceptual Organization.* Hillsdale, N.J.: Erlbaum.

Spelke, E.S. (1982). Perceptual knowledge of objects in infancy. In J. Mehler, E.C.T. Walker and M. Garrett (Eds.), *Perspectives on Mental Representation.* Hillsdale, N.J.: Erlbaum.

Sperry, R.W. (1950). Neural basis of the spontaneous optokinetic response produced by visual inversion. *Journal of Comparative and Physiological Psychology, 43,* 482-489.

Stent, G.S. (1981). Strength and weakness of the genetic approach to the development of the nervous system. *Annual Review of Neuroscience, 4,* 163-194.

Stern, D.N., Hofer, L., Haft, W. & Dore, J. (1985). Affect attunement: the sharing of feeling states between mother and infant by means of inter-modal fluency. In T.M. Field and N.A. Fox (Eds.), *Social Perception in Infants.* Norwood, N.J.: Ablex.

Sylvester-Bradley, B. (1985). Failure to distinguish between people and things in early infancy. *British Journal of Developmental Psychology, 3,* 281-292.

Thelen, E. (1985). Developmental origins of motor coordination: leg movements in human infants. *Developmental Psychobiology, 18,* 1-22.

Thelen, E., Bradshaw, G. & Ward, J.A. (1981). Spontaneous kicking in month-old infants: manifestation of a human central locomotor program. *Behavioral and Neural Biology, 32,* 45-53.

Thelen, E. & Fisher, D.M. (1982). Newborn stepping: an explanation for a disappearing reflex. *Developmental Psychology, 18,* 760-775.

Tinbergen, N. (1963). On aims and methods of ethology. *Zeitschrift für Tierpsychologie, 20,* 410-433.

Trevarthen, C. (1974). The psychobiology of speech development. In E.H. Lenneberg (Ed.), *Language and Brain: Developmental Aspects (Vol. 12 Neurosciences Research Program).* Boston: Neurosciences Research Program.

Trevarthen, C. (1978). Modes of perceiving and modes of acting. In H.L. Pick and E. Saltzman (Eds.), *Modes of Perceiving and Processing Information.* New York: Wiley.

Trevarthen, C. (1979a). Communication and cooperation in early infancy: a description of primary intersubjectivity. In M. Bullowa (Ed.), *Before Speech: the Beginning of Interpersonal Communication.* Cambridge: Cambridge University Press.

Trevarthen, C. (1979b). Instinct for human understanding and for cultural cooperation: their development in infancy. In M. von Cranach, K. Foppa, K. Lepenies and D. Ploog (Eds.), *Human Ethology.* Cambridge: Cambridge University Press.

Trevarthen, C. (1980a). The foundations of intersubjectivity: development of interpersonal and cooperative understanding in infants. In D.R. Olson (Ed.), *The Social Foundations of Language and Thought.* New York: Norton.

Trevarthen, C. (1980b). Neurological development and the growth of psychological functions. In J. Sants (Ed.), *Developmental Psychology and Society.* London: Macmillan.

Trevarthen, C. (1982). The primary motives for cooperation. In G. Butterworth and P. Light (Eds.), *Social Cognition.* Brighton: Harvester Press.

Trevarthen, C. (1984). How control of movement develops. In H.T.A. Whiting (Ed.), *Human Motor Actions- Bernstein Reassessed.* Amsterdam: North-Holland.

Trevarthen, C. (1985). Facial expressions of emotion in mother-infant interaction. *Human Neurobiology, 4,* 21–32.

Trevarthen, C., Murray, L. & Hubley, P. (1981). Psychology of infants. In J.A. Davis and J. Dobbing (Ed.), *Scientific Foundations of Paediatrics.* London: Heinemann.

Turvey, M.T. & Shaw, R. (1979). The primacy of perceiving: an ecological reformulation of perception for understanding memory. In L.G. Nilsson (Ed.), *Perspectives on Memory Research: Essays in honor of Uppsala University's 500th. anniversary.* Hillsdale, N.J.: Erlbaum.

Turvey, M.T., Shaw, R.E., Reed, E.S. & Mace, W.M. (1981). Ecological laws of perceiving and acting: in reply to Fodor and Pylyshyn (1981). *Cognition, 9,* 237–304.

Vinter, A. (1984). The role of movements in eliciting early imitations. Report, Zentrum für Interdisziplinäre Forschung, Universität Bielefeld.

Vries, J.I.P. de, Visser, G.H.A. & Prechtl, H.F.R. (1982). The emergence of fetal behaviour, I: qualitative aspects. *Early Human Development, 7,* 301–322.

Vygotsky, L.S. (1962). *Thought and Language.* Cambridge: MIT Press.

Walker, A.S. (1982). Intermodal perception of expressive behaviors by human infants. *Journal of Experimental Child Psychology, 33,* 514–535.

Watson, J.S. (1979). Perception of contingency as a determinant of social responsiveness. In E.B. Thoman (Ed.), *Origins of the Infant's Social Responsiveness.* Hillsdale, N.J.: Erlbaum.

Webster, G. & Goodwin, B. (1981). History and structure in biology. *Perspectives in Biology and Medicine, 25,* 39–62.

Werner, H. (1948). *Comparative Psychology of Mental Development.* New York: International Universities Press.

Wolff, P.H. (1984). Discontinuous changes in human wakefulness around the end of the second month of life: a developmental perspective. In H.F.R. Prechtl (Ed.), *Continuity of Neural Functions from Prenatal to Postnatal Life.* Oxford: Blackwell.

Wulfften-Palthe, T. van & Hopkins, B. (1984). Development of the infant's social competence during early face-to-face interaction: a longitudinal study. In H.F.R. Prechtl (Ed.), *Continuity of Neural Functions from Prenatal to Postnatal Life.* Oxford: Blackwell.

SECTION 6
ESTABLISHING A BASE FOR PERCEPTION AND ACTION

ESTABLISHING A FRAME OF REFERENCE FOR ACTION

B.M. Owen and D.N. Lee

Moving through the environment and interacting with or avoiding objects and other organisms requires picking up information about the position, orientation and movement of the body and body parts relative to the environment and to objects. A major source of the information is the optic array at the eye. Thus a fundamental step in establishing a basis for action is the development of efficient head-eye coordination in order to pick up the information. This we examine in Sections 1 and 2. In Section 3 we consider another prerequisite for effective action- the proprioceptive linking of the different parts of the body - and examine the role vision plays in this process. Section 4 considers the problem of stabilising the head and body to form a physical base for actions. Finally, in Section 5, we examine how, through prospective control, actions are tailored to fit the spatio-temporal constraints of the environment.

1. LOOKING WITH THE HEAD AND EYES

It is commonly assumed that the organ of sight is the eye. This is an oversimplification. Rather we see "with the eyes in the head on the shoulders of a body that gets about" (Gibson, 1979). This means that picking up adequate visual information for controlling manipulative and locomotor actions first and foremost requires controlling the direction of gaze with respect to a shifting base.

Seeing entails inter-relating three principal bodily frames of reference and the environmental frame. The frame of reference of the eye (considered as fixed to the eye with origin at the nodal point of the lens) can swivel and translate relative to the head frame, as can the head frame relative to the trunk frame and the trunk frame relative to the environmental frame. The combined movements of the trunk, head and eyes serve, in general, to translate and rotate the eye relative to the environment.

The optic array at an eye moving in this general way comprises an optic velocity field with two components (taken relative to the frame of reference fixed in the eye). There is the translatory component, due to the translation of the nodal point of the lens, and there is the rotary component, due to rotation of the eyeball with respect to the environment. The translatory optic velocity field consists of a set of vectors which, when considered projected on a sphere, lie along lines of longitude (Figure 1a, 1b, 1c). The magnitudes and positions of the vectors provide the organism with information about the layout of the environment and about the organism's

288

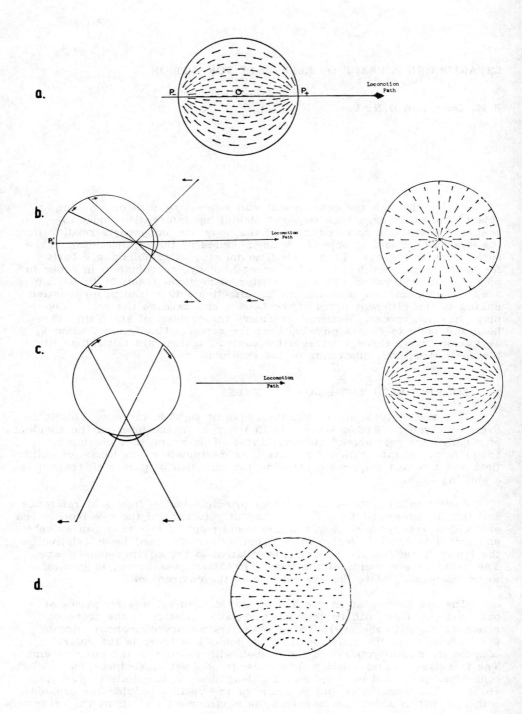

Fig. 1. The locomotor Optic Flow Field.

A When a point of observation, 0 (i.e., a point where the nodal
point of an eye could be placed) moves linearly in the
environment, there is an optic flow field at the point. The
rays of the optic array trace out planes which all pass
through the locomotion path of the point of observation.
Therefore, the points where the rays intersect a sphere
centred on the point of observation move along lines of
longitude through the "locomotor poles", P+ and P-.

B When the head moves forward, the eye samples the positive
polar region of the optic flow field. Thus, with the eye
stationary in the head, the retinal image (as seen from the
pupil) expands. The image elements flow outward, along
lines of longitude, from the image of the locomotor pole,
until they disappear because of occlusion by the nose and
eye orbit. Conversely for backward movement of the head.

C When the head moves laterally, the eye samples an equatorial
region of the optic flow field. Again, the images on the retina
flow along lines of longitude through the locomotor poles
(though, with the eye in its normal resting position, the poles
are not imaged on the retina), until they disappear because
of occlusion by the nose and eye orbit.

D Rotating the eye with the head stationary does not change
the optic array, and the pattern of image flow on the
retina is quite different to when the head is moving.
The images flow along lines of latitude defined with respect
to the axis of rotation of the eye. The flow pattern, in
fact, specifies an eye rotation. When the eye is rotating
at the same time as the head is moving the flow pattern
on the retina has two components: a longitudinal flow
component specifying the head movement and a latitudinal
flow component specifying the eye rotation.

translatory movement through the environment (Lee, 1980). In contrast, the rotary component of the optic velocity field, which, when seen projected onto a sphere, consists of vectors aligned along lines of latitude (Figure 1d), affords the organism much less information about the environment; in the main, it simply specifies how the eye is rotating with respect to the environment.

It is to an organism's advantage, therefore, to optimise pick-up of information from the richly endowed translatory component of the optic velocity field. This entails stabilising gaze - i.e. controlling rotation of the eye so that the optic velocities relative to the retina, which are the vector sum of the translatory and rotary optic velocity fields, lie in a detectable range.

A simple action which entails stabilising gaze is turning the head to face a point off to the side. The normal sequence of events is that first the eyes make a saccade to look at the point and then, as the head turns, the eyes counter-rotate in order to maintain gaze on the point. The initial eye saccade and the head movement appear to be triggered together in that EMG discharge from the neck muscles occurs at the same time as the start of the eye saccade (Biguer, Jeannerod & Prablanc, 1982). That the movement of the head normally lags the eye is probably due to the greater inertia of the head.

The counter-rotation of the eyes as the head turns is generally considered to be controlled by the vestibular system, via the so-called vestibular ocular reflex, and also partly by vision (Robinson, 1981). However, in spite of much experimentation, the relative contributions of vestibular and visual information to gaze stabilisation is unclear. This is probably due to an overemphasis in the literature on the (assumed) role of the vestibular ocular "reflex".

The term reflex is misleading insofar as it imputes a fixed relationship between degree of head rotation and degree of counter-rotation of the eyes. The relationship is, in fact, labile. The ratio of eye velocity to head velocity in the dark, which is a measure of the gain of the "reflex", can be substantially increased by simply asking the subject to do mental arithmetic and can be increased yet further by asking the subject (in the dark) to look at an imaginary spot on the wall in front of them (Barr, Schultheis & Robinson, 1976). The gain can even be reversed in sign (so that, instead of counter-rotating, the eyes rotate in the same direction as the head) by the subject visual adapting to wearing left-right reversing prisms (Melvill Jones, 1977).

Furthermore the vestibular system can only act as an aid in stabilising gaze: it cannot specify exactly what counter-rotation of the eyes is required to maintain fixation on a target. Only vision can do that. The reason is shown in Figure 2. The angle the eye has to counter-rotate does not depend simply on the angle turned through by the head (which could, in principle, be registered by the vestibular system) but also on the distance away of the target. Figure 2b shows how the eye has, in general, to rotate more than the head, the more so the closer the target and the larger the head movement (see also Biguer & Prablanc, 1981).

Coordinated head and eye movements also occur in tracking a moving object, as when watching a tennis match. They also occur in stabilising gaze

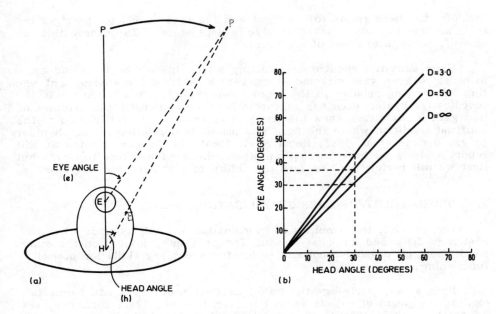

Fig. 2. Showing how the eye movement required to compensate for
a head movement does not depend simply on the head
movement, as is often assumed, but also on the distance of
the target. In (a), E is the centre of rotation of an eye,
H the centre of rotation of the head. The axes of rotation
are taken to be vertical. Initially, H and E are aligned
with target point P and gaze is directed at P. When the
target moves to the right, first the eye turns through
angle e to fixate the target and then, as the head turns
through angle h to point at the target, the eye counter-
rotates through angle e. Note that eye angle e will always
be greater than head angle h. The difference between the
angles is greater the closer the target and the larger the
head or eye angles. This is seen by applying the sine rule
to triangle HEP, which gives $\sin(e)/\sin(e-h)= HP/HE= D$
(say), where $e= \tan^{-1} (D \sin(h)/(D\cos(h)-1))$. This function
is plotted in (b) for different values of D: D=3 corresponds
to close reading distance, D=5 to comfortable reaching
distance, D=∞ to the horizon.

with respect to the environment when the trunk is moving. For example,
when walking, running, cycling, canoeing and so on, the trunk twists and
sways. If the head were fixed to the trunk and the eye were fixed to the
head then the eye would move along with the trunk, and so the optic
projection on the retina would jiggle like the movie image from a camera
strapped to the chest of a photographer. In practice, however, the eyes do
not jiggle with the trunk. Instead, the optical motion is dampened and vision
made clear by coordinated movements of the head and eyes. One can get a
feel for the fine coordination between head and eyes by reading a notice-
board while twisting the trunk from side to side. As the trunk rotates to

the left, the neck twists to the right and the eyes swivel to the right in their sockets in such a way that gaze is kept steady. To observe this in oneself, perform in front of a mirror.

Many activities require coordinating movements of the head and eyes in order to keep gaze directed at relevant aspects of the environment when they are moving relative to the trunk. Surprisingly, this fundamental coordinative system does not appear to have been investigated; studies of how gaze is stabilised when the trunk is rotating have been limited to the artificial condition where the head was immobilised relative to the shoulders (e.g., Herman et al, 1982; Regal et al, 1983). In the next section we will report a study we have carried out where the head was free to move, but first we will review work on how the ability to stabilise gaze develops.

2. DEVELOPMENT OF GAZE STABILISATION

For an adult the problems of coordination are only obvious when the system is disturbed for some reason. The developing infant, on the other hand, must continually learn and refine the necessary skills for normal functioning.

From a very early age the infant uses its head, eyes and hands to explore the world of objects around it (von Hofsten, 1982; Bullinger, 1981; Trevarthen, 1975, 1984b). In order to do this effectively it must not only coordinate different parts of the body, but must also have a sense of the body in relation to the rest of the world so that objects can be located with respect to the self (Hein, 1974). The infant therefore has to develop a hierarchy of stabilised systems; trunk, head and eyes must work in conjunction to be directed at interesting objects, forming a general, stable orientation to allow effective use of the arms and hands as part of the exploratory system (Trevarthen, 1984b).

The work on the development of gaze stabilisation has, with some exceptions, been limited to the same questions as the adult research and consequently embodies the same problems. The control of gaze when fixating and compensating for body movement has been investigated primarily at the level of the eyes rather than the head and eyes. Thus research has concentrated on examining vestibularly driven 'reflex' compensatory eye-movements for externally imposed head movements. This emphasis on vestibular reflex activity (Eviatar, 1979) has two important shortcomings. First, it presupposes that stabilisation principally occurs at the highest level of the hierarchy (the eyes), and ignores the fact that for adults the head compensates for a lot of the movement of the trunk, as we have pointed out above. Second, it neglects the fact that vision is essential in stabilising gaze, as shown in Figure 2.

The main problem is that the experiments have not been set in the context of functional tasks. Although it may be useful to know facts such as the gain of the vestibular-ocular reflex in the dark, the optimal velocity for optokinetic nystagmus, etc., these system specifications do not capture the essence of the overall functional process. Descriptions of eye movements need to be set in the context of overall coordination during activities such as orientation, exploration, interaction and reaching.

Young infants exhibit patterns of coordination that are clearly not

reflex (Bower et al, 1970; Trevarthen, 1975, 1984a). Different elements
seem to be innately linked to form 'prefunctional' units (Trevarthen, 1975).
Coordinated head and eye movements have been observed as young as three
days and several researchers have reported early arm movements under
some degree of visual control (Bower et al, 1970; Bullinger, 1983; von
Hofsten, 1982; White et al, 1964). In order to look and reach effectively,
posture must be appropriate (Bower, 1974). As Forsstrom and von Hofsten
(1982) found, in neurologically impaired children a common problem in
reaching is abnormal postural fixation.

Bullinger (1983, 1981) has described the developmental sequence from
2 to 17 weeks which shows the importance of postural control and
stabilisation for effective action. Early object tracking is achieved by
rotation of the whole trunk; it appears that infants restrict the degrees of
freedom by using a trunk related frame of reference only. At the next
stage the shoulders and arms move independently of the trunk and finally
the head alone can be used "with the torso serving as a stable reference".
By this stage then infants appear to be developing the ability to function
within several frames of reference as an adult does. Early looking behaviour
can therefore be relatively successful, albeit limited. Early in this period
visual control of head posture is also apparent (Butterworth, 1983; Jouen,
1985).

At the level of head and eye coordination those few studies which have
not restricted head movement have shown a variety of patterns of coordination in which the head plays an active role. Two main findings emerge:
head and eye movements are quite well coordinated in the infant and smooth
looking patterns involving head and eyes occur before the smooth pursuit
system of the eyes alone. Therefore there can be functional orienting by a
relatively immature system. Tronick and Clanton (1971) have described four
different patterns of looking during free exploration of a static visual field.
All the patterns involved smooth integration of head and eyes. They
emphasised the importance of the head as part of the orienting system and
described it as serving a place-holding function while the eyes explore small
areas of the visual field, or as acting under visual guidance to shift the
line of regard in the visual field. The imprecision of the calibration system
used in this study though has lead to some doubt as to the exact descriptions
of the different patterns (Maurer et al, 1979; Salapatek, 1975), but it does
show the importance of the head both for tracking and for maintaining
fixation.

Although several studies have looked at compensatory eye movements
incident on head movement (Goodkin, 1980; Roucoux et al, 1983; Regal et
al, 1983), none has investigated the pattern of compensation for externally
imposed body movement. For babies this is a very common experience.
Much useful visual information would be lost if a baby were unable to use
the visual system effectively while being carried. In order to examine the
development of looking behaviour in this kind of situation we measured the
eye and head coordination of several babies. The infants were strapped
safely into a padded Britax car seat, 50 cm from a small toy which acted as
a target. Once the child's attention was fixed on the target it was possible
to either gently rotate the child's chair from side to side while keeping the
target fixed or to fix the chair while moving the target from side to side
in an arc at a constant 50 cm from the subject. Rotations of the head and
chair or target were monitored by a Selspot system: infra-red leds were

294

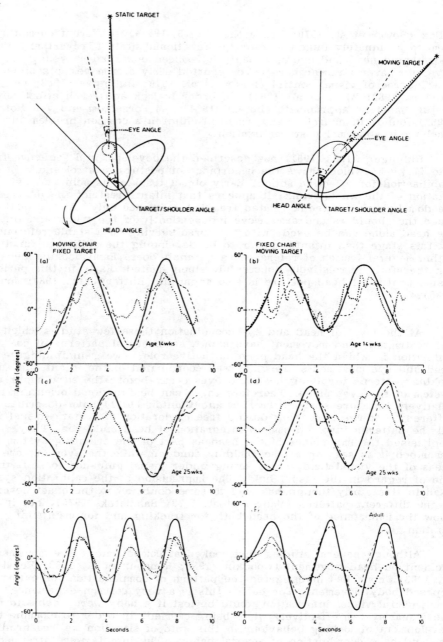

Fig. 3. Showing how a 14 week old infant (a), a 25 week old infant (c),
and an adult (e) coordinated head and eyes to maintain gaze on
a static target while seated on a chair which was oscillating
about a vertical axis. (b), (d) and (f) - the same subject but
on a stationary chair and maintaining gaze on a target moving
on a horizontal circular arc radius 50 cm centred on the axis of
the head. Solid lines, target/shoulder angle; dashed lines, head
angle; dotted lines, eye angle.

mounted above the eyes, on each side of the chair and on the target, and were viewed by an overhead camera with it's optical axis coincident with the vertical axis of rotation of the chair. Eye movements were recorded using electro-oculography.

Figure 3 shows the results for a 14 week old, a 25 week old and an adult. It can be seen that even in the younger infant the head plays an important part both in compensating for the rotation of the body and in tracking a moving target. Referring to Figure 3 and Table 1, two differences between head and eye control may be noted: (1) By 25 weeks of age, the head movement is as smooth as the adult's, whereas eye movements are more jerky. (2) By 25 weeks the head-target coupling (the zero-lag cross-correlation between head angle and target/shoulder angle) is as high as the adult's, whereas for eye movements it is lower.

Table 1. Cross Correlations, Lags and Gaze Errors

SUBJ	AGE	Head-target correl.		Head-target lag (ms)		Eye-target correl.		Eye-target lag (ms)		SD of gaze error	
		MC	MT	MC	MT	MC	MT	MC	MT	MC	MT
NORMAL											
MF	14wk	.80	.77	358	333	.81	.65	-192	- 96	11	26
SF	25wk	.97	.93	141	210	.69	.53	-384	-672	7	9
BO	25yr	.96	.97	-38	-90	.90	.60	160	384	1	2
BRAIN DAMAGED											
CG	21wk	.75	.44	0	600	.82	.57	-224	800	8	-
CG	28wk	.66	.62	1000	448	.95	.50	- 96	-320	8	-

Notes: MC means moving chair and fixed target
MT means moving target and fixed chair
Correl. is the zero-lag cross correlation between the head (or eye) angle and the target/shoulder angle (see Fig. 3 for definitions of the angles).
lag is the lag yielding the maximum time-lagged crossed correlation between the head (or eye) angle and the target/shoulder angle. A negative lag means the head (or eye) was leading the target movement.
Gaze error means the observed eye angle minus the eye angle which was required to fixate the target. In all cases, the mean gaze error was less than 0.7 in absolute value. Gaze error could not be computed for C.G. in the moving target case because of eye calibration problems.
Computations based on data presented in Figures 3 and 4.

Thus head tracking appears quite mature at 25 weeks, whereas eye tracking is less mature. What information is used in coupling the head to the target? When the target is stationary, visual and vestibular information might be used: when the target is moving, only vision specifies the head movement required. The fact that the head-target correlations were about equal in the two situations and improved together with age (Table 1) suggests that vision predominantly guides the head.

That the 25 week old's head-target correlation was as high as the adult's though its eye-target correlation was lower indicates that there is adequate information for stabilising the head in the optic flow on the retina, without it being necessary to foveate the target. This makes sense if one assumes that the function of the head movement is to point the eyes in the general direction of the target where they can foveally explore it. In fact, the infants kept the head pointing more or less at the target, (Bizzi, (1981) found the same in monkey with a moving target), whereas the adult made more use of the eyes to stabilise gaze when the trunk was rotating.

The infants did not couple their heads to the target in quite the same way as the adult. The adult's head movement slightly anticipated the movement of the target or chair, demonstrating prospective control. The infant's head, however, lagged behind, particularly at 14 weeks (Table 1 & Fig. 3). Infants clearly have to learn how to use predictive information in tracking.

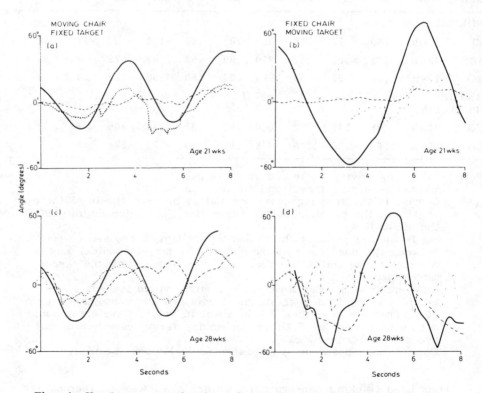

Fig. 4. Head-eye coordination of a brain-damaged infant, plotted as in Figure 3.

The study of functional head and eye movements can give insights into abnormalities of early development that could later affect movement control in a broad way. As a result of pneumococcal meningitis soon after birth, C.G. was diagnosed as having suspected right-sided hemiplegia and right-sided neglect. From Figure 4(a) and (b) it is apparent that at 21 weeks he was not controlling his head either to compensate for body movement or when tracking an object of interest. By 28 weeks (Figure 4 (c) and (d)), head control was improving but the head-target correlations were lower than those of the normal 14 week old and the head-target lag was longer (Table 1). Eye movements when tracking a moving target were also jerkier than normal (Fig. 4). The weakness of head/eye control carried through to an inability to keep the trunk erect when the child was at the normal age for sitting. Thus studies of this kind could help in pinpointing particular problems in the development of control, and aid early diagnosis of such problems.

3. LINKING FRAMES OF REFERENCE

We turn now to the problem of directing actions toward objects in the environment. When the effector is part of the head, as for an infant suckling, then visually orienting the head frame of reference to the target automatically orients the effector. This is not so, however, when an upper limb is the effector, as in many human actions. Visual guidance here requires registering, by proprioception, the relation between the frames of reference of the eye and head, of the head and trunk, and of the trunk and limb.

The proprioceptive links between the frames of reference can be established through the mechanical receptors in the joints and muscles or through vision. The mechanical proprioceptors have the advantage that they are never turned off and so continually provide information. On the other hand, it is apparent that mechanical proprioceptive systems are subject to drift and need to be tuned periodically by vision (Lee, 1978).

To understand how perceptuo-motor skill develops, it is therefore important to understand how the different parts of the body are proprioceptively linked during infancy and the role that vision plays in this. The question has not been investigated systematically, but there are some pointers. In learning to stabilise gaze the infant must at the same time be establishing proprioceptive links between the eyes and head and between the head and trunk. Thus when starting to reach and grasp objects at around 4-5 months of age, the infant will already have forged much of the proprioceptive chain between the eye and hand. The remaining proprioceptive linkage between the trunk and hand might also be partly established prior to reaching for objects by, for example, touching other parts of the body and making "pre-reaching" movements - i.e. movements similar in form to normal reaches but not directed at anything (Trevarthen, 1982). There is also evidence for rudimentary visually directed "reaches" in neonates (von Hofsten, 1982). Von Hofsten concluded that the function of neonatal "reaches" is attentional rather than manipulative. They could well serve the purpose of building proprioceptive links between the eye and hand.

An experiment which has some bearing on the question of visual tuning was carried out by Laskey (1977). He found that preventing sight of the upper limbs adversely affected the performance of $5\frac{1}{2}$-$6\frac{1}{2}$ month olds in reaching for a visible object, but did not affect the performance of $2\frac{1}{2}$-$4\frac{1}{2}$ month olds. This could suggest that visual tuning of mechanical proprioception in the upper limbs starts at around 5 months of age, giving rise to improved reaching. An alternative explanation is that infants older than 5 months can improve their reaching by visually guiding their hands whereas younger infants cannot. While the visual tuning explanation seems the more likely, given that McDonnell (1975) found visual guidance capability in 4 month olds, further experiments are required to clarify the issue. The results could have important consequences for the treatment of blind infants. They are normally retarded in developing perceptuo-motor skills and this is likely to be due in part to lack of visual tuning. If more were known about the tuning role of vision it should be possible to design better therapy for blind infants to help them compensate for lack of vision.

4. STABILISING THE HEAD AND BODY

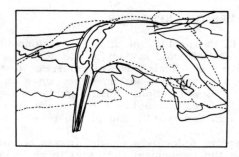

Fig. 5. A pied kingfisher keeping its head locked to the environment while hovering over its prey.

In practising head/eye control, the infant is setting up a basis for many activities in addition to reaching. The head is a natural frame of reference for action: since it houses most of the perceptual systems it has the closest informational links with the environment. Thus by visually coupling the head to the environment or to a moving object a stable base for action is established. A pied kingfisher demonstrates this beautifully when hovering over water intent on spearing a fish (Figure 5). Though its body waves up and down with the flapping of its wings, by fine neck adjustment it keeps its bill anchored to within about half a degree to the vertical (Lee & Young, 1986). The octopus provides a nice aquatic example: when its visible environment is rotated, it turns to stabilise its head on the environment (Packard, 1969). In human behaviour, a spinning ballerina elegantly demonstrates the point. To control balance and guide locomotion while spinning, the dancer keeps gaze fixed on an object in the environment until the head and eyes can turn no further, and then rapidly counter-rotates the head and eyes to catch the object again. By fixating an object, the high-speed rotary component of the optic flow field at the eye is removed, which makes translatory movement of the head and rotation about other axes more detectable visually. Somersaulting, high-board divers do the same when they "spot" the water prior to entry. This gives them a frame of reference for controlling their angular deceleration so that they enter at the right angle. Maintaining balance in one place is generally characterised by stability of the head; this is so even when the rest of the body is in vigorous

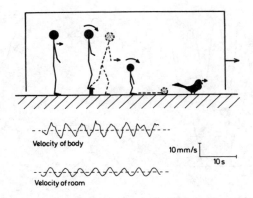

Fig. 6. Visual control of static balance. See text for details.

motion, as when a gymnast is on a pommel horse. The control of static
balance is the first step an infant must take towards independent locomotion.
Vision plays a major part in stabilising the head and body as Figure 6
illustrates. A subject stands on a fixed floor while the walls and ceiling of the
surrounding "room" are, for example, moved forward. This provides misleading visual information that the head is moving backward and so the
subject compensates by swaying forward. A toddler standing within the
"room" can be literally bowled over by the visual information (Lee &
Aronson, 1974) and an infant who has recently learnt to sit unsupported
will sway abnormally (Butterworth & Hicks, 1977). An infant as young as
two months will move its head with the room (Butterworth, 1983). A dove,
too, will bob its head, visually anchoring it to the moving room (Friedman,
1975). A standing adult human is very sensitive to the misleading visual
information: the head and body can be visually driven by 3 mm oscillations
of the room, as the graphs in Figure 6 show (from Lee & Lishman, 1975).
However, unlike an infant, an adult is not usually knocked off balance by
the misleading visual information when standing normally. This is probably
because the infant has poorer information through the ankles and feet than
the adult, since if the information is made less precise for an adult - e.g.
by balancing crossways on a beam, which allows the feet to tip (Fig. 6) -
then balance can be disturbed visually, as for the infant (Lee & Lishman,
1975).

It thus appears that a child in the early stages on its feet relies on
visual and/or vestibular information for balance control and, through
practice using this information in standing, walking and running, tunes the
ankle-foot information. Recent evidence indicates that much of the tuning
occurs between the ages of 4 and 6 years (Shumway-Cook & Woollacott,
1985). Vision is likely to assume the lead role in this tuning. Firstly, vision
affords more sensitive information than the vestibular system (Lee & Lishman,
1975). Secondly, absence of vision results in less efficient tuning; thus
Edwards (1946) found that blind adults standing normally sway about twice
as much as sighted adults with their eyes closed. Stable movement of the
head with respect to the environment, apart from being a general feature of
static balance, is also a general feature of locomotion. In running, ski-ing,
canoeing, cycling, swimming, driving and the many other forms of human
locomotion, the trunk and limbs move in a wide variety of ways relative to

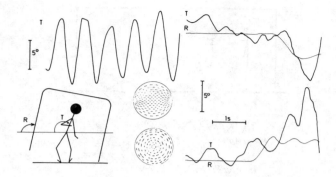

Fig. 7. Visual control of balance of an adult running on a
treadmill. See text for details.

the environment, while the head maintains a relatively straightforward
course. The steady movement of the head establishes a stable frame of
reference which facilitates the pick-up of information for controlling
locomotion. Some of this information is necessary for controlling dynamic
balance. For example, when a person runs, the trunk tilts from side to
side. Vision helps keep the tilt within stable bounds. This is shown by the
experiment illustrated in Figure 7, carried out with Michael Anderson and
David Young (Lee & Young, 1986). The moveable room (2.7 m long x 1.8 m
wide x 2.1 m high) was supported over a treadmill. As an adult ran on the
treadmill, the room was unexpectedly tilted through 4° about a horizontal
axis roughly through the ankles. A Selspot system monitored the inclination
of the room and the subject's trunk, defined by the line joining nape of
neck to coccyx. The curve on the left in Figure 7 shows the oscillations of
the trunk as the subject ran with the room stationary. These oscillations
were subtracted from the trunk movement which occurred in the neighbour-
hood of a room rotation to reveal how the rotation affected the pattern of
trunk movement (right-hand graphs). The subject tilts with the room,
apparently compensating for the visually simulated body tilt in the opposite
direction.

We recently tested sixteen 3-5 year old children in a similar set up,
except that the children walked on a solid floor within the moveable room
and their movements were video-recorded. Each child walked down the
middle of the room from the open end to the closed end in order to stick
a toy onto a stationary stand about the height of the child. They did this
twelve times and, as they were walking, the room was tilted, in random
order, to the right on three occasions, to the left on three occasions and
was kept stationary on six occasions. Two independent judges, ignorant of
the order of the test trials, viewed the resultant video-recordings, which
were played back in such a way that movements of the room could not be
seen. Test trials were scored +1 or -1 when the child showed a clear loss
of balance movement to the right or left respectively, and $+\frac{1}{2}$ or $-\frac{1}{2}$ when
there was a weaker effect. No visible effect was scored zero. Average
scores were then computed for each subject for the three trials when the
room was tilted left, for the three when it was tilted right and for the six
when it was kept stationary. The results (Figure 8) show that, as for the

adult running, the children had a strong tendency to tilt with the room, in accord with the misleading visual information.

TILT OF VISUAL SURROUNDINGS

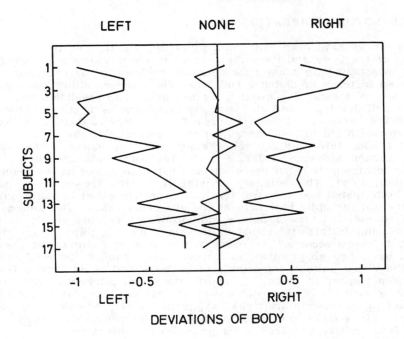

Fig. 8. Visual control of balance of 3-5 year old children walking. See text for details.

Stabilising the head is not only important for static and dynamic balance, but also in performatory actions relative to the environment, such as throwing and hitting. Thus Ripoll, Bard and Paillard (1986) found in basketball that the efficiency of head and eye stabilisation on the target significantly affects the success of shooting. Bahill and LaRitz (1984), like-wise, found very precise head/eye orientation to the target in baseball batters. The same would appear to be true in driving off at golf, playing a tennis shot, kicking a football, pitching a baseball and many other skills, where the accepted golden rule is to keep one's eye on the target. Most of these skills remain to be analysed, however. They offer a fertile field for investigation.

Stabilising the head on a target does not necessarily entail pointing the head directly at it. Biguer, Prablanc and Jeannerod (1984) found that when adults pointed the hand to a visible target with the hand out of sight, they turned the head only about 60% of the way to the target, their eyes turning the remaining 40%. As the authors suggested, the reason could be to keep the deviations of the head and eye within accurately detectable zones so that the perceived direction of the target relative to the trunk (the sum of head and eye deviations) is as precise as possible. Registration of the head and eye deviations is facilitated by visual proprioception: subjects point more accurately with an unseen hand to a small luminous target in the light than in the dark (Conti & Beaubaton, 1980).

5. VISUO-MOTOR CALIBRATION

Thus far we have been concerned primarily with the control of orientation of the body and its parts relative to the environment. Equally important in establishing a basis for action is calibrating the perceptuo-motor system in terms of distance and time. Visuo-motor calibration appears to get underway around five months, by which age accommodation and acuity are well developed and stereo-acuity is as fine as 1 min arc (Banks, 1980; Braddick, Atkinson, French & Howard, 1979; Birch, Gwiazda & Held, 1982). Five month old infants can adjust their reaching to the distance of the object (Field, 1976) and can see whether or not an object is of graspable size (von Hofsten & Spelke, 1984). Four to five month olds also show prospective control: they can reach out and catch an object as it passes (von Hofsten, 1979). This entails perceiving the future trajectory of the object in both spatial and temporal terms. Information about distance and time is given in the optic flow field at the eye (Lee, 1980). The information is not, of course, in units of metres and seconds, which are simply human conventions, but in intrinsic visual units, which we may think of as "visual metres" and "visual seconds". In order to see when and how far to reach the infant has, through practice, to discover and establish the relationship between the visual units and the units of its body and of its actions (e.g., arm length and speed of reach). In short, the visual information has to be body/action scaled. This visuo-motor calibration takes time. At four months of arc reaching movements are jerky, suggesting a step-wise approach to the object, but by eight months movements have become progressively smoother (von Hofsten, 1979). Timing precision also improves with age and by nine months can be as fine as 50 ms (von Hofsten, 1983). Perceptuo-motor calibration is not a once-and-for-all event. Any skilled athlete, musician and so on must have fine calibration and must keep it so by constant practice. Also, since calibration entails scaling perceptual information in terms of the spatio-temporal dimensions of actions, learning a new skill requires new perceptuo-motor calibration. Take, for example, crossing the road. Crossing in the gap between two approaching vehicles requires perceiving the temporal size of the gap in terms of the time it will take to cross the road. That is, it requires perceiving the *affordance* of the gap, the fit between the putative action and the spatio-temporal constraints of the situation (see Gibson, 1979 for the theory of affordances). A measure of the affordance of a gap is obtained by taking the difference between the time to contact, t_1, of the first vehicle with the planned crossing line and the time to contact of the second, t_2, and dividing by the crossing time. As illustrated in Figure 9, if the affordance $(t_2-t_1)/$(crossing time) is greater than unity, then it is safe to cross, providing one perceives the time to contact of the first vehicle and starts walking as soon as it passes. Crossing time equals distance across the road, d, divided by walking speed, s, and so the affordance of the gap equals $s [(t_2-t_1)/d]$. The extero-specific component, $(t_2-t_1)/d$, is specified optically and, through practice, has to be calibrated in terms of the propriospecific component, walking speed.

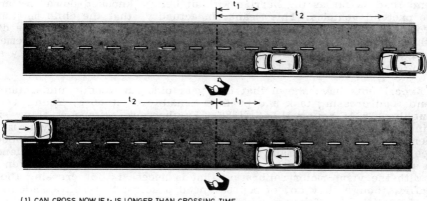

(1) CAN CROSS NOW IF t_1 IS LONGER THAN CROSSING TIME

(2) CAN CROSS AFTER FIRST VEHICLE IF GAP ($= t_2 - t_1$)
IS LONGER THAN CROSSING TIME

Fig. 9. Timing a safe crossing between vehicles.

An experienced adult maintains visuo-motor calibration through daily use of the roads and is not usually aware of doing so until calibration has to be changed as when carrying a heavy bag or when temporarily lame. Children, on the other hand, need to calibrate from scratch. Ideally, they need a safe situation in which to practice and explore their capabilities and limitations, like a pilot has in a flight simulator. A simple road-crossing simulation, using a "pretend road", is shown in Figure 10. The pretend road

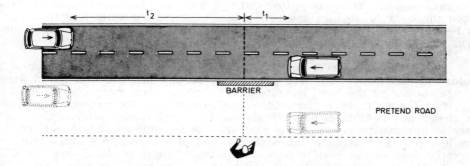

BARRIER

PRETEND ROAD

Fig. 10. Pretend road crossing: a training method for children.

is simply a stretch of pavement alongside a road. An adult chooses a suitable site which allows adequate view down the road and erects a short barrier alongside the kerb. The child stands where indicated and pretends that for each vehicle seen coming along the real road there is one in a corresponding position on the pretend road (the pretend road vehicles are indicated by dotted outlines in Figure 10). The child's task is to cross the pretend road as far as the barrier without being "knocked down" by any of the pretend vehicles. This means, in actuality, that the child must not be crossing the pretend road when a vehicle passes the barrier. The child can thus easily see how well he/she is performing and where improvement is needed. The adult supervisor can likewise assess the child's ability and judge when it is safe to introduce the child to crossing real roads.

Experiments have shown that five year olds can readily understand the pretend road crossing task and perform sensibly on it (Lee, Young & McLaughlin, 1984; Young & Lee, 1986). Furthermore, after but a few short training sessions, the children improved markedly in their ability to make efficient use of gaps in the traffic. In general, five year olds developed a degree of competence normally shown in older children, whose experience on roads put them at lower risk. The results indicate that young children can cope with the visuo-motor calibration that is necessary for crossing the road in traffic, though they do, of course, need practice to reach an adequate level of proficiency. The results thus argue against the commonly held view, put forward by Sandels (1975), that under the age of about ten years "children do not have the sensory or cognitive ability to cope with modern traffic". This proposition, however, was based mainly on the results of laboratory tests. In order to get a realistic assessment of the child's potential one has to measure performance on the actual task.

6.   CONCLUSIONS

In this chapter we have attempted to delineate some of the principles underlying the development of perceptuo-motor coordination and skill.

1) Analysis of the optic flow field at the eye reveals that information for controlling action is principally given in the component of the optic flow field that results from the translatory movement of the eye through the environment. Thus, to optimise the pick-up of visual control information when the body is moving, the rotary component of the optic flow field has to be minimised. This is achieved by coordinated rotations of the head and eyes.

2) The head/eye coordinative system is one of the first perceptuo-motor systems to develop. Our preliminary studies indicate that by 25 weeks of age control of the head is quite mature but eye movement control is lagging. The information controlling head/eye movements during body and/or object movement is principally visual, since only vision affords the precise information required for control. The possible secondary role of the less precise vestibular information is not clear, despite a number of investigations of the vestibular-ocular reflex. This is because very few of the studies have allowed natural movements of the head and eyes. Such experiments need to be done for they would cast light on how coordinative systems develop. The information would be of practical value in the early diagnosis and treatment of brain damage.

3) Visually coupling the head to the environment or to a moving object of interest establishes a perceptual frame of reference for action. However, in order to carry out an action with a limb within the frame of reference of the head, the frame of reference of the limb needs to be proprioceptively linked to that of the head. The forging of proprioceptive links between different parts of the body is fundamental to perceptuo-motor development.

How this proceeds during infancy has not been adequately studied, however. What evidence there is suggests that vision tunes the mechanical proprioceptive systems.

4) To provide a physical base for action when sitting, standing or locomoting the body has to be kept stable - i.e., the movement of the body relative to the environment needs to be controlled and predictable. Vision plays a major part in stabilising the head, and thence the body, particularly in the early stages of development when mechanical systems are not well tuned.

5) Having established a stable frame of reference, the infant can tackle the problem of regulating actions to fit in with the spatio-temporal structure of external events. This requires prospective control and entails calibrating the visuo-motor system - i.e., scaling visual information in terms of actions. Calibration of reaching and grasping appears to start around 5 months of age. In general, perceptuo-motor calibration continues throughout life as new skills are learnt and existing skills refined.

ACKNOWLEDGEMENTS

We thank Dave Young for help with the experiments. We also thank him, Colwyn Trevarthen and Robert Minns for much valuable discussion, and the parents of the infants who acted as subjects. The work was supported by the Medical Research Council, the Science and Engineering Research Council, General Accident and the Scottish Health Education Group.

References

Bahill, A.T. & LaRitz, T. (1984). Why can't batters keep their eyes on the ball? *American Scientist, 72,* 249-253.

Banks, M.S. (1980). The development of visual accommodation during early infancy. *Child Development, 51,* 646-666.

Barr, C.C., Schultheis, L.W. & Robinson, D.A. (1976). Voluntary, non-visual control of the human vestibuloocular reflex. *Acta Oto-Laryngol, 8,* 365-375.

Biguer, B. & Prablanc, C. (1981). Modulation of the vestibulo-ocular reflex in eye-head coordination as a function of target distance in man. In A.F. Fuchs and W. Becker (Eds.), *Progress in Oculomotor Research.* Amsterdam: North Holland Publishing Co.

Biguer, B., Jeannerod, M. & Prablanc, C. (1982). The coordination of eye, head and arm movements during reaching at a single visual target. *Experimental Brain Research, 46,* 301-304.

Biguer, B., Prablanc, C. & Jeannerod, M. (1984). The contribution of coordinated eye and head movements in hand pointing accuracy. *Experimental Brain Research, 55,* 462-469.

Birch, E., Gwiazda, J. & Held, R. (1982). Stereoacuity development for crossed and uncrossed disparities in human infants. *Vision Research, 22,* 507-513.

Bizzi, E. (1981). Eye-head coordination. In *Handbook of physiology.* Section 1, Vol. 2, Part 2. Bethesda: American Physiological Society.

Bower, T.G.R. (1974). *Development in Infancy.* San Francisco: Freeman.

Bower, T.G.R., Broughton, J.M. & Moore, M.K. (1970). Demonstration of intention in the reaching behaviour of neonate humans. *Nature, 228,* 679-681.

Braddick, O., Atkinson, J., French, J. & Howland, H.C. (1979). A Photo-refractive study of infant accommodation. *Vision Research, 19,* 1319-1330.

Bullinger, A. (1981). Cognitive elaboration of sensorimotor behaviour. In G. Butterworth (Ed.), *Infancy and Epistemology: An Evaluation of Piaget's theory.* The Harvester Press.

Bullinger, A. (1983). Space, the organism & objects, their cognitive elaboration in the infant. In A. Hein and M. Jeannerod (Eds.), *Spatially Oriented Behaviour.* New York: Springer-Verlag.

Butterworth, G. (1983). Structure of the mind in human infancy. In L.P. Lipsett (Ed.), *Advances in Infancy Research.* Vol. 2. Norwood, NJ: Ablex.

Butterworth, G. & Hicks, L. (1977). Visual proprioception and postural stability in infancy. A developmental study. *Perception, 6,* 255-262.

Conti, P. & Beaubaton, D. (1980). Role of the structural visual field and visual reafference in accuracy of pointing movements. *Perceptual and Motor Skills, 50,* 239-244.

Edwards, A.S. (1946). Body sway and vision. *Journal of Experimental Psychology, 36,* 526-535.

Eviatar, L. & Eviatar, A. (1979). The normal nystagmic response of infants to caloric and perrotatory stimuli. *The Laryngoscope, 89,* 1036-1044.

Field, J. (1976). The adjustment of reaching behaviour to object distance in early infancy. *Child Development, 47,* 304-308.

Forsstrom, A. & Hofsten, C. von (1982). Visually directed reaching of children with motor impairments. *Develop. Med. Ch. Neurol., 24,* 653-661.

Friedman, M.B. (1975). Visual control of head movements during avian locomotion. *Nature, London, 255,* 67-69.

307

Gibson, J.J. (1979). *The ecological approach to visual perception*. Boston: Houghton Mifflin.

Goodkin, F. (1980). The development of mature patterns of head-eye coordination in the human infant. *Early Human Development, 4*, 373-386.

Hein, A. (1974). Prerequisite for development of visually guided reaching in kitten. *Brain Research, 71(2-3)*, 259-263.

Herman, R., Maulucci, R. & Stuyck, J. (1982). Development and plasticity of visual and vestibular generated eye movements. *Experimental Brain Research, 47*, 69-78.

Hofsten, C. von (1979). Development of visually directed reaching: The approach phase. *Journal of Human Movement Studies, 5*, 160-178.

Hofsten, C. von (1982). Eye-hand coordination in the newborn. *Developmental Psychology, 18*, 450-461.

Hofsten, C. von (1983). Catching skills in infancy. *Journal of Experimental Psychology: Human Perception and Performance, 9*, 75-85.

Hofsten, C. von & Spelke, E.S. (1985). Object perception and object-related reaching in infancy. *Journal of Experimental Psychology: General, 114*, 198-212.

Jouen, F. La contribution des recepteurs visuels et labyrinthiques à la detection des deplacements du corps propre chez le nourrisson. To be published in Annee Psychologique.

Lasky, R.E. (1977). The effect of visual feedback of the hand on the reaching and retrieval behaviour of young infants. *Child Development, 48*, 112-117.

Lee, D.N. (1978). The functions of vision. In H.L. Pick Jr. and E. Saltzman (Eds.), *Modes of Perceiving and Processing Information*. Hillsdale, NJ: Erlbaum Associates.

Lee, D.N. (1980). The optic flow-field: the foundation of vision. *Phil. Trans. R. Soc. London B, 290*, 169-179.

Lee, D.N. & Aronson, E. (1974). Visual proprioceptive control of standing in human infants. *Perception & Psychophysics, 19*, 529-532.

Lee, D.N. & Lishman, R. (1975). Visual proprioceptive control of stance. *Journal of Human Movement Studies, 1*, 87-95.

Lee, D.N. & Young, D.S. (1985). Visual timing of interceptive action. In D. Ingle, M. Jeannerod and D.N. Lee (Eds.), *Brain Mechanisms and spatial vision*. Dordrecht: Martinus Nijhoff.

Lee, D.N. & Young, D.S. (1986). Gearing action to the environment. In C. Fromm and H. Heuer (Eds.), *Generation and Modulation of Action Patterns*. Heidelberg: Springer-Verlag (in press).

Lee, D.N., Young, D.S. & McLaughlin, C. (1984). A roadside simulation of road crossing for children. *Ergonomics, 27*, 1271-1281.

Maurer, D. & Lewis, T.I. (1979). A physiological explanation of infants' early visual development. *Canadian Journal of Psychology, 33*, 232-252.

McDonnell, P. (1975). The development of visually guided reaching. *Perception & Psychophysics, 18(3)*, 181-185.

Melvill Jones, G. (1977). Plasticity in the adult vestibulo-ocular reflex. *Arc. Phil. Trans. R. Soc., Lond. B., 278*, 319-334.

Packard, A. (1969). Visual acuity and eye growth in *Octopus vulgaris* (Lamark). *Monitore Zoologico Italiano (N.S.), 3*, 19-32.

Regal, D.M., Ashmead, D.M. & Salapatek, P. (1983). The coordination of eye and head movements during early infancy: a selective review. *Behav. Brain Research, 10*, 125-132.

Ripoll, H., Bard, C. & Paillard, J. (1986). Stabilisation of head and eyes on target as a factor in successful basketball shooting. *Human Movement Science* (in press).

308

Robinson, D.A. (1981). Control of eye movements. In, *Handbook of Physiology*, Section 1, Vol. 2, Part 2. Bethesda, MD: American Physiological Soc.

Roucoux, A., Culee, C. & Roucoux, M. (1983). Development of fixation and pursuit eye movements in human infants. *Behavioral Brain Research, 10,* 133-139.

Salapatek, P. (1975). Pattern perception in early infancy. In L.B. Cohen and P. Salapatek (Eds.), *Infant Perception: From Sensation to Cognition.* Vol. 1. NY, SF, LON: Academic Press.

Sandels, S. (1975). *Children in traffic.* London: Elek (Translated from Swedish, 1968).

Shumway- Cook, A. & Woollacott, M.H. (1985). The growth of stability: Postural control from a developmental perspective. *Journal of Motor Behavior, 2,* 131-147.

Trevarthen, C. (1975). Growth of visuomotor coordination in infants. *Journal of Human Movement Studies, 1,* 57.

Trevarthen, C. (1982). Basic patterns of psychogenetic change in infancy. In T. Bever (Ed.), *Regressions in Mental Development: Basic Phenomena and Theories.* Hillsdale, NJ: Erlbaum.

Trevarthen, C. (1984a). Biodynamic structures, cognitive correlates of motive sets and the development of motives in infants. In W. Prinz and A.F. Sanders (Eds.), *Cognition and Motor Processes.* Berlin: Springer-Verlag.

Trevarthen, C. (1984b). How control of movement develops. In H.T.A. Whiting (Ed.), *Human Motor Actions: Bernstein Reassessed.* Amsterdam: North Holland Publishing Co.

Tronick, E. & Clanton, C. (1971). Infant looking patterns. *Vision Research, 11,* 1479-1486.

Warren, D.H. (1970). Intermodality interactions in spatial localization. *Cognitive Psychology, 1,* 114-133.

White, B.L., Castle, P. & Held, R. (1964). Observations on the development of visually-directed reaching. *Child Development,* 349-364.

Young, D.S. & Lee, D.N. (1986). Training children in road crossing skills using a roadside simulation. *Accident Analysis and Prevention* (in press).

CONTRIBUTION OF HEAD MOVEMENT TO THE ACCURACY O
AIMING AND COINCIDENCE-TIMING TASKS

C. Bard, M. Fleury

Many motor skills require a performer to aim at a fixed target or to visually track a moving stimulus while executing a response that is linked both temporally and spatially to the stimulus available. In this paper, we will report experimental data on the head/eye control system in adults and children pointing at a fixed target, and in children intercepting a moving stimulus at a specific location in space.

Spatial encoding of visual cues relies heavily on proprioceptive signals of several origins. Foveal acquisition of the visual target in the retinal co-ordinate system has to be plotted within the head-centric coordinate system by taking into account both proprioceptive information from extraocular musculature about eye position in the orbit, and proprioceptive information of labyrinthine origin about head position in the gravitional field. Finally, the evaluation of body position, deriving from neck proprioceptive information, allows the spatial encoding of the location of a visual target within a body-centric system or coordinates (Roll et al, submitted for publication).

Hand pointing at a visual target, located in the near space of the prehension field, has been extensively studied. It has been shown that the foveation process is so precise that the directional accuracy of the pointing program of the arm is assumed to depend mainly on the calibration of eye position in the head (Biguer, 1981; Carlton, 1979, 1981; Conti & Beaubaton, 1976; Jeannerod & Prablanc, 1983). However, when unexpected targets are presented in an eccentric position in the visual field, a coordinated pattern of eye and head movements is observed. The final gaze orientation seems independent of neck proprioceptive information, provided that the vestibular system is intact (Abrahams, 1977; Bizzi, 1980). In contrast, the directional accuracy of arm pointing is heavily affected after cervical dorsal root section in monkey (Cohen, 1961). In man, the accuracy of pointing is improved when the head is free to move when compared to an head-fixed condition (Bard et al, 1982; Biguer, 1981; Biguer et al, 1982; Marteniuk, 1978; Roll, 1981).

Previous studies have shown that the combination of head and eye movements varies with stimulus eccentricity and predictibility of target position. According to different authors, the eccentricity of the target at which head rotation accompanies eye movement varies from 10-15° (Bartz, 1962; Mackworth & Mackworth, 1958). The functional contribution of head orientation to the overall behavioural performance obviously requires clarification.

The studies presented herewith aim at analysing the role of head orientation in the spatial encoding of the location of a distant target, within body-centric-space coordinate system. An aiming task has been used in preference to a classical pointing task for three reasons. (1) Distance coding is eliminated as a source of variance in performance accuracy. (2) The feed-forward programming of the aiming task is assumed to be better timed than that of a pointing task. (3) The aiming task has some ecological value; many every-day tasks consist of aiming rather than pointing (e.g., swinging at a golf ball, throwing a dart or a ball at a target).

In a first study (Roll et al, 1981), we showed an increase in the aiming error with target eccentricity, and a larger undershooting when the head is fixed. Analysing the amplitude of head movement in the head-free condition, we found a large variability of head movement amplitude among subjects, suggesting the existence of a prevailing typology which differentiates between head and eye movers. In a subsequent experiment (Bard et al, 1982), two groups of adults were selected on the basis of their eye/head strategy. Subjects were seated in front of a black curved board which supported the targets. The targets were a line of vertical pieces of plexiglas lighted by green light emitting diodes (LEDs); targets were 10 cm high, 0.5 cm wide, set 5 degrees apart, and located at 30 cm from the resting position of the subject's arm. Aiming movements were horizontal extension of the arm towards the target. Accuracy was measured at target level, but the subject's hand could overshoot the target. In order to perform the task the subject held in his hand a vertical levermounted at the ground level on a double universal joint (with minimal friction). Two potentiometers fixed at the base of the lever were used to record frontal and lateral displacements. The filtered signals were digitalised by a micro processor Data General MP 100. The targets locations used in this study were 10, 20, 30, and 45 in the right hemifield. Aiming accuracy was measured according to three head conditions, head fixed in the sagittal plane, head free, and head lined up with the target. Absolute and constant spatial error, as well as latencies for eye, head and arm movements, were recorded.

Results showed that eye movers were more precise than head movers over all, and for each head condition (Fig. 1). Here again, accuracy deteriorates with target eccentricity. However, in a head-fixed condition, accuracy

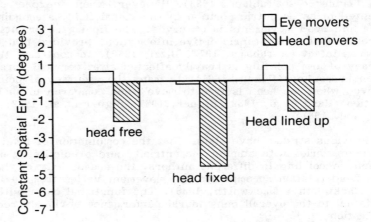

Fig. 1. Constant spatial error according to typology of head behaviour and head condition in adults.

in pointing deteriorates beyond 30° in eye movers, whereas for head movers pointing error increases significantly beyond 20° (Fig. 2).

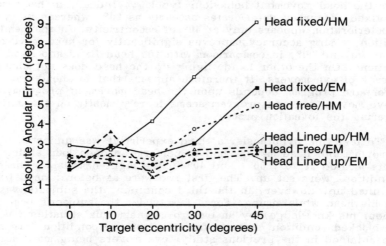

Fig. 2. Absolute angular error according to target eccentricity, head condition, and typology of head behaviour.

It was also found that head latency differed significantly between the two groups in the head-free condition (Fig. 3); the head movers moving their head much earlier than the eye movers. However, with head lined up, that is when the subject is instructed to move his head in the direction of the target, no difference is any longer observed between both groups of subjects.

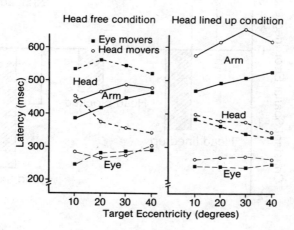

Fig. 3. Arm, head, and eye latencies according to target eccentricity, head condition, and typology of head behaviour in adults.

This second experiment supports the finding that aiming accuracy for eccentric targets depends upon head movements. However, the angle beyond which this contribution becomes effective lies upon the subject's classification under the head-movement behaviour typology. Indeed, in head movers with head fixed, accuracy deteriorates as early as 20°, whereas in eye movers the deterioration appears only at 40° of eccentricity. In the head-lined up condition, aiming accuracy improves significantly for head movers with targets beyond 20°, in comparison with the head-fixed and head-free conditions. On the other hand, lining up the head does not change the accuracy of eye movers. It therefore appears that for head movers the arm feedforward program depends upon the head movement program, whereas for eye movers the arm program seems to rely mostly on the retinal signal triggering the foveation process.

To test this hypothesis, a third experiment was undertaken wherein eye movers and head movers had to perform an open-loop aiming task at targets located at 20°, 30°, and 40° in the right hemifield. Three experimental conditions were set up. The first two were as before: head fixed and head lined up. However, in the third condition, the subjects was asked to move his head while aiming. For a few trials, the subject's head was blocked (without his knowledge) by an electro-magnet; this situation was called the head-blocked condition. Results for the first two conditions are similar to those obtained in the previous study; eye movers being more accurate than head movers (Fig. 4). The direction of error is different for each group, eye movers have a tendency to overshoot the targets, whereas the opposite tendency characterised head movers. However, it was found that both groups are more accurate in their aiming when the head is blocked in comparison with the head fixed. In both situations, the head does not move but in spite of all, in the head-blocked condition the subject was committed to program his head movement.

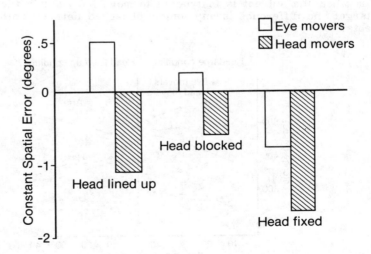

Fig. 4. Constant spatial error according to typology of head behaviour and head condition in adults.

These results suggest that head programming, at least for eccentric targets, is part of the aiming act. It supports the hypothesis presented by Biguer et al (1982) that "neural commands forwarded to different moving segments (e.g., eye, head, arm) implicated in the same act of reaching are generated in parallel... One possibility could be that the commands would in fact be released by a signal from a common generator".

The same question of head contribution to accuracy of aiming was approached from an ontogenetic point of view. Movement control in reaching and pointing is well documented in infants (Bower et al, 1970; Hofsten, 1979, 1980; McDonnell, 1979; McGraw, 1941; Trevarthen et al, 1975); in contrast, few authors have specifically analysed pointing in children from 5 to 10 years of age (Bard et al, 1985; Bard & Hay, 1983; Hay, 1978, 1979, 1981, 1984; White et al, 1964).

The task used is the same as for adults: a directional aiming at a target, without stopping under the target. We tested 6 groups of children (6, 7, 8, 9 and 10 years of age). Two head conditions were selected: head free and head fixed. Aiming was done without visual feedback of the arm trajectory. The absolute spatial error (ASE) recorded. The analysis of variance revealed a significant effect of age, 6-year olds being less accurate than all other groups of children. Target location significantly affected ASE; children were less accurate for eccentric than for central targets. The head factor was not significant, however, from Figure 5 it can be seen that younger children seem to be more precise in head-free condition than older ones. After nine, children perform equally well in both conditions.

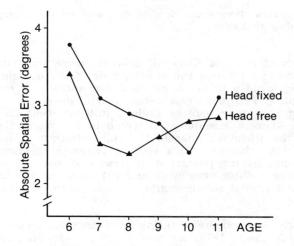

Fig. 5. Absolute spatial error according to age and head condition in the aiming tasks.

The analysis of execution time (arm reaction time + arm movement time) revealed an age x head significant interaction, showing that younger children are slower in the free-head than in the head-fixed condition (Figure 6). It appears that in the 6- and 7-year-old groups, the head programming is not yet perfectly integrated to the aiming mechanism, leading

314

to an overload of the central processing capacity. The execution time is therefore significantly slowed down.

These results suggest that the programming of aiming movement matures earlier than the pointing program, however, when head programming is sollicited, both the programming and execution times are still very slow.

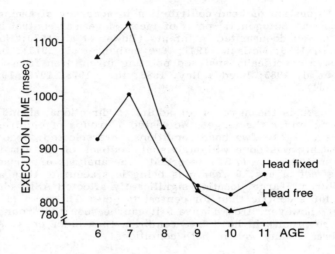

Fig. 6. Execution time according to age and head condition in the aiming tasks.

On the basis of the same issue of head movement contribution to visuo-motor coordination, we studied the development of the coincidence-anticipation ability of children aged 6 to 11. Head condition and visual feedback were manipulated . This perceptual motor task, usually called coincident-timing behaviour, can be divided into different components: (1) a sensory phase where a stimulus is detected in the visual field followed by the tracking of the stimulus, wherein the child attempts to identify the speed and direction of the stimulus; (2) a sensory-motor integration phase, in which the individual, once having predicted the time and place of arrival of the stimulus, programs a motor response; and (3) an execution or motor response phase. Timing and spatial requirements are thus both present (Bard et al, 1981).

Only recently has coincident-timing behaviour been studied in children (Dorfman, 1977; Dunham, 1977; Haywood, 1980, 1983; Stadulis, 1971; Thomas et al, 1981; Wade, 1980; Wrisberg & Mead, 1981, 1983). Various factors have been shown to influence performance, e.g., the speed of the stimulus, the complexity of the response, the training experience. However, the role of head movement in the accuracy of performance has not yet been studied specifically in coincidence timing.

A fourth experiment was conducted wherein three groups of children aged 6, 9 and 11 years were tested. Children were seated in front of a stimulus runway 440 cm long, fixed on a support 1 m 25 high, and located 2 m away. The runway presented 89 photodiodes (.6 cm in diameter), 5 cm apart. An apparent movement was created through successive switching on of the diodes: it came randomly from right or left and ended at the centre of the runway, that is 2 m 20 from an extremity. Subjects holding in hand a joy stick, had to execute an horizontal arm extension in the sagittal plane (amplitude = 30 cm), and had to terminate their movement in coincidence with the end point of the moving stimulus. The joy stick was mounted on a double universal joint, and two potentiometers fixed at the base of the stick and connected to a computer were used to give information on spatial deviation of arm movement. Velocity of apparent movement, direction of movement, and timing data, were controlled by a micro-computer. Two head conditions were selected: head fixed and head free to move. Three dependent variables were considered: the absolute temporal error (absolute difference between the moment of illumination of the last light and the end of arm movement), the absolute spatial error (absolute difference between the location of the last light of the runway and the terminal position of the arm), and the movement time of the arm.

For absolute temporal error, it was found that 6-year-old children are temporally less accurate than the other two groups. Head condition significantly affects all groups, subjects being more precise whenever their head is fixed. However, the head movement deteriorates performance more drastically in the 6-year-old (Fig. 7). For spatial error, head condition does not affect accuracy. Finally, the arm movement is significantly slower when the head is moving and for all groups (Fig. 8).

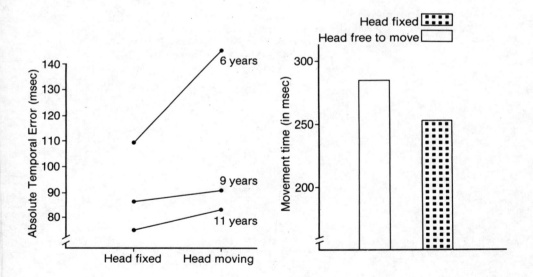

Fig. 7. Absolute temporal error according to age and head condition in the anticipation coincidence task.

Fig. 8. Arm movement time according to head condition.

As for the aiming task, younger children seem unable to accurately coordinate eye-head movements to adequately evaluate the speed of the stimulus and to anticipate the arrival of the stimulus in a specific spatial location. It also seems that the head program overloads the central processing capacity and slows down the different phases of the motor output.

In conclusion, with this type of task cephalic stabilisation seems to be a contributive factor to efficient performance. The present results are in agreement with the findings of Ripoll et al (in press), who used a basketball throw for their study.

In contrast with an aiming task at fixed targets where the head movement is leading the eye to its optimal working zone, in the coincidence-timing task cephalic stabilisation insures a postural control of the body in relation to the moving environment. Children do not seem to escape these constraints, however the contribution of the head is not yet as efficient as in adults.

References

Abrahams, J.C. (1977). The physiology of neck muscles: their role in head movement and maintenance of posture. *Canadian Journal of Physiological Pharmacology, 55,* 332-338.

Bard, C., Fleury, M., Carrière, L. & Bellec, J. (1981). Components of the coincidence-anticipation behavior of children aged 6 to 11. *Perceptual and Motor Skills, 52,* 547-556.

Bard, C., Paillard, J. & Fleury, M. (1982). Contribution of head movement to the projective aiming accuracy in adults. *Society for Neuroscience Abstracts.* Minneapolis.

Bard, C. & Hay, L. (1983). Etude ontogénétique de la coordination visuo-manuelle. *Journal Canadien de Psychologie, 37,* 390-412.

Bard, C., Hay, L. & Fleury, M. (1985). Contribution of vision to the performance and learning of a directional aiming task in children aged 6, 9 and 11. In J.H. Humphrey and I.E. Clarke (Eds.), *Selected Research in Motor Development, vol. 1.* Princeton: Book Comp. Pub.

Bartz, A.E. (1962). Eye movement latency, duration and response time as a function of angular displacement. *Journal of Experimental Psychology, 64,* 318-324.

Biguer, B. (1981). Coordination visuo-motrice: séquence d'activation et contrôle des mouvements visuellement guidés. Thèse de 3e cycle. Université de Lyon I.

Biguer, B., Jeannerod, M. & Prablanc, C. (1982). The coordination of eye, head and hand movements during reaching at a single visual target. *Experimental Brain Research, 46,* 301-304.

Bizzi, E. (1980). Central and peripheral mechanisms in motor control. In G.E. Stelmach and J. Requin (Eds.), *Tutorials in Motor Behavior.* Amsterdam: North Holland.

Bower, T.G.R., Broughton, J.M. & More, M.K. (1970). Demonstration of intention in the reaching behaviour of neonate humans. *Nature, 228,* 689-681.

Carlton, L.G. (1979). Control processes in the production of discrete aiming responses. *Journal of Human Movement Studies, 5,* 115-124.

Carlton, L.G. (1981). Processing visual feedback information for movement control. *Journal of Experimental Psychology, 7,* 1019-1030.

Cohen, L.A. (1961). Role of the eye and neck proprioceptive mechanisms in body orientation and motor coordination. *Journal of Neurophysiology, 24,* 1-11.

Conti, P. & Beaubaton, D. (1976). Role of structured visual field and visual reafference in accuracy of pointing movements. *Perceptual and Motor Skills, 50,* 239-244.

Dorfman, P.W. (1977). Timing and anticipation: A developmental perspective. *Journal of motor Behavior, 9,* 67-79.

Dunham, P. (1977). Age, sex, speed, and practice in coincidence-anticipation performance of children. *Perceptual and Motor Skills, 45,* 187-193.

Hay, L. (1978). Accuracy of children on an open-loop pointing task. *Perceptual and Motor Skills, 46,* 1079-1082.

Hay, L. (1979). Spatial-temporal analysis of movements in children: Motor programs versus feedback in the development of reaching. *Journal of Motor Behavior, 11,* 189-200.

Hay, L. (1981). The effect of amplitude and accuracy requirements on movement time in children. *Journal of Motor Behavior, 13,* 177-186.

Hay, L. (1984). Discontinuity in the development of motor control in children. In W. Prinz and A. Sanders (Eds.), *Cognition and motor processes.* Berlin, Heidelberg: Springer-Verlag.

318

Haywood, K.M. (1980). Coincidence anticipation accuracy across the life span. *Experimental Aging Research, 6,* 451-462.

Haywood, K.M. (1983). Responses to speed changes in coincidence-anticipation judgments after extended practice. *Research Quarterly, 54,* 28-32.

Herman, R., Herman, R. & Maulucci, R. (1981). Visually triggered eye-arm movements in man. *Experimental Brain Research, 42,* 392-398.

Hofsten, C. von (1979). Development of visually directed reaching: The approach phase. *Journal of Human Movement Studies, 5,* 160-178.

Hofsten, C. von (1980). Predictive reaching for moving objects by human infants. *Journal of Experimental Child Psychology, 30,* 369-382.

Jeannerod, M. & Prablanc, C. (1983). Visual control of reaching movements in man. In J.E. Desmedt (Ed.), *Motor Control Mechanisms in Health and Disease.* New York: Raven.

Mackworth, J.F. & Mackworth, N.H. (1958). Eye fixations recorded on changing visual scenes by the television eye marker. *Journal of the Optical Society of America, 48,* 439-445.

Marteniuk, R.G. (1978). The role of eye and head positions in slow movement execution. In G.E. Stelmach (Ed.), *Information processing in motor control and learning.* New York: Academic Press.

McDonnell (1979). Patterns of eye-hand coordination in the first year of life. *Canadian Journal of Psychology, 33,* 253-257.

McGraw, M.B. (1941). Neural maturation as exemplified in the reaching-prehensile behavior of the human infant. *The Journal of Psychology, 40,* 30-38.

Ripoll, H., Bard, C. & Paillard, J. (1985). Oculo-cephalic stabilization on target as a factor of success of throw in basketball shooting. *Journal of Human Movement Science* (in press).

Roll, R. (1981). Influence des mouvements céphalogires sur l'adjustement visuo-moteur chez l'homme. Contribution à l'étude de la perception de l'espace. Thèse de IIIe cycle. Université Aix-Marseilles II.

Roll, R., Bard, C. & Paillard, J. (1981). Rôle des mouvements céphalogires sur la précision d'un adjustement visuo-moteur chez l'homme. *Journal de Physiologie* (Paris) *77,* 44A.

Roll, R., Bard, C. & Paillard, J. (1985). Head orienting contributes to the directional accuracy of aiming at distant targets. Submitted for publication.

Stadulis, R.D. (1971). Coincidence-anticipation behavior of children. Unpublished doctoral dissertation. Columbia University, Teacher's College.

Thomas, J.R., Gallagher, J.D. & Purvis, G.J. (1981). Reaction time and anticipation time: Effects of development. *Research Quarterly, 52,* 359-367.

Trevarthen, C., Hubley, P. & Sheeran, L. (1975). Les activités innées du nourrisson. *La recherche, 6,* 447-458.

Wade, M.G. (1980). Coincidence-anticipation of young normal and handicapped children. *Journal of Motor Behavior, 12,* 103-112.

White, B.L., Castle, P. & Held, R. (1964). Observations on the development of visually directed reaching. *Child Development, 35,* 349-364.

Wrisberg, C.A. & Mead, B.J. (1981). Anticipation of coincidence in children a test of schema theory. *Perceptual and Motor Skills, 52,* 599-606.

Wrisberg, C.A. & Mead, B.J. (1983). Developing coincident timing skill in children: A comparison of training methods. *Research Quarterly, 54,* 67-74.

VISUO-MANUAL COORDINATION FROM 6 TO 10: SPECIFICATION, CONTROL
AND EVALUATION OF DIRECTION AND AMPLITUDE PARAMETERS OF
MOVEMENT

L. Hay, C. Bard and M. Fleury

1. INTRODUCTION

This article describes research on visuo-manual coordination in children
performing aiming movements at targets. The aim of this study was two-fold:
first to investigate how the various spatial parameters of a visually directed
movement are specified and controlled, and, second to analyse the relationship between the accuracy of the actual aiming action and the accuracy of
children's perceptual evaluation of their own performance.

Reaching a visual goal in the prehension space requires that the
direction and extent of the hand movement be correctly specified and
controlled. The two spatial dimensions, direction and amplitude, which have
been extensively discussed by Paillard (1985a), have to be distinguished
from different view points. With regard to movement programming, several
studies on Choice Reaction Time have shown, either by varying uncertainty
on one of these two dimensions (Megaw, 1972; Fiori, Semjen & Requin, 1974),
or by means of a precuing technique (Rosenbaum, 1980; Bonnet, Requin &
Stelmach, 1982), that directional programming is more time consuming than
amplitude programming, which suggests that on-line regulations might be
applied more to amplitude than to direction. With regard to feedback
progressing, it seems that, depending on whether the task requirements
focus on direction or amplitude, visual feedback can be integrated within
different temporal ranges (Hay, Beaubaton, Bard & Fleury, 1984), and during
different phases of the trajectory - initial phase under directional control
(Bard, Hay & Fleury, 1985), and final phase under amplitude control (Carlton,
1981; Beaubaton & Hay, 1986). From an ontogenetical point of view, directional regulation seems to be an earlier acquisition than amplitude regulation.
Von Hofsten (1982), when discussing his results on neonate eye-hand coordination, concluded that the reaching space of the newborn shows a cruder
distance structuring, if any, than direction structuring, since the gain in
distance accuracy when reaching watched objects over unwatched objects was
not very large. In children performing movement without visual feedback,
programming seems to reach its highest efficiency quite early (at about 7
years of age) when directional requirements only are imposed (Bard & Hay,
1983), whereas it takes longer to develop in pointing tasks in which both
requirements are involved indiscriminately. Therefore it seems logical to
investigate the development of programming and feedback-based control
capacities, using tasks in which a clear distinction was made between the
direction and amplitude components.

Goal-directed movements involve ballistic and feedback control processes.
Developmental studies on Fitt's Law using reciprocal tapping tasks have shown
that the interception coefficient decreases with increasing age, which suggests
that a developmental reduction in the "homing" (feedback processing) time

takes place while ballistic distance covering time remains constant at all ages (Kerr, 1975; Sugden, 1980). Nevertheless some of these studies have also shown a reduction in slope coefficient (Hay, 1981; Salmoni & Pascoe, 1979), suggesting that both ballistic and feedback processes could undergo developmental changes. Schellekens, Kalverboer and Scholten (1984), on the basis of a detailed spatio-temporal analysis of visually controlled tapping movements, have shown that the ballistic phase of movement improves in accuracy (closeness of approach) with age while the same duration is maintained constant, which results in a reduction in duration and number of movement elements during the homing phase, and probably facilitates further integration into a smooth approach movement. Other studies using experimental situations, in which visual feedback was distorted or not involved in online regulation, have shown the existence of a sort of developmental alternation between the feedforward and feedback components of action, both in infants (McDonnell, 1975; McDonnell & Abraham, 1981; Mounoud & Hauert, 1982) and in children (Hay, 1979; Gachoud, 1983), suggesting that younger subjects have difficulty in integrating feedback information in the ongoing action.

Apart from on-line feedback, information about the result of action, which cannot be used to correct the ongoing response, may be used in the amendment of subsequent motor programs. If no external information about the result of action is available, the subject is confined to rely on an "internal" evaluation. The question of the relationship between the accuracy of this evaluation and the accuracy of the action itself seems to be relevant from an ontogenetical point of view. The notion of a possible functional dissociation between information processing channels has been put forward and documented by Paillard (1985b), who stressed that "the discriminating capacity of perceptual evaluation is often cruder than that of sensorimotor processing". If the visuo-motor loop is interrupted by removing visual feedback of movement, the accuracy of the spatial correspondence between the visually located target position and the terminal position of the hand might vary depending on whether this correspondence is established through the subject's action or through some comparative evaluation, which we attempted to measure from the subject's performance without any verbal mediation. The point was therefore to describe the respective development of the acuity of the action program and the acuity of action evaluation; our hypothesis was that these two abilities do not develop synchronously, and that the relationship between them depends on whether direction and amplitude is the task parameter.

2. METHOD

2.1. Subjects

Three groups (four boys and four girls per group) of 6-, 8-, and 10-year-old children, were used in this study. All were right-handed and had a normal scholastic level. The exact mean age of each group was 5.9 years, 8.1 years, and 10.2 years, respectively. A group of eight adult subjects was also tested as control, but will be referred to only occasionally for comparative purposes.

2.2. Apparatus

The subject sat astride an adjustable seat, with his/her chest leaning against a vertical support. In front of this support and between the subject's legs, was a vertical lever with a hilt reaching a position below the subject's chin when in resting position. The lever was equipped with a double universal joint at floor level. Two potentiometers perpendicularly attached to the basis of the lever and connected to a Micro Nova MP100, allowed the recording of all frontal and lateral displacements. The potentiometric values corresponding to lever positions were automatically translated into angular or amplitude values. In front of the subject at eye level, a horizontal support could be fitted with the target sets. Behind this support a vertical curved screen served as a visual background. Both were painted matt black in order to maintain some visual homogeneity in the experimental environment. Two target sets could be fitted into the apparatus, just above the top lever hilt level: in the first set the targets were placed in a horizontal line at an equal distance (30 cm) from the starting point (resting position), 0°, 20° and 40° to the right of the subject. In the second set the targets were placed on the sagittal plane at the level of the subject's eyes, at 20 cm, 25 cm and 30 cm from the starting position. The targets were 0.5 cm-wide, 10 cm-high vertical tubes, tapering at the bottom, made of translucent plexiglass and lit by green diodes.

2.3. Task and experimental conditions

Each subject had to perform three types of visuo-manual aiming tasks, holding the lever hilt in his/her right hand and moving back to the resting position at the end of each trial (see Fig. 1). In the first, purely directional task (1), the first set of targets was used, and the subjects were required to move the lever in the direction of the lit target and to overshoot it, moving their arm from a flexed position to full extension. Angular error and movement time were recorded as the hand crossed the target line. The second task, a pure amplitude task (2), was performed with the second set of targets. In this case the lever was laterally locked and could only move in the sagittal plane along the target line. The subjects were then required

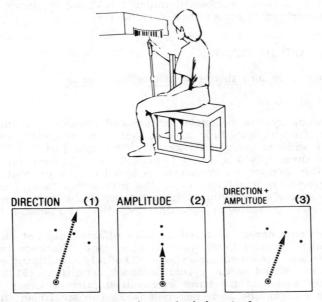

Fig. 1. Schema of the experimental aiming tasks.

to push the lever until reaching a position just below the target with their hand. The amplitude error was recorded as soon as the hand stopped. In the third task (3), the direction and amplitude requirements were combined. Using the first set of targets, the subjects had to move the lever in the accurate direction and stop just below the target. In this case, the aiming error was recorded in terms of both direction and amplitude.

All three tasks were performed under two visual conditions: one allowing vision of the hand trajectory, and the other without vision of the hand. Vision of the hand trajectory was precluded by a black horizontal screen which covered the area of the hand displacements. Under the condition without vision an additional requirement was introduced: at each trial, immediately after the subjects reached the final position and before they return to the resting position, they were required to correct their aiming movement by making a small readjustment in order to improve their terminal accuracy. This second phase of the trial was punctuated by an auditory signal, triggered one second after the end of the aiming movement and lasting two seconds, allowing the subjects to readjust their final position. In the purely directional task, the readjustment consisted of drawing the hand back slightly behind the target and crossing the target line again in order to improve directional accuracy. At the end of the readjustment, the error was again recorded in terms of direction, amplitude, or both, depending on the task performed.

In all tasks and under all conditions, the three targets were randomly presented five times each. The three tasks were performed by all subjects, in a varied order within each age group, with a resting period between them. The non-visual condition was always applied before the visual condition. Without specification on the movement speed, the subjects, nevertheless, were required not to perform movement times out of a range of approximately 300 to 800 ms, in order to avoid too great a disparity. Familiarisation trials were performed under the visual feedback condition, before each experimental series on a specific task.

3.   RESULTS AND DISCUSSION

3.1. Spatial accuracy and timing of aiming movements

3.1.1. Spatial accuracy

Aiming accuracy was measured in terms of absolute terminal errors. For both direction and amplitude errors, scores were allotted on the single tasks (1 or 2) and the combined task (3). The data (see Fig. 2) were subjected to a three-way 3 x 2 x 2 (Age x Task x Vision) analysis of variance. In this analysis of variance, as in all others presented in this paper, the error-term was taken to be the interaction factor/subjects, which allows additional analysis within each condition, since the error-term used in any comparison is treatment specific (Hoc, 1983; Rouanet & Lepine, 1977).

The directional error, in terms of main effects, did not change significantly with age and there was no significant difference between tasks with the single and combined dimensions. The only significant change in performance was related to the visual feedback conditions ($F_{1,21} = 46,62$, $p < .001$), since vision of the hand improved angular accuracy in all age groups and on both single and combined tasks (no significant interaction

appears between these two factors and Vision). Nevertheless a specific
analysis per condition showed that under the visual condition, Age had a
significant effect (F2,21 = 6.37, p < .01), since accuracy improved as shown
by a significant linear component (F1,14 = 7.30, p <.025), reflecting a
significant increase in accuracy between the age of 6 and 8 (F1,14 = 10.33,
p <.01) followed by a stabilisation of performance between the age of 8 and
10.

More main effects were found on amplitude error, as shown by Figure
2. Age significantly affected performance (F2,21 = 3.96, p <.05), and so
did Task (F1,21 = 7.77, p <.025) and Vision (F1,21 = 83.63, p <.001).
But these effects were essentially due to modifications in performance under
the non-visual condition, as shown by interactions between Age and Vision
(F2,21 = 5.76, p <.025) and between Task and Vision (F1,21 = 4.87, p <
.025). In the same way, the Age x Task interaction (F2,21 = 4.93, p <.025)
was apparent only under the non-visual condition as shown by the triple
Age x Task x Vision interaction (F2,21 = 5.45, p <.025). Thus the age
effect consisted of a decrease in error without vision between 6 and 10 years
of age as shown by a linear trend under this condition (F1,14 = 8.08, p <
.025), but with an intermediate maximum at 8 years of age in the single
amplitude task (2) for which a significant quadratic trend was found (F1,21
= 7,48, p <.025).

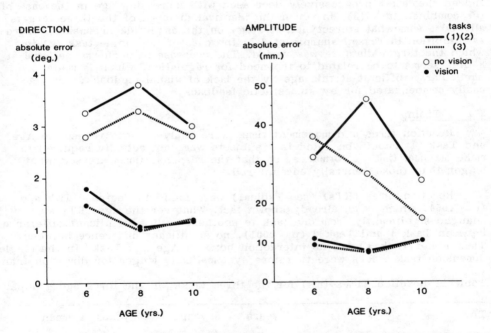

Fig. 2. Direction and amplitude error of movement, with respect
to age, task and visual conditions.

Thus specification of the directional parameter in the absence of visual
feedback seems to be fairly accurate early on during development, since
mean error was only around three degrees at 6 years of age and did not
show any major changes afterwards. In agreement with previously mentioned

studies, directional accuracy thus seems to depend on quite elementary and early functional mechanisms. This does not exclude the possibility that directional accuracy may be subjected to a developed type of control such as visual guidance. This type of control is in fact the only one which improves slightly with age. Introducing an additional amplitude requirement (Task 3) does not affect directional accuracy whatever the visual feedback condition, which suggests the existence of specific channels. In the case of the visual feedback condition, this compatibility could moreover be attributed to the fact that visual regulation of the two dimensions does not involve the same phases of movement trajectory, as suggested by the studies on adults already mentioned.

Regulation of amplitude seems to develop in a different manner, with respect to terminal accuracy. Specification of the amplitude parameter in the absence of visual feedback shows age-related changes which take the form of non-monotonic development, as previously encountered with pointing tasks in which both requirements were combined; in contrast, visually controlled movements tend to be equally accurate at all ages. In fact most of the amplitude errors made without visual feedback were undershooting errors. However, the different scores obtained in the two tasks (2 and 4) at 8 and 10 years of age suggest that the particularly marked undershooting error at 8 was not only due to the increasing effect of a general motor inhibition. Indeed the latter progressively decreased with increasing age in the case of the combined task (3), in which the identical distance of the three targets allowed a somewhat stereotyped strategy on the amplitude dimension, whereas inhibition increased sharply at 8 in the case of the single task (2) in which the target distance was varied. The decrease in performance level at 8 thus seems to be related to the need for regulation, which is made particularly difficult at this age by the lack of visual feedback, not yet easily compensated for by kinaesthetic feedback.

3.1.2. Timing

Reaction times and movement times were analysed with respect to Age and Task. It should be noted that subjects were not actually required to make maximal time performance, so that the response times are somewhat longer than those generally encountered.

Reaction times (RTs) (see Table 1) were found to decrease with age (p < .05), which is an already known fact. Whatever the age, RTs also changed significantly from one task to another, with a significant difference between Task 1 and Task 2 (p < .001), no significant difference between Task 1 and Task 3, and no interaction between Age and Task. In the single-dimension tasks, RTs were therefore systematically longer for direction than

Table 1. Reaction Times (ms) for the three tasks, in the three age groups.

TASK	6 years	8 years	10 years	mean
DIRECTION (1)	753	639	616	669
AMPLITUDE (2)	626	585	514	575
COMBINED (3)	742	602	600	648

for amplitude, and an additional amplitude requirement did not cause any increase in RTs over the single directional dimension task. These data are consistent with the previously mentioned notion that the specification of direction and amplitude parameters of movement could mainly involve different stages of the response process.

Movement times (see Fig. 3) were anlaysed together for Tasks 1 and 3 in which the target distances were identical, and separately for Task 2 in which the target distance was varied. The data from the tasks with a single target distance were analysed by means of a three-way 3 x 2 x 2 (Age x Task x Vision) analysis of variance. Significant effects were found for Age ($F_{2,21}$ = 4.68, p < .025), Task ($F_{1,21}$ = 25.98, p < .001), and Vision (F $_{1,21}$ = 6.19, p < .025), and a significant interaction was found between Age and Task (2,21 = 5.07, p < .025). The data from Task 2 were analysed by means of a three-way 3 x 3 x 2 (Age x Targets x Vision) analysis of variance. It revealed significant effects for Age ($F_{2,21}$ = 9.25, p < .01) and Targets ($F_{2,21}$ = 60.40, p < .001), and no effect for Vision. The interactions were significant between Age and Targets ($F_{4,42}$ = 2.74, p < .05) and between Age and Vision ($F_{2,21}$ = 8.39, p < .01).

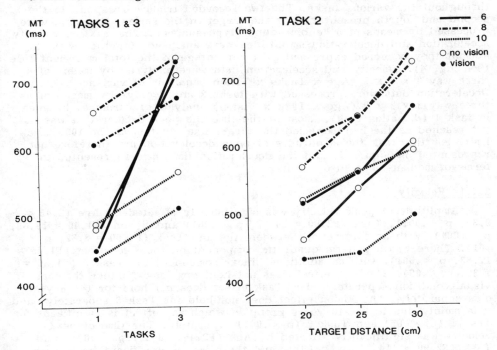

Fig. 3. Movement time in the three tasks, with respect to age and visual conditions.

Unlike the Reaction Times, the Movement Times (MTs) did not change monotonously with age. On average the 8-year-olds performed with the longest MTs, the 10-year-olds with the shortest, and the 6-year-olds had intermediate MTs. In both tasks with the same target distance (1 and 3),

326

MTs were systematically shorter in the single direction task (1), which is not surprising since this task can be performed without final braking, and since MTs (which were recorded as the hand crosses the target line) did not include any final braking phase. But the differences in MTs between Tasks 1 and 3 were much more pronounced with the 6-year-olds, so that this age group behaved like the 10-year-olds in the single direction task (1) and like the 8-year-olds in the combined task (3) involving braking and stopping on the target. In the single amplitude task (2), the target distance affected MTs at all ages and under both visual feedback conditions. But the slope function was less marked for the 10-year-olds than for the two younger groups, which is consistent with the age-related differences found in MTs in Task 3, and suggests an increasing efficiency in ballistic distance covering phase between 8 and 10.

3.2. Patterns of aiming movements

The potentiometric values were recorded during the whole hand trajectory with a 6 msec pace, for two trials in each series. The recorded trajectories were aimed at the 0° target of tasks 1 and 3 and at the 30 cm distant target of task 2, so that identical trajectories could be compared throughout the various tasks. The two recorded trials correspond to the second and fourth presentation of the target in the series. The data were processed by means of a "cubic spline" type analysis. The maximal velocity, acceleration and deceleration amplitudes were analysed, together with the moment they occurred expressed as a percentage of the total movement time (see Fig. 4). Velocity and acceleration data were analysed by means of a three-way 3 x 3 x 2 (Age x Tasks x Vision) analysis of variance. Deceleration data were processed with tasks 2 and 3 only, by means of a three-way 3 x 2 x 2 (Age x Task x Vision) analysis of variance, because in task 1 (direction task), most of the time the peak deceleration was not yet reached as the hand crossed the target line, that is at the 100% time limit. For this task the amplitudes of peak deceleration are therefore not represented on Figure 4, and the deceleration times are represented in terms of medians instead of means.

3.2.1. Velocity

Amplitude of peak velocity was significantly affected by Age (2,45 = 9.34, p < .001), Task (F2,90 = 13.67, p < .001) and Vision (F1,45 = 19.69, p < .001), with an interaction between Age and Task (F4,90 = 3.82, p < .01). There was a general quadratic component on the Age effect (F1,45 = 17.63, p < .001), with an additional linear component for Task 3 (F1,30 = 7.33, p < .05). The Age effect does not hold for Task 2 under the non-visual condition separately. The Task effect does not hold for the 8-year-olds separately. The Vision effect does not hold for Task 3 separately, and it is mainly due to the 10 years group in which the effect is significant for Task 1 (p < .05) and Task 2 (p < .001) separately. The time of peak velocity was significantly affected by Age (F2,45 = 8.29, p < .001) and Task (F2,90 = 114.04, p < .001), and there was a significant interaction between both factors (F4,90 = 3.64, p < .01); Vision had no effect. When considering tasks separately, the Age effect was not found to be significant for Task 2; it took the form of a quadratic trend (F1,45 = 8.57, p < .01) for Task 1 and a linear trend (F1,20 = 24.20, p < .001) for Task 3.

3.2.2. Acceleration

Amplitude of peak acceleration was significantly affected by Age (F2,45

327

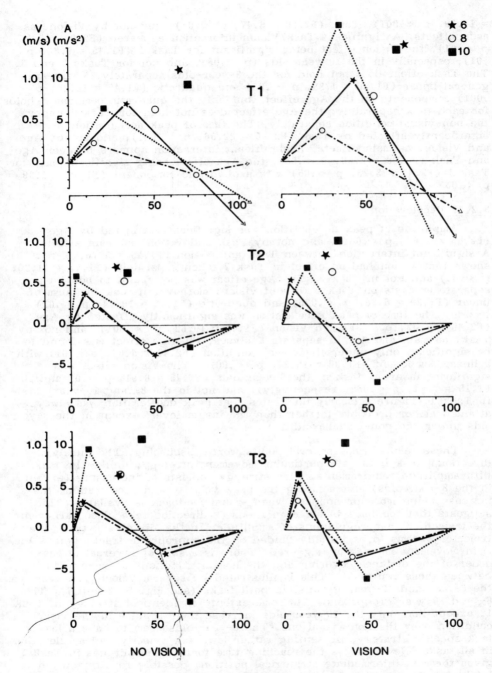

Fig. 4. Peak velocity (isolated points), peak acceleration and
deceleration (points joined by lines), and their time of
occurrence (in percentage of movement time), with
respect to age and visual conditions.

= 13.19, p < .001), Task (F2,90 = 6.47, p < .01), and not by Vision, as main effects. A significant Task/Vision interaction appeared (F2,90 = 5.35, p < .01), the Vision effect being significant for Task 1 (F1,45 = 7.84, p < .01), especially in the 10-year-olds (p < .05), and not for Tasks 2 and 3. The Task effect does not hold for the 8-year-olds separately. There are general linear (F1,30 = 4.88, p < .05) and quadratic (F1,45 = 19.20, p < .001) components on the Age effect, but only the quadratic component holds for each task separately; the Age effect does not hold for Task 2 under the non-visual condition separately. The time of peak acceleration was significantly affected by Task (F2,90 = 32.56, p < .001), and not by Age and Vision, as main effects. A significant interaction appears between Age and Task (F4,90 = 2.60, p < .05), the Age effect being significant only for Task 1 (F2,45 = 3.25, p < .05) with a quadratic component (F1,45 = 4.39, p < .05).

3.2.3. Deceleration

Amplitude of peak deceleration was significantly affected by Age (F2,45 = 9.69, p < .001), and not by Task and Vision, as main effects. A significant interaction between Task and Vision (F1,45 = 5.76, p < .025) shows that Vision had an effect in Task 2 taken separately (F1,45 = 11.20, p < .01) and not in Task 3. The Age effect was not found to hold in a separate analysis on Task 2 without vision; moreover it took the form of linear (F1,30 = 6.38, p < .025) and quadratic (F1,45 = 10.44, p < .01) trends. The time of peak deceleration was significantly affected by Age (F2,45 = 7.02, p < .01) and Vision (F1,45 = 19.62, p < .001), and not by Task, as main effects. In separate analyses, the Age effect was found to be significant only under the visual condition (F2,45 = 5.62, p < .01) with a linear component (F1,30 = 16.28, p < .001). The Vision effect was significant in every task in the 6-year-olds (F1,45 = 8.91, p < .01 and F1,15 = 7.61, p < .025, respectively), and not in the 8- and 10-year-olds. In Task 1, Figure 4 clearly illustrates that peak deceleration was always attained at, or probably farther than the target level, except in the 8-year-olds under the non-visual condition.

These results raise several points worth discussing. The purely directional task induces a particular movement strategy, unlike the tasks with amplitude requirements. This strategy consists of increasing (except in the 8-year-olds) and delaying the peak velocity and acceleration, the increase being more pronounced when visual feedback is available. This suggests that feedback-based regulations of direction take place earlier in the trajectory than regulations of amplitude. In the directional task, the trajectory seems to be initially guided on the appropriate track, before the main movement impulse is triggered. There is a sort of reversal in the order of the distance covering and the homing functions of movements between these two tasks. This is illustrated by several velocity curves from the 6-, 8- and 10-year groups, in both tasks (see Fig. 5, 6 and 7). The 6- and 10-year groups show, to some extent, an identical strategy in Task 1, except that only the 10-year-olds increase their impulse in the visual condition over the non-visual one. The 8-year-olds seem to have a less task-specific strategy, presenting rather low peak velocity and acceleration in all tasks. Nevertheless the reaching time for peak amplitudes in Task 1 gives them an intermediate strategical position, possibly resulting in an inhibitory overcontrol. In most cases, the peak deceleration in Task 1 is reached passed the target line which is consequently crossed at a still rather high speed, except for 8-year-olds in the non-visual condition

TASK 1 (DIRECTION)   6 yrs.   TASK 2 (AMPLITUDE)

NO VISION   VISION   NO VISION   VISION

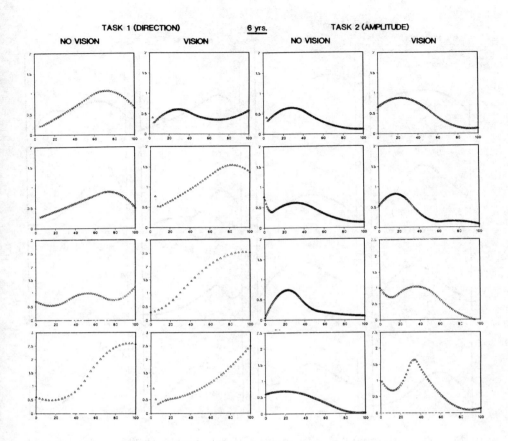

Fig. 5. Individual velocity curves of 6-year-old children, in
Tasks 1 and 2, under the two visual conditions.

who begin to brake their movement clearly before reaching the target level.
This confirms the idea of an overcontrol at this age, particularly in a
situation where visual feedback is not available. This precautionary strategy
at 8 in the absence of vision suggests a persistent difficulty in using
kinaesthetic feedback.

The second point of concern is the difference between the pure
amplitude task (2) and the combined dimensions task with the same
amplitude (3). Under the non-visual condition, both tasks differed in that
there were no age-related differences in all peak amplitudes in Task 2,
whereas the 10-year-olds increased their peak amplitudes over the two
younger groups in Task 3. Under the visual condition, the age-related
differences in peak amplitudes were identical in both tasks and consisted
of minimal amplitudes at 8 and variably increased amplitudes among the 6-
and 10-year-olds. This suggests that when visual feedback is available,
the ballistic distance-covering character of movements achieved at 10 has

330

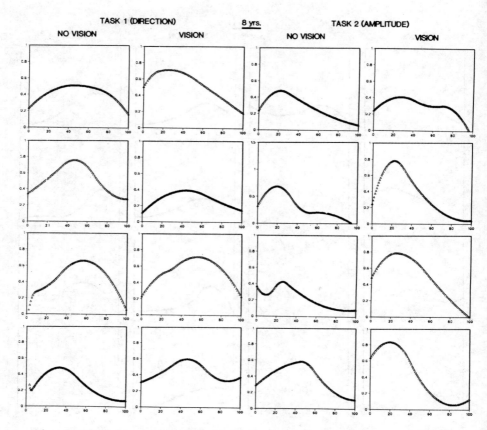

Fig. 6. Individual velocity curves of 8-year-old children, in Tasks
1 and 2, under the two visual conditions.

increased over the previous years whether or not amplitude regulation is
necessary, whereas it does not increase when amplitude needs to be regulated
through kinaesthetic feedback in the absence of vision.

The last point concerns the changes in peak deceleration times with
respect to age and visual conditions. Relative time of peak deceleration is
the only one to change with visual conditions. In Tasks 2 and 3, the
availability of visual feedback generally hastened the beginning of braking,
with a particularly marked effect at 6, and a weak effect at 8. This results
in different trends in the Age effect depending on the visual conditions.
Under the non-visual condition, there was a tendency for the duration of
the terminal braking phase to decrease between 6 and 10, with an intermediate maximum at 8. This tendency is consistent with a previous study on
movement patterns performed without visual feedback (Hay, 1979), but here
it does not reach statistical significance. In contrast, with visual feedback,
the braking phase clearly decreases with increasing age, which is consistent
with the age-related decrease in the visually guided homing time found by

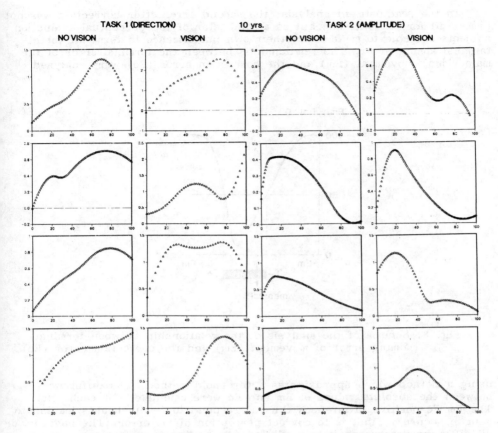

Fig. 7. Individual velocity curves of 10-year-old children, in
Tasks 1 and 2, under the two visual conditions.

Schellekens et al (1984). Thus the development of movement patterns seems
to differ depending on whether visual or kinaesthetic feedback only is
available.

3.3. Perceptual evaluation of movement accuracy

The readjustments were analysed using the constant error. Negative
directional errors refer to aiming to the left, and positive errors refer to
aiming to the right of the target. For amplitude errors, undershooting is
referred to as negative error, and overshooting is referred to as positive
error. It should be noted here that the main difference between mean
absolute and constant errors was encountered at 10 for directional error
under the non-visual condition, where constant error approximated zero.
This means that absolute errors at 10 expressed only dispersion around a
central point near zero, and the nearly identical absolute error found in
the younger age-groups reflects an approximately identical dispersion around
a systematic error.

332

In the readjustment analysis, the second error after correction was not processed for its own sake but as an indicator of the perceptual evaluation subjects are able to make about their own performance in terms of their terminal aiming error. The relationships between the terminal error of the main aiming movement (Em) and the correction error (Ec) were analysed

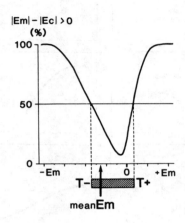

Fig. 8. Schema of the analysis of the relationship between terminal aiming error of movement (Em) and the correction error (Ec).

using a method which approximates a threshold method. The difference between the absolute values of Em and Ec were calculated for each trial. The Em-Ec positive differences thus correspond to readjustments leading to gain in accuracy, that is to correct perception of Em error. The negative or nil differences correspond to readjustments leading to a decrease (or no improvement) in accuracy, that is to a wrong (or no) perception of Em error For each class of Em constant error, the percentage of positive 'Em - Ec' differences over the total number of responses was calculated. A curve of frequency of positive differences with respect to Em was plotted, defining two absolute thresholds, one for the negative Em values, and the other for the positive Em values (see Fig. 8). Thus the two Em threshold values circumscribe a sub-liminal range, within which terminal error is not perceived judging from the corrections performed by the subjects. The aim of this analysis was to study the age-related changes in the extent of this sub-liminal range and its relationships with the mean terminal aiming error (Em). Figure 9 presents for each age group the extent and location of the sub-liminal range in relation to the mean and intraindividual dispersion of constant error (Em), for both single tasks (1 and 2) and for the directional dimension of the combined task (3). The amplitude dimension of Task 3 is not represented on the figure because amplitude was not varied in this task, which makes the comparison with the single amplitude task less relevant than it is for the directional dimension. The data from the adult group are shown for the sake of comparison.

333

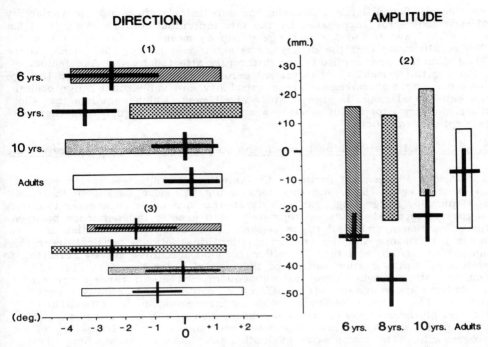

Fig. 9. Mean (short black crossbars) and variability (long black
lines) of the terminal movement error (Em), and sub-liminal
range of Em perception (grey and white strips), with respect
to age, for direction and amplitude dimensions.

3.3.1. Extent of the sub-liminal range and variability of movement accuracy

In the case of the directional dimension, it was found that the age-
related changes in the sub-liminal range were not monotonous. At 6 and 10,
the range is approximately the same in both tasks, and at 8 it reaches a
minimum in the single task (1) and a maximum in the combined task (3). The
8-year-old group was therefore the only one of the three in which involving
amplitude as an additional dimension seems to overload the perceptual
evaluation system. In the case of amplitude, the extent of the sub-liminal
range does not change in the same way since it decreases between 6 and 8
and remains at the same level thereafter.

The intraindividual variability of movement error (Em) was analysed on
each dimension by means of a two-way 3 x 2 (Age x Task) analysis of
variance (the adults were not included in the analysis). For the directional
dimension, the results show no significant main effect of Age and Task; but
a significant interaction between both factors ($F_{2,21} = 4.31$, $p < .05$) reveals
a significant Age effect for the single task (1) ($F_{2,21} = 5.18$, $p < .05$) and
not for the combined task (3). The Age effect in Task 1 consists of a greater
variability in the 6-year-olds than in the two older groups ($F_{1,14} = 6.50$, $p
< .025$ and 5.57, $p < .05$, respectively), the latter being identical in this
respect. The Task effect was significant specifically in the 8-year-olds
($F_{1,7} = 13.45$, $p < .01$). For amplitude, no main or specific significant effect

was found. The difference between the sub-liminal range and the variability of movement error (expressed by the intraindividual confidence limits of Em at p = .05) was tested for each age group by means of Student's t-test. The results show that the difference is significant at p < .001 in all groups. Thus direction and amplitude are differently affected by the Age factor, including the variability of movement error. Nevertheless, whatever the age-related changes in movement error variability and sub-liminal range occur, the sub-liminal range is always wider at all ages, which suggests that the discriminatory capacity of sensori-motor processing is higher than that of perceptual evaluation.

3.3.2. Spatial relationships between the sub-liminal range and the movement error

Among the general findings, the sub-liminal range was rarely centred on terminal error (Em), and this decentering was more marked in the case of amplitude, suggesting, particularly on this dimension, a greater tendency to correct terminal errors appropriately, and greater independence between the evaluation system and the movement. The perceptual evaluation of motor performance and the various relationships between terminal error (Em), sub-liminal range, and target position, can be accounted for by referring to a classical and simplified schema of the sensori-motor loop (see Fig. 10). For evaluating terminal error for subsequent correction, three sources of information are available: visual afferences continuously defining target position, kinaesthetic feedback providing information on hand position at the end of the movement, and a representation of the movement end point (final goal), which has been associated with the choice or triggering of its programming. The comparative evaluation thus consists of matching visual afferences with either one or the other movement-related type of information, or both. If information derived from movement programming is privileged in the matching (Comparison 1), this should result in a sub-liminal range centred on the aiming error of movement (Em). If kinaesthetic feedback information is privileged in the matching (Comparison 2), the sub-liminal range should be centred on the target position (zero).

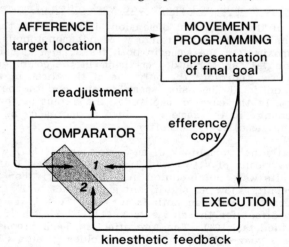

Fig. 10. Schema of sensori-motor loops possibly involved in corrective activities.

With regard to direction, a rather wide sub-liminal range can be found at age 6 for both tasks, including both terminal error and zero. Two possible interpretations are suggested: 1) the subjects might privilege Comparison 2, but without being able to successfully implement this strategy because of inadequate spatial calibration of kinaesthetic feedback, which results in a sub-liminal range including Em error, on account of its wideness; 2) both Comparison 1 and Comparison 2 systems are involved, which results in a sub-liminal range centred between terminal error and target position, and including both of them. A definite conclusion cannot be reached on the basis of our results alone. Other data suggest a possible weakness in spatial calibration of kinaesthetic feedback information at 6, such as the absence of relationships between movement time and accuracy of directional aiming without vision of the hand at this age, in contrast with older ages (Bard, Hay & Fleury, 1985b). However, the co-activation of a Comparison 1 system, referring to an egocentric type of strategy at this age, is also plausible. At 8, it is obvious that subjects exclusively function with Comparison 2 system since their sub-liminal range in the single dimension task (1) is exactly centred on zero; moreover this system is discriminatory, its range being much narrower. The 8-year-old children, while making the greatest aiming error, are able to perceive their error most accurately. Thus this age group shows the most marked discrepancy between accuracy of programming and acuity of evaluation, because of both motor inaccuracy and perceptual acuity. Moreover in the 8-year-olds, amplitude evaluation is also based on Comparison 2 as we will see later. So it might be thought that adding an amplitude requirement as in the combined dimension task (3) overloads the directional evaluation system, resulting in a considerable extension of the sub-liminal range as observed at this age. This extension can be interpreted either as a decreased efficiency of Comparison 2 system because of its overloading, or as an attempt to solve the problem of overloading by working with both comparison systems together. At 10 years of age, programming becomes more accurate since constant error approximates zero. But the sub-liminal range is still rather wide, and it is unpredictably centred according to the model. It is most improbable that the acuity of kinaesthetic perception itself may have decreased. Maybe the kinaesthetic regulation of the on-going movement is not the same at 10 as at 8, as suggested by differences in movement patterns, which could result in a bias in the evaluation of final position. Besides the sub-liminal range at this age is differently centred in the case of the combined dimensions task (3) involving terminal braking. In any case, it should be noted that relationships between the terminal directional error (Em) and the sub-liminal range were exactly the same for the 10-year-olds as for the adults, in both single (1) and combined (3) dimension tasks.

Regarding the amplitude task (2), the sub-liminal ranges of all age-groups are mainly centred on zero, suggesting that the amplitude task involves a type 2 comparison whatever the age. Nevertheless the sub-liminal range at age 6 is wide enough to include terminal error, again suggesting a less accurate kinaesthetic perception. At 8 and 10 years of age, the sub-liminal range is smaller, allowing subjects to perceive their terminal error, even with lower values than the mean value. This is not only the case in the 8-year-olds whose terminal error reflects a strong inhibition in the approaching movement, but also in the 10-year-olds whose terminal error is the smallest among all these groups of children. Lastly it should be noted that, in contrast with direction, the development of relationships between terminal error and sub-liminal range is not complete at 10, since the sub-liminal range in adults is centred on mean terminal error which approximate to zero.

4.   CONCLUSION

Specification of the spatial parameters of aiming movements seems to undergo a longer and more complex development with regard to amplitude than to direction, with important changes of strategy occurring around the age of 8. Both dimensions seem to be predominantly specified at different stages in the response process, which is consistent with previous studies in adults. Specification of direction seems to predominantly load the preparatory stage of the response, compared to amplitude specification. Amplitude seems to be more dependent on on-going regulations than direction, and hence on the maturation of braking which allows a modulation of velocity as required by integration of feedback information. A particular difficulty in braking is apparent at 6, from the differences in MTs observed between tasks. On-line regulations based on feedback seem to take place predominantly at different phases in movement execution for both dimensions. Nevertheless the contrast between amplitude and direction varies with respect to age; the 8-years-olds show greater propensity for feedback control on both dimensions as shown by their over-inhibited approach without vision leading to an important undershoot, and further illustrated by their improved visual control on direction. This results in an improvement in the efficiency in the distance covering phase occurring only between 8 and 10, as shown by the MTs slopes with respect to target distance. It seems therefore that, with increasing age (and particularly at 10), amplitude specification tends to be handled to a greater extent by the feedforward process. This is specially noticeable when the homing phase is visually controlled, as shown by the peak deceleration times in Tasks 2 and 3. When visual feedback is not available, children seem to have difficulty, even at 10 years of age in the case of amplitude regulation, in matching kinaesthetic and visual information in order to kinaesthetically control movements towards a visually defined goal.

Amplitude seems to undergo more corrective readjustments than direction which suggests that the spatial system of reference involved is different, since more depending upon the coding of the final position. For both direction and amplitude the execution accuracy is higher than the range of perceptual evaluation would lead to predict. Moreover, some evidence has been obtained that perceptual evaluation of movement accuracy may rely on two kinds of matching with visual information from the target: one depending on a representation of the movement end point associated with the prescription of the aiming movement program, the other depending on kinaesthetic information about the real final position of the hand. This may result in two spatial coordinate systems, variably distinct depending on age. Finally the duality in spatial coding stressed by Paillard in terms of "where" and "how to go" (here one might rather say "how to go" and "where did I get to") seems to also have an ontogenetic history, involving the asynchronous development of both capacities, and a partial dependence of the modes of evaluating upon the modes of controlling movement.

References

Bard, C. & Hay, L. (1983). Etude ontogénétique de la coordination visuo-manuelle. *Revue Canadienne de Psychologie, 37,* 390-413.
Bard, C., Hay, L. & Fleury, M. (1985a). Role of peripheral vision in the directional control of rapid aiming movements. *Canadian Journal of Psychology, 39,* 151-161.
Bard, C., Hay, L. & Fleury, M. (1985b). Contribution of vision to the performance and learning of a directional aiming task in children aged 6 to 11. In J.H. Humphrey and J. Clark (Eds.), *Current selected research in motor development, Vol. 1.* Princeton, N.J.: Princeton Book Co.
Beaubaton, D. & Hay, L. (1986). Contribution of visual information to feedforward and feedback processes in rapid pointing movements. *Human Movement Science,* (in press).
Bonnet, M., Requin, J. & Stelmach, G. (1982). Specification of direction and extent in motor programming. *Bulletin of Psychonomic Society, 19,* 31-34.
Carlton, L.G. (1981). Processing visual feedback information for movement control. *Journal of Experimental Psychology, 7,* 1019-1030.
Fiori, N., Semjen, A. & Requin, J. (1974). Analyse chronométrique du pattern préparatoire à un mouvement spatialement orienté. Résultats préliminaires. *Le Travail Humain, 37,* 229-248.
Gachoud, J.P. (1983). Acquisition d'une habileté motrice chez l'enfant de 6 à 9 ans: étude cinématique et électromyographique. Thèse de l'Université de Genève.
Hay, L. (1979). Spatial-temporal analysis of movements in children: motor programs versus feedback in the development of reaching. *Journal of Motor Behavior, 11,* 189-200.
Hay, L. (1981). The effect of amplitude and accuracy requirements on movement time in children. *Journal of Motor Behavior, 13,* 177-186.
Hay, L. (1984). Discontinuity in the development of motor control in children. In W. Prinz and A. Sanders (Eds.), *Cognition and motor processes.* Berlin, Heidelberg: Springer-Verlag.
Hay, L., Beaubaton, D., Bard, C. & Fleury, M. (1984). Control and correction of pointing movements at different speeds, with direction and amplitude requirements. *Society for Neuroscience, Abstracts, 10,* 342.
Hoc, J.M. (1983). *L'analyse planifiée des données en psychologie.* Paris: Presses Universitaires de France.
Hofsten, C. von. (1982). Eye-hand coordination in the newborn. *Developmental Psychology, 18,* 450-461.
Kerr, R. (1975). Movement control and maturation in elementary-grade children. *Perceptual and Motor Skills, 41,* 151-154.
McDonnell, P.M. (1975). The development of visually guided reaching. *Perception & Psychophysics, 18,* 181-185.
McDonnell, P.M. & Abraham, W.C. (1981). A longitudinal study of prism adaptation in infants from six to nine months of age. *Child Development, 52,* 463-469.
Megaw, E.D. (1972). Directional errors and their correction in a discrete tracking task. *Ergonomics, 15,* 633-643.
Mounoud, P. & Hauert, C.A. (1982). Development of sensori-motor organization in young children: grasping and lifting objects. In G. Forman (Ed.), *Action and thought: from sensori-motor schemes to symbolic operations.* New York: Academic Press.

Paillard, J. (1985a). Espace et structures d'espace. In J. Paillard (Ed.), *La lecture sensorimotrice et cognitive de l'expérience spatiale. Directions et distances. Comportements.* Paris: Editions du Centre National de la Recherche Scientifique.

Paillard, J. (1985b). L'encodage sensori-moteur et cognitif de l'expérience spatiale. In J. Paillard (Ed.), *La lecture sensorimotrice et cognitive de l'expérience spatiale. Directions et distances. Comportements.* Paris: Editions du Centre National de la Recherche Scientifique.

Rosenbaum, D.A. (1980). Human movement initiation: specification of arm, direction, and extent. *Journal of Experimental Psychology, 109,* 444-474.

Rouanet, H. & Lepine, D. (1977). L'analyse des comparaisons pour le traitement des données expérimentales. *Informatique et Sciences Humaines, 33-34,* 9-123.

Salmoni, A.W. & Pascoe, C. (1978). Fitts' reciprocal tapping task: a developmental study. In C.G. Roberts and K.M. Newell (Eds.), *Psychology of Motor Behavior and Sport.* Champaign, Il: Human Kinetics.

Schellekens, J.M.H., Kalverboer, A.F. & Scholten, C.A. (1984). The micro-structure of tapping movements in children. *Journal of Motor Behavior, 16,* 20-39.

Sugden, D.A. (1980). Movement speed in children. *Journal of Motor Behavior, 12,* 125-132.

SECTION 7

COGNITION AND ACTION

CONSTRAINTS ON THE DEVELOPMENT OF COORDINATION

K.M. Newell

The development of coordination is one of the most important and fascinating problems in the study of both development and action. Indeed, Weiss (1941) has characterised the ontogeny of coordination as being essentially *the* problem of the ontogenetic origin of behaviour. The significance of coordination in physical activity is most apparent in infancy because it is during this period that many of the basic patterns of posture and movement appear. These basic patterns of coordination are usually called phylogenetic activities because they are seen as fundamental to the continued survival of the human species. Ontogenetic activities, in contrast, reflect more socially driven skills and the shorter term demands of groups or individuals which vary with the culture. Traditionally, these distinct classes of activities have promoted different theoretical formulations regarding the acquisition of coordination in action.

The domain of motor development has focused primarily on the patterns of coordination that support engagement in phylogenetic activities, such as sitting, standing, walking, running and grasping. The early work of Gesell (1929), Ames (1937), McGraw (1943), Shirley (1931) and others charted the chronological milestones in the emergence of prone progression and the other fundamental activities of posture, locomotion and manipulation. These developmental studies are also important, however, because collectively they represent one of the few attempts to study the acquisition of coordination in humans. This situation has arisen because studies in motor learning with adults have focused either on tasks that require the performer to constrain only a single degree of biomechanical freedom, which by definition excludes a coordination problem at the behavioural level of analysis, or, on tasks that demand a pattern of coordination that the subject can produce on the first trial of learning (cf. Newell, 1981, 1985). Thus, the early motor development work by Gesell and other developmentalists holds potential significance from the general perspective of formulating theoretical notions about the acquisition of coordination per se.

Theoretical discussion of the development of coordination is traditionally couched in terms of the maturation vs. learning debate, or more generally, the nature-nurture issue (cf. Bower, 1974). The drawing of a sharp distinction between the impact of endogenous and exogenous factors in the development of coordination has waned in recent years (cf. Connolly, 1981), as indeed it has generally in developmental psychology. Consistent with this trend, it is primarily the similarity of the maturation and learning theories with respect to the development of coordination that is of interest here, rather than the traditional focus on their differences.

The maturation and learning theory approaches to motor development

342

share an important assumption regarding the development of coordination. Namely, that the coordination of activity is specified by instructions from either a genetic code or through some instance of learning theory formulations In other words, both the maturational and learning perspectives assume that the development of coordination is due to the development of prescriptions for action, where "prescriptions" is taken as a general label for symbolic knowledge structures at some level of representation prescribing the course of action. Furthermore, recent cognitive orientations to motor development (e.g., Bruner, 1970 , 1973; Connolly, 1970a; Zelazo, 1983), essentially reflect a modern prescriptive version of a learning theory approach to the acquisition of coordination in children's physical activity (Newell & Barclay, 1982).

The traditional and contemporary prescriptive orientations to the development of coordination stand in opposition to the coordinative structure theory of action advanced by Kugler, Kelso and Turvey (1980, 1982). On this view, coordination emerges not from prescriptions for action but as a consequence of the constraints imposed on action. That is, constraints eliminate certain configurations of response dynamics, with the resulting pattern of coordination a reflection of self-organising optimality of the biological system, rather than specifications from some prescriptive symbolic knowledge structure.

In this paper, the prescriptive and coordinative structure orientations to coordination are briefly contrasted as a background to outlining the general significance of constraints to the development of coordination. It will be argued that the ubiquity of order and regularity in the developmental progressions of children's fundamental movement patterns is determined in large part by the constraints imposed on action. A general theme to emerge from the ensuing synthesis is that a research strategy that manipulates to the extremes the interaction of organismic, environmental and task constraints could prove useful in distinguishing the utility of, on the one hand, the traditional prescriptive orientations to motor development, and on the other, the coordinative structure perspective. In addition, an understanding of the significance of constraints to action opens the door to thinking about the acquisition of coordination as a general theoretical problem, independent of the class of activity and developmental stage of the individual.

The Motor Development Sequence

The development of coordination has been taken as synonomous with the development of fundamental movement and posture patterns. The ubiquity of order observed in the development of these coordination patterns has promote the idea of a sequence of stages or steps in motor development. For example, Gesell (1946, p. 302) defined stages as a series of postural transformations. In discussing postural transformations and the development of coordination Gesell recognised that concepts of morphology can be extended from physical phenomena to the phenomena of behaviour. In short, Gesell assumed that behaviour has shape. Specifically, Gesell (1946, p. 297) proposed "a morphological approach leads to the description and measurement of specific forms, the systematic study of topographic relations and correlations of such forms, their ontogenetic progression and involution, their comparative features among individuals and among species". It seems that Gesell has an appreciation of the significance of the topological features of the response dynamics although he and other scholars in this early period of motor development never pursued this approach formally with respect to the development of coordination. Some discussion of both the definition and measurement of the terms stage and coordination is essential to a theoretical consideration of the development of coordination.

Motor Stages: Progressive sequences of coordination?

The construct of 'stage' has had a checkered history in developmental psychology (cf. Brainerd, 1978; Kessen, 1962; Wohlwill, 1973). Problems have arisen from its use or misuse as both a descriptive and/or explanatory construct. In addition, the breadth of behaviours encompassed by the stage construct has made it difficult to apply a consistent definition. Although many developmentalists would agree with Flavell and Wohlwill (1969) that stage attains its maximal usefulness when it is used in reference to a set of behaviours intermediate in specificity between the case of an isolated response (e.g., crawling) and the case of a completely non-specific array of behaviours associated with a given age (e.g., infancy), this is not the interpretation generally given to discussions of the stage construct in motor development (cf. Roberton, 1978).

Typically, "stages of motor development" is the phrase used in reference to the order and regularity of the emergence of specific phylogenetic movement patterns in infancy and the early years of childhood. Shirley (1931), on the basis of observing 25 infants, identified five sequential stages in the "development" of upright locomotion: postural control of upper body; postural control of entire trunk and undirected activity; active efforts at locomotion; locomotion by creeping; and postural control and coordination of walking. Similarly, McGraw (1943) categorised seven stages of prone progression from the newborn state to the acquisition of a characteristically human gait. More recently, the development of ultrasound technology has allowed the charting of the emergence of fetal movements *in utero* (Ianniruberto & Tajani, 1981; Reinold, 1976; de Vries, Visser & Prechtl, 1984).

Early motor development researchers, therefore, defined 'stage' in terms of the specific movement patterns of children, with the implicit or explicit maturational prediction of an invariant and universal sequence of movement patterns emerging in the developing child. Although the notion of an invariant developmental movement sequence is generally accepted there have been a number of documented departures from this sequence. The primary example is that of variations in the individual rate of developmental progression that has been shown in cross-cultural (cf. Super, 1981) and training studies (e.g., Zelazo, Zelazo & Korb, 1972). However, individual differences in rate of development are not seriously damaging to the maturational perspective as long as the invariant order of the coordination sequence is preserved. Of more significance from a theoretical standpoint are examples of omissions (e.g., Robson, 1970; Touwen, 1971), and reversals (e.g., Touwen, 1971; Zingg, 1942) in the developmental movement sequence. Exceptions to the developmental movement sequence are rarely emphasised in theoretical discussions of the development of coordination, and where they are broached, they are often dismissed due to the unreliability of the data (e.g., feral children).

The discrepancy in the breadth of behaviours encompassed by current cognitive and motor interpretations of the stage construct has also been recognised (Roberton, 1978). In response to this differential use of the term

344

stage, Roberton proposed that the specific intra-task developmental
movement sequences be referred to as steps, allowing stage to be reserved
for the broader interpretation of a common approach to a set of motor tasks.
This caveat has not generally been heeded.

Gesell (1929, 1946, 1952) was instrumental in providing a maturational
interpretation of the developmental movement sequences exhibited in phylogenetic skills. Essential characteristics of the maturation process were
considered to be: 1) the appearance of new patterns of behaviour without
the benefit of practice; 2) consistency in these new patterns of behaviour
across subjects within the same species; and 3) an orderly and invariant
sequence in the development of these behaviours. Gesell (1929) did not
deny the influence of the environment but endogenous factors were viewed
as more critical than exogenous factors in the development of coordination.

The maturational perspective on motor development has been criticised
to the extent that it has now lost much of its impact as an explanatory
construct (cf. Connolly, 1970b). In spite of this trend, and the emergence
of cognitive orientations to motor skill development (e.g., Bruner, 1970;
Connolly, 1970a; Piaget, 1950, 1970), maturation is implicit, if not explicit,
in current accounts of the development of coordination. Consider, for
example, the systematic research by Roberton (1982) charting the invariant
steps in development of throwing actions in young children.

In summary, the "stage" construct in motor development has generally
referred to the specific patterns of coordination exhibited by infants and
individuals in early childhood, rather than a disposition toward a general
set of motor behaviours. The primary, although not exclusive, theoretical
account of these developing movement patterns has been the maturational
formulation, after Gesell (1929, 1946).

Behavioural Manifestation of Coordination

The development of an explanatory construct for the order and regularity
observed in the progressive sequences of children's coordination patterns
has also been hampered by the imprecise methods traditionally utilised to
describe veridically the developmental movement patterns. Furthermore, the
theoretical and operational definitions of the term coordination have usually
been formulated as verbal descriptions of movement sequences. These descriptions have related at various times to: anatomical units and; the
relative positions of the body and limbs with respect to the environment.
Verbal accounts of the changes in these variables in phylogenetic skills
inevitably lose the precision required to formulate theoretical constructs of
the development of coordination.

Attempts to provide a precise theoretical and operational framework for
analysis of the development of the behavioural unit in action may be enhanced
by a distinction between the terms coordination, control and skill (Kugler et
al, 1980, 1982; Newell, 1985). Briefly, Kugler et al (1980) propose that:
coordination is the function that constrains the potentially free variables
into a behavioural unit; control is the parameterisation of this function; and
skill is the optimal parameterisation of this function. The language of the
coordination function, that is, the essential variables that are being constrained, remains one of the fundamental unknowns in the theory of action.
Formal accounts of the behavioural unit or activity may, nevertheless, be

developed independent of the concern with the essential nature of the basic organisational principles of movement control.

Recent studies of the visual perception of biological motion (cf. Cutting & Profitt, 1982; Johansson, von Hofsten & Jansson, 1980) show that relative motion of limb segments takes priority over the observer's perception of the absolute motion of the limbs and torso in various activities. One can elaborate from this work to suggest that any activity may be defined by a unique set of topological characteristics of relative motions of the torso and limbs (Newell, 1985). In other words, it is the topological characteristics of movement, those that remain invariant in the face of transformations of scale, that distinguish patterns of coordination, and hence, the labelling of physical activities. The scaling of the set of relative motions is taken as an index of control. This operational approach provides a more rigorous basis to examine the development of coordination in general, and the traditions of stage theory approaches to motor development in particular, whereby the acquisition of fundamental skills, such as posture, locomotion and manipulation is viewed to follow a series of invariant steps with increments of chonological age.

It is proposed that the coordination patterns commonly construed as stages in the development of action are, therefore, specified by unique sets of relative motions (see Newell & Scully, in press, for an elaboration of this position). Given this perspective, it is not surprising that the concept of stage or step has been introduced in assessments of the development of action because the measurement scale used in the categorisation of relative motions is nominal. The observation of motor stages is, therefore, an instance of the general problem of categorical perception. Hence, observation of discontinuity in the development of action, as reflected by the terms stages or steps, is as much a product, if not more so, of the approach to measurement, as it is to changes in behaviour itself (cf. Emde & Harmon, 1984). With this proviso and, the general claim that it is the topological characteristics of the response dynamics that specify a pattern of coordination, I move on to contrast the constraints and prescriptions orientations to the development of coordination.

Constraints vs. Prescriptions for the Development of Action

As it was remarked earlier, the traditional (e.g. Gesell, 1929) and more recent cognitive (e.g., Bruner, 1970) approaches to the development of coordination in action each assume that coordination is specified by symbolic knowledge structures at some level of representation. In contrast, the coordinative structure theory (Kugler et al, 1980), proposes that the patterns of coordination that emerge during infancy and early childhood are due to the changing constraints imposed on action, rather than the acquisition of prescriptions for action. The issue of constraints versus prescriptions is central to any comparison of the coordinative structure theory with other formulations of the development of action (see also Kelso, 1981).

Gesell (1929) postulated that maturation refers to those phases and products of growth that are wholly or chiefly due to innate and endogenous factors. In short, maturation is mediated by genes (Gesell, 1952, p. 48). The traditional maturation theory of development offers a form of genetic predeterminism for the control of development in general, and in regard to the focus of this paper, the development of coordination patterns in particular

The central consequences of this position are that the sequence of development is predictable and is approximately the same for all children, although the rate at which developmental changes take place may vary from child to child.

The maturation viewpoint of development rests on the idea of genetically coded instructions prescribing progressive sequence of coordination patterns such as those observed in phylogenetic skills. However, Gesell's maturation theory also emphasised the notion of biological constraints on development. In discussing the developing child Gesell remarked that "his biological equipment sets the primary limits, directions, and modalities in which he reacts to his personal environments" (1952, p. 60). In spite of the above viewpoint, Gesell, and subsequent proponents of the maturational view of development, have largely failed to distinguish the contribution of prescriptions and constraints to be observed progressions in children's motor behaviour. While it can be argued that prescriptions are a special class of constraint, it seems more useful to reserve the term prescriptions for symbolic rule based knowledge structures. Thus, it is not clear from Gesell's writings to what extent the order and regularity observed in children's progressions of coordination are due to the "read-out" of prescriptions from the genetic code or the changing status of organismic constraints, although the prescriptive perspective is always emphasised in maturation theory.

Interpretations of the role of maturation theory in motor development (e.g., Gesell, 1946; McGraw, 1943) have emphasised the genetic code basis to maturation and, as a consequence, a programming notion to the patterns of behavioural development. Indeed, as Prechtl and Connolly (1981) have remarked, we have been left with the legacy of maturation as a substitute notion for the genetical control of development in general. This legacy also includes to some lingering degree a predetermined formulation of genetics and its prescribed framework for motor development rather than a probabilistic view of the pathways travelled in development on the epigenetic landscape (Waddington, 1957).

There have been attempts to characterise the genetic information coded in DNA as a constraining rather than prescribing process (e.g., Goodwin, 1970). Indeed, Kugler et al (1980) have elaborated these arguments from the micro level of analysis in proposing scale-independent physical principles to account for the development of coordination. Their general claim is that "order in biological and physiological processes is primarily owing to dynamics and that the constraints that arise, both anatomical and functional, serve only to channel and guide dynamics; it is not that actions are caused by constraints, it is rather that some actions are excluded by them" (1980, p. 9). This position allows a different interpretation of the strong preformationist maturation hypothesis because genetic information can be viewed as permissive, rather than deterministic, in relation to the development of movement patterns.

Although the traditional maturational perspective has failed to distinguish between prescriptions and constraints there is no doubt that the idea of biological constraints (broadly conceived) is central to the maturation view. In contrast, traditional learning theory and its modern cognitive counterparts, have typically ignored or played down the significance of biological constraints to the development of coordination. In particular, cognitive notions of the development of action have been largely neutral with respect to the role of biological constraints to action. Furthermore, as Kugler et al (1980, 1982) have emphasised, modern cognitive notions place a heavy reliance on computatinal solutions to the degrees of freedom problem in action (Bernstein, 1967), and in effect, claim to accommodate every posisble action circumstance by means of intelligent executive action.

This divergence of emphasis on biological constraints by the maturational and cognitive approaches may be due in part to the respective focus of these research programs on phylogenetic and ontogenetic skills. However, Zelazo (1983), has argued that even the onset of voluntary locomotion is reflective of a general cognitive shift that occurs at around the chronological age of one year. This cognitive change is viewed as a necessary although not sufficient condition for the onset of locomotion. It is of interest to note that the reverse causal sequence of mental and motor activity has been proposed with the onset of self-produced locomotion being viewed as the organiser of many psychological processes (Berthenthal, Campos & Barrett, 1985). There is no convincing evidence that the problems of coordination in the development of so-called phylogenetic and ontogenetic skills reflect fundamentally different processes, although the constraints on action clearly change with growth of the child. The differing emphasis on the significance of biological constraints reflects an apriori theoretical bias rather than an emphasis resulting from the experimental focus on a certain set of activities.

In summary, the significance of the constraints perspective to action advanced by the coordinative structure theory (Kugler et al, 1980, 1982) has not been fully explored with respect to the order and regularity observed in the development of young children's fundamental posture and movement patterns. The emphasis on constraints by the maturational perspective has largely been implicit whereas the cognitive orientation has been neutral on this issue. The explicit role of constraints in the coordinative structure theory stands, therefore, in marked contrast to traditional and contemporary accounts of motor development that emphasise the role of prescriptions in the development of coordination.

Constraints on Action

Constraints may be viewed as boundaries or features that limit motion of the entity under consideration. In engineering parlance, constraints reduce the number of possible configurations of a system. Constraints exist at various levels of analysis of the organism and its interaction with the environment (e.g., biochemical, biomechanical, morphological, neurological). Furthermore, constraints may be relatively time dependent or time independent. That is, the rate with which constraints may change over time varies considerably with the level of analysis and parameter under consideration. Kugler et al (1980) have argued that descriptions of constraints are essentially no more than alternative accounts of the degrees of freedom, although constraints may or may not reduce the number of degrees of freedom. Formal kinematic descriptions can be applied to the space-time properties of the constraints on coordination (see McGinnis & Newell, 1982).

The significance of the coordinative structure theory is not simply its recognition of the role of constraints on degrees of freedom in the development of action, but rather, the emphasis it gives to constraints in determining the development of coordination. In emphasising the dynamical processes of action, it proposes that constraints eliminate certain configurations of response dynamics. The resulting patterns of coordination reflect the propensity towards self-organising optimality in biological systems.

348

Constraints are not accommodated by reparameterising a knowledge structure
that symbolises these constraints, as would be reflected, for example, by
the schema theory of motor learning (Schmidt, 1975). Rather, the optimality
principles reflect the search for a stable pattern of coordination and control
that accommodates the prevailing constraints.

It is proposed that there are three categories of constraints that
interact to determine for a given organism the optimal pattern of coordination
and control for any activity (Newell, 1984a). These are organismic constraints,
environmental constraints and task constraints (see Figure 1). The first two
categories are based on familiar principles but the latter category of task
constraints requires justification and elaboration. The impact of organismic,
environmental and task constraints to the development of coordination is
now considered in some detail.

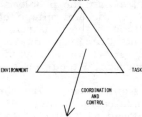

Fig. 1. A schematic diagram of the categories of constraints
that specify the optimal pattern of coordination and control.

Organismic Constraints

Constraints reside at each level of analysis of the organism. Relatively
time independent organismic constraints are typically interpreted as
structural constraints whereas the relatively time dependent constraints are
viewed as functional constraints. For example, at the macro level of analysis,
body weight, height and shape are assumed to be structural constraints to
the development of coordination because of their very slow (although
systematic) rate of change with development. In contrast, the development
of synaptic connections is often taken as a functional constraint. The
structural-functional distinction is not as qualitative as it first appears,
due to the qualifier that constraints are *relatively* time dependent or
independent.

It is clear that a variety of organismic constraints converge to specify
the appropriate pattern of coordination for the developing child. In spite
of this realisation, certain classes of biological constraints have been over
and underplayed in accounts of the development of coordination and control.
For example, the status of the child's central nervous system has long been
the basis for the increasing behavioural organisation exhibited by the
developing child. The evidence for a direct link between neural development
and the onset of new patterns of coordination is considerably less than might
be assumed from most developmental text books, although it should be
evident that methodological problems dictate that neurological evidence is
invariably gleaned from species or from preparations other than normal
healthy infants.

Prechtl (1984) in summarising evidence for a link between neural development and motor development offers two important observations. First, growth and differentiation of the nervous system do not consist of an autonomous 'read-out' of genetic instructions, but involve an intimate inter- action with extrinsic factors in an extremely complex epigenetic process. Second, neural development is not a simple linearly progressive increase in the number of elements and their interconnections, and hence in complexity, but also includes retrogressive processes for matching and removing transient age-specific adaptations. These observations capture the difficulty of mapping a causal relationship between neural constraints and the development of coordination.

At the whole body level, a key problem to be resolved is how the motor system accommodates to the changes in growth that occur throughout the life span. Changes in growth and form (Thompson, 1917) are particularly evident in infancy and the early years of childhood. These changes have a strong impact on, among other parameters, the biomechanical constraints to action. Cognitive notions to the development of coordination implicitly accommodate growth changes through a rescaling of the designated knowledge structure and its attendant burden on computational function. The coordina- tive structure theory handles the change in growth and form through the concept of constraints on the emergent dynamics of coordination.

A major consequence of children's growth is the change in the absolute and relative size of respective bodyparts. These changes in body size lead to changes in the biomechanical constraints on the system. An important biomechanical parameter in posture and movement is the moment of inertia of each body segment, but there have been very few studies of the rate with which moments of inertia of body segments vary as a consequence of growth. An exception is the study of Jensen (1981) who examined the effect of 1 year's growth on the moment of inertia of children's body parts. 12 caucasion boys were studied with one endomorph, one mesomorph and one ectomorph at each age of 4, 6, 9 and 12 years. The children were somato- typed and the principal whole body moments of inertia calculated at the beginning and end of a 12 month period.

The results of Jensen's (1981) study showed that as a consequence of growth, the moment of inertia of the centroidal transverse axis reflected individual increases from 12% to 57% (mean 30.8%), while the increments for the longitudinal centroidal axis ranged from 8% to 92% (mean 33.5%). These percentage changes in the moments of inertia far exceeded the percentage changes in age, height (mean 4.7%) and mass (mean 15.8%). The best predictor of the constraints on rotational movements imposed by growth was the product of mass multipled by the square of the standing height. This index showed an average subject increase of 27.7% over the 12-month time span. Interestingly, Jenson found no relationship between body type and amount of change in the moment of inertia. The changes observed in the moments of inertia need to be accommodated by systematic (although non- proportional) changes in strength of the individual if the same function for coordination and control is to be appropriate for a given individual.

A more direct example of the influence of macro bodyparameters on the development of coordination can be found in Shirley (1931) and Bayley and Davis (1935). They showed that children with proportionately longer legs who were not overweight tended to walk earlier than did children with proportionately shorter legs. Norval (1947) also found that an increase in body length of 1 in led on average to a 22 day advantage in the onset of voluntary walking. Changes in body form could also be strong contributors to the differences in gait pattern produced by children between 1-7 years (Bernstein, 1967; Grieve & Gear, 1966). The establishment of an adult-like gait pattern at about 7 years tends to correlate with the emergence of adult-like proportions to body segments. A similar relationship exists for the development of stance (Sinclair, 1978).

Although it is clear that many organismic constraints influence the development of coordination, it is difficult to provide a direct operational test of the prescriptions versus constraints view of coordination. Indeed, a recent pair of papers on the development of upright voluntary walking in infants reflects both the theoretical contrast and the methodological problem. Zelazo (1983) argues that the onset of upright walking can largely be accommodated by understanding the biomechanical constraints on walking.

A compelling and challenging line of evidence implicating the significance of self-organisation principles in coordination is the shift of gait pattern observed in the centipede (lithobius) when various combinations of its legs are amputated (von Holst, 1973). That is, the normal wavelike leg motion of the centipede is instantaneously replaced by the asymmetric gaits of quadrupeds when all but two pairs of legs are amputated and the gaits of six-legged insects emerge when all but three pairs of legs are amputated. As Kugler et al (1980) indicated, the cognitive programming perspective has considerable difficulty handling the instantaneous onset of these new patterns of coordination. Of course, this kind of direct manipulation is not possible with humans although accidents and illnesses can create similar human circumstances for study.

The coordinative structure theory would also find support in Thelen's (1983) empirical demonstrations of shifts in locomotor coordination patterns of the infant. It would be inferred that the onset of walking in human infants reflects the self-organising optimality in biological systems. This position is difficult to uphold empirically, but as prescriptive formulations of the development of coordination do not address biological constraints in a predictive manner, it would seem that the demonstration of a relationship of patterns of coordination to biophysical principles would provide evidence consistent with the coordinative structure viewpoint. It should be noted, however, that without a direct link to biophysical principles, interpretations of the development of coordination in terms of optimality theory in biological systems are likely to be as hollow as many of the cognitive claims to mental processes and the like.

Environmental Constraints

Environmental constraints are generally recognised as those constraints that are external to the organism. Any constraint on the organism-environment interaction that is not internal to the organism can be viewed as an environmental constraint. It is useful, however, to distinguish between environmental constraints that are general and those that are task specific. Environmental constraints and task constraints are not mutually exclusive as their definition depends on the nature of the task.

Generally, environmental constraints are those that are not manipulated by the experimenter and are relatively time independent. Environmental constraints may include gravity, natural ambient temperature, natural light and other environmental features that are not usually adaptations of the task. However, these environmental features can be manipulated for a given individual by changing the environment in which the activity takes place. Shifts in geographical location on earth change the impact of gravity on the performer, in addition to the natural ambient temperature and light. Extreme changes in the influence of gravity on performance occur when moving an individual to a space vehicle or submerging him in water.

There have been very few tests of the influence of environmental constraints on the development of coordination. One important environmental contrast is the prenatal versus post-natal development period (e.g., Hooker, 1969; Ounsted & Ounsted, 1973), but few direct prenatal examinations of the development of coordination have been undertaken until the recent use of ultrasound technology (e.g., de Vries et al, 1984). As indicated earlier, this technology has allowed a mapping of the movements of the developing fetus *in utero*. There appears to be a systematic order to the development of voluntary action in the fetus. However, it is interesting to note that this order does not follow the cephalo-caudal trend established for post-natal phylogenetic activities. This may be due to the fact that the constraints of gravity in the womb are only about one third of those facing the neonate. The shift from the womb to the outside environment presents additional qualitative shifts in environmental constraints, rather than mere scaling changes of a given environmental parameter (such as gravity).

Qualitative shifts in environmental constraints influence the patterns of coordination exhibited by infants. In the buoyant medium of water infants display coordinated movement patterns long before they can support themselves posturally on land (McGraw, 1939). Similarly, rats can swim as soon as they are born whereas it takes one week or so for them to locomote on terra firma (Bekoff, 1978). Interestingly, the movement patterns exhibited in water by infants and rats are similar to those that they produce respectively on land. This suggests that the initial failure of infants and rats to locomote on land after birth is largely due to the severe biomechanical constraints on the onset of voluntary locomotion.

Thelen (1983) has demonstrated the interaction of organism and environmental constraints in the development of upright walking in infants. The stepping reflex typically disappears in infants between the age of 4 to 16 weeks and this change is often attributed to maturation and neurological development. However, Thelen (1983) showed that the stepping reflex 'reappears' when the infant is supported in water. This suggests that the disappearance of the stepping reflex is influenced by the environmental constraints of the medium in which the action takes place. In this case, supporting the child's limb in water served to counteract gravitational force.

A more extreme test of environmental constraints on the development of coordination are reflected in the traditional studies on the effect of specific rearing patterns (Gesell & Thompson, 1929; McGraw, 1940). Another broader example is the impact of different cultural backgrounds on the development of fundamental motor skills (cf. Super, 1981). These training and cross-cultural studies are often interpreted as tests of the maturation and learning perspectives of motor development, although the manipulation is not as clear cut as is generally assumed (cf. Bower, 1974). More importantly, from the perspective of this paper, is the proposal that these studies are primarily manipulating task constraints rather than environmental constraints, as the key feature of the rearing and cross-cultural studies is the specific task interactions that the child experiences rather than the effect of the relative time independent constraints of the environment per se. The cross-cultural studies primarily reveal variations in the timing of the onsets of the steps of the developmental movement sequence rather than systematic shifts in the order of the developing movement sequences (cf. Super, 1981). This finding suggests that the general experience of interacting with the environment may not be as influential as the various physical constraints (organismic, environmental and task) in determining the optimal patterns of coordination.

Task Constraints

There have been a variety of definitions and classifications of tasks (cf. Fleishman & Quaintance, 1984). These attempts at definition vary on many dimensions, particularly with respect to their narrowness/breadth and their inclusion or exclusion of performer perceptions. The performer's perception of the task constraints and the optimal patterns of coordination for the task will be discussed subsequently. Environmental constraints reflect the ambient conditions for the task, whereas the focus of task constraints is the goal of the activity and the specific constraints imposed. Three categories of task constraints are proposed. These relate to: 1) goal of the task; 2) rules specifying or constraining response dynamics; and 3) implements or machines specifying or constraining response dynamics.

All tasks have goals that relate to the product or outcome of the action. In the majority of tasks the way in which the performer may satisfy the out-come of the act is not specified. That is, most tasks do not specify the pattern of coordination to be utilised by the performer. In some ontogenetic skills, however, task constraints specify or limit the kinematic or dynamic nature of the response that a performer is able to produce.

In a number of closed sporting skills, for example, the rules of the event specify that a specific pattern of coordination must be produced. Indeed, as indicated earlier, some tasks are defined solely by a given pattern of coordination. A Yamashita vault in gymnastics has a unique set of topological characteristics dependent upon a set of relative motions. As a consequence, the performer either executes a Yamashita or does not.

In other tasks the rules merely constrain the range of response dynamics that can be produced in pursuit of the task goal *without* dictating a specific pattern of response dynamics. For example, the sporting events of shot put, breaststroke swimming, and tennis, provide boundaries to the action patterns that can be generated by the performer without specifying an appropriate or optimal pattern of coordination. The performer's task is to optimise performance within the imposed task constraints (Newell, 1985).

When the task constraints merely limit the range of coordination patterns that can be produced, the issue of what the optimal pattern of coordination is for a given individual becomes paramount. Skilled performance, as reflected in the optimal pattern of coordination and control, will be determined in the interaction of the organismic, environmental and task constraints. As a consequence, the optimal pattern of coordination and control for a given task will be individual specific. Sometimes, however, individuals interpret the imposed constraints differently, leading to the production of different patterns of coordination for the same set of task constraints. By the same token, individual differences in organismic constraints can lead to different optimal patterns of coordination for the same set of environmental and task constraints

An interesting example of the significance of the interpretation of task constraints occurred many years ago in the swimming event of breaststroke. One of the rules (task constraints) indicated that the legs and arms should be moved simultaneously and symmetrically. The rule, however, did not mention whether the arms and legs could be brought out of the water. A swimmer in the 1930's recognised that increased power could be gained from an out of the water arm and leg recovery and the butterfly stroke was born (see Wallechinsky, 1984). Indeed, in the breaststroke final at the 1952 Helsinki Olympic Games 7 out of 8 finalists in the men's event swam the butterfly stroke. World records for the breaststroke event were broken frequently as a consequence of this technique change. After the Helsinki games, the administrators of the swimming associations separated the breaststroke and butterfly events. In doing so, they effectively specified different task constraints for the two events.

This example of task constraints in swimming reflects how the performer's interpretation of the task constraints can influence the pattern of coordination produced. Of course, in many sporting events the search for the optimal pattern of coordination continues and formal approaches to optimisation in human motion are being developed. Progress in the area of biomechanical optimisation has largely superceded the traditional 'champion's model' approach (Hatze, 1983).

The goal of the task, together with the constraints that specify or limit the response dynamics for a given task, reflect rules that are implicit to the task. Task rules are not physical barriers or limitations that physically eliminate certain responses, nevertheless, they influence the pattern of coordination produces by an individual in a given task. The champion's model alluded to above is an instance where an innovative individual has produced a widely accepted solution to the problem of optimising performance within the task constraints.

The third category of task constraints listed is a physical constraint in that it represents implements or machines that are indigenous to the task and that specify or constrain the response dynamics. These might be construed as a narrow interpretation of environmental constraints but it seems useful to preserve the distinction between task and environmental constraints. As mentioned earlier the distinction is task specific. An object could be a task constraint in one activity and an environmental constraint in another. In the main, however, objects used for grasping, implements used in task interactions, and machines such as lawn mowers, cars, bicycles, etc., will be viewed as imposing task constraints. These physical objects specify or constrain the response dynamics in a manner similar to the rule based constraints discussed above.

The size and weight of task objects or machines relative to the body size of the individual, reflect physical constraints on the optimal pattern of coordination in relation to the task goal. There have been very few tests of task by organismic constraint interactions on the pattern of coordination. For example, while object size is often implicated as a significant factor in prehension, the classical normative data on the development of prehension is severely restricted with respect to the range of object size manipulated. Indeed, the continued reliance on the Halverson (1931, 1932) project as reflective of the normative data on the development of prehension seems unwarranted. In the main, the impact of body scale on the development of coordination has been underemphasised, in spite of the early writings of

Thompson (1917) and the recent analysis by Kugler et al (1982).

Other task constraint limitations to investigations of the development of prehension have been exposed by von Hofsten (1979, 1982, 1983; von Hofsten & Lindhagan, 1979). When 2 week-old infants have appropriate postural support they reach and make contact with a brightly colored moving object in a manner consistent with anticipatory behaviour. This kind of infant catching skill (von Hofsten, 1983) is counterintuitive to traditional notions about the development of coincident timing behaviour and prehension.

In practice, the impact of task constraints on the development of coordination is slowly being acknowledged. An increasing number of toy manufacturers and sporting associations are body scaling the task constraints, which generally means reducing the size of implements and activity boundaries for younger children. The establishment of physical principles of body size to implement size ratios specifying a given pattern of coordination remains an interesting possibility and one that would be consonant with the co-ordinative structure theory. Dimensionless body scaled ratios that correspond to shifts in gait pattern (cf. Alexander, 1984) and the perception of affordances (Warren, 1984) have been reported.

Summary

The optimal pattern of coordination and control for a given individual is specified by the interaction of organismic, environmental and task constraints. The relative impact of these three categories of constraint on the pattern of coordination varies according to the specific situation. Interestingly, in terms of whole-body mechanical constraints, appropriate changes in two or three of the constraint categories, can preserve the relative effect of forces on a given pattern of coordination.

The extant theories relating to the development of coordination recognise to some greater or less degree the significance of constraints on action although the theoretical interpretation given to constraints varies. Traditionally, it is the organismic immaturity of the neurological system that is taken as *the* limiting factor in the development of coordination. It is proposed that a research strategy that manipulates to the extreme the interaction of organismic, environmental and task constraints could prove useful in tests of the prescriptions versus constraints perspectives to the development of coordination. Theoretical orientation aside, it would appear that the impact of task constraints in relation to the body scale of the subject is an overlooked factor in descriptive accounts of coordination in general, and the progressions of the developmental movement sequence in particular.

Concluding Remarks

The current synthesis suggests that a more extreme manipulation of the constraints on action than heretofore undertaken might provide a strong test of current notions of the development of coordination. A key point is the recognition that the optimal pattern of coordination is specified by the *interaction* of the three sources of constraints, namely, organismic, envir-onmental and task. The impact of task constraints may primarily reside in the development of ontogenetic skills, although prehension is clearly influenced by task factors.

In a general sense, the manipulation of constraints holds some similarities to the early tests of the maturation and learning theory accounts of development. However, the theoretical significance given to constraints in the coordinative structure theory (Kugler et al, 1980, 1982) is very different. Even on a descriptive level, the elaboration of the constraints perspective offered here is much broader than traditional tests of maturation and learning theory and seems a more viable approach to determine the degree to which departures from the traditionally accepted norms of motor development can occur. A major problem is that the bandwidth of the stability of the co-ordination patterns for the phylogenetic skills is so robust that it is difficult to engender shifts in the pattern of coordination.

The manipulation of constraints in studying the development of co-ordination should not proceed in isolation with respect to children. Indeed, manipulation of constraints with adults will offer a basis to understand the generality of the principles advanced. One problem is that adults are typically seen as the "norm" or "bench mark" for comparison with children. If organis-mic constraints influence coordination patterns along the lines suggested here, children will not necessarily exhibit adult-like patterns of coordination and control for the same set of environmental and task constraints. Indeed, if they did, concerns might be expressed about the integrity of the central nervous system. This philosophy for comparing child and adult patterns of coordination is counter to traditional prescriptive views of development which have been driven by the maturational perspective. One can probably change or reverse the developmental progression of coordination by the manipulation of mechanical constraints and induce adults to generate coordination patterns that are typically dubbed as immature or child-like.

In summary, the emphasis of constraints in the coordinative structure perspective (Kugler et al, 1980, 1982) offers a firm theoretical base to re-examine the traditional notions of motor development. In particular, the constraints perspective forces a different interpretation of both the developmental movement sequence and the traditional distinction between phylogenetic and ontogenetic activities. Arising from such a reexamination is the notion that principles of the acquisition of coordination may cut across class of activity and developmental maturity of the individual.

The constraints perspective suggests that the ubiquity of order and regularity in the development of coordination is due to the similarity of constraints imposed on the infant and young children rather than a conse-quence of a common set of genetic prescriptions for the human species. The range of constraints manipulated in the infant to date has not been sufficient generally to engender significant shifts in the developmental movement sequence. It is not surprising, therefore, that the universality of an invariant developmental movement sequences gives prima-facie evidence for the maturational theory of motor development.

It would appear that only strong manipulations of the physical con-straints to action are likely to give rise to patterns of coordination different to those of the traditional developmental movement sequence. In the main, the manipulations required will not be the norm for societies of any culture, and, therefore, it is unlikely that many naturally emerging examples of new patterns of coordination will be generated that depart from the traditional developmental sequence. However, as it was documented earlier, exceptions

356

to the developmental movement sequence already exist. The constraints perspective suggests that these departures need to be considered more seriously than they typically are. Furthermore, stronger manipulation of the constraints to action would provide additional evidence of departures from the developmental sequence and the emergence of new patterns of co-ordination. Broadening the range of constraints to action would help promote and test the idea that it is the influence of constraints that is important rather than an emphasis on either endogenous or exogenous factors. These intrinsic and extrinsic factors to the development of coordination cannot be separated via an analysis of variance model to motor development.

The constraints perspective also leads to the postulation that the traditional distinction between activity classes does not carry with it any significance for theoretical principles regarding the acquisition of co-ordination per se. From the constraints perspective, phylogenetic activities are common to the species because of the ubiquity of the constraints imposed to the development of coordination.

The distinction between phylogenetic and ontogenetic activities has been at the heart of the division between the fields of motor development and motor learning. Eliminating the basis of the distinction between these classes of activity opens the door to the establishment of principles for the acquisition of coordination per se, independent of activity class and stage of individual development.

Author Notes

This work was supported in part by the National Science Foundation Award BNS 83-17691. R. van Emmerik, D.M. Scully and W.A. Sparrow provided helpful comments on an earlier version of the manuscript.

357

References

Alexander, R. Mc. (1984). Walking and running. *American Scientist, 72,* 348-354.

Ames, L. (1937). The sequential patterning of prone progression in the human infant. *Genetic Psychology Monographs, 19,* 409-460.

Bayley, N. & Davis, F.C. (1935). Growth changes in bodily size and proportions during the first three years: A developmental study of sixty-one children by repeated measurements. *Biometrika, 27,* 26-87.

Bekoff, A.A. (1976). A neuroethological approach to the study of the ontogeny of coordinated behavior. In G.M. Burghardt and M. Bekoff (Eds.), *Comparative and evolutionary aspects.* New York: Garland.

Bernstein, N. (1967). *The coordination and regulation of movement.* New York: Pergamon.

Berthenthal, B.I., Camps, J.J. & Barrett, K.C. (1984). Self-produced locomotion: An organizer of emotional, cognitive, and social development in infancy. In R.N. Emde and R.J. Harmon (Eds.), *Continuities and discontinuities in development.* New York: Plenum.

Bower, T.G.R. (1974). *Development in infancy.* San Francisco: Freeman.

Brainerd, C.J. (1978). The stage question in cognitive-developmental theory. *The Behavioral and Brain Sciences, 1,* 173-214.

Bruner, J.S. (1970). The growth and structure of skill. In K.J. Connolly (Ed.), *Mechanisms of motor skill development.* London: Academic Press.

Bruner, J.S. (1973). Organization of skilled action. *Child Development, 44,* 1-11.

Connolly, K.J. (1970a). Response speed, temporal sequencing and information processing in children. In K.J. Connolly (Ed.), *Mechanisms of motor skill development.* London: Academic Press.

Connolly, K.J. (1970b). Skill development: Problems and plans. In K.J. Connolly (Ed.), *Mechanisms of motor skill development.* London: Academic Press.

Connolly, K.J. (1981). Maturation and the ontogeny of motor skills. In K.J. Connolly and H.F.R. Prechtl (Eds.), *Maturation and development: Biological and psychological perspectives.* Philadelphia: Lippincott.

Cutting, J.E. & Profitt, D.R. (1982). The minimum principle and the perception of absolute, common and relative motions. *Cognitive Psychology, 14,* 211-246.

Emde, R.N. & Harmon, R.J. (Eds.) (1984). *Continuities and discontinuities to development.* New York: Plenum.

Flavell, J.H. & Wohlwill, J.F. (1969). Formal and functional aspects of cognitive development. In D. Elkind and J.H. Flavell (Eds.), *Studies in cognitive development.* New York: Oxford University Press.

Fleishman, E.A. & Quaintance, M.K. (1984). *Taxonomies of human performance: The description of human tasks.* New York: Academic Press.

Gesell, A. (1929). Maturation and infant behavior pattern. *Psychological Review, 36,* 307-319.

Gesell, A. (1946). The ontogenesis infant behavior. In L. Carmichael (Ed.), *Manual of child psychology.* New York: Wiley.

Gesell, A. (1952). *Infant development.* New York: Harper and Brothers.

Gesell, A. & Thompson, H. (1929). Learning and growth in identical twins: An experimental study of the method of co-twin control. *Genetic Psychology Monographs, 6,* 1-124.

Goodwin, B. (1970). Biological stability. In C.H. Waddington (Ed.), *Towards a theoretical biology (Vol. 3).* Chicago: Aldine.

Grieve, D.W. & Gear, R.J. (1966). The relationship between length of stride, step frequency, time of swing and speed of walking for children and adults. *Ergonomics, 5,* 379-399.

Halverson, H.M. (1931). An experimental study of prehension in infants by means of systematic cinema records. *Genetic Psychology Monographs, 10,* 107-283.

358

Halverson, H.M. (1932). A further study of grasping. *Journal of Genetic Psychology, 7,* 34-63.

Hatze, H. (1983). Computerized optimization of sports motions: An overview of possibilities, methods and recent developments. *Journal of Sport Sciences, 1,* 3-12.

von Hofsten, C. (1979). Development of visually directed reaching: The approach phase. *Journal of Human Movement Studies, 5,* 160-178.

von Hofsten, C. (1982). Eye-hand coordination in the new born. *Developmental Psychology, 18,* 450-461.

von Hofsten, C. (1983). Catching skills in infancy. *Journal of Experimental Psychology: Human Perception and Performance, 9,* 75-85.

von Hofsten, C. & Lindhagan, K. (1979). Observations on the development of reaching for moving objects. *Journal of Experimental Child Psychology, 28,* 158-173.

von Holst, E. (1973). *The behavioral physiology of animals and man.* Coral Gables, FL: Univesity of Miami Press.

Hooker, D. (1969). *The prenatal origin of behavior.* New York: Hafner.

Ianniruberto, A. & Tajani, E. (1981). Ultrasonographic study of fetal movements. *Seminars in perinatalogy, 5,* 175-181.

Jensen, R.K. (1981). The effect of a 12-month growth period on the body moments of inertia of children. *Medicine and Science in Sports and Exercise, 13,* 238-242.

Johansson, G., Von Hofsten, C. & Jansson, G. (1980). Event perception. *Annual Review of Psychology, 31,* 27-63.

Johnston, F.E., Roche, A.F. & Sussane, C. (Eds.). (1980). *Human physical growth and maturation: Methdologies and factors.* New York: Plenum.

Kelso, J.A.S. (1981). Contrasting perspectives on order and regulation in movement. In J. Long and A. Baddley (Eds.), *Attention and performance IX.* Hillsdale, NJ: Erlbaum.

Kessen, W. (1962). "Stage" and "structure" in the study of children. *Monographs of the Society for Research in Child Development, 28,* 2, (Whole No. 83).

Kugler, P.J., Kelso, J.A.S. & Turvey, M.T. (1980). On the concept of coordinative structures as dissipative structures: 1. Theoretical lines of convergence. In G.E. Stelmach and J. Requin (Eds.), *Tutorials in motor behavior.* Amsterdam: North-Holland.

Kugler, P.N., Kelso, J.A.S. & Turvey, M.T. (1982). On the control and coordination of naturally developing systems. In J.A.S. Kelso and J.E. Clark (Eds.), *The development of movement control and coordination.* New York: Wiley.

McGinnis, P.M. & Newell, K.M. (1982). Topological dynamics: A framework for describing movement and its constraints. *Human Movement Science, 1,* 289-305.

McGraw, M.B. (1939). Swimming behavior of the human infant. *Journal of Pediatrics, 15,* 485-490.

McGraw, M.B. (1940). Neural maturation as exemplified in achievement of bladder control. *Journal of Pediatrics, 16,* 580-590.

McGraw, M.B. (1943). *The neuromuscular maturation of the human infant.* New York: Columbia University Press.

Newell, K.M. (1981). Skill learning. In D.H. Holding (Ed.), *Human Skills.* New York: Wiley.

Newell, K.M. (1984a, May). *The development of coordination: Significance of task constraints.* Paper presented at the meeting of the American Association for the Advancement of Science, New York, NY.

Newell, K.M. (1984b). Physical constraints to development of motor skills. In J.L. Thomas (Ed.), *Motor development during childhood and adolescence*. Minneapolis: Burgess.

Newell, K.M. (1985). Coordination, control and skill. In D. Goodman, I. Franks and R.B. Wilberg (Eds.), *Differing perspectives in motor learning, memory, and control*. Amsterdam: North-Holland.

Newell, K.M. & Barclay, C.R. (1982). Developing knowledge about action. In J.A.S. Kelso and J.E. Clark (Eds.), *The development of movement control and coordination*. New York: Wiley.

Newell, K.M. & Scully, D.M. (in press). Steps in the development of coordination: Perception of relative motion? In J.E. Clark and J.H. Humphrey (Eds.), *Motor development: Current selected research* (Vol. II). Princeton: Princeton Book Co.

Norval, M.S. (1947). Relationship of weight and length of infants at birth to the age at which they begin to walk alone. *Journal of Pediatrics, 30,* 676-678.

Ounsted, M. & Ounsted, C. (1973). *On fixed growth rate*. Philadelphia: Lippincott.

Piaget, J. (1950). *The psychology of intelligence*. New York: International Universities Press.

Piaget, J. (1970). Piaget's theory. In P.H. Mussen (Ed.), *Carmichaels manual of child psychology*. New York: Wiley.

Prechtl, H.F.R. (Ed.). (1984). *Continuity of neural functions from prenatal to postnatal life*. Oxford: Blackwell.

Prechtl, H.F.R. & Connolly, K.J. (1981). *Maturation and development: Biological and psychological perspectives*. Philadelphia: Lippincott.

Reinold, E. (1976). *Ultrasonics in early pregnancy*. Karger: Basel.

Roberton, M.A. (1978). Stages in motor development. In M.V. Ridenour (Eds.), *Motor development: Issues and applications*. Princeton, NJ: Princeton.

Roberton, M.A. (1982). Describing "stages" within and across motor tasks. In J.A.S. Kelso and J. Clark (Eds.), *The development of movement control and coordination*. New York: Wiley.

Robson, P. (1970). Shuffling, hitching, scooting or sliding: Some observations in 30 otherwise normal children. *Developmental Medicine and Child Neurology, 12,* 608-617.

Schmidt, R.A. (1975). A schema theory of discrete motor skill learning. *Psychological Review, 82,* 225-260.

Shirley, M.M. (1931). *The first two years: A study of twenty-five babies. Vol. 1. Postural and locomotor development*. Minneapolis: University of Minnesota Press.

Sinclair, D. (1978). *Human growth after birth*. London: Oxford University Press.

Super, C.M. (1981). Cross-cultural research on infancy. In H.C. Triandis and A. Heron (Eds.), *Handbook of cross-cultural psychology: Developmental Psychology (Vol. 4)*. Boston: Allyn and Bacon.

Thelen, E. (1983). Learning to walk is still an "old" problem. A reply to Zelazo (1983). *Journal of Motor Behavior, 15,* 139-161.

Thompson, D.W. (1917). *On growth and form*. Cambridge: Cambridge Univesity Press.

Touwen, B.C.L. (1971). A study of the development of some motor phenomena in infancy. *Developmental Medicine and Child Neurology, 13,* 435-446.

de Vries, J.I.P., Visser, G.H.A. & Prechtl, H.F.R. (1983). Fetal mobility in the first half of pregnancy. In H.F.R. Prechtl (Ed.), *Continuity of neural functions from prenatal to postnatal life*. Oxford: Blackwell.

360

Waddington, C.H. (1957). *The strategy of the genes*. London: George, Allen & Unwin.

Wallechinsky, D. (1984). *The complete book of the Olympics*. New York: Viking Press.

Warren, W.H., Jr. (1984). Perceiving affordances: Visual guidance of stair climbing. *Journal of Experimental Psychology: Human Perception and Performance, 10,* 683-703.

Weiss, P. (1941). Self-differentiation of the basic patterns of coordination. *Comparative Psychology Monographs, 17,* 1-96.

Wohlwill, J.F. (1973). *The study of behavioral development*. New York: Academic Press.

Wyke, B. (1975). The neurological basis of movement - A developmental review. In K.S. Holt (Ed.), *Movement and child development*. Philadelphia: Lippincott.

Zelazo, P.R. (1983). The development of walking: New findings and old assumptions. *Journal of Motor Behavior, 15,* 99-138.

Zelazo, P.R., Zelazo, N.A. & Kolb, S. (1972). Newborn walking. *Science, 177,* 1058-1059.

Zingg, R.M. (1942). Feral man and cases of extreme isolation. *American Journal of Psychology, 53,* 487-517.

MOTOR COORDINATION: CONSTRAINTS AND COGNITION
A reaction to K.M. Newell

P.C.W. van Wieringen

1.   DICHOTOMIES IN PSYCHOLOGY

In 1962 the philosopher Suzanne Langer remarked that:

> In every age, philosophical thinking exploits some
> dominant concepts and makes its greatest headway
> in solving problems conceived in terms of them.

A number of psychologists have revealed that such dominant concepts are
not only characteristic of philosophy. I will quote only one as an illustration:
Sigmund Koch, best-known as editor of the handbook 'Psychology, a study
of a science', which appeared in the late fifties, early sixties, and one of
the most remarkable sceptics in the field of psychology.

About ten years ago he ventured his pessimism about the state of the
art in psychology in stating that 'the pooled pseudo-knowledge that is much
of psychology can be seen as a congeries of alternate - and exceedingly
simple - 'images' around each of which one finds a dense, scholastic cluster
of supportive research, 'theorising', and methodological rhetoric' (Koch,
1974, p. 7).

With the images in question Koch refers to conceptualisations of man,
giving the following impressive list of examples:

> 'cockroach, rat (...) dog (...) a telephone exchange,
> a servo-mechanism, a binary digital computer, a reward
> seeking vector, a hyphen between an S and R process,
> a stimulation-maximising game-player, a status-seeker, a
> mutual ego-titillator, a mutual emotional (or actual)
> masturbator, or a hollow cocoon seeking extasy through
> the liquidation of its boundaries in the company of other
> cocoons similarly seeking extasy' (Koch, 1974, p. 7).

While Koch evaluated the *whole field* of psychology, at about the same time
A. Newell (1973) evidenced comparable feelings with respect to *experimental*
psychology. He complains about the research in this area being 'phenomenon
driven', the phenomena in question being conceptualised in terms of binary
oppositions like nature versus nurture, peripheral versus central and analog
versus digital (Newell refers to 21 more oppositions, see p. 288).

In evaluating this state of affairs, Newell writes:

'It seems to me that clarity is never achieved.
Matters become muddier and muddier as we go
down through time (...). This form of conceptual
structure leads (...) to an ever increasing pile
of issues which we weary of or become diverted
from, but never really settle' (p. 289).

Some pages later he draws attention to the fact that

'We never seem in the experimental literature to
put the results of all the experiments together
(...). We do (...) relate sets of experiments.
But the linkage is extraordinary loose. One picks
and chooses among the qualitative summaries of a
given experiment what to bring forward and
juxtapose with the concerns of a present treatment
(Newell, 1973, p. 298).

Now it might be objected here, and, indeed, I think such objection has some
justification, that the dichotomies referred to by Newell are a rational
starting point for research in generating conflicting hypotheses and testing
the explanatory power of either, or both, dichotomised points of view. However, one should realise quite clearly that in the majority of the phenomena
studied (and here I refer to Fentress' contribution to this book) such
dichotomies only highlight the *logical* extremes of the organisational
polarities under consideration, dynamic gradients having much greater
biological import.

Some nice illustrations of this thesis are to be found in the report on
grooming behaviour in mice in Fentress' paper (this book).

Stressing dichotomies for too long a time may easily lead to more or less
sterile discussions, the participants giving the impression of being aboard
ships that pass in the night. In my opinion one very clear instance of such
a discussion is highlighted in 'The Behavioral and Brain Sciences' (1980)
where proponents of either 'direct' or 'indirect' perception comment on Ullman'
leading article in defense of 'indirect' perception. Turvey, Shaw, Reed and
Mace (1981) have drawn attention to the fact that because the ecological
approach (in defense of the 'direct' perception view) is concerned with the
perceiving that goes with acting, its canonical examples are very different
from those of the Establishment (as the authors choose to call the cognitivist
approach favouring 'indirect' perception). Where the latter's kind of
perception is whatever eventuates in perceptual judgement or belief, the
ecologist's (Gibsonian) kind of perception eventuates in adjustment of activity
oriented to the various levels of the environment.

Without implying that I agree with their treatment, Turvey at al's (1981)
diagnosis seems to make good sense (and reinforces A. Newell's evaluation
referred to earlier). Recent attempts to reconcile the two positions have been
made by Shepard (1984) and Strelow (1985), arguing that, although in limiting
cases mobility in humans may indeed be completely controlled by visual
stimuli in the optic array, generally speaking cognitive variables, like
expectations, schema's and images contribute to this control.
Shepard's contribution to the discussion is, at least to me, especially
convincing and can be welcomed as an important step in overcoming too rigid
and one-sided perceptual theories.

2. CLOSER INSPECTION OF ONE OF THE DICHOTOMIES

Coming now to the notion of development (and closer to K.M. Newell's ball park) some remarks in the same spirit as the aforementioned considerations will be made with regard to the 'nature-nurture' question. They are not new, but they are worth reiterating.

Although there is now almost universal agreement that influences due to maturation and influences due to environmental factors interact during development, the full implications of this almost trivial fact are not always realised. Let me start with a very nice illustration of the interaction in question (see Fig. 1), derived from Krafka (1919), by Gottesman (1974)

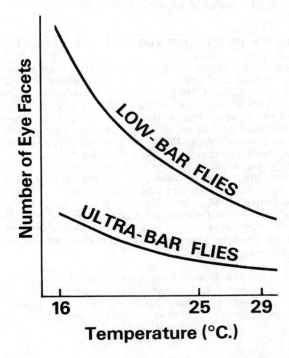

Fig. 1. *Drosophila* eye facet number as a function of temperatures at which larvae are reared (Adapted from Gottesman, 1974).

Plotted in Figure 1 are the number of eye facets in two, genetically different, types of Drosophila, 'Low-Bar flies' and 'Ultra-Bar flies', as a function of an environmental variable, namely the temperature at which the larvae are reared. As Gottesman (1974) notices, the strong interaction effect is suggestive of differential buffering or differential sensitivity of the two genotypes to temperature changes. Fig. 1. graphically shows clearly how similar genotypes can have different phenotypes, and how similar phenotypes can be the expression of different genotypes.

Now let us, for the sake of argument, carefully substitute humans for drosophilae, behaviour for eye facets, and differential sensitivity to all kinds of environmental influences, including those potentially influencing learning (e.g. reward and punishment), for differential sensitivity to warmth. If we now, after this exercise in mental plastic surgery, also realise that (1) differences in environmental sensitivity (i.e. the developmental responsiveness of an organism to environmental variation), may, themselves, be under genetic control and, with Gottlieb (1983), (2) that many different levels of organisational complexity (molecule → tissue → organ → organ system → organism) must be traversed to get from the genes to the overt behaviour of an organism, one is left with the same insecurity about the exact meaning of the two phrases 'genetically determined' and 'environmentally determined'. For further discussion of this whole issue the reader is referred to Gottlieb's (1983) illuminating article. With the above-sketched perspective in mind, I will now address K.M. Newell's paper.

3.   NEWELL'S VIEW ON THE DEVELOPMENT OF COORDINATION

In his paper, K.M. Newell argues that, while the maturational versus learning (nature versus nurture) debate has recently waned, both of these viewpoints about development (e.g. of motor coordination) might be contrasted with a third approach which stresses the importance of constraints which might be imposed on action. Where the first two perspectives assume the development of coordination to be due to the development of prescriptions for action - prescriptions being taken as a label for symbolic knowledge structures - the third perspective takes coordination to be a consequence of constraints imposed on action. These constraints (organismic, environmental and task constraints) do not (and here Newell refers to Kugler, Kelso & Turvey, 1980, 1982) *cause* the actions, but rather *eliminate* certain configurations of response dynamics, with the resulting pattern of coordination being a reflection of the self-organising optimality of the biological system. Newell notices that prescriptions *could* be seen as a special class of constraints, but he prefers reserving the term for symbolic rule-based knowledge structures.

From his perspective Newell also argues against a difference between what are sometimes called 'phylogenetic' and 'ontogenetic' or 'natural' and 'cultural' skills, the necessary coordinations for *both* types of skill being a consequence of constraints. The rest of this paper can be read as a comment on these notions.

4.   PRESCRIPTIONS FOR FOETUSES

A new video film by Prechtl on the development of motor behaviour in human foetuses very convincingly shows that, already, at a very young age (about 11 to 12 weeks) very well coordinated movement patterns are apparent. This motor behaviour is spontaneously generated, in the sense of not being triggered by any identifiable external stimulus. How do these coordinated movements emerge, what is their cause? That is not an easy question. What seems to be clear is that there is a massive increase in the excitatory axodendritic synapses of motoneurones at about eight or nine weeks (Prechtl, this book). It is also clear (even from a logical point of view) that the patterned muscle activity manifesting itself in the coordinated foetal movement patterns is crucially dependent on patterned neural activity in, maybe relatively simple, neural circuitry developing on a strong genetic base.

Now, I hesitate, here, to speak about a knowledge structure, possibly being wired into the system on the basis of a genetic code, but this hesitation has only to do with reservations about too broad a use of the term knowledge. In principle I see neither logical nor empirical arguments against a description of the functioning of the neural circuitry *as if* embodying procedural knowledge, or prescriptions for action, these prescriptions having important implications for post-foetal possibilities. What we have to realise at the same time, however, is that the organisation of the neural circuitry and the functional role of neurons in that circuitry are not invariant. They change throughout ontogeny in a manner which is, and here I refer to Varela (1979), subordinated to the ontogeny of the organism, because these changes are both caused by, and are a cause of, the changes in both the neuronal networks and the organism of which these networks are components.

Here, one might pursue the operational consequences of this state of affairs along the lines of Varela (1979), treating the nervous system and organisms as autopeietic systems closed in themselves, thus getting rid of the whole question of prescribed versus constrained. However, I have the impression that this approach, or, if you like, way of description, will not prove very fruitful when we want to account for questions, arising later, about behavioural effects of, say, psychologically relevant variables. Even for framing such questions the latter viewpoint has to be replaced by one treating the organism (and its nervous system) as open to its environment.

We seem to be left with no alternative to an open system, with all the intricacies I referred to earlier, in the interactions between genetically and environmentally induced changes.

4.   INFANTS ON THE MOVE

At about nine months after its inception, the open system will enter extra-uterine life with many well developed motor patterns being ready to be displayed. If, and when, this will occur depends not only on state variables, but on context variables as well.

Smith (1977) drew attention to the fact that, contrary to what earlier ethologists seemed to imply, releasing signals, even in lower species like birds, do not automatically elicit particular responses, but that the effect of the same signal varies with the environmental situation in which it is presented. In several of the papers in these proceedings is made clear how important are, for example, postural variables in eliciting stepping movements (Thelen) or movements directed towards a target. Von Hofsten discusses the latter movements in an evolutionary framework, reminiscent of earlier accounts of the development of sensory-motor mechanisms (Judd, 1910). A number of perception-action systems developed during evolution and are functional in narrowly defined ecological contexts. According to Von Hofsten it is cheaper to pay for such 'special purpose devices' or 'smart mechanisms', to borrow Runeson's (1977) term, in genes than in learning currency. Here again I think there are no objections against speaking in terms of genetically based prescriptions, although in this case the prescriptions have more to do with the control under which already established coordinations are brought, than with such coordinations *per se*.

When the infant continues its motor development, it displays, on a descriptive level, an orderly sequence of what is called developmental 'stages' the latter term having been used to refer to either motor behaviour in general, in specific tasks or even in task components (Roberton, 1978). Where the invariance in the sequence of stages has traditionally been interpreted as supportive for a maturational, prescriptive point of view, Newell suggests that the observed order results from uniformities in constraints imposed on the motor behaviour in question.

According to him, experimental manipulation of those constraints to a stronger degree than is usually done in natural or laboratory situations, could prove useful in testing the prescription versus constraint perspectives to the development of coordination.

Now let's assume, and I think that is surely not improbable, that if we tighten up some constraints further than usual, other coordinations and movement patterns indeed show up, and maybe even some stage transitions will occur. We should realise, however (and this is a consequence of what was said earlier with respect to nature-nurture interactions), that adoption of a prescriptive viewpoint does not imply that, irrespective of constraints, the same coordinations should always been seen. To put it another way: Prescriptions by 'species-typical' genomes require a species-specific environment (species-specific constraints) to lead to, say, 'species-typical behaviour'

These considerations make me wonder, if, for the same reasons as the nature-nurture debate, the prescriptions-constraints debate might not wane in the same way. Of course, that does not rule out the importance of research directed at establishing the effects of manipulating the three kinds c constraints on motor behaviour and coordination. And, the coordinative structure theory (Kugler, Kelso & Turvey, 1980, 1982) might lead us to expect that, given the characteristics of biological systems, relatively simple changes in control signals can lead to adaptive changes in coordination in newly constrained situations.

5.   CHILDREN DO MIND

The child is a little older now, let us say it has reached the age of five, as my daughter Rosa did two years ago, when she started her dancing-lessons. I, being a model parent, bought her a book with drawings about positions and postures in ballet. After having quickly leaved through it, Rosa put the book on a low table and, using the table edge as the barre, tried to imitate the postures, looking to and from the illustrations and her body members. Sometimes she left the table, tried to realise a specific posture and then ran back to the book to have a look at the "model".

Something like this, of course, goes on in learning processes directed at mastering all kinds of 'ontogenetic skills', not only in the dance and sport domain, but in every day life as well. Moreover, the children are instructed verbally, look at video's, use mirrors to evaluate their performance etc. In many cases teachers will serve as models for either simultaneous or delayed imitation. Often, also, the children use verbal codes, either aloud or covert, to guide their behaviour, like counting in dance, or verbalising ballet phrases, like 'plié, relevé, plié, glissade etc.'. In doing this the children are trying to reach their goal. This goal really implies new *coordinations* (in Newell's sense of relative motions, new forms of movement) and surely not only new *control* in the sense of new parameterisations of already established movement forms.

What the children are doing, and here I fully agree with Newell, is searching for a stable pattern of coordination and control that accommodates the constraints defined by the rules of the game. These constraints can be very tight, like the ones for, say, an entrachet, a fouetté, or a grand jété. But, beware: although the task constraints here eliminate almost all configurations of response dynamics except the optimal one, the search for the optimal configuration (a new coordinative structure, if you like) takes months or years of training.

Moreover, the search process in question, and this is a crucial characteristic of this process, a *guided* search, a search mediated by cognitive processes and mental representations of both the actual and intended performance.

In ballet classes (as well as in many other teaching situations) cognitive 'plans' are transmitted from teachers to their pupils, and this is, according to Miller, Galanter and Pribram (1960), one of the fundamental differences between such teaching processes and the operant conditioning of animals, where the plan guiding the learning process is only that of the teacher and is not transferred to the animal.

It will be clear by now that I have no hesitation whatsoever in referring to the human learning processes in question as being guided by prescriptions in the sense of a rule-based knowledge structure.

By making use of such knowledge structure culturally loaded movement patterns can be transmitted from one generation to the other. Initially this knowledge will often be conscious and explicit, later, when some degree of 'automatisation' has been reached, it may lose its explicit character and become more procedural and unconscious.

6. CONCLUSION

Maybe the difference in emphasis between K.M. Newell and myself can be best illustrated by Figure 2. This figure has been derived from Newell's paper, with only one addition: the central nervous system. The organism has a central nervous system, and, in the case of humans, a nervous system with a well developed brain. This has fundamental implications for the development of motor coordination, as one example may illustrate.

As Oster and Ekman (1978) have stipulated, the newborn infant already shows a full-blown gusto-facial reflex when the tongue is stimulated with bitter or sour taste stimuli. Both of these expressions have many of the components of adult disgust patterns. There are some suggestions in the literature about these patterns having a subcortical basis, because they have also been observed in anencephalic children. Also 'basic' patterns of emotional expressions, like smiling, laughter and crying do not seem to be learned, in any traditional sense of the word, these patterns being also displayed by congenitally blind infants and infants born blind and deaf. Later on, these expressions can be modified by cultural influences; such observations gave rise to Ekman's (e.g., 1977) 'neuro-cultural' theory of facial expression of

368

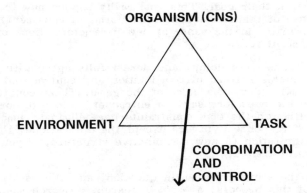

ORGANISM (CNS)

ENVIRONMENT

TASK

COORDINATION
AND
CONTROL

Fig. 2. Categories of constraints that specify the optimal pattern
of coordination and control (Adapted from K.M. Newell (this
book), the central nervous system (CNS) having been added).

emotions.

Unlike the involuntary displaying of emotional expressions in natural
settings, voluntary expression of these facial movements, as on command, is
not an easy task. But, mimes and Kathakali dancers, after years of training,
eventually gain conscious control and use of all the muscles of the face,
followed by some degree of automatisation of repeatedly displayed patterns.
And after many rehearsals an actor can end up with, for example, two sad
facial patterns, one as Lear, carrying the body of his beloved Cordelia over
the stage, and one when detecting some minutes later that his money has
been stolen from the dressing room. The first-mentioned facial pattern has
been reached by another way, and the search for it was guided by other
'prescriptions', than the latter 'natural' one. It is for this reason that a
distinction between ontogenetic and phylogenetic skills might be both
justifiable and useful.

Drawing this reaction to a close, I conclude that cognitive processes,
and, in Newell's terms, prescriptions in terms of symbolic knowledge
structures, cannot be dismissed from theorising about developing motor skills
If we were to do so, the influence of all kinds of variables, as mentioned in
these proceedings by, for example, Reid, Roy and Wall, simply could not be
accounted for.

Of course a theory of motor actions in which an important role is
ascribed to cognitive processes (or some analogon), is not without its
problems. The most basic one has to do with the jumping from one level of
description to another. Cognitive psychologists sharing the 'Establishment'
view tried to account for the rules representing cognitive processes in
formal models, which, preferably, were to be implemented in artefacts like
computers. The fate of Chomsky's (1965) theory of linguistic competence has
taught us to be hesitant in supposing that such rules functioning in formal
models should be represented in the functioning of the human brain, or even
at a more molar psychological level, in any literal sense. Or, in the words
of the Dutch classicist, Guèpin (1983, p. 264) (in my translation): 'While
Chomsky may suppose that I am, unconsciously, following the rules of his

grammar, I prefer to think that these rules are conciously in his head, but not, for that reason, also unconsciously in mine'*. I am all but sure that the description level problem can be solved in a really satisfying way. Neither classical reductive theories on the one hand, nor system-theoretical approaches on the other have led to such solutions. I think as psychologists we have to live with this problem, generating theories in which both 'bottom-up' and 'top-down' processes are invoked to account for our data.

7. SUMMARY

In motor skills, constraints imposed on action do eliminate configurations of response dynamics. That does not imply, however, that the resulting patterns of coordination should be described merely in terms of the self-organising optimality of biological systems. For an adequate description, both the genetically determined neural organisation and cognitively represented rules underlying the motor skills have to be taken into account.

---

* Just in passing: the Chomsky-Skinner debate on language development formed, in my opinion, one of the clearest examples of unjustified dichotomising: the existence of hard-ware based universals is not intrinsically incompatible with environment based learning processes at all (see also Eysenck, 1979).

370

References

Chomsky, N. (1965). *Aspects of the theory of syntax*. Cambridge, MA: M.I.T. Press.

Ekman, P. (1977). Biological and cultural contributions to body and facial movement. In J. Blacking (Ed.), *Anthropology of the body*. New York: Academic Press.

Eysenck, H.J. (1979). Behavior therapy and the philosophers. *Behavior Research & Therapy*, *17*, 511-514.

Gottesman, I.I. (1974). Developmental genetics and ontogenetic psychology: overdue détente and propositions from a matchmaker. In A.D. Pick (Ed.), *Minnesota symposia on child psychology*, *Vol. 8*. Minneapolis: The University of Minneapolis Press.

Gottlieb, G. (1983). The psychobiological approach to developmental issues. In P.H. Mussen (Ed.), *Handbook of Child Psychology*, *Vol. II*. New York: Wiley.

Guépin, J.P. (1983). *De beschaving*. Amsterdam: Bert Bakker.

Judd, C.H. (1910). Evolution and consciousness. *Psychological Review*, *17*, 77-97.

Koch, S. (1974). Psychology as science. In S.C. Brown (Ed.), *Philosophy of psychology*. London: Macmillan.

Krafka, J. (1919). The effect of temperature upon facet-number in the bar-eyed mutant of drosophila. Part I. *Journal of General Physiology*, *2*, 409-432.

Kugler, P.N., Kelso, J.A.S. & Turvey, M.T. (1980). On the concept of coordinative structures as dissipative structures: I. Theoretical lines of convergence. In G.E. Stelmach and J. Requin (Eds.), *Tutorials in motor behavior*. New York: North-Holland.

Kugler, P.N., Kelso, J.A.S. & Turvey, M.T. (1982). On the control and co-ordination of naturally developing systems. In J.A.S. Kelso and J.E. Clark (Eds.), *The development of movement control and co-ordination*. New York: Wiley.

Langer, S. (1962). *Philosophical sketches*. Baltimore: John Hopkins Press.

Miller, G.A., Galanter, E. & Pribram, K.H. (1960). *Plans and the structure of behavior*. New York: Holt, Rinehart & Winston.

Newell, A. (1973). You can't play 20 questions with nature and win: Projective comments on the paper of this symposium. In W.G. Chase (Ed.), *Visual information processing*. New York: Academic Press.

Oster, H. & Ekman, P. (1978). Facial behavior in child development. In W.A. Collins (Ed.), *Minnesota symposia on child psychology*. *Vol. 11*. Hillsdale, New Jersey: LEA Publishers.

Pattee, H.H. (1982). The need for complementarity in models of cognitive behavior: A response to Fowler and Turvey. In W.B. Weimer and D.S. Palermo (Eds.), *Cognition and the symbolic processes*. *Vol. II*. Hillsdale: LEA Publishers.

Roberton, M.A. (1978). Stages in motor development. In M.V. Ridenour (Ed.), *Motor development*. Princeton: Princeton Book Company.

Runeson, S. (1977). On the possibility of 'smart' perceptual mechanisms. *Scandinavian Journal of Psychology*, *18*, 172-179.

Shepard, R.N. (1984). Ecological constraints on internal representation: resonant kinematics of perceiving, imagining, thinking and dreaming. *Psychological Review*, *91*, 417-447.

Smith, W.J. (1977). *The behavior of communicating*. Cambridge: Harvard University Press.

Strelow, E.R. (1985). What is needed for a theory of mobility: direct perception and cognitive maps - lessons from the blind. *Psychological Review*, *92*, 226-248.

Turvey, M.T., Shaw, R.E., Reed, E.S. & Mace, W.M. (1981). Ecological laws of perceiving and acting: In reply to Fodor and Pylyshyn. *Cognition, 9*, 237-304.

Ullman, S. (1980). Against direct perception (Followed by peer commentary). *The Behavioral and Brain Sciences, 3*, 373-415.

Varela, F.J. (1979). *Principles of biological autonomy*. New York: North Holland.

ACTION AND COGNITION
Cognitive and motor skills in a developmental perspective

P. Mounoud

We would like to discuss in this chapter the relationships between motor and cognitive skills, usually considered as two separate categories of behaviour. Although it is not usual to speak in terms of "cognitive skills", the idea is not new. Bartlett (1958) already suggested that "thinking is an advanced form of skilled behaviour"; but he made, however, a sharp distinction between "bodily skills" and "thinking skills". Weimer (1977), expanding on the idea, considers that "the processes underlying human knowledge are (pace Bartlett) skilled actions". Similarly, Gelman and Gallistel (1978) speak of counting skills, or classification skills. Fischer (1980) has also adopted the notion of hierarchical skills in his developmental theory. Beilin (1983) considers the actual use of this term as a feature of contemporary functionalism. We will use the "skill" lable in this chapter in order to facilitate the comparison between so-called cognitive and motor behaviours or tasks and also to make more explicit the point of view that will be adopted. We shall try to demonstrate, if not the equivalence between motor and cognitive skills, at least that the processes and mechanisms underlying them are the same. This is an important issue, in our view, since for several years now, we have been using motor tasks (skills) to study cognitive development (Hauert, 1980; Mounoud, 1970; Mounoud & Hauert, 1982). In a not too serious strain, we would suggest that this approach may be considered as "cognitivist behaviorism".

The relationships between action and cognition have been widely discussed recently (Arbib, 1980; Prinz & Sanders, 1984; Shaw & Bransford, 1977). Nevertheless little has been written on this topic in relation to development, the only exceptions being the chapters of Hay, Pick and Trevarthen in the book edited by Prinz and Sanders. We shall start this paper by paraphrasing Herb Pick's formula (this volume), according to which "we perceive in order to act and we act in order to perceive", in the following way: "we act by means of our knowledge and we know by means of our actions, by means of what we experience through our actions".

It is perhaps first necessary to specify that our knowledge and cognitive capacities are not necessarily conscious. Our cognitive skills are based mainly upon unconscious processes (in other words, cognition and consciousness do not have any necessary connections) and we are not usually conscious of the rules, relations, operations, schemas and representations (frequently qualified as mental) which determine our cognitive or motor skills.

For the purpose of this chapter, we shall consider cognitive skills and motor skills separately. Then, using our own field of research we shall try to define the links between them. Particular attention will be paid to "seriation" skills, from both a motor point of view and a cognitive one. A large number of studies have been carried out from the latter point of view in order to discover how children succeed in seriating objects or events according to a given property (size, weight, etc...). Attention is paid both to the final product (the order introduced among objects) and to the procedure, i.e. the strategy used to produce the series. We have studied, from a motor point of view, together with Hauert, Gachoud, Viviani and Corbetta how children manage to seriate certain parameters of their actions (intensity, amplitude, force, etc) in relation to the variations of different properties (aspects) of the objects upon which the action is applied (grasping and lifting of objects of different weight, size, etc) or in relation to the variations in size of objects generated by the action itself (for example drawing circles of different sizes).

It is usual in all these experimental situations to interpret children's performances in terms of plans, programs, strategies that are qualified as more or less local or global (locally or globally defined), more or less integrated, coordinated or juxtaposed or fragmented in a piecemeal way. We shall examine children's skills in different situations - these skills being qualified sometimes as cognitive, sometimes as motor - in order to improve our understanding of children's behaviour as an adaptive tool for interacting with the environment.

The major problem in this kind of study is to know whether these plans (cognitive labels) or programs (motor labels) qualify an unique entity, whether they have the same underlying mechanisms or whether, on the contrary, they are different kinds of seriation skills.

1. COGNITIVE SKILLS

We shall first deal with so-called cognitive skills. We consider these to be the capacity to organise the relationships (spatial, causal, logical) between objects with respect to their different properties, or the capacity to organise the relationships between different parts of an object or yet again the capacity to organise the relationships between the subject and the objects he is confronted with. In our opinion, such a definition of cognitive skills necessarily includes perceptual skills. Cognitive skills can be both concrete material behaviour applied to objects, like sorting or seriating things, and internal or mental behaviour.

We will first consider free *classification or sorting skills* as a prototype of cognitive skills which organise relationships between objects. Sorting skills cannot be considered separately from class inclusion skills. The initial description in three phases given by Inhelder and Piaget (1964) starts with figural collections. These are typical of children aged from 4 to 5 year (objects are organised in spatial configurations as part of a whole). In a second phase ($5\frac{1}{2}$ to 7 years), children construct non-figural collections (objects are put together in small groups, based on more or less fluctuating and overlapping criteria). In a third phase (8 to 9 years), children are able to form well-articulated classes which are no longer juxtaposed but hierarchically organised. According to Inhelder and Piaget, children at this level fully grasp class-inclusion relationships, in other words the "all" and "some" relation.

From this initial description, it is possible as for the other cognitive skills to distinguish between two lines of research: one centered on early competences, the other on late incompetences (Case, 1985). There are good reviews on this topic (see in particular Gelman & Baillargeon, 1983; Schol-nick, 1983; Sugarman, 1983; Winer, 1980).

Studies done on "early competences" (e.g. Denney, 1972a,b; Fischer & Roberts, 1980; Rosch et al, 1976; C.L. Smith, 1979; L.B. Smith, 1984; Sugarman, 1979, 1981, 1983) all describe a series of steps or phases between 1 and 4 years. According to these authors, three-year-olds for example are able to sort objects according to a stable criterion, without any remainder or overlap. Preschool children can construct consistent and exhaustive classes: they are able to reason about inclusion relations, to embed classes within one another. We fully agree with J.M. Mandler's comment "it is hard to imagine a hierarchically arranged system that did not imply *some* under-standing of class inclusion" (1983, p. 469).

Studies done on "late incompetences" (e.g. Bideaud, 1979; Carbonnel, 1978; Lautrey et al, 1981; Markman, 1978; Markman et al, 1980; Ribeaupierre et al, 1985; Rieben et al, 1983; Thornton, 1982) show the limits of 8 and 9-year-olds' classification skills, and in particular the tendency of children up to 11 years to base class inclusion judgments on empirical rather than logical factors.

If we leave aside classification in action, i.e. the sensori-motor or practical form of classification based upon the assimilation mechanism, it would seem that there are two moments when children's classification skills seem to reach some kind of optimal level: a first one at around $3\frac{1}{2}$ or 4 years and a second one at around 9 to 11 years. As far as the transition between these two steps is concerned, we would especially like to mention the systematic research done by Markman (Markman, 1973; Markman & Seibert, 1976; Markman et al, 1980). Her results demonstrate clearly that 6 to 7-year-old children tend to organise objects in terms of collections (collective nouns such as family, forest, etc...) and part-whole relations, rather than in terms of classes or class-inclusion relations. How should one interpret this preference for collections as opposed to classes? Markman considers, for example, that collections have a higher psychological coherence than classes. It is, in fact, true that collective nouns are useful to particularise a class as a whole, to singularise it, to concretise it, to increase its intention. Collective nouns make it easier to keep the whole (the super-ordinate class) in mind while paying attention to its subparts.

Thornton (1982) studied children from 5 to 10 years in a classification task. She considered the age of 7 years as a transitional phase in which children actively elaborate relations between classes. We prefer to say "re-elaborate" since early competences already presuppose such an elaboration at a much earlier age (between 2 and 3 years). From our point of view, these two successive elaborations are done by means of different types of coding systems (Mounoud, 1976, 1981, 1985).

We now propose to consider another category of cognitive skills: the *seriation skill*. It can be defined as the capacity to order objects or events with respect to one or several of their properties such as height, weight or duration of water flow (Inhelder & Piaget, 1964; Piaget, 1946; Piaget & Szeminska, 1952; Piaget & Inhelder, 1974). This behaviour has been studied not only from the point of view of the final product (how successful the child has been in ordering objects) but also from the point of view of the strategies used by the child to carry out the seriation. In some recent studies on classification skills, sorting strategies have also been

376

considered (Langer, 1980; Sugerman, 1983). This study of strategies takes us a step in the direction of motor skills. Reid (this volume) includes the study of strategies in the field of motor skills. The task usually evoked is one studied by Piaget. In the size seriation task, children were asked to arrange ten rods differing by .8 cm, from the "shortest" to the "longest" (Piaget & Szeminska, 1941). Although, some 5-year-old children succeeded in correctly ordering the ten rods by a trial-and-error strategy, it is only at around eight years that they were able, according to Piaget and Szeminska, to seriate the ten rods in a systematic way, from the smallest to the largest. These children were also successful in subsidiary tasks such as the insertion of additional elements into an already-formed series and the correction of the placement of an additional element that had been incorrectly inserted. For Piaget, the use of a systematic strategy means that the child *anticipates in advance the complete series*. In the same way, as inclusion for classification skills, the operational ability to seriate is formally unseparable from success on transitivity judgments.

Other experiments, some of which are contemporary to that of Piaget and Szeminska, have shown that much younger children can correctly seriate objects with regard to their size, in a systematic way. As for classification skills, *early competences* in three to four-year-old children have also been demonstrated in seriation tasks (Greenfield et al, 1972; Koslowski, 1980; Meyer, 1940; Sugarman, 1983). The same goes for transitive inferences (de Boysson-Bardies & O'Regan, 1973; Bryant & Trabasso, 1971; Harris & Bassett, 1975).

Edith Meyer, in her study of the understanding of spatial relationships between objects in preschool children, studied in 1940 already "the fitting together of forms" (the nesting of boxes). She gave children a set of five triangular boxes. They were asked to take the boxes out of each other and then to put them back again in the correct order. Behaviours were classified by Meyer in three stages.

During a first stage (typical from one-and-a-half to two-and-a-half years), children show *no appreciation of the forms and sizes of the objects* they want to put together. In the second stage (typical from 3 to 3-and-a-half years) children learn from experience to adjust the forms to each other. They succeed in holding the boxes so that their axes fit correctly (in such a way that the axis of one prolongates the axis of the other). They are *"not aware of all the relations beforehand" but they adjust to them through experimentation*. They cannot complete the series without making errors. Their planning is limited.

In the third stage (typical from 4 to 4-and-a-half years) children choose the right sizes and adjust the position of the boxes so that they will slide together easily. *They plan* their actions *beforehand and do not only adjust empirically*.

The description given by Meyer in 1940 still seem relevant today. It could be relabelled in terms of feedback and feedforward mechanisms.

Thirty years later, Greenfield, Nelson and Saltzman (1972) studied the manipulation of different sized cups by 11 to 36-month-old children, drawing a parallel between the development of action-manipulative strategies and grammatical construction. Moreover they establish a parallel between the stages described by Piaget between 4 and 8 years and the stages they discovered between 1 and 3 years.

In this task, five cups with a circular section were used. Instead of presenting already-nested boxes to the child, the experimenter proceeded to nest the cups. The demonstration started with the smallest cup and proceeded to the next largest, yielding a seriated structure (strategy usually considered as the most advanced). After the demonstration the cups were placed one by one in front of the child. Three distinct strategies were identified.

In the first strategy (typical of one-year-old children) a single cup was placed in or on a second cup and most often immediately withdrawn from this cup. The child constructs one pair or successive pairs of cups. This strategy is compared to the binary division of the sticks into "big" and "little" described by Piaget and Szeminska (1952).

In the second strategy, called the "pot" method (typical at 2 years of age), two or more cups are placed in or on another cup. The child success-ively holds a number of cups which move into or onto a single stationary cup. The stationary cup functions as a "pot" holding the mobile cups. This strategy is compared to the second stage described by Piaget starting at age six in which series can be constructed by trial and error, but in which an additional intermediate element cannot then be inserted.

In the third strategy typical of the 3 year-old called the subassembly method, a previously constructed structure consisting of two or more cups is moved as a unit into or onto another cup. The critical feature of this strategy is that each cup or cup structure has a double role: it makes the transition from being acted upon to acting; each multicup unit functions as a single moving or acting cup. This strategy is compared with the third and final stage identified by Piaget characterised by the ability to insert a new element in an already formed series.

Between the stages described by Meyer (1940) and those described by Greenfield et al (1972) there is approximatively a one-year decalage. This decalage is partly due to the material and partly to the method. As far as the material is concerned, it is definitely easier to nest cups than boxes with triangular sections. As to the method, it would seem that the demonstration done by Greenfield et al, although it did not determine the use of a specific strategy as the results indicate, probably maximised the child's performance, which was the result the authors had set out to obtain. We particularly mention this decalage in order to relativise the ages mentioned in this presentation. Ages are not and cannot be considered in too strict or rigid a perspective. But it is possible to conclude on the basis of the empirical evidence that children of around 3 to 4-year-old are capable of correct seriation and insertion with a set of nesting cups or boxes, using of a systematic strategy. These preschool children planned beforehand or anticipated the successive actions to be produced in a similar way to the 8 or 9-year-old children in the classical size seriation task.

Early competence has also been demonstrated among 3 and 4-year-old children for transitive inference (de Boyssons-Bardies & O'Regan, 1973; Bryant & Trabasso, 1971; Harris & Bassett, 1975; Riley & Trabasso, 1974). For Halford and Kelly (1984) it is only around 4-and-a-half to 5 years of age that children show a real understanding of transitive inference. There is a strong controversy between the different authors (for an overview of

378

the topic, see Breslow, 1981; Breslow et al, in press).

As was the case for classification skills, seriation skills and transitive inference have also been considered from the point of view of late incompetences. Researchers have demonstrated the limits of understanding capacities among 8 to 9-year-old children (Bullinger, 1973; Gilliéron, 1976; Retschitzki, 1978). Using ingenious masking techniques to eliminate perceptual indices, some horizontal decalages, e.g. between seriation of length and seriation of weight, were suppressed (for a discussion see also Montangero, 1980). In addition, in certain experimental conditions, the operational strategy (called the choice of the biggest) is not used by children before 11 or 12 years of age. We would like also to mention the paper recently published by Retschitzki (1982) stressing the large variability in the strategies used to solve seriation problems even at a given developmental level.

For classification and seriation skills, as for inclusion and transitive inference, two levels of success seem to emerge clearly from the empirical findings: a first one around 3 to 4 years of age and a second one around 9 to 11 years of age, with a certain variability due to the experimental conditions. Most of the authors base their explanations upon mental structures But some of them consider that there is a *structural transformation* between these two levels of performance (this Piagetian explanation is adopted in particular by Breslow, 1981; Breslow et al, in press) whereas for others there is *structural invariance*, and the explanation of change is to be found elsewhere. Authors in favor of the structural invariance consider that children from very early on have the logical competence to solve classification and seriation tasks.

Several hypothesis have been suggested to explain the change between the two levels of performance. For example:
- the ability to apply the logical competence to more and more complex arrays improves in time (Gelman & Baillargeon, 1983)
- the transformation of memory space or of language capacities (Trabasso, 1975; 1977)
- the degree of conscious awareness of categorical relations the tasks require (Mandler, 1983)
- the emergence of new coding capacities (Mounoud, 1981).
We would like to suggest that the first level of success at 3 to 4 years of age could be achieved by means of the perceptual coding system; whereas the second level of success at 9 to 11 years of age depends on (involves) the conceptual coding system. We previously considered perceptual organisation to be achieved around the age of two years. Thus we would be more inclined to consider the success of the 3 to 4 year-olds as a late achievement of the perceptual organisation and not as a first step in the conceptual organisation.

2.   MOTOR SKILLS

We shall now discuss the development of motor skills. Motor skills can be considered as based upon the capacity to organise the spatial-temporal and physical aspects of a movement and its different components in relation to - or in correspondence with - the spatial-temporal and physical aspects of a given situation. This type of organisation can be demonstrated by the invariance or systematic variation of the movement parameters involved in motor skills behaviour. This was basically the method adopted by Piaget for his study of some of the major aspects of cognitive development. In the field of motor skills, many invariants were identified by researchers at the end of the last century already, but these invariants are usually described as laws, principles, tendencies such as the Fitt's law or Isogony Principle and not as resulting from compensatory mechanisms produced by an active organism engaged in an adaptative relationship including action and perception.

As we already mentioned, we shall consider seriation skill from the motor skill point of view. In the experimental situation called weight seriation, the subjects were asked to lift objects of different weight and size. Weight variations can be inferred, at least partly, from variations in size. To accomplish the task in an optimal way, subjects must be able to vary the amount of force in relation to variations in the objects' weight so as to produce more or less similar movements whatever the weight of the object. In other words, the total duration of the lifting movement will be more or less constant and more or less invariant. We carried out various experiments in order to see at what ages children are able to organise their movement in such a way, and which are the different solutions they propose to solve this problem. We are not going to present the initial studies we did with 6 to 16 month-old babies on grasping for objects of different weights (Mounoud, 1973; 1974; Mounoud & Bower, 1974; Mounoud & Hauert, 1982).

We next studied children from 2 to 5 years of age in collaboration with Hauert (Hauert, 1980; Hauert et al, 1980, 1981). Children had to lift each object of a five-objects series three times in two different conditions with and without abutment. We will only mention that the 3 and a half to 4 year-olds were more able than the other children to compensate weight variations by corresponding variations of some parameters of their movements. However, these compensations were relative and partial. In the condition without abutment, they succeeded in keeping the amplitude of their movements roughly constant, the other parameters varying in proportion to the weight variations. In the condition with abutment, i.e. when the amplitude was externally imposed, they kept the movement duration constant. It is also at this age that one finds the highest proportion (80%) of continuous movements, according to Brooks et al's criterion (Brooks, Cooke & Thomas, 1973). Continuous movements are usually interpreted as the sign or the index of an overall planning of action.

Thus, in the motor skill version of the seriation problem, the performances of 3 to 4-year-old children show a peak, an optimum level as was the case for the cognitive version.

We will now present in more detail some of the results obtained in a study done with children from 6 to 9 years of age and adults, in collaboration with Gachoud (Gachoud, 1983; Gachoud, Mounoud, Viviani & Hauert, 1983).

The subjects were forty boys aged from 6 to 9 years and ten young male adults. They were seated in front of an object laying on a table, with their forearm horizontally placed and the half-prone hand grasping the object. The objects to be lifted were parallelepipeds of constant square section (4x4 cm), varying in height from 3 to 19 cm (by steps of 2 cm). The movement required was a simple flexion of the forearm so as to bring the wrist into contact with a fixed abutment; during the whole movement, the elbow stayed in contact with the table. The subjects could choose when to start, as well as the velocity of the movement. They were asked to perform the movements in what they felt to be the most natural manner. Each object was attached to a rod connected to an angular potentiometer.

Electromyographic activity in the main agonistic and antagonistic muscles (biceps, triceps and deltoid) was recorded.

Adults lifted the entire series of nine objects from the lightest to the heaviest six times. Children only lifted the seven lightest objects in the series in the same order as the adults.

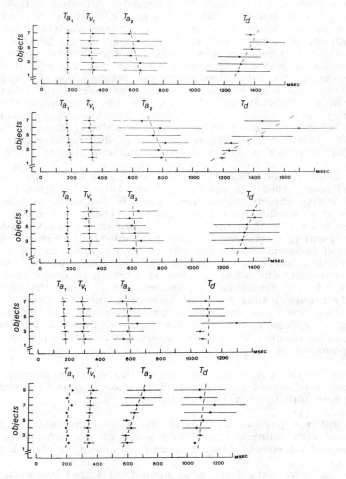

Fig. 1. Times of occurrence of the velocity and acceleration peak values (see text) in an object lifting seriation task. From the top: 6, 7, 8, 9 year-old children and adult subjects. Bars indicate the standard deviations.

We shall briefly summarise the results. Firstly, adult performance is characterised by a clear tendency to invariance with respect to the considerable changes in the external conditions. Figure 1 illustrates this tendency. It shows the time of occurrence of the first two peaks of acceleration (Ta1, Ta2), of the first peak of velocity (Tv1), and the total duration of the movement (Td), as a function of the object rank order in the series. Note that the value Ta1, Tv1 and Td do not vary with the weight of the object.

If we now look at children's performances on the timing of the kinematic parameters, we see that for the 6, 8 and 9 year-olds, the times of occurrence are constant for all parameters. Although the trends are not statistically significant, the duration parameter (Td) increases more for the 6 and 8 year-olds as a function of the object weight than it does for the 9 year-olds. For the 7 year-olds, the times of occurrence of Tv1 and Ta2 are constant. The time of occurrence of the first peak of acceleration (Ta1) decreases linearly with weight. In contrast, the duration parameter (Td) increases linearly with the objects weight. The different phases of the movement (acceleration and deceleration) are not completely coordinated. Taking into consideration other parameters such as the amplitude of the kinematic parameters and the emg data, it appears that the 9 year-olds children master the task in an optimal way: they fully compensate the variations of weight throughout the movement, including the deceleration phase.

We are not going to discuss the differences between children and adults. This has been done in detail in a recent paper (Gachoud et al, 1983). It is sufficient for our purpose to note that the 7 year-olds show simultaneously an overcompensation in relation to the increase in the weight of the objects in the first phase of acceleration, followed by a partial compensation in the deceleration phase. Such data are very illustrative of the nature of regulations and relations which are established at this age between the spatial-temporal characteristics of the movements and the object's properties. These regulations can be considered as analogous to those which appear in classification skills (elaboration of relations between hierarchical classes).

As for cognitive skills, motor skills seem to reach an optimum level at the age of 9. However, this achievement is probably dependent on the nature of the situation. Indeed, if the task were to consist of lifting objects in a random order of weight, we would probably have to study older children to get similar compensations in action.

We will now briefly outline the main results of an ongoing research on graphomotor activities in the developmental perspective (a study in collaboration with Viviani, Corbetta & Hauert). This research also involves a "motor seriation" task: subjects are asked to draw circles with various perimeters from the largest to the smallest. As early as 1893, Binet and Courtier presented evidence of invariants in the organisation of graphic movements. In particular, they suggested a direct relationship between the amplitude of the movement and the average speed of execution which, they noted, implies the relative invariance of the total execution time. More recently, Viviani and Terzuolo (1982) have demonstrated that the figural parameter that relates directly to the tangential velocity is the total linear extent of the trajectory, irrespectively of the overall size and shape of the trajectory. They also showed that total execution time is relatively insensitive to total linear extent (Isochrony Principle). A striking feature of this compensatory regulation of speed in adults, as noted by Binet and Courtier, is the independence of visual feedback and its apparently involuntary nature. One could assume that this principle is an intrinsic characteristic of the neuromuscular system and that it is independent of development and active experience. In order to study this problem, we asked children aged from 5 to 9 years to draw circles of different perimeters. They used an Edison pen which burns a sensitive paper at a constant rate, in order to characterise the spatio-temporal parameters of their productions. Subjects were shown four circles (perimeter: 24, 18, 12, 6 cm) presented side by side on a board. They were asked to reproduce the four models in order of decreasing size. The models were not visible during the execution phase. In one experimental condition, subjects could monitor their movements visually. In a second condition they were blindfolded. Conditions were counterbalanced across subjects. Let us first examine the data collected concerning the amplitude of the movement, i.e. concerning the seriation of the perimeters.

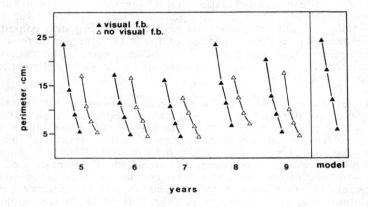

Fig. 2. Relation between theoretical (model) and experimental mean values of the perimeter in each condition.

Figure 2 shows the mean value (10 subjects in each age group) of the perimeters of the circles drawn in both experimental conditions. In all cases, the movement amplitudes clearly correlate with model size. But, in terms of *error* (quadratic error between model sequence and movement sequence), the analysis shows that the best performance is produced by the 8 year-old children in the experimental condition with visual feedback, followed by the 5 year-olds. The 7 year-old children present the greatest error in their reproduction of the models. However, if one considers the *regularity* of the differences in movement amplitude - i.e. the regularity of the seriation per se -, the 7 year-old children present the best performances in the experimental condition in which visual feedback is unavailable. They tend to keep the difference between successive circles almost invariant, as in the template. It is also at this age that the circles are restituted most regularly with respect to their curvature.

If we now look at the isochrony principle, it can be seen from Figure 3 that at all ages and in both experimental conditions a linear correlation exists between perimeter and duration. The slope of the regression, however,

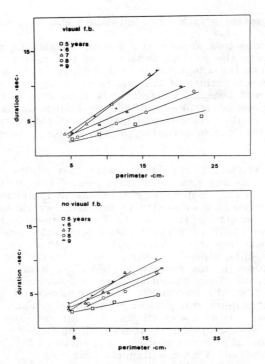

Fig. 3. Relation (regression) between perimeter and duration.

varies with age. When the slope is shallow, as at 5 years, the velocity
compensation – the isochrony – is quite good. At 6 and 7 years, the slope
is much steeper: duration increases almost linearly with the perimeter. At
these ages, isochrony is practically absent: the subjects move their hand at
a relatively constant and low velocity. At 8 and 9 years of age, isochrony
tends to reappear. Let us note finally that similar results can be obtained
in a circle cutting situation (Corbetta & Mounoud, 1985).

The ease with which such a figure as a circle for example can be
produced under different biomechanical conditions is well-known. This fact
is often advanced as evidence that the motor programs or engrams underlying
the movements are to be considered as abstract. In this context, it is
interesting to note that the performance of the 5 year-old children in the
circle seriation clearly shows the existence of such an abstract representation
of the movement, allowing the subject to control, in particular, the temporal
aspects of the movements. The representation of the 6 to 7 year-old children
differs from the previous one in that it allows the control of the spatial
aspects of the seriation movements via a constant velocity strategy.

The age-related evolution of behaviours in the situation of motor
seriation we have studied is very close to that Hay obtained in several of
her experiments (1978, 1979, 1984), particularly in a manual pointing task
without visual feedback. While children of 5 years present rapid and direct
pointing movements, with a very low error, children of 6 and 7 years
demonstrate slow and discontinuous movements with high error rates (under-

shoots). Error decreases afterwards, between 8 and 11 years of age.

The modifications that appear with age in the development of motor skills seem to concern the control modalities of the movements. These modifications increase the adaptation of the actions to the various characteristics and constraints of the environment. In the object-lifting task, for example, the child becomes progressively more able to adjust the acceleration and deceleration phases of his movements accurately. In the data Hay presents in this volume, she insists on the fact that 7 year-old children try to master the interruption of the action (a particular phase of their movements).

Jeannerod (1984, and this volume) claims that adults are able to plan the transport and grasping phases of their manual prehensile behaviours in a fully organised and anticipatory way. Prehension is organised as a whole by means of representations or abstract schemas, which Jeannerod calls "visual maps" and "proprioceptive maps". The movement can therefore be successfully produced with or without visual feedback. Isochrony appears to be one of the most important characteristics of these organisation: Jeannerod's experimental subjects compensate the amplitude variations of the movement by variations of the movements' velocity. Such a compensation results, in our opinion, from an anticipatory processing of the characteristics of the situation and of the movement. However, at certain stages of ontogenetic development, the transport and grasping phases of prehensile movements are not coordinated. During these stages, one can consider that the child is actively processing the spatial, temporal, cinematic, etc.., information relative to his action and to the situation (Mounoud, 1983, in press; Mounoud & Vinter, 1981; Mounoud, Vinter & Hauert, 1985).

3. RELATIONSHIPS BETWEEN COGNITIVE AND MOTOR SKILLS

We have tried, in this survey, to show the synchrony of the stages characterising the development of a set of cognitive and motor skills, and the similarity between the problems the child has to solve to master these skills. In our theoretical perspective, this synchrony and this similarity are evidence of a common underlying process, consisting of the *ability to establish relationships between the different properties of the objects (or situations) and actions*. These relationships can be established, partially or wholly, before the onset of the movement and, in this case, we speak of a *beforehand planification* (anticipatory planning) of action by means of central abstract representations (feedforward). But, these relationships can also be built up during the movement. In this case, we can speak of *adjustments* via retroactive loops, combined with a partial planning of the movement. These two modes of functioning tend to confirm the proposition we made at the beginning of this chapter: "we act by means of our knowledge (beforehand planification or anticipatory planning) and we know by means of our actions, by means of what we experience through our actions (empirical adjustments)". However, it is important to consider that these planning abilities depend to a critical degree on developmental and learning processes. In this sense, it is no longer possible to distinguish between different kinds of abilities. There is a general *Cognitive Ability* underlying all types of behavioural abilities. It can be considered the equivalent of Weiner's "skilled actions", considered as processes underlying local knowledge. However, we would like to emphasise that new knowledge does not simply consist of sampling information from the environment: it involves the *adjustment* of this information to previously existing schemas. In all cases, it is the initial knowledge which allows the planning of action, followed or not by adjustments. We have seen that such a process concerns both so-called cognitive and motor skills, and their acquisition.

The question now is: do motor skills necessitate less "skilled actions", less general processing abilities than cognitive skills? Our answer is no. The objection could be raised that we have chosen, for our demonstration, motor skills which particularly need cognitive activities to be performed. But, do motor activities exist - such as professional, musical or sporting activities - which do not involve mediation by cognitive activities? Let us take as an example the highly-regulated run-up in long jumping (Laurent, 1981; Lee, Lishman & Thomson, 1982). The strides can be considered as seriated backwards from the last one. As in a cognitive task such as the seriation, it is always necessary for the subject to master some parameters of his/her action (amplitudes, durations, etc...) in an orderly manner, in correlation with the increase or decrease of certain dimensions of the situation involved.

In this connection, we would like to stress again the unconscious nature of these activities. At the beginning of this chapter, we clearly rejected the equation "cognitive activities=conscious activities". The human subject is unconscious of a very large part of the internal processing that is involved in all his/her cognitive, motor and affective behaviours.

An other objection could be that, when a behaviour becomes a skill, cognitive activities are no longer necessary. In other words, cognitive activities play a role only during the acquisition phases of a skill. Once the skill is acquired, the behaviour becomes irreflective. This question - the automatisation of behaviours - is one of the greatest challenges put to contemporary psychology. It should be remarked in this connection that, if it is usual to speak of a irreflective behaviour in the case of a skill, it is curiously unusual to speak in terms of thoughtful behaviour during the acquisition phases of a skill. Authors say then that the behaviour is actively controlled or corrected. However, it remains evident that when a behaviour is being acquired, it is slow and awkward, and that a fully-achieved behaviour is rapid and elegant.

Now, for years, psychologists have associated the time of response to the complexity of the processing involved. It is clear that in such a perspective, a sports' champion or a musical virtuoso is a irreflective person. Psychologists have imperatively to change some of their points of view if they wish to avoid being qualified as ...mindless.

Motor development and cognitive development have been considered during this century as based mainly on the capacity to coordinate elementary behaviours called sub-routines or elementary and partial representations in a broader organisation (see Bernstein, Piaget & Bruner). These coordination or chunking operations involve mainly a gain of time and memory, and they can be considered as being at the root of the automatisation of behaviours. Such automatisation does not reduce the importance of the computations the subject has to do but makes them simpler and faster. In this sense, "thought" increases rather than decreases. Without underestimating the importance of this mechanism, we have personally placed the accent, in our works, on the complementary process of dissociation and segmentation of complex, highly organised behaviours into elementary behaviours. Indeed, this process is

386

often neglected by theories of development.

ACKNOWLEDGEMENTS

We would like to thank warmly Daniella Corbetta, Claude-Alain Hauert, Marie-Paule Michiels, Annie Vinter-Cioni, Paolo Viviani, Angela Wells-Cornu and Pier-Giorgio Zanone for their help and Mary Smyth and Michael Wade for their comments and reactions during the Maastricht Conference.

387

References

Arbib, M.A. (1980). Perceptual structures and distributed motor control. In V.B. Brooks (Ed.), *Handbook of Physiology (vol. III): Motor Control.* Bethesda, Maryland: The American Physiological Society.

Bartlett, F.C. (1958). *Thinking.* New York: Basic Books.

Beilin, H. (1983). The new functionalism and Piaget's program. In E. Scholnick (Ed.), *New trends in conceptual representation: Challenges to Piaget's theory?* Hillsdale: Erlbaum.

Bideaud, J. (1979). Etude génétique de la quantification en situation d'emboitements concrets. *Enfance, 2,* 133-148.

Binet, A. & Courtier, J. (1893). Sur la vitesse des mouvements graphiques. *Revue Philosophique, 35,* 664-671.

Boysson-Bardies, B. de & O'Regan, K. (1973). What children do in spite of adults' hypotheses. *Nature, 246,* 531-534.

Breslow, L. (1981). Reevaluation of the literature on the development of transitive inferences. *Psychological Bulletin, 89,* 325-351.

Breslow, L., Pastuszek, M., Nosbush, L. & Oakes, L. Structure and process in logical development: transitive inferences. Monograph. In press.

Brooks, V.B., Cooke, J.D. & Thomas, J.S. (1973). The continuity of movements. In R.B. Stein, K.G. Pearson, R.S. Smith and J.B. Redford (Eds.), *Control of posture and locomotion (Vol. 7).* New York: Plenum Press.

Bryant, P.E. & Trabasso, T.R. (1971). Transitive inferences and memory in young children. *Nature, 232,* 456-458.

Bullinger, A. (1973). *Comparaison, mesure et transitivité.* Genève: Editions Médecine et Hygiène.

Carbonnel, S. (1978). Classes collectives et classes logiques dans la pensée naturelle. *Archives de Psychologie, 177,* 1-19.

Case, R. (1985). *Intellectual development: Birth to adulthood.* New York: Academic Press.

Corbetta, D. & Mounoud, P. (1985). Circles cutting out in 6 to 10 year-old children: motor planification and bimanual coordination. *Cahiers de Psychologie Cognitive, 5,* 297. (Abstract Poster Presentation, Eighth Biennial Meeting of the ISSBD).

Denney, N.W. (1972a). A developmental study of free classification in children. *Child Development, 43,* 221-232.

Denney, N.W. (1972b). Free classification in preschool children. *Child Development, 43,* 1161-1170.

Fischer, K.W. (1980). A theory of cognitive development: the control and construction of hierarchies of skills. *Psychological Review, 87,* 477-531.

Fischer, K.W. & Roberts, R.J. (1980). A developmental sequence of classification skills in preschool children. Unpublished manuscript. University of Denver.

Gachoud, J.P. (1983). *Acquisition d'une habileté motrice chez l'enfant de 6 à 9 ans: étude cinématique et électromyographique.* Genève: Imprimerie Nationale.

Gachoud, J.P., Mounoud, P., Hauert, C.A. & Viviani, P. (1983). Motor strategies in lifting movements: a comparison of adult and children performances. *Journal of Motor Behavior, 15(3),* 202-216.

Gelman, R. & Baillargeon, R. (1983). A review of some Piagetian concepts. In J.H. Flavell and E. Markman (Eds.), *Cognitive development.* Vol. 3 of P. Mussen (Ed.), *Carmichael's manual of child psychology.* New York: Wiley.

Gelman, R. & Gallistel, C.R. (1978). *The child's understanding of number.* Cambridge: Harvard University Press.

Gilliéron, C. (1976). Le rôle de la situation et de l'objet expérimental dans l'interprétation des conduites logiques. Les décalages et la sériation. *Archives de Psychologie, 44,* 1-152 (Monogr. 3).

Greenfield, P.M., Nelson, K. & Saltzman, E. (1972). The development of rulebound strategies for manipulating seriated cups: a parallel between action and grammar. *Cognitive Psychology, 3,* 291-310.

Halford, G.S. & Kelly, M.E. (1984). On the basis of early transitivity judgments. *Journal of Experimental Child Psychology, 38,* 42-63.

Harris, P.L. & Bassett, E. (1975). Transitive inferences by 4-year-old-children? *Developmental Psychology, 11,* 875-876.

Hauert, C.A. (1980). Propriétés des objets et propriétés des actions chez l'enfant de 2 à 5 ans. *Archives de Psychologie, 185(48),* 95-169.

Hauert, C.A., Mounoud, P., Mayer, E. & Erkohen, M. (1980). Programmation des activités de soulèvement d'objets chez l'enfant de 2 à 5 ans. In J. Requin (Ed.), *Anticipation et comportement.* Paris: Editions du C.N.R.S.

Hauert, C.A., Mounoud, P. & Mayer, E. (1981). Approche du développement cognitif de l'enfant de 2 à 5 ans à travers l'étude des caractéristiques physiques de son action. *Cahiers de Psychologie Cognitive, 1,* 33-54.

Hay, L. (1978). Accuracy of children on an open-loop pointing task. *Perceptual and Motor Skills, 47,* 1079-1082.

Hay, L. (1979). Spatio-temporal analysis of movements in children: motor programs versus feedback in the development of reaching. *Journal of Motor Behavior, 11(3),* 189-200.

Hay, L. (1984). Discontinuity in the development of motor control in children. In W. Prinz and A.F. Sanders (Eds.), *Cognition and motor processes.* Berlin: Springer-Verlag.

Inhelder, B. & Piaget, J. (1964). *The early growth of logic in the child.* New York: Norton (Original French version: 1959).

Jeannerod, M. (1984). The timing of natural prehension movements. *Journal of Motor Behavior, 16(3),* 235-254.

Koslovski, B. (1980). Quantitative and qualitative changes in the development of seriation. *Merrill-Palmer Quarterly, 26(4),* 391-405.

Langer, J. (1980). *The origins of logic: Six to twelve months.* New York: Academic Press.

Laurent, M. (1981). Problèmes posés par l'étude du pointage locomoteur d'une cible visuelle. *Cahiers de Psychologie Cognitive, 2,* 173-197.

Lautrey, J., Ribaupierre, A. de & Rieben, L. (1981). Le développement opératoire peut-il pendre des formes différentes chez des enfants différents? *Journal de Psychologie, 4,* 421-443.

Lee, D.N., Lishman, J.R. & Thomson, J.A. (1982). Regulation of gait in long jumping. *Journal of Experimental Psychology: Human Perception and Performance, 8(3),* 448-459.

Mandler, J.M. (1983). Representation. In J.H. Flavell and E. Markman (Eds.), *Cognitive development.* Vol. 3 of P. Mussen (Ed.), *Carmichael's manual of child psychology.* New York: Wiley.

Markman, E.M. (1973). Facilitation of part-whole comparisons by use of the collective noun "family". *Child Development, 44,* 837-840.

Markman, E.M. (1978). Empirical versus logical solutions to part-whole comparison problems concerning classes and collections. *Child Development, 49,* 168-177.

Markman, E.M. & Siebert, J. (1976). Classes and collections. Internal organization and resulting holistic properties. *Cognitive Psychology, 8,* 561-577.

Markman, E.M., Horton, M.S. & McLanahan, A.G. (1980). Classes and collections: principles of organization in the learning of hierarchical relations. *Cognition, 8,* 227-241.

Meyer, E. (1940). Comprehension of spatial relations in preschool children. *The Journal of Genetic Psychology, 57,* 119-151.

Montangero, J. (1980). The various aspects of horizontal decalage. *Archives de Psychologie, 48,* 259-282.

Mounoud, P. (1970). *Structuration de l'instrument chez l'enfant.* Neuchâtel & Paris: Delachaux & Niestlé.

Mounoud, P. (1973). Les conservations physiques chez le bébé. *Bulletin de Psychologie, 312(13-14),* 722-728.

Mounoud, P. (1974). La construction de l'objet par le bébé. *Bulletin d'Audiophonologie, 4,* 419-438.

Mounoud, P. (1976). Les révolutions psychologiques de l'enfant. *Archives de Psychologie, 171,* 103-114.

Mounoud, P. (1981). Cognitive development: Construction of new structures or construction of internal organizations. In I.E. Sigel, D.M. Brodzinsky and R.M. Golinkoff (Eds.), *New directions in piagetian theory and practice.* Hillsdale, N.J.: Lawrence Erlbaum.

Mounoud, P. (1983). L'évolution des conduites de préhension comme illustration d'un modèle du développement. In S. de Schoenen (Ed.), *Les débuts du développement.* Paris: P.U.F.

Mounoud, P. (1985). Similarities between developmental sequences at different age periods. In I. Levin (Ed.), *Stage and structure.* Norwood: Ablex.

Mounoud, P. L'utilisation du milieu et du corps propre par le bébé. In J. Piaget, P. Mounoud and J.P. Bronckart (Eds.), *La Psychologie.* Encyclopédie de la Pléiade, Paris: Gallimard (in press).

Mounoud, P. & Bower, T.G.R. (1974). Conservation of weight in infants. *Cognition, 3(1),* 29-40.

Mounoud, P. & Hauert, C.A. (1982). Development of sensori-motor organization in young children: grasping and lifting objects. In G. Forman (Ed.), *Action and thought: From sensori-motor schemes to symbolic operations.* New York: Academic Press.

Mounoud, P. & Vinter, A. (1981). Representation and sensori-motor development. In G. Butterworth (Ed.), *Infancy and Epistemology: An evaluation of Piaget's theory.* Brighton: The Harvester Press.

Mounoud, P., Vinter, A. & Hauert, C.A. (1985). Activités manuelles et développement cognitif. In P.M. Baudonnière (Ed.), *Etudier l'enfant de la naissance à 3 ans.* Paris: C.N.R.S., Collection Comportements.

Piaget, J. (1946). *Le développement de la notion de temps chez l'enfant.* Paris: P.U.F.

Piaget, J. & Inhelder, B. (1974). *The child's construction of quantities.* London: Routledge & Kegan Paul (Original French version: 1941).

Piaget, J. & Szeminska, A. (1952). *The child's conception of number.* London: Routledge & Kegan Paul (Original French version: 1941).

Pick, H.L. (1984). Cognition and action in development: a tutorial discussion. In W. Prinz and A.F. Sanders (Eds.), *Cognition and motor processes.* Berlin: Springer-Verlag.

Prinz, W. & Sanders, A.F. (1984). *Cognition and motor processes.* Berlin: Springer-Verlag.

Retschitzki, J. (1978). L'évolution des procédures de sériations. *Archives de Psychologie, 46,* Monographie 5.

Retschitzki, J. (1982). Vers l'explication de la variabilité des stratégies de sériation. *Cahiers de Psychologie Cognitive, 2(1),* 3-17.

Ribaupierre, A. de, Rieben, L. & Lautrey, J. (1985). Horizontal decalages and individual differences in the development of concrete operations. In V.L. Shulman, L.C. Restaino-Baumann and L. Butler (Eds.), *The future of piagetian theory. The Neo-Piagetians.* New York: Plenum Press.

Rieben, L., Ribaupierre, A. de & Lautrey, J. (1983). *Le développement opératoire de l'enfant entre 6 et 12 ans.* Paris: Editions du C.N.R.S.

Riley, C.A. & Trabasso, T.R. (1974). Comparatives, logical structures and encoding in a transitive inference task. *Journal of Experimental Child Psychology, 17,* 187-203.

Rosch, E., Mervis, C.B., Gray, W.D., Johnson, D.M. & Boyes-Braem, P. (1976). Basic objects in natural categories. *Cognitive Psychology, 8,* 382-439.

Scholnick, E.K. (1983). *New trends in conceptual representation: Challenges to Piaget's theory?* Hillsdale: Erlbaum.

Shaw, R. & Bransford, J. (1977). *Perceiving, acting and knowing. Toward an ecological psychology.* Hillsdale: Erlbaum.

Smith, C.L. (1979). Children's understanding of natural language hierarchies. *Journal of Experimental Child Psychology, 27,* 437-458.

Smith, L.B. (1984). Young children's understanding of attributes and dimensions: a comparison of conceptual and linguistic measures. *Child Development, 55,* 363-380.

Sugarman, S. (1979). Product and process in the evaluation of early pre-school intelligence. *The Quaterly Newsletter of the Laboratory of Comparative Human Cognition, 1,* 17-22.

Sugarman, S. (1981). The cognitive basis of classification in very young children: an analysis of object-ordering trends. *Child Development, 52,* 1172-1178.

Sugarman, S. (1983). *Children's early thought. Developments in classification.* Cambridge: Cambridge University Press.

Thornton, S. (1982). Challenging "early competence": a process oriented analysis of children's classifying. *Cognitive Science, 6,* 77-100.

Trabasso, T.R. (1975). Representation, memory and reasoning: how do we make transitive inferences? In A.D. Pick (Ed.), *Minnesota Symposia on child psychology.* (Vol. 9). Minneapolis: University of Minnesota Press.

Trabasso, T.R. (1977). The role of memory as a system in making transitive inferences. In V. Kail and J.W. Hagen (Eds.), *Perspectives on the development of memory and cognition.* New York: Halsted.

Trevarthen, C. (1984). Biodynamic structures, cognitive correlates of motive sets and the development of motive in infants. In W. Prinz and A.F. Sanders (Eds.), *Cognition and motor processes.* Berlin: Springer-Verlag.

Viviani, P. & Terzuolo, C. (1982). The organization of movement in hand-writing and typing. In G. Butterworth (Ed.), *Language production (Vol. 2): Production of language in non-speech modalities.* London: Academic Press.

Weimer, W.B. (1977). A conceptual framework for cognitive psychology: motor theories of the mind. In R. Shaw and J. Bransford (Eds.), *Perceiving, acting and knowing.* Hillsdale: Erlbaum.

Winer, G.A. (1980). Class-inclusion reasoning in children: a review of the empirical literature. *Child Development, 51,* 309-328.

RELATING COGNITION AND ACTION: REACTION TO MOUNOUD

Mary M. Smyth

To respond to a paper on "Cognition and Action" implies some understanding of the nature of action, the nature of cognition and the relationship
between the two. I have some difficulties with both terms, and I have
considerable anxiety about their relationship. What I hope to do in this
reaction is to make a few comments on the terms 'action' and 'cognition' and
then raise some questions about the relationship. I have no answers.

If we say, as von Hofsten did in his presentation, that action is
concerned with intentions and ends, not with movements themselves, what
do we study? In most cases we study movement. We are not interested in why
the child reaches for the toy, but only in how does it do it. We ask if the
hand is open throughout the movement or if there is a swipe, and so on. A
theory of action starts with ends but studies movements and seems to be
very different from what many psychologists would think of as a psychology
of human action.

In comparing a psychology of human action with a psychology of human
behaviour, Harre and Secord (1972) argue that action has significance and
meaning and occurs in a social context, so that there is no way of reducing
action to movement. They compare these two versions of the same event:
a) Her arm moved rapidly forward and made contact with his face.
b) She slapped him angrily.
The behavioural description does seem to remove some of the social meaning.
We might elaborate (a) into an account of the perceptual information specifying
the distance from his face, a kinematic description of her arm trajectory, the
force of the slap, the position of her fingers during the transport phase, but
we would still be describing the movement, not the action. The fact that she
could have moved her arm in many different ways in order to slap his face
does not justify the study of movement as the study of action.

The kind of action theorists who are concerned with intentions and
meanings are more interested in motive than mechanism (Harre, Clarke & de
Carlo, 1985) that is, in the study of the why, rather than the how. This
would probably mean recognising that getting course credit for participation
in an experiment is what the *person* we are studying is doing, even if the
subject is moving her/his forearm about the elbow. This digression is not
intended to be critical of our use of the term action, but to remind us that
having a definition of a term does not mean that we use that term in
accordance with the definition.

Action is not the only term which has different meanings in different
research areas. 'Cognition' can mean the content of beliefs as well as the
processes by which people make sense of their world. However, in motor

control cognition seems to be equated with a rather slow serial serious minded kind of information processing. When we can show that we don't use such information processing then we can throw away cognition, or can we? Try this problem.

In Figure 1 there are 4 cards, each of which has a number on one side and a letter on the other. Here is a rule about these cards: If there is an A on one side of the card then there is a 3 on the other. Now, which of the cards would you turn over in order to verify the rule?

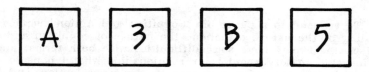

Figure 1. The four card selection task.

Most people pick A, some also go for 3, occasionally even the 5 gets picked. A slightly easier version of the same problem is in Figure 2. This time the cards represent people in a bar, each of whom has a drink and an age. The rule this time is: If a person is drinking beer then that person is over 21. Now, what would you turn over to verify the rule?

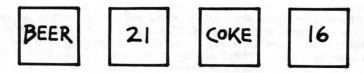

Figure 2. A realistic selection task.

This time it is fairly clear that the person with a beer should be looked at and so should the person who is 16, the person who is 21 and the person drinking coke are irrelevant - anybody can drink coke, and a person over 21 can drink anything. This problem is easier than the first one, yet it is the same problem, and the correct answer to the first problem is that the A card must have a 3 on the other side and the 5 card must NOT have an A on the other side, so you would turn over those two. The 3 and the B are irrelevant because there is nothing in the rule which says anything about what should be on the other side of 3s or Bs.

Most people would agree that when you do these problems you do cognition -whatever it is. That is, we can label some kinds of activity as cognitive and get a high agreement about them. Thinking and reasoning - solving problems in your head - is cognitive. But if we take the beer and age problem, do you know how you did it? Did the answer 'just appear' or did you have to construct it slowly? You can explain why it is correct, but you may find you could do this and not the A/3 version, partly because you know already that 16 year olds should not drink beer in bars (at least in the

U.K. and North America) and this knowledge allows you to choose the correct response (Griggs & Cox, 1982). When the content has no meaning for you errors occur. These suggest that many adults cannot apply the logical rule which says that when p implies q (if p then q), then the absence of q means the absence of p (-q, therefore -p) (Wason, 1968). A great deal of work on the way in which people solve such problems suggests that there is more to thinking and reasoning than the automatic application of logical rules and that logics may not be very useful for explaining how human thought processes work.

Piaget was very influential in the growth of logicism in psychology. The developing child constructs logical thought by internalising actions and reflecting on them. What is eventually to be explained is knowledge which has necessity, like logic or mathematics. "Reasoning is nothing more than the propositional calculus itself" say Inhelder and Piaget (1958, p. 305). This is not the place to discuss the nature of objectivity as a social concept and scientific thought, logic or mathematics as particular rationalities rather than the only rationality. However, it is perhaps appropriate to point out that in the psychology of adult human reasoning there is a continuing debate over whether the role of logic is as a tool for the analysis of knowledge, not for reasoning by intelligent agents. There is increasing evidence that an account of human reasoning must take account of fallacious inferences, the relation of content to form, and the role of extra-logical heuristics in the production of inferences (Johnson-Laird, 1983).

One of the reasons for giving the four card task at the beginning of this paper was to get some consensus that what is going on is cognition. A second is to ask, in a spirit of mischief, whether one version of the task is more 'ecological' than the other. It should be clear that the realistic version with beer and ages, allows subjects to perform very well while the abstract version does not. We might even say that the beer-age version demonstrates abilities which the abstract version somehow masks. That is, most people can solve the problem when the appropriate operations are cued from experience, but cannot access those operations otherwise. BUT, the difference in performance has to be explained, and if part of the goal of explanation is to account for how people come to be able to do tasks which are free of normal content, whether in reasoning or in target acquisition, then the difference may even be more informative than the 'ecological' situation alone. We should at least be asking ourselves "What is ecological for an organism that plays games?"

A third, and less mischevious reason for presenting the four card task, is to demonstrate that cognition does not have to mean 'effort', 'conscious-ness', 'explicit' or any of the other words which seem to get attached to 'cognitive' processes in motor learning. How do you know that you should turn over the card with 16 on it? Did you construct the answer or did it pop up? Indeed, how did you know what the problem was about? Did you have to concentrate to read the words, to comprehend the task and provide the solution? Implicit and explicit inferences are both necessary for thinking (Johnson-Laird, 1983), and reading can be as automatic as any well learned motor skill (LaBerge & Samuels, 1974). Cognition is not to be equated with effortful and in cognitive development changes do not occur because the child becomes *aware* of knowing that objects can continue to exist even if out of sight or that number remains the same even if the array is lengthened. Indeed, "much the greater part of human information processing is undoubtedly unconscious" (Allport, 1980, p. 48), and even more dogmatically "practically all psychologically interesting cognitive states are unconscious" (Fodor, 1983, p. 86). Questions about how we acquire knowledge which we cannot report are not special to motor learning, they are central to most of cognition.

Conceptual knowledge and practical knowledge

For Piaget in 1947 "The structures of intelligence have to be entirely rebuilt before they can be completed – knowing how to reverse an object does not imply that one can represent a series of rotations in thought" (p. 122), that is, there is a large distinction between sensori-motor and conceptual knowledge. In 1974 he recognises that after the sensori-motor period practical intelligence – solving problems by doing – coexists with conceptual intelligence, but nevertheless, they are separate and conceptualisation derives its elements from actions "as a result of cognizance". The representations which develop after the sensori-motor period are not representations as commonly used in information processing cognition, they are knowledge structures which serve abstract thought and so allow us NOT to act. First logic is in action (I have already commented on the importance of logic for Piaget), then it is somewhere else.

In this view of the relation of action and knowledge we are talking about action, not about movements. The schemes of the sensori-motor period are structural in that they are not specific to particular situations or objects (a sucking scheme, or a grasping scheme). These schemes are important as fore runners of concepts rather than as plans for movement. However, for the developing child acquiring knowledge by acting in a world of objects and people a great many different kinds of knowledge are developing. Some of these have their origins in early patterns of activity, and some of them do not. By interacting with the world we come to know about the nature of that world and how to act in it as well as how to think about it. Is the distinction between conceptual knowledge and practical or action knowledge a correct one?

Mounoud argues that it is not. The developing child is constructing not structures but representations or internal organisations of contents. Reflective abstraction is a process of construction of representations not of the construction of logical structures. Action schemes are not independent of content. The term representation is how being used differently. "A representation is a realisation by way of a code of a translation of objects and their properties" (Mounoud & Hauert, 1982). Several types of code arise during development and a new code leads to new representations. Action procedures or schemes exist in the infant at birth, but new procedures are worked out during development on the basis of new representations. The action program which allows the child to interact with objects is produced from representations of the object's physical characteristics (size, weight, etc.) and from the action itself in terms of exteroceptive and proprioceptive information. If the representation is incomplete then the program will not be correctly adjusted and will require correction. The action is to be seen as controlled by representation in anticipation and as part of the construction of new representations.

Representations as contents not structures are fairly common in information processing psychology. Palmer (1978) has identified visual codes, verbal codes, spatial codes, physical codes, name codes, image codes, analog representations, digital representations, propositional representations, first order isomorphs, second order isomorphs, multi dimensional spaces, templates, features, structural descriptions, relational networks, multi-component vectors, and even holograms, as kinds of things in the head. It is only when we try to be fairly specific that we find people turning to formal schemes with rules for operating them and content as a higher level description of them (Marr, 1982). However, even if representation is used to mean what people want it to mean, there is considerable agreement that there is persistence over time of something which is known.

Earlier, I used a reasoning task to get some agreement on what can be called cognitive. We can use tasks involving movement to try to get similar agreement. Van Wieringen did just this in his presentation when he described a child trying hard to learn positions in ballet. This gives us a good example of someone guiding the search for the optimal configuration of body parts, but nevertheless involving knowledge structures which we can call representations. Perhaps it is the arbitrariness of the pattern and its position within a cultural framework which allows us to accept that cognition is involved. The example of teaching a child handwriting has some of the same effect. Many of us will probably agree that dealing with the shape to be produced, the organisation of the strokes, the general process of copying, imitating and understanding, require processes which are cognitive. The use of these examples allows us to avoid definitions to get some consensus on the involvement of cognition, but it does, of course, break down if pushed too far. The tasks which Mounoud has used, like lifting weights and drawing circles, probably do push too far for some. You don't need cognition to lift an object, or do you?

While, we may be reasonably happy with culturally determined activities, such as dancing or writing, involving cognition, we may feel that babies lift objects, gorillas lift objects, lobsters probably even lift objects. Gorillas may have some cognition, but lobsters? Does this mean that we have to separate off the developing child's ability to lift things from its other abilities? Even if we agree that development in many domains goes through periods of stability and instability, and that we can characterise these as changes in the use of an organisation which allows another organisation to develop, we may still have to argue that some such changes are cognitive and others are not. The child's motor control, conceptualisation, language abilities and interaction with others are all changing. If gorillas don't have the same conceptual, social and linguistic development do we take the child's lifting of objects as being more like the gorilla's or more like the other activities in the child itself? This is the first of the questions about the relationship between cognition and action.

Mounoud's work places the development of lifting firmly within the context of conceptual development as whole. The chief argument for this is that around 6 to 7 years old performance in many activities deteriorates on some measures and does not completely recover until about the age of nine. (If correct seriation of weight occurs at a particular period, then the ability to seriate is presupposed by the ability to lift objects accurately). In other work Mounoud has compared motor tasks with other cognitive tasks such as the ability to segment speech into phonemes. At 4 and 5 years old children can tap out the number of syllables in a word, but they can not break it into smaller units. This ability is around age 6 and is accelerated by learning to read. Adult illiterates can segment speech into phonemes about as well as 6 year olds with 3 months schooling. The capacity to consider language as an object and break it into parts may be dependent on the development of literacy, but it is also dependent on a general ability to relate wholes to parts. Literacy does not cause the segmentation but depends upon it. Mounoud argues that we are seeing here the development of a new organisation of action. If we than relate it to other changes such as those in circle drawing in which 5 and 9 year olds are not powerfully controlled by vision, while 7 year olds are, then can we create a general developmental mechanism which is coming into play in many domains, probably at slightly different times depending on whether other aspects of a domain limit its expression.

Clearly, there are major developmental issues which relate to the way in which the infant's early experience of action and perception leads to both adult action and adult knowledge of objects, of one's own body, and of logical relations. Given that the infant is much more capable at birth than Piaget supposed, the relation between perception and action has to be understood in a different way (Butterworth, von Hofsten, this conference). However, it is not clear what the relation is between general cognition and movement, even within the framework which Mounoud proposes. In earlier work, (Mounoud, 1985) it is suggested that the child up to two years uses representations which are basically perceptual, from 2 to 10 years representations are conceptual, and at 10 plus representations are formal or semiotic. Within such a post Piagetian framework it still seems that what is developing is formal knowledge and it is still possible to ask what kind of a representation, or what kind of knowledge, is used to reach for an object. If action in the world provides knowledge both of the world and of how to act in it, what is the difference between these two, and how do the differences arise? If you can think about an object, say you can solve a problem using its physical characteristics, but you don't have to touch it in order to come to the answer, is the knowledge you use in thought the same as that you use when you pick up the object? That is, is knowledge for lifting available for other purposes or not? This is the second of the questions about the relationship between cognition and actions, and to consider it we need to look more closely at proposals which suggest that it is possible to use information in one, and only one, system.

Modules for actions

Jeannerod (1981) has described visuo-motor sub systems which link the size or spatial position of an object with the correct pattern of grasp or with distance transported. It is possible that such a visuo-motor 'organ' would not share information with any other system or with knowledge in general and so we could argue that reaching for an object did not involve general cognition. Such a system would be encapsulated, or modularised in the way proposed by Fodor (1983), and indeed, Marshall (1984) has suggested that Jeannerod's visuo-motor organ is a module of the cognitive system in exactly this way. But does this help us to understand the place of information about the weight of objects? To do this we have to consider what modules might be.

Modularity has been a popular term in many areas for the last few years. The idea is based on the view that an extremely complex information processing system is unlikely to be designed in such a way that a small change in one place has consequences in many other places (Marr, 1982). The sub division of human information processing into components or modules is widespread but there are many different types of division. One of the strongest accounts available is that put forward by Fodor (1983) who is chiefly concerned to argue that input processes are distinct from general cognitive ones. The input processes are between transducers and central processes and they represent the world to make it accessible to thought. Central processes (which are the cognitive system proper) are isotropic and Quineian systems which cannot be encapsulated. They are isotropic because in principle any thing that is known is relevant in determining the fixation of belief – just as in scientific discovery any thing that is known may be relevant to the development of a new theory. Analogical reasoning is, for Fodor, pure isotropy. Quineian is related to isotropic, but they aren't quite the same. Two scientific theories might make the same predictions, but one is judged to be better than the other on the basis of principles like simplicity, or conservatism. These principles are derived from the global properties of belief systems, so not only can any piece of information be related to hypotheses about the current problem but in addition, acceptance of confirmation is related to the belief system as a whole. Fodor's account of scientific confirmation and discovery is "by no means untendentious" as he says himself. However, it gives one very strict account of what general cognitive processes are, and how they relate to domain specific ones.

The modules Fodor proposes are vertical ones, that is they are domain specific. (Horizontal modules are a kind of mechanism – a faculty of judgement would be the same faculty whether what was being judged was a legal question, a practical question or a moral question. That is, "a horizontal faculty is a functionally distinguishable cognitive system whose operations cross content domains" (p. 13)). Domain specificity is the first of the properties of a vertically modular system. This does not mean that they are sense specific. The early development of visual and verbal language perception (e.g. Studdert-Kennedy, 1983), reflects a language domain not a domain of sensory input.

A second characteristic of modular systems is that they are mandatory – you can't help hearing words (in a language you know) as words, even if asked to attend to the acoustic phonemic properties of the input (Marslen-Wilson & Tyler, 1981). You may however be able to avoid hearing at all. In addition, central processes have limited access to the interlevels within a module. Perceptual processing goes from bottom to top and access goes from top to bottom, so that in general, central processes have access only to the outputs of perceptual processes. Modules are also fast, associated with fixed neural architecture, have characteristic breakdown patterns and develop according to fixed endogenously determined patterns, under the impact of environmental releasers.

One of the largest claims about modules is that they are informationally encapsulated. That is, they are not able to share information. Fodor is not asking about what computational resources are or are not shared between systems, but about what access an input process has to information which is shared with other systems. It is information encapsulation which allows speed. Language processing however, does seem to present situations in which context interacts with the physical signal, that is, top-down information is available. Fodor considers that encapsulation is maintained if the high level information is regarded as module internal, although this does not deal with accounts which suggest that individual recognition units can have their thresholds lowered by central processes (e.g. Morton, 1979).

If central cognition is general but input modules are formationally encapsulated, what other kinds of modules could there be? Fodor isn't particularly bothered with output, although the example of apparent motion when the eye is pushed with a finger is used as an example of "modularity with a vengeance" (p. 67). However, using the fairly strict criteria for modularity which Fodor has put forward we can ask whether there are modular output systems, and whether there are systems which are modular but go all the way from sensory transducers to motor output. These are different questions, though they can get confused.

As Fodor is operating within a computational framework we can take a computational example of how an output system might be encapsulated, such as Hinton's (1984) work on parallel computations for controlling an arm. This is based on the need to develop computational models for motor control which are plausible for implementation of a system composed of large slow processors like neurons. The system can compute the torques necessary to follow a desired trajectory and can also compute a non-optimal trajectory using heuristic rules. However, the development of rules for producing good trajectories, or those with particular spatio-temporal forms, occurs over time and experience with reaching, which "needs to be boiled down into a set of easily applied heuristics". Knowing the correct trajectory to bowl in cricket is equivalent to using heuristics to generate a good trajectory, but the computation of the torques is left to a separate module, and the problem of how to set the length-tension characteristics of the muscles to produce the torques is also left to a separate module. A minimum amount of information is necessary via a look up memory or transferred from another part of the system. The problem of dealing with the mass of objects is one which may, however, require look up (Raibert, 1978).

Putting together the components of an action like bowling in cricket, in terms of where to pitch the ball, length, speed, swing and so on, happens before the selection of a spatio-temporal pattern. Presumably these require wide knowledge of the game of cricket. After this stage however the further computations necessary to arrive at muscle length-tension configurations are not available to the general cognitive system. That is, just as encapsulated input systems wring as much as possible from the input before presenting it to higher processes, so the output system requires only a small amount of information from higher levels and is not itself available to them. This account puts modularised output processes after central processes, but there are other suggestions for action specific systems, to which we now turn. These emphasise the perception and action links.

Fodor suggests that modules are like computationally complex reflexes, so we should expect them to have both input and output processes. Of course the more complex reflexes get the more they look like modules. We could think here of the separate encapsulated systems for perception and action in frogs (Arbib, 1981). Information for avoiding obstacles or predators has no way of affecting the system for catching prey. Catching prey is fast, virtually mandatory, and no matter how often you tell a frog that fresh dead flies are good to eat it will starve to death if they don't move in the way live flies do, so information is encapsulated. Are there aspects of human action which are like this?

Before we consider reaching and the weight of objects again, we could consider the suggestion that the balance system is a modular system of a Fodorian kind. Complex, multimodal, but encapsulated, endogenously specified, associated with fixed neural architecture, and fast. Balance is easily fooled by illusions and adapts to being at sea in such a way that knowing you are no longer at sea does not prevent a negative after effect. This does not mean that the balance system is not flexible and that posture is not affected by other tasks which are being performed (Cordo & Nashner, 1982), but that the system only has access to their consequences for posture and balance. Even when postural adjustments are dependent on the subject's response set (Marsden, Merton & Morton, 1981) this does not mean that the balance system is penetrable but that it takes input from the central processes which is used for subsequent computations. Balance is also one of the crucial components of skills which people say are never forgotten - like bicycle riding. If the rule for how not to fall off a bike is "adjust the curvature of the bicycle's path in proportion to the ratio of unbalance over the square of the speed" this is subdoxastic belief which is encapsulated within a system which does not have access to other knowledge.

Marshall (1984) suggests that walking may also be understood to be modular, largely because its development is endogenously specified and seems to require no other input than the goal of walking. How far the control of walking is cognitively penetrable, is however, a different question from how far it *is* penetrated, but it is a possibility. I have already mentioned that Jeannerod's proposal that there is a visuo motor organ for reaching could also be a module proposal in this sense. Information about the distance and size of an object could be available for use in reaching before it is available for the higher levels of the perceptual system which allows the fixation of belief. This would be a little bit like the frog, but not necessarily fast, and not mandatory.

Reaching for an object can be shown to be affected by the object's size. If reach includes lifting then the weight of the object is important too. As I have said, Mounoud's work directs us to whether the knowledge of how heavy an object is, which is used in judging how to lift it, is the same knowledge as that used to decide whether the object could be used as a pendulum in Maier's string task. That is, the knowledge which is available for thought may also be the knowledge which is available for action. How would we find out if there is one piece of information about weight or two? Runeson and Frykholm (1981), did a pilot experiment for a study on subjects' reports on their perception of the weight of objects which others were lifting. They showed that knowledge can be used to alter the way in which same-size objects of different weights are picked up. Observers judged the weights which other subjects lifted simply by watching them lift. When the lifters knew in advance what weights they would be lifting, the observers were not able to discriminate between the weights but they could discriminate when the lifters only knew the weight after they had picked up the object. The lifters were using non-visual knowledge of the weight of the objects to control the way in which they lifted. So even a comparatively simple action, like picking up a box, is probably accessible by knowledge which is not given perceptually

Skill, cognition and action

Some of the more interesting bits of human action are those which are related to the advanced status of humans as tool and language users. (Advanced does not mean superior - an organism with a tool to destroy the rest of the world and itself is not necessarily a better organism). A complex intentional organism which has culturally transmitted knowledge of a high level, both explicit and implicitly acquired, is a lot more than a co-ordinated, well balanced locomotor. Yet culturally transmitted knowledge may be used in such a way that the person who is dancing, driving a car, or simply reading a book, seems to have little need to control or intervene in the running of the activity. Surely well learned skills are modular and do not interact with the rest of the cognitive system?

This has been a popular reply to Fodor (Schwartz & Schwartz, 1984; Sternberg, 1985) in the discussion of his book, and the question of whether skill develops modules is a relevant one which we can address in several ways. As modules are associated with a fixed neural architecture, neuro-psychologists have considered whether disorders resulting from brain damage are typically associated with domains which can be modules. Language disorders occur without deficits in spatial processing or non-verbal memory, the inability to name objects can be associated with good performance on drawing of the same objects, spatial skills may be affected and language skills spared, and so on. It can even be argued that memory does not seem to be a horizontal faculty which behaves in exactly the same way no matter what is being dealt with. Retrograde amnesia spares both motor skills and language, anterograde amnesia can preserve the ability to carry out procedural tasks of many kinds (Graf, Squire & Mandler, 1984). However, not everyone agrees that a dissociation between different domains following brain damage is attributable to the destruction of a localised module (Shallice, 1984), and no one seems to want to suggest a dance module, or a cardriving module, which will be selectively affected following brain damage.

Even if learned motor skills aren't likely to be selectively affected by brain damage we can ask if there are other ways in which they are modular. Schwartz and Schwartz (1984) suggest that in driving a car, the components are domain specific, fast, mandatory and without conscious access. Abbs, Gracco and Cole (1984) also use the lack of attention required in car driving to argue for specifically motor learning in this task. I have already pointed out that there isn't any reason why central processes must be conscious. The components may be fast but they are not mandatory, and they are probably not encapsulated. The important question here is whether you can alter the activity. If you can get into a car which you know as a higher clutch point than your normal one, can you change? The fact that you don't always get it right doesn't mean that the system is cognitively impenetrable. Most learned skills, including motor skills, remain penetrable. They are better not penetrated, but they are penetrable. "A bit more of this, and a bit less of that" makes a change to the movement selected. How it continues from there may take us back to the genuine modularity of the motor output system, but in general automaticity isn't modularity.

One way to investigate the development of independent processing subsystems (whether vertical modules or not) is to look at the lack of interference in dual task studies as evidence for independent processing activity and do something else at the time, but it is not always the specifically motor nature of the skill which is relevant here. Any learned activity may be separable from any other, so, for example, it may be possible to read and write different messages simultaneously (Spelke, Hirst & Neisser, 1976). However, it is unlikely that the linguistic and semantic knowledge required to carry out one of these tasks is duplicated so that it is available separately for the two tasks. That is, the development of effective strategies for separating two kinds of input-output combination does not mean that the information used is in principle available for only one activity. In addition, because 'soft' modules can be acquired for tasks which are not primarily motor, we cannot use the independence argument to show that skilled action is different from cognition.

Perhaps an example will help to make the point that both motor and non-motor activities can be skilled. The amnesic patients mentioned earlier can learn to do motor tasks without being able to report that they have learned them, but this also applies to reading mirror reversed text and to solving the Tower of Hanoi problem, both of which involve procedural knowledge which is not specifically motor (Cohen & Squire, 1980; Graf, Squire & Mandler, 1984). In the Tower of Hanoi problem four discs of increasing in size are stacked on a stick, largest on the bottom. There are two empty sticks and the task is to move the discs one at a time on to the second of the empty sticks without ever putting a large disc on top of a smaller one. This is a problem to solve, but when it is well known it can be done quickly, without effort, either in the head or in the world. If we ask someone who has learned to solve the Tower of Hanoi to learn a sequence of movements, like a waltz step with a whisk and syncopated shuffle, how would our description of the two skilled activities differ? Both are executed by routine procedures although one is a movement task and the other a problem solving task. Perhaps we have to decide that we cannot distinguish action from cognition on the basis of the autonomous nature of skill.

Skill has become very important in cognitive psychology in the last few years (e.g. Anderson, 1985) and skilled action can contribute to the understanding of skill in general (Neisser, 1985). If we consider the three stages of skill acquisition proposed by Fitts (1964) - cognitive, associative, and autonomous - we find that they apply to skill in general and that 'cognitive' is a misnomer. We can call the early stage 'cognitive' because at the beginning of learning one thing, anything else you know may be relevant. What learning does is to exclude some aspects of the task, of the world, of the response domain, from consideration. That is, it sets up procedures which allow relevant knowledge to be used more effectively. In doing a crossword, for example, all knowledge may be relevant but the expert solver also has a whole set of heuristics for finding the correct answer. There is nothing about a general cognitive system which makes it unable to become expert. (Fodor is too pessimistic about the possibility of studying central processing, but that is another story).

Explanatory systems for cognition and action

I used Hinton's computational account of arm movements in discussing the modularity of a purely output system because it was appropriate for the computational view of overall cognition which Fodor discusses. This assumes that explanations for central cognitive and output systems should not be of different types. We can consider handwriting as an example here. Ellis (1982) described a model of the organisation of sequential output in handwriting in which successive stages transformed the initial thought or idea into a form in which it would be turned over to motor processes. Using data from the errors made in normal handwriting he suggested that sequences of abstract letter codes, or graphemes, are made more specific by the selection by the particular forms or allographs, which are appropriate for the context. Following this, a specific series of strokes is retrieved for each allograph and the output becomes suitable for transfer to a motor system. This cognitive model is mute about further levels of output processing but later work has elaborated two more response stages (Van Galen & Teulings, 1983). This approach regards the stroke pattern as a program which is not specific for particular muscle groups, or for the size of letters, or the speed at which they are produced. The final two stages are the substitution of parameters for size and scale so that speed and size are controlled, and finally, the translation into nerve impulses for specific muscle groups. When the two accounts are combined we have a coherent sequence of processes using explanations of the same type at different levels. There is no clear point at which cognition stops and motor processes start.

Is the decision about where cognition stops and motor processes start one which we should try to make? When someone becomes so skilled at writing that a continuous stream of auditory input can be converted into marks on a page with no subjective experience of effort, do we conclude that they no longer use cognitive process because the motor output is so skilled? More importantly, if we develop accounts of the control of the human body as a physical system which do not attach to accounts of the human being as a knower, we may be unable to account for the activities which are ecologically real for a language and tool using organism.

I have raised four questions about the relationship between cognition and action. They are: Are developmental processes similar across domains so that motor development cannot be studied independently of cognitive development? Is the information used for a motor activity like lifting separate from that used to solve problems concerned with weight? Is skilled motor action non-cognitive because it is modular? Do we need different explanatory systems for cognition and action? I said at the beginning that I have no answers to these, but I have subsequently argued that the answer to the third question is 'No'. For the others I can only raise the issues. I hope that I have raised some doubts about the view that cognition and action should be studied in isolation from one another. If a new theory of action is to develop it may have to produce a new theory of cognition too, otherwise it will be in danger of studying a physical system which can act but which can not know.

References

Abbs, J.H., Gracco, V.L. & Cole, K.J. (1984). Control of multimovement coordination: sensorimotor mechanisms in speech motor programming. *Journal of Motor Behaviour, 16,* 195-231.

Allport, A. (1980). Attention and performance. In G. Claxton (Ed.), *Cognitive psychology: new directions.* London: Routledge and Kegan Paul.

Anderson, J.R. (1985). *Cognitive psychology and its implications.* New York: W.H. Freeman.

Arbib, M.A. (1981). Perceptual structures and distributed motor control. In V.B. Brooks (Ed.), *Handbook of physiology - the nervous system vol. II.* Bethesda MD: American Physiological Society.

Cohen, N.J. & Corkin, S. (1980). Preserved learning and retention of pattern-analysing skill in amnesia: Dissociation of know and how and knowing that. *Science, 210,* 207-210.

Cordo, P.J. & Nashner, L.M. (1982). Properties of postural adjustments associated with rapid arm movements. *Journal of Neurophysiology, 47,* 287-302.

Ellis, A.W. (1982). Spelling and writing (and reading and speaking). In A.W. Ellis (Ed.), *Normality and pathology in cognitive functions.* London: Academic Press.

Fodor, J.A. (1983). *The modularity of mind.* Cambridge MA: MIT/Bradford Books.

Fitts, P.M. (1964). Perceptual-motor skill learning. In A.W. Melton (Ed.), *Categories of Human Learning.* New York: Academic Press.

Graf, P., Squire, L.R. & Mandler, G. (1984). The information that amnesic patients do not forget. *Journal of Experimental Psychology: Learning Memory and Cognition, 10,* 164-178.

Griggs, R.A. & Cox, J.R. (1982). The elusive thematic-materials effect in Wason's selection task. *British Journal of Psychology, 73,* 470-520.

Harre, R., Clarke, D. & De Carlo, N. (1985). *Motives and mechanisms: an introduction to the psychology of action.* London: Methuen.

Harre, R. & Secord, P.F. (1972). *The explanation of social behaviour.* Oxford: Basil Blackwell.

Hinton, G. (1984). Parallel computations for controlling an arm. *Journal of Motor Behavior, 16,* 171-194.

Inhelder, B. & Piaget, J. (1958). *The growth of logical thinking from childhood to adolescence.* London: Routledge and Kegan Paul.

Jeannerod, M. (1981). Specialised channels for cognitive responses. *Cognition, 10,* 135-137.

Johnson-Laird, P.N. (1983). *Mental models.* Cambridge: Cambridge University Press.

LaBerge, D. & Samuels, S.J. (1974). Toward a theory of automatic information processing in reading. *Cognitive Psychology, 6,* 293-323.

Marr, D. (1982). *Vision.* San Francisco: W.H. Freeman.

Marsden, C.D., Merton, P.A. & Morton, H.B. (1981). Human postural responses. *Brain, 104,* 513-534.

Marshall, J.C. (1984). Multiple perspectives on modularity. *Cognition, 17,* 209-242.

Marslen-Wilson, W. & Tyler, L. (1981). Central processes in speech understanding. *Philosophical Transactions of the Royal Society, B295,* 317-322.

Morton, J. (1979). Word recognition. In J. Morton and J.C. Marshall (Eds.), *Psycholinguistics series, vol. 2.* London: Elek.

404

Mounoud, P. (1985). Similarities between developmental sequences at different age period. In I. Levin (Ed.), *Stage and structure*. Norwood NJ: Ablex Publishing Corporation.

Mounoud, P. & Hauert, C.A. (1982). Development of sensorimotor organisation in young children: grasping and lifting objects. iN G.E. Forman (Ed.), *Actions and thought*. New York: Academic Press.

Nashner, L.M. & Cordo, P.J. (1981) . Relation of automatic postural responses and reaction-time voluntary movements of human leg muscles. *Experimental Brain Research, 43*, 395-405.

Neisser, U. (1985). The role of theory in the ecological study of memory: comment on Bruce. *Journal of Experimental Psychology: General, 114*, 272-274.

Palmer, S.F. (1978). Fundamental aspects of cognitive representation. In E.H. Rosch and B.B. Lloyd (Eds.), *Cognition and categorisation*. Hillsdale NJ: Erlbaum.

Piaget, J. (1950). *The psychology of intelligence*. London: Routledge and Kegan Paul (Originally published in French, 1947).

Piaget, J. (1976). *The grasp of consciousness*. London: Routledge and Kegan Paul (Originally published in French, 1974).

Raibert, M.H. (1978). A model for sensorimotor control and learning. *Biological Cybernetics, 29*, 29-36.

Runeson, S. & Frykholm, G. (1981). Visual perception of lifted weight. *Journal Experimental Psychology: Human Perception and Performance, 7*, 733-740.

Schwartz, M.F. & Schwartz, B. (1984). In defence of organology. *Cognitive Neuropsychology, 1*, 25-42.

Shallice, T. (1984). More functionally isolable subsystems but fewer "modules"? *Cognition, 17*, 243-252.

Spelke, E., Hirst, W. & Neisser, U. (1976). Skills of divided attention. *Cognition, 4*, 215-230.

Sternberg, R.J. (1985). Controlled versus automatic processing. *Behavioral and Brain Sciences, 8*, 32-33.

Studdert-Kennedy, M. (1983). On learning to speak. *Human Neurobiology, 2*, 191-195.

Van Galen, G.P. & Teulings, H.L. (1983). The independent monitoring of form and scale factors in handwriting. *Acta Psychologica, 54*, 9-22.

Wason, R.C. (1968). Reasoning about a rule. *Quarterly Journal of Experimental Psychology, 20*, 273-281.

COGNITION AND ACTION: A reply to Mounoud

M.G. Wade

The issues raised over the past eight days of the Institute highlight
two philosophical positions concerning problems of coordination and control.
Before I present my comments on Professor Mounoud's paper, I think a brief
reminder is in order, relative to the theoretical and philosophical positions
that drive traditional cognitivism and direct realism.

Historically, the development of what is often referred to as motor
learning has its roots in cognitive theory and has developed from the
psychological models of the forties, to the present day when it now possesses
its own theoretical paradigms built upon those earlier models. *Action systems*
are a much more contemporary view and can trace their roots back to the
ideas of the physiology of activity proposed by Nicolai Bernstein (1967) and
in the ecological psychology proposed by James Gibson (1966). Perhaps more
important than tracing the theoretical development of these two positions and
some of the constructs upon which they rest, it is important to recognise
the constructs upon which they rest, it is important to recognise the
philosophical underpinnings on which each position is predicated.

Orthodox cognition, from which traditional theories of motor learning
have their philosophical foundation, adheres strictly to the Lockean view
that the development of motor coordination is achieved through, and explained
by a special class of "things" that are inter-mediary between the world and
the organism. Locke referred to these "between things" as "ideas" and they
are seen as interfacing the organism and the environment. Contemporary
cognitive theorists addressing motor learning issues refer to these as
"representations", "programs", "reference schemas", etc., etc. Irrespective
of what they are called, they refer to some sort of device which acts as an
intermediary between the organism and the environment. Action theorists
rely on an important point of departure philosophically; namely, they have a
commitment to realism. This view eliminates the Lockean notion of "ideas" and
promotes a direct relationship between the organism and the environment.
Thus, for the realists the model construct for coordination and control is
that it is autonomous, self-organising and possesses no "between things".
The realists seek a single theory for action, and *perception is part of that
theory*.

From a philosophical perspective, the two positions have developed from
different origins. The differences in the two views may be seen not only in
their initial philosophical underpinning but also in the nature of the empirical
activity which has evolved from the two viewpoints. Traditional motor skills
research has developed its empirical activity by borrowing heavily from
traditional information processing models, or by testing ideas of closed loop
theory or the more recent schema theory of motor behaviour. All of these

usually involve the recording and evaluation of error scores based on performance of a laboratory based task and all of this encompassed in the traditional experimental design using control groups and groups who receive different levels or different degrees of some experimental treatment. The experimental activity for the ecological approach to the problems of co-ordination and control produces what Turvey and Carello (1982) have referred to as "an eccentric way of doing science". The experiments carried out are non-traditional in the sense that control groups are often unnecessary, the experiments generally do not require extensive data manipulation. The scientific activity for action systems seem to be more in line with the demonstration of styles of control, with reliance on careful observation and a level of analysis that focuses more on the descriptive topology of the activity to explain elements of control and coordination, rather than the measurement of error scores.

The work presented by Mounoud is interesting for it relies on a traditional view of cognitivism for its theoretical base. Yet, the data present topological descriptions of motor skill performance in both children and young adults. Professor Mounoud's paper focuses on perhaps one of the most inviting and potentially satisfying ideas relative to the functional activity of Homo sapiens; namely, the complementarity between cognitive activity and motor activity. Certainly such an idea is both intuitive and potentially seductive in trying to explain under one common umbrella the two major components of human activity, thinking and moving. While they are clearly sets of very different skills, Professor Mounoud has presented in the first half of his paper considerable research evidence on the developmental aspects of cognitive activity. It is therefore, an inviting idea to take the development of cognitive skills in children and present parallels in the motor domain. The research reviewed by Mounoud in the first part of his paper focuses on the levels of success that children have for classification and seriation skills. The research suggests that somewhere between the ages of 3-4 years and between the ages of 9-11 years there appear two fairly distinct levels of performance. Accounting for these differences has produced some diversity of interpretation for explaining these phenomena. Some consider that there is structural transformation between the two levels of performance and this is clearly a Piagetian explanation, whereas others tend to rely more on a structural invariance explanation with performance differences being found elsewhere. Proponents of structural invariance argue that from a very early age children have the logical competence to solve the classification and seriation tasks, but the change from one level to the other is explained in several ways. An improved ability in logical competence over time; the transformation of memory space or language capacities; and the emergence of new coding capacities, the latter explanation favoured by Mounoud (1981). Mounoud explains success at the 3-4 year level based on perceptual coding and improvements at the second level of success (9-11 years) on a conceptual coding system.

Professor Mounoud is clearly attracted, as I suspect are many of us, to this interesting area of motor development, which attempts to produce evidence that parallels in the cognitive domain exist in the motor domain. He presents two sets of data. First, some earlier work that was published in the *Journal of Motor Behavior* (Gachoud, Mounoud & Hauert and Viviani, 1983), and second some preliminary data on children's circle drawing performance. The first data set required both boys of 6-9 years and young adults to lift objects of different weight with the idea being that to accomplish the task in an optimal way subjects must be able to vary the amount of force in relation to variations in the object's weight so as to use more or less similar movements whatever the weight of the object. To quote Mounoud, "the total duration of the lifting movement will be more or less constant and more or less invariant". Just as Piaget in his earlier studies of cognitive development argued for cognitive invariance so Mounoud is attempting to parallel this with invariance in the motor domain. Mounoud alludes to principles of invariance in the motor domain. For Mounoud, this type of invariance is exemplified by the principle of isogony (e.g. Fitt's Law) for the lifting experiments and for the second data set (circle drawing) the principle of isochrony (Binet & Courtier, 1893). For the latter data, the assumption is that relative to the size of the circles to be drawn, execution time will be essentially invariant.

To define parallels in the motor domain to research already reported in the cognitive domain presents no small challenge, and Professor Mounoud should take considerable credit for pursuing this line of research. The question and task posed to this reactor is to determine the degree to which his data argues for such a proposed parallel between the motor and cognitive domains, and to make some comments relative to the experiments presented and the conclusions from these data. My role here is not to be critical for the sake of being critical, but rather to try and hone the arguments so that we might bring to bear a clearer focus on the problem under attack which, I think we all agree is both fascinating and challenging. Let us now consider Professor Mounoud's presentation from both a theoretical viewpoint and from the data, that he has presented. The questions that I pose are mostly of a methodological nature that arise from the problem of the invariance principle that appears to be a cornerstone of his presentation.

From the theoretical point of view, Mounoud's perspective is cognitive and supports a representational view that seeks a complement between what he refers to as motor invariance, and cognitive invariance or equivalence. I understand the point he is trying to make here which is perhaps a richer, conceptualisation of the world enhancing learning and performance in a variety of domains - including the motor domain. I remain, however, unconvinced that Mounoud has developed sufficiently the logic that describes the precise relationship between motor and cognitive invariants and further I am not sure the evidence he presents necessarily illustrates the invariance principle he seeks to demonstrate.

The study presented on lifting movements by Gachoud, Mounoud and Hauert and Viviani (1983) is consistent with Mounoud's quest to illustrate that differences in the kinematics (no difference) and electromyographic records (differences between children and adults) is evidence of a developing representational schemata that distinguishes cognitive elements of the activity reflected in the motor performance. Mounoud's data appear to satisfy his hypothesis that differences in the performance of children and young adults is due to a less well developed representational schemata (cognitive) of the properties of the motor system. Again, my point here is not to criticise the experiments but to raise questions which will hopefully sharpen future empirical activity.

Mounoud reports, "profound differences" between the adult subjects and the children. I think these conclusions should recognise the following reservation: The experimental protocol which demands that both adults and children (6-9 years) perform on the same apparatus under all but two of the same conditions (not 8 and 9) suggests that the task is scaled in favour of the adult performers for at least three reasons:

   (i)   Object weight as a percentage of subject's weight.
  (ii)   The relative size and muscle mass of the limbs.
(iii)   The dimension and scale of the apparatus.

     Rather than use the same weights for both sets of subjects, it might be interesting to use sets of weights for each group that are relative to the subjects body weight and skeletal and muscle mass of the involved limbs, this would ensure scalar invariance of the experimental protocol. The only safeguards Mounoud seems to have taken were to omit the two heaviest conditions for the children (8 and 9); not to include the last weight in one sequence to the first weight in the next (heaviest to lightest); reduce repetitions and duration time. These modifications suggest a recognition by Mounoud of the potentional fatigue problems that might beset the 6-9 year olds. These safeguards, however, may not have been sufficient to preclude fatigue effects and certainly the co-contraction effects exhibited in the EMG records of the children may not be so surprising. Certainly the problems of lack of scaling of the task between adults and children needs to be addressed if Mounoud is to feel confident in his conclusions.

     Mounoud's second study is relatively new and by his own recognition is preliminary. It promotes a theme noted in the kinematic data of the first study (Gachoud, Mounoud, Hauert & Viviani, 1983). Namely the principle of isochrony. Broadly defined subjects exhibit consistent velocity (temporal invariance) across the drawing of circles of different sizes. Certainly there is evidence of this in handwriting (Viviani & Terzuolo, 1982) and in the temporal characteristics of some complex movement activities (Shapiro, 1977). My comments on the circle drawing data focus on three issues.

   (i)   The robustness of the isochrony principle;
  (ii)   The nature of the instructions offered subjects;
(iii)   The role of vision in the reported experiments.

If the principle of isochrony is generalisable (a law?) then we must ask whether or not the principle holds up if the task is constrained or perhaps the boundary conditions change.

     Figure 1, Part A represents the circles the children were asked to draw in the study reported by Mounoud (this volume). Part B are my suggestions as to possible task constraints which may produce results that do not support the isochrony principle. In addition, asking subjects to use whole-arm movements (shoulder-girdle) rather than movements which are finger controlled, may produce different results.

     My second point relates to the instructions given to the subjects. What was actually said to the subjects by way of instruction is only briefly reported by Mounoud. It is possible that the information contained in the instructions may key subjects as to the kind of performance expected by the experimenter. There is evidence that instructions have an effect on the outcome of Piagetian experiments. Research by William Schiff (Schiff, 1983; Schiff & Saarni, 1976) suggest this is a potential problem. Schiff has noted that:

> Pre-operational children do not fail to conserve length
> because of misleading perceptual information or immature
> cognitive operations... it appears that linguistic immaturity

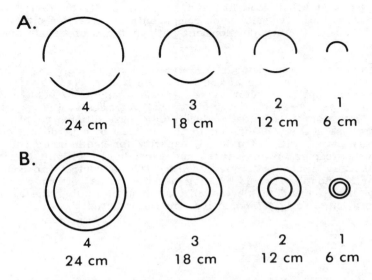

Fig. 1. Part A illustrates circles used in Mounoud's task,
(perimeters noted in centimeters). Part B are
Wade's suggested constraints to the task.

and perceptual-cognitive immaturity leads to failures to
conserve length in Piaget's verbal task (p. 1503).

Schiff has elegantly demonstrated that it is not perception that, "leads
them astray". Schiff suggests that children's length-relations words may be
initially mapped on alignment features of length conservation displays, but
mappings (Schiff's emphasis) change with age. Not to belabor the point,
suffice to say instructions may have a significant effect on children's
performance on such tasks as the one used by Mounoud. Schiff's work on
conservation of length and volume clearly show that older children interpret
instructions differently than younger children.

My third point concerns the manipulation of vision. I am unsure why
this was manipulated. In the discussion of the data, Mounoud notes that 7
year old subjects performed less well than 8 year old subjects. Yet, in the
non-vision condition, 7 year olds produced the best "regularity" in circle
drawing. What is the theoretical significance of this?

My comments are not to deny the role of cognition in motor or any other
behaviour - the challenge is to conduct experiments which reflect a theory
that seeks an important role for non-dynamic constraints that enhance
developmentally, motor skill and control. We seek the logic that links the
motor - cognitive invariance. We have heard throughout this conference
pleas from some quarters to consider a not so strict view of cognition as a
concrete representation of conceptual ideas but rather a less rigid view.
Kugler (this volume) has suggested we view a cognition made up of *properties*
rather than *propositions*, certainly a theory of motor control and coordination,
in or out of a developmental context, will require some role for cognition. The

question is what will it look like and what will be its building blocks? The integration of both dynamic motor components and complementary cognitive components need further development both in terms of theory and empirical work.

My opening remarks about the style of inquiry suggest this may not be an easy task. The style of control of the human motor system is to say the least puzzling. The motor system appears capable of behaving in a variety of ways thereby satisfying a variety of models, the majority of which seem to have their theoretical underpinning in traditional cognitivism. This can lead those seeking a solution to the problem of control and coordination down many paths. With its inherent capacity for redundancy this makes the motor system capricious in nature, and exceedingly difficult to formulate and empirically demonstrate one absolute style of control and coordination. Professor Mounoud's work is exciting because he has attempted to meet the challenge head-on and tackle the difficult task of finding the evidence that promotes a singularity for cognitive and motor activity.

411

References

Bernstein, N. (1967). *The coordination and regulation of mvoements*. London: Pergamon Press.

Binet, A. & Courtier, J. (1983). Sur la vitesse des mouvements graphiques. *Revue Philosophique, 35,* 664-671.

Gachoud, J.P., Mounoud, P., Hauert, C.A. & Viviani, P. (1983). Motor strategies in lifting movements: A comparison of adult and child performance. *Journal of Motor Behavior, 15(3),* 202-216.

Gibson, J.J. (1966). *The senses considered as perceptual systems*. Boston: Houghton Mifflin.

Mounoud, P. (1981). Cognitive development: Construction of new structures or construction of internal organizations. In I.E. Sigel, D.M. Brodzinsky and R.M. Golnikoff (Eds.), *New directions in Piagetian theory and practice*. Hillsdale, N.J.: Erlbaum.

Schiff, W. (1983). Conservation of length redux: A perceptual-linguistic phenomenon. *Child Development, 54,* 1497-1506.

Schiff, W. & Saarni, C. (1976). Perception and conservation of length: Piaget and Taponiar revisited. *Developmental Psychology, 12,* 98-106.

Shapiro, D.E. (1977). A preliminary attempt to determine the duration of a motor program. In D.M. Landers and D.W. Christina (Eds.), *Psychology of Motor Behavior and Sport*. Urbana, IL.: Human Kinetics.

Turvey, M.T. & Carello, C. (1982). Cognition: The view from ecological realism. *Cognition, 10(1081),* 313-321.

Viviani, P. & Terzuolo, C. (1982). The organization of movement in handwriting and typing. In B. Butterworth (Ed.), *Language Production (Vol. 2): Production of Language in Non-speech Modalities*. London: Academic Press.

SECTION 8

CONTRIBUTION OF THE NEUROSCIENCES TO AN
UNDERSTANDING OF MOTOR DEVELOPMENT

DEVELOPMENT AND ACQUISITION OF MOTOR SKILLS: A CHALLENGING PROSPECT FOR NEUROSCIENCE

J. Paillard

In the last session of our meeting and, as it were, the last act of the play, I am reminded of a well known opera by Georges Bizet in which one of the central characters is called 'l'Arlésienne'. The "Arlésienne" is an enigmatic and supposedly very attractive young lady, who is permanently behind the whole action but never physically present on the scene. In retrospect, I have the feeling that the brain has been somewhat "l'Arlésienne" of our meeting and that what is expected from me at the end of the play is to try to entice this protagonist out of the green-room in order to illuminate some aspects of its role in the development and acquisition of motor skills.

There has been such an impressive expansion of the neurosciences in contemporary studies of developmental neurobiology and the neurophysiology of motor control that I could not possibly hope to encompass all of these new developments. Focussing on the discussions of the meeting, I have been struck by the fact that many speakers have explicitly aligned themselves in terms of a rather sharp contrast between two views of motor development: the so-called "preordered prescriptions" and the "dynamic constraints" approaches.

Right from the start, I would like to emphasise that, whereas the large corpus of data derived from the study of living systems can be evenly divided to support either view, the two explanations are clearly not mutually exclusive but patently complementary. Prominence can be given to one or to the other, depending on the level of organisation at which the living process is observed and the time scale of its evolution.

Thus, it appears self-evident for a biologist to claim that environmental constraints have dynamically moulded the morphogenesis of living systems in the course of evolution and led to the selection and improvement of the coordinative processes that allow their survival in adverse surroundings. Equally, we can point to an obvious evolutionary advantage for organisms which confront rather stable constraints and predictable environmental changes in stabilising successful adaptations in the hard core of their structural organisation. Hence, they avoid permanent and costly recourse to the energy-dissipating (but otherwise efficient) process of a continuous dynamic affordance to changing environments.

It is an incontrovertible fact of contemporary neurophysiology that a consolidated repertoire of motor capacities, either inherited (and developed during growth) or acquired (and secondarily engrammed in the nervous circuitry), exists in all animals. Likewise, it is clear that the processes of coordination and control involved in the working out of this inbuilt machinery, remarkably mimic *cybernetic modes of regulation* . The developing and functioning brain must instantiate the dynamic processes that are required to select, assemble and coordinate the interacting elements of a systematic circuit, thus reflecting some kind of *self-organising process*.

My basic position is to reject the frequently invoked "either-or" dilemma. Instead, I would like to emphasise the logical necessity of two interacting modes of functioning in neural organisation: one dealing with the structurally organised part of the brain machinery and its well-defined nervous activity circulating in precisely and rigidly wired networks of inter-connected elements; the other concerned with the labile and plastic part of the machine and thus its potential for reorganisation by way of dynamic organising processes yet to be defined (Paillard, 1977).

Within this framework, we shall discuss some of the neurobiological processes that underpin the development of motor skills and present some examples of neural mechanisms that may be involved in the acquisition and retention of learned motor activity. It will emerge that both these approaches illustrate the complementary role of the two contrasting modes of functioning that characterise the working brain.

1.   THE CONTRIBUTION OF DEVELOPMENTAL NEUROBIOLOGY

We will first consider the field of developmental neurobiology, focussing on some novel concepts that have recently emerged and that could revise our conventional image of brain organisation.

Three general principles must be taken into account. The first concerns the precise ordering of neural connections that emerges from a drastic selection process among superabundant basic elements (due to a remarkable overproduction of neurons and connecting fibres at the early stages of neurogenesis and synaptogenesis). We will refer to it as a *principle of Darwinian selection*. The second concerns the identification of an elementary anatomical unit as a basic component of the whole neocortex. From the clustering of such units in columnar organisation emerges a mosaic of functional modular structures. We will refer to it as the *module concept*. Finally, we will examine the concept of a basic operation, common to all parts of the cortex, that could account for the stabilisation of coactive synapses and hence the engramming, in neural circuitry, of invariant or covariant features of the environment. This is referred to as the *principle of covariance detection*.

1.1. A Darwinian model of neuronal selectivity during development

The development of the vertebrate nervous system, not unlike the growth of all other tissues and organs in living organisms, was long considered to be an ordered sequence of phenomena reflecting the progressive and cumulative addition of the features that finally compose the mature functioning brain. They include the mitotic production of primitive neuroblasts, their migration to their definitive location, their selective aggregation with other neurons and their phenotypic diversification according to local environmental constraints. Then, with regard to their final morphology, there is the differentiation of their membrane properties in relation to their mode of synaptic transmission, together with the growth, orientation, distribution and myelination of their connecting fibres. The latter ultimately compose the complex network of interconnections that characterises the nervous system.

These progressive developmental events are so striking that they have contributed, to a large extent, to divert attention from both massive and widespread regressive events that occur during neurogenesis. These regressive events have only recently been understood to play a major role in establishing the final organisation of neural networks in the adult nervous system. A rapidly growing body of experimental evidence demonstrates surprisingly extensive neuronal cell death and an intriguing elimination of certain of the morphological and functional features of developing neurons (reviewed by Cowan et al, 1984). Such evidence reveals the applicability to neurogenesis of a general principle of Darwinian selection, under the pressure of endogenic as well as exogenic constraints. Among these phenomena we shall first examine two which are clearly dependent on endogenic factors: neuronal death and the elimination of axon collaterals.

1.1.1. Although the occurence of *neuronal death* and the role of cell death as morphogenetic features in neurogenesis have long been recognised, it is only recently that experimental data, derived mainly from new labelling procedures in modern neuroanatomy, have shown that during the development of most regions of both the central and the peripheral nervous system there is a distinct phase of neuronal regression during which an astonishing proportion of existing neurons die and are rapidly wiped out by the surrounding glial cells. Hence neuronal death appears to be an ubiquitous phenomenon in the developing brain. (Pontine nuclei, locus coeruleus, red nucleus and part of the hippocampal formation, for reasons as yet unknown, seem to be the only structures that escape the slaughter, at least in the avian brain). More than half of the neurons that are generated die at some stage between the initial aggregation of cells in the constitutive nucleus ganglion or cortical layer and its final maturation.

In the motor columns of the spinal cord of chick embryo, 40% of the motoneurons die between days 5 and 9 of incubation; in the mesencephalic nucleus of the trigeminal nerve 75% of the motoneurons die between days 9 and 13; 50% of the neurons of the ciliary ganglion degenerate between days 8 and 14. In most of these cases, almost all of the condemned neurons had an axon that had already reached the target field (i.e. the muscle) before the onset of cell death. The activation of postsynaptic muscular cells has been shown to be involved in the regulation of the survival of motoneurons. Curare treatment of embryos during the cell death period reduces or prevents entirely the naturally occurring cell death (Oppenheim, 1985). Moreover, synchronous activity of pre- and post-synaptic cells is held to confer a competitive advantage for neuron or synapse survival whereas asynchronous activity is postulated to be disadvantageous.

This overproduction of neurons and the subsequent elimination of a substantial proportion of them obviously have the characteristics of a selective process. The fate of each neuron seems to depend on the success or failure of its axon to occupy a "vital territory" on the membrane of the target neuron where it competes with others, either for limited synaptic sites or (more plausibly according to recent research) for limited trophic material within the target cell. The relevant trophic factor has been identified as the celebrated nerve growth factor (NGF) in only two classes of neurons, sympathetic and sensory ganglion cells, both originating from the primitive neural crest formation. But presumably a large amount of specific trophic material associated with different classes of neurons remains to be identified.

With regard to the functional significance of this cell death, three hypotheses, which are not mutually exclusive, have received experimental support: first, a merely *random matching* of cell number to the magnitude of its target field; second, a more *selective elimination* of neurons whose axons grow to a wrong target area or terminate in the wrong region within the target field, hence serving a mechanism to "fine tune" neuronal wiring; third, a *programmed elimination* to terminate specific neuronal lineage.

1.1.2. The extensive *elimination of long axon collaterals* constitutes the second unexpected revelation of recent developmental studies. Many initially formed connective fibres are later eliminated without the death of the parent cells. Neuroanatomical investigations involving long-term retrograde labelling procedures by fluorescent dyes show a widespread process of selective degeneration of long axon collaterals, leading to large scale elimination of early-formed pathways while preserving some selected axonal branches of the parent cell.

The first indication of this phenomenon came from studies of developing callosal projections in the mammalian brain (Innocenti & Caminiti, 1980). Similar observations have since been reported for the somatosensory cortex of rodents and for parietal and frontal association areas in monkey. But especially relevant for our topic are recent studies of the development of pyramidal tract projections in the rat: there is reported to be an unexpectedly widespread occurrence of transient cortico-spinal axonal projections into the bulbar pyramids, which are later eliminated during the first few weeks of postnatal life. It thus appears that pyramidal neurons in the fifth layer of the occipital cortex, labelled (post-natal day 2) by an early dye injection in the pyramidal decussation, are still present at post-natal day 25. They cannot, however, be doubly labelled by later injections (post-natal day 20) of another dye into the pyramidal decussation. Nevertheless, they maintain early established connections to the region of the pontine nuclei or the superior colliculus. The process which governs this strange reorganisation of cortical projection systems is still unknown as well as its overall functional role in cortical development (Ebbesson, 1984).

Whether this phenomenon, discovered relatively recently, occurs in the brain of all mammals – even in man, remains to be established but current evidence suggests that it is a general and major feature of cortical development.

Thus, both neuronal death and elimination of early-formed axonal collaterals appear as selection processes oriented by endogenic factors (chemoaffinity, local trophic factors or some general or permissive influence of hormonal origin). They serve the fine tuning of neural connections and the sculpturing of long efferent tracts. Such processes extend over several weeks during the post-natal period in rat, which implies months or years if transposed on the scale of early human development. Moreover, if we have to consider the specification of "addresses" – namely, the destination of fibres to precise target sites – as representing one of the most important aspects of coding in the nervous system, together with time and frequency codes (Paillard, 1983), we are led to conclude that the strange struggle for life that opposes neuronal populations (competing for synaptic sites) and the extensive loss of long axon collaterals (that occurs during the early post-natal period) might have consequences, still largely unexplored, for the interpretation of early forms of motor activity in human infants. Coarse tuning of axonal addresses is, in a sense, comparable to a kind of noise introduced in the processing of the information that is incorporated in the structural code of synaptic linkages.

Two additional selection mechanisms, occurring at a later stage of development, might also intervene to increase further the adaptive capacity of the developing nervous system. In contrast with the preceding one, they are mainly oriented by activity-dependent exogenic factors. These two mechanisms will be referred to as *selective stabilisation of synapses* and *selective modulation of transmission strength* respectively (see Fig. 1).

1.1.3. The selective stabilisation of synaptic structures with the subsequent elimination or withdrawal of unused axon terminals is now recognised as a widespread phenomenon during neural development. Although clearly related to the elimination process described above, it occurs appreciably later than the well-identified phase of cell death. Moreover, in contrast with the process of collateral elimination, it appears to be tightly coupled with neuronal activity elicited by environmental stimuli. Hence it underlies an epigenetic process of moulding transitory plastic neural connections (the sensitive period concept) in accordance with the early experience of the organism, which is of adaptive value for its affordance to future environmental conditions (see Fig. 1.).

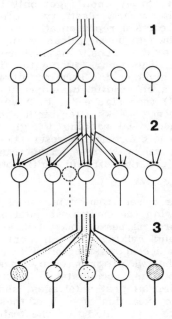

Fig. 1. Epigenesis of neural networks by selective stabilisation
of synapses. 1. Axonal growth. 2. Transitory redundancy
of developing synapses. 3. Selective stabilisation of
neuronal connections (from Changeux et al, 1973).

Interestingly, the first evidence of this selective process came from studies of developing neuromuscular junctions. Although in mature rat (and in many other mammals) most muscle cells receive one single axon with one single junction, they are usually innervated during the first weeks after birth by as many as five or six separate axons with corresponding junctions. The progressive elimination of the supernumerary axons occurs relatively late and usually long after the period of naturally occurring motoneuronal death at the spinal level. Moreover, the stabilisation of the single remaining junction seems to depend on neuronal activity.

It soon became evident that this phenomenon occurs widely in both the peripheral and central nervous system. The best known experimental models are those elaborated by Hubel and Wiesel (1979) in the mammalian visual system, by Van der Loos and Woosey (1979) in the somaesthetic projection area of rodents (barrels related to vibrissae structures) and by Mariani (1983) in cat and Crepel (1982) in mouse cerebellar cortex. The elegant studies of Hubel and Wiesel on the visual system and their bearing on the neuro-biological basis of the "sensitive period" concept do not need to be re-capitulated here. The interesting finding in relation to our topic, specifically because of its presumptive occurrence in the post-natal period in man, concerns the early plasticity of efferent connections comparable to that observed on the afferent side.

There exist to date, to my knowledge, only two experimental demonstrations of transitory early plasticity of efferent connections. First, in the kitten where the cortical representation of the contralateral forelimb motor area has been shown to be significantly expanded (in comparison with the corresponding area of the opposite hemisphere), provided that the forced exercise imposed on that limb occurs during the first weeks of post-natal life. The same exercise given in the same condition after this sensitive period does not lead to a differential development of the cortical motor areas (Spinelli & Jensen, 1979) (see Figure 2). In A and B kittens were trained with the left forelimb from 4 weeks after birth and in C only from 11 weeks. Comparison between the cortical mapping of right and left motor areas shows a clear extension of the left forearm representation in the right motor cortex of kitten trained from 4 weeks whereas kitten trained from 11 weeks do not show any asymmetry between the left and right motor areas (Spinelli & Jensen, 1979).

The second example comes from an ingenious study on infant rabbits that was carried out during the early post-natal period press). Two different programmes of locomotion are used by the rabbit: hopping with in-phase and walking with opponent-phase extension of the two hind limbs. A special device allows the rabbit to be intensively trained with activation of either of the two programmes by passively mobilising its hind limbs in the two corresponding combinations. Preliminary results, using animals spinalised at different post-natal ages, show that specific neural networks involved in the execution of each of these two programmes may be independently consolidated, provided that the training exercises are given before the first 18 days of post-natal life, thus reflecting a sensitive period comparable to that observed in the developing visual system.

Undoubtedly, this fascinating field of research will be extensively exploited during the next few years and shed new light on the adaptive capacity of the early developing motor system.

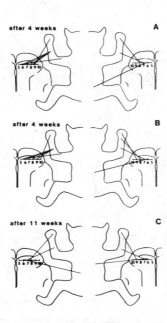

Fig. 2. Mapping of the cortical representation of the different
segments of the forelimb obtained by electrical stimulation
of the postcruciate cortex along a line perpendicular to the
middle sagittal plane, 1.5 mm posterior to the cruciate sulcus.
Electrode penetrations are marked in millimetres lateral to
the midline. Lines are drawn from each penetration site to
the part of the body, which is set to move by electrical
stimulation of that site. Kittens are trained during 10 weeks
to raise their left forelimb and to hold it up in order to
avoid electrical shocks delivered when their forepaw is in
contact with a metallic plate (Spinelli & Jensen, 1979).

1.1.4. Finally, we have to take into account the *selective modulation of
the strength of synaptic transmission* which, in contrast with selective
stabilisation, appears to be a reversible process. The plastic properties
of certain synapses can last for a life time although such properties
probably decline with age. This mechanism provides the foundation for
most theories of learning and memory. The theoretical and practical
importance of this matter makes the study of the mechanisms that account
for plasticity of synaptic transmission, one of the major targets of contemporary neurobiological research (Viana di Prisco, 1984) (see Figure 3).
By the same token, recent studies have concentrated on putting theories
of cerebellar synaptic plasticity to experimental test. In particular, they
examine the ability of climbing fibre activity to alter durably the efficiency
of the parallel fibre/Purkinje cell synapses during the acquisition of motor
skills. Given the fact that the cerebellum is now believed to play an

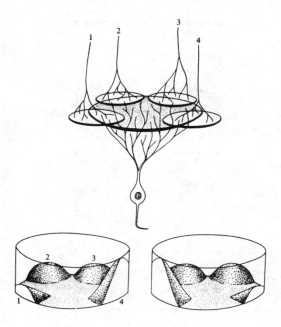

Fig. 3. Changing pattern of connection strength. Input fibres 1 to
4 make connections with a common neuron. The strength of
connections is represented on the three-dimensional graphs
below, with synaptic efficacy on the vertical axis and the
area of connection corresponding to a horizontal section of
the dedritic tree on the horizontal axes. On the left is the
expected pattern of efficacy if fibre 4 is used more than the
others, on the right the pattern if fibre 1 were the most
frequently used connection (from Mark, 1974).

important role in the learning of motor tasks, we shall revert to this matter
in a later section.

Let me now turn to the second principle that has emerged from
contemporary studies of brain organisation.

1.2. The "module-concept" as an organising principle for the developing brain

The striking homogeneity of the monkey cortex up to three to four
months of gestation led Mountcastle (1979) to suggest that a repetitive
basic anatomical unit may in fact exist at an early stage of neocortical
development in all mammals. It is only after 110 days in the monkey that
the extrinsic connections afferent to and efferent from the neocortex begin
to develop, with the subsequent progressive differentiation of the
cytoarchitectonic features that are associated with the segregation of the
cortex into its classic topological areas.

In support of this idea is the demonstration by Rakic (1972) of the role of basal glial cells that emit, at the stage of proliferation of the neuroblasts in the germinal zone of the neural tube, long parallel radial filaments. These connect the internal zone to the external boundaries of the neural tube, hence constituting an array of radially distributed glial filaments to each one of which a fixed number of 110 neurons will migrate, successively stopping at different distances from the base so that each neuron has its predetermined location in the future laminar organisation of the cortex. This primitive arrangement has two remarkable features. First, it gives rise to a regular juxtaposition of identical repetitive units in a vertical column of 30 microns diameter. Second, it seems to be similar in size and number of constituent neurons for all species of vertebrates. Hence, the neocortex would appear, at its embryonic stage, to be like a cristalline structure of redundant basic units, all similar in shape, whose specification depends on the later selective distribution of their extrinsic afferent inputs. Then, what differentiates at this stage a human neocortex from the homologous structure of a more primitive mammal is simply the greater number of redundant units that is potentially available for the future development of the human brain.

The grouping of several hundred of these basic units into clusters of wider columns 350 microns in diameter, has recently been recognised as the basis of modular organisation in the neocortex. Structural and functional modules are now becoming the salient target of current neuroanatomical, neurophysiological and neurochemical research.

We have to appreciate the epistemological stake in this new conception of brain organisation. If we can accept the idea that the hypercomplexity of the brain - conceived of until recently as an intricate network of 10^{11} neurons with 10^{15} connections - can be resolved into elementary packages of basic anatomical units of 110 neurons, whose intrinsic connections may be repetitively similar from one unit to another, then the understanding of the developing and functioning brain in terms of its elementary operations is no longer out of the reach of scientific experiment although the task remains formidable. A comprehensive paper (Phillips et al, 1984) has recently summarised the import of this relatively new picture of nervous organisation with the important questions that it raises for future research.

There is impressive evidence that this modular organisation is not limited to the neocortical columns but occurs widely in both peripheral and central structures of the nervous system in the form of discs, slices, stripes or segregated lattice arrangements. This evidence includes the following: vertical columns in the tectum, cortico-nuclear micro-complexes (envisaged as the constituent anatomo-functional units of the cerebellum), the digitation of the striatum into longitudinal stripes, and the ordered slices of the hippocampal formation. Even the bulbomesencephalic reticular formation, long considered as prototypical of stochastic networks, reveals a patchy organisation of neuronal ensembles in repetitive, coin-shaped, transverse discs within which both the dendrites of cells and the entering axon terminals are rather strictly confined. The central and dorsal horns of the spinal cord can be considered as appendages to such columns of discs that characterise the organisation of the central core of gray matter. Finally, functional evidence derived from invertebrate and vertebrate studies attests to the reality of inbuilt preorganised networks, along the spinal cord and brain stem, whose electrical stimulation releases a complete set of co-ordinated, behaviourally significant muscular actions. Thus, the concept of motor programmes has emerged with its pervasive influence on current models of motor coordination and control.

More generally, the nervous system can be seen as having evolved in vertebrates, as in other organisms, in the form of segregated networks of vertical sensorimotor channels that connect parallel modular units distributed in different areas, and that are brought into play for performing unified, coherent, goal-directed behavioural acts. Therefore, the segmentation of sensorimotor performance into component functional operations, serially ordered for the execution of behavioural acts, appears as a fruitful research strategy for the identification and analysis of the underlying neural mechanisms (Goodale, 1983). But the utility of such a strategy (the core of the traditional analytic scientific approach) clearly presupposes that the system under study can be carved "at its natural joints", hence the importance of the precise anatomical delineation in the nervous system of its modular arrangements and of their functional identity.

Similarly, the "module concept", now extended to the organisation of the neocortex, suggests that the same strategy should henceforth be applied to the study of cognitive operations, incorporated in the modularity of the brain (Fodor, 1983). This idea is currently invading the contemporary approach to the architecture of cognition, with the fascinating prospect of having at its disposal all the resources of CT scan, position emission tomography and nuclear magnetic imaging that permit "in vivo" visualisation of the functioning human brain.

Let me turn now to the third general principle which follows directly from the existence of a Darwinian selection of nervous connections and of a modular organisation of neuronal assemblies.

1.3. A basic operation: covariance-detection

If we accept the premiss of the modular organisation of the neo-cortex with functional differentiation among redundant basic units (based on the pattern of local connections that characterises their inputs and the corresponding addresses that define their outputs), then we must be prepared to look for a common process that accounts for the selective strengthening and stabilisation of specific configurations of presynaptic inputs and that would support a basic operation common to all areas of the cerebral cortex.

One important function performed by the cortex is that of the redistribution of information from one area to another or, more precisely, from one given class of modules to higher order classes of layered modules. Redistribution means here that the information "encapsulated" in each modular unit and thus representing an abstract description of some characteristic features will be combined with information from other sources to give rise in the collecting module to a new description at a still higher level of abstraction.

What characterises a column or cluster of cells that constitutes a module is that it aggregates neurons sharing some common property. Input neurons of the module on which converge information from lower-order modules must be specifically set in their synaptic assortment in order to detect, among the impinging inputs, those whose configurational characteristic fits the specific features described by the module. Hence the pre-setting of the synaptic assortment defines the configuration of inputs that will normally be accepted by the module as matching the specific role assigned to it in the chain of information processing.

The mechanism of selective stabilisation of synapses, that characterises the early stage of development including its "sensitive period", could certainly account for the shaping of the first repertoire of feature detectors that have now been identified in primary projection areas (notably in the visual cortex). But most modules throughout the cortical association areas remain open to selective operations of this kind throughout a life-time. Relatively reversible changes in the strength of synaptic transmission could here account for such a selective operation. The optimum response of the module is then obtained when the most active inputs are connected to synapses having maximum strength of connectivity.

Without discussing here the many attempts to formulate rules which changes in connection strength might obey, suffice it to say that the prevalent hypothesis is that changes result primarily from frequently occurring combinations of coincident inputs. The change in connection strength could, furthermore, depend on the co-occurrence of these time-locked pre-synaptic activities with post-synaptic events. The latter intervene like a contingent permissive factor for the whole operation and appear to depend on local state-control (Byrne, 1985). Regarding this last point (somewhat reminiscent of the earlier concept of the "now print signal"), it has been suggested that inputs to layer one of the laminar organisation of the cortex could possibly effect such a state-control modulation of the constituent neurons of the module, either by way of diffuse aspecific nervous activity and/or by regional neurohormonal impregnation. The two most attractive hypotheses that are currently influencing research in this field invoke either long-term changes in calcium ionic channels or trophic changes induced at the presynaptic level by a presumptive "rewarding factor" released by the target neuron (analogous to the trophic factor for which impinging axons compete at an earlier stage of synaptogenesis).

Whatever the final explanation for this basic operation, its overall significance for our understanding of the higher abstract functions of the brain is obvious. Such a simple mechanism could account for the astonishing capacity of all nervous systems to extract regularity and invariant or co-variant features of their changing surroundings. It provides living organisms with the finely tuned adaptivity that is required for survival in an adverse environment. It has to be considered as a primitive basic function of neural networks.

Moreover, it could explain the evolutionary necessity of the enormous expansion of the neocortex once the brain undertook the task of detecting the significantly covariant inputs that are needed to generate an internal neural representation of the world in terms accessible to further processing by higher mental processes, including their translation into new systems of symbolic indexation.

Whether it is necessary to postulate for these higher mental processes, as suggested by Fodor (1983), non-modular superstructures comprising a "central system" inaccessible to a traditional analytic scientific approach – precisely because of its non-modularity and indivisible structure – obviously remains speculative and highly controversial (Fodor, 1985).

Leaving these developmental aspects, let us now consider the crucial problems involved in an attempt to understand learning processes and the acquisition of motor skill.

2. MOTOR SKILL ACQUISITION AND THE LEARNING PROCESS

The concept of motor learning, that has long been the Cinderella of general learning theories, is now often replaced by that of motor skill acquisition. Accordingly, a shift of experimental interest can be observed. The careful analysis of the regulatory mechanisms that underlie the evolution of the learning process during the acquisition of a new skill now takes precedence over the search for empirical laws that predict the course of learning curves. A proliferation of new theoretical models of motor control systems has ensued, mostly originating from cognitive psychologists; their interest contrasts sharply with the attitude of the neurophysiologists who are activily engaged in the investigation of motor control systems, while showing little concern, until recently, with motor learning problems.

Most current neurophysiological studies of motor control (despite impressive new techniques for observing the working nervous system at the minute scale of single neuron activity, in unanaesthetised, awake, behaving animals) have used overlearned stabilised motor performance in order to reduce variability in the search for correlations between behavioural and neural parameters. Psychological research, on the other hand, has increasingly focussed on hypothetical constructs such as plans, programs and schemata that remain difficult to instantiate in nervous tissue, within the framework of our existing knowledge of brain architecture and function. The present impetus in neuroscience, however, seems to offer novel theoretical approaches and potent new experimental tools to address the issue of motor learning.

Having devoted a recent paper to the neurophysiology of motor control in relation to disorders of higher brain functions (Paillard, 1982), I will concentrate here mainly on two points specifically related to the acquisition of motor skills, that stem from the argument of the preceding section of this paper.

First, a basic fact has to be kept in mind when addressing the problem of the neural basis of motor skill acquisition - namely that the muscular keyboard does not allow a new original kinetic melody to be played immediately. The central command is bound to operate upon the spinal keyboard through the pre-existing arrangements of its inherited or habitual repertoire of action. To execute purposefully a new act, of which the aim is beyond the limit of flexibility of the existing repertoire, a complex selective operation is involved that characterises the initial phase of every learning process. The main concern for our understanding of the underlying nervous mechanisms is that this selective operation is limited in setting up new patterns of action by the extent of its capacity to remodel or abolish the existing ones. It follows that motor learning capacity must be closely related to the degree of refinement in the connections between the higher and lower level neural networks involved in the shaping of skilled acts. In this perspective, we shall first examine how recent advances in our knowledge of the hodology and neurophysiology of corticospinal pathways may suggest

a new image of the evolutionary development of a pyramidal tract that is
specifically devoted to the skilful use of motor instruments, thus complementing the parallel development and refinement of the analytic power of sensory
instruments.

Once the difficulties encountered by the central command in shaping
the newly planned act have been resolved, a second important phase of the
learning process begins. It concerns the cleaning and polishing of the new
action in order that performance becomes progressively faster, smoother,
more economical and more accurate. It then becomes what we may call a
skill.

Where then can the stabilisation of this newly acquired component of
the motor repertoire be located in nervous structures? Is the question even
answerable today or are neuroscientists still engaged in the unending quest
for the engram? I would like to suggest that recent investigations of the
role of the cerebellum in the motor learning process point toward the
direction in which decisive advances can be expected in the not too distant
future.

2.1. Pyramidal function and the shaping of motor skills

The relationship between pyramidal function and manual skill has been
well documented by data from both phylogenetic and ontogenetic sources
(Paillard, 1960). Anterior limbs, when no longer exclusively required for
locomotor purposes, have become progressively elaborate tools for living
organisms to handle their physical environment. The appearance and
development of a pyramidal tract seem to follow the same progression as the
use of fore-limbs for non-locomotor function and especially the even more
refined use of the five-fingered hand inherited from the primitive reptiles.
The first point to make is that this conventional image of pyramidal tract
function needs substantial revision. The often repeated assertion that man
is unique among mammals in having an impressive number of pyramidal tract
fibres has proved to be misleading. Man has, in fact, the expected number
of pyramidal tract fibres for a mammal of his size and of his brain weight.

2.1.1. A morphometric analysis of the pyramidal tract has been carried out
in 69 species of mammals (Heffner & Masterton, 1975) in order to establish,
on a comparative basis, the role of the pyramidal system in the skilful use
of the hand. Variations in digital dexterity were ranked in terms of
mechanical features of the hand (e.g. independence of the digits, opposition
of the thumb, etc.). These variations were related to various morphological
features of the pyramidal tract of the species considered (e.g. number and
size of fibres, depth of caudal extension of the tract down the spinal cord,
etc.).

The highest correlation with the practical dexterity index was obtained
with the level of termination of the fibre tracts within the laminate
organisation of the spinal cord – a clear indication of the extent of direct
cortico-motoneural connections. Correspondingly, the lowest correlation was
found with body weight. In contrast, number and size of tract fibres in
the pyramidal decussation did not contribute as much as expected to the
correlation with hand dexterity. The following formula allows the calculation
of a theoretical index of dexterity.

$Di = (.65)Cm + (.49) EC + (.16)P - (.30)S$ where Di is the calculated
dexterity index; Cm: the estimated amount of corticomotoneural connection;

Lc: the caudal extension of the tract down the spinal cord; P: the body weight; S: the section area of the pyramids.

The correlation between the calculated and the practical dexterity index was found to be .815.

An interesting feature of this study is the presence at the top rank of the classification of some mammals endowed with a large and well-distributed pyramidal system but devoid of digital dexterity. Thus, the seal occupied the third rank just behind man and chimpanzee. It is also strange to find the dog or, more surprisingly, the goat before the gibbon in the same classification; and the dolphin before the maccaca. We may therefore ask whether the emphasis that has been placed on the obvious relationship between pyramidal function and *manual* skill has not tended to obscure its possible association with *postural* skill not directly involving the distal segments of the body. The ability of certain mammals to learn astonishing postural skills (the juggling seal, the acrobatic elephant, the dancing horse or the cycling bear) seems to justify their high rank in terms of pyramidal tract equipment despite a low rank on the scale of digital dexterity. Such postural skills obviously require very elaborate control of basic inbuilt programmes of posture and movement. We have then to explain how the pyramidal tract contributes to both the skilful use of the delicate motor instrument of the five-fingered hand and the enrichment of the primitive repertoire of posturokinetic skills.

2.1.2. The organisation of corticospinal connections

The ability to generate discrete movements obviously depends on the specificity with which the *spinal* keyboard responds to cortical commands and thus on the refinement of the organisation of the *cortical* keyboard that generates the descending commands. More generally, it depends on the relative strength of connectivity between these two structures.

A modular cortical motor map. The somatotopic topography of the motor cortex is traditionally considered to correspond to the size of the cellular field that, in turn, correspond to elements of the "upper-motoneuron" keyboard. The size of each area and hence the number of independent keys increase in proportion to the complexity and the delicacy of the movements which they generate.

The micro-organisation of the cortical keyboard with its mosaic of columnar arrangements is beginning to emerge more clearly from research combining controlled microstimulation of neurons located in different laminae of the motor cortex and sophisticated new techniques for tracing the microcircuitry inside the modular structure. Recent work has defined the subtle concentric distribution around the digit areas of the cortical modules controlling the wrist, elbow, and shoulder joints that govern the movement of the contralateral forearm in monkey (Kwan et al, 1978). A striking finding here is the existence of two separate hand areas, each one surrounded by its wrist-joint columnar arrangement. The two areas differ with regard to the prevalent sensory modality of their afferent projections. The more caudal representation of the hand is mainly afferented by cutaneous information, the more rostral by proprioceptive information (Strick & Preston, 1982). This suggests a segregation of modules that separately control a "tool-hand" able to power-grip and a "palpatory-hand" tuned for the tactile exploration of the world: a striking illustration of modular specification.

A direct cortico-motoneuronal pathway. Regarding the connections that link the motor cortex to the spinal motor machinery, a unique feature of the pyramidal tract is certainly the presence, at least in mammals endowed with manipulatory activity of their forelimb, of a direct monosynaptic path-way linking large pyramidal cells of the fifth layer to spinal motoneurons. Monosynaptic connections permit the discrete and independent control of the most distal segments. This pathway could account for the development of manual dexterity as assessed by Heffner and Masterton's study (1975). This notion is corroborated by a developmental study of Kuypers (1962) in monkey: labelling techniques showed that pyramidal fibres established their direct connections with motoneurons of the ventral horn as late as seven months after birth and that this period precisely corresponded to the acquisition by the infant monkey of independent control of its digits. It is worth mentioning here that the direct corticomotoneuronal tract includes only 3% of the contingent of pyramidal tract fibres. It is nevertheless composed of the largest and fastest conducting fibres that link the motor cortex to the spinal keyboard. What then is the destination of the 97% remaining fibres of the tract?

A profuse distribution of axon collaterals. Histological and electro-physiological evidence have shown that pyramidal axons, on their way down the spinal cord, give off numerous collaterals to several neuronal systems (Armand, 1982). Hence, our conventional picture of the distribution of corticospinal tracts has been completely transformed (see Fig. 4) and should be further modified to take into account recent developmental data – especially those concerning the late regression of long axon collaterals. Setting aside the well identified cortico-motoneuronal tract (group 1 in Figure 4), three additional arrangements may be tentatively proposed for the distribution of the main contingent of corticospinal fibres (Paillard, 1978).

The first concerns the internal control of the pre-wired networks of the inherited repertoire located throughout the spinal cord and brain stem structures (group 2 in Figure 4).

The second deals with the control or the supply of neocerebellar feedback loops through axon collaterals that project to nucleus reticularis lateralis, pontine nuclei and olivary complex (group 3 in Figure 4).

The third system controls several relay stations that carry information upstream to the somatosensory and cortical association areas. It includes the sensory nucleus of the thalamus, brain stem structures, dorsal column nuclei and the spinal trigeminal nuclei (group 4 in Figure 4).

How, then, can we envisage the functional role of this distributed organisation of pyramidal tract fibres? As this topic has been extensively reviewed elsewhere (Paillard, 1978), we will focuss here only on the contribution of the pyramidal tract to the shaping of new motor skills.

2.1.3. The contribution of the pyramidal tract to motor skill acquisition

A suggested property of the pyramidal tract resides in its capacity to break up components of the primitive inbuilt motor repertoire in order to organise both new programmes of action and the control of the feedback

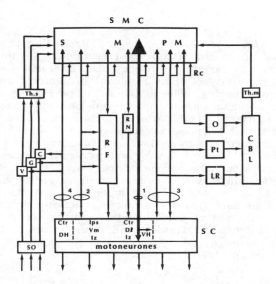

Fig. 4. Functional distribution of corticospinal tracts. SMC: sensori-
motor cortex; S: somato-sensory areas; M: motor areas; PM:
premotor areas; Th.s: sensory thalamus; Th.m: motor thalamus;
Rc: recurrent collaterals; RN: ruber nucleus; RF: reticular
formation; O: olive; Pt: pontine; LR: lateralis reticularis;
CBL: cerebellum; C: cuneatus; G: gracilis; V: trigeminal;
SC: spinal cord; Ctr: contralateral; Ips: ipsilateral; Vm:
ventromedial; Dl: dorso-lateral; Iz: intermediate zone; DH:
dorsal horn; VH: ventral horn; SO: sensory organs (from
Armand, 1982). See comments in text.

loops of servo-assistance that provide these programmes with the required
flexibility in their execution.

We have here to consider two possible roles of the pyramidal system in
the acquisition of new motor skills: either pyramidal commands bypass the
established repertoire of inbuilt motor programmes and then play their own
original kinetic melody on the spinal keyboard; or pyramidal commands are
able to rearrange the existing programmes, thus generating new sets of
coordinated activity by tuning older ones. We suggest that both systems
can operate and that they are complementary.

The by-passing mode of operation. Newly learned programmes could well
be channelled by cortico-motoneural pathways. Given the known distribution
of these pathways, skilled movement of the hand would be mainly concerned
with this first mode of operation. Independent command of finger movements
has been shown to be suppressed after pyramidotomy. Data from experimental
or therapeutic muscle-tendon transposition also point clearly in this direction.
Sometimes, operations are such that tendinous attachments are reversed so
that muscles, that are normally activated in synergy with flexor muscles of
a joint, must function as antagonists of the same muscles in order to perform
an adaptive limb movement. Depending on the animal species and on the

joints involved in such operations, the success of this kind of adaptive learning seems to rely on the existence of direct cortico-spinal projections. Tendons of distal muscles (around digits or wrist joints) can be transplanted in man so as to exert antagonistic function with regard to their primitive use. Surprisingly, they adapt rapidly to their new function. The rich supply of these distal muscles in direct cortico-motoneuronal fibres probably accounts for this success. In the same vein, the known absence of direct connections may explain the failure of certain animals to recover the correct use of their operated limb after similar tendon transpositions. Pyramidal commands, however, may also contribute to rearrange the existing circuitry.

The tuning-mode of operation. The capacity of pyramidal commands to break up the inbuilt blocks of the primitive repertoire remains presumptive and, as yet, lacks the support of systematic experiment. A study by Ioffe (1973) with dogs seems, however, to point in the right direction. Two dogs were trained to keep one foreleg raised (in order to gain access to food) and to hold it in this position during feeding. The access to food was allowed with either a nose-up or nose-down tilt of the head, depending on the position of the food-delivery system. Both animals learned the task, whatever the position (high or low) of the food distributor. After pyramidotomy, however, both operated animals, although capable of raising the leg in response to a signal and of holding it with a nose-up tilt of the head, failed dramatically with a nose-down tilt. Ioffe concluded that inhibition of the lowering reaction of the leg, when feeding with head down, required control of inbuilt programmes by pyramidal command whereas the other condition allowed the use of a combination of movements compatible with the existing synergies in the inbuilt repertoire. We do not yet know whether long practice of such a newly acquired motor activity could result in a stabilised automatic response that would survive pyramidal section.

Whatever the mode of pyramidal mediation, the question arises as to where new programmes of action or of tuning are generated and consolidated.

A working hypothesis. One of the most intriguing discoveries regarding pyramidal tract function was the observation by Tower (1940) that a bilateral pyramidotomy in monkey had only the minor consequence of impairing the ability to move the digits independently. It did not have the drastic effect on motor performance and on voluntary control that might have been expected from the suppression of a massive descending tract (of about one million fibres in monkey) widely considered to be the main instrument of voluntary control upon the spinal machinery. It has since been established that normal motor habits or acquired conditioned responses are unaffected by pyramidotomy (Wiesendanger, 1969). This fact has certainly contributed to divert attention from the pyramidal tract as a possible candidate for the mediation of motor learning processes.

With this in mind, the following hypothesis was formulated: could it be that "the pyramidal output chiefly contributes to increase the motor repertoire by acquisition of new skills and that, once acquired, these new programmes can be retrieved and triggered by other routes?" Hence, pyramidotomy would not be expected to impair the inborn repertoire or even the expression of newly learned consolidated motor skills. "It could, however, impair the capacity to solve unusual new motor problems not necessarily restricted to manipulative skills but involving postural skills, as well". This working hypothesis, formulated seven years ago (Paillard, 1978), seemed logically compatible with a critical reappraisal of the rather confusing state

432

of neurological and physiological studies of pyramidal function at that time.

Interestingly, a recent comprehensive publication by Ito (1984) devoted to "The cerebellum and neural control" brings powerful support in favour of such a view. He adopts the two-stage model of motor learning in which the cerebellum is presumed to intervene in the transitional process that transforms an attentionally controlled, newly acquired motor skill into an automatised motor habit. We will now consider this final point.

2.2. Cerebellar function and the consolidation of motor habits

A functional distinction between two levels of information processing by the nervous system has been suggested (Paillard, 1985). One concerns the direct dialogue that the organism entertains with the part of the physical world to which it is attuned by virtue of its sensori-motor apparatus. The other is related to cognitive activities that operate on mental representations of physical reality embodied in memory stores. The general idea is that the progressive evolution of the cognitive apparatus has created new control systems of action that enlarge the adaptive capacity of the organism but without, at the same time, undermining the more primitive and far more economic mode of automatic control that characterises the sensorimotor level (Paillard, in press).

Consequently, we would like to suggest here that the acquisition of new motor skills implies an attentionally-controlled phase involving all the resources of cognitive processing followed by a progressive delegation of action control to the processing modes of the sensorimotor level.

A distinction between adaptive processes that operate automatically at a subconscious level and learning processes that require the intervention of cognitive levels of processing seems apposite. Whether a further distinction has to be made between the automatisation process of a newly learned action corresponding to the consolidation process of the new programme and the adaptive process that tunes an already consolidated programme to transitory changes in environmental conditions remains an open question.

Let us first examine the adaptive process which undoubtedly comes within the competence of the sensorimotor system and for which evidence of a cerebellar contribution is now accumulating.

2.2.1. The cerebellum and adaptive changes of motor performance

It must be borne in mind that the fundamental framework of the sensorimotor machinery is made up of an assembly of neurons rigidly ordered in patterns of interconnection that constitute a basic inbuilt motor repertoire. A common characteristic of the hierarchical modular organisation of this design logic is the existence of feedback loops that provide each working unit, at all levels of this hierarchy, with its own private servo-assistance device. Thanks to this autonomous self regulation, each unit disposes of a given range of flexibility that allows it to tolerate some deviation outside its usual mode of functioning. The hierarchy of control levels incorporates a cascade of corrective devices whereby higher levels may intervene to compensate for the failure of lower level mechanisms. Once a unit is cut off from its own self-adjustment capabilities by external constraints, a higher-order unit is called into action to bring it back into the margin within which its self-regulation capacities can operate. This remarkable property may account for the overall flexibility of motor performance which, in other respects, is strictly dependent on rigidly prearranged patterns of neuronal interconnection. Thus, the motor machinery can automatically adjust its functioning to the changing constraints of the environment without modifying its inbuilt circuitry. This cybernetic self-regulation, however, has its own limitations. Once it is unable to operate effectively with its own resources, a new adaptive process must then intervene.

The adaptive process operates in general by durable modification of the internal parameters of the system, supported by durable changes in synaptic strength. Hence, gain and phase shift are usually involved. The paleocerebellar structures are known to play an important role in this type of automatic adjustment which is itself comparable to a learning process.

This has been illustrated by recent studies, namely: the adaptation of the vestibulo-ocular reflex which allows compensatory eye movements during head turning to an ever-changing visual environment; the automatic adaptation of motor commands to match changes in the bio-mechanical constraints that overwhelm the self-regulating capacity of the system; and the adaptive postural corrections associated with the execution of new motor skills.

The study of the vestibulo-ocular reflex has been especially productive; it has shown that the cerebellar circuit is involved in the automatic gain and phase shift that results from the adaptive process. Durable changes at the synaptic junction between parallel fibres and the Purkinje cells (see Fig. 5) have been demonstrated. An hypothesis originally formulated by Marr (1969), then modified by Albus (1971), postulating a coincidence-detection process that intervenes during conjunctive activation of parallel and climbing fibres (converging on the somato-dendritic surface of the Punkinje cells) and leads to durable changes in the strength of parallel fibre synapses has been experimentally confirmed (vide Gellman & Miles, 1985).

According to this model, each inferior olivary cell receives a signal derived from cortical command and conveys it by way of a climbing fibre to a Purkinje cell that also receives (through the profuse distribution of parallel fibres) contextual information concerning the circumstances in which the olivary cell has been activated. This contextual information is provided by signals that record parameters such as muscle length and tension, joint angles and skin pressure associated with the movement, as well as proprioceptive signals concerning the overall postural state of the body. Every covariant signal that regularly activates a parallel fibre synapse coinciding with the arrival of the climbing fibre signal will change the strength of the parallel fibre synapses.

Two important features of this model are worth mentioning. First, it provides a remarkable illustration of the covariance-detection principle that accounts for the specification of neocortical modules. Second, it allows the extrapolation of the module-concept to the cerebellar structure. Ito has proposed that each Purkinje cell together with its satellite grain and golgi cells, its parallel fibres and its single climbing fibre (as extrinsic input) and the nuclear cells connected to that Purkinje cell (as output channel of this neuronal assembly) constitute the functional basic unit of the cerebellum labelled a "cortico-nuclear micro-complex" (C.N.M.C.).

Many recent experiments (reviewed by Andersen, 1982) have examined

434

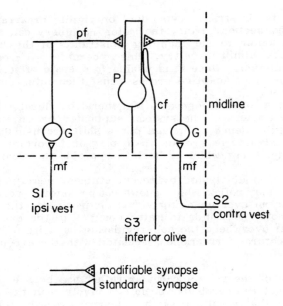

Fig. 5. Simplified diagram of the cerebellar cortex. Ito and Kano (1982)
have demonstrated long-lasting reduced efficiency of the
synapses between the parallel fibre (pF) and floccular
Purkinje cells (P) following a conjoint stimulation (duration
25 s.) at 4 Hz of the inferior olive (S3), giving rise to
activation of the climbing fibres (cf) and at 20 Hz of the
ipsilateral vestibular nerve (S1) giving rise to activation
via mossy fibres (mf) of granule cells (G) and parallel
fibres (pf). The response to stimulation of the contralateral
vestibular nerve (S2) which was not paired with the olivary
stimulation, was used as control (from Andersen, 1982).

the presumptive role of the cerebellum not only in adaptive processes but
more generally in the learning of motor tasks. It appears that the general
concept of "learning process" in its current use is not devoid of ambiguity
and that a clarification of its operational content is still badly needed. In
this context, an advance in understanding the mode of operation of the
cerebellum in the acquisition and retention of new motor skills has been
made by Ito.

2.2.2. Ito's model

The schema proposed by Ito (1984) makes a clear distinction between
two stages of the motor learning process. Within the constraints of the
experimental data currently available on the structure of cerebellar control-
systems, Ito suggests the following flow diagram (see Fig. 6) to account for
the transitional process that transforms an attentionally-driven new motor
performance into an automatically-released motor programme that is
consolidated in the neural circuitry.

Briefly, Ito suggests that the initial phase of acquisition involves mainly the cortico-corticospinal pathways that include neocortical association areas and premotor and motor areas, with the pyramidal tract as the main descending output. The late consolidation phase bypasses cortico-cortical processing and implicates a more or less direct triggering of the cortico-rubrospinal pathways, either at the cortical level or even by a direct activation of the ruber nucleus structure. Both circuits are thought to share a common cerebellar "sidepath" presumably involving the same C.N.M.C. (vermal-interpositus micro-complex).

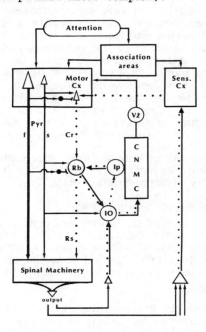

Fig. 6. Schematic illustration of Ito's hypothesis on motor learning. The dotted lines indicate the circuits assumed to be involved in the automatic driving of learned motor skills. CR: cortico-rubral; Rb: ruber nucleus; RS: rubrospinal; IO: inferior olive; Ip: interpositus; CNMC: cortico-nuclear micro complex. The hypothetical comparator of Ito's model (not included in the schema) is assumed to be a preolivar structure. Fast (f) and slow (s) fibres of the pyramidal tract (Pyr) are thought to intervene in the initial stage of motor learning together with the CNMC and its retroactive loop on the motor cortex (Motor Cx) via the ventro-lateral nucleus (Vl). This stage is under the control of attentional processes. See comments in text.

More precisely, it is suggested that the initial execution of a new voluntary movement (in response to a set of sensory signals) requires the mobilisation of attentional and "cognitive" processes at the level of neo-cortical structures. Then the parametric prescription of the movement may be forwarded from premotor to motor cortex and thereafter to cortico-spinal and cortico-rubral pyramidal cells. Both pathways have collaterals that activate the corresponding C.N.M.C. of the cerebellum (i.e. the paravermal-interpositus complex) through cortico-ponto cerebellar pathways. The neo-cerebellar loop then contributes, through its return projection to the pre-motor cortex (via the ventrolateral nucleus of the thalamus), to the on-going adjustment of the programme of the planned movement. While the movement is still unskilled, attentional mechanisms would allow fast conducting cortico-spinal fibres to be activated. Activity of the corresponding pyramidal cells inhibits both the slowly conducting cortico-rubral cells and the rubro-spinal tract cells, such that signals flowing through the cortico-rubro-spinal pathway are blocked. The cerebellar C.N.M.C., common to both cortico-spinal and cortico-rubral tracts, would then be tuned to allow an increasingly precise execution of the voluntary movement through the fast cortico-spinal cells. After repeated practice, the withdrawal of attentional processes is assumed to block the cortico-corticospinal pathways as well as the return pathways of the neocerebellar loop via the VL. The central command is then conveyed through the cortico-rubro-spinal pathways that are now provided with the "already learned" C.N.M.C. that is commonly shared by both descending pathways. The cortico-rubral pathway now becomes able to display automatically an "already learned skill".

This general sketch is, of course, only speculative and awaits experimental confirmation. Nevertheless, several predictions of the model seem to be supported by already existing data.

2.2.3. Experimental validation of Ito's model

First, a central feature of the model concerns the role of the C.N.M.C. The strengthening of synaptic connections between parallel fibres and the Purkinje cell is known to depend on the coactivity of a climbing fibre issuing in the inferior olive nucleus (IO). An interruption of the connection between the IO and the cerebellum would then be predicted to impair the learning process.

In fact, Llinas et al (1975), had observed in cat that recovery from motor abnormalities (generated by unilateral labyrinthine lesions) was prevented by selective chemical lesion of the IO by 3Acetylpyridine. More-over, animals that had already recuperated from the labyrinthine lesion showed, within two hours of the injection of the drug into the IO, a complete recurrence of the symptoms. Llinas and his coworkers concluded that the olivo-cerebellar system was necessary for both the acquisition and the retention of that type of motor learning.

A second prediction of Ito's model concerns the role of the cerebro-thalamo-cortical feedback loop in the initial phase of the learning process and its exclusion during the final phase of automatisation.

An experiment by Fabre and Buser (1980) had already shown that cats trained to catch a moving visual target with their forepaw were prevente from learning that task if a bilateral lesion of the VL was performed *before training*. Subsequently, the animals never achieved normal scores. In contrast, the same bilateral lesions made *after training* surprisingly did not impair performance.

A third prediction of the model concerns the presumed transfer of cortico-spinal commands from the fast pyramidal pathways to the cortico-rubro-spinal pathways. The only experimental data pointing in this direction

are those obtained by Massion's group (reviewed by Massion, 1979) in
Marseilles. They studied the compensatory postural adjustment associated
with a forelimb-placing task in cat. The lifting of the forelimb entails a
new distribution of the supporting forces among the three other limbs.
Retroactive feedback could well account for this corrective adjustment but
Massion and his team have shown that postural compensation may in fact
anticipate the lifting movement. The initial commands for limb placement
are then presumed to include (together with the limb-lifting programme)
predictive commands (feedforward) related to the associated corrective
posture. Furthermore, this group has established that the same limb
movement, elicited by electrical stimulation of the corresponding motor
cortex area, also gives rise to the anticipatory postural correction. Moreover, a pyramidotomy does not suppress either the lifting movement or the
postural adjustment (Nieoullon & Gahery, 1978). In accordance with Ito's
model, we could interpret this result as showing that overlearned postural
compensation associated with a relatively simple movement (i.e. belonging
to the repertoire of frequently used motor activities of the animal) is
commanded via the cortico-rubro-spinal pathways.

It remains, however, to be established whether unusual postural
constraints that necessitate the learning of a new pattern of postural
correction are critically dependent, during the initial phase of learning, on
the integrity of cortico-spinal pathways and whether a lesion of the rubro-
spinal tract would impair overlearned corrective adjustment.

As to the supposedly crucial role of the ruber nucleus in the learning
process, it is interesting to note the first demonstration by Tsukuhara et
al (1982) of a morphological change of cortico-rubral synapses consequent
upon the overlearning of a motor task in cat.

In conclusion, it is patently clear that this attempt to approach the
problem of motor learning at the level of neurophysiological mechanisms is
still speculative and incomplete. Most of the evidence currently available
concerns mechanisms that intervene at a late stage of the acquisition
process: namely, at the sensorimotor level of information processing where
the paleocerebellar structures intervene for the adaptive tuning of already
learned programmes (Brooks, 1984). The initial reorganisation process that
produces a programme in conformity with the goal prescription of the
intended plan is the province of the neocortical cognitive mode of information-
processing; it involves both the neo-striatum and the neocerebellar loops,
together with the association areas of the neocortex (vide Paillard, 1982).
Single unit recording techniques are now available and extensively used to
explore this new field of higher cortical functions where the models and concepts
of neurological and psychological studies are becoming increasingly relevant
for neurophysiological investigations.

Recent advances in neuroscience have produced an impressive amount
of new information - notably about microstructures and micromechanisms. In
contrast, we still lack coherent models that can integrate these data in a
way that is meaningful at the behavioural level.

Further progress will depend on our capacity to integrate the mass of
information about local mechanisms that is so rapidly accumulating into models

of how we imagine the whole system works. Thus it depends on our willingness to speculate about the brain's most significant functions and then submit such speculations to the verdict of carefully designed experiments: a challenging prospect indeed for the neurosciences in the immediate future.

439

References

Albus, J.S. (1971). A theory of cerebellar function. *Math. Biosc.*, *10*, 25-61.
Andersen, P. (1982). Cerebellar synaptic plasticity. Putting theories to the test. *Trends in Neurosc.*, *5*, 324-325.
Armand, J. (1982). The origin, course and terminations of corticospinal fibres in various mammals. In H.G.J.M. Kuypers and C.F. Martin (Eds.), *Descending pathways to the spinal cord. Progress in Brain Research*, *57*, 329-360.
Brooks, V.B. (1984). The cerebellum and adaptive tuning of movements. *Exp. Brain Res.*, *19*, 170-183.
Byrne, J.H. (1985). Neural and molecular mechanisms underlying information storage in Aplysia: implications for learning and memory. *Trends in Neurosc.*, *8*, 487-492.
Changeux, J.P., Courrège, P. & Danchin, A. (1973). A theory of epigenesis of neural networks by selective stabilization of synapses. *Proc. Nat. Acad. Sci. USA*, *70*, 2974-2978.
Cowan, W.M., Fawcette, J.W., O'Leary, D.D.M. & Stanfield, B.B. (1984). Regressive events in Neurogenesis. *Science*, *225*, 1258-1265.
Crepel, F. (1982). Regression of functional synapses in the immature mammalian cerebellum. *Trends in Neurosc.*, *5*, 266-269.
Ebbesson, S.O.E. (1984). Evolution and ontogeny of neural circuits. *Behav. Brain Sc.*, *7*, 321-366.
Fabre, M. & Buser, P. (1980). Structures involved in acquisition and performance of visually guided movement in the cat. *Acta Neurobiol. Exp.*, *40*, 95-116.
Fodor, J.A. (1983). *The modularity of mind*. Cambridge, MA: MIT Press.
Fodor, J.A. (1985). Multiple book-review of the modularity of mind. *Beh. Brain Sc.*, *8*, 1-33.
Gellman, R.S. & Miles, F.A. (1985). A new role for the cerebellum in conditioning. *Trends in Neurosc.*, *8*, 181-182.
Goodale, M.A. (1983). Vision as a sensorimotor system. In T.E. Robinson (Ed.), *Behavioural approaches to Brain Research*. Oxford University Press.
Heffner, R.S. & Masterton, R.B. (1975). Variation in form of the pyramidal tract and its relationship to digital dexterity. *Brain Behav. Evol.*, *12*, 161-200.
Hubel, D.H. & Wiesel, T.N. (1979). Brain mechanisms of vision. *Sc. Amer.*, *241*, 150-162.
Innocenti, G.M. & Caminiti, R. (1980). Postnatal shaping of callosal connections from sensory areas. *Exp. Brain Res.*, *38*, 381-394.
Ioffe, M.E. (1973). Pyramidal influences in establishment of new motor coordinations in dogs. *Physiol. Behav.*, *11*, 145-153.
Ito, M. (1984). *The cerebellum and neural control*. New York: Raven Press.
Ito, M. & Kano, M. (1982). Long lasting depression of parallel fibre-Purkinje cell transmission induced by conjunctive stimulation of parallel fibers and climbing fibers in the cerebellar cortex. *Neurosc. Lett.*, *33*, 253-258.
Kuypers, H.G.J.M. (1962). Corticospinal connections: postnatal development in the rhesus monkey. *Science*, *138*, 678-680.
Kwan, H.C., MacKay, W.A., Murphy, J.T. & Wong, Y.C. (1978). Spatial organization of precentral cortex in awake primates. II. Motor outputs. *J. Neurophysiol.*, *41*, 1120-1131.
Llinas, R., Walton, K., Hillman, D.E. & Sotello, C. (1975). Inferior olive. Its role in motor learning. *Science*, *190*, 1230-1231.

440

Loos, H. van der & Woolsey, T. (1973). Somatosensory cortex: structural alterations following early injury to sense organs. *Science, 179*, 395-398.

Mariani, J. (1983). Elimination of synapses during the development of the central nervous system. *Prog. Brain Res., 58*, 383-392.

Mark, R. (1974). *Memory and Nerve Cell Connections*. Oxford: Clarendon Press.

Marr, D. (1969). A theory of cerebellar cortex. *J. Physiol. London, 202*, 437-470.

Massion, J. (1979). Role of motor cortex in postural adjustments associated with movement. In H. Asanuma and V.V. Wilson (Eds.), *Integration in the nervous system*. Tokyo: Igaku-Shoin.

Mountcastle, V.B. (1979). An organizing principle for cerebral function. The unit module and the distributed system. In G.M. Edelman and V.B. Mountcastle (Eds.), *The Mindful Brain*. Cambridge, MA: MIT Press.

Nieoullon, A. & Cahery, Y. (1978). Influence of pyramidotomy on limb flexion movements induced by cortical stimulation and on associated postural adjustment in the cat. *Brain Res., 149*, 39-52.

Oppenheim, R.W. (1985). Naturally occurring cell death during neural development. *Trends in Neurosc., 8*, 487-493.

Paillard, J. (1960). The patterning of skilled movements. In Handbook of Physiology. Section I. *Neurophysiology, Vol. III, 67*, 1679-1708.

Paillard, J. (1977). La machine organisée et la machine organisante. *Revue Educ. Phys. Belge, 217*, 19-48.

Paillard, J. (1978). The pyramidal tract: two millions fibres in search of a function. *J. Physiol. Paris, 74*, 155-162.

Paillard, J. (1982). Apraxia and the neurophysiology of motor control. *Phil. Trans. R. Soc. London, B298*, 111-134.

Paillard, J. (1983). The functional labelling of neural codes. *Exp. Brain Res., 7*, 1-19.

Paillard, J. (1985). Les niveaux sensorimoteur et cognitif du contrôle de l'action. In M. Laurent and P. Therme (Eds.), *Recherches en activités physiques et sportives*. Editions Centre de Recherches UEREPS. Un. Aix-Marseille II.

Paillard, J. (in press). Sensorimotor versus cognitive encoding of spatial information. In P. Ellen and C. Thinus-Blanc (Eds.), *Cognitive processes and spatial orientation in animal and man*.

Phillips, C.G., Zeki, S. & Barlow, H.B. (1984). Localization of function in the cerebral cortex. *Brain, 107*, 328-361.

Rakic, P. (1972). Mode of cell migration to the superficial layers of foetal monkey neocortex. *J. Comp. Neurol., 145*, 61-84.

Spinelli, D.N. & Jensen, F.E. (1979). Plasticity: the mirror of experience. *Science, 203*, 75-78.

Strick, P.L. & Preston, J.B. (1982). Two representations of the hand in area 4 of a primate. III. Somatosensory input organization. *J. Neurophysiol., 48*, 150-159.

Tower, S.S. (1940). Pyramidal lesion in the monkey. *Brain, 63*, 36-90.

Tsukahara, N., Fujito, Y., Oda, Y. & Maeda, J. (1982). Formation of functional synapses in the adult cat red nucleus from the cerebellum following cross-innervation of forelimb flexor and extensor nerves. *Exp. Brain Res., 45*, 1-12.

Viala, D., Viala, G. & Fayein, N. (in press). Plasticity of locomotor organization in infant rabbits spinalized shortly after birth. In A. Gorio and M.E. Goldberger (Eds.), *Development on plasticity of the mammalian cord*.

Viana di Prisco, G. (1984). Hebb synaptic plasticity. *Progress in Neurobiol., 22*, 89-102.

Wiesendanger, M. (1969). The pyramidal tract. Recent investigations on its morphology and function. *Ergebn. Physiol.*, *61*, 73-136.

THE CONTRIBUTION OF THE NEUROSCIENCES TO UNDERSTANDING THE DEVELOPMENT OF REACHING

E.A. Roy, J. Starkes and J. Charlton

Two issues are of particular interest in considering the contribution that the neurosciences might make to understanding motor development. The first concerns whether changes in motor function observed in development are reflected or related to maturational changes in underlying neural systems. Considerable work in the development of vision (Boothe, Dobson & Teller, 1985) in both humans and monkeys and in the development of bird song (Konishi, 1985) supports the notion of parallel development in neural and behavioural processes. With regard to vision, for example, it appears that grating acuity is about 1 cy/deg in very young infants, more than two orders of magnitude below the 30 to 60 cy/deg shown by adults. Acuity improves slowly and monotonically over the early postnatal months until it reaches its adult level at three to five years postnatally in children and about one year in monkeys. Much of the normal development of acuity depends on maturation of neural elements lying in the retina and lateral geniculate nuclei which receive projections from the central visual field. Extrapolating from this work to motor development there is reason to predict that changes in motor development could be related to underlying changes in neural systems.

The second issue concerns how our present conceptualisation of the organisation of neural systems subserving perceptual motor functions might contribute to understanding the development of motor competencies. Clearly, the model depicting the organisation of neural systems underlying motor control may provide insight into developmental changes in these systems which in turn, may assist in comprehending changes in motor behaviour observed over development.

Both of these issues will be considered here through a focus upon the specific motor skills of reaching and grasping. Such a limited scope is necessary to make comments in reasonable space. Further, the kinematic aspects of these movements have been studied carefully in both adults (Jeannerod, 1984; Prablanc, Eschallier, Komilis & Jeannerod, 1979) and children (Von Hofsten, 1979, 1984) and the neurophysiological substrates of reaching have been the focus of much research (e.g., Humphrey, 1979).

Discussion begins with a review of the components of reaching observed in adults. A brief review of the development of reaching observed up to two years follows. We then discuss the relationships between development in neural systems and ontogenetic changes observed in reaching and grasping, with a particular focus on the issues alluded to at the outset of the paper. Finally, consideration is given to other issues which are thought important in comtemplating the contribution of neurosciences to understanding motor development.

COMPONENTS OF REACHING

Prehensile movements represent advanced, multi-joint complex co-ordination tasks involving integration of visual and kinesthetic information in order to reach a point in body-centred space and to adjust hand grasp in accordance with the size, shape and weight of the object. Furthermore, the co-ordination of not only hand and eye movements, but head and trunk posture is thought to contribute significantly to the control of prehensile movements.

Much of the work on prehensile movements suggests that there are three components involved (Prablanc et al, 1979; Paillard, 1982). One is related to eye and head movements directed toward the target. The other two components involve movement of the arm and hand. The first component, transport, involves propelling the arm toward the target with an initial fast or ballistic movement followed by a slower phase in which visual information is used to direct the hand to the target. The second component here, manipulation, involves grasping the object at the target location. Tactual and kinesthetic information are important sources of information in this phase.

While there are three separable components, they are integrated. The onset of EMG controlling eye, head and hand movements in reaching for the target coincide temporally (Prablanc et al, 1979). Further, accuracy in pointing at targets is greatly improved when the head and eyes are free to move in the direction of the target suggesting that signals generated by head and eye movement may facilitate at some level in the central nervous system the organisation of target-directed hand movements (Biguer, Prablanc & Jeannerod, 1984).

Paillard and Amblard (1985) have cited convincing evidence for the contribution of two parallel and semi-independent visual channels operating in the control of spatially oriented movements. Central vision, they propose, is highly sensitive to position cues and plays an essential role in the final homing-in phase in pointing tasks. In this respect, central vision codes rate of change of location of the moving hand. In a complementary role, the peripheral retina picks up movement cues related to the velocity and direction of the hand trajectory.

Finally, there is an apparent coupled timing relationship between the transport and manipulation components in reaching. Jeannerod (1984) maintains that up until peak velocity in the transport component, the fingers extend to accommodate the target object. The onset of finger closure in the manipulation component follows and is highly correlated with the beginning of the low velocity phase in the transport component. Vision apparently plays little role in this temporal co-ordination since the synchrony of finger closure with the low velocity phase remains when vision of the moving hand is not present during reaching.

DEVELOPMENT OF REACHING

In considering the development of reaching we will not extensively review the literature but rather focus on specific aspects which will serve as points for discussion later on. Research into the development of reaching (see Hay, 1984 for a review) has focused on the neonatal period (e.g. Trevarthen, Murray & Hubley, 1981) to three months of age, the postnatal period to about eighteen months (e.g. Von Hofsten, 1979) and much later in a period beginning at about five years of age (e.g. Hay, 1981). The reach and grasp pattern in neonates has been termed prereaching (Trevarthen et al, 1981; Bower, 1974). Under certain conditions infants as young as 6-11 days can perform reaching movements. These movements appear to have the characteristics of reaching movements observed in adults, although they are much more variable. There appear to be distinct transport and manipulation phases in which the opening and closing of the hand is coupled to the end of arm extension and upward rotation of the wrist. Wrist flexion and the degrees of hand opening appear to be varied and unpredictable. Examination of the temporal aspects of the transport component of these movements reveals that they are composed of a succession of ballistic elements which have the same fundamental cadence as the saccades seen in visual scanning. There appears to be some co-ordination with head and eye movements and compensation for postural changes.

The clearest deficiencies in prereaching in addition to it being un-predictable is that it is stereotyped and capable of only very limited modulation to adjust for object position or size, and the movement is some-what erratic and affected by reflex perturbations. The influence of reflexes is evident in a study of Amiel-Tison and Grenier (1980, reported in Hay, 1984, p. 256) who showed that once involuntary reflex responses had been inhibited, a new "liberated motor behaviour" emerged in which reaching movements were slower and more co-ordinated, similar to those seen in older children. While involuntary reflexive movements may interfere with reaching during this period, there is some evidence to suggest that some reflexes may also facilitate reaching (De Schonen, 1977). In reaching for objects with one hand there is a compensatory flexion of the other arm toward the body. De Schonen (1977) suggests that this movement of the other arm results from the asymmetric tonic neck reflex which serves to maintain postural equilibrium enabling transport of the arm in the reaching movement.

While there appear to be separate transport and manipulation components in prereaching, work by Bower (1974; Bower, Broughton & Moore, 1970) examining the latency of grasp following contact with the object suggests that these components are not completely separable until after five months. In reaching for real objects, neonates coincided their grasp with object contact. Infants at least five months old, however, demonstrated on average a contact to grasp delay of approximately 450 msec. The hand stayed open, and after the arm was transported, made exploratory movements. Further, in reaching for virtual objects neonates closed their hands on what they thought was the object, while infants older than five months inhibited such hand closures. These findings may suggest that in the neonate, the trans-port and manipulation components of reaching are preprogrammed together and occur despite environmental cues indicating the object is not graspable (i.e. only a virtual object). An alternate interpretation, however, is that upon touching the object at the end of the reaching movement, the grasp is triggered, resulting in automatic grasping of the object.

Toward the end of this period (third month) the temporal co-ordination between transport and manipulation in reaching becomes disrupted. The "rather fluid stereotype of arm extension and retraction, and the associated hand opening and closing, become blocked or broken up into irregular fragments" (Trevarthen et al, 1981, p. 219). The infant may fail to reach at all, or may make incoherent swipes which do not have the co-ordinated pattern seen in prereaching. Toward the beginning of the fifth month reaching and grasping become more integrated such that the infant acquires a more refined level of control not seen in prereaching. Adjustments to compensate for changes in object position and size now appear possible.

Several investigators have studied movements in the period from five to approximately eighteen months. Wishart, Bower and Dunkeld (1978) studied infants 6-11 months of age, reaching for objects when lights were left on versus suddenly shut off during a reach. At five months infants had no trouble locating the object on the first reach, whether lights were on or off. With older infants, however, the probability of precise contact increased with lights on. The reliance upon visual information to guide and project the hand to the object thus appears to increase with age. If this is true we should see significant changes in transport and trajectory of the arm in older infants. In fact such changes were observed in studies by McDonnell (McDonnell, 1975; McDonnell & Abraham, 1981).

In these two studies by McDonnell, infants 4-10 months of age were examined for their abilities to reach for objects during prism adaptation. Both studies found that even the youngest infants were able to adapt to prisms and acquire the object. Visual guidance appeared to peak around 7 months of age. With the increased reliance on visual cues, arm trajectory was significantly altered. In a study of these trajectory changes McDonnell (1979) was able to illustrate developmental changes in transport of the arm. From 4-5 months infants used "sweeping" movements employing only the shoulder. This resulted in an immature ballistic approach of the arm. By 7 months the trajectory was "parabolic", using the shoulder and some elbow control. This parabolic approach reflected the use of visual corrections. Finally by 9 months of age the child was able to use a "straight" approach. All joints of the arm were co-ordinated to provide a smooth ballistic approach to the object.

Further study of proximal changes was conducted by Von Hofsten (1979, 1980). He studied infants 3 to 8 months and found that with age there was a decrease in the number of submovements involved in reaching. Von Hofsten's basic assumption is that each submovement represents a trajectory change based on a visual correction. A second finding was that age alters the first submovement; it increases in length, covers more distance, and reflects the greatest acceleration component of the movement. Clearly older infants are creating a more efficient movement trajectory and using less, but more critical visual feedback. Von Hofsten also found (1979) that smooth grasping did not appear until after arm transport had been stabilised at 5 to 6 months of age.

While the previous studies address the issue of arm transport and proximal control, several studies have also dealt with the effects of maturation on distal control. The most obvious links between the functions are the earlier reported findings of Von Hofsten, and the finding that, in reaching, the forward extension of the arm is often accompanied by the synergic opening of the hand. (Trevarthen, 1974; Von Hofsten, 1982). Another study by Von Hofsten (1984) demonstrated that this synergic response of the hand during forearm extension is found in infants older than four months. However, this behaviour was only apparent when the object was visually fixated. While the hand opening appears to be a genuine form of adaptive behaviour in the infant it too appears to be initially under the influence of visual guidance.

Perhaps the finest study so far of distal control in infants is by Von Hofsten and Fazel-Zandy (1984), who studied the development of visual guidance in adjusting the hand and fingers to the orientation of an object. Infants studied were 4 ½ to 8 ½ months. Subjects were presented with vertical or horizontal rods. Hand orientation while reaching for the rods was measured during the last 540 msec of the approach. They witnessed dramatic stabilisation of the motor system of the arm during this period. Smoother, straighter approaches to the object were seen, that must have had corollary effects on the infant's ability to control the hand during the approach. More specifically, 4 ½ month olds crudely adjusted hand orientation prior to object contact. Therefore tactual guidance of grasping did not precede and was not a prerequisite to visual guidance. Adjustments before or during the early part of the reach appeared to be as important as those during the later, measured part. Presumably early or prior adjustments, like hand rotation, limit the degrees of freedom to be controlled during the movement.

STRUCTURE-FUNCTION RELATIONS

Having selectively reviewed the development of reaching in infants, we now turn to a consideration of whether changes in neural structures over development may relate to the changes in reaching behaviour. One of the clearest points regarding neural organisation is that there are phylogenetically newer structures which we do not share with species lower down on the phylogenetic scale. If we expand our concept of development for a moment to consider development from a phylogenetic perspective, we might predict that as we move up the phylogenetic scale there would be changes in motor function associated with the proliferation of neocortical structures.

Indeed, there is some evidence to indicate that moving up the phylogenetic scale there is a progressive increase in the ability for fine manipulative movements with the upper limbs (Weisendanger, 1981). The progressive ability to carry out such fine movements is correlated with the development of the corticospinal motor system both at the cortical level as well as in its projections to the motor neuron pools in the spinal cord. Indeed most animals with an ability for fine control have monosynaptic connections from the cortical representation of the corticospinal system (Brodman's Areas 1, 2, 3, 4) and the motor neuron pool. Thus, the progression through the phylla in the ability for fine control of reaching and grasping seems related to progressive development in the neural system subserving this ability.

This phylogenetic evidence provides some basis for postulating that human postnatal development may relate to maturational alterations in brain structures. Indeed, humans are altricial species meaning that they are born with considerable structural development of the brain yet to be completed (Rose, 1980). Thus, there is the potential for a relationship between neural and behavioural development.

Evidence that the development of neocortical structures in moving up the phylla affords increasing precision in the control of reaching and grasping movements suggests that ontogenetic changes in reaching may reflect this phylogenetic trend, that is, an increasing contribution of newer brain structures to control throughout development. There is considerable evidence that phylogenetically newer neocortical structures undergo myelination later than the older, subcortical structures (Yakolev & LeCours,

1967). Myelination is frequently thought to be an indication of the functional maturity of brain structures, thus providing some structural evidence for the increasing contribution of neocortical and neocerebellar structures to reaching movements throughout ontogeny.

There are several suggested indicators of an increasing cortical control. At approximately 3 or 4 months many reflexes drop out of the infant's behaviour, presumably as a result of increasing inhibition of lower centres by cortical structures. Before integration between cortical and subcortical regions, stimulation elicits involuntary, subcortically mediated reflex responses. As cortical centres mature and become integrated with subcortical areas, primitive reflex behaviour is inhibited, and the infant progresses to a more mature, integrated neurological state (Woodruff, 1978).

Another indicator of increasing cortical control is the onset of organised rhythmic activity in occipital areas in 3 to 4 month old infants. Given that the occipital lobes are the primary cortical projection area of the visual system, this increase is thought to reflect the onset of cortical visual function. Indeed behavioural evidence suggests that infants younger than 9 - 10 weeks use different visual information than older infants. The younger infants are sensitive to information such as the size or number of elements of the stimulus, a largely quantitative aspect. Older infants, however, are sensitive to more qualitative aspects of the stimulus such as form or pattern which have been thought to be associated with the development of cortical visual function (Bronson, 1974; Woodruff, 1978). The parallels between EEG alpha onset and the disappearance of primitive reflexes, then, provide evidence that normal infants are functionally subcortical organisms. Through development there is an increasing contribution made by phylogenetically newer brain structures.

In considering our own discussion of the development of reaching, several indications of the increasing contribution of neocortical and neo-cerebellar structures through development are evident. First, De Schonen (1977) suggests that the onset of accurate, well coordinated reaching appears associated with the dropping out of the tonic neck reflex. Recall that this reflex is apparently used to enable the infant to stabilise his body during the reaching movement. It is possible that the elimination of this reflex is associated with an increasing contribution of sensorimotor cortex to postural stabilisation during reaching (Weisendanger, 1981).

The increasing use of a ballistic, feed-forward mode of control observed by Von Hofsten (1979) may provide another line of evidence for the contribution of phylogenetically newer structures in reaching. The use of such a predictive mode of control would seem to involve the contribution of neocerebellar and basal ganglia structures (Marsden, 1984). Evidence that this is the case comes from the observation that cerebellar patients, while able to use such predictive control, are notoriously inaccurate. On the other hand patients with basal ganglia disorders seem unable to use this type of feed-forward control at all (e.g. Flowers, 1978). Much like Von Hofsten's younger infants they use a series of small movements which seem to be predominantly visually guided.

The use of this type of predictive control would also require accurate postural stabilisation prior to the reaching movement. This postural stabilisation may be afforded by the increasing control exhibited by prerolandic motor areas over spinal motor neural pools, a point previously made in reference to De Schonen's work in the dropping out of reflexes (Weisendanger, 1981).

The increasing precision in the control of reaching movements may reflect the contribution of the corticospinal tract in the control of distal musculature. As well, there may be an increasing contribution of what Trevarthen (1968) has termed focal vision subserved by the phylogenetically newer geniculostriate visual system. The use of this system could account for the increasing importance of visual information (e.g. McDonnell, 1979) in reaching and the increasing precision in the use of this information in directing reaching movements. Indeed, Bronsun (1974) has argued that infants in the first months of life rely on the phylogenetically older second visual system. In the third month the newer cortical or focal visual system begins to function.

This idea that phylogenetically newer brain structures play an increasingly important role in development emphasises the point that in a complex functional system (e.g. Roy, 1978) it is conceivable for different components in the system to play increasingly more important roles throughout development. More generally, different components may develop at different rates and so become functionally mature at different times. This notion is exemplified well in Goldman's (1972) studies of the effects of lesioning different regions in the frontal lobes on monkeys at different stages in development on subsequent adult behaviour. She has shown, for instance, that lesions in dorsolateral prefrontal areas of infant and juvenile monkeys have little or no effect on behaviour when compared to adults. As adults, however, these early lesioned monkeys do show the expected deficits. Early lesions in the orbitofrontal region, however, are associated with deficits at this point in development, but the deficits dissipate over development.

Goldman (1972) argues that the difference in recovery patterns here relates to the functional maturity of the undamaged brain areas in a given region. Areas which mature early and so are "committed" to a functional role may not be able to compensate for damage to another region. On the other hand areas which mature later and are relatively "uncommitted" functionally at an early stage of development may be able to assume the role of the damaged areas. Using this logic she reasoned that the dorsolateral area may mature later than the orbitofrontal area. The decreasing deficit with orbitofrontal lesions over development, she thought, reflected the relatively "uncommitted" dorsolateral area assuming the function of this region. The increasing deficit observed with dorsolateral lesions, she proposed, reflected the fact that this area was functionally immature early in development and that the early maturing orbitofrontal region, being functionally committed, was unable to assume the function of the dorsolateral region.

This idea that different brain structures, and, thus, the different components they subserve develop at different rates may provide some basis for understanding the relatively non-monotonic trend observed in motor development. That is, components which appear early in development drop out only to reappear later. One example from reaching is the early appearance of a dissociation between the transport and manipulation components in prereaching. This dissociation seems to break down around the third month. There is a dropping out of the grasp or manipulation component along with a loss of precision in the control of the reaching movement. About one month later the grasp reappears and is well coordinated with the reaching or transport component (Trevarthen et al, 1981). This pattern suggests that the neural systems subserving proximal and distal motor control are developing at different rates. Proximal control develops early. Around the second or third month there may be increasing development in the neural system (corticospinal) subserving distal control. At this point the components of the reaching movement subserved by this neural system, grasping, become disorganised. Following the development of maturational changes in this system which may relate to myelination (Yakolev & LeCours, 1967) there is a reappearance of this component in the reaching movement.

Not only does the grasping component reappear at this time but also this component is better coordinated with the transport component. Given that myelination is beginning in the neocerebellar and neocortical circuits, this increased coordination could reflect the increasing contribution of neo-cerebellar areas to control.

Another line of evidence relating behavioural changes to changes in neural systems comes from work examining the effects of altering sensory input on neuronal development. Given the perception action linkage described by Arbib (1972, 1981) it would seem that while the basic neuronal structures may be largely present at birth, perceptual experience may be critical to the complete development of the behaviour subserved by the neural system concerned. Indeed, work by Wiesel and Hubel (1985) with kittens showed that deprivation of form vision led to a selective degeneration of cells in the striate cortex responsive to form or pattern of a visual stimulus. Research work such as this by Wiesel and Hubel suggests that genetic programs controlling maturational changes in the nervous system specify so called critical periods during which the conditions of input determine permanent characteristics of the nervous system.

To further elaborate using an example of direct relevance to reaching, Held (Held & Hein, 1963; Hein & Held, 1967; Held & Bauer, 1967) demonstrate that kittens and monkeys reared without sight of their forelimbs, but not restrained otherwise either visually or manually, were unable to guide the hand or paw to grasp or strike objects. Given the work of Hubel and Wiesel it is possible that depriving the animals of sight of the moving hand may have prevented the development of neuronal connections subserving visually guided reaching. Considering that disruption of the cortico-cortical connections between parietal (Area 7) and premotor areas in monkey leads to an impairment in visually directed reaching (Haaxma & Kuypers, 1975) and in humans leads to an impairment termed optic ataxia (Damasio & Benton, 1982) it is possible that preventing the animal from viewing its moving hand disrupted development of these cortico-cortical connections.

The importance of early experience in developing the potential for eye hand co-ordination is exemplified in the long and intense period infants spend in looking at their moving hand prior to actually using it in visually directed reaching. A second example of the importance of this experience is provided in an anecdote by Arbib (1981). Arbib described a friend who had cataracts removed after the first twenty years of his life. There was apparently a time shortly after removal of the cataracts in which he spent long periods just watching his moving hands.

The fact that the cataract patient as well as Held's monkeys are event-ually able to learn to visually guide their hands to targets once visual information of hand movement is available suggests that the deprivation of visual information of hand movement may not have prevented the development of the cortico-cortical pathways. Rather, the deprivation may have prevented the animal from *learning* to use these pathways. Thus, there may be a form of critical period for this type of learning. If the organism is not availed of this experience during this period, experiences at a later point may not lead to as effective use of these pathways. Commenting on this issue Arbib (1981) argues that following a period of exposure to visual feedback about hand movement, the formerly visually-deprived animals, in reaching for targets, developed a set of isolated reach commands associated with each target (e.g. A-reach, B-reach, C-reach) which were each paired with a different visual stimulus for head and eye direction for looking at each target. In contrast the normal non-visually-deprived animals may have used a single command, "reach (X)", with a parameter, the visual coordinate X of the target.

THE CONTRIBUTION OF THE NEUROSCIENCES: ISSUES TO CONSIDER

Within the context of the models described above depicting the organisation of the neurobehavioural system for coordinated action we have proposed some parallels between changes in neural systems and changes in reaching behaviour through early development. Such structure-function correlates reflect one contribution neuroscience may make to understanding motor development. There are a number of other important issues eminating from structural and functional principles of neural organisation, however, which must be considered in order to more fully appreciate the contribution of the neurosciences.

Many of the issues to be discussed here relate to the notion that action involves the operation of functional systems. Roy (1983a) has argued that the control of action involves both conceptual and production systems. The conceptual system provides a knowledge base for action. The production system comprises the mechanisms for the control of movements involved in actions. Control is thought to be exerted at a number of levels involving both top-down and bottom-up processes. The top-down processes are thought to involve the operation of cognitive processes in the conceptual system and generalised motor programs in the production system, while the bottom-up processes involve the interface between the performer and the environment. Performance of actions involves a balance of control between levels subserving top-down processes which demand attention and levels subserving bottom-up processes which involve much less attention demands (Roy, 1982, 1983a; Roy & Square, 1985).

Using this notion of a functional system it is possible that levels and components in the system may develop at different rates. Accordingly, it would seem important to design tests which would enable one to study the contribution of these levels and components separately to determine whether they follow different time courses in development. Using an action sequencing task Roy (1981, 1983a) has found that different types of errors reflect disruptions of different processes in learning the sequence. For example, in studying patients with left or right hemisphere damage, substitutions observed in sequencing errors revealed a conceptual disorder in the aphasic but not in the non-aphasic left-hemisphere patients, although both left-hemisphere groups made many more sequencing errors that did the right-hemisphere patients.

David (1985) has adapted the task developed by Roy (1981) to study sequence learning in children from kindergarten to grade three. Basically, she found that third graders were able to learn the task more quickly and proficiently than the kindergarteners. Further, the kindergarteners tended to employ kinesthetic cues for recall, while the third graders used verbal rehearsal more often. David suggests that these differences observed between the kindergarten and third grade groups supports a model (Roy, 1983a) of praxis development which encompasses changes in both conceptual and production systems. Younger children had more difficulty remembering the serial order, she argues, since they had not yet developed the capacity to rehearse verbal labels. These observations reinforce the idea that different processes develop at different rates and we need to design tasks to measure these changes more precisely.

Considering the proposal that action involves conceptual and production systems and David's (1985) findings regarding sequence learning in children, it would seem important to examine higher cognitive/conceptual structures and processes in skill development. The fact that we are able to imitate the use of common objects outside the context in which they are normally used and without actually holding them suggests that such cognitive or knowledge structures exist. There is some evidence that disruption of these processes may underly impairments in sequence learning in certain patients (e.g. Roy, 1981, 1983a). Further, David (1985) suggests that the increasing availability of these structures and processes through development may facilitate the learning of movement sequences.

Another point related to the need to consider cognitive processes in development of skill concerns the strategies used in performance (e.g. Roy, 1983b; Roy & Elliott, in press). With advancing development, additional strategies for performance may become available, thus affecting the quality, efficiency and consistency of skill learning. In support of this notion, David (1985) found that younger children used kinesthetic information to code the action sequence, while the older ones employed a more verbal strategy which seemed to enable more proficient learning of the sequence. Along with the availability of more diverse strategies with development, metacognitive processes also emerge fostering a greater awareness of what strategies are available. Metacognition has been studied in tasks such as reading and problem solving (e.g. Flavell, 1976) but has received relatively little consideration in motor skill learning (see Das, Reid & Wall, this volume).

Somewhat related to the notion of strategies is the idea of task demands. To some extent the demands of a task constrain the strategies which may be useful in performance. In addition there is some evidence suggesting that the demands of a motor task may relate to the selective activation of various brain regions (Roland, Larsen, Lassen & Skinho, 1980). For example, in Roland's work single finger tapping principally engaged the primary motor area. Sequential finger tapping involved activation of both the primary and supplementary motor areas. Sequential target pointing using the whole arm engaged not only these motor areas but also parietal areas. Given these data, task demands may not only constrain available strategies, but may also relate to activity in selective brain regions; thus, the availability of certain strategies with advancing development may relate to the development of these brain regions.

The notion that action may be controlled through functional systems comprised of interacting components seems reflected in the columnar organisation of the neocortex (e.g. Goldman-Rakic, 1984). The cortex is thought to be organised into modular columns in a vertical orientation. These modules are formed into integrated networks which communicate through patterns of inhibition and excitation. Neurons in association cortex neither receive input directly from, nor do they project directly to motor neurons. These types of neurons could take on "computational" functions as described by Arbib (1981). The potential for combination and recombinations between input and output provides a highly adaptive and plastic mechanism for information processing. Further, the "spatial parcellation of cortex into smaller and more tractable cellular units with knowable inputs and outputs should at the least facilitate the analysis of structure function relationships of association cortex, long deemed inaccessible to neurobiological analysis" (Goldman-Rakic, 1984). Such an opportunity for studying structure-function correlates may greatly enhance the precision with which one may trace the course of the development of neurobehavioural functions in motor control.

This principle of columnar organisation also affords a system which is self-organising (e.g. Fentress, 1984). Indeed, one feature of development may be an increasing propensity for self organisation. Work by Warner and Karrer (1984) and Todor and Lazarus (in press) provides some support for this contention in that there appears to be an increasing tendency toward inhibition of associated movement through development.

A final consideration here relates to the role that the environment plays in development. According to the model alluded to above (Roy, 1983a), the performer and the environment in which he performs mutually relate in such a way that movements meet the demands of the environment. This relationship is defined by a system of constraints which are internal (i.e., in the performer) and external (i.e., in the environment). This notion of contraints has important implications for development. Throughout development the internal constraints are changing. Muscle and bony mass increase, thus affecting the forces and mechanical advantages involved. Furthermore, increasing neocortical and neocerebellar control through development serve to facilitate differentiation and integration among body and limb segments used in movement. These internal changes in constraints serve to alter the nature of constraints in the environment (e.g. forces required to move in a given environment change), a fact which immensely complicates the study of the interface between the child and his environment.

In summary we have provided some evidence that patterns in the development of reaching in infants relate to maturational changes in underlying brain function. The tendency through development toward the co-ordination of postural control with reaching movement, along with greater feedforward control in reaching and precision in the control of distal muscles in grasping, may all relate to the increasing contribution of cortical and neocerebellar areas to behaviour. Much additional work with both human infants and animals using tasks sensitive to changing control strategies over development needs to be done in order to more clearly understand the neurobehavioural bases of motor development.

ACKNOWLEDGEMENTS

Preparation of this manuscript was supported through grants to Dr. Eric Roy from the Natural Sciences and Engineering Research Council and National Health Research Development Program, Health & Welfare, Canada.

454

References

Arbib, M.A. (1972). *The Metaphorical Brain: An Introduction to Cybernetics as Artificial Intelligence and Brain Theory*. New York: Interscience.
Arbib, M.A. (1981). Perceptual structures and distributed motor control. In J.M. Brookhart and V.B. Mountcastle (Eds.), *Handbook of Physiology, Vol. II:2*. Bethesda, Maryland: American Psychological Society.
Biguer, B., Prablanc, C. & Jeannerod, M. (1984). The contribution of coordinated eye and head movements in hand pointing accuracy. *Experimental Brain Research, 55,* 462-469.
Boothe, R.G., Dobson, V. & Teller, D.Y. (1985). Postnatal development of vision in humans and nonhuman primates. *Annual Reviews of Neuroscience, 8,* 495-545.
Bower, T.G.R. (1974). *Development in Infancy*. San Francisco: Freeman.
Bower, T.G.R., Broughton, J.M. & Moore, M.K. (1970). Demonstration of intention in the reaching behaviour of neonate humans. *Nature, 228,* (5272): 679-681.
Bronsun, G. (1974). The postnatal growth of visual capacity. *Child Development, 45,* 873-890.
Damasio, A.R. & Benton, A. (1979). Impairments of hand movement under visual guidance. *Neurology, 29,* 170-178.
David, K.S. (1985). Motor sequencing strategies in school-aged children. *Journal of the American Physical Therapy Association, 65, (6),* 883-889.
De Schonen, C. (1977). Functional asymmetries in the development of bimanual coordinations in human infants. *Journal of Human Movement Studies, 3,* 144-156.
Fentress, J.C. (1984). The development of coordination. *Journal of Motor Behavior, 16 (2),* 99-134.
Flavell, J.H. (1976). Metacognitive aspects of problem solving. In L.B. Resnick (Ed.), *The Nature of Intelligence*. Hillsdale, N.J.: Lawrence Erlbaum Associates.
Flowers, K. (1978). Some frequency response characteristics of Parkinsonism on pursuit tracking. *Brain, 104,* 167-186.
Goldman, P.S. (1972). Developmental determinants of cortical plasticity. *Acta Neurobiologica Experimentalis, 32,* 495-511.
Goldman-Rakic, P. (1984). Modular organization of prefrontal cortex. *Trends in Neurosciences, 7,* 419-429.
Haaxma, R. & Kuypers, H.G.J.M. (1974). Role of occipito-frontal and cortico-cortical connections in visual guidance of relatively independent hand and finger movements in rhesus monkeys. *Brain Research, 71,* 361-366.
Hay, L. (1979). Spatial- temporal analysis of movements in children: Motor programs versus feedback in the development of reaching. *Journal of Motor Behavior, 11, (3),* 189-200.
Hay, L. (1981). The effect of amplitude and accuracy requirements on movement time in children. *Journal of Motor Behavior, 13,* 177-186.
Hay, L. (1984). The development of movement control. In M.M. Smyth and A.M. Wing (Eds.), *The Psychology of Human Movement*. London: Academic Press.
Hein, A. & Held, R. (1967). Dissociation of the visual placing response into elicited and guided components. *Science, 15,* 390-392.
Held, R. & Bauer, J.A. Jr. (1967). Visually guided reaching in infant monkeys after restricted rearing. *Science, 155,* 718-720.
Held, R. & Hein, A. (1963). Movement-produced stimulation in the development of visually-guided behaviour. *Journal of Comparative Physiological Psychology, 56,* 872-876.

Hofsten, C. von. (1979). Development of visually directed reaching: The approach phase. *Journal of Human Movement Studies, 5,* 160-178.

Hofsten, C. von. (1980). Predictive reaching for moving objects by human infants. *Journal of Experimental Child Psychology, 30,* 369-382.

Hofsten, C. von. (1982). Eye-hand coordination in the newborn. *Developmental Psychology, 18,* 450-461.

Hofsten, C. von. (1984). Developmental changes in the organization of prereaching movements. *Developmental Psychology, 20, (3)* 378-388.

Hofsten, C. von & Fazel-Zandy, C. (1984). Development of visually guided hand orientation in reaching. *Journal of Experimental Child Psychology, 38,* 298-219.

Humphrey, D.R. (1979). On the cortical control of visually directed reaching: Contributions by non-precentral motor areas. In R.E. Talbott and D.R. Humphrey (Eds.), *Posture and Movement.* New York: Raven Press.

Jeannerod, M. (1984). The timing of natural prehension movements. *Journal of Motor Behavior, 16,* 235-254.

Jeannerod, M. & Prablanc, C. (1983). Visual control of reaching movements in man. In J.E. Desmedt (Ed.), *Motor Control Mechanisms in Health and Disease.* New York: Raven Press.

Konishi, M. (1985). Birdsong: From behaviour to neuron. *Annual Reviews of Neuroscience, 8,* 125-170.

McDonnell, P.M. (1975). The development of visually guided reaching. *Perception & Psychophysics, 18,* 181-185.

McDonnell, P.M. (1979). Patterns of eye-hand coordination in the first year of life. *Canadian Journal of Psychology, 33,* 253-267.

McDonnell, P.M. & Abraham, W.C. (1981). A longitudinal study of prism adaptation in infants from six to nine months of age. *Child Development, 52,* 463-469.

Paillard, J. (1982). The contribution of peripheral and central vision to visually guided reaching. In D.J. Ingle, M.A. Goodal and R.J.W. Mansfield (Eds.), *Analysis of Visual Behaviour.* Cambridge: Massachusetts: MIT Press.

Paillard, J. & Amblard, B. (1985). Static versus kinetic visual vues for the processing of spatial relationships. In D.J. Ingle, J. Jeannerod and D.N. Lee (Eds.), *Brain Mechanisms of Spatial Vision.* La Haye: Martinus Nijhoff.

Prablanc, C., Eschallier, J.F., Komilis, E. & Jeannerod, M. (1979). Optional response of eye and hand motor systems in pointing at a visual target. Spatio temporal characteristics of eye and hand movement and their relationships when varying the amount of visual information. *Biological Cybernetics, 35,* 113-124.

Roland, P.E., Larsen, B., Lassen, W. & Skinhoj, E. (1980). Supplementary motor area and other cortical areas in the organization of voluntary movement. *Journal of Neurophysiology, 43,* 118-136.

Rose, D. (1980). Some functional correlates of the maturation of neural systems. In D. Caplan (Ed.), *Biological Studies of Mental Processes.* Cambridge, Massachusetts: MIT Press.

Roy, E.A. (1981). Action sequencing and lateralized cerebral damage: Evidence for asymmetries in control. In J. Long and A. Baddley (Eds.), *Attention and Performance, IX,* New Jersey: Erlbaum.

Roy, E.A. (1982). Action and Performance. In A. Ellis (Ed.), *Normality and Pathology in Cognitive Function.* London: Academic Press.

Roy, E.A. (1983a). Neuropsychological perspectives on apraxia and related disorders. In R.A. Magill (Ed.), *Advances in Psychology, Volume 12, Memory and Control of Action.* Amsterdam: North-Holland Co.

Roy, E.A. (1983b). Manual performance asymmetries and motor control processes; subject-generated changes in response parameters. *Human Movement Science,* 271-277.

Roy, E.A. & Elliott, D. (in press). Manual asymmetries in visually aimed movements. *Canadian Journal of Psychology.*

Roy, E.A. & Square, P.A. (1985). Common Considerations in the study of limb verbal and oral apraxia. In E.A. Roy (Ed.), *Advances in Psychology, Volume 23, Neuropsychological Studies of Apraxia and Related Disorders.* Amsterdam: Elsevier Science Publishers B.V. (North-Holland).

Todor, J.L. & Lazarus, J.C. (in press). Inhibitory influences on the emergence of motor competence in childhood. In C. Fuchs, L. Zui and L. Zaichowsky (Eds.), *The Psychology of Motor Behavior.* Wingate, Israel: Wingate Institute Press.

Trevarthen, C. (1974). The psychobiology of speech development. In E.H. Lenneberg (Ed.), *Language and Brain: Developmental Aspects, Vol. 12.* Boston: Neurosciences Research Program.

Trevarthen, C., Murray, L. & Hubley, P. (1981). Psychology of infants. In J.A. Davis and J. Dobbing (Eds.), *Scientific Foundations of Paediatrics.* London: William Heinemann Books Ltd.

Warren, C.A. & Karrer, R. (1984). Movement-related potentials during development: A replication and extension of relationships to age, motor control and I.Q. *International Journal of Neuroscience, 24,* 81-96.

Wiesendanger, M. (1981). The pyramidal tract: Its structure and fucntion. In A.L. Towe and E.S. Luschei (Eds.), *Handbook of Behavioral Neurobiology, Volume 5, Motor Coordination.* New York: Plenum Press.

Wiesel, T.N. & Hubel, D.H. (1985). Comparison of the effects of unilateral and bilateral eye closure on cortical unit responses in kittens. *Journal of Neurophysiology, 28,* 1029-1040.

Wishart, J.G., Bower, T.G.R. & Dunkeld, J. (1978). Reaching in the dark. *Perception, 7,* 507-512.

Woodruff, D.S. (1978). Brain electrical activity and behavior relationships over the life span. In P. Baltes (Ed.), *Life Span Development and Behavior, Volume 1.* New York: Academic Press.

Yakolev, P.I. & Le Cours, A. (1967). The myelogenetic cycles of regional maturation of the brain. In A. Menkowski (Ed.), *Regional Development of the Brain in Early Life.* Philadelphia: Davis.

457

SECTION 9

EPILOGUE

A MORPHOLOGICAL PERSPECTIVE ON THE ORIGIN AND EVOLUTION OF MOVEMENT PATTERNS*

P.N. Kugler

> The waves of the sea, the little ripples on the shore, the sweeping curve of the sandy bay between the headlands, the outline of the hills, the shape of the clouds, all of these are so many riddles of form, so many problems of morphology (D'Arcy Thompson, 1917).

INTRODUCTION

One of the most striking and intriguing aspects of a living system is its ability to continually assemble and disassemble long range correlations among collections of 'atomistic-like' cellular units (such as cells, organs, muscles, etc). Perhaps the most interesting aspect of this phenomena is that only a small number of *well-defined correlational states* ('macroscopic patterns') tends to be assembled. In addition, the developmental sequences that converge onto these macroscopic patterns can originate from a variety of initial conditions and are stable with respect to perturbation. Nowhere is this process more readily apparent than in the assembling, sustaining, and dissolving of biomechanical movement patterns. The precision and accuracy of the process is attested to by the actions of a performing artist or skilled athlete. The subtlety of the process is revealed in the actions of an infant discovering the organisational capabilities of its own movement system (see Figure 1). Identifying the design principles underlying this process is fundamental to movement science; it is the topic of this paper.

---

* There are no concepts in this paper that do not bear the conceptual efforts of my long standing relationship with Professor M.T. Turvey. Anything original has emerged out of this collaboration. A further treatment of topics covered in this paper can be found in a recent monograph by Professor Turvey and myself, *Information, Natural Law and the Self-Assembly of Rhythmical Movement: Theoretical and Experimental Investigations*, Erlbaum Press, Hillsdale: New Jersey, 1986.

DEVELOPMENTAL (ORIGINS) QUESTION:

WHAT IS THE ORIGIN OF THE CONSTRAINTS
THAT TRANFORM A BIOMECHANICAL MOVEMENT
SYSTEM FROM AN UNCOORDINATED MOVEMENT
PHASE TO A COORDINATED MOVEMENT PHASE ?

DEVELOPMENTAL TRANSFORMATION

SOURCE OF CONSTRAINTS ?

UNCOORDINATED MOVEMENT PHASE   COORDINATED MOVEMENT PHASE

Fig. 1. The origins problem.

1. BERNSTEIN'S PROBLEM: THE CO-ORDINATION AND REGULATION OF MOVEMENT (Bernstein, 1967; Whiting, 1984).

1.1. The degrees of freedom problem

The human body (in childhood and in maturity) has on the order of 790 muscles that act almost always in combination to generate and degenerate kinetic energy over 100 mobile joints. These joints vary in the kind of anatomical pieces that they link (e.g., cartilages, bones) and in the number of axes over which they can change (for example, hinge joints like the elbow are uniaxial whereas the ball-and-socket joints like the hip are tri-axial). A conservative estimate of the body's mechanical degrees of freedom, assuming the existence of only hinged joints, would suggest a system of 100 or so mechanical degrees of freedom. Relatively little is known about how to control systems of this order of complexity. This much is certain: Regulation of an action defined over 100 mechanical degrees of freedom is not a function of individually instructing 100 processes; control of a multi-variable system is achieved in more subtle ways.

The subtlety in question – the principles that shape movement organisations – can be approached from two broadly defined orientations (see Kugler, Kelso & Turvey, 1980, 1982; Kelso, 1981). One perspective (termed *artifactual-machine)* equates the solution with the resolution of the engineering problem of how to effectively control the behaviour of a multivariable system. Designing artificial control systems that regulate many independent variables quickly results in, what Bellman (1961) terms, 'the curse of dimensionality', or, what Bernstein (1967) and Turvey (1977; Turvey, Shaw & Mace, 1978) refer to as, 'the degrees of freedom problem': the number of states in the control space exponentially increases with the dimension of the problem. A second perspective (termed, *natural-physical)* approaches the problem in terms of (i) geometric principles that give 'shape' or 'qualitative form' to flow processes and (ii) physical principles that cause 'breaks' in the symmetry of flow processes. The geometric principles have their historical roots in the natural sciences that address the general problem of morphology - the origin and evolution of 'form'. The physical principles draw their substance from the physical sciences that address the problem of 'why things flow' - the origin and evolution of irreversible transport processes.

These two perspectives differ dramatically with respect to their concern for the system's degrees of freedom. The former (artifactual-machine) perspective sees degrees of freedom as a curse, to be eliminated; the latter (natural-physical), see degrees of freedom as a necessity, to be exploited. The artifactual-machine perspective is the more popularly held.

1.2. The artifactual-machine perspective

> The first clear biomechanical distinction between the motor
> apparatus in man and the higher animals and any artificial
> self-controlling device, ..., lies in the enormous number
> (which often reaches three figures) of degree of freedom
> which it can attain both in respect to the kinematics of
> the multiple linkages of its freely jointed kinematic chains,
> and to the elasticity due to the resiliences of their
> connections - the muscles (N. Bernstein, 1967, p. 125).

The conceptual roots for the artifactual perspective are buried in the engineering sciences that promote the technical design of machines. Much of the appeal is captured by the engineer's ability to build physically realisable machines that can mimic the behaviour of a *small set* of state variables. If a machine generates patterns similar to those commonly associated with living organisms, then the machine is likely to attract the attention of scientists of this persuasion. This strategy dominated the modelling attempts in the eighteenth and early nineteenth century. So impressed were Descartes and LaMettrie by the similarity in the macroscopic patterns of motion generated by mechanical puppets, that they proposed a theory of biological movement organisation based on the personification of mechanical puppets. Technological progress, however, made these models unfashionable, only to be replaced by the latest version of technological gadgetry that generates 'human-like' patterns. The significance test for artifactual-modelling rests fundamentally on the requirement of an aesthetic similarity (see Figure 2) in the macroscopic 'patterns' generated by the machine, as if to assume that a sufficient criterion for modelling living processes is the duplication of a macroscopic pattern, independent of the sustaining, microscopic, substrate).

The contemporary candidates are artifactual machines in which movement patterns are generated either through (a) a pre-established arrangement among components, here termed 'cybernetic machines' - machine constructs in which the signals controlling skeletomuscular kinetics derive from reference values or set-points (Adams, 1971; Greene, 1972; Powers, 1973, 1978; Roland, 1977) or (b) a pre-established arrangement among specific instructions, here termed 'algorithmic machines' - machine constructs in which the signals controlling the skeletomuscular kinetics derive from stored

462

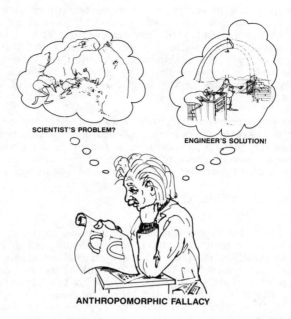

SCIENTIST'S PROBLEM?

ENGINEER'S SOLUTION!

ANTHROPOMORPHIC FALLACY

Fig. 2. A pathetic fallacy is a literary device portraying inanimate
nature as having human feelings and character (the angry
sea, a stubborn door). The anthropomorphic fallacy is
similarly an attribution of human-like qualities to nonhuman
entities. In the case of the latter, explanatory intent is
invoked, whereas in the former only descriptive clarification
is the motive. In both instances aesthetics are involved, but
for differing reasons. In attempting to understand how a
collection of workers can become organised so as to construct
an arch, the wiley scientist is attracted by the idea that his
collection of social creatures might build their arches
according to the same design principles that are used by
engineers to build bridges. The solution seems obvious enough
- social creatures build arches in the same manner that
engineers build arches! This is the artifactual-machine
solution. See Section 5.2 for the natural-physical solution
to this problem.

rules, programs, look-up tables or schemas (Arbib, 1980; Hollerbach, 1982;
Rosenbaum & Patashnik, 1980; Schmidt, 1975; Shaffer, 1980). In these
machines (i) the body's many degrees of freedom are a 'curse'; (ii) coordination and control are impositions on the skeletomuscular apparatus;
and, relatedly, (iii) the central nervous system is the source of the coordinating and control signals and is sharply distinguished from the high-
powered, energy-converting skeletomuscular system that is the recipient of
these signals. These machines are designed so that the central nervous
system (CNS) is the source of the signals that 'inform' the skeletomuscular
kinetics, and it is the site of the information on which the signals are based.
The actions at the level of muscle-joint kinetics are viewed as problems

involving standard physics and chemistry. The actions of the CNS, however, are viewed as problems that do not come under the purview of
physical theory. They are viewed as constraints that are *independent* of
physical theory and the goal of this perspective is to provide the details
of those 'extra-physical', engineering, ordering principles.

> Serious errors in experimental model-making arise from a
> tendency of authors to project their models upon their
> material, and to think that they have succeeded in re-
> producing some function of a living prototype when in
> fact they are engaged in constructing a fictitious proto-
> type based on some naive or primitive hypothesis. As a
> result, when what purports to be a program of the living
> prototype is laid out in symbols or in hardware, it is
> really only the conceptual model of the living prototype
> which has been reproduced. It is not surprising that
> the authors of such models are invariably satisfied with
> the accuracy of their analogies. Indeed, their situation
> is the same as that of a man who is seized with delight
> to meet a familiar acquaintance only to realize at the
> last moment that he is looking into a mirror (N. Bernstein,
> 1967, p. 186).

1.2.1. Large-scale patterns are stabilised by small-scale pattern generators

The artifactual-machine perspective assumes a fairly direct correspondence
between external patterns of motion (external coordinates of motion) and
internal events associated with the causal substrate that creates, sustains
and dissolves the macroscopic patterns (see Bernstein, 1965; Turvey, 1977
for discussions on the inapplicability of this assumption). By assuming this
correspondence, the scientist can proceed to identify an internal (neural)
substrate that exhibits the same patterns (at a smaller dynamic scale). The
identification is either empirical, such as central pattern generator ('CPG'),
or hypothetical, as in 'frames', 'schemas', 'motor programs', etc. In either
case, the establishment of macroscopic patterns is viewed as a process of
relating small-scale internal dynamics to large scale movement patterns (see
Figure 3). The postulation of these explanatory constructs is derived from
two related premises: (i) external regularities are derivative effects of
internal regularities; and (ii) solving the internal regulation problem, solves
the external regulation problem, *ipso facto*. Once these small-scale pattern
generators have been identified the interface with the high-energy, muscle-
joint actuators is assumed to be mere chemistry and physics.

It is difficult to imagine that these internal constructs will not fall prey
to the same set of problems initially addressed, once the challenge of
explaining their origin and evolution is pursued. These mechanisms are as
complicated, conceptually, as the external phenomena they purport to explain.
In addition, the identification of the location of a pattern is not the same as
the identification of a theory of pattern generation. Patterns are ubiquitous
to all scales of nature. Merely locating a pattern does not solve the problem
of how the pattern is generated. The concept of pattern generation owes no
allegiance to scale or material substrate, and as such, its independence must
be respected at each scale of observation. The concept of pattern formation
owes its primary allegiance to a generalised theory of morphogenesis; one

464

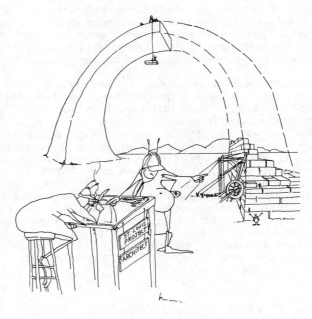

Fig. 3. Artifactual-machine solution for the construction of an arch.
The long range correlations required for the 'cooperative'
building of the arch is accomplished by a small scale 'blueprint' ('plan', 'frame', 'schema', etc.) of the large scale
project. The actions of the individual workers are constrained
according to restrictions specified in the blueprint. External
regularity is intimately tied to internal regularity of
the blueprint. Of particular importance is the fact that the
blueprint must exist *prior to* and *independent of* the actual
construction. In general it takes an agent (i.e., an architect)
more complicated than the phenomena being explained to
account for the origin of the blueprint.

that accounts for the geometrical origin of 'form' (see Section 3.) and the
physical origin of the 'symmetry-breaking instabilities' that creates the
'change' in form (see Section 4.).

1.3. The end of the 'honeymoon'

The artifactual-machine conception has assumed in recent decades an
unprecedented status as *the* perspective on order and regulation (Kugler
et al, 1982). This has been due in large part, to the fact that the
development of automata theory, information theory, and cybernetics have
fostered the concept of 'machine' so as to appear on *prima facie* grounds
to be of special relevance to the 'puzzles' of biology and psychology (Carello
et al, 1984). In automata theory the abstract mathematical notion of a machine
has been given an explicit reading by tying it to both recursive function
theory and the digital computer. Recalcitrant natural phenomena – such as
the cognitive abilities of humans – are viewed as analogous to the machine
capabilities and explicable in machine terms (Fodor, 1975; Minsky & Papert,

1972; Pylyshyn, 1980). The formal conception of information, as expressed by Shannon and Weaver (1949), has given a precise and mathematical way of describing communication situations. Moreover, the way in which information theory links information to probability theory has provided a basis for great generality – a theory adaptable, in principle, to many systems and to many phenomena. The fixing of a biologically and psycho- logically useful conception of 'machine' by automata theory and information theory has been further abetted by cybernetics which provided an under- standing of machine behaviour as goal-directed (see Weir, 1984). Thus in biology and psychology the cybernetic closed-loop device that includes a constant reference input (the goal) and negative feedback is a commonplace explanation of conserved values (see Yates, 1984; Tomovic, 1978 for informed discussions).

Despite the great popularity of the artifactual-machine perspective there are good reasons for believing that it is inapplicable to biological and psychological phenomena and that 'the *honeymoon* between the two sciences might be over': (see Belinski, 1976; Bernstein, 1967; Bertalanffy, 1973; Haken, 1977; Iberall, 1969; Prigogine & Stengers, 1983; Yates, 1982).

> The entire period from the publication of Wiener's work right up to the present day is full of the search for and use of analogies between living and artificial systems – analogies which, on the one hand, have aided physiologists in working out system interrelationships in the organism, and have, on the other hand, provided technologists with valuable new ideas on the construction of automatic systems.
>
> It is difficult to say whether or not the 'honeymoon' between these two sciences is over, and with it their common quest for and use of analogies and other similarities, but problems that suggest an opposite line of development have been increasingly coming to the fore in recent scientific literature: is there, after all, a fundamental difference in principle between living and non-living systems, and if there is, where does the 'watershed' forming the boundary between them lie? (N. Bernstein, 1967, p. 181).

While Bernstein (1967) had frequently promoted engineering designs using self-controlling systems as candidate solutions for the biological movement problem (see Chapter IV; Some Emergent Problems of the Regulation of Motor Acts), his later writings (see, Chapter VI, Trends in Physiology and their Relation to Cybernetics, and Conclusion) emphasised a dissatisfaction with the 'artificial perspective' with its search for analogs between manmade machines and living systems.

> Recent research has led to re-formulations of the concepts of organisms, which are in many respects different from the formulations of the classical period – in which the organism was treated as a reactively equilibrating or self-regulating system. An organism must be considered to be an organization possessing two determining features.
>
> Firstly, it is an organization which preserves its own (systematic) identity in spite of the continuous flow of

energy and substrate matter passing through it. Despite
the fact that not a single individual atom in the organism
is retained in the cell structure for longer than a certain
and (with few exceptions) comparatively brief space of
time, the organism remains the same now as it was previously
and its present life activity is determined by its previous
life (and, of course, not only previous).

Secondly, the organism is continually in a set
direction at all stages of its existence. The fact that
thousands of examples belonging to the same animal or
plant type develop into species that are identical in all
their basic determining features (in spite of the often
enormous differences in living conditions between the various
individuals) is ample proof of this directional trend in ontogenetic evolution (N. Bernstein, 1967, p. 173-4).

1.4. Unity of movement science with the physical sciences

Inspired by the work of Gel'fand and Tsetlin (1962) and recent
advances in the physical sciences, Bernstein foresaw an opportunity to
model 'the basic forms and phenomena of real, and not fictitious, life
processes' (1967, p. 186) in terms of anti-entropic processes of open system
and thereby provide a unity between movement science and physical science.

As early as the 18th century, when militant mechanistic
materialism firmly defined its scientific positions, natural
science was faced with a choice which appeared un-
avoidable (and also for a long time afterwards). On the
one hand, the contrast between the phenomena of life
activity and the then-known processes of inanimate
nature was so striking that some explanation was
demanding. On the other hand, the store of knowledge
concerning deep-seated physio-chemical processes,
biophysical and biochemical principles on the molecular
level, was still very small. The result was that many
scientists, finding that their physio-chemical knowledge
did not offer them an adequate means of explaining the
specificity of life, put forward the notion of a non-
material life force by way of explanation; this was
completely satisfactory for the ones who readily enter-
tained notions on all sorts of non-material factors and
entities, and who consequently joined the idealist camp.
The materialists, however, could generally do nothing
but repudiate all research into vital specificity which
could not be supported by the physics or chemistry of
the day. Meanwhile, during the more recent past, a
great deal of fresh information has been collected and
this has permitted a close enquiry into the nature of
many processes, ... Nothing was known the last century
about stochastic processes...; nor was anything known
about anti-entropic processes in open systems, or under
what conditions they took place and how they could be
regulated... (N. Bernstein, 1967, pp. 181-182).

Bernstein's last paragraph in this monograph *The Co-ordination and Regulation of Movement* proclaimed an appeal for the unification of the biological and physiological sciences with the physical sciences (see Agarwal & Gottlieb, 1984; Arbib, 1984; for commentaries on Bernstein's final commitment towards a physical biology):

> The great problem confronting physiology, and the biological sciences as a whole, is the discovery of those definitive and wholly materialistic characteristics of living things and principles of their organization which underlie and actively control the directional development and planned activity which we observe throughout the entire range of living creatures, from bacteria to *homo sapiens socialis* (N. Bernstein, 1967, p. 187).

Within the last twenty years since Bernstein's death there have been significant advances made in the physical sciences concerning the problem of long range correlations in field processes. There is a generality about the nature of these processes that owes little allegiance to the particular material substrate that embeds them. The result of these studies is an understanding of how macroscopic patterns can be temporarily assembled, sustained, and dissolved with no *apriori* set of (internal or external) constraints that causally specify any detailed description of the patterns. What is emerging is a theory of self-organising systems that directly addresses the problem of morphogenesis. The central concepts of the theory are being drawn from geometrical and physical considerations. The geometric concerns focus on the identification of intrinsic symmetries (similitudes) and how they are sustained (structurally stable) under some scale changes and annihilated (structurally unstable) under others, - see Section 3. The physical concerns focus on the identification of the symmetry-breaking mechanisms that initiate qualitative changes in cause-effect relations, - see Section 4. These concepts will then be generalised to the problem of movement organisation - see Sections 5 and 6. Before introducing these concepts, however, a few comments are required about the generalisation of physical and geometric ordering principles to living processes and the required existential commitment.

2. EXISTENTIAL COMMITMENTS: ONE ONTOLOGY OR MANY?

2.1. The program of physical science

The program of physical science involves the formulation of descriptive accounts of order and regularity of natural phenomena through the use of a minimal set of first principles. The strategy is to discover the simplest and most general self-contained description of natural events. Physics does not purport to explain nature. Its interest is in the identification of a minimum set of global symmetries (conservations, universal constants, etc.) and ordering principles (second law of thermodynamics, Boltzmann's ordering principle, etc.) that when combined can be used to predict events. Symmetries and universal constants reveal themselves as correlations among descriptions that are invariant from region to region. The ordering principles identify changes in the correlations. Physical laws are formal expressions

468

that specify those transformations that sustain correlations and those that annihilate correlations. The generality of local regularity to other regions in space and time is commonly referred to as *physical order;* and, the laws that define changes in the correlations are referred to as *physical ordering principles.*

2.2. Failure of the Enlightenment program

One of the hopes of the Age of Enlightenment, especially in the works of Saint-Simon and Comte, resting on the physics of Galileo and Newton, was to account for phenomena of living systems according to the laws and regularities of natural science (see Yates & Kugler, 1984). This program failed chiefly because of its inability to come to terms with the principles governing the origin and evolution of auxiliary constraints (initial and boundary conditions). The identification of the invariance of physical laws over frames of reference can succeed only to the extent to which the initial and boundary conditions can be provided. If these conditions are time-independent, they will appear only as constants in the equations of motion and can be factored out; their etiology will not affect the invariance of the law under evaluation. But the independence of laws from initial and boundary conditions can be expensive at the level of ontology.

2.2.1. Newton's four ontologies: initial conditions, geometry, time and mechanical laws

At the foundation level, physics' only ground-rule pertains to parsimony: Keep the number of required first principles to a minimum. Avoid the introduction of unnecessary concepts that implicate new ontologies – no *deus ex machina,* no *élan vital,* no smart homuncular elements. The Newtonian program provided the first formal benchmark for explanatory parsimony. It required a minimum of four ontologies: (i) one defining the laws of matter in motion; (ii) one defining the geometric laws of space; (iii) one defining the structure of time; and (iv) one defining the 'initial configurational layout' of the universe. Collectively, they defined *classical mechanics.* Awareness that these laws might be applicable to scales other than that of celestial activity gave rise to a scientific ideal that received its most celebrated expression in the writings of Laplace in the eighteenth century; namely, that it was possible to regard the behaviour of any physical system as ultimately determined by the laws of Newtonian mechanics. Laplace's only requirement was that full knowledge be available, at some instant of time, of the composite force configuration. Given this knowledge, it was thought that all future and past events could be completely determined merely by applying the laws of mechanics (with the exception of three body collisions). Laplace's argument was the classical foundation of the so-called *mechanistic perspective* on natural phenomena (cf. Bohm, 1957). The working hypothesis of this mechanistic perspective stated that ultimately any set of phenomena could be reduced, completely and unconditionally, to nothing more than the effects of some definite and bounded set of *fixed* laws which *determined* completely and precisely the phenomena. The conclusion drawn from the hypothesis was that systematic behaviour on any scale of analysis, and under any set of conditions, could be fully analysed, requiring only the specification of a set of auxiliary boundary conditions (assumptions about initial conditions, geometry and time).

2.2.2. Einstein's two ontologies: geometry and initial conditions

Newton's four ontologies stood invincible for more than two centuries until Einstein showed that the laws of matter-energy, motion, space and time could all be unified under a single set of geometric principles. Einstein's universe, however, required, as had Newton's and Laplace's before, an orderly set of configurational preconditions - the initial conditions. The new geometric framework required a time-independent vessel, a container, that was bounded at both ends by singularities. These singular states defined the creation and annihilation of a physical layout, a topological distribution of matter-energy. The laws of general relativity defined transformations of the distributional layout that were continuous and deterministic between the singular states. Thus, an analysis of any intermediary state (between singularities) allows for an inexorable determination of past and future events. Temporal discontinuities only occurred at the singular states. Between the singular states the trajectories were perfectly time-symmetric - future and past events could be causally exchanged. Einstein's universe was without any historical 'arrow of time'.

Even Einstein's grand geometric scaffolding, however, could not derive the universe's initial conditions from his geometric ontology. Einstein's mechanistic construct provided a theory of state transitions for matter and energy which was indifferent to the concept of 'organisation'. Once a system emerged from the singular state its organisation remained unchanges. (There are some solutions to Einstein's equations without singularities, such as those used to study the *Big Bang*. These go *back* from regular states and not forward from where the manifold structure (and hence the equations) breaks down. They do not, however, address the problem of temporal or spatial symmetry-breaking mechanisms).

2.3. The relationship between physics and biology: general to special?

A primary distinction between physical systems and biological systems concerns the role of auxiliary conditions. In simple, physical systems all time-dependent observables are a function of the laws of mechanics. In contrast, biological systems can involve observable time-dependent states that involve *both mechanical laws and auxiliary conditions* resulting in time-dependent behaviours that are not dominated solely by the current causal effects of mechanical laws. The auxiliary conditions are associated with historical and evolutionary aspects of the system as well as intentional, informational, linguistic or communicative aspects, all of which are outside the province of mechanical laws (see Yates & Kugler, 1984). For these systems, auxiliary conditions actively compete with physical laws. The introduction of auxiliary conditions does not necessarily imply the inapplicability of physical laws. It merely implies that the invariances (symmetries) associated with these laws will require additional knowledge in order to observe their influence. The excessive role of auxiliary conditions in biology is one of the major challenges confronting the analysis of biological organisations.

> For a long time, theoretical physics has concerned itself
> with the articulation of universal and of general laws.
> From that perspective, biology seems limited to a rather
> small class of very special systems, indeed *inordinately*
> special systems. Clearly, then, organisms are not the sort
> of thing that physicists seeking universal principles would
> look at. To a physicist, what makes organisms special is
> conceived as a plethora of constraints, initial conditions
> and boundary conditions which must be superimposed upon

the true, general physical laws, and which must be
independently stipulated before those laws bear directly
upon the organic realm. Physicists rightly felt that the
determination of such supplementary constraints was not
their job. But no physicist has ever doubted that, since
physics is the science of material nature in all of its
manifestations, the relationship of physics to biology
is that of general to particular (R. Rosen, 1984).

Traditionally, physics has not been concerned with the identification
of the origin and evolution of the 'special auxiliary conditions'. It has
focused, instead, on the understanding of the 'general conditions' –
universal symmetries (conservations of mass, energy momentum, charge, etc.)
universal constants (speed of light, Planck's constant, Boltzmann's constant,
gravitational curvature, etc.) and the relations (laws) that relate the
symmetries to constants. Biological events, however, are 'shaped' more by
local symmetries and invariants than by global ones. When confronted with
the origin and evolution of these 'local constraints' it has not been un-
common to propose etiologies requiring *extraphysical ordering principles*.
(See Elasser, 1958 and Raven, 1961 for contrasting views on the nature of
ordering principles in biology). While physical laws are assumed to have a
global, incorporeal, character, the localisation of biological order suggests
the requirement of a local 'embodiment' of the ordering principle(s). The
embodied principles provide a nonphysical source of constraints that
harness the 'free dynamics' associated with the more global physical laws.

2.3.1. Pattee's complementarity problem: how do auxiliary conditions ('constraints') relate to laws?

It has been argued by Pattee (see 1972a, b, 1973, 1977) that the
relationship between laws and constraints constitutes a fundamental
complementarity principle: *Constraints are not reducible to laws*. In
addition, he proposes that this complementarity principle provides a rationale
for the concepts of *symbols* and *information* in biology. The reasoning
behind the complementarity of these two (ontologically distinct) modes of
description has been summarised by Turvey (Kugler, Kelso & Turvey, 1982;
Turvey & Kugler, 1984a, b) as follows:

1. The microscopic degrees of freedom of all systems, inanimate and animate,
   abide by the laws of motion and change, that is, dynamical laws.

2. To harness these laws to produce specific and reliable macroscopic
   functions requires constraints which selectively reduce degrees of
   freedom.

3. Constraints that persist for durations that are relatively long in compariso
   to the phenomena of interest may be termed structural: they are said
   permanently to freeze-out degrees of freedom. Constraints with relaxation
   times that are relatively short in comparison to the phenomena of interest
   may be termed functional: they are said effectively to select one trajectory
   from among the virtual trajectories that a system might exhibit. The latter
   type of constraint is a control constraint and it is the one of major interes

4. Unlike the dynamical laws which are expressible as functions of rate, i.e.,
   as derivatives of some variable with respect to time, the constraints that
   harness these laws are rate-independent. This is the fundamental in-
   compatibility of laws and constraints qua rules.

5. Constraints are unlike dynamical laws in two other ways: they must have a specific material embodiment (laws are incorporeal) and they are local (laws are universal).

6. Because the microscopic degrees of freedom of the physical embodiment of a constraint must abide by the laws of dynamics, the details of their individual motions must be completely determined. Therefore, the only sensible interpretation of a constraint is that it is an alternative description of the behaviour of the individual degrees of freedom.

7. Synonymously, a constraint is a classification of the microscopic degrees of freedom; it is a reduced, less detailed description. Being less detailed it is less complex and therein lies its utility: in terms of control a constraint is simple and efficient because it makes the fullest use of the dynamical context without being a description of that context.

8. Constraints are not only extremely simple with respect to the dynamics that they control but the structure of their physical embodiment has no direct relationship to those dynamics just as the structure of a written injunction (say, STOP) has no direct relationship to the structure of the activities that it might be associated with. Constraints are therefore like symbols – they are arbitrary with respect to that which they signify.

9. Being arbitrary and just symbol vehicles, individual control constraints assume definite meaning only in the context of a system of constraints. This is tantamount to saying that a co-ordination of symbols – a generalised language structure or syntax – defines the informational basis for the control of dynamical processes.

10. There are, therefore, two descriptions of a complex system. One description is of the system's states of affairs as infinite, continuous and rate-dependent (the dynamical description) and the other description is of the system's states of affairs as finite, discrete and rate-independent (the informational or linguistic description). These two descriptions are incompatible but complementary.

2.3.2. Fodor and Pylyshyn's 'impenetrability' problem: how do mental states relate to physical states?

Phenomena of biological science, especially those studied by psychologists, do not readily reduce to physical-law-based accounts. It is difficult to refer the predicates of psychological and abstract physiological explanations to physical laws. The standard form of *type physicalism* construes the physical types to which psychological and physiological types are to be reduced as orthodox physical properties (see, Kugler & Turvey, 1986). In the standard form type physicalism has not fared well, giving the impression that it may not fare well in any form (Fodor, 1975). *Token physicalism*, which is less demanding, has fared better. It claims that any particular psychological or abstract physiological state is a token physical state. Significant among the implications of token physicalism is the indifference of psychological and abstract physiological states to the materiality of the system that expresses them (Fodor, 1981). The material instantiation of a system could be silicon-based as readily as carbon-based. The difference in materiality is not a difference that counts. What does make a difference is that the psychological and physiological states have a symbolic-basis that can be ordered or manipulated according to rules, similar to the rules of arithmetic (see Fodor, 1981; Fodor & Pylyshyn, 1981; Pylyshyn, 1984; see also the reply by, Turvey, Shaw, Reed & Mace, 1984). Of particular importance is the 'impenetrability' of these 'cognitive states' by 'physical laws': Pylyshyn

(1980, 1984) has referred to this requirement as the *cognitive impenetrability requirement* (see Kugler, Turvey & Shaw, 1982, for an extended commentary on this requirement). The act of coordinating 'material' properties that are ontologically independent of 'mental' properties resurrects Brentano's problem:

> As materialists we must ask how behavioral regularities such as those captured by statements that mention extrinsic but causally unconnected entities (or perhaps nonexistent objects) are possible in a world governed by physical laws. How is it possible for properties of the world to determine behavior when the properties are not causally related in the required sense to the functional states of the system, which is what we seem to be claiming when we say, for example, that what determines the person's behavior in rushing to the phone is something like his anticipation of, or desire to obtain, help? This conondrum is sometimes called 'Brentano's problem', after the psychologist who first anticipated its force. Brentano saw no way out of the puzzle except by accepting that mental events are not governed by physical laws but by their own mental principles. The answer I ultimately give to this puzzle is that the causes of the behavior are not literal numbers, anticipated future events, or other 'intentional objects' but rather some physically instantiated *internal representation* of such things, that is, a physical code or a symbol (Z. Pylyshyn, 1984, pp. 25-26).

2.3.3. Turing's machine: a physical substrate for instantiating mind-body causality?

Brentano's coordination problem addresses the issue of how to instantiate a causal substrate for mental properties, if their organising principles are independent of the organisational principles associated with the material substrate that embodies the mental properties. Fodor and Pylyshyn's solution suggests that the necessary causal requirements can be found in the design principles of devices that manipulate symbols via rules. A general version of such a symbol manipulating device, in a logical and mathematic sense, is the Turing machine – a *class* of abstract machines originated by Turing to clarify, in part, the implications of Goedel's incompleteness proof. According to Goedel's proof any logical formalism complicated enough to include arithmetic, contained true theorems which could not be proven. And, if a proof could be formulated within the formalism, then the formalism was inconsistent! Turing's construct was in effect an abstract machine capable of processing symbols in a manner simulating the Goedelian proof process. Turing's abstract machine could be used to simulate any other machine whose state transitions could be logically specified. Turing's machine, given a properly encoded description of a machine logic, and an encoded version of the data on which the latter was to operate, would produce an encoded version of what the arbitrary machine would produce. Turing's machine could simulate any arbitrary machine processing arbitrary data according to logical operations.

The generality of the design of Turing's machine (and all of its practical limitations, unsolvability, halting problems, N-P completeness problem, execution time, etc.) as a mechanism that adequately accounts for psychological and biological phenomena will ultimately depend on whether the assumptions that are fundamental to the arithemetic formalism can be validly carried over to the system being modelled. If the Turing machine is to be used as a universal machine, capable of modelling any set of phenomena, then the question must be raised as to whether physical phenomena suffer from the same limitations: Are the problems of a Turing machine unique to the arithmetic formalism or are these problems universal and realisable in all forms of its instantiation – formal or physical? The 'strong explanatory' version of the Turing construct rests on the assumption that the predicate calculus maps isomorphically onto the set of all events (physical, nonphysical, etc.). Weaker versions of the construct view the relationship between arithmetic and physical events as less than an identity and, in this regard, view the construct more as a means or method for 'simulating' events through discrete logical operations; that is, the model is merely a *description* of the physical event in terms of (i.e., in the language of) analytic functions.

2.3.4. Logical positivism, Turing's machine and representational realism

The following question can be considered: Is the causal status ascribed to logical formulae by token physicalism/Turing reductionism *real?* Causal relations hold that causation is a category of connections and relations corresponding to the actual traits of the physical world. The causes ascribed by token physicalism/Turing reductionism are more nearly Humean, that is, categories of relations among ideas. There is a closeness between token physicalism/Turing reductionism and the tradition of logical positivism that merits consideration.

As an orientation to scientific explanation, logical positivism rejected causal realism. It viewed the scope of science as limited to the collection of data and the linking of these data together in a formally closed system. According to logical positivism, it is logic that provides the connections, and enables the scientist to make predictions about new data. The ultimate antecedents are the logical predictates postulated in advance by the scientist. Conceived as abstract logical entities, independent of observables, these 'causal' antecedents need not refer to anything physical.

Token physicalism/Turing reductionism's attitude toward scientific explanation continues the tradition of logical positivism in its emphasis upon explaining phenomena through logical formulae, logically connected in a formally closed system. It is, at the same time, discontinuous with that tradition in that it ascribes ontological status to the logical formulae. The Church Thesis claims that if a set of events can be expressed as logical formulae then those events can be simulated by a Turing machine. The 'software' (symbols and rules) both 'explains' the phenomenon and is physically realisable. In this sense token physicalism/Turing reductionism goes beyond logical positivism: it aspires to raising the status of explanation from merely logical to real. The instantiation of logical operations with a material substrate operating on 'real' (physically embodied) symbols constitutes a new form of epistemological realism, termed *representational realism*, that allows psychological states to causally connect with 'real' properties – physical materials that 'represent' abstract symbols and concatination rules. What is not clear from this account, however, is how the symbols are 'interpreted' (its semantics) without postulating an additional set of symbols

474

with an additional set of rules as the interpreter, which requires an additional set of symbols and an additional set of rules for its interpretation, ..., *ad infinitum!*

2.3.5. The cognitive impenetrability methodology: a 'rich man's' game of science

The cognitive impenetrability assumption claims to distinguish between phenomena explainable functionally in terms of the physical constraints and actions of the machine substrate, and those explainable in terms of rules and representations. This proposal further claims to provide an operational methodology for distinguishing regularities whose ontology resides in the domain of physical states and those requiring an appeal to a separate psychological ontology (the machine substrate's beliefs and goals). According to the impenetrability criteria, processes connected with the functional architecture have a physical ontology (principles of physical geometry) that is independent of the semantic ontology (principles of rules and represent-ations). Pylyshyn summarises the methodological procedure for securing ones 'belief' in these cognitively impenetrable states as follows:

> First priority goes to explaining the regularity in question
> in physical or biological terms, that is at the physical level.
> If, under a description of a behavior that captures the
> regularity in question, that regularity can be subsumed
> under biological or physical principles, we need go no
> further; we do not posit special principles when the
> universal principles of physics will do. This application
> of Occam's razor prevents us from ascribing beliefs and
> goals to streams, rocks, and thermostats. Of course, if
> the system is a computer, there will be some descriptions
> of its input-output behavior (namely, the descriptions
> under which the system is seen as executing a program)
> that will not be explainable by appeal to physical laws.
> The explanation of the machine's production of a certain
> output symbol when the machine is given a certain input
> symbol is not explainable at the physical level...
> (Z. Pylyshyn, 1984, pp. 131-132).

A careful application of Occam's razor in the manner suggested by Pylyshyn would, in fact, lead directly to the ascription of 'beliefs and goals' to 'streams, rocks and thermostats' for there are indeed many phenomena associated with the material states of these systems for which physical science has incomplete descriptions. The complex fluid flow of a turbulent stream is only beginning to be understood, yet Occam's razor would suggest a degree of patience on the part of the scientist before it would suggest a new ontology. The microscopic (quantum) organisational states of materials has only received a formal treatement by physicists in this century, yet Pylyshyn's strategy suggests that previous scientists should have sought explanatory constructs from a second ontology. The scaffolding of physical science involves a complex blending of geometric and physical concepts. Occam's razor applied at the level of theory construction (as opposed to Pylyshyn's application at the level of phenomena) would argue against the view that any theoretical scaffold be viewed as absolute and complete. Instead, it would suggest, when new phenomena are observed that fall outside the existing framework that the framework be readjusted to accommodate the phenomena, rather than adjusting the ontological classification of phenomena to accommodate the existing scaffold. To suggest that any theoretical framework is complete is indeed a grand claim. To further suggest that they have observed phenomena outside of this framework and want to propose a new ontological basis to account for it is a *rich man's* game of science, in general, and of ontology, in particular

3. THE 'NATURAL' PERSPECTIVE: THE ORIGIN AND EVOLUTION OF 'FORM'

3.1. The principle of similitude (Kugler, Kelso & Turvey, 1982)

It has long been respected that the earth's gravity plays a significant role in designing terrestrial animals: the forms (morphologies) and function that animals assume vary as a function of the gravitational constant (see Thompson, 1917/1942). Imagine a doubling in the magnitude of gravity: the upright posture that marks *homo sapiens* would be rendered inoperative, and the largest surface locomoting creatures would be reduced to short-legged creatures with bodies very close to the ground or to legless, snake-like creatures with bodies in contact with the ground. In contrast, a halving of gravity's strength would yield tall and slender creatures requiring less by way of energy and equipped with metabolic organs – heart, lungs, etc. - of comparatively diminutive size or maybe the same size, using less power consumption.

The effects of scale changes against the backdrop of a gravitational constant owe no allegiance to biology, they are similarly present in inert systems. For example, consider the scale transformation associated with the design of a bridge. Suppose that an engineer, after constructing a strong and durable bridge is then confronted by the problem of building a much larger bridge. To save time, the engineer repeats the earlier design by simply applying a scale factor to the bridge's linear dimensions (such as the lengths of its struts and girders). Unfortunately, this new, larger bridge, though geometrically identical to its smaller counterpart, does not match the structural stability of the smaller bridge. The resistance of a supporting structure to a crushing stress – its strength – varies as the square of a linear dimension (say, its length) whereas the weight of the structure varies as the cube; thus the larger of the two geometrically similar bridges is dis-proportionately heavier for its strength and is, therefore, more prone to collapse. At the smaller scale the geometric form represents a stable configuration of forces whereas at the large scale that same form, in terms of forces, is configurationally unstable. Stability of forces at the larger scale necessitates a change in the geometric form. Similarly, the forces that determine an organism's form vary, some as one power and some as another power of the organism's dimensions such as, for example, its height or its volume. That is to say, forces do not configure independently of dimensions: a scale change in the dimensions is accompanied by a change in the relative values of the forces. Necessarily, form as a diagram of forces changes with a change in scale.

Changes in form as a function of the strength of the force of gravity is one manifestation of the Principle of Similitude (see Bridgman, 1922; Thompson, 1917/1942). The principle of similitude (principle of similarity relations) historically provides the first methodology for qualitatively

476

classifying systems. Systems are classified as 'similar' if they share a small set of qualitative properties (see Section 3.3.1.).

3.2. Dimensional analysis

3.2.1. Fundamental and derived parameters

In mechanical systems, all scales are fixed by the scales in which the basic quantities of mass, length and time are measured; in nonmechanical sysems other basic quantities, such as temperature, charge, etc., may be required. For mechanical systems, in general, it is possible to choose three of the observables of the process, say x_1, x_2, x_3 as *fundamental parameters*, for example mass (M), length (L) and time (T), respectively. Given the fundamental parameters x_1, x^2, x^3, the remaining parameters x_4,... x_n can be derived from the scales of the fundamental parameters. These *derived parameters* are expressed as monomials in the units in which the fundamental parameters are measured. Suppose that mass (M), length (L), and time (T) are taken as the fundamental dimensions (identified with x_1, x_2, x_3), then additional parameters (x_4,... x_n) can be derived from various combinations of product-ratios of the fundamental dimensions. For example, frequency (T^{-1}), velocity (L/T), and force (ML/T^2) are derived parameters built out of the fundamental dimensions of M, L, and T. In an experimental paradigm the fundamental and derived parameters can be arranged to correspond to the independent and dependent parameters, respectively.

3.2.2. The equation of state

The dimensional structure of derived variables (and, ultimately, laws) is built up from products of powers of the fundamental variables. Because the derived variables are built out of the fundamental variables the numerical scales of the derived variables are set by the fundamental variables. Put simply, the fundamental variables scale the derived variables. The formal study of the dimensional structure of these variables is the subject of dimensional analysis (Bridgman, 1922; Duncan, 1953; Kline, 1965; Langhaar, 1967; Rosen, 1978). The first normal treatment in its modern form, was offered by Buckingham in 1915, and was based on the principle of *dimensional homogeneity* introduced by Fourier and emphasised by Maxwell. The theory of dimensional homogeneity provides a method for deriving an estimate of the form of the equation of state with a limited amount of knowledge about the actual quantitative details of the process under inquiry. Suppose that the goal is to describe a physical process that depends on a certain number of physical quantities, or observables; then the law governing the process must be expressible as some functional relation between the observables that are involved in it; i.e., it must be of the form:

$$\text{Equation of State: } \emptyset \ (x_1, \ldots x_n) = 0$$

whereas x_i's are the observables in question. The only knowledge required is an identification of the dimension associated with the physical quantities and constants involved. This relation is called the *equation of state* of the process.

3.2.3. Dimensionless ratios and the Buckingham π-theorem

Within the framework of dimensional analysis it may be postulated that any law of nature must satisfy the property of being *dimensionally in-*

variant. (For an exact treatment of this issue see Krantz, et al, 1971; Rosen, 1978). A law of nature is dimensionally invariant because the form of the law does not rest on the choice of units. The central concept about laws being dimensionally invariant is that the dimensions involved can be grouped into several products of powers that are *dimensionless* and the law depends only on these dimensionless quantities. These dimensionless quantities are termed π-numbers in recognition that π = (circumference/radius) = 3.14... is a dimensionless ratio) and are built out of product-ratios between the fundamental and derived parameters. The only criterion for the product-ratios is that their dimensions all cancel out, resulting in a *pure number*. The equation of state can then be written in a dimensionless form:

Dimensionless Equation of State: $\emptyset$ (π_1, π_2,... π_p) = 0.

The number (p) of dimensionless coefficient groups π_i that define the dimensionless equation of state can be derived from the π-theorem of Buckingham (1915). The π-theorem states that:

> If there are m *derived parameters* required to define
> the system of interest, and these require n { where n < m}
> independent *fundamental parameters* for their specification,
> then there are m-n independent dimensionless groups
> required for the equation of state.
>
> $\emptyset$ [f_1, f_2,..., f_n; d_1, d_2,..., d_m] = 0
>
> Fundamental Parameters: [f_1, f_2, ..., f_n]
>
> Derived Parameters: [d_1, d_2, ..., d_m]
>
> π-Theorem: m-n = p

The critical requirement for the success of the π-theorem concerns the property of *independence*. A fundamental parameter is independent of other fundamental parameters if it cannot be formed from the sum or product of the remaining fundamental parameters. likewise, a dimensionless product group π_i is not independent of other groups if it can be formed from them by taking sums, products, and powers of other groups.

Dimensionless numbers are important in the description of degenerate behaviour, that is, transition regions where the system's behaviour suddenly changes from one stable mode to another. Transitions through the regions of degeneration identify qualitative changes in the macroscopic behaviour of the system that are associated with sudden changes in the structural stability of the underlying geometric structure. The π-numbers identify dimensionless quantitative values that can be used to predict precisely where a qualitative transition region will occur. And the π-theorem predicts the number of qualitative transitions for a particular system.

3.3. Qualitative classifications of systems: an historical review

3.3.1. Similarity analysis

Classifying systems according to a small set of invariant properties ('similarities') is the hallmark of the theory of modeling. In general there is a point-to-point correspondence between a model and its prototype. Two points that correspond to each other are *homologous*. Figures or parts of the model and the prototype are said to be homologous if they are comprised of homologous points. Euclid's (300BC) principle of *geometric similarity*

478

forms one of the earliest attempts to classify systems in this manner. Two systems are said to be *geometrically similar* if homologous parts of the systems are in a constant ratio. Any deviation from the above restriction will annihilate or distort certain shared geometric qualities.

Extending Euclid's geometric similarity, Galileo (1564-1642) formulated the first theory of dynamic similarity. Two systems are *dynamically similar* if, in addition to the constant ratio between the linear dimensions, the corresponding ratios of mass and work are also constant. It then follows that the forces at corresponding points relate as a certain ratio dependent on the other three ratios. Newton (1642-1727) proposed the principle of kinematic similarity. Invariant space-time relationships are used to define similarities. Two systems are said to be *kinematically similar* if homologous parts of the system lie at homologous points at homologous times (e.g., corresponding components of velocity and acceleration are invariant from model to prototype). If kinematically similar systems also shared similar mass distributions, they also satisfied dynamic similarity.

3.3.2. Poincaré's qualitative dynamics

Towards the end of the nineteenth century Poincaré proposed a more abstract classification method for organising qualitative properties. By inventing topology, Poincaré conceived of a new qualitative study of differential equations (i.e., $dx_i/dt = f(x_1, ... x_n)$), called *qualitative dynamics*. Poincaré found that even if quantitative solutions were impossible, it was still possible to derive qualitative information. For example, qualitative statements such as 'the solution is periodic' are readily revealed, whereas quantitative statements such as 'the solution has a period of 2.5432' are not available without elaborate computational procedures. In fact exact quantitative solutions often defy computation. Using the methods of differential topology, Poincaré identified qualitative properties of dynamic systems (e.g., periodicity, equilibrium points, types of stable regions, etc.). Whereas the earlier Principles of Similitude are based in a theory of modeling (preservation of a given set of qualities from a prototype to a model), Poincaré's theory of qualitative dynamics was concerned with understanding the nature and origin of the qualitative properties within a system.

3.3.3. D'Arcy Thompson's theory of 'growth and form'

Based on an appreciation of qualitative dynamics and the earlier principles of similitude, Thompson (1917/1942) proposed a theory of *growth and form*. Thompson argued that the form an object takes on is intimately linked to the dynamic properties of stability. Moreover, stability is not to be understood merely as the sum total of interacting forces, but rather requires a close examination in terms of the qualitative properties inherent in the system's geometry. The exact nature of these stabilities, however, eluded Thompson's mathematics. Once the qualitative properties are manifest by the system, various transformations (affine, shear, cardioidal, etc.) can be imposed on the system without annihilating them. Growth is explained as a modeling process in which certain qualitative properties are preserved under continuous transformations. This allowed for an explanation of how systems grow and still maintained certain kinematic, geometric, and dynamic similarities. Thompson suggested that the similarity in forms between animate and inanimate systems is the result of the systems sharing similar stable configurations. In short, the fundamental nature of stable configurations is insensitive to material composition. Whether in a cloud in the sky or an amoeba in a pond, the qualitative form realised by these dynamic structures is understandable as a stable configuration. Force and material composition can only affect the form in the quantitative fashion of similarity transformations.

3.3.4. Rashevsky's theory of relational biology

Later, Rashevsky (1938/1950) proposed a theory of *relational biology* based on the qualitative properties of functions. His insight is the recognition that biology is directly interested in the qualitative aspects of dynamic function and behaviour, and not the quantitative study of static structure. Rashevsky opposed the traditional reductionist view that 'structure implies function'. In contrast, he viewed biological design as 'function implying structure'. Motivated by a commitment to function, Rashevsky attempted to create a mathematical framework in which function, organisation, and behaviour could be directly characterised and studied apart from any material or structural basis. Through an understanding of qualitative properties of biological functions, Rashevsky hoped to gain insight into the corresponding organisational constraints manifest in a behaving system. Relational biology was grounded in the realisation that the qualitative properties of a function could be expected to place corresponding quantitative constraints on the organisation of biological systems.

3.3.5. Gel'fand and Tsetlin's theory of 'well-organised' functions

In attempting to mathematically model biological life spaces, Gel'fand and Tsetlin (1962) proposed that the functions used to model a biological system should have an intrinsic qualitative organisation, and that this organisation should facilitate its exploration without any requirement of *prior knowledge*. The underlying assumptions were (i) that the biological organisms discover the organisation of the functional space by performing actions whose outcomes involve a *single evaluation value* (i.e., a one degree of freedom control system) and (ii) that the expediencies by which the organism searches its 'functional life space' are *gradient-based*. Functional spaces are classified as 'well-organised' if the variables defining the space can be perceptually partitioned into two classes: essential and inessential. A variable is classified as *inessential* if a small variation in the variable results in a large variation in the evaluation value. The identification of evaluation values for these variables is carried out comparatively simply and quickly. In contrast, a variable is classified as *essential* if a large manipulation in the variable is associated with a small variation in the evaluation value. While not all mathematical functions can be partitioned into inessential and essential variables, Gel'fand and Tsetlin were of the opinion that the 'overwhelming majority' of biological functions were organised in this manner.

3.3.6. Thom's catastrophe theory

More recently, Thom's theory of catastrophes (1970, 1975) offers the most formal analysis of qualitative complexity in dynamic systems. Thom's analysis provides a classification scheme for analysing degeneracies in the macroscopic organisation of a system. Thom is interested primarily in qualitatively classifying the transitions themselves. Thom's analysis uses the techniques of Poincaré's differential topology to extract properties of a function's form. For a problem involving dynamic (time-dependent) variables,

480

qualities such as 'tendencies' to *converge* or *diverge* around 'critical regions' are of importance, and may be readily revealed using the techniques of differential topology. If the flow tends to converge on a small region, the region is termed an *attractor;* and conversely, if the flow tends to diverge, the region is referred to as a *repellor*. The basic building materials are the qualities of convergence, divergence, attractors – regions in which flows 'terminate' – and repellors – regions in which flows are 'initiated' (see Thom, 1983). Stable states (in the classical, not structural, sense) are associated with the attractor regions. The ability to reveal these qualitative properties, however, is only achieved by giving up quantitative concepts such as rate, distance, and magnitude. This allows a topologist to search multidimensional spaces for stable regions with relative indifference to any quantitative measures. The area of multidimensional spaces with their various equilibrium points constitutes the basic building materials for Thom's theory of catastrophes (see Section 3.4.).

Thom's theory of catastrophes provides a qualitative analysis of a system's behaviour of a system during transitions. The critical event associated with a transition region is the creation or annihilation of a singularity (i.e., equilibrium state). Thom's analysis focuses on the qualitative nature of the discontinuities and their geometric unfolding. Whereas the π-theorem and dimensionless numbers identified the number of discontinuities and their quantitative locations, Thom's theory of catastrophes ventures into the transition itself and provides a generic classification scheme for transitions associated with the creation and annihilation of singular (equilibrium) states.

3.4. The problem of morphogenesis: identifying the origin and evolution of singular states

3.4.1. Classical stability theory

Classical stability theory is concerned with understanding the dynamical properties associated with certain systems of differential equations. The stability associated with these systems is often represented by the analogy of a marble rolling on a surface. Equilibrium states are defined when the net resultant of the horizontal forces is zero. Displacements in any direction creates as force resultant that tends to return the ball to the equilibrium position. Conventionally these changes are associated with a potential function (whose values are assigned by the Z-axis). Potential functions can come in a variety of 'forms'. The particular shape of these forms determines the stability of the system. Figure 4 identifies a bowl-shaped potential function.

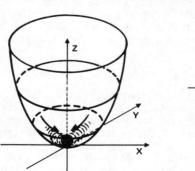
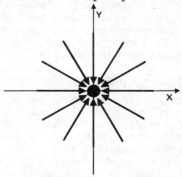

Fig. 4a. Stable Equilibrium Point.   Fig. 4b. Motion in X-Y Plane.

A single equilibrium point occurs at the bottom of the bowl (where the potential function is minimum). At this location (in space) the net horizontal forces are symmetric and equal to zero. Displacements of the ball from the minimum result in the development of a resultant force structure which tends to return the ball to the minimum – at the equilibrium point the force resultant becomes zero. The equilibrium point is referred to as stable if small perturbations are counteracted by resultant forces that tend to return the ball to the equilibrium condition. Such equilibria are referred to as *attractors*.

Figure 5 identifies an inverted bowl-shaped potential function. The top of the inverted bowl identifies an equilibrium state that is *unstable*. At this point there are no resultant forces (satisfying the equilibrium requirement). In this instance, however, if the ball is perturbed away from the equilibrium state, a resultant force developes that tends to move the ball *away* from the equilibrium state. The motion of the ball in the vicinity of this equilibrium point is unstable and the equilibrium point is referred to as a *point repellor*.

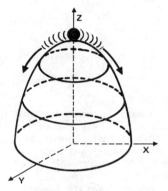
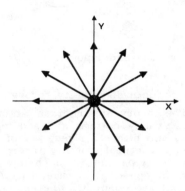

Fig. 5a. Unstable Equilibrium   Fig. 5b. Motion in X-Y Plane.
Point.

Figure 6 identifies a 'saddle-shaped' potential function. An equilibrium point, termed a *saddlepoint*, is defined at the 'seat' of the saddle. It is a combination of an attractor and a repellor. It is a stable attractor for perturbation in the x-plane and an unstable repellor for movements in the y-plane. (This equilibrium point is not realisable by a one-dimensional potential function).

Classifying equilibria through the perturbation of a marble-like entity on a potential surface provides the conceptual back-drop for conventional stability theory. The attractor, repellor and saddlepoint are the only building material used in conventional stability theory. Structural stability provides an alternative method for exploring and classifying equilibria states In structural stability theory parameters of the potential function are perturbed (instead of particular states of the system). The equilibria are then classified by the response patterns of the equilibria states to the parameter perturbations.

482

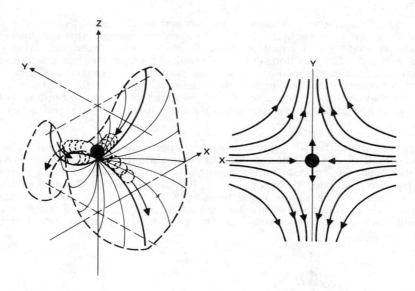

Fig. 6a. Saddlepoint.   Fig. 6b. Motion in X-Y Plane.

3.4.2. Structural stability theory

The theory of structural stability theory extends beyond the simple hilltops, valley bottoms and saddlepoints offered by conventional stability theory, and offers a richer set of building material for dynamical landscapes. Structural stability theory provides a methodology for analysing the *qualitative* nature of change in a system's dynamical character as various independent parameters (which serve to define the dimensions of a system) are changed. Whereas conventional stability theory deals with local response patterns to perturbations, structural stability theory deals with global changes in the dynamical landscapes.

A system of differential equations is referred to as *structurally stable* if the dynamical landscape remains qualitatively unaltered in the course of changes in the independent parameters (i.e., the numerical descriptions of its trajectories may change, but the overall pattern of its stabilities remains unchanged). This change identifies a region in which a certain similitude is preserved invariant, a *preservation* of qualitative form over a scaling-up in magnitude. The system is *structurally unstable* if the similitude is annihilated. Only for an exceptionally small region of parameter space does the system exhibit structural instability - this small submanifold region constitutes the *bifurcation set* or *catastrophe set*. Slight changes in parameters across this region can result in a 'catastrophe' - a catastrophe is the annihilation of one similitude and the creation of another, a shift in the landscape's qualitative form such as when a peak coalesces with a valley resulting in its annihilation (see Figure 7). This region of instability may be likened to a dissimilitude region or a *change* in qualitative form over a scaling-up magnitude. In these critical regions continuous changes in micro variables which define the system's dimensions may suddenly become associated with dramatic 'jumps' in a system's description on a more macro level. The sudden transition or jump appears to be discontinuous not because

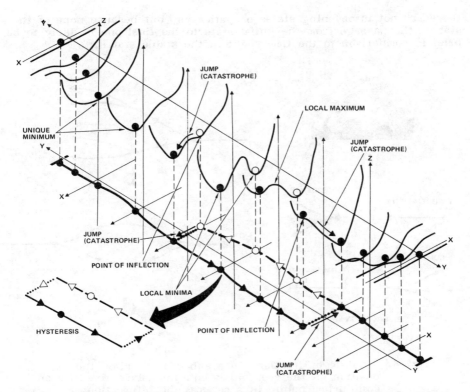

Fig. 7. The set of stable and unstable points changes as a function
of variations in the Y-parameter. The manifold is initially
flat with no equilibrium points. Changes in the Y-parameter
result in the emergence of a minimum (a 'valley'). The ball's
trajectory follows the minimum point as Y is changed. Further
changes in Y result in the appearance of a small perturbation
on the right side wall of the valley, eventually, evolving into
an 'inflection point'. The inflection point is then annihilated
with the emergence of two new singularities, a second minimum
and a maximum. Throughout this evolutionary sequence the
ball remains in the original minimum, forbidden access to the
other singular states by the intervening gradient to its right.
The next stage of evolution involves the coalescing of the
maximum ('peak') with the original minimum (valley), resulting
in a mutual annihilation. The ball's position on the manifold
becomes unstable, resulting in a sudden 'jump' of the ball to
a new stable equilibrium point located a short distance off to
the right. The dotted line identifies the path of the ball. No
equilibrium points are defined on the dotted line. The term
'catastrophe' was introduced by Thom to refer to these 'jumps'
across regions in which no equilibrium points are defined. The
dashed line indicates the path that the ball would take if the
evolution proceeded in the other direction (moving from right
to left). A jump or catastrophe will occur at the point of
inflection. A hysteresis loop can result.

484

there are not intervening states or pathways, but because none of them is stable; the passage from the initial state to the final one is likely to be brief in comparison to the time spent in the stable states.

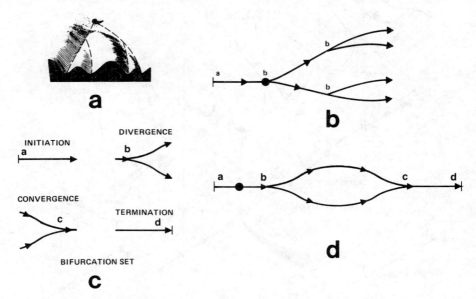

Fig. 8. A subtle bifurcation. In a subtle bifurcation the ball's position on the manifold is continuously defined by an equilibrium point. In a catastrophe bifurcation, an equilibrium point is *not continuously defined*. Panel (C) identifies bifurcations involving both subtle and catastrophic change: convergence (c) and divergence (b) of flows are associated with subtle bifurcations; initiation (a) and termination (d) of flows are associated with catastrophes. Panels (A), (B) and (D) identify examples of bifurcation sequences.

3.4.3. Thom's theorem of elementary catastrophes

The theory of catastrophes addresses the problems of (i) how many qualitatively different ways solutions can approach and exit singular states, and (ii) what 'forms' the solutions assume. Thom's theorem of elementary catastrophes is a classification theorem that identifies the number and qualitative nature of these transitions (see Poston & Stewart, 1978 for a very readable account). It is based on the following assumptions: (i) a system of interest is structurally stable, that is, its 'form' (defined topologically) remains essentially unchanged during small perturbations of the underlying vector field that describes the system's motion and (ii) the system's motion is governed only by *scalar-valued potential functions*. A scalar potential is a function that relates the underlying state space to the (one-dimensional) real numbers; that is, it is a function that assigns a single real number to each point in the state space.

A system is said to be driven by a scalar potential if there is a scalar potential V that has the property that at every point in time the system's evolution is in the direction of steepest increase of V. Put simply, the time evolution of a system driven by a scalar potential always follows a trajectory that maximises the increase of V. Increases and decreases in the values defined by the potential function are referred to as *gradients* of the potential. Singular states in the potential function identify *equilibrium states*. The theorem describes the seven simplest ways for such transitions to occur. According to the theorem, the types of catastrophes which may be associated with a particular system are finitely bounded by the dimension of the control space, regardless of the system's dimensions. In short, each number of control parameters has a distinct number of catastrophes associated with it (for example, there are seven distinct catestrophes or bifurcations associated with four dimensions of control, see Thom, 1975).

Essentially, Thom has created a mathematical language - catastrophe theory - built on the assumptions of structural stability and qualitative regularity. He proposes that the development of form is completely 'independent of the substrates of form and the nature of forces that create them' (1975, p. 8). Furthermore, 'the only stable singularities are determined solely by the dimensions of the ambient space' (1975, p. 8). In short Thom has proposed a theory of form based principally on an appreciation of potential stable points and the dimension of the control space. The properties of force and material substance are primarily associated with scalar transformations (affine, shear, cardioidal, etc.) on the system's stable dynamic form. Due to the abstract nature of form and stability, the same pattern of stable points could be manifest by a wide variety of systems. Once again, this commonality could account for the wide similarity in form between many animate and inanimate systems. Because of this fact Thom argued, as Thompson had earlier, that a qualitative study of form should proceed from the mere study of force and substance to the abstract study of form itself.

3.4.4. 'Building materials' for flow fields: attractors, repellors, basins and separatrices

A flow field consists of a field of tangent vectors, termed the *vector field* X, on a state space, termed the *smooth manifold* S. Analytically, the vector field can be viewed as a 'flow' (or group of motions of the space of states upon itself). Viewed quantitatively the flow field can be decomposed into a number of sets defining *basins,* each of which contains a single state termed an *attractor, saddle,* or *repellor*. The region that separates one basin from another defines a set called a *separatrix*. A description in terms of these sets is referred to as an *attractor-basin portrait* of the flow field. (An introduction to the concept of attractor-basin portraits and their structural stability can be found in Abraham and Shaw's visual math series on *Dynamics: The Geometry of Behavior* volumes I, 1982; II, 1984; III, 1985).

The qualitative 'forms' associated with these sets mathematically identify equivalence classes of solution to differential equations. The individual members of a particular solution space - or equivalence class - are referred to as having *qualitative similarity*. The solution space can be very large or very small, the smallest set containing a single point and identifying a *singular state*. All neighboring states differ quantitatively from the singular states (in solution space). The singular states identify attractor and repellor regions. They are low-dimensional subsets of the state space to which the motion of a system settles or from which it departs; they serve, roughly, as the mathematical definition of form.

Complex flow field patterns or morphologies can be assembled by arranging a *layout* of attractors, repellors, and their connecting basins and separatrices (see Figure 9).

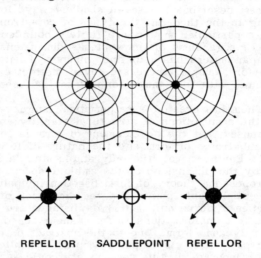

REPELLOR   SADDLEPOINT   REPELLOR

Fig. 9. An example of a flow pattern generated when two
repellors are brought into competition for neighboring
flows. The result is the emergence of a saddle point.

The qualitative properties of the patterns will vary as a function of (i) the number of singular states in the pattern and (ii) the nature of the qualitative continuation assumed by the solution in entering and exiting the singular state. For example, a solution can enter a singular state in qualitative form X (increasing gradient) and take on the qualitative form Y (no gradient) defined by the singular state. Upon exiting the singular state the qualitative form of the solution can either (i) return to the state X associated with the approach state (characteristic of an attractor or repellor region) or (ii) enter a new state Z associated with a new solution space (characteristic of a saddle region).

The structural stability of the potential function ($\emptyset$), however, does not necessarily imply structural stability of the flows ($x = - \nabla \emptyset$) that approach and depart from function's singular set. The structural evolution of the singular set defines one manifold and the structural evolution of the derivative flows that converge or diverge from the singular set defines a second manifold. The second manifold (derivative flows) is organised by the first manifold (singular set). The time rate of evolution of these respective manifolds need not be coupled. One can change slowly while the other changes rapidly. For example, if the time-evolution of the singular set is slow relative to the time-evolution of the derivative set, then the former is termed a *slow manifold*, and the latter a *fast manifold*.

3.5. Symmetry-breaking mechanisms that create and annihilate singular states. Is there a purely geometric account?

The geometric theory of morphogenesis has made significant advances in the last century. Starting with Poincaré's first formulation of topology, it has been clear that the submanifold of a dynamic system's singular states plays a central role in the structural and functional 'form' assumed by a system's behaviour. Geometrically, the study of *form* or *morphology* has been reduced to the studies of the singular set and its effects on the system's macroscopic behaviour. Thom's theory of catastrophes provides an account of the qualitative classes of change in singular sets of dimension four or less. While Thom's theory defines the necessary conditions (in terms of the dimension of the control space) for the existence of singular states, it does not address the issue of the physical mechanisms that create or annihilate the singular states. There is as yet, no purely geometric account of these *symmetry-breaking mechanisms*.

While no geometric account has been forthcoming, identifying these symmetry-breaking mechanisms is currently on the agenda in the area of nonlinear, nonequilibrium, thermodynamics. The strategies underlying the creation, sustaining, and annihilation of singular states in thermo-dynamic processes is fundamental to Prigogine and his colleagues' theory of *dissipative structures* (1967; Nicolis & Prigogine, 1971; Glansdorff & Prigogine, 1977).

4. THE PHYSICAL PERSPECTIVE: SYMMETRY-BREAKING MECHANISMS, IRREVERSIBLE FLOWS, AND SELF-ORGANISATION

4.1. Statistical mechanics: a bridgework linking micro and macro states

The laws of quantum mechanics provide precise descriptions of micro behaviour at the atomic or molecular scale and the principles of classical (and relativistic) mechanics have proven equally successful at predicting the behaviour or large scaled (macro) objects. The behaviours at these two scales, however, are of a strikingly different character. Statistical mechanics has been developed as a bridge-work for linking these two scales of analysis.

Statistical mechanics is a theoretical bridgework that relates the microscopic dynamical laws to the macroscopic dynamical laws through the use of distribution functions. These distribution functions provide a mapping of states between the microscopic phase space descriptions and the macro-scopic state space descriptions. The use of distribution functions, however, has proven to be a less than ideal bridge. The mapping function from the micro phase space into the macro state space specifies the existence of a unique correspondence in the direction of the micro-physical to the macro-physical. The mapping states that 'to every micro state there corresponds one and only one macro state'. The reverse of this statement, however, is *not* true. The statement 'to every macro state there corresponds one and only one micro state' is *false* (see Balescu, 1975). The reason for this is that not all macroscopic qualities can be expressed in the form of a dynamical function weighted by a distribution function. Put simply, there is a one to many mapping from micro to macro and a many to one from macro to micro.

4.2. Introduction of thermodynamic variables

The mapping function would be symmetrical if the micro states were independent of one another. If, however, the micro states interact, then the mapping function is asymmetrical and the previous set of mechanical variables no longer suffice to completely characterise the behaviour of the system. With particle interaction a new set of state descriptions emerge that do not exist at the scale of a single particle. Variables that come into, and go out of, existence with the creation, and annihilation, of interactive states are termed *thermodynamic*. Temperature, pressure and entropy are examples of thermodynamic variables. It is not possible to speak of a single particle's temperature, pressure or entropy. Only with reference to an ensemble of particles do these states have meaning. These variables contrast mechanical variables, such as energy, momentum and mass which can be assigned as states of a single particle. Thermodynamic variables are, however, similar to the classical variables in terms of their sensitivity to conservational constraints: Temperature is sensitive to the energy constraint, pressure to the momentum constraints, volume to the mass constraint, etc. Following the traditional physical format systems are isolated by boundaries, preventing the flow of the conservations, and equations of state are formulated that describe time-symmetric (reversible) processes. These processes define the equilibrium states.

Systematic linking together of ensemble variables into equations of state, similar to the mechanical equation of state, forms the scaffolding of thermodynamics. The thermodynamic equations provide a means for predicting correlations among observables and establish a framework within which patterns of ensemble behaviour can be organised and tested for self-consistency. These equations of state have proven to be as successful at predicting ensemble behaviour as classical and quantum mechanical equations are for individual particles.

4.3. The origin of temporal irreversibility

The introduction of ensemble descriptions into physical models brought with it a surprise unparalleled in the physical sciences. When events associated with ensemble behaviour are analysed, an irreversible ordering of temporal states can be observed and a state variable *(entropy)* can be measured that is *not* time-symmetric. The entropy of a system is observed to increase unidirectionally along the time axis. The observation of an intrinsically defined, temporal ordering tendency, leads to the formal recognition of the second law of thermodynamics. The second law defines a natural tendency of ensemble systems to distribute or partition conserved entities equally among all available microscopic degrees of freedom. In isolated systems the tendency to equipartition conserved entities always evolves in time toward the state of uniform distribution, the equilibrium state. An intrinsically defined *arrow of time* can always be assigned by identifying the temporal direction associated with increases in the system's entropy. All events can be assigned a temporal ordering according to whether the entropy is increasing or decreasing.

Classical thermodynamics (Zemansky, 1937) defines the equipartition tendencies in terms of the distribution functions. Equilibrium and non-equilibrium states can be distinguished by monitoring these distribution functions. Equilibrium states are defined when the conserved entities are equally distributed among the degrees of freedom, e.g. when the Maxwell-Boltzmann distribution of velocities or energy is uniform. Alternatively, nonequilibrium states are defined when the conserved entities are in the process of being distributed, e.g. when the Maxwell-Boltzmann distribution of velocities or energy is *not* uniform. The tendency of ensemble states to convergence onto equilibrium states is a function of the stability of the global distribution relative to local fluctuation (see Kugler & Turvey, 1986). The strength of the distributional tendency defines the (nonequilibrium) thermodynamic field potential.

4.4. Lyapounov stability: time-dependent equilibrium and nonequilibrium attractor states

The basic concept of a stability analysis for a thermodynamic system is that of Lyapounov stability (see Minorsky, 1962). Lyapounov stability is defined by the assertion that solutions (final states) that relate to neighboring initial states evolve in the neighborhood of each other. This notion of stability explicitly refers to the limit (t-- >∞) and implies the notion of a direction of time. The concept of asymptotic stability further implies that any finite perturbation will eventually be damped back onto the original state through dissipative (entropy producing) processes.

An asymptotically stable state defines an *attractor state* in the state space evolution of the system's dynamics. Physically this refers to the asymptotic convergence of the source and sink concentrations (for t-- >∞) onto a concentration defining the equilibrium state. In an isolated system the equilibrium state identifies an attractor for all other states. Displacements from equilibrium result in the creation of forces that tend to drive the system back to equilibrium. For example, uniform distribution of temperature defines thermal equilibrium, uniform distribution of mass and momentum defines mechanical equilibrium, uniform distribution of chemical potential defines chemical equilibrium, etc. Displacements from the equilibrium state results in the generation of a gradient-dependent dynamic whose forcing function is reduced as it approaches the equilibrium condition. The geometrical meaning of the attractor state, and the asymptotic convergence, is illustrated in Figure 10.

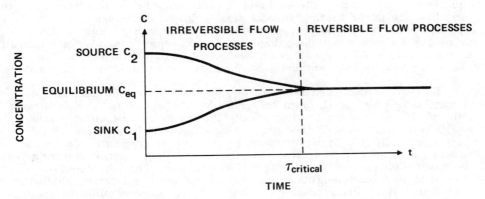

Fig. 10. Time evolution plot of conservational distribution. The second law of thermodynamics identifies equilibrium as a time-dependent attractor state for isolated systems. At equilibrium, the field potentials are uniformly distributed (according to the equipartition theorem) over all available degrees of freedom).

The second law of thermodynamics can be restated using the language of stability theory: For all physical processes a Lyapounov function exists with global (thermodynamic) equilibrium or steady-states that act as *attractors* for neighboring nonequilibrium states (see Planck, 1932; Prigogine, 1980). The time-dependent dynamic, predicted by the second law (e.g., production of entropy with time), can be used to distinguish among processes: (i) those processes that produce entropy are *irreversible* and their associated states were *nonequilibrium;* and, (ii) those processes that produced no entropy are *reversible* and all their states are at *equilibrium.*

4.4.1. Regions of reversibility and irreversibility

The production of entropy is related to *change* in the concentration of a conserved entity (e.g., *gradients).* If the concentration is uniform throughout the field, e.g., *no gradients,* then the distribution function describing the partitioning process in constant. Regions in which the system's dynamics are *not gradient-dependent* are termed *regions of reversibility.* If the concentration is not uniform, resulting in gradients, then (according to the second law) the distribution function will change with time, a symptotically approaching a well-defined equilibrium or steady state condition. Regions in which the system's dynamics are *gradient-dependent* are termed *regions of irreversibility.*

4.5. Nonlinear, nonequilibrium, thermodynamics: far from equilibrium conditions

Within the last few decades the development of thermodynamics has been characterised by attempts to introduce nonlinear processes into the formalism. Classical reversible thermodynamics was principally concerned with thermal, mechanical and chemical equilibrium states. The next phase of thermodynamics addressed problems concerning small displacements from equilibrium states. For these displacements the dynamical equations describing the irreversible, nonequilibrium, processes were linearised with respect to the quantities (forces and fluxes) describing the deviation from equilibrium. By limiting the analysis to small equilibrium displacements, the formalism for linear thermodynamics was defined. There are many thermo-dynamic processes, however, that are associated with nonequilibrium processes which are not describable by macroscopic thermodynamic quantities that are linearisable. These processes occur farther from equilibrium and are addressed by the formalisms of nonlinear, nonequilibrium, thermodynamics

In systems displaced far from equilibrium, by a continous flow of energy and/or matter through the operational components, the density of internal interaction can be dramatically increased by competitions among and between irreversible flow processes. At *critical densities of inter-action* (identifiable by a π -number) the internal structure can *suddenly* undergo a *reorganisation* whereby new correlations emerge resulting from the elimination of microscopic degrees of freedom. The correlated state acts to attract neighboring states in the same manner in which the equilibrium state attracted neighboring states in near equilibrium conditions. An example of a *nonequilibrium attractor* is the ensemble state of a burning flame. The 'flame' persists even through it has a continuous input and output of matter and energy. The internal states of the flame are organised by a nonequilibrium attractor. Other examples include hydrodynamic flow patterns such as the Benard convection and Taylor instability. Section 5.2. provides a detailed analysis of the origin and evaluation of these nonequilibriu attractors in a biological setting.

4.5.1. Benard convection and Taylor instability

The Benard convection is the result of a competition between a temperature gradient, as a driving force for heat flow, and a gravitation field, as a force field that resists convective flows. A large scale flow pattern emerges when a fluid layer is heated from below, keeping a fixed temperature on the top surface. This creates a temperature differential resulting in forces that tend to push the fluid's molecules in the direction of the cooler upper surface. The convective motion of the molecules is resisted by internal friction and gravity. When the thermal gradient is small, only heat-energy is conducted along the gradient. The molecules remain local, their motion dominated by random thermal motion. The convective forces generated by the thermal gradient, which tend to force the more bouyant hot liquid to the top surface, are damped by the frictional and gravitational forces. If the strength of the thermal gradient exceeds the damping forces, a convective motion of molecules can occur that has a macroscopic spatial and temporal scale. Further increases in the thermal gradient can evolve additional macro patterns, such as hexagonal flow cells, as the dominating roles of competing transport processes change (see Koschmeider, 1977).

Taylor instability occurs when fluid is trapped between two cylinders rotating in opposite directions. The fluid is caused to rotate by shear forces transmitted by the cylinders. At rotation speeds below a critical value the fluid flow is laminar; above that value, the flow becomes turbulent progressing toward stable, organised vorticies. The patterns are the result of a competition between friction and centrifugal force. From an initial unordered macroscopic state, a well-ordered spatial pattern can suddenly emerge. With further gradient increases, the spatial pattern can become oscillatory, periodically returning to the same state (once they have reached the so-called *limit cycle*). These macroscopic patterns (long range coherences) can be continuously assembled and disassembled by changing a single parameter (referred to by Haken, 1977, as an *order parameter*, see Figure 11). The self-assembly process is: (i) stable and reproducible – i.e., the same patterns can be repeatedly assembled and once assembled they resist perturbation; (ii) generically generative – a finite set of patterns are assembled that are strictly determined by the dimension of the flow field and the number and layout of the attractor states (see Section 4.4.3); (iii) a low dimension control system – patterns can be assembled and disassembled through variation in a single control (of order) parameter; and (iv) self-organised via irreversible flows towards nonequilibrium attractor states – requires no *apriori* specification of constraints.

4.7. Open and closed systems, nonequilibrium attractors, and self-organisation: a summary

The behaviour of thermodynamically open and closed systems is markedly distinct from isolated systems. Isolated systems exhibit a natural tendency to evolve towards an attractor state defined by thermodynamic equilibrium. The second law identifies the time-evolution tendency to approach the equilibrium attractor. Open and closed systems, in contrast, need not evolve toward equilibrium. Under appropriate conditions the orientational tendency of the system can switch and become oriented toward a well-defined non-equilibrium state. The nonequilibrium attractor constrains the time evolution of the dynamics in the same manner as the previous equilibrium attractor. With the emergence of nonequilibrium attractors comes a natural

492

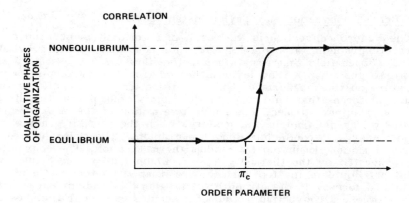

Fig. 11. If a system is displaced sufficiently far from equilibrium
the stability of the equilibrium branch of thermodynamic
states can become unstable. The local attractiveness
previously associated with the equilibrium state can
suddenly be replaced by a 'well-defined' nonequilibrium
state. This is a nonequilibrium attractor. The attractiveness of the state is *not* strictly a function of boundary
conditions, it is resistant to perturbations. The attractor
is defined by a set of long range correlations that play
the same orientational role as the mean velocity plays in
a Maxwellian distribution. The bifurcation points are
associated with dimensionless π-numbers (see Section
3.2.3). The movement can be controlled by changes in
a single *(control)* parameter. In the Benard convection
the control parameter was temperature, and, in the Taylor
instability, it was rotational velocity. The ordinate is a
measure of relative correlations. Equilibrium defines a
state of minimum correlation. Nonequilibrium states are
defined by increased long range correlation.

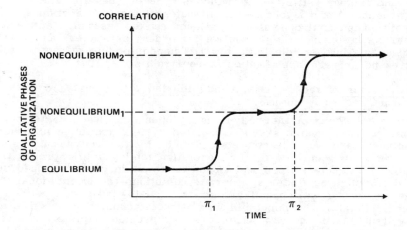

Fig. 12. Time evolution of a self-organising system.

tendency to create (long range) order and a reversal of the classical evolutionary tendency towards (long range) disorder - the system exhibits a natural tendency to self-organise (see Figure 12).

5.   SELF-ORGANISING INFORMATION SYSTEMS

5.1. Interactions involving biological atomisms

Interactions between simple Newtonian particles and their surroundings are dominated by descriptions that involve the mass dimension. Ordinary interactions are said to occur through forces (the dimension of force is ML^2T^{-2}). In contrast, interactions between complex biological particles and their surroundings are dominated by descriptions in which the mass term is absent - whether hormonal, pheromonal, neural, optical, acoustical, or verbal the interaction is low in energy, momentum and mass (see Figure 13).

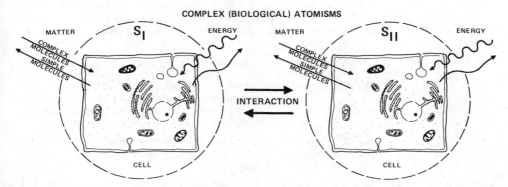

Fig. 13*. Informational interactions: Kinematic singularities, symmetries, and invariants are fundamental descriptors for sustaining interactions. Particles with large numbers of interior (molecular) constraints can time-delay energy flows from the interior to the exterior. The result is the emergence of thermodynamic flow processes. These flow processes will vary as a function of the number of internal constraints. The time-delaying of exterior---> interior--> exterior... energy flows dramatically changes the particle's external mode of interaction: the particle is no longer a 'slave' to external force fields. The time-delaying of internal (thermo-dynamic) energy flows provides a 'particle-based' source of forces that can actively compete with the external forces. As the internal force field increases with respect to the scale of the external force field, the role of the mass dimension becomes successively less relevant for sustaining interactions. What remains relevant, however, are the fundamental dimensions of length and time. These nonforce dominated interactions are termed 'informational interaction' and are viewed as being methodologically continuous with elastic and inelastic interactions. Informational interactions are the physical consequence of particles with complex interiors that can time-delay large amounts of energy relative to external force fields.

* Figure reproduced, with permission, from Kugler and Turvey, 1986.

These descriptions are kinematic (space/time), geometric (space) and/or spectral (time). Indeed, interactions that do not involve mass-based descriptions or observables might be taken as the hallmark of systematic behaviour at the ecological scale (see Table 1). At the ecological scale interactions are largely informational not forceful. The significance of this fact is that suppression or removal of the mass dimension from the state description eliminates the 'interactive violence' associated with the shock waves and impulses that strain the internal constraints and ultimately lead to internal fracture and 'organisational death'.

Table 1. Alternative field descriptions: The field descriptions are macroscopic. They do not include microscopic descriptions such as
charge, spin and other attributes of interaction at the electro-
magnetic and quantum scale (adapted from F.E. Yates and P.N.
Kugler, Signs, singularities and significance: a physical model
for semiotics, *Semiotica*, 49-77, 1984). The scale of interaction
of interest is the ecological scale where the particles of interest
have complex interiors that time-delay energy flows.

Descriptions	Dimensions	Properties
Kinetic (Newtonian Mechanics)	M, L, T	Forces - violent interactions; conservations such as mv^0, mv^1, mv^2 symmetries; potentials; constraints; singularities; X, $\dot{X}$ phase space
Kinematic	L, T (no mass)	Non-violent interactions; singularities; constraints; symmetries; X, $\dot{X}$ phase space
Geometric	L	Geometries, forms, boundary conditions initial conditions
Temporal	T	Spectra, frequencies; functions initial conditions

An historical challenge for the physically-minded scientist has been the removal of vitalism from explanatory accounts of biological systems. A less heralded but no less important challenge is the removal of the interactive violence associated with mass-dominated interactions. A physical pursuit of this latter challenge brings to the forefront the centrality of the concept of information and puts a 'non-Newtonian life' back into biology. This challenge was anticipated by J.J. Gibson (1950, 1966, 1979) in his pursuit of a kinematic flow-field analysis (see also Reed & Jones, 1982). Gibson's methodology focused on the physical and functional significance of nonmass interactions in a manner that is continuous with the theory of collisions (see Kugler, Turvey, Carello & Shaw, 1985 for an extended discussion). By focusing on nonmass field descriptions a natural transition can be made from the physical theory of self-organisation to a theory of self-organising 'information systems'.

5.2. Insect nest-building: a self-organising information system (Kugler & Turvey, 1986)

The periodic assembling of a nest by a population of social insects using pheromone gradients provides an illustration of how nonequilibrium attractors can emerge and orient cooperative activities among several million insects. The analysis focuses on the nature of various field couplings (macro/micro, flow/force) and the strategic role each assumes. The nest-building activity is significant in that it exemplifies a self-organising system, dominated macroscopically by 'kinematic flow field' properties, and microscopically by 'force field' properties. The microscopic motion of a pheromone particle is constrained by a Newtonian *force* field description (fundamental dimensions M, L, and T, see Figure 14a). In comparison, the motion of an insect is constrained by a non-Newtonian *flow* field descriptions (fundamental dimensions L and T, Figure 14b). Two features distinguish the (pheromone)

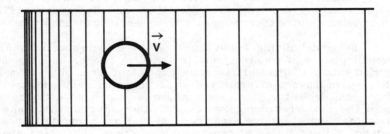

Fig. 14a*. Irreversible force field gradient. The particle's motion is
a *reaction* to external forces. The mass of the particle
plays a significant role in the scale of the forces. The
particle's motion is completely determined by the force
gradient generated as a function of the particle's external
coordinates of motion.

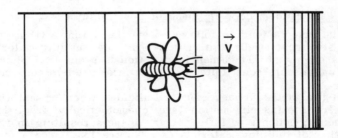

Fig. 14b*. Irreversible flow gradient. The insect's (loco)motion is an
action generated in response to a (kinematic) flow gradient.
The motion of the insect up the gradient is a function of
forces that are generated from the particle's interior. These
internally generated forces can actively resist or complement
external forces. The regulation of these forces can be
through either internal or external coordinates of motion.

* Figure reproduced, with permission, from Kugler & Turvey, 1986.

particle's motion from the insect's motion. First, the particle moves *down* a gradient towards a region of minimum concentration. In contrast, the insect moves *up* a gradient towards a region of maximum concentration. Second, the microscopic motion of the pheromone particle is a function of *external forces only*. These forces are generated solely as a function of the particle's external coordinates of motion. In contrast, the macroscopic motion of the insects is a function of both *internal and external forces*. The insect's interior actively contributes forces that can supplement external forces.

The nest-building activity involves a population of social insects, such as African termites. The activity involves the coordination of several million termites, resulting in the building of a nest that stands more than twenty feet high and weighs several tons. The principal notions expressed in the analysis are derived from Grassé's (1959) and Bruinsma's (1977) naturalistic observations and a thermodynamic treatment advanced by Deneubourge (1977)

The nest-building behaviour consists of a number of qualitatively distinct phases of construction. In the first phase, building materials are carried into the site and randomly deposited. This phase comes to an end with the emergence of preferred sites that number far fewer than the number of original deposits. The second phase is associated with the material build-up of the preferred deposit sites until they take on the shape of pillars. When the pillars achieve a certain size and are separated by a critical distance a third phase of construction emerges. The third phase is characterised by a mutual 'curvature' of two neighboring pillars towards a 'virtual mid-point'. This phase is complete when the two pillars meet at the mid-point, forming an arch. A final phase is marked by the construction of an arching dome that extends from the top of the arches. The completion of the dome marks the end of the building cycle. The building begins with the random deposit phase.

The primary questions are: (i) What is the origin of the constraints that restrict insect trajectories to those that converge on preferred locations; and (ii) What is the nature of the description that links the behaviour of the insects (a macroproperty) to the pheromone field (a microstructure)?

5.2.1. The random deposit phase of nest-building

The insects tend to follow two simple dictums (i) move in the direction of the strongest smell; and, (ii) deposit the building material where the smell is strongest. The smell in question is a chemical pheromone that the individual insects contribute to the material used to construct the nest.

In the earliest phase of nest-building, when no materials have been deposited, the insects' motions are 'chemotactically' free. There are no pheromone gradients to influence the insects resulting in the random depositing of building materials (see Figure 15). Once a few deposits have been made, the pheromone diffuses into the air, creating a gradient field whose highest point of concentration is at the center of the deposit. The diffusion gradient orients nearby insects towards regions of higher pheromone concentration. The regions of highest concentration identify *singular regions;* at these regions the gradient is annihilated.

5.2.2. A threshold restriction on macro-micro couplings

The pheromone attractant diffuses throughout the building site according to Fick's law (rate of diffusion is proportional to density). An insect flying

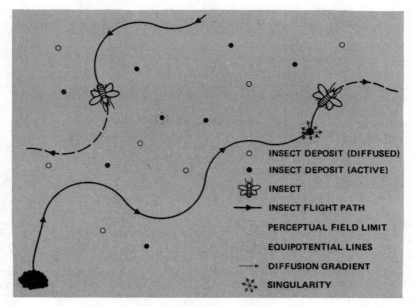

Fig. 15*. Random flight pattern. The behaviour of the insects is
at equilibrium during this phase – e.g., the motion of
each insect is independent of other insects, there are
no long range correlations between the motions of insects.

into the area can become *oriented* by this gradient. While the pheromone
diffusion extends throughout the building site, the insect's motion is only
influenced by the gradient if the pheromone concentration exceeds a
critical value determined by the insect's sensitivity threshold (Figure 16).
This threshold is a *symmetry-breaking* mechanism that partitions the
insects' activity space into *gradient-dependent regions,* where the insects
are influenced by the pheromone, and *gradient-independent regions,* where
the insects are uninfluenced by its presence. The former are *regions of
irreversibility* and the latter are *regions of reversibility.* The
partitioning of the space into reversible and irreversible regions is continuous
with the classical partitioning of dynamic processes identified in Section
4.4.1. Insects in the region of reversibility are at equilibrium, there are no
correlations between insects' external coordinates of motion. *At equilibrium
the motion of an insect is independent of other insects.* In contrast, insects
in the region of irreversibility are in a nonequilibrium state, there are long
range correlations between insects' external coordinates of motion. *In a
nonequilibrium state the motion of an insect is not independent of other
insects.*

5.2.3. The development of preferred sites

When there are only a few deposits in the building area, the pheromone
concentration remains low and it exharts very little influence on the insects.
The majority of the building site is defined by regions of reversibility –

* Figure reproduced, with permission, from Kugler and Turvey, 1986.

498

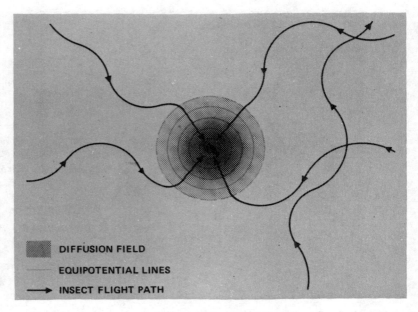

DIFFUSION FIELD

EQUIPOTENTIAL LINES

INSECT FLIGHT PATH

Fig. 16*. 'Perceptual limit' of the field. Insects in areas where the
pheromone gradient falls below the perceptual limit exhibit
no correlations among their actions; they are at equilibrium.
Insects in areas where the gradient is above the perceptual
threshold, exhibit correlations among their motions; they
are displaced from equilibrium.

the insects' motion is not gradient dependent and therefore it is at
equilibrium. At equilibrium, any locale is as attractive as any other; there
are no preferred sites. These conditions can persist indefinitely if the
number of insects depositing remains small. If the number of insects is
increased, however, the likelihood that an insect will move into the vicinity of
recent pheromone deposits and become influenced by their orienting gradients
will increase (see Figure 17,a,b). The greater the number of random
deposits within a given interval of time, the greater the probability that
an individual insect will pass into a pheromone field defined by a previous
deposit. As the number of recent deposits makes the site more attractive,
more insects contribute deposits, which in turn makes the site even more
attractive, leading the following sequence of events: (i) an increase in
concentration level, followed by (ii) an increase in probability of deposit,
followed by (iii) an increase in deposits, followed by (i)--> (ii)--> (iii)--> (i)
etc. A cyclic sequence of the preceeding kind is referred to as an *autocatalytic reaction:* The rate of accumulation of material at X is in
proportion to the material at X. Below a critical number of insects the
diffusive character of pheromones eliminates the possibility of any of the
attractant persisting long enough to support the development of a preferred
site. Above a critical number, the diffusive character of the pheromone
field can amplify (becoming autocatalytic) and take on a macroscopic space
and time scale. As the gradient region amplifies, the corresponding insect
organisation becomes successively displaced from equilibrium: the insects
develop successively greater amounts of long range correlation, there is a
tendency to self-organise.

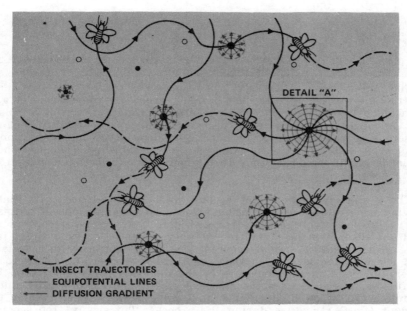

Fig. 17a*. Development of preferred sites. The development of a
preferred site marks a sudden transition in the correlational
state of the insect population. As the size and number of
preferred sites increases correlations begin to develop
among the insects' external coordinates of motion. The
behaviour of the insects is no longer at equilibrium (independent of one another), it evolves into nonequilibrium
states of increased correlation.

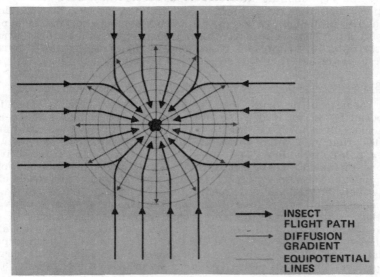

Fig. 17b*. Macro-micro, flow-force, informational coupling. The flow
pattern of the insects becomes constrained by the kinematic
properties of the diffusion field through a perceptual-motor
coupling.

* Figure reproduced, with permission, from Kugler and Turvey, 1986.

5.2.4. The emergence of a time-dependent structure as a function of the second law of thermodynamics

The second law of thermodynamics underlies the process that distributes the attractant throughout the nest building area. The pheromone at a material deposit defines a chemical potential, a concentration of a conserved entity. Accordingly, each deposit is a local source of instability that diffuse the pheromone molecules into neighboring regions according to partioning principles. A stable distribution of molecules is achieved when the chemical potential is partitioned uniformly throughout the medium enveloping the building area.

The customary image of the second law of thermodynamics is that of dissolving constraints, of rendering structured organisations of atomisms into structureless aggregations. For example, in the present context the second law eliminates the clustering of pheromones at a given site – it breaks up a particular spatial organisation. It is customary to associate the second law with the loss of spatial structure with time. It is less common, however, to focus on the structure of the diffusion processes itself. While the diffusion process lowers the chemical potential towards a more uniform distribution (i.e., lower order of spatial structure), its also creates time-dependent (flow) structure during the process. Put simply, the second law results in the break-down of spatial structure, at the expense of the creation of temporal flow structure. What was previously spatial structure, is transformed into a temporal structure that has 'properties' that persist for bounded regions of time. These temporal structures are annihilated when the process reaches equilibrium. In the case of the insects building nests, it is this temporal flow structure that provides the source of 'informational constraints' that restrict the insects' motions. The flow structure is sustained by the replenishing of fresh deposits. If they were not replenished, the temporal flow structure would be annihilated as the chemical field approached equilibrium. In a most important sense, the nest is a product of the second law. That is to say, this coherent time-independent structure (the nest) owes its origin and characteristic features, in large part, to the dissipative processes that the second law engenders.

5.2.5. Successive point attractors and the development of pillars

On the site of an original deposit a pillar may develop (see Figure 18). The process by which it does so illustrates the point about the second law as a source (ultimately) of time-independent structural organisations. It is noteworthy that as a pillar grows its uppermost region at each new height acts as a point attractor. (The pillar's top is always the most active site of pheromone diffusion). This means that in the course of construction here is a continuous succession of point attractors or singularities, each characteristi of a relatively short-lived dissipative field. A pillar, therefore, can be viewed as a structural vestige – or, more abstractly, an alternative description – of properties defined temporarily in the geometry of pheromone diffusion fields. It is important to make the parenthetical remark about 'alternative descriptions'. A great deal of puzzlement has been expressed (e.g. Pattee, 1972, 1979) about the origin of rate-independent structures in biology that constrain rate-dependent dynamics (see Section 2.3.1.). The pillars of the termite nests are structures that restrict the trajectories of the insect builders. Similar to biological constraints, the pillars function to select one trajectory from among many virtual trajectories – to constrain the insect dynamics in a certain way at a certain time - but their physical origin is not mysterious; roughly, they arise from the play of the second law in the context of an open system, as outlined above.

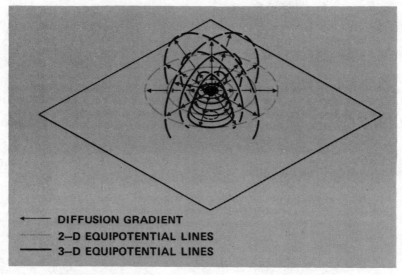

Fig. 18*. Development of a pillar.

To summarise: Pillars are included among the time-independent structures that constrain the dynamics of nest-building. These structures, however, are erected on the basis of *time-dependent* geometries carried in diffusive flow fields. Is this a crude blueprint for the evolution of biological constraints in general? The advantage of the strategy sketched is that no extra-physical principles (consistent with but not reducible to physical principles) are implicated in the origin of biological constraints.

5.2.6. Saddlepoint attractors and the development of arches

If two pillars are constructed sufficiently close to each other so that their diffusion fields interact within the perceptual limit of the insects, then a new type of singularity emerges in the flow field geometry (see Figure 19a). The interaction of the diffusion fields results in a saddlepoint singularity whose location is midway between the two pillars. Insects entering the pheromone field from certain angles will find the geometry of the field similar to that of a single, isolated pillar. Insects entering the pheromone field midway between the two pillars, however, encounter a flow gradient that takes them to a singular state marking a point roughly midway between the two pillars. After following the gradient into this singularity the insects encounter even steeper gradients that lead out of the singularity towards the two active pillar sites. The significance of the saddlepoint is that it introduces a depositing bias toward a region between the two pillars; the result is the building of an arch. The significance of the saddlepoint,

---

* Figure reproduced, with permission, from Kugler and Turvey, 1986.

502

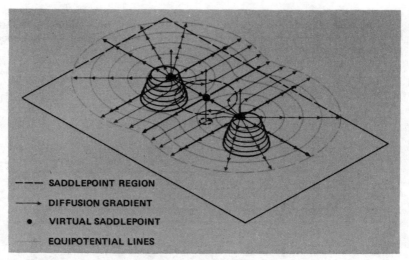

Fig. 19a*. Emergence of a saddlepoint.

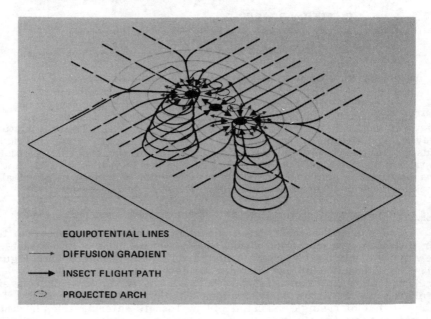

Fig. 19b*. Building of an arch. The emergence of the saddlepoint
marks a further increase in the distance associated with the
long range correlations. During pillar building the
correlations were restricted to the activity around each
pillar. The coordinates of motion of insects were not
correlated from one pillar to the next. During the building
of the arch correlation relating the insects are extended
to a region defined over the two pillars. Arch-building is
a phase of organisation that is further away from equilibrium
than the pillar-building.

* Figure reproduced, with permission, from Kugler and Turvey, 1986.

relative to the insect coordination problem, is that it is a low dimensional description, one that 'alternatively describes', and one that plays back causally upon a dynamic of high dimensionality. The result is a stable and reproducible solution to the arch building problem.

5.2.7. The final phase: the construction of a dome

the completion of the arch is associated with the coalescing of the two pillar singularities with the saddlepoint, resulting in the annihilation of the saddlepoint and the emergence of a new singularity whose attractiveness is a function of the combined attractiveness of the two pillar singularities (see Figure 20).

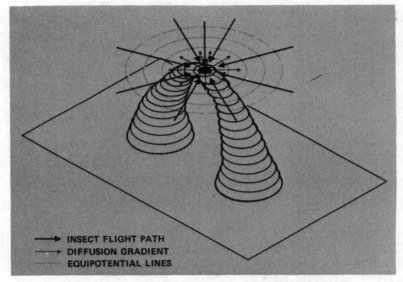

Fig. 20*. Completion of the arch and the annihilation of the saddlepoint.

The new singularity can interact with other local singularities resulting in the emergence of an intricate pattern of new saddlepoints. These saddlepoints and their associated gradient fields provide constraints that are used in the construction of a domed roof (see Figure 21, 22). Upon completion of the roof a new cycle begins with random deposits on the upper surface of the roof (see Figure 23).

5.3. A circular causality of self-assembled flows and forces

The assembling of a pheromone flow field is kinetically based. Two forces are largely responsible: The force exerted muscularly by the individual insects in pursuing a given trajectory and in depositing material at a given site; and the 'generalised' force sustained by the nonuniform distribution of potential. The former force (see Figure 14a) is responsible for the concentrations of matter within the building area; the latter force (see

---

* Figure reproduced, with permission, from Kugler and Turvey, 1986.

504

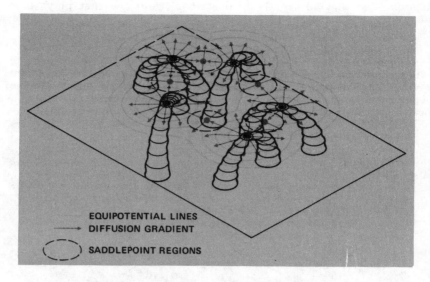

Fig. 21*. Interactions of singularities evolve new saddlepoints.

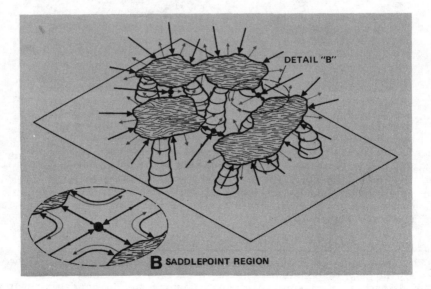

Fig. 22*. Saddlepoints are used to build a dome.

* Figure reproduced, with permission, from Kugler and Turvey, 1986.

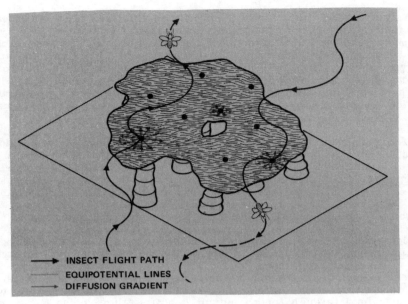

Fig. 23*. A roof is formed and a new random depositing phase
begins. The insect organisation return to its initial
equilibrium condition and starts the cycle over; a
new level of structure begins.

Figure 14b) is responsible for irreversibly dispersing the pheromone
attractant uniformly throughout the neighboring medium (by definition, at
'chemical equilibrium' force and flow vanish). How forces that are sustained
by the conservation gradients can drive flows is a question addressed by
the Onsager (1931) relations. Such force-to-flow couplings are obviously
of significance to the nest building activity, but they do not constitute the
whole story.

The above analysis reveals that the loci at which matter is deposited
are the major determinants of the structure assumed by the field of diffusing
pheromones. Individual insects flying in the nest building area must generate
particular forces in order to deposit at these select loci. What constrains
the action of the muscular forces as to restrict the behaviour of the
insects to small well-defined regions in the building site? The answer is:
'kinematic properties of the pheromone flow field'. There is, therefore, a
heterodox kinematic (pheromone) flow---- > kinetic (muscular) force coupling
that complements the orthodox Onsager force---> flow coupling. This
heterodox coupling is not addressed by the Onsager relations.

Understanding this heterodox coupling is primarily a matter of coming
to terms with alternative descriptions of pheromone diffusion. To begin with,
pheromone diffusion defines a chemical kinetic field and as such it can be
assigned an energy value. The magnitude of this value is very small, however, relative to the energy of the metabolic processes that drive the limbs
and wings of the insect builders. Pheromone diffusion is a low energy field,

* Figure reproduced, with permission, from Kugler and Turvey, 1986.

506

relatively speaking. What is the implication of this fact vis-a-vis insect locomotion? Simply that at the macroscopic scale of locomotory activity the pheromone gradient cannot function as a force gradient. The approach by an insect to a deposit site is not a movement against a force gradient. Moreover, it is plainly *not* the case that departures of an insect from the chemical kinetic field's maxima and minima give rise to forces that drive the insect back onto those states. The significant properties of pheromone diffusion for insect locomotion are found in its kinematic flow patterns or morphologies.

The details of the heterodox coupling can be summarised as follows: It is a low-energy flow-force coupling. It might be termed a *perceptual coupling,* and the topological properties (i.e., singularities, gradients, saddlepoints, etc.) carried in the kinematic flow field might be termed *informational constraints* (cf.; Lee, *This Study Section;* Lee & Young, 1985; Koenderink, 1985; Lackner, 1985; Nakayama, 1985; Runeson, 1977/83; Runeson & Frykholm, 1983). The intrinsic, dissipative, geometry of the chemical flow field (that is, patterned layouts of singular and gradient states) provides a set of low-energy informational constraints that classify or restrict the high-energy force outputs generated by the insect's movement system.

The behaviour of the insects both contributes to and is constrained by the structural properties of the pheromone field. Insects contribute to the pheromone field through their frequent deposits, they act as a *thermodynamic pump* that creates and maintains *chemical potential.* These potentials generate patterned diffusion fields that, in turn, constrain the depository activities of the insects. In this regard the evolving insect nest is exemplary of a 'self-reading' and 'self-writing' system. The system's 'behaviour' is both guided by - in the sense of 'self-reading' - and a contributor to - in the sense of 'self-writing' - the structure of the flow field. There is a 'circular causality' of the following kind: force field ---> flow field --- > force field --- > flow field ..., which can be described, alternatively, as an action --- > perception --- > action --- > perception ... cycle (see Figure 24). While the cycle is closed, by definition, in terms of complementary forces and flows, it is *open* in terms of the properties that constitute the descriptors of the flows, namely, the informational constraints. The primitives

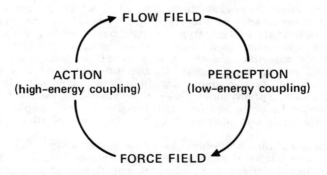

Fig. 24*. Perception/action cycle.

* Figure reproduced, with permission, from Kugler and Turvey, 1986.

of the nest-building process (flow field properties that govern its phases) arise *during* the force-flow cycles. Nest-building is a self-complexing phenomenon; the governing properties of the diffusion field self-assemble and dissolve in conjunction with the expedient behaviours of the insects. The various ideas expressed in the present subsection are collected in Figure 25 as a means of summarising the concept of *a self-organising information system*.

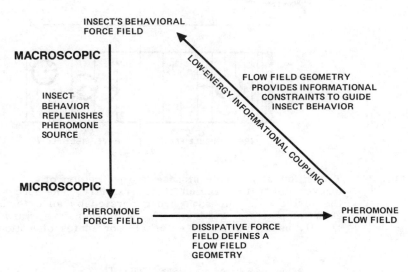

Fig. 25*. Self-organising information system.

5.4. Self-organisation and the co-mutation of micro/macro field constraints

It was remarked at the outset of this discussion that two perspectives can be taken on the pheromone field – one macroscopic, the other microscopic What is happening from the microperspective? Obviously a change is taking place. Constraints that bind the molecules together – that trap the molecules within a certain circumscribed area (viz. a deposit site) – are continuously undergoing fracture in accordance with the second law of thermodynamics. When viewed microscopically the field of pheromones is subject to *entropic mutation* – the gradual removal of all potential gradients. What is happening from the macroperspective? Again a change is taking place. But it is a change of a drastically different kind: Macroscopically, the field processes are 'building gradients', resulting in the emergence of large scale patterns defined over the pheromone flow lines. From the macroperspective, with the emphasis on large-scale kinematic and geometric effects, the field is subject to *negentropic mutation*.

Traditionally the focus of physics has been microscopic mutations. This focus led to the formulation of thermodynamics' second law. In contrast, the traditional concern of biology has been macroscopic mutations. This concern spawned the formulation of a special theory of the evolution of form and

* Figure reproduced, with permission, from Kugler and Turvey, 1986.

508

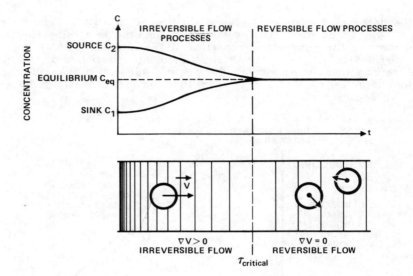

Fig. 26*. Transition of a simple atomism from a region of irreversibility to a region of reversibility. The forces that drive these atomisms are generated by an external chemical potential gradient ∇V, and, therefore, vary strictly as a function of external coordinates of motion.

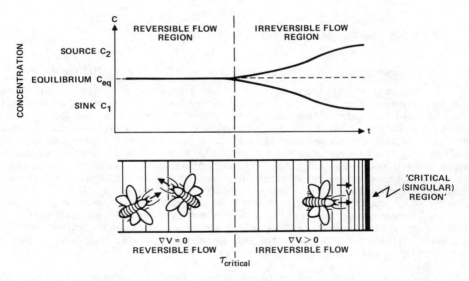

Fig. 26b*. Transition of a biological atomisms from a region of reversibility to a region of irreversibility. The forces that power these atomisms are a function of both internal and external potentials, and can be varied by internal coordinates of motion.

* Figure reproduced, with permission, from Kugler and Turvey, 1986.

509

Caption for entire Figure 26:

Reversible and irreversible time evolution of field processes.
The time course of evolution for an open system need not evolve
towards a state of total time reversibility. Insect nest-building
provides an example of a time evolution process in which an
initial reversible flow evolves into an irreversible flow. The
initial reversible state is defined during the random flight phase
of the nest-building. The emergence of preferred sites marks
the transition *in time* from reversible (gradient-independent)
insect activity to irreversible (gradient-dependent) insect
activity.

function. However, the nest-building example suggests that these two
historically distinct concerns – entropic and negentropic change – may be
intimately connected. This is one of the implications currently emerging
in the domain of nonequilibrium thermodynamics: A physics of self-
organisation might rest fundamentally on a theory of *organisation through
co-mutation,* where co-mutation refers to an entropic microstructure and a
negentropic macrostructure linked through circular causality (see Figures
26a, b).

5.5. Crossing the Rubicon from a physics of 'dead' coordinate spaces to a physics of 'living' coordinate spaces

The insect nest-building activity defines a closed periodic orbit of
macroscopic organisational modes. The closure is a function of a ringing
together of successive stabilities and instabilities. A full cycle is completed
when a set of (arbitrarily defined) initial conditions have been recovered.
For instance, define the initial conditions as the random deposit phase of
insect behaviour. Then it is apparent that this set of initial conditions is
recovered after the completion of the roof-building phase of construction.
The recovery of the initial conditions, so defined, marks the closure of
the building cycle.

The successions of stabilities and instabilities are associated with the
creation and annihilation of singularities in the topology of the pheromone
flow field. Stabilities are associated with the processes in which the layout
of singularities is invariant and instabilities are associated with the transition
region in which singularities are created or annihilated. Each topologically
distinct layout of singularities is associated with a qualitatively distinct,
macroscopic, mode of organisation. Figure 27 identifies the organisational
phases associated with the nest-building behaviour.

A succession of symmetry-breaking instabilities exemplifies the
developmental sequence of a self-organising system. Each symmetry-breaking
instability is associated with the creation or annihilation of a singular state(s).
At the molecular scale the singularities are defined in the kinetic (force-
fundamental dimensions, M, L, and T) regimes generated by the distribution
of chemical potential. At the insect scale the singularities are defined in
the kinematic (flow-fundamental dimensions L and T) regimes abstracted from
the chemical gradients. Macroscopic flow morphologies emerge as a function
of the number and layout of singular states. These *flow morphologies* define
an intrinsic set of coordinate spaces around the behaviour of insects and
which pheromone molecule are oriented. The process of self-organisation is in
essence the process of *self-organising coordinate spaces.* Biological phenomena

510

is characterised by the origin and evolution of 'living coordinate spaces' that change with time. These 'living coordinate spaces' stand in sharp contrast to 'dead extrinsic coordinate spaces' (time and space independent) that have traditionally been used to describe natural phenomena.

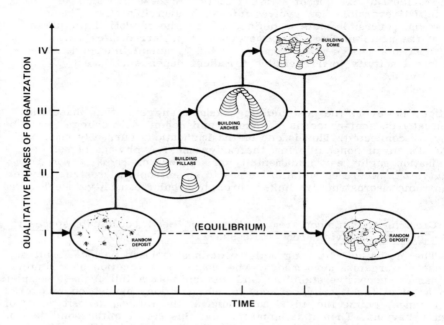

Fig. 27. Developmental sequence of nest-building modes.

6. DEVELOPMENTAL TRANSITIONS FROM RANDOM TO COORDINATED PHASES OF ORGANISATION

6.1. Perceptual-motor loops

The role of an insect's nervous system is to map kinematic information arising from interactions with kinetic force fields back into the world of kinetic force fields through adjustment of the insect's flight machinery. The kinematic operations are found in the neural substrate; the kinetic processes are both in flight muscles and in the diffusion field of the pheromones. The kinematic field *constrains* the kinetics of flight through soft couplings (neural) and, thereby, becomes *causal* without being forceful. The construction of insect nests is lawful - but this system does not fit the Newtonian model of causality. The causality is not a function of forces, rather it is a function of the lawful structuring of kinematic, geometric and spectral constraints by singularities that emerge in the soft coupling between kinetic force fields and kinematic flow fields (see Yates & Kugler, 1984; Kugler & Turvey, 1986).

The generation of these kinematic flow field properties by kinetic processes, and their playing back as constraints on those kinetic processes, yields a circularly causal process of force---> flow--- > force--- > etc. that is the hallmark of perceptual-motor loops (see Figure 28, 29 and 30):

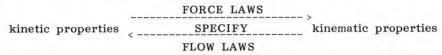

kinetic properties $\xrightarrow{\text{FORCE LAWS}}$ kinematic properties
$\xleftarrow{\text{SPECIFY}}$
FLOW LAWS

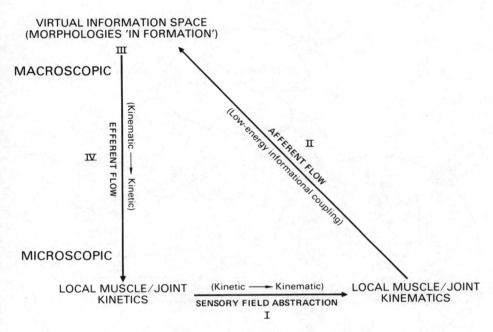

Fig. 28*. A self-organising, execution driven, biomechanical system dominated by low-energy informational couplings.

(i) Flow field descriptions are abstracted from the kinetics of the local muscle-joint complex via a (reasonably compact) field of sensory endings;

(ii) The abstracted flow field descriptions radiate centrally via an irreversible (neural propogative) transport mode. During the radiational spreading the field description remains compact;

(iii) Muscle/joint flow field descriptions from different regions of the biomechanical system converge centrally on a localised region evolving new qualitative properties (morphologies) in the interference patterns. The qualitative properties that evolve from the interaction 'specify' (in the informational sense) organisational constraints that can be used to coordinate those muscle-joint complexes that are currently contributing to the interference patterns.

(iv) Perceptual sensitivity to these evolving constraints allows for them to be mapped back into the local muscle-joint complexes via efferently radiating neural propogation setting up new boundary conditions for the kinetics of the muscle-joint complexes.

* Figure reproduced, with permission, from Kugler and Turvey, 1986.

512

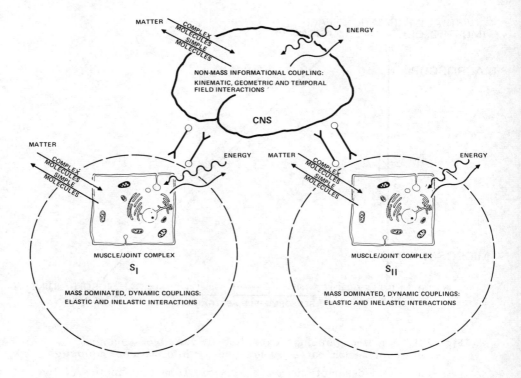

Fig. 29*. A lattice of muscle–joint complexes that form a
hybrid kinetic/informational system. Elastic and
inelastic interactions dominate the local transport
processes and information interactions dominate
the global transport processes.

* Figure reproduced, with permission, from Kugler and Turvey, 1986.

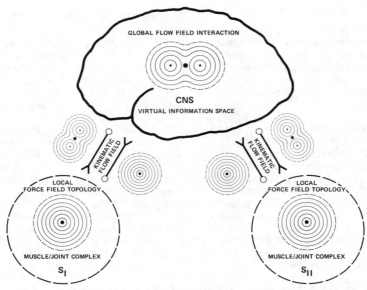

Fig. 30*. An example of a low dimensional qualitative morphology that
emerges during a field interaction. Motions (especially
oscillatory) about the muscle-joint complexes generate stress/
strain patterns that are specific to the local 'layouts' of
elastic and gravitational potentials. These locally generated
patterns spread centrally via the irreversible flow processes
associated with neural radiation. The descriptions that are
flowing centrally are field descriptions defined over the
fundamental dimensions of length and time (kinematic flow
fields). Of particular interest are the low-dimensional
qualitative flow patterns (morphologies) that are induce by
transformation on the stress/strain field in time. These
patterns can define an intrinsic coordinate space around
which movements can be organised and stabilised. There
are a number of types of flow dynamics that can result in
pattern formation: (i) local flow morphologies that are
characteristic of the potential (source-sink) layout; (ii)
summation properties that result from field interactions –
global cooperative interactions; (iii) subtractive properties
that result from field interactions – global competitive
interactions. The example presented identifies local flow
morphologies that converge centrally, interact, and form a
new flow pattern as a result of competitive and cooperative
processes. The local singularities could be the singular states
defining a 'preferred' limit cycle during an oscillatory task
involving the coordination of two oscillating limbs. The limit
cycle would define a small annular region in phase plane, the
cross section of which is a singular point with a gradient
basin surround. The interaction between two limit cycles will
generate a morphology associated with the phase relating the
two amplitudes. A saddlepoint can emerge from this interaction
and be used to 'orient' the system with respect to a 'preferred
phase relation'.

* Figure reproduced, with permission, from Kugler and Turvey, 1986.

6.2. A self-organising, execution-driven, biomechanical system

The movement construct outlined in Figures 28, 29 and 30 views singular (attractor) states and their surrounding gradients (basins) as a primary source of the constraints around which macroscopic movement patterns can be organised. These attractor portraits originate in a *self-assembly process* that occurs during the actual execution of the movement; the assembly process does *not* occur prior to the movement. Such a process is termed an *execution-driven, self-assembly, process* (see Figure 28).

An execution-driven control strategy has particular application for movements in which the phase space of motion can be partitioned into singular regions (*attractors: regions of reversibility)* and surrounding gradient regions *(basins: regions of irreversibility)*. Following Gel'fand and Tsetlin (1962), functional organisations that can be partitioned into gradient-independent dynamics (regions of reversibility) and gradient-dependent dynamics (regions of irreversibility) are *well-organised* (see Section 3.3.5). Variables responsible for orienting the system throughout regions of reversibility have been referred to as *control variables* and variables responsible for orienting the system about regions of irreversibility have been termed *coordination variables* (Kugler, et al, 1980; Newell, *This Study Institute)*.

In an *execution-driven* system future states are more dependent on the system's current configurational states than on prior (stored) states. Only crude initial conditions are required to initiate the process; once started, the process becomes parasitic upon, and driven by, flow field structures that emerge from current (biomechanical) state configurations. The only 'memory' requirement of the system is that of a crude, 'ball-park' knowledge of initial conditions.

6.3. Crude ('ball-park') initial conditions can be self-organised into precise final conditions ('equifinality')

The crude initial condition, identified above, are associated with the basin that surrounds an attractor. If the initial conditions put the system in the attractor's basin, then the movement system can be (self) organised by the flow tendencies associated with the basin so as to converge onto the small singular (attractor) region. The stability and reproducibility of the movement pattern is a function of the structural stability of the attractor and its surrounding basin (conjointly defining the attractor portrait). The size of the ball-park initial condition varies as a function of the nonlinear cut-off value associated with the system's perceptual sensitivity threshold. For system's with a high sensitivity threshold the initial ball-park can define a large region of the state space. Decreases in the sensitivity level will require a greater amount of precision in defining the initial condition.

The attractor portraits provide a minimal organisational back-drop around which large scale functional movements, such as locomotion, can be assembled. The precision of the system's behaviour is not dependent upon the specification of precise initial conditions; instead, it is a function of the system's *self-sensitivity* to the 'critical features' (singular regions) of the unfolding flow morphology. Stability and reproducibility of movement patterns is conditioned solely by: (i) the system's self-sensitivity to the flow patterns; and, (ii) the structural stability of the flow patterns themselves.

515

6.4. The importance of threshold nonlinearities in biology

Irreversibility begets irreversibility as threshold nonlinearities beget self-organisation. The concept of irreversibility is intimately tied to the concept of threshold nonlinearities, both of which are central to biology and self-organisation. The ubiquitity of threshold nonlinearities in biology rivals the ubiquity of irreversibility in physical processes. If systems exhibit irreversibility, organisational changes are occurring. If the irreversible flows are small the organisational states evolve towards disorder. If the flows are sufficient, then synchronisation of microstates can occur which result in the emergence of macroscopic patterns – the system tends to self-organise. This synchronisation process is a function of threshold nonlinearities. At critical flow rates atomistic components will reach thresholds at the same time. The atomisms will suddenly change state in a synchronised fashion. The synchronisation occurs without individual connections or instructions, it occurs because of the similarities (geometric, kinematic, dynamic, etc.; see Section 3.1.) shared by the atomisms. Similar atomisms will be synchronised by sharing the same threshold level and the same flow rate. Large scale synchronisation can be achieved by merely varying the rate of flow.

A membrane constitutes one of the most fundamental symmetry-breaking mechanisms in biology. It is a device that breaks the input --- > output flow symmetry. For example, consider a membrane that is designed to allow fluid to pass through only when a critical input pressure is reached. A continuous input pressure will result in a discontinuous output flow. At low input pressures, there will be no output flow. As the input pressure increases, an output flow can suddenly emerge at a critical value. At even greater input pressures, the output flow can even become saltatory, pulsing in a limit cycle, manner. A field of these membranes that share the same critical value and the same field pressure can result in the creation of a synchronised flow pattern without any individual connections between the atomistic units. The field coupling and the threshold nonlinearity provide the building materials for the synchronisation process. The action potential of a nerve cell exemplifies the process. Continuous input depolarisation results in a saltatory chemical wave that suddenly passes down the axon towards its synaptic endings. Fields of neurons can become quickly synchronised if they share threshold similarities (geometric, kinematic, dynamic, etc.) and similar field couplings.

6.5. Symmetry-breaking mechanisms and the violation of Curie symmetry

The Curie symmetry principle states that *output states are symmetric with input states*. A symmetry-breaking mechanism, however, is a device whose input states are not symmetric with its output states. Their input-output relations do not satisfy Curie symmetry. The Curie principle is fundamental to the physical sciences approach to the problem of causation. Input-output symmetry allows for input causation to be inferred from (measurable) output states. Causation can be inferred by effects only to the degree that Curie symmetry is satisfied. Symmetry-breaking devices involve nonmonotonic, nonlinear, transfer functions relating input to output. A self-organising system exemplifies a device that violates the Curie principle: Its output states can have a greater degree of long range correlation than its input states. For these systems a sequence of input states (i.e., an input flow) having only short range correlations can be transformed by a symmetry-breaking mechanism into a stable and reproducible sequence of output states (i.e., an output flow) that exhibits long range correlations. The stability and reproducibility of the correlation associated with the output states are *not* causally tied to the input correlations, i.e., the input-output *symmetry* violates Curie Symmetry.

6.6. The perceptual-motor loop as an open, self-organising, flow system

The perceptual-motor control loop is sustained by a high-dimensional chemical wave (defined over a neural bundle) that irreversibly transports input and output correlations through the neuromuscular actuators. Kinematic properties of the wave are irreversibly transported, in a radiational manner, globally. The kinetic effects that sustain the wave, however, have only local effects. No work is generated globally by the wave's action. The wave exhibits soliton characteristics (e.g., no residual global work cycle and preservation of structural properties of the wave through interactions).

The chemical wave may require a high dimension state space for its characterisation. Under certain open flow conditions, however, long range correlations can emerge in the output wave. These long range correlations identify tendencies of the output flows to converge or diverge from a set of *critical (singular) states*. Macroscopically, these flow tendencies can reveal geometric 'patterns' that can be classified according the number and layout of singular regions; and, the number of dimensions needed to define the singular region need not be very large (D < 5).

The neuro-muscular (perceptual-motor) control system is viewed as exemplary of a self-organising information system. The input to the system defines afferent flows and the output defines efferent flows. Asymmetries between input and output flows can arise as a function of threshold nonlinearities occurring among the internal operational components (sliding friction limits, elastic tissue limits, perceptual-motor resolution limits, etc.). Energy, matter (fundamental dimensions M, L, and T) and information (fundamental dimensions L, and T) flows through these symmetry-breaking mechanisms can result in the emergence of a small set of 'preferred' output states that is characterised by long range correlations (i.e., a correlation can appear across widely separated motor units, muscles, muscle-joints complexes, etc.). (The concept of 'preferred' output states has received an extensive theoretical and experimental treatment in a recent monograph by Kugler and Turvey, 1986). These preferred states do not constrain the system in terms of rigid mechanical constraints. Instead, they tend to softly 'orient' the current state of the system towards these states through gradients that radiate out from the preferred (attractive) states. The flow patterns or morphologies that emerge define a *self-organising informational substrate* that can be used to guide, or softly constrain, movement organisations.

6.7. The generality of self-organisation

The process by which movement patterns are created, sustained and dissolved has been the topic of this paper. It has concerned the origin and evolution of long range correlations among various combinations of atomistic-like entities, ranging from social insects to cooperative muscle-joint complexes. The problem has been couched around the more general issue of self-organisation. The benchmark of self-organisation is a progression of symmetry-breaking instabilities that transform an initially random phase of organisation into progressively more ordered phases (see Figure 31). The problem of self-organisation owes no allegiance to material constituents. The requirements are strategic, not material. They apply with equanimity across scale and material instantiation; they are universal design principles that are

517

reductionistic only to the degree that they rquire a minimum set of
conditions: 'openess to flow', 'partitioning tendencies', 'availability of
degrees of freedom' and 'threshold nonlinearities'. If these conditions are
present, and the flow through the system is sufficient, then it is possible
that the system can undergo a sudden instability that drives the system
into a new stable state that exhibits more long range order than its prior
state.

DEVELOPMENTAL TRANSITIONS FROM RANDOM
TO COORDINATED PHASES OF ORGANIZATION

RANDOM PHASE   **COORDINATED PHASE**

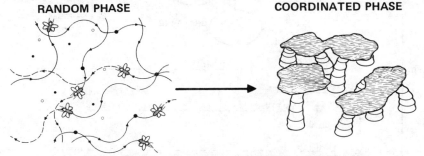

INSECT ARCHITECTURAL DEVELOPMENT

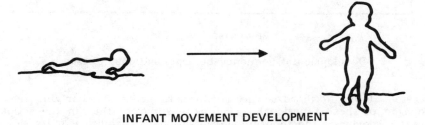

INFANT MOVEMENT DEVELOPMENT

Fig. 31.

6.8. A morphological perspective on the origin and evolution of movement patterns

The perspective advanced here suggests that the stability and
reproducibility of the macroscopic movement patterns, and their sequential
unfolding, is a function of the inherent structural stabilities (morphologies)
of evolving field processes. The developmental sequences associated with an
infant discovering locomotion, is viewed as exemplary of the process. A small
number of well-defined patterns unfold (see Gesell, 1929; Ames, 1937; McGraw
1943; Shirley, 1931), each with progressively longer range correlations among,
and within, muscle-joint complexes (see Figure 32). These patterns are viewed
as the result of an evolving geometry of flow patterns - a living coordinate
space (flow geometry) that can become structuralised in hard (bone,
cartilage, etc.) and soft tissues (organs, neurons, etc.) or remain functional
and self-sustained by low energy media (neuronal, hormonal, pheromonal,
acoustical, optical, etc.). In either case patterns or more generally,
morphologies, receive their birth and death in the mixing of reversible and

518

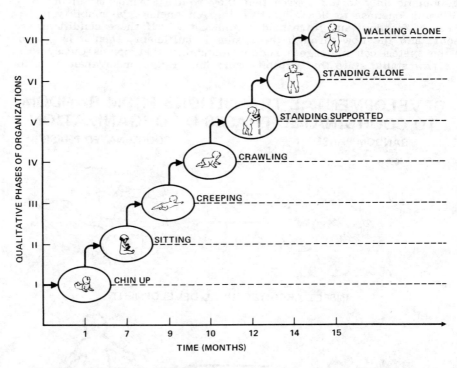

Fig. 32. Developmental sequence of organisational phases.

irreversible flows. Nowhere is the development process underlying the
development of these functional spaces more apparent than in the actions of
an infant discovering the inherent organisational capabilities of its movement
system: the progressive development of long range correlations first within,
then between muscle-joint complexes, as the movement system slowly evolves
large scale functional movement patterns.

   The role of geometrical representations in classical physics
   is well known. Classical physics is based on Euclidean
   geometry, and modern developments in relativity and other
   fields are closely related to extensions of geometric concepts.
   But take the other extreme: the field theory used by
   embryologists to describe the complex phenomena of
   morphogenesis. It is a striking experience, especially for
   a nonbiologist, to attend a movie describing the development
   of, for example, the chicken embryo. We see a progressive
   organization of a biological space in which every event
   proceeds at a moment and in a region that make it possible
   for the process to be coordinated as a whole. The space is
   functional, not geometrical. The standard geometrical space,
   the Euclidean space, is invariant with respect to translations
   or rotations. This is not so in the biological space. In this

space the events are localized in space and time and
not merely trajectories. (Ilya Prigogine, *From Being
to Becoming*, xiv, 1980).

7. A SUMMARY

A major problem in biological organisation is to account for the
systematic occurrence of long range correlations among a system's component
parts ('atomisms'). A collection of independent 'atomisms' (such as, cells,
organs, muscle-joint complexes, etc.) can suddenly become constrained so
as to exhibit long range correlations among its coordinates of motion. In a
biomechanical system the process is revealed in the assembly, sustaining
and dissolving of movement organisations that are distributed over many
mechanical degrees of freedom. While assembled out of a skeletal basis
composed out of many fine-grained degrees of freedom, these macroscopic
cooperativities require only a very few coarse-grained degrees of freedom
for their regulation. A movement construct is suggested that addresses the
degrees of freedom problem in terms of the physical principles of *cooperative phenomena*. It draws heavily on topological principles of qualitative
dynamics, bifurcation and catastrophe theory; partitioning principles of
irreversible thermodynamics; and informational principles of perceptual
realism. The construct is derived from the following assumptions:

1. Units of action are assembled out of 'generalised'
   reversible (gradient-independent) and irreversible
   (gradient-dependent) transport processes that
   compete for spatial and temporal boundaries - i.e.,
   the system oscillates at well-defined spatial and
   temporal scales;

2. Neural networks provide a compact low-energy, low-
   mass, medium dominated by irreversible transports -
   i.e., neural sensing irreversibly radiates throughout
   the CNS; forming, field-like, flow patterns;

3. Competition between and within field processes can be
   described by a finite number of converging and diverging
   flow regions, that originate or terminate in singular states
   - i.e., flow fields 'build' low-dimensional topological
   portraits;

4. Flow patterns (portraits) can be classified according
   to the number and layout of singular states (potential
   sources or sinks) and the dimension of the space in which
   the flow occurs - i.e., portraits can be classified according
   to theorems;

5. The singular set provides a low-dimensional, control space,
   description that can be mapped into a high-dimensional,
   machine space, description to form an efficient control
   system - i.e., a low-dimensional 'informational description'
   constrains a high-dimensional muscle-joint description;

6. Nonlinear thresholds characterising perceptual-motor
   couplings are symmetry-breaking devices that partition
   (categorise) control spaces into regions of reversibility
   (gradient-independent) and regions of irreversibility
   (gradient-dependent) - i.e., symmetry-breaking mechanisms

qualitatively categorise field processes;

7. Neural sensing is a mapping ('abstraction') process that preserves certain properties and annihilates others by reducing the number of fundamental dimensions defining the field (M, L, T kinetic descriptions _map_ > L,T kinematic or L-geometric or T-spectral descriptions) - i.e., movements are organised via a process that abstracts properties that have 'real' signifiers rather than an encoding process that defines 'formal', symbolic, referents as the signifiers;

8. New informational properties (flow patterns) can emerge centrally, from the creation or annihilation of singular states, and can be mapped back into the system as constraints for local, muscle-joint, kinetic spaces - i.e., the movement system internally self-organises.

ACKNOWLEDGEMENTS

I would like to thank Professors M.G. Wade and H.T.A. Whiting for their invitation to attend the Advanced Study Institute, their hospitality, and the provision of NATO support to cover travel expenses. I acknowledge the generous financial assistance provided by the Crump Institute for production of artwork, and Mike Gold, for securing the funds. My thanks to E. Deland, T. Poston and J. Parker for helpful comments; P. Etevenon and R. Thom for timely discussions; and, finally, special thanks to Scott Dudevoir who generously assisted me in all phases of manuscript preparation, both conceptually and materially.

References

Abraham, R.H. & Shaw, C.D. (1982). *Dynamics: The Geometry of Behavior, Part One - Periodic Behavior*. Santa Cruz, California: Aerial Press.

Abraham, R.H. & Shaw, C.D. (1984). *Dynamics: The Geometry of Behavior, Part Two - Stable and Chaotic Behavior*. Santa Cruz, California: Aerial Press.

Abraham, R.H. & Shaw, C.D. (1985). *Dynamics: The Geometry of Behavior, Part Three - Bifurcation Behavior*. Santa Cruz, California: Aerial Press.

✳ Adams, J.A. (1971). A closed-loop theory of motor learning. *Journal of Motor Behavior, 3*, 111-150.

Agarwal, G.C. & Gottlieb, G.L. (1984). Control theory and cybernetic aspects of motor systems. In H.T.A. Whiting (Ed.), *Human Motor Actions: Bernstein Reassessed*. Amsterdam: North-Holland.

Ames, L.B. (1937). The sequential patterning of prone progression in the human infant. *Genetic Psychology Monographs, 19*, 409-460.

Apter, M.J. (1966). *Cybernetics and Development*. London: Pergamon Press.

Arbib, M.A. (1980). Interacting schemas for motor control. In G.E. Stelmach and J. Requin (Eds.), *Tutorials in Motor Behavior*. New York: North-Holland Publishing Co.

Arbib, M.A. (1984). From synergies and embryos to motor schemas. In H.T.A. Whiting (Ed.), *Human Motor Actions: Bernstein Reassessed*. Amsterdam: North-Holland.

Balescu, R. (1975). *Equilibrium and Nonequilibrium Statistical Mechanics*. New York: Wiley.

Bellman, R.E. (1961). *Adaptive Control Processes*. Princeton, NJ: Princeton University Press.

Berlinski, D. (1976). *On Systems*. Boston: MIT Press.

✳ Bernstein, N.A. (1967). *The Coordination and Regulation of Movements*. London: Pergamon Press.

Bertalanffy, L. von. (1973). *General System Theory*. Harmondsworth, England: Penguin.

Bohm, D. (1957). *Causality and Chance in Modern Physics*. London: Routledge and Kegan.

Bridgman, P.W. (1922). *Dimensional Analysis*. New Haven, CT: Yale University Press.

Bridgman, P.W. (1941). *The Nature of Thermodynamics*. Cambridge, MA: Harvard University Press.

Bruinsma, O.H. (1977). An analysis of building behavior of the termite macrotermes subhyalinus. *Proceedings of the VIII Congress IUSSI*, Wageningen.

Buckingham, E. (1915). On physically similar systems. *Physiological Review, 4*, 345-370.

Carello, C., Turvey, M.T., Kugler, P.N. & Shaw, R.E. (1984). Inadequacies of the computer metaphor. In M. Gazzaniga (Ed.), *Handbook of Cognitive Neuroscience*. New York: Plenum.

DeGroot, S.R. & Mazur, P. (1962). *Non-equilibrium Thermodynamics*. Amsterdam: North-Holland.

Deneuborge, J.L. (1977). Insects Sociaux, 23, 329.

Duncan, W.J. (1953). *Physical Similarity and Dimensional Analysis*. London: Edwald.

Elasser, W.M. (1958). *The Physical Foundation of Biology*. Oxford: Pergamon Press.

Fodor, J.A. (1975). *The Language of Thought*. New York: Thomas Y. Crowall.

Fodor, J.A. (1981). *Representations*. Cambridge, MA: MIT Press.

Fodor, J.A. & Pylyshyn, Z.W. (1981). How direct is visual perception? Some reflections on Gibson's 'Ecological Approach'. *Cognition, 9,* 139-196.

Gel'fand, I.M. & Tsetlin, M.L. (1962). Some methods of control for complex systems. *Russ. Math. Surv., 17,* 95-116.

Gesell, A. (1929). Maturation and infant behavior pattern. *Psychological Review, 36,* 307-319.

Gibson, J.J. (1950). *The Perception of the Visual World*. Boston: Houghton Mifflin.

Gibson, J.J. (1966). *The Senses Considered as Perceptual Systems*. Boston: Houghton Mifflin.

Gibson, J.J. (1979). *The Ecological Approach to Visual Perception*. Boston: Houghton Mifflin.

Glansdorff, P. & Prigogine, I. (1971). *The Thermodynamic Theory of Structure, Stability and Fluctuations*. New York: Wiley-Interscience.

Grasse, P.P. (1959). Insectes Sociaux, 6, 127.

Greene, P.H. (1972). Problems of organization of motor systems. In R. Rosen and F. Snell (Eds.), *Progress in Theoretical Biology*, Vol. 2. New York: Academic Press.

Gregory, R.L. (1974). *Concepts and Mechanisms of Perception*. New York: Scribner.

Haken, H. (1977). *Synergetics*. Heidelberg: Springer-Verlag.

Helmholtz, H. von. (1925). In J.P. Southall (Ed. and trans.), *Treatise on Psychological Optics*. Rochester, NY: Optical Society of America.

Hollerbach, J.M. (1982). Computers, brains and the control of movement. *Trends Neurosci., 6,* 189-192.

Iberall, A.S. (1969). A personal overview, and new thoughts in biocontrol. In C.H. Waddington (Ed.), *Toward a Theoretical Biology*, 2. Chicago: Aldine.

Iberall, A.S. & Soodak, H. (1978). Physical basis for complex systems - some propositions relating levels of organizations. *Collect. Phenom., 33,* 9-24.

Kelso, J.A.S. (1981). Contrasting perspectives on order and regulation in movement. In J. Long and A. Baddeley (Eds.), *Attention and Performance*, Vol. 9. Hillsdale, NJ: Erlbaum.

Kline, S.J. (1965). *Similitude and Approximation Theory*. New York: McGraw-Hill.

Koenderink, J.J. (1985). Space, form and optical deformations. In D.J. Ingle, M. Jeannerod and D.N. Lee (Eds.), *Brain Mechanisms and Spatial Vision*. Dordrecht: Martinus Nijhoff Publishers.

Koschmieder, E.L. (1977). Instabilities in fluid dynamics. In H. Haken (Ed.), *Synergetics: A Workshop*. New York: Springer-Verlag.

Krantz, D., Luce, R., Suppes, P. & Tversky, A. (1971). *Foundations of Measurement*, Vol. I. New York: Academic.

Kugler, P.N., Kelso, J.A.S. & Turvey, M.T. (1980). On the concept of coordinative structures as dissipative structures: I. Theoretical lines of convergence. In G.E. Stelmach and J. Requin (Eds.), *Tutorials in Motor Behavior*. New York: North-Holland.

Kugler, P.N., Kelso, J.A.S. & Turvey, M.T. (1982). On the control and coordination of naturally developing systems. In J.A.S. Kelso and J.E. Clark (Eds.), *The Development of Movement Control and Co-ordination*. New York: John Wiley and Sons.

Kugler, P.N. & Turvey, M.T. (1986). *Information, Natural Law, and the Self-Assembly of Rhythmic Movement: Theoretical and Experimental Investigations*. Hillsdale, NJ: Lawrence Erlbaum.

Kugler, P.N., Turvey, M.T., Carello, C. & Shaw, R.E. (1984). The physics of controlled collisions: a reverie about locomotion. In W.H. Warren and R.E. Shaw (Eds.), *Persistence and Change: Proceedings from the First Conference on Event Perception*. Hillsdale, NJ: Erlbaum.

Kugler, P.N., Turvey, M.T. & Shaw, R. (1982). Is the 'cognitive impenetrability' criterion invalidated by comtemporary physics? *Behav. Brain Sci., (5)2*, 303-306.

Lackner, J.R. (1985). Human sensory-motor adaptation to the terrestrial force environment. In D.J. Ingle, M. Jeannerod and D.N. Lee (Eds.), *Brain Mechanisms and Spatial Vision*. Dordrecht: Martinus Nijhoff Publishers.

Langhaar, H. (1967). *Dimensional Analysis and Theory of Models*. New York: Wiley.

Lee, D.N. & Young, D.S. (1985). Visual timing of interceptive action. In D.J. Ingle, M. Jeannerod, and D.N. Lee (Eds.), *Brain Mechanisms and Spatial Vision*. Dordrecht: Martinus Nijhoff Publishers.

McGraw, M.B. (1943). *The Neuromuscular Maturation of the Human Infant*. New York: Columbia University Press.

Minorsky, N. (1962). *Nonlinear Oscillations*. Princeton, NJ: D. van Nostrand

Minsky, M. & Papert, S. (1972). Artificial intelligence. *Artificial Intelligence Memo*, 252. Cambridge, MA: Artificial Intelligence Laboratory, MIT.

Mishra, R.K. (1984). *The Living State*. New York: Wiley.

Morowitz, H.J. (1978). *Foundatins of Bioenergetics*. New York: Academic.

Nakayama, K. (1985). Extraction of higher order derivatives of the optical velocity vector field: Limitations imposed by biological hardware. In D.J. Ingle, M. Jeannerod and D.N. Lee (Eds.), *Brain Mechanisms and Spatial Vision*. Dordrecht: Martinus Nijhoff Publishers.

Nicolis, G. & Prigogine, I. (1977). *Self-Organization in Nonequilibrium Systems: From dissipative structures to order through fluctuations*. New York: Wiley-Interscience.

Onsager, L. (1931). Reciprocal relations in irreversible processes. *Psychological Reviews, 37*, 405.

Pattee, H.H. (1972a). Physical problems of decision-making constraints. *International Journal of Neuroscience, 3*, 99-106.

Pattee, H.H. (1972b). Laws and Constraints, symbols and languages. In C.H. Waddington (Ed.), *Towards a Theoretical Biology*. Chicago, IL: Aldine.

Pattee, H.H. (1973). Physical problems of the origin of natural controls. In A. Locker (Ed.), *Biogenesis, Evolution, Homeostasis*. Heidelberg: Springer-Verlag.

Pattee, H.H. (1977). Dynamic and linguistic modes of complex systems. *International Journal of General Systems, 3*, 259-266.

Pattee, H.H. (1979). The complementarity principle and the origin of macromolecular information. *Biosystems, 11*, 217-226.

Planck, M. (1932). *Theory of Heat* (translated by Brose). New York: Macmillan.

Poston, T. & Steward, I. (1978). *Catastrophe Theory and Its Applications*. London: Pitman.

Powers, W.T. (1973). *Behavior: The Control of Perception*. Chicago: Aldine.

Powers, W.T. (1978). Quantitative analysis of purposive systems: Some spadework at the foundations of scientific psychology. *Psychological Review*. Prigogine, I. (1978). Time, structure and fluctuations. *Science, 201*, 4358.

Prigogine, I. (1980). *From Being to Becoming: Time and Complexity in the Physical Sciences*. San Francisco: Freeman and Co.

524

Prigogine, I. & Stengers, I. (1984). *Order Out of Chaos*. Toronto: Bantam Books.

Pylyshyn, Z.W. (1980). Cognition and computation: issues in the foundations of cognitive science. *Behavioral and Brain Sciences, 3, 1,* 111-132.

Pylyshyn, Z.W. (1984). *Computation and Cognition: Toward a Foundation for Cognitive Science*. Cambridge, MA: MIT Press.

Rashevsky, N. (1938/1950). *Mathematical Biophysics: Mathematical Foundation. of Biology*. New York: Dover Publications.

Raven, C.P. (1961). *Oogenesis: The Storage of Development Information*. London: Pergamon Press.

Reed, E. & Jones, R. (1982). *Reasons for realism: selected essays of James J. Gibson*. Hillsdale, NJ: Lawrence Erlbaum Associates.

Rock, I. (1975). *An Introduction to Perception*. New York: Macmillan.

Roland, P.E. (1977). Sensory feedback to the cerebral cortex during voluntary movement in man. *The Behavioral and Brain Sciences, 1, 1,* 129-171.

Rosen, R. (1978). *Fundamentals of Measurement and Representation of Natural Systems*. New York: North-Holland.

Rosenbaum, D.A. & Patashnik, O. (1980). Mental clock setting process revealed by reaction times. In G.E. Stelmach and J. Requin (Eds.), *Tutorials in Motor Behavior*. New York: North-Holland Publishing Co.

Runeson, S. (1983). On visual perception of dynamic events. *Acta Universitatis Upsaliensis: Studia Psychologia Serial Number 9* (originally published 1977 as dissertation).

Runeson, S. & Frykholm, G. (1983). As an informational basis for person and action perception: Expectation gendre recognition and deceptive intention. *J. Exp. Psych: General, 112,* 585-619.

Schmidt, R.A. (1975). A schema theory of discrete motor skill learning. *Psychological Review, 83,* 225-260.

Shaffer, L.H. (1980). Analysing piano performance: a study of concert pianists. In G.E. Stelmach and J. Requin (Eds.), *Tutorials in Motor Behavior*. New York: North-Holland Publishing Co.

Shannon, C.E. & Weaver, W. (1949). *The Mathematical Theory of Communication* Urbana: University of Illinois Press.

Shirley, M.M. (1931). A schema theory of discrete motor skill learning. *Psychological Review, 82,* 225-260.

Thom, R. (1970). Topological models in biology. In C.H. Waddington (Ed.), *Towards a Theoretical Biology* (3). Chicago: Aldine.

Thom, R. (1975). In D.H. Fowler (trans.), *Structural Stability and Morphogenesis*. Reading, Mass.: Benjamin.

Thom, R. (1983). *Mathematical Models of Morphogenesis*. New York: Wiley.

Thompson, D.W. (1917/1942). *On Growth and Form*. London: Cambridge University Press.

Tomovic, R. (1978). Some central conditions for self-organization - what the control theorist can learn from biology. *American Journal of Physiology: Regulatory, Integrative and Comparative Physiology, 3,* R205-R209.

Turvey, M.T. (1977). Preliminaries to a theory of action with reference to vision. In R. Shaw and J. Bransford (Eds.), *Perceiving, Acting and Knowing: Towards an Ecological Psychology*. Hillsdale, NJ: Lawrence Erlbaum.

Turvey, M.T. & Kugler, P.N. (1984a). An ecological approach to perception and action. In H.T.A. Whiting (Ed.), *Human Motor Actions: Bernstein Reassessed*. Amsterdam: North-Holland.

Turvey, M.T. & Kugler, P.N. (1984). A comment on equating information with symbol strings. *Am. J. Physiol.: Regulatory Integrative Comp. Physiol., 15,* R925-R927.

Turvey, M.T., Shaw, R. & Mace, W. (1978). Issues in a theory of action: degrees of freedom, coordinative structures and coalitions. In J. Requin (Ed.), *Attention and Performance*. Hillsdale, NJ: Erlbaum.

Turvey, M.T., Shaw, R.E., Reed, E.S. & Mace, W.M. (1981). Ecological laws of perceiving and acting: In reply to Fodor and Pylyshyn. *Cognition*, *9*, 237-304.

Whiting, H.T.A. (1984). *Human Motor Actions: Bernstein Reassessed* (Editor). Amsterdam: North-Holland.

Yates, F.E. (1981). Temporal Organization of Metabolic Processes: A Bio-spectroscopic Approach. *Carbohydrate Metabolism: Wualitative Physiology and Mathematical Modeling*. R.N. Bergman and C. Cobelli (Eds.). New York: John Wiley and Sons.

Yates, F.E. (1982). Outline of a physical theory of physiological systems. *Can. J. Physiol. Pharmacol.*, *60*, *3*, 217-248.

Yates, F.E. & Kugler, P.N. (1984). Signs, singularities and significance: a physical model for semiotics. *Semiotica*, *52*, *1/2*, 49-77.

AUTHORS INDEX

534

SUBJECT INDEX

542

biomechanical 87
biomechanical factors 35
biophysical perspective 199, 200
bipedal locomotion 114
blind 298
blind infants 297
blind subjects 143
body constraints 114
body play 240
body schema 30
body/action scaled 302
both 84
bottle-feeding 268
bottom-up 35
boundaries 84, 92, 101
boxes 376
brain 81
brain physiology 71
brain-damaged infant 295
breast 268
breathing movements 58
Buckingham-theorem 479

canids 81
canis lupus 87
canonical babbling 226
catastrophe theory 478
catch 302
catching 168, 192
caudal 351
central core of the brain 215
central pattern generator 268
central predisposition 93
central programming 93
central states 93
central vision 444
cephalic stabilisation 316
cephalo 351
cerebellum 211, 421, 423, 431, 434
cerebral 211
cerebral mechanisms governing expressions 226
cerebral regulatory structures 249
cf 90
chained reflexes 27
change versus stability 80
change-stability 86
changes in perception and motor coordination
  239
chreods 11, 12, 14
chreods generative assimilative 17
chronically implanted oral cannulae 93

chunking 385
Church Thesis 473
circular causality 503
circular reactions 234
cirtical period 451
classes of action 91
classical stability theory 480
classification 54, 373 375, 378, 406
classify 90
closed environment 44
closed 84
clusters 89
co-activation of separate parts of the body 215
co-articulation 95
co-ordered 80, 82
co-orderings 83, 84, 95, 130
coactive 226
coding 418
coding capacities 378
coding systems 375, 378
cognition 391, 392
cognitive 373
cognitive ability 384
cognitive activities 385
cognitive competence 10
cognitive control 36
cognitive development 182, 250, 379
cognitive impenetrability requirement 472
cognitive mediation 149
cognitive processes 435
cognitive resources 36
cognitive skills 374
cognitive stage 154, 159
cognitivism 406
cohesions 83
coincident-timing behaviour 314
collections 375
collective nouns 375
collectives 200
columnar organisation 453
combinations 86
combinatorial functions 86
combinatorial sequences 88
combined actions 87
command structure 94
common movement principle 273
communicating brains 207
communicating movements 207
communication 87, 215, 216
communication systems 216
communicative mode 271, 272

engagement of expressive behaviours 224
engrams 383
entrainment 66
environment 79, 87
environmental 350
environmental disturbance 93
environmental modification 194
environmentally impoverished conditions 92
epigenesis 264, 265, 419
epigenetic 346
epigenetic events 265
epigenetic landscape 10, 13, 16, 17
equation of state 478
ergotropic 212
Eshkol-Wachmann 95
ethological research 81
ethologists 81, 85
ethology 66
evaluation 319, 320, 331-336
evaluations of objects 249
evaluative aspect of motor transactions 212
evaluative relationships 212
excitatory foci 92
execution-driven, self-assembly, process 514
existential commitment 467
expectancies 275
experience 97-99
expert-novice differences 40, 44
exploration 93
exploratory and performatory adjustments to
    objects 239
exploratory interest in surroundings 239
expressions 219, 249
expressions specifically indicative of distress
    229
expressive behaviours 222
expressive contexts 88
expressive hand gestures 226
expressive movements 224, 255, 264
expressive system 135
extension 172
extensor strength 114, 115
external environment 88
extraphysical ordering principles 470
extrinsic influences 83
eye and head coordination 292
eye contact 227
eye movements 66, 68, 139, 294, 296
eye movers 310

face 90

facial grimaces 232
facial grooming 93
facilitate 92
facilitation 92
facilitative precursor 267
failure of contact 230
failure of maternal emotional support 230
familiar partners 248
fear of strangers 248
fearful behaviour towards strangers 248
fearfulness 247
features of music 222
feedback 45, 160, 172, 319, 320, 336, 376,
    382, 384
feedforward 87, 376, 384
feeling movement and emotion in sound 220
fetal behavioural development 269
fetal motility 53
fetal motor activity 65, 68
fetal motor development 65
fetal movements 53, 65, 66, 231
fields 211
fine-grained analyses 95
Fitt's law 379
flexibility 89, 90, 431
flexible 96
flow morphologies 509
flow patterns 97
fluency 160
fluency of movement 162
focus 92, 97
focussed 92
foetuses 364
forelimb movements 90
form 85, 90, 94, 95, 160, 349
forward-looking subjectivity 275
fractionated movements 170
frame of reference defined 89
frames of reference 287, 292, 296, 297, 299
frames or contexts of interaction 274
framework 77
frontal association areas 418
frontal lobes 449
function 82, 85, 90
functional categories 99
functional dynamics 70
functional interconnections 266
functional orienting 292
functional specificity 191, 192
functional system 449, 451, 452
functionalism 373

550

554